If you are wondering why you should buy this new edition of *The World is a Text*, here are six great reasons.

- **38 new or enhanced selections** are featured on timely, engaging topics like the Internet, movies, television, public space, race, and gender. Over **90 new images** are presented as texts or to enhance texts.

- **Four entirely new clusters of readings** help you write papers incorporating multiple points of view: the Campus Suite in Chapter 3, the Obama Suite in Chapter 4, the *Avatar* Suite in Chapter 6, and the Google Suite in Chapter 9.

- Throughout this edition, **expanded attention to the purpose and process of writing** helps you compose more effective, insightful essays about the texts in this book and about the world around you.

- Ten selections are complemented a **new "How I Wrote This" feature,** a question-and-answer interview about how individual authors anthologized in *The World is a Text* planned and composed their pieces, illustrating the diversity and commonalities among successful writers' processes.

- An **annotated essay** in Chapter 2 helps you better understand active reading, and a photograph in Chapter 7 is now accompanied by a **discussion of visual analysis** to assist in active viewing.

- The authors present **two new photo essays:** one on college campuses in the United States and abroad in Chapter 3, and one in the "Interchapter" following Chapter 5 on the kinds of signs you see every day, like road signs, billboards, and restaurant signs, to name only a few.

PEARSON

The World is a
TEXT

FOURTH EDITION

The World is a
TEXT

Writing, Reading, and Thinking about Visual and Popular Culture

Jonathan Silverman
University of Massachusetts Lowell

Dean Rader
University of San Francisco

Prentice Hall

Boston   Columbus   Indianapolis   New York   San Francisco   Upper Saddle River   Amsterdam
Cape Town   Dubai   London   Madrid   Milan   Munich   Paris   Montreal   Toronto   Delhi
Mexico City   Sao Paulo   Sydney   Hong Kong   Seoul   Singapore   Taipei   Tokyo

Senior Editor: Brad Potthoff
Editorial Assistant: Nancy C. Lee
Senior Supplements Editor: Donna Campion
Senior Marketing Manager: Sandra McGuire
Senior Media Producer: Stefanie Liebman
Associate Managing Editor: Bayani Mendoza de Leon
Senior Managing Editor: Linda Mihatov Behrens
Project Coordination, Text Design, and Electronic
    Page Makeup: Electronic Publishing Services Inc., NYC

Senior Manufacturing Buyer: Mary Ann Gloriande
Art Director, Cover: Pat Smythe
Cover Designer: Miguel Ortiz
Cover Image: © Julian Cash
Printer and Binder: RRDonnelley-Crawfordsville
Cover Printer: Color Graphics Services, Inc.

Library of Congress Cataloging-in-Publication Data

Silverman, Jonathan.
  The world is a text: writing, reading, and thinking about visual and popular culture / Jonathan Silverman, Dean Rader.—4th ed.
      p. cm.
  Includes bibliographical references and index.
  ISBN-13: 978-0-205-83446-4 (paperbound)
  ISBN-10: 0-205-83446-9 (paperbound)
  1. English language—Rhetoric. 2. Culture—Problems, exercises, etc.
  3. Readers—Culture. 4. Critical thinking. 5. College readers. 6. Report writing.
  7. Semiotics. I. Rader, Dean. II. Title.
PE1408.S48785 2011
808'.0427—dc22

                                            2010042363

1 2 3 4 5 6 7 8 9 10—RRD—14 13 12 11

Prentice Hall
is an imprint of

www.pearsonhighered.com

ISBN-13: 978-0-205-83446-4
ISBN-10:   0-205-83446-9

Contents

2 Reading and Writing about Television   126

3 Reading and Writing about Public and Private Space   186

4 Reading and Writing about Race and Ethnicity   **270**

5 Reading and Writing about Movies   **318**

Alternative Table of Contents

Below are the readings in *The World Is a Text* grouped according to subject matter, genre, or style of writing. They offer cross-chapter ways of reading individual works.

Social and Economic Class

College/University

Comparison/Contrast

Definitional Essays

Fun!

Games (Sports and Other)

Gay & Lesbian Issues

Gender/Sexuality

Images, Visual Culture & Non-Traditional Texts

Personal (Uses First Person)

Race/Ethnicity

Preface

Welcome to *The World Is a Text IV: The Wrath of Rhetoric* or *(IV: Meta-tacular!)*. In this edition, as in the last three, *The World Is a Text* relies on a modified semiotic approach as its pedagogical theory; it is based on the assumption that reading occurs at all times and places. It also relies on traditional critical skills employed by literary scholars and the generally contextual approach employed by cultural studies scholars. The book also features a sophisticated way of thinking about texts, writing, and the rhetorical moment. Taking as its major theoretical framework Kenneth Burke's notion of rhetoric as the "use of language as a symbolic means of inducing cooperation in beings that by nature respond to symbols."

The World Is a Text considers how various texts enact rhetorical strategies and how students might begin not only to recognize these strategies but use those strategies for their own writing. Textual analysis (reading) and textual formation (writing) jointly contribute to the larger process of knowledge making. Thus, *The World Is a Text* is interested in helping students to ask not simply what something means but how something means.

And because knowledge making requires knowledge of how we make arguments and sentences and theses and assertions, this book goes one step further than similar readers. In our experience, writing remains a secondary concern for most similar books. One of our goals is to make the writing experience a vital part of the entire book from the introduction, to the section on writing, to each individual reading. For instance, Section I, The World Is a Text: Writing takes a comprehensive approach to the various stages of the writing process. We walk students through selecting a topic, brainstorming, outlining, developing a thesis, and revising. We offer help with research and citation. We even provide a unique chapter on making the transition from high school to college writing. One of our goals is to help students make these connections between reading and writing, thinking and writing, revising and re-visioning.

The World Is a Text also has its focus in encountering media and texts in general; each chapter has questions that encourage students not only to respond to readings, but the texts and media themselves. Every chapter has an introduction that focuses on reading media and individual texts (not the readings themselves). In the readings that follow, each piece features questions geared toward both reading and writing. And its general apparatus in the form of worksheets and classroom exercises encourages students to use the readings as a starting point for their own explorations of television, race, movies, art, and the other media and texts we include here.

On a more theoretical level, we show how language in text and context functions to produce meaning. And we talk about how writing is fundamentally linked to other aspects of critical inquiry like reading, listening, thinking, and speaking. Just as Burke argues that all literature is a piece of rhetoric, we suggest that all texts are rhetoric, and that every moment is a potential moment for reading and therefore for writing.

As always, we have tried to keep in mind that what we are asking is for our students to see the world in a new way, and that such efforts can be difficult. But we think that such efforts will be repaid many times over in the way you engage the world. And we thank you for using our book.

If you have suggestions for the fifth edition, or if you have student essays you'd like us to consider, please let us know. We are always looking for good new essays about popular culture, especially essays on TV, film, and music. So please feel free to send us an email recommending particular essays. Or feel free to pitch us one of your own. We love hearing from colleagues and students.

WHAT'S NEW

With each new edition, we have made discreet revisions in attempt to improve certain aspects of the book. This time we have chosen to foreground the writing process. To that end, we have reoriented our introduction to accentuate both the purpose and process of writing, and we have added a new feature called "How I Wrote This," in which some of the authors discuss how they put together their pieces. We also revised each chapter introduction in an attempt to provide specific writing instruction for that particular chapter.

Even though we ramped up the writing component, we also paid attention to the practice of reading. Over the past couple of years, we heard from a few instructors that some of their students can have trouble reading and comprehending some of the more complicated essays. So, we included another annotated essay, but this one, using one of our favorite articles, Katherine Gantz's "Not That There is Anything Wrong with That: Reading the Queer in Seinfeld" to focus on the reading process of a scholarly essay. Along these same lines, photographer Cheryl Aaron takes one of her photographs, discusses how it came to be, and then discusses how it can be read.

We have also added essays and suites that focus more on the student experience. Our new Google suite discusses the way the popular website has impacted students (with perhaps not even knowing it.) We have added material about the way college campuses work in a suite, including a new photo essay about campuses both in the United States and abroad. We have also taken the idea about signs and semiotics more literally—this edition has a photo essay devoted to signs. And with a new president who has inspired a symbolic storm (as well as a political one), we have devoted a new suite based on the semiotic response to President Barack Obama. Additionally, we feature a fabulous photo essay by Judith Taylor that focuses entirely on dolls and mannequins. These images raise a number of provocative questions about gender and semiotics. Lastly, we offer a special essay, new to this edition, by award-winning architect Liz Swanson, who offers an introduction to reading architecture.

INSTRUCTOR'S MANUAL

The Instructor's Manual to accompany *The World Is a Text*, Fourth Edition, offers practical tips and detailed notes to each reading as well as suggested answers to the questions found after each selection. We also share own personal and detailed strategies for teaching popular culture and writing in their "World Notes" section. In addition, this Instructor's Manual contains a variety of sample syllabi that show how the book can be taught in different contexts. Instructors may download this manual from its catalog page at www.pearsonhighered.com. Of course, your local Pearson representative is always available for help, too. Visit our Facebook page or send us an email at WorldIsAText@gmail.com

Acknowledgments

We would like to acknowledge more people than can comfortably fit, but here's a start. First, we want to express our gratitude to everyone at Prentice Hall, especially our editor, Brad Potthoff, and his helpful assistant, Nancy Lee. We also want to thank Leah Jewell, Brandy Dawson, and Corey Good (our first editor on this project). We thank Lake Lloyd and everyone at EPS for putting the manuscript together. Thanks go out to the various authors who wrote original pieces for the book, gave us the rights to reprint things at a reduced rate, and made helpful suggestions. We also appreciate the impressive feedback from professors and students who used the book. We really aren't joking; please email us if you have questions or suggestions.

We are also grateful for the advice, critiques, and suggestions from the people who graciously agreed to review and comment on *The World Is a Text* in manuscript: Lauren Ingraham, University of Tennessee; Steven Bidlake, Central Oregon Community College; Kelly Sassi, University of Michigan; Greg Barnhisel, Duquesne University; Pat Tyrer, West Texas A&M University; Adrienne Bliss, Ball State University; Jason Walker, San Francisco State; Mitra Ganley, San Francisco State; Loren Barroca, San Mateo Community College; Denise Cummings, Rollins College; Leslie Taylor Collins, University of Tennessee at Chattanooga; Linsey Cuti, Kankakee Community College; Karen Gardiner, University of Alabama; Amy Lawlor, Pasadena City College; David Moutray, Kankakee Community College; Patricia Webb, Arizona State University; and Lynn Wright, Pasadena City College. We thank reviewers for this manuscript: Michalle Barnett, Gulf Coast Community College; Laurie A. Britt-Smith, University of Detroit Mercy; Hugh Culik, Macomb Community College; Margaret Lazarus Dean, University of Tennessee; Rodney F. Dick, Mount Union College; Robert Imbur, The University of Toledo; Robyn Lyons-Robinson, Columbus State Community College; and Matthew T. Usner, Harold Washington College. And we also thank previous reviewers of the manuscript: Leslie Taylor Collins, University of Tennessee at Chattanooga; Linsey Cuti, Kankakee Community College; Karen Gardiner, University of Alabama; Amy Lawlor, Pasadena City College; David Moutray, Kankakee Community College; Patricia Webb, Arizona State University; and Lynn Wright, Pasadena City College. We also thank Cherelyn Willet, who composed a great poem entirely of passages from *The World Is a Text*. We are now convinced she knows the book better than we do.

We are appreciative of the many scholars who read and commented on the first and second editions of the book but who are not mentioned here. We also thank Johnny Cash, Beck, Nirvana, Radiohead, Cat Power, Aimee Mann, Lyle Lovett, The Fountains of Wayne, De La Soul, Cornershop, Sufjan Stevens, Badly Drawn Boy, Bonnie "Prince" Billy, The Last Town Chorus, Aimee Mann, and Loop!Station who unknowingly provided the soundtrack for the writing process of this new edition. Of course, we thank our students at VCU, USF, Pace, and UMass Lowell for giving us feedback and providing constant inspiration.

For their help with the reading gender chapter, we thank Rachel Crawford, Nicole Raeburn, and Jill Ramsey; for the reading race and ethnicity chapter, Katherine Clay Bassard; for reading the technology chapter, Michael Keller; and for the introduction, Patty Strong. We also thank Miles McCrimmon for reading an early version of the proposal and for his work on the instructor's manuals. We are also grateful to Judith Taylor, Liz Swanson, and Phil West for providing original material for this edition.

Lisa Mahar, author of *American Signs,* was of great help. We're still grateful to Rigo of San Francisco for his murals. We also thank all of the authors in Chapter 1 who contributed original pieces. We also thank Steve Grody for his special introduction to the images of graffiti. Thanks, too, to the students—especially Anna Rose Tull whose essay is new to this edition—who submitted and contributed their work.

In areas of institutional and collegial support, the following were of special help: Catherine Ingrassia, Marcel Cornis-Pope, Richard Fine, Margret Vopel Schluer, Sharon Call Laslie, Ginny Schmitz, Bill Tester, Tom De Haven, Laura Browder, David Latane, Nick Sharp, Elizabeth Savage, Randy Lewis, Emily Roderer, Pat Perry, Elizabeth Cooper, Elizabeth Hodges, Bill Griffin, James Kinney, Marguerite Harkness, Michael Keller, Leslie Shiel, Nick Frankel, Faye Prichard, Angier Brock Caudle, Traci Wood, Walter Srebnick, Carol Dollison, Geoff Brackett, Jeannie Chiu, Kristin di Gennaro, Martha Driver, Steven Goldleaf, Tom Henthorne, Todd Heyden, Eugene Richie, Mark Hussey, Karla Jay, Helane Levine-Keating, Amy Martin, Sid Ray, Walter Raubicheck, William Sievert, Michael Roberts, Nira Herrmann, Katie Henninger, Kathie Tovo, Frank Goodyear, Anne Collins, Jan Lisiak, Teresa Genaro, Suzanne Forgarty, Michael Tanner, Dan Marano, Elisabeth Piedmont-Marton, Jeffrey Meikle, Mark Smith, Greg Barnhisel, Fouzia Baber, Anne Darby, Matt Compton, Matt King, Carlease Briggs, Virginia Colwell, Rita Botts, Sarah Hawkins, Whitney Black, Tracy Seeley, Eileen Chia-Ching Fung, Alan Heinemann, Patricia Hill, Carolyn Brown, Carolyn Webber, Sean Michaelson, John Pinelli, Robert Bednar, Wendy McCredie, Leonard Schulze, Jean-Pierre Metereau, Steven Vrooman, Beth Barry, Amy Randolph, T. Paul Hernandez, Chris Haven, Brian Clements, George McCoy, Michael Strysick, Brian Brennan, Mike Henry, LeAnne Howe, Brian Dempster, Cary Cordova, Monica Chiu, Andrew Macalister, Aranzazu Borrachero, Cecilia Santos, Vamsee Juluri, Jeff Paris, Christopher Kamrath, Susan Steinberg, Susan Paik, Peter Novak, Heather Barkley, Colleen Stevens, Freddie Wiant, Mark Merrit, Brian Dempster, Zachary White, Marika Brussel, Loren Barroca, Michael Bloch, T-Bone Needham, Jonathan Hunt, Brandon Brown, Katherine Conlon, Melissa Pennell, Marlowe Miller, and Nina Coppens.

In addition, we thank the English department at the University of Massachusetts Lowell, the staff at the O'Leary Library at UMass Lowell, the English Department at Pace University, the Henry Birnbaum Library at Pace University, English Department at Virginia Commonwealth University, the VCU James Branch Cabell Library, the Andover Summer Session, and the Department of English and the Dean's Office of the University of San Francisco, particularly Provost Jennifer Turpin, former Associate Dean of the Arts & Humanities Peter Novak, and current Associate Dean Lois Lorentzen. Also, thanks to the excellent staff of the Dean's Office in the College of Arts and Sciences. A special nod goes out to John Pinelli and his crew.

Finally, we thank Melvin Silverman, Beverly Silverman, Joel Silverman, Alba Estanoz, Jason Silverman, Christian Leahy, Ginger Rader, Gary Rader, Barbara Glenn, Amy Rader Kice, Adam Kice, Isabella Kice and the twin cousins of Simone Kice and Gavin Rader. Dean also thanks his wife, Jill, for, you know, everything.

We are most grateful to all of you who adopted this book for your classes, and a particularly hearty thank you to all of the students who made, for better or worse, this text a part of your world.

Jonathan Silverman
University of Massachusetts Lowell

Dean Rader
University of San Francisco

Email us at:worldisatext@gmail.com and visit us on our World Is A Text Facebook page

About the Authors

Jonathan Silverman and Dean Rader conceived the idea of *The World Is a Text* while commuting to their job outside Austin, Texas. Frustrated with the textbook they were using in their freshman composition courses, they set out to write a book that merged rhetoric and writing with popular and visual culture. In 2008, Jonathan and Dean also began *Semiobama*, a blog that uses the concepts laid out in this book to offer "readings" of Barack Obama in popular culture through the lens of semiotics.

Jonathan is an assistant professor of English at the University of Massachusetts at Lowell, where he teaches composition, journalism, and literature. He recently served as a Fulbright Roving Scholar in Norway. He is the author of *Nine Choices: Johnny Cash and American Culture.*

Jonathan Silverman

Dean has published widely in the fields of American Indian Studies, American poetry, and composition studies. He is also an award-winning poet. His book *Works & Days* won the 2010 T. S. Eliot Poetry Prize and *Engaged Resistance: American Indian Art, Literature, and Film* is forthcoming from The University of Texas Press. Dean is a professor of English at the University of San Francisco. He curates the arts and culture blog, *The Weekly Rader,* and writes a regular column for the City Brights section of The *San Francisco Chronicle.*

Dean Rader

The World Is a Text

INTRODUCTION

Writing, Reading, Culture, and Texts: An Introduction to the Introduction

The following chat took place on March 15, 2010 between the two authors of this book—Jonathan Silverman and Dean Rader. The exchange has been edited slightly for grammar and clarity, but not much.

13:07 Jonathan: Hi Dean.

13:07 Dean: Hi Jonathan.

Jonathan: I think we should talk about the introduction.

13:08 Dean: Has it been misbehaving again?

Jonathan: Yes. It's being pedantic and irrelevant.

13:10 Dean: Well, I'm not sure that's the introduction's fault. It's our fault. What do you think we should do about it?

Jonathan: I think we should rewrite it focusing more on what concerns both students and teachers—writing.

13:14 Dean: It's true that our introduction begins by addressing reading. But, it's impossible to talk about writing without linking it to the process of reading.

13:18 Jonathan: I agree. What we need is to get to the heart of the reading/writing issue a bit quicker. Maybe we should talk about audience?

13:19 Dean: What do you mean?

13:21 Jonathan: I think students do interpretation and reading of what we call non-traditional texts all the time, but writing for an audience is different than conversation.

13:22 In other words, students might evaluate and discuss movies, television shows, and video games all the time, but they are not always asked to write about them. I think our book is trying to help them with this.

13:23 Dean: So, you're talking about process—the process of writing a paper vs. the process of casually interpreting what someone is wearing or trying to figure out the vibe of a coffee shop.

13:26 Jonathan: Yes. But they don't have to be separate. We've talked about this before, but I think students are often intimidated by trying to write about anything, but especially things they are not used to writing about.

13:30 Dean: Yeah. The topics and format of our book must be a little startling to some students. On one hand, we write about things they already know well, but on the other hand, we are asking them to write about things they've probably never written about. So, we need to do a better job of ushering them into the writing process.

The World Is a *Really Big* Text at the Unisphere, Queens, New York.

13:33 Jonathan: I agree. One thing I would say that makes this process different is that the process of discovery through writing is often different than it is through personal communication—we can read clues into the way people discuss movies and television shows, avoiding strong opinions or allowing conversation to dictate interpretation. We talked yesterday about whether you had liked *Crazy Heart*, because in our conversation, I could not tell immediately.

In writing, we are forced to come to grips with what WE think in starker terms. That's why I believe in prewriting and freewriting as a way of establishing our own ideas about a particular subject.

13:36 Dean: As you know, I agree. And, as you also know, I'm particularly concerned that our book be really helpful for students. I hear from other professors who use *The World is a Text* (and from my own students) that the hardest part of writing a paper for a college class is getting started—knowing where to begin. So, maybe we can make the beginning of our introduction similar to how students might begin a paper.

Jonathan: I think we're doing that! Right now!

13:37 We don't exactly know how we want to begin our introduction, so we're getting our ideas out through writing about them.

Sometimes when I'm stuck on writing about something, I pose questions to myself to get the material flowing.

13:40 Dean: I often tell my students that writing is dialogue—with yourself and with the audience you imagine to be reading your work. Yesterday, you said you liked that E. M. Forester quote, something like "How do I know what I think until I see what I say?" Writing is thinking.

13:43 Jonathan: But if students are nervous about starting, they should be. It's hard work writing—even for more experienced writers—but it can only begin by beginning.

13:44 Dean: You're pretty smart—not like they say!

13:58 Dean: The smart thing you said was that this exchange—this goofy chat we are doing right now—is a kind of model for how one might begin a writing assignment. So, why don't we put this in the book? Let's make this chat how we begin our introduction.

14:01 Jonathan: Done!

While we do not recommend you begin your papers as we just did, there is something to our chat that might be worth thinking about as you write your own papers. We wrote informally, as part of a dialogue, even though, you might have noticed, our topic may have seemed rehearsed. It was; we wanted to mimic the process of discovery and often informality that often guides our own writing and thinking. And as we are writing here, we move to a more formal mode; when we publish, we have to write formally for our audiences to take us seriously. But almost no writing we do begins complete—the process we undergo in order to get our thoughts in order often begins haphazardly, nonlinearly (not in a straight line) but in fragments and in writing down ideas.

Some of you by now have been introduced to the idea of brainstorming and freewriting by high school or college teachers; almost all of you will be. While we have always endorsed this process when writing about anything, such an approach seems particularly appropriate for writing about non-traditional texts such as movies, television, race, public space, and so on because it mimics the way we do actually begin our discussions about these texts. Many of you have had heated discussions about the bands and television shows you like, have read postings on the Internet about movies, and even used text messaging or Facebook posts to comment on things or other people. These informal ways of arguing can themselves be the beginning of more formal arguing—and paper writing.

This book hopes to build on some of the skills you already have and work on new skills in writing and interpretation. We think it is important to learn how to write a good paper, whether it is about *The Simpsons* or Shakespeare. But we think writing about popular culture has a few advantages that writing about other subjects may not. For one, writing papers develops skills you may often use in everyday life—both in terms of your informal critiques AND your more formal writing process. By now, you may also be tired of writing informational research papers and literary analysis. Looking at a fresh subject can also help you re-think your writing process.

Because we want you to both write and read better, this book is both a guide to writing and a collection of essays about popular culture. In the first part, we talk about semiotics as a way of interpreting popular culture, move to a detailed explanation of how the writing process works, and then keep a focus on writing as we move to chapters on a variety of subjects. In a way, this chapter is not only the result of a dialogue between us but between our readers, both teachers and students, and us. We want the book to serve your interests as students and ours as teachers. That is why we think dialogue, discussion, as well as more formal writing, are key to this process.

As you can tell from the chat above, we're eager to make sure you understand the main objective of our book and this introduction. If that objective was not clear, we'll restate it here: our goal is to help you read and write about **texts** (movies, pieces of art, experiences, people, places, ideas, traditions, advertisements, etc.), in much the same way you would read and write about traditional texts. Many of these texts are visual or have visual elements, and past tendencies probably have been to "see" them rather than "read" them—that is, you likely simply regarded them rather than *interpreted* them. In this book, however, instead of looking through texts by not actively interpreting, we ask you to look *at* them—to slow down and decode texts in ways you may not have done previously. In addition, we want you to try formalizing this reading process. What we mean by "formal" here is the process we undertake when analyzing literature (or, depending on your training, math formulas, a painting, or research data). One of the primary elements of formal reading is the breaking down of a text into smaller elements and interpreting them. Analyzing a short story for themes, character development, and figurative language (symbols, metaphors, etc.) is formal reading, as is the process of poring over a Supreme Court decision. Explicating a poem is a classic example of formal "decoding." Looking at a poem's rhyme, meter, symbolism, tone, structure, and design is a formal process that involves posing questions about what the poem is trying to do and how it does it. Although it may feel natural to think of reading or decoding poems in this way, approaching an advertisement or a television show or a gender may feel a bit foreign at first. Over the course of reading this book, we hope that this process ceases to feel alien and begins to seem natural, especially as you become more familiar with analyzing the elements associated with these cultural and visual texts.

To sum up, the traditional analytical work you have done in English classes is something we want to imitate here. We believe that texts, including those that are nontraditional such as public spaces, songs, and advertisements, have meanings that can be uncovered through the exploration of their elements. You may know a public space seems ugly—but we want you to understand *why*. You may already sense that advertisements use sex to sell products, but we want you to understand *how*. The idea is not only to slow the interpretive process down, but also to make more conscious your meaning-making, a process you undertake all the time—whether you intend to or not. Understanding how texts make meaning is the most important step toward writing your own texts about this world.

SEMIOTICS: THE STUDY OF SIGNS (AND TEXTS)

All reading we do, perhaps anything we do, is backed up by various ideas or theories—from the simple idea that the acts we undertake have consequences both good and bad, to the more complex theories about relativity and gravity. In this book, we rely on a theory that the world itself is open to interpretation—that we can make meaning out of just about anything. The notion that the world is a text open to interpretation is itself a theory, which has a strong connection to **semiotics**, the study of signs. In this part of the introduction, we elaborate on the idea of semiotics as a way of having you understand some of the assumptions we made when writing this book. You can use the rest of the book without focusing too much on the theory, but you may find that this section will prove helpful when taking notes or drafting for your assignments.

In semiotics, the main idea is that everything is a sign. You already know what signs are, because you encounter them everywhere. There are traffic signs, signs telling whether something is open or closed, signs in your classroom urging you not to smoke, or cheat, or informing you where the exit is. You do very little work in trying to understand these signs, which seemingly need no interpretation. Once you understand what "stop" means, or that red in fact means "stop," or that green means "go," or that yellow means "slow down" or "caution," there is little need to stop, think, and interpret these signs each time you see them. Of course, you did not always know what these signs meant; at some point in your childhood, you picked up the ideas behind these signs and now take them for granted. The important thing to realize, however, is that our culture has come to a common understanding that a number of random signs and symbols—a cross, a red octagon, a round green light, a stick figure with the outline of a skirt—stand in for or symbolize specific concepts.

We have a broader idea of signs (or texts) in this book, although how we talk about signs here is based on the most rudimentary cultural symbols. A *sign* is an object or idea or combination of the two that refers to something besides itself, and it depends on others to recognize that it is a sign. The red octagon and the letters S–T–O–P mean "Stop" to most of us through the combination of the shape, color, and letters; a blue diamond with "HALT" on it would catch our attention, but we would not treat it in the same way, despite

the fact that *halt* and *stop* are synonyms, or that a blue diamond is a perfectly fine combination of color and shape. The stop sign as we now know it carries a meaning beyond a simple combination of word, color, and shape. It carries the weight and force of history, law, and ubiquity.

Another example: We know an "Open" sign at a store means the store is transacting business. But "Open" itself is an arbitrary sign, unique to English-speaking cultures. The symbols O–P–E–N are characters English speakers have identified as "letters," and those letters, when put together in a certain way, create "words." If we were to put these symbols together, "Δ•≠»" and hang them on the door of a coffee shop, we would just confuse people because our culture has not assigned specific meanings for these symbols. But what if we came across this sign: ABIERTO? In Spanish, "abierto" means "open." So, if we read Spanish, then we can decode the sign. Or, if we live, say, in San Diego, and we have grown up knowing these seven letters mean "open" in Spanish, then we can also decode it. And in some places, a sign contains both *abierto* and open to indicate that it is signifying to two different sets of clientele. "Open" and "abierto" can both be signs, but so can their presence together be a sign. If we saw an abierto and an open sign in one place, we might draw conclusions about where we were (a neighborhood where English and Spanish are spoken), who owned the restaurant or store (bilingual owners?), and who their audience was (primarily speakers of Spanish and English). In other words, the presence of both signs is itself a sign—taken together they create meaning.

Semioticians ("sign-studiers") have a more formal way of referring to signs. Ferdinand de Saussure, a Swiss linguist working in the nineteenth and twentieth centuries, believed that signs contained two elements: the **signifier** and the **signified**, which, when taken together, often create meaning. The signifier is the object that exists, and the signified is what it means. In other words, the letters O–P–E–N are the signifier, and the message that a place is open for business is the signified, and the external reality is that the store or restaurant is open for business. Similarly, using our stop sign example, the actual red sign with the STOP written in white letters is the signifier. The signified is the message that you must bring your car to a complete halt when you approach this sign.[1]

SYSTEMS OF READING: MAKING SENSE OF CULTURAL TEXTS

Sometimes the same signifiers (physical signs) can have different signifieds (meanings). For instance, what do you think of when you see the word "pan"? Most of you probably imagine an item for cooking. Or you might think of a critic "panning" or criticizing a bad movie. However, a Spanish speaker who saw the word *pan* in our bilingual store would most likely imagine bread. The signifier "pan" in Spanish cultures refers not to an item for cooking but to what English speakers think of when they see the signifier "bread." Thus, people from both cultures would experience the same signifier, but what is signified would be entirely different.

However, we do not even need other languages for there to be various signified meanings for the same signifier. Photographers may think of a pan or wide-angle shot. Scholars of Greek mythology may think of the Greek god who is half goat and half man. The letters p–a–n remain the same, but the meanings change; the sign—the word "pan"—has different meanings. We also can have the same signified but with different signifiers. For example, "soda," "pop," or "Coke" are all different signifiers that different people from different parts of the country use to refer to a flavored carbonated drink.

So when we talk about signs, we are not talking only about physical signs but also about a system of reading. In this system, we can interpret images, words whose letters are arbitrarily assigned meaning, and experiences—really just about anything. Sometimes we make these interpretations with little or no effort and sometimes with a lot of work. Many semioticians believe that everything is a sign, including the way we are writing this introduction. The words are signs, and so is the way you are reading them (it is simply a more complex way of saying that everything is a text).

And more complex signs of course do not reveal themselves so easily. For example, let us consider a very famous sign (or text)—the *Mona Lisa*. Its power in some part comes from its simplicity and its *unreadability*. We do not know why she is smiling, we only have a vague idea of who she is, and we will likely never know. That smile, or half-smile, has become so famous that its life as a sign has transcended even its power as an image. The painting is a signifier, but its signified is ambiguous and difficult to determine. If we look at the various images of the *Mona Lisa* on shirts, mouse pads, posters,

---

[1]The terms signified and signifier are well known; a good introduction to the work of the complicated idea of semiotics is Daniel Chandler's *Semiotics: The Basics* (New York: Routledge, 2002)—a discussion of signifiers and signifieds is on page 19.

even variations of the original (we like the version where Mona Lisa has a big black moustache), we can agree that the *Mona Lisa* has become a symbol of something 1) traditional, 2) artistic, 3) commercial, and yet 4) universal, and perhaps 5) modern. We can agree that something about its power has not diminished despite or because of its age. But our signified—our mental concept of what "*Mona Lisa*–ness" is—depends on what perspective we bring to the reality of this artwork. Does it signify our definition of a masterpiece? A commodity? A self-portrait by the artist?

We do not know exactly (but people guess all the time). And that's why sometimes sign reading is so frustrating. Some signs are easy to read and understand, so easy that we do not even know that we are reading. Others, like paintings—and more importantly, human relationships—are more difficult. One of the most complex components of

Source: Leonardo da Vinci (1452–1519). *Mona Lisa*, oil on canvas, 77 × 53 cm. Inv. 779. Photo: R. G. Ojeda. Louvre, Paris. Reunion des Muses Nationaux/Art Resource, NY.

reading texts is suspending judgments about a text's values. In your initial semiotic analysis—your initial reading of a text—try to consider all aspects of a text before applying a label like "good" or "bad" (or "interesting" or "boring"). Such labels can come only after a thorough reading of the text under question. Later, if you want to argue that a text has problems, then you would use the details, the information you gleaned from your reading, to support these assertions in your papers. In attacking the *Mona Lisa*, for example, it would be acceptable to most professors for you to guess about what you thought da Vinci meant in painting her if you can defend your guess. Reading visually, in fact, often means such guessing is a natural part of writing any sort of paper.

Overall, the basic idea behind semiotics should not be foreign to you—on a fundamental level, it simply means reading and interpreting nontraditional objects like you would a short story or a poem.

THE "SEMIOTIC SITUATION" (OR THE "MOVING TEXT")

As you may have guessed, you do this type of work all the time. You read people and relationships every day, having developed this skill over your years of reading the world. For instance, let us say you are walking down Wall Street in New York City. You see a man dressed in a suit, talking on a cell phone, carrying a copy of *The Wall Street Journal,* and yelling "Sell Microsoft at 42! Sell! Sell! Sell!" What would you assume his profession is? He could be a lawyer. He could be a banker. But given the context (where you are, Wall Street), what he's talking about (stocks), and how he's dressed (a suit), the best interpretation of this text might be that he is a stockbroker. You could be wrong, but based on the clues of the text, that is a pretty good reading.

We perform this work constantly. For example, on first dates we try to read the other person for cues of attraction and enjoyment; quarterbacks read a defense before every play and pass; we read a classroom when we enter it; we read a friend's house, and especially his or her room, by scanning posters, its cleanliness, its odor, and the collection of books and music. These moments are what we call **semiotic situations**—when we try to make sense of our surroundings or interpret one aspect of our surroundings based on the signs or texts of our situation. The copy of *The Wall Street Journal,* the cell phone, the man's comments—all are signs that represent a text that can be read. And when we put these signs together, they help us make sense of the larger text (the man) and the larger text (Wall Street) and an even larger text than that (America). As you may have guessed by now, this act of reading can even help you make sense of the largest text of all—the world—in both literal and mythical ways.

Because we are always trying to make sense of the world, because we are always reading, we often find ourselves in semiotic situations. This book builds on your own methods of reading and tries to sharpen them so that you become more critical and thoughtful readers of the complex text that is our world. We keep returning to the reading metaphor because it aptly describes the process of making sense of our surroundings, and because it is the first step toward crafting an excellent essay. When we read a poem or a short story, we pay attention to detail: we look for symbols, metaphors, and hidden themes. We "read between the lines," meaning that we read not only what is there, but also what's *not* there. We do this frequently as well; we "read into things." Beer commercials never come right out and suggest that attractive, straight, single women will immediately become attracted to straight men if the men drink a certain kind of beer, but that is implied in almost every ad. People we are interested in dating may not tell us what kind of people they are, where they come from, what kind of music they like or what their political leanings are, but by paying attention to the clothes they wear or the comments they make, or the bumper stickers on their cars, we may be able to begin to piece together a better interpretation of the text that is this person. In other words, we already know how to read books and poems, and we also know how to read the world itself. This book will help you merge your experiences from formal and informal, as well as conscious and unconscious reading.

TEXTS, THE WORLD, YOU, AND YOUR PAPERS

We hope by now that you understand what we mean by reading the world as a text, and that this notion seems both comfortable and interesting to you. However, you are probably wondering how any of this figures into your writing course. As you have no doubt figured out by this time in your academic career, writing is fundamentally connected to reading and thinking. To our knowledge, there has never been a great writer who was not also a great thinker. What's more, to be a great thinker and a great writer, we must also be great readers. Writing is so intimately tied to thinking and thinking so intimately tied to the act of reading the world and one's surroundings, that the three form a kind of trinity of articulation and expression:

Of course, by "reading" we mean not only reading books and newspapers and magazines, but also the semiotic situation or the nontraditional text, the practice of reading the world. Writing, thinking, and reading are a symbiotic process, a cycle in which they feed off and influence each other. Thus, if we are reading and thinking, then the chances are we will be better prepared to do good writing.

RHETORIC: WRITING'S SOUNDTRACK

Good writing is also grounded on solid rhetorical principles, as is good reading (as we have broadly defined reading so far). **Rhetoric** comes from the Greek word *rhetorik*. Its literal definition means speech or speaking. In English, "rhetoric" has come to refer to the art of speaking or writing effectively—usually with an emphasis on persuasion. This book considers rhetoric broadly, exploring how it works not only in cultural and visual texts but also how you can apply rhetorical principles and strategies to your writing to make your papers more effective.

The history of rhetoric is a long and complicated one, and it is worth knowing a little about its background. Generally, scholars link the birth of rhetoric with the Sophists (Greek thinkers from the fifth century B.C.E.), who first began studying and theorizing the concept of public speech. Later, rhetoric became one of the three pillars of the liberal arts and a foundation for classical education. The great Greek philosopher Plato (437–347 B.C.E.) had issues with rhetoric being considered an art; for him it was more of a cheap skill—essentially, fancy flattery. He considered medicine a true art and compared rhetoric to cooking. Given the current popularity of *Top Chef*, that is not so bad, but at the time, it was a bit of an insult. Ultimately, Plato argued that rhetoric could never be an art, because it had no subject; it had nothing to ground it. Thus, when you hear a pundit describe a political speech as "all rhetoric," the pundit is using rhetoric in much the same way Plato saw it—as empty, content-free verbiage.[2]

---

[2]Much of the work on rhetoric can be found in a variety of sources, including James L. Golden et. al, *The Rhetoric of Western Thought: From the Mediterranean World to the Global Setting* (Dubuque: Kendall Hunt Pub Co, 2007).

However, Aristotle (384–322 B.C.E.), also a famous Greek philosopher and Plato's student, argued that rhetoric was one of the great arts and that its subject was all things. In fact, Aristotle found the subject of medicine and warfare rather narrow, whereas, in his mind, rhetoric had no bounds. For him, rhetoric cast the widest net and because it could encompass so much, it was worthy of study. In fact, in his famous study *On Rhetoric*, Aristotle advances a concept of rhetoric ("the art of finding the possible means of persuasion in reference to any given situation") that informs current rhetorical theory and much of this book.

Indeed, with the advent of the modern media, advertising, and visual culture, rhetoric has grown to encompass all persuasive techniques, strategies, and approaches beyond mere speaking and writing. One of the main goals of our book is to help you to detect various strategies of persuasion in any situation, whether it is an advertisement, a movie, a building, or fashion. To that end, *The World Is a Text* is interested in both cultural and visual rhetoric—how cultural and visual texts make arguments. As you will see, we discuss the "rhetorical moment" or the "rhetorical situation" a great deal. By this, we mean the many different situations Aristotle refers to that will require you to use new interpretive skills. You cannot read all texts the same way—you must adjust your reading to meet the signs of the text. For example, commercials for heart medication may make different arguments than those for Match.com. Beer ads in *Maxim* rely on an entirely different set of images, codes, and associations than those for Diet Coke in *Cosmopolitan*. Thus, the rhetorical tools advertisers use and that readers (like you) employ can change dramatically in any given situation.

In addition, the study of rhetoric carries with it a sense of the *polis* (Greek for city or public) that the authors of this book find utterly appealing. Originally linked to public oratory, rhetoric now subsumes under its umbrella political speeches, public art, television shows, commercials, billboards, and now, the Internet. Plato and Aristotle could never have imagined the degree to which rhetoric has been stretched. Nevertheless, rhetorical approaches help make sense of everything from grafitti to buildings to video games to movies to clothing. In short, any text designed to make meaning or have an effect incorporates some aspect of rhetoric. An awareness of the history, reach, and goals of rhetoric make you better readers of the world. Ultimately, rhetoric is about civic engagement.

The World Is a Text is a visual and cultural rhetoric, meaning that this book is a kind of treatise, a playbook, a how-to manual of rhetorical principles, with emphases on texts and approaches that make meaning in both cultural and visual realms. It is primarily about writing, but it argues that no good writing can happen without good reading skills. In the remaining pages, we address both. We offer strategies for decoding cultural texts; we provide various strategies for reading and writing; and we offer step-by-step instructions on both reading and writing. Later in this introduction, we discuss various ways of making arguments and provide strategies for identifying how other texts make arguments with the ultimate goal of rounding out your vocabulary and your facility in regard to persuasion in discourse. One of the most famous scholars of rhetoric, Kenneth Burke, describes rhetoric as the "use of language as a symbolic means of inducing cooperation in beings that by nature respond to symbols."[3] Burke's emphasis on symbols points to the importance of signs, signifiers, and the

---

[3]Burke's quote appears in Golden, *The Rhetoric of Western Thought* and many other sources.

visual language on which so much of the communication in our world relies. His interest in cooperation reveals the degree to which rhetoric is woven into the fabric of a culture, part of the garment that humans wear in the world. The visual and cultural implications of rhetoric and their importance for undergraduate education and writing undergird the larger scope of this book.

FROM RHETORIC TO WRITING

As you have no doubt gleaned by now, our goal is to help you learn to see the rhetorical strategies of various texts and also to get you started writing your own. We are firm believers that textual analysis (reading) and textual formation (writing) jointly contribute to the larger process of knowledge making. Thus, we are interested in helping you to ask not simply *what* something means but *how* something means. This is why reading will help your writing: it teaches you how to be savvy consumers and producers of texts. You will get to know texts from the inside out, so that when it comes to writing your essay, you will know, intimately, how arguments work.

Here is also where our instructions about reading and your assignments for writing intersect, because learning to identify rhetoric in cultural and visual texts better enables you to use rhetoric in your papers. In fact, writing is itself an important component of interpretation. Writers and thinkers have long seen writing as a means of helping us arrive at ideas. When we think abstractly, we tend to gloss over ideas so fast that we do not slow down and articulate them. They are more sensations than thoughts. To put them down on paper, to compose them into sentences, ideas, and reasons, is harder than thinking. Indeed, if you have done freewriting exercises, you may have had no idea what you thought about something until you wrote it down. It is no surprise that journaling or keeping a diary is vitally important to writers. The act of writing can often be an act of unlocking: the door opens and ideas, reactions, fears, and hopes walk right out of your head and on to the page and say, "Here I am!" Sometimes, we wish they had stayed inside, but this is where the interesting work happens, and here is where learning to read the world as a text can help you learn to write on a college level. Learning to write well allows us to move into the world of ideas, interaction, and exchange. And learning to read outside our traditional ideas of what it means to read will expand your mind even further.

Writing about the world as a text may not only facilitate writing and thinking, but also writing and feeling. Although we certainly do not want to diminish the logical aspect of writing, we want to pay attention to a component of writing that is often overlooked, and that is the emotional component. Franz Kafka, Emily Dickinson, Pablo Neruda, and dozens of other writers turned and continue to turn to writing because it helps them get a handle on the world and relieves anxiety. Writing is or can be rewarding, refreshing, rejuvenating. In part, writing means sharing, participating in a community of language and ideas. We learn about others and ourselves through writing because writing is simultaneously self-exploration and self-examination. We see ourselves in a larger context. Of course, we may not always like what we discover (perhaps traces of sexism or racism or classism), but uncovering those elements of our personality and understanding them is an extremely rewarding experience. Writing that is honest, candid, and reflective attracts us, because those are traits we value.

At the same time, we do not want to neglect the idea that writing is a difficult process to master. Between us, we have authored thousands of papers, articles, handouts, tests, reports, and now, this book. In almost every case, we went through multiple drafts, stared at the computer screen, cursed whatever picture was on the wall for its interference, and struggled at various points along the way. In fact, this very introduction went through between fifteen and twenty drafts. In some ways, writing is very much like exercising: It does not always feel great when you are doing it, but when you are finished, it is both rewarding and good for you. We are drafters by nature—we believe that whereas writing is a form of thinking, several drafts are often needed to convert that thinking into something worth showing the public.

By now, you should be beginning to see some direct connections between writing and reading. Only by reading well can you write well. A good essay makes sense of a topic using detail, insight, and purpose—the same traits one uses to read. We believe that the readings and questions in this book are a good springboard for that writing process. Some of the essays may anger you, but that is okay. Some will make you laugh, some will confuse you, and some will make you see a movie or a place or a gender in ways you never have before. We hope that these readings and images not only show you what writing can do, but also that the texts in this book spark your imagination and push you toward the writing process so that your own work will be as vigorous and as provocative as the texts presented here.

In the next section, we provide you with some hands-on examples of visual and cultural rhetorical readings so that you can see firsthand how you might make the transition from the act of reading to the act of writing.

READING THE WORLD AS A TEXT: WRITING'S OVERTURE. THREE CASE STUDIES ON INTERPRETATION

In this section, we walk you through the act of interpretation, of reading semiotically; that is, we help you read certain texts in ways that you may find unfamiliar. However, as stated earlier, we believe that living critically in the world means living as an informed, questioning, and engaged person. Learning to read the world as a text is a good way to begin, and it is critical for writing a solid paper.

CASE STUDY 1 Reading Public Space: Starbucks

One of the most familiar places in our modern world is the coffee shop, and in particular, Starbucks. As a ubiquitous presence, it could make for an interesting "read"—many ideas about the world could come from reading a Starbucks. With this in mind, we sat down one morning in a Starbucks and did a reading. We began with note taking, just writing down what we saw and thought. This is a transcribed version.

Note taking: brown, green, red, brown patterned carpet.
Green
Lighting non-fluorescent
Curves

Wood—metal

Tables different types

Products art—decoration

Logo "coffee-related art" photos

Baby chairs, modern garbage cans

Advertisements, baskets, games, "Cranium" wood

Handicapped bathrooms—*The New York Times,* windows, mahogany, metal door handles, pull to get in, push

Music: "cool," varied

With this information, we can begin to construct a series of observations that could develop into ideas:

Starbucks relies on moderate earth tones for decoration.

Their seating places are made of durable materials.

Their artwork is a mix of coffee photographs and advertisements.

There is lots of light. The lighting they use is bright but not harsh, avoiding fluorescent light.

Their advertisements are prominent within the store. Their products are geared to the middle and upper classes both by design and content. (Oops—an argument slipped in!)

As you can see by the last statement, in the process of writing down observations, arguments about the text itself may present themselves, which is what we were hoping for. In this case, the idea that Starbucks is geared toward a particular target audience is an argument, and potentially one that you might pursue in a paper. How could you make this a paper? You could expand the idea of a target audience into multiple paragraphs: one about products, another about décor, maybe one about music, and perhaps another about the location of the particular Starbucks you are in.

If we were going to construct a thesis statement, it might sound like this: "Starbucks appeals to the middle and upper classes through a combination of its décor, music, products, and location."

Well, that thesis statement is okay and would work to organize a paper, but it is still pretty vague. We could ask why Starbucks wants to sell its wares to a particular demographic through its design. We know the answer to this already—they are a commercial venture. But the question of "how" still raises itself—we can see the target audience and the tools, but how they are using them is a different story. Maybe another question is this: What is Starbucks trying to sell *besides* coffee? What experience can someone hope to get by entering Starbucks? We would argue that Starbucks is trying to sell an idea of "cool" or "hip" to its customers. And for its target audience of middle- and upper-class people, cool is something these people may feel they need to buy. So a new thesis could be: "Starbucks tries to sell its idea of cool to the middle and upper classes through its hip music; sturdy, smooth décor; and its sleek and streamlined products."

This could still improve, but notice that this thesis gives you an automatic organization of paragraphs about décor, music, merchandise, and location. From here, you could work on incorporating the details of your observations as evidence for the points you are making. For example, you could describe in some detail the nature of the furnishings, the various songs that play over the loudspeaker, and the general location of this particular Starbucks. If you wanted to, you might research how companies use these elements to make their businesses more profitable.

We hope, through this example, that you can see how this sort of thing might work. We began with a trip to Starbucks and ended up talking about demographics and public space. Not all such experiences could end up as papers, but you would be surprised how many can.

CASE STUDY 2 Reading Fonts: How Type Can Say a Lot About Type

Although you are only a few words into this section, the shift in font has already altered your reading experience. We associate many things with certain fonts; more than we might expect. Even though you know this is a book for a class, the simple change of font may have made you think of Throne of Blood 99 or some older European manuscript, although no reference to either appeared until just now. **If we were to ask you what fliers written in this font were advertising, what would you say? Even if you have never been to a jazz concert or a Broadway play, you would likely guess one of those two options.** *Similarly, if an invitation appeared in your mailbox engraved in this script, what would you think? Does this font suggest a luau? An American Idol watch party? Probably not. In fact, we are willing to bet that your attitude, your general happiness, even your basic anxiety level has altered a bit simply through an alteration of font.* For example, those of you who have relied on Courier to make your essays appear longer may be visited with a sense of joy, nostalgia, or anxiety at seeing it here, in a textbook, where it is just not supposed to be.

In truth, we had several conversations about the most appropriate font for *The World Is a Text*. We wanted to express seriousness and scholarly competence, but at the same time, we hoped for a font that would convey a sort of contemporary edginess that we thought the book embodied. THAT FONT PROBABLY WOULD HAVE LOOKED MORE LIKE THIS THAN WHAT WE SETTLED ON, BUT ULTIMATELY, WE DECIDED THAT THIS IS A FONT FOR ADVERTISING OR MENUS—NOT A BOOK. PLUS, THE ALL-CAPS SITUATION MAKES IT LOOK LIKE WE ARE YELLING AT THE READER. That something as small as font can carry so many associations, hang-ups, and biases speaks to the unspoken power of semiotics and the importance of visual rhetoric.

Fonts tell us how the designers of a text want to be seen. Retailers, advertisers, designers, T-shirt manufacturers, sports franchises, and alcohol producers take full advantage of fonts to influence the public. For example, what if the Oakland Raiders began the 2010 football season with the same famous black and silver pirate logo, but with all the lettering on the uniforms, helmets, and memorabilia in this font:

The Oakland Raiders

Or, if The Raider Nation, considered by sports aficionados to be the craziest, rowdiest fans of any professional American franchise, suddenly changed their promotional and Web font to

THE RAIDER NATION
Win, Lose or Tie, Raiders til We Die!!!

In both cases, the groups would lose all credibility—even if the play of the team or the insanity of the fans remained the same—because neither of these fonts suggest dominance, fear, or aggression. The first evokes silliness; the second, old-school cursive or cross-stitch.

These two examples reveal yet another truism about semiotics—signs are almost never value free. This is certainly the case for fonts. Every font carries associations and assumptions. Take the examples used previously. One reason they seem so ludicrous is that both are somewhat stereotypically feminine. The humor comes in the gap between the values we associate with professional football and the values we associate with curly font. **THE OAKLAND RAIDERS AND THE RAIDER NATION** might work, because we tend to associate this Stencil font with the military, and we tend to associate the military with masculinity, force, power, strength, and victory. THE OAKLAND RAIDERS AND THE RAIDER NATION probably would not work because this Desdemona font calls up art déco, France, and all kinds of associations that are antithetical to the image of American football. Thus, how serious we take a font is often related to its perceived femininity or masculinity. Consider what traits in font we might link with femininity and which we might consider masculine. Pay attention to flourishes, curls, and fat and wide lines.

Just as fonts often carry gender values, they also frequently carry cultural values as well. For example, why would this sign seem incorrect?

Jean Luc's French Bistro

For better or worse, when we see this font, we tend to think of one kind of cuisine, but when we think of French food, we never consider this font as even a remote possibility for an effective medium of communication. Similarly, we may also carry prejudices toward cultures without even knowing it. To some, an odd juxtaposition of appearance and content can come off not simply as discordant, but offensive as well.

God Bless the United States of America

Even though the sentiment may be genuine and completely in line with traditional American Christian values, the Arabic font—a source of fear and anxiety to some Americans—somehow sends a different message than if the same phrase appeared in a less loaded font:

God Bless the United States of America

or

God Bless the United States of America

If both of these last two examples feel more appropriate than the Arabic-influenced font, it might be useful to examine how and why this might be.

In the introduction, we distinguish between the signified and the signifier, and the font/message equation is a perfect example of this complex linguistic and visual coding. If fonts carry positive or negative associations, it is because, over time, a culture has imbued them with meaning—a kind of stereotyping. Our culture would like to think of words and language in nonvisual terms, but the font issue points to ways in which even the written word sends messages.

One final example. Let us say there is a restaurant called "Beverly's." Based on the font used in the sign in front of the restaurant, think about what kind of food and ambiance is suggested by each sign:

BEVERLY'S

Beverly's

BEVERLYS

Beverly's

Beverly's

BEVERLY'S

Guessing what kind of place the various fonts evoke is relatively easy and fun, but the harder part is figuring out why a certain font sends the message it does. The Beverly's signs are another instance when cultural and visual rhetorics merge. For your papers, if you decide to read an advertisement or a commercial or a movie poster or a building, remember that a font is not merely a means of delivering the written message, it is also a visual cue along with photographs, logos, brands, and illustrations that underscores the larger argument the text is making.

CASE STUDY 3 Can We Laugh? Reading Art and Humor in Geico Commercials

Geico is funny. From the talking gecko with the undetermined British accent (Cockney?) to the celebrity "interpreters," to the caveman series, Geico has made viewers laugh perhaps harder than any other advertiser in recent memory.

But . . .

Geico is a commercial enterprise that makes us laugh only to sell us something. Is there anything wrong with this? And more importantly, how might we write about such a phenomenon? Thinking about the Geico ads raises all sorts of questions about art, entertainment, and commerce, not to mention the nature of humor.

In sitting down to write this, we thought about how we might take our reaction to Geico's commercials and convert it into an argument for an essay. We already know that the commercials engage topics that are popular targets of semiotic analysis—art and advertising. A number of influential writers have read billboards, ads in magazines, and television commercials—especially those broadcast during the Super Bowl—in an attempt to make sense of corporate strategies, cultural mores, and common assumptions about race and gender. But the Geico ads complicate these lenses. In fact, the caveman ads have very little to say about Geico at all, so selecting the right lens for reading these commercials is important. To help you make sense of the Geico ads, we have provided a sample semiotic reading, taking as our point of departure their most obvious trait—humor.

One way of beginning a reading of the Geico commercials might be to inquire into why these commercials are funny, and to do that, we should determine what types of humor they use. In this situation, as in any such reading, we begin with the obvious. In this case, it is the gecko. The gecko himself has made it clear that he's a pitchman for the company solely because of the similar name. "Because Geico sounds like gecko—that's the only reason I'm here," he says in one commercial. From the start, then, the commercial is asking to be read through a lens of comedy. Despite their charm, geckos do not know anything about car insurance. They cannot even drive. The gecko does not provide price quotes or reliability statistics; Geico's use of the gecko is merely for humor's sake. What makes this interesting is that the Geico commercials derive their humor from the fact that they are commercials about commercials. In other words, the commercials in many ways are advertising themselves with only a secondary hook to the product of insurance.

So part of the humor is *meta-commentary*. Meta-ness simply means acknowledging the subject of what you are talking about as you are talking about it. When the gecko refers to his role in the commercial during the commercial, it is a form of a meta-commentary. Part of the humor here has to do with the way we perceive advertising, as something that is supposed to be forced on us to pay for the television we are watching or the periodical we're reading.[4] Instead, Geico lets us know that we are indeed watching a commercial, and that the commercial may not tell us anything useful about the product.

In turn, this suggests that Geico is not trying to deceive the customer. You might ask yourself whether this is actually true, or whether it matters, or whether Geico is being "honest"—or even whether this question matters in trying to evaluate the commercials. To do this, you should consider what kind of appeal the commercial makes. In the language of rhetoric, one might argue that Geico appeals to both our *ethos*—our common sense, our sense of ethics, or the credibility of the company itself—as well as our *pathos*, our emotions—it is making us laugh. The *logos*, or logic, of the appeal is less apparent; indeed, what we are doing here is trying to decode the logos, so one could argue that its appeal is minimal if we cannot readily perceive it. (We talk more about ethos, pathos, and logos later

---

[4]Which is why some people are outraged at the commercial ads shown before movies—we have already paid for the movie!

in this introduction—**"How Do I Argue About Popular Culture Texts? A Guide for Building Good Arguments"** [Part IV].)

The commercials' ethos appeal builds through a cumulative trust of a company that so willingly makes light of itself. Such an appeal thirty years ago might not have been as effective, because these commercials might have conveyed the idea that a company that jokes about itself cannot be taken seriously, but to increasingly savvy consumers, such an approach punctures our usual resistance to companies that do nothing but brag about their products (almost *all* car companies' commercials use this appeal). Geico trusts its viewers to understand the commercials on multiple levels.

You also might ask why it is important to laugh at insurance commercials. To do that, inquire into the cultural associations surrounding insurance. We often perceive insurance salesmen and insurance companies negatively. Insurance generally is often associated with misfortune; no one calls an insurance company unless something terrible happens. So, when anything insurance-related makes us laugh, the company has already broken down some viewer resistance because so little about insurance is positive, funny, or engaging.

A closer reading of these commercials shows other humorous appeals. The "celebrity interpreter" commercials pair a celebrity with a "Geico customer," who is labeled on-screen as a "real person," whereas the celebrity is labeled as an "actor," or in the case of Burt Bacharach, a "celebrity." The commercial humorously implies Burt Bacharach is not a real person and entertains the notion that celebrities are somehow more equipped to endorse products rather than real users. That Geico plays with this idea has little to do with insurance but rather entertainment. Of course, in these commercials, celebrities are silly—Bacharach's second line is the hilarious, but nonsensical, "Lizard licks his eyeball," which is, again, a meta-commentary, as it refers to previous Geico commercials when the gecko does, in fact, appear to lick his eyeball. And other celebrities are similarly of no help in validating Geico's competency as an insurance company, like Charo, Little Richard, and Don La Fontaine, the famous announcer for action movie trailers. We likely laugh at these commercials because of the juxtaposition (re-ordering) between traditional ideas of insurance and an absurdist humor, but we could only come to that conclusion through a process of thinking and writing. If we were making this into an actual paper, we might start with a summary of the commercials (it is better to be specific in the introduction rather than general), have a thesis about this juxtaposition, and perhaps write paragraphs about humor, insurance, the specific humor involved in the commercial, and the way the two aspects combine. Taking notes on all of these things, writing down your reactions (no matter how silly they may seem) is a way of applying language to association. It is a form of articulating what you are thinking and feeling.

You might also think about Geico ads as a larger project that involves research. Watch past commercials on YouTube. Track down Geico sales numbers. Read articles about their ad campaigns. From this perspective, it is clear that Geico has established a reputation through humor—the reality show parody (*Tiny House*), the gecko himself, and the Caveman series, all of which emphasize branding over information. Geico likely hopes humor, a form of absurdity, will emphasize the importance of consumers for the company, but it is also mainly designed to help emphasize the Geico name, building brand awareness. The messages can be somewhat contradictory—does Geico want its customers to laugh or purchase? Is humor consonant with good insurance service? In a business sense, the Geico ads have paid off, adding two million customers from 2002 to 2006, for a total of seven million.[5]

We know why Geico made these commercials, but why do we laugh—and buy? And should we be laughing at something that is so explicitly commercial? In writing a paper, you could argue either side of the question that underlies this—whether commercials are art—pretty convincingly. On the negative side, you could argue that you should be skeptical of the motives of a producer of art that means to sell you something—it means that the art is not "pure." This is a variation of an argument that has been made many times over the years. Some even argue that the Geico ads are not art but commerce. This raises even more complicated questions about the interplay between commerce and entertainment. What if the Geico commercials are substantially more fun than the tedious reruns of *King of Queens*?

However, you could point to the fact that people like one of the co-authors—who does not drive—have no financial stake in the ads, and so the ads are really just entertainment for those viewers. Others could argue that most, if not all, art does not have a pure basis, and that to be entertained is a primary consideration in terms of whether to evaluate a piece of art. In the suite appropriately titled "Is It Art?" we tackle this question in more depth.

READING THIS TEXT AS A TEXT: TIPS ON USING THIS BOOK

We hope that our book is written with insight, knowledge, and openness, just as we hope that you read it with such. To augment this, we are going to give you a brief overview of the rest of the book, so that you can become a particularly good reader of the text that is *The World Is a Text*. To that end, we arranged the book to help you with the writing and the reading processes.

■ The World Is a Text: Writing

This section begins on page 25 and provides numerous strategies for writing, drafting, researching, and persuading. Let us be clear at the outset that we designed our section on writing as an *introduction* to the writing process. By no means should you consider this section a comprehensive guide to constructing papers. Our section here is merely an overture to the symphony that is your paper. Virtually no other book of this kind discusses the difficult process of transitioning from high school writing to college writing. *The World Is a Text* is unique in this regard, as we begin our section on writing with a short explanation of how college essays differ from high school essays. The segment entitled "How Do I Write a Text for College? Making the Transition from High School Writing," by guest author Patty Strong, is not so much a nuts-and-bolts essay as it is a description of how your thinking (and therefore your writing) process must change to do college-level writing. We think you will find this segment very helpful, and we recommend that you read it first.

One of the most difficult challenges facing beginning college writers is figuring out what they want to say in their papers. Actually settling on a thesis can be frustrating. Sadly, there is no guaranteed remedy for the malady of the elusive thesis; however, we provide some steps that should make the thesis process slightly less anxiety provoking in the next segment. "**From Semiotics to Lenses: Finding an Approach for Your Essays**" and "**How Do**

---

[5]Theresa Howard, "Gecko Wasn't First Choice for Geico," *USA Today*, July 16, 2006, <http://www.usatoday.com/money/advertising/adtrack/2006-07-16-geico_x.htm>.

I Write About Popular Culture Texts? A Tour through the Writing Process" walk you through the entire paper-writing process, from thinking about ways to approach your topic, to understanding the assignment, to freewriting, to outlining, to building your opening paragraph. We also added information on constructing a good thesis and on making and building arguments. Finally, we include an annotated student paper in which we walk you through what a student writer does well in an actual undergraduate writing assignment.

We say this throughout *The World Is a Text,* but we will restate it here—always listen to your professors in regard to your assignments. Their requirements may differ from our recommendations. You should first and foremost follow your professor's advice—even if it is different from ours.

It is quite common for instructors to assign a personal essay as the first major assignment in a first-year writing class. To help you with this assignment, we provide an overview of the personal essay. "**How Am I a Text? On Writing Personal Essays**" suggests the ways in which you are a text, worthy and ready to be read. You have a wealth of experiences and a mind full of ideas. This segment offers some very solid advice that should facilitate the move from private topic to public writing.

Finally, we end this segment with some information on researching popular culture texts. The simple act of going to the library and figuring out how and where to look can be intimidating, but we break it down into a manageable process.

Even though we think this section provides a good entrée into the book as a whole, there is a wealth of information out there. Online writing labs like those at Purdue University and the University of Texas are accessible on the Internet and have more detailed information than we can provide here. For more complete descriptions of writing, rhetoric, and the construction of papers, consult our sister publication, *Strategies for Successful Writing: A Rhetoric, Research Guide, Reader, and Handbook,* edited by James A. Reinking, Andrew W. Hart, and Robert von der Osten (published by Pearson).

■ The World Is a Text: Reading

This section begins with Chapter 1 on page 78. Of course, it is the most important section of the book—the part where you will spend most of your time. To make navigation of these chapters easy for you, we designed each chapter the same way, so you should have no trouble maneuvering through the readings, the worksheets, or the questions. You will find the following in each chapter:

    I. Introduction
   II. Worksheet
  III. Readings
      a. Chapter Readings
        1. Questions (This Text: Reading/Your Text: Writing)
      b. Suite of readings
        1. Questions (This Text: Reading/Your Text: Writing)
  IV. Reading Outside the Lines
      a. Classroom exercises
      b. Essay ideas

We have several goals in this book. First, we want you to become a better writer. Second, we want to help you become a better reader of the world generally and a better reader of texts like television and movies specifically. We also want to make you a better reader of essays about those topics. We remain confident that your increased abilities as a reader will, of course, translate into better writing.

To help with these missions, the book focuses both on the texts like public space and art and readings about these texts. Our introductions orient you to the text being read and to some basic questions and issues surrounding these areas of study. Following the introduction in each chapter is a worksheet that focuses on both the readings in the chapter and interpretation of the general text (such as gender or public space). Read these worksheets closely before you read the rest of the chapter. In this edition, we have added "quick guides" to writing about these texts outside of the textbook; we hope they are useful when your professors ask you to analyze nontraditional texts for papers.

Each chapter contains essays that focus on different aspects of texts, such as television and race, and then a group of texts about a particular topic—called "suites"—such as reality television (television) or censorship (visual arts). These grouped essays are to show the different ways you might approach a topic, with the hope that you can use some of these ideas in approaching your own interpretation of television shows or paintings. In analyzing these essays, you will develop a better sense of how writers write.

As you read, your primary objective is to identify the author's main points, the argument or arguments she or he tries to make. This is called the author's "rhetorical strategy," and deciphering a rhetorical strategy is just like reading any other kind of text. Pay attention to the evidence that the author uses to make his or her point. Does the author use statistics, personal experience, research, rumor, or the experiences of others? Read each entry at least twice. On the first reading, make notes. If there is a word you do not recognize or an idea that puzzles you, underline or highlight it. Try to find the author's thesis, and mark that. Underline other important points throughout the piece. On your second read, take your level of analysis one step further by asking questions about the passages you underlined. This process will help your transition into writing.

After each entry there are two sets of questions. The first set, called "**This Text: Reading**," is designed to help you understand the text you just read. The second set, entitled "**Your Text: Writing**," will help get you started writing about the text (public space, music, race, etc.) or the article itself.

Following the texts are some supplemental items that should help with class discussion and will assist you in thinking about a paper topic. In many of the chapters, we have also included a sample student paper (or two). These are papers written by our students on the same topics and texts as you, so that you can see how someone in a similar semiotic situation might turn a text to read into a text to be written. We are not suggesting that you mimic these papers; we want to give you an idea of how such a paper might look. Not all are examples of stellar writing, but if you and your instructors go over them in class, they will help you visualize your own papers.

Finally, because you worked your way through this rather long introduction to reading texts, we thought it might be useful for you if we read our own text. We like this book a lot; in fact, we feel strongly about its premise: that you can become a better writer, a better student, that you can be in the world more fully if you are a critical, thoughtful, insightful reader of the world around you.

Our book relies on the premise that we are always reading and interpreting. *The World Is a Text*'s goals are primarily to help you understand the relationship between reading traditional texts such as novels, short stories, and poems, as well as other less-traditional texts such as movies, the Internet, artworks, and television. Equally important, we also want you to discover that perhaps the most valuable way of learning about the world is through writing about it. Finally, and perhaps most important, we want you to learn to read your surroundings actively. The first two premises are geared more toward academic achievement; the third is oriented toward helping you become a better citizen of the world and a more active participant in the world in which you live.

Some of you may take exception to specific aspects of this book. Particular images, individual essays, or even parts of our introductions may make you mad, they may upset you, and they may challenge some of your most secure assumptions. We think that is good. We believe critical inquiry is part of the college experience. Another kind of problem that you or your instructor may have with our book is what is not in it. We understand that there are many texts we could have included in these chapters. It pains us to think of all the great stories, essays, poems, and artworks that we had to leave out. There are also many different texts we could have read, such as sports, cars, business, and families. But we wanted to leave some things out there for you to explore on your own. Such is the nature of textbooks.

In this edition, we expanded the possibilities for reading by including a special opening chapter constructed entirely of original commissioned essays written especially for this edition of *The World Is a Text*. In addition, we provide links to additional readings as part of our completely online technology chapter.

A note on format: This book is formatted in Modern Language Association style, known by most scholars and teachers as "MLA style." Throughout the book, however, you will see several other styles of formatting, including American Psychological Association (APA), Chicago or Turabian, and Associated Press (AP) style. Each discipline, such as English or history or psychology, has its own preferred form. Because the book covers so many different types of texts and crosses disciplines, and our readers come from many disciplines, we decided to keep to the original style of the article or book portion we are reprinting whenever possible.

The World Is a Text

WRITING

This section provides a number of resources specifically designed to help you with the actual paper-writing process. If you have been in any large bookstore, you have probably seen the dozens, even hundreds, of books devoted to writing, which suggests that there are many different approaches to writing. Not surprisingly, these approaches have changed over time, and it is possible that in the future our suggestions here will seem outdated. That said, you should feel reassured that there is a lot of overlap among those who both teach and write about writing concerning the most effective ways to teach writing. And although every professor is different and every assignment has its own quirks, we are confident that the information here will be of use to you in many ways.

PART I. HOW DO I WRITE A TEXT FOR COLLEGE? MAKING THE TRANSITION FROM HIGH SCHOOL WRITING

by Patty Strong

Writing is thinking. This is what we teachers of college writing believe. Hidden inside that tiny suitcase of a phrase is my whole response to the topic assigned me by my colleague, Jonathan Silverman, one of the authors of the textbook you are currently reading. Knowing my background as a former teacher of high school English, Dr. Silverman asked me to write a piece for students on the differences between writing in high school and writing in college. I have had some time to ponder my answer, and it is this: Writing is thinking. Now that's not very satisfactory, is it? I must unpack that suitcase of a phrase. I will open it up for you, pull out a few well-traveled and wearable ideas, ideas that you may want to try on yourself as you journey through your college writing assignments.

Writing is thinking. I suggest that this idea encompasses the differences between high school writing and the writing expected from students on a college level, not because high school teachers do not expect their students to think, but rather that most students themselves do not approach the writing as an *opportunity to think*. Students might construct many other kinds of sentences with writing as subject: Writing is hard. Writing is a duty. Writing is something I do to prove that I know something.

When I taught high school English, I certainly assigned writing in order to find out what my students knew. Did they, for example, know what I had taught them about the light and dark symbolism in Chapter 18 of *The Scarlet Letter*? Did they know precisely what Huck Finn said after he reconsidered his letter to Miss Watson ("All right, then, I'll *go* to hell!") and did they know what I, their teacher, had told them those words meant in terms of Huck's moral development? Could my students spit this information back at me in neat, tidy sentences? That's not to say I did not encourage originality and creativity in my students' writing, but those were a sort of bonus to the bottom line knowledge I was expecting them to be able to reproduce.

College writing is different precisely because it moves beyond the limited conception that writing is writing what we already know. In college, students write to discover what they do not know, to uncover what they did not know they knew. Students in college should not worry about not having anything to write, because it is the physical and intellectual act of writing, of moving that pen across the page (or tapping the keyboard) that produces the thoughts that become what you have to write. The act of writing will produce the thinking. This thinking need not produce ideas you already know to be true, but should explore meanings and attitude and questions, which are the things that we all wonder and care about.

My discussion of these matters has so far been fairly abstract, caught up in the wind of ideas. Practical matters are of importance here, too, so I will address some points that as a college student you should know. First, your professors are not responsible for your education—you are. While your teachers may in fact care very much that you learn and do well in your coursework, it is not their responsibility to see that you are successful. Your college teacher may not do things you took for granted like reminding you of assignments and tests and paper deadlines. They probably won't accept your illness or the illness of a loved one or a fight with a girlfriend as legitimate excuses for late work. Sloppy work, late work, thoughtless work, tardiness, absences from class—these things are the student's problems. Successful college students accept responsibility for their problems. They expect that consequences will be meted out. Successful students do not offer excuses, lame or otherwise, although they may offer appropriate resolutions. Successful students understand that their education is something they are privileged to own, and as with a dear possession, they must be responsible for managing it. If you wrecked your beloved car, would you find fault with the person who taught you how to drive?

On to the writing task at hand. You will want to write well in college. You probably want to write better and more maturely than you have in the past. To do this, you must be willing to take thinking risks, which are writing risks. I read an interesting quote the other day that I shared with my writing students because I believed it to be true and pretty profound. The American writer Alvin Toffler wrote that "The illiterate of the twenty-first century will not be those who cannot read and write, but those who cannot learn, unlearn, and relearn." And so it is true that when you come to the university for your "higher education," you must be willing to unlearn some old things and relearn them in new ways. That is probably true for just about every academic subject you will explore during your university career, and it is certainly true about the writing courses you will take.

Writing is thinking. Writing will lead you toward thought. Your college writing teachers will expect more of your thinking, thinking you have come to through the process of writing and rewriting. In order to get where you need to be, you must relearn what writing is. You must see that writing is not duty, obligation, and regurgitation, but opportunity, exploration, and discovery. The realization that writing is thinking and that thinking *leads* to writing is the main idea behind this book—the simple notion that the world is a text to be thought and written about. The successful college writer understands that he or she writes not just for the teacher, not just to prove something to the teacher in order to get a grade, but to uncover unarticulated pathways to knowledge and understanding.

PART II. FROM SEMIOTICS TO LENSES: FINDING AN APPROACH FOR YOUR ESSAYS

by Dean Rader and Jonathan Silverman

In the beginning of this book, we talk a great deal about semiotics as that pathway to knowledge and understanding. Formal and informal decoding of cultural and visual cues can be pretty interesting stuff, but you may be wondering what bearing this has on college, grades, and your class. You are going to have to write some papers for this course, and these concepts will help you land on a topic for your paper. Your next step, however, is to select an approach for that paper. Only rarely can essays be simply observational; most of the time you have to turn those observations into arguments. Thus, in order to make an argument, you have to have an approach, or what talk show host Jim Rome might call a "take." There are any number of **approaches** or **lenses** when writing about nontraditional/popular culture/visual texts. We began with **semiotics** as it explains how texts make meaning through signification and connotation. But there are other ways of thinking about texts beyond their theoretical components. In the second part of this introduction, we devote a great number of pages to helping you with the micro aspects of your arguments, but the following paragraphs give you a broad introduction to the macro aspects of your papers by providing some of the language you need in order to approach these texts.

The main approaches we consider here are those of lenses, microscopes, and windows; language and elements of literary interpretation; context, historical and otherwise; social and political approaches, such as race, class, gender, sexual orientation, region, age—and more; and finally, academic disciplines.

LENSES, MICROSCOPES, AND WINDOWS

The idea of a lens is a metaphor for "putting on" a particular point of view in order to think, read, and write about it, in much the same way you might put on sunglasses or reading glasses to see the world in a different way. Aside from the major lenses of race and gender, which we address later, there are other lenses you may put on when reading texts, such as college student or consumer; Democrat or Republican (or Independent); rural, urban, or suburban; Western or Eastern European or Asian; queer (as in Katherine Gantz's essay about *Seinfeld* in Chapter 2 (p. 134), and so on. By thinking either with or through your own perspective or someone else's, you can put into words the point of view you may have already been using.

A microscope takes something small and makes it bigger. In much the same way, you might take a portion of a text or short contained text, examine it closely, and reveal some larger truths. For example, one might examine a particular image, such as Lady Gaga's clothes, or Lisa Simpson's pearls, or the images in your university logo and write about how they represent a particular idea. Such an approach can be part of a larger paper or an examination of its own. For instance, one could write an entire paper on the border of the beach and the forest as a means of understanding the complexities, fears, and tensions of *Lost*.

A window allows one to look outward from a particular perspective, also as a way of exploring a larger truth. One could look at a television show as a way of writing about race or ethnicity or politics. You might, for example, use cable news as a window for the way Americans view politics, a popular CD as a window for a way young people view gender attitudes, or a new shopping mall as a window for how Americans currently view consumption. Later in this introduction, we talk about the movie *Office Space* as a window onto the mind-numbing corporate job.

Your professor may point out that these approaches overlap with some of the ones we discuss further—that's true. But we find that sometimes we as scholars and students get untracked when trying to apply the language of traditional interpretation to nontraditional texts.

LANGUAGE AND ELEMENTS OF LITERARY INTERPRETATION

In a sense, each text has an argument and narrative that invites interpretation, whether it is a movie, an advertisement, or a building. One way of thinking about this is to figure out the "grammar" of whatever the text is. If stories are made up of words and sentences, buildings are made up of beams and concrete, which are almost always chosen deliberately for effect. Movies are made up of scenes, advertisements of discrete images, specific editing choices, camera angles, and soundtracks that when taken together, create a kind of cinematic grammar. Now, think about what a particular element of a building could mean. For example, what effect does a new building constructed entirely of brick have on the viewer? What connotations or meanings do bricks have? Why might a designer put in columns? Why build a new building to look like an old warehouse? When a movie character wears a cowboy hat, what does it mean? A critic in *Rolling Stone* makes the argument that the trumpets in Sufjan Stevens' "Casimir Pulaski Day"—an ode to a dead childhood friend—signal Stevens' displeasure with God. For the critic, that particular sound—the blast of trumpets, which are mentioned in the Bible—is similar to a way a writer might use a description of landscape to make a larger point in a novel or short story.[6]

Metaphor remains one of the most popular approaches to any text. A metaphor is a part of a narrative or text that can be taken for the whole of the text itself or as a small indicator of a larger trend. For example, commentators often describe reality shows as metaphors for the decline in quality television (some suggest such shows reflect a culture's lack of interest in story in favor of spectacle) or as metaphors for the postmodern world we live in (everything is edited, everything is performance). Some argue that *Lost* is a metaphor for the sense of directionlessness and entrapment felt by young people today. In the '90s, grunge music became a metaphor for Generation X's need for controlled catharsis. The Washington Monument, you might argue, is a metaphor for America's soaring ambitions, its towering strength, and, as some have argued, its masculine value system. One could even argue that the movie *The Hangover* is a wacky metaphor for waking up in a post 9-11 world in which nothing makes sense. Metaphors can be tricky, because sometimes they lead an author to read too much into a text or to overinterpret, but metaphor can be an excellent lens for making sense of a popular text.

CONTEXT, HISTORICAL AND OTHERWISE

Reading a work through the lens of context is another way of making sense of a text and of establishing an argument about that text. For instance, understanding the historical situation of the Old South, slavery, and black/white relations helps make sense of *The Adventures of Huckleberry Finn*. Knowing a bit about William Randolph Hearst and the newspaper business in the '20s, '30s, and '40s makes viewing *Citizen Kane* more meaningful. To place something in context means in essence to put something in perspective, often through comparison. If you were writing about *The Cosby Show*, you could put the show into any

---

[6]Rob Sheffield, rev. of *Illinois* by Sufjan Stevens, *Rolling Stone*, 28 July 2005 <http://www.rollingstone.com/reviews/album/7370215/review/7471685/Illinois>. .

number of contexts: family sitcoms, comedies that featured African American characters, the 1980s generally, sitcoms, working-parent shows, comedies that featured former stand-up comedians, and so on. The reason you put nontraditional texts, or all texts for that matter, into context is to gain perspective by looking at similar items. Typically, we think of context in historical or temporal terms—comparing a building to others built in the same era, for example—but context could also mean comparing all baseball stadiums in terms of their playability, seating, and vistas. Finally, context can also refer to genre—the "kind" of text it is. For instance, if you want to write about Metallica, you probably would not compare them to Kronos Quartet, Iron and Wine, or Celine Dion, because those acts are all operating in different genres. For the purposes of your paper, it would be most fruitful to place Metallica in context—perhaps reading them alongside AC/DC, Nirvana, or Kings of Leon.

RACE, CLASS, GENDER, SEXUAL ORIENTATION, REGION, AGE—AND MORE

One's experiences affect one's perspective. As we see in Chapter 4, about race and ethnicity, and Chapter 6, concerning gender, people often write from the larger perspective of these groups, which have been historically discriminated against. But discrimination does not need to drive one's group perspective. Some examples can be found in our suite on Barack Obama images in the chapter on race. As a college student, you probably see things differently from your professor; if you come from a working-class background, you may see things from a different perspective than someone from a more wealthy background. In a famous essay on economic class, critic Michael Parenti reads *Pretty Woman* through the lens of class, arguing that the movie upholds traditional upper-class patriarchal values. On the opposite end, the wonderful British comedy *The Full Monty* can be read as a celebration of working-class men and women. You will see such readings throughout this book, both in the gender and race chapters but in other chapters as well. One of the funniest essays in *The World Is a Text* is Gantz's piece on *Seinfeld*, in which she reads the popular sitcom through the lens of queer theory.

ACADEMIC DISCIPLINES

This book might be part of a course called "Writing Across the Disciplines." Although there are different definitions of what that means, generally it signals that your professor or department wants you to learn to write in your chosen discipline or major. Social scientists read texts differently than artists. Scientists approach information in a distinct way, as do semioticians, literary scholars, and cultural critics. In Chapter 1, physicist Brandon Brown reads a science lab. His lens is informed by an entirely different set of criteria than if an architect were reading the same lab or if the reader were an insurance adjuster. The accoutrement of disciplinary readings is vocabulary, prose style, and citation. Sometimes this simply means that you need to be attuned to the citation style of your discipline; English departments, for example, use the Modern Language Association style, known as MLA, whereas psychology departments use the American Psychology Association style, or APA. History departments often use Chicago (or Turabian), whereas other disciplines may have their own styles.

Disciplinary approaches can also affect issues of subjectivity and objectivity. For example, in literary studies, film studies, and media studies, writers often ground their writing in argument, interpretation, and insight. But, in many social sciences, soft sciences, and the hard sciences, scholars rely on data and objective proof. Thus, a scientist, a film scholar, and a political scientist would each read Al Gore's movie *An Inconvenient Truth* through three very different lenses, because they work in three utterly distinct disciplines.

But this might also mean a larger issue than of writing style or content. This book contains writing more focused on English-related subjects, but throughout, you find writings done in other disciplines as well. *The World Is a Text* is proud to offer a mix of various disciplinary readings, each reflecting the format of the field.

LANDING ON AN APPROACH: AN ENTRÉE TO THE ESSAY ITSELF

Your professor may have a specific approach in mind for you, but he or she may not. In general, the approach you take will probably mirror your own lenses. If you were raised on a farm in Ohio, you will likely always, in some way or another, look at people, places, and things through the Ohio-rural-farm lens. Thus, you may read a movie like *Field of Dreams* (even though it is set in Iowa) quite differently than a baseball player who grew up in Puerto Rico. As you try to land on an approach for your essay, think about what sort of lenses you tend to look through on a daily basis.

But we would also be lax if we did not suggest that such essential perspectives can be changed. For example, most people who live or work in Manhattan will tell you that New York has transformed them, has made them look at the world differently—even if they came from small towns in the Midwest. Perhaps more important is your willingness to try on approaches or lenses. One of the foremost experiences one of your authors had was learning about others developed, theoretical perspectives on the world around them; fellow graduate students were feminists, or had race-oriented perspectives, or were highly political, or had completely absorbed even more obscure perspectives. By trying to understand others' perspectives, both through reading and discussion, one can become a better reader of texts.

PART III. HOW DO I WRITE ABOUT POPULAR AND VISUAL CULTURE TEXTS? A TOUR THROUGH THE WRITING PROCESS

We begin by underscoring how important being a good reader is for the writing process. Both processes are about discovery, insight, ordering, and argument. The process of writing, however, differs from the product of writing. When we say product, we mean the produced or finished version—the completed paper that you submit to your instructor. The writing process is the always complex, sometimes arduous, often frustrating, and frequently rushed series of events that eventually lead you to the finished product. There are a lot of theories about writing, so we will not bore you with an overview of all of them. Chances are your instructor or your institution's writing center has a series of handouts or guidelines that will help you along the way, but we thought we would take you on a quick tour of what we see as the highlights of the writing process, with an added emphasis on building a good first paragraph and building sound arguments.

Of course, your process may not be exactly the same as this one nor might be the same for every assignment. In this edition, we have added a series of questions and answers with our writers—they are scattered throughout the book. One thing that stands out in reading them together is how differently people approach assignments. For example, Katherine Gantz describes writing her essay about *Seinfeld* as a process that lasted almost a month, while Alessandro Portelli, writing about the country singer Loretta Lynn, said he wrote his essay with one big effort. You might imagine yourself more Portelli than Gantz, but the majority of our writers here said that writing an essay took time—from settling on an approach to a topic, doing research if appropriate, and then writing a draft. Some writers wrote a draft without stopping, while others stopped and edited along the way. But almost all the writers here got feedback from others, and even after we accepted them, some of them received feedback from us. The lesson we learned from reading our writers' comments about their process is that while everyone has an individual approach to writing, most recognized that constructing a paper is actually made up of several interrelated tasks that often overlap. You probably know this yourself from putting together your own paper.

That begins with understanding the assignment.

UNDERSTANDING THE ASSIGNMENT

This is usually the easiest part of the writing process, but it, too, is important. And because you are learning how to be savvy readers of various texts, this task should be easy for you. First, you should read the assignment for the paper as you would read a poem or an advertisement. Look for textual clues that seem particularly important. In fact, we recommend making a list of questions about the assignment itself, such as:

- What questions do I have to answer in order to complete or answer the assignment? Do I have a research or writing question that my paper must answer?
- Does my assignment contain any code words, such as "compare," "analyze," "research," "unpack," or "explore"? If so, what do these terms mean?
- What text or texts am I supposed to write about? Do I understand these texts?
- What is my audience? For whom am I writing?
- What are the parameters of the assignment? What can I do? What can I not do? Is there anything I do not understand before beginning?

One of the biggest mistakes students make is paying too little attention to the assignment. Like any text, it contains textual cues to help you understand it.

FREEWRITING AND BRAINSTORMING

Freewriting and brainstorming are crucial to the writing process because they generally produce your topic. Freewriting involves the random and uncensored act of writing down anything that comes into your mind on a particular topic. There are any number of ways to freewrite; some teachers and students like visually oriented methods, whereas others prefer a straightforward "Write all you can down in five minutes" approach. Some of our students set a stopwatch at two minutes, and within that two minutes, write down anything and everything that pops into their heads. When the two minutes are up, they review the list to see if any pattern or ideas emerge. From this list of random stuff, you can generally narrow down a topic. Let us say your assignment is to analyze the film *The Return of the King*, and you see that you jotted down several things that have to do with the way the movie looks. From that, you could decide that you want to write on the innovative "look" of the movie.

At this point, you can move on to brainstorming. Here, you take a blank piece of paper, or sit down in front of a blank computer screen, and write the topic of your paper across the top: The "look" of *The Return of the King*. Now, write down everything that pops into your head about the look of *The Return of the King*. See if you can come up with 10 to 20 ideas, observations, or questions. When you are done, look closely at your list. Does a pattern emerge? Are there certain questions or ideas that seem to fit together? Let us say you have written "cool effects," "lots of action," "scary creatures," "mythical overtones," "religious symbols," "good vs. evil," "darkness vs. light," "beautiful scenery," "the camera angles were very unique," "very serious," "it felt like fantasy," and "good wins, evil loses." Based on these observations, it looks like you could write a paper about good versus evil, or perhaps certain symbols in the film, like light and dark or white and black. Or, you could take things in a different direction and talk about how the "look" of the movie (camera angles, the setting, the colors, and the effects) make a certain argument or contribute to the theme in some way. Yet another possibility is to combine these observations into a paper that looks at the theme *and* the form.

The goal here is to try to home in on your topic—the overall subject of your paper. At this point, your topic does not have to be perfectly formulated, but you should be getting an idea of how you might narrow your topic down to something that you can feasibly write a paper about. It is possible—even likely—that as you start plotting an outline, a more defined topic will emerge.

OUTLINING

Once you have your topic, you need to organize your paper. Outlines are helpful because they provide a visual map of your paper so that you can see where you're going and where you have been. An outline is also useful in helping you see if your ideas fit together, if the paper is coherent, and if the paper is equally distributed among your various points. If you find yourself getting stuck or suffering from writer's block, an outline might help push you along. In addition, an outline presents your ideas in a logical format, and it shows the relationship among the various components of your paper.

The truth is that deciding on these various components is a process of trial and error. We change our minds all the time. So, as authors of this text, we are reluctant to say that one approach is better than another. Writing is always an organic process—that is, it grows at its own pace in its own way, and as a writer, you will likely need to adjust to accommodate where your ideas want to go.

No doubt, your instructor will talk a great deal about developing a **thesis** (which is the main argument or focus of your essay—what you argue about your topic), and he or she may encourage you to make this thesis part of your outline. This is a common strategy. The only problem is that you may make an outline with an idea of a thesis, finish the outline, and decide you need to change your thesis. At that point, you should make yet another outline. During the writing process, you may hone your thesis yet again, at which point, you will probably want to draft another outline so that you stay on course given your new thesis. Our point here is that there is no clearcut process when you are talking about the very fuzzy beginning stages of writing a paper. You should do whatever works for you—whatever leads to the most organized product.

Unlike most other books, we decided to combine a section on outlining and thesis-making because for us, the two go hand in hand. Most suggest that writers figure out a thesis *before* doing an outline. Our experience, however, tells us that arriving at a thesis is often hard, and we do not always know exactly what we want to say about our topic until we get a visual map of the paper. In fact, most of the time, you arrive at your thesis after the first draft of the essay. Just remember that the first outline you make does not have to be the last outline—you can and should change it as you see fit.

Now, to that visual map. Traditionally, an outline states your topic (maybe states your thesis), enumerates your main points and supporting arguments in Roman numerals and, beneath the Roman numerals, lists your evidence in letters. For an essay with two main points, an outline might look something like this:

THE TITLE OF MY ESSAY
    I. Introduction (1–2 paragraphs)
        Thesis: This is my thesis statement, if I have one at this point
    II. My first point (2–4 paragraphs)
        a. My supporting evidence
        b. My supporting evidence
    III. My second point (2–6 paragraphs)
        a. My supporting evidence
            1. Further evidence, graphs, statistics, perhaps
        b. My supporting evidence
            1. Further evidence
    IV. My smart conclusion (1–2 paragraphs)

Notice how the outline helps flesh out an organizing idea, even if it is in the most general way. The final outline almost never matches up with the first version, but an outline can help you see the strengths and weaknesses of your organization, and it can help you think in an organized way.

Still, outlining in this manner may not suit everyone. Some students (and professors) do not like outlining, because they do not refer to the outline when writing, and they feel like the whole process is a waste of time. Others like to outline at various stages of writing; some outline after they have written a draft to make sure they have covered everything they wanted to cover. Those approaches are okay as well; so is writing an outline that is less formal in nature. At various times, we have written outlines that are barely outlines—just a mere list of points. Other times, we have written outlines with topic sentences of every one of our paragraphs. The approach you take will depend not only on class requirements, but also on the topic of your paper, your knowledge of the topic, and the amount of research required.

The reason we are committed to outlining is that it separates to some degree the thinking and composing stages of writing; if you know more or less what you want to say before you start putting words on paper, the more likely you are to write a clear and thoughtful draft, one that needs less extensive revision. The thinking aspect of outlining is why it is at once difficult and rewarding.

CONSTRUCTING A GOOD THESIS

Now that you have an idea of the work an outline can do, we can move on to helping you construct a **thesis**. As stated earlier, a thesis is the argument that you make about your topic. It is the main point, the assertion, you set forth in your essay.

We should say at the outset that the term "thesis" is only one possible term for the paper's argument. Some instructors like the term "claim," some like "focus," still others like "controlling idea." Regardless of what term you use, the concept is the same. The thesis is the idea you propose in your paper—it is not a statement of fact, but rather a claim, an idea.

The most important first step is to distinguish among a **topic**, **a thesis**, and **a thesis statement**. One of the great mistakes students make is that they assume a topic is a thesis. A topic is merely the avenue to the freeway that is the thesis, the appetizer to the main course. Let us say you are writing a paper about Affirmative Action. The topic is what you write about, which is Affirmative Action. Your thesis is the argument you make about Affirmative Action. Your thesis statement is the actual articulation, the statement or statements in which you unpack or explain your thesis. Now, a thesis statement does not have to be (nor should it be) one simplified sentence; in fact, it could and probably should be two or three sentences, or even a full paragraph. (A book can have a thesis statement that goes on for pages.)

We might break down these three components as follows:

Topic: What you are writing about (Affirmative Action)

Thesis: What you argue about your topic (Affirmative Action is a necessary law)

Thesis statement: The reason or explanation of your overall thesis—this usually appears in the first or second paragraph of your essay. For example: (Affirmative Action is a necessary law because it prevents discriminatory hiring practices. Minorities, women, people with disabilities, and gay and lesbian workers have suffered discrimination for decades. Affirmative Action not only redresses past wrongs, but also sets a level playing field for all job applicants. In short, it ensures democracy.)

Generally, the topic causes you the least anxiety. Your instructor will help you with your topic and may even provide one for you. In any case, you cannot start a paper without a topic.

The real task is figuring out your **thesis**. Many students feel anxious if they do not have a thesis when they begin the writing process, but that is normal, and in a way preferable in the quest to find a solid argument. Sometimes it is enough to have what we might refer to as a thesis question—a question that when answered through writing and research, actually reveals to you your thesis. Or you might have what we call a "working thesis," one that is too broad for a final paper, but is specific enough to guide you through the writing process. Often you must write a first draft of your essay before a thesis finally emerges. Remember that writing is exploration and discovery, so it may take some freewriting, brainstorming, outlining, and drafting before you land on a thesis. But stay with the process—you will eventually find what you want to say.

Perhaps the most confusing aspect of the thesis for students is the realization that a good thesis means you might be wrong. In fact, you know you are on the road to a good thesis if you think someone might be able to argue against your point. Writing is grounded in rhetoric, which, as we discussed earlier, is the art of persuasion. Your goal in your papers is not necessarily to change your audience's mind, but to get them to consider your ideas. Thus, your thesis needs to be something manageable, something reasonable that you can argue about with confidence and clarity.

The most effective strategy we found with helping our students understand a thesis is to use the example of the **hypothesis**. As most of you know, a **hypothesis** is an educated guess. A thesis is the same thing. In Greek, thesis means "a proposition" or "an idea"; hypo is Greek for "under" or "beneath." So, literally, a hypothesis is a "proposition laid down." Your thesis is the same thing. It is not a fact; it is not a statement. It is an idea, a proposition that you lay down on paper and then set out to support. You are not absolutely sure that Affirmative Action is a necessary law, but you believe it is. You are pretty confident in your stance, but you also know that someone could write an essay arguing why Affirmative Action should be abolished. This possibility of disagreement is how you know you have a good thesis, because you must provide sound reasons and convincing examples to support your assertion about the necessity for Affirmative Action.

Why must a thesis be an educated guess? Because if a thesis is a statement of fact, there is literally nothing to argue. If your thesis is "Affirmative Action is a law that was designed to prevent discrimination," you have simply stated a fact. There is nothing at stake, nothing to debate. Even a thesis like "Affirmative Action is an important law" is rather weak. Virtually no one would suggest that Affirmative Action is not important. It has been extraordinarily important in American culture. So, again, that is not the best thesis you could come up with, although it remains better than our first example. However, arguing that it is a *necessary* law makes your thesis more provocative, more risky. Therefore, it is likely to draw interest and get people excited. Readers will want to see your reasons and think about the examples you provide.

Let us break it down even further, using an example from this book. Say you are writing about visual art. Your topic is censorship and the *Sensation* exhibit—our book features a reproduction of the painting exhibited at the Brooklyn Museum that prompted Mayor Rudolph Giuliani to threaten to shut down the exhibit—Chris Ofili's *Holy Virgin Mary*. We also print Diana Mack's discussion of the exhibition in the "Is It Art?" suite. Here are some sample theses for that topic.

Weak thesis: The *Sensation* exhibit in New York raised a lot of questions about censorship and public money.

This is a weak thesis statement because it is a statement of fact. No one would debate this point.

Better thesis: The *Sensation* exhibit in New York deserved to run its course despite public opinion.

This is a better thesis statement because it proposes something a bit controversial. Many people, including the mayor of New York at the time, could argue against this thesis. That tells you that you are on the right track.

Even better thesis: It is important that the *Sensation* exhibit in New York was allowed to happen without being censored, despite political opposition to the content of some of the pieces. Freedom of speech and freedom of expression are critical parts of American ideas of liberty, and silencing works of art meant for public consumption is in violation of our most basic rights.

This thesis statement is even better because it provides a bit more precision, and it gives a reason for the author's stance. It is easier, then, for this writer to prove the thesis because the reason is already articulated. Homing in on a good thesis is the foundation for building a good paragraph—which, in turn, is the foundation for building a good essay.

BUILDING AN OPENING PARAGRAPH: A CASE STUDY

The opening paragraph for your essay does a great deal of work, both for your essay and for your audience. For your audience, it sets up your argument and informs them what is going to happen in the remaining pages. In the paper, it functions as the road map, pointing readers down certain avenues, and telling them to avoid others. If your reader is confused after the first paragraph, she may remain confused for a good bit of your essay, and that is never what you want.

An opening paragraph should do a number of things—it should engage the reader's interest with an entertaining or provocative opening sentence, and it should provide the road map for the rest of the paper. In addition, your opening paragraph is typically the home for your thesis statement (although some professors might have different preferences on whether your thesis must go in the first paragraph). It is also the face for your paper, so it should be well organized, moving from a general observation to the more-specific thesis statement (think of an upside down pyramid—broad going down to narrow). For the writer, the opening paragraph is critical because it provides the formula for working through the issues of the essay itself. A vague opener provides too little direction; a paragraph that tries to argue three or four different topics never gets on the right track; and a paragraph that does not make an argument has a tendency to go nowhere, because it keeps restating facts instead of staking out a position and making an argument.

The purpose of this section is to avoid these pitfalls. Here, we give you some models of opening paragraphs before and after revision to show you how a thorough revising process can improve your opening paragraph, strengthen your thesis, and provide a good entrée into your essay.

Let us say you are writing about the movie *Office Space*. You know that you like the movie. You think it is funny, and all of your friends think it is funny. During parties and over lunch, you trade lines with each other. You all agree that the movie speaks to your generation in some odd way, but you are having trouble figuring out *exactly* what you want to say about it. You decide (wisely) to make a list of all possible observations and some questions about those observations:

- *Office Space* speaks to people of my generation. (Why is this important?)
- *Office Space* is funny. (But that's not an argument). *Office Space* is the funniest movie of the last 5 years. (But how would I prove that?)
- *Office Space* makes a connection with college students like no other movie. (Is this true? What about *Lord of the Rings* or *Caddyshack*?)
- *Office Space* was not a huge box office hit, but it is wildly popular among college students. (Maybe its biggest audience is college students?)
- We like *Office Space* because it is funny.
- We like *Office Space* because it is about rebellion.
- It is anti-establishment, anti-corporate.
- Maybe we identify with it because it is also anti-institution, like school or college.
- *Office Space* appeals to college students because they can identify with the anti-institution theme. (But we are all part of institutions—school, jobs.)
- We like *Office Space* because it is anti-institution and yet not. (It is kind of subversive, but not *really*. The people in it are kind of lazy.)

This is a pretty good list. We can likely get some kind of argument from it.

The trick is finding something that is truly an argument. Saying that *Office Space* is funny is not much of an argument. Most would agree with this, and really, who cares if it is funny or not? That does not help us understand the movie any better. Arguing that college students like it is also overstating the obvious. The key is to explain why this particular movie appeals to college students at this particular time. Of course, one could talk about the fantasy of stealing a million dollars or getting a date with Jennifer Aniston, or the bigger fantasy of enjoying working construction over being in a cubicle, but those kinds of ideas occur in other movies. What sets this movie apart is the idea of being subversive (sort of) in an institutional setting. You want your paper to be unique, and you want it to tell your readers something they might actually find compelling. Readers can usually tell after an opening paragraph if there is anything in there for them, so as you craft your essay, ask yourself—Am I giving pertinent information? Is my argument interesting?

So, the first try at an opening paragraph might look like this:

> *Office Space,* directed by Mike Judge, has become a classic movie for college students. It's funny plot, it's witty dialogue and stance on corporate life appeals to students across disciplines and states. One might wonder why a movie that was not a box-office sensation has become a cult sensation among college students, but it's clear that *Office Space* appeals to students in a number of ways. Perhaps the biggest way is the movie's theme of rebellion. Students can identify with the movie's anti-corporate message.

Okay, so what do we see here? On a micro level, there are some problems with the prose: the rogue apostrophe in *it's* (first and second sentences) has to go; the phrase "across disciplines and states" is vague and not really helpful; "box-office sensation" is a cliché and also vague; "number of ways" also does not do much work. Still, there is also a great deal of information here to work with. The beginnings of our thesis probably rest in the last two sentences—it is there that we make our argument. On closer examination, however, it would appear that the last sentence is not really an argument. Almost no one would disagree with that statement, so proving it would be easy but, ultimately, pointless. Essays that merely sum up what everyone agrees with do little to further our understanding of the issue or topic at hand. From an entertainment perspective, a good opening paragraph needs to give us reasons to keep reading, so the next version should incorporate some reasons why the movie appeals to students. It should also be a bit more sophisticated and precise. So, in the next version, list some reasons the movie appeals to college students, and give the date of the film, for starters. And do a bit of research and see what you can come up with.

Draft two might come out like this:

> *Office Space* (1999), directed by Mike Judge of *Beavis and Butthead* fame, has become an underground classic among American college students. It is not uncommon to overhear students quoting entire passages from the movie, and there is even an *Office Space* drinking game. Though the movie features a couple of funny subplots involving dating and stealing a million dollars, the real draw of the movie lies in the fact that it is rather anti-establishment. The main character of the film does not simply quit his job—he actually stops working. What's more, he gets rewarded for it through a promotion. Thus, *Office Space* sends a message to college students that when they enter the same corporate environment, they too can be rewarded for rebelling against the corporate mindset.

Wow, what happened here? On one hand, the paragraph is much stronger. Notice the increased specificity: American college students, examples of how students enjoy the movie, more active verbs instead of being verbs (is, are); even some details from the movie itself. But, beyond all that, the thesis has gone off in a different direction! Our argument was that students relate to the movie's theme of rebellion; now, it would appear that we are arguing that students like the movie because they will get rewarded for rebelling. Is that what we want to argue? Is that the reason students like the movie? Does the appeal of the movie lie in the fact that students relate to it, or that it gives them hope? What if it is both? Is there a way to work both into the thesis? Generally, the more precise you are, and the more thorough your thesis is, the better; however, yours has gone off in a different direction! In truth, probably both things appeal to students, so why not strengthen the thesis and the essay by making arguments about both?

The resulting third draft:

Mike Judge took slacking to new heights with his hilarious cartoon *Beavis and Butthead,* which chronicled the lives of two under-achieving teen-age boys who had a great deal of fun doing a great deal of nothing. Judge's first movie involving real humans is also about doing nothing, but this time it is recent college graduates who find themselves working in cubicles for a mind-numbing corporation. Despite the fact that *Office Space* (1999) was not a huge hit at the box office, it has become an underground classic across university campuses. Students quote entire scenes to each other from memory, *Office Space* T-shirts abound, and there is even an *Office Space* drinking game. One might wonder why a movie with no real stars except for Jennifer Aniston has made such an impact on this generation of students. Though there are some funny subplots involving dating and stealing a million dollars from a corporation, the main action of the movie comes when the main character, Peter, decides to stop working but winds up getting a promotion. Thus, the movie appeals to students not simply because it champions rebelling against the man, but it suggests one might get rewarded for doing so. On one hand, students identify with the desire to completely stop working, and they like the idea that things might turn out better for them if they do. Ultimately, students are drawn to *Office Space* because it tells them they can be anti-establishment and successful at the same time.

This version is better not because it is longer, but because it provides detail, it is precise, and it features a thorough three-sentence thesis statement. Readers know from this opening paragraph that we are going to read an essay that 1) makes an argument and 2) makes an argument about the two ways/reasons the movie appeals to college students.

Because we have a focused thesis, we can now go into a lot of detail in the rest of our paper about how and why students related to specific scenes and concepts, and we can also make some interesting observations about "safe rebellion" and rewards. From here on, the writing process involves "proving" and elaborating on the thesis we just wrote.

A note here on opening paragraphs: One of the authors believes that writing the opening paragraph should come closer to the end of the composing process rather than the beginning. Although getting a thesis early is important, writing an opening paragraph before you know what you want to say might mean you must extensively revise the paragraph or scrap it altogether. Some writers, however, need to "begin with beginning"—they cannot go on until they know exactly what their argument is going to be. Ultimately, your preference regarding the writing process is less important than the finished product.

Finally, avoid writing a clichéd introduction. Do not use phrases like "since the beginning of time," which is much too general and tells us little. Also, resist using a dictionary definition of an important word. These two strategies should almost never be used in college writing. If you want to use a time construction, confine it to specific knowable time, such as "the recent past" or "in the 1990s." If you find yourself drifting toward a dictionary definition, try defining it yourself, looking in a more specialized source such as a book about the subject (but be careful to cite), or engaging the definition you find by arguing with it or refining it. *Never* write: "The dictionary defines [your subject here] as . . ." — there are many different dictionaries, all of which define words differently.

If you take your opening paragraph seriously, use it as a method of organization, and make it interesting, you will be off to a good start with your paper.

BUILDING GOOD PARAGRAPHS

Building a good paper is relatively simple, once you understand the formula. By formula, we do *not* necessarily mean a standard five-paragraph essay. Instead of thinking of your paper in terms of numbers of paragraphs, think in terms of **points** or **reasons**. By "points," we mean ideas, concepts, observations, or reasons that support the argument you make in your thesis. The units that help you organize these points are the paragraphs themselves. This section helps you get a handle on how to structure your paragraphs so that you make the most of your supporting points.

For a typical undergraduate paper, you do not want too many or too few points. If you are arguing about Affirmative Action, how many reasons do you want to include in your paper to support your thesis? Do you want seven? No, that's too many. One? That's too few. Generally, we suggest two to four points or reasons for a standard three- to six-page paper. For a longer paper, like a research paper, you may want four or five points to drive home your argument. But the danger of including too many points in your paper is that, unless you can supply ample evidence for each point, an overabundance of points winds up having the opposite of the intended effect. Rather than bolstering your argument by the sheer number of reasons, you tend to weaken your argument because you dilute your points through an overabundance of reasons and a lack of evidence. In other words, it is better to write three or four paragraphs for one or two points than to write five paragraphs for five points. Write more about less as opposed to less about more.

The key to making and supporting your assertions is the paragraph. Paragraphs are the infrastructure of your essay; they frame and support the arguments you make. Every paragraph is like a mini-essay. Just as your essay has a thesis statement, so does your paragraph have a **topic sentence**—a sentence in which you lay out the main idea for that paragraph. Once you write your topic sentence, then you have to provide evidence to support the claim you have made in your topic sentence. Each paragraph has its own topic and its own mini-assertion, and when taken together, all of these paragraphs work together to support the overall thesis of the entire essay.

Topic sentences should establish the mini-argument of your paragraph. Try to make them assertive and focused, because they serve as a small map to the theme of your paragraph. Some examples:

> ***Weak topic sentence:*** This is a plan one finds in the library.
> ***Weak topic sentence:*** *Family Guy* first aired in 2002.

These are weak topic sentences because they simply state facts rather than advance an argument. Note the topic sentences of the previous two paragraphs. Neither are over-the-top in terms of making an argument, but they both make assertions. Following are topic sentences from a freshman essay on the overuse of medication in the United States:

- The increasing over-use of medication has been made possible by the "quick-fix" mentality that has become prevalent in our society.
- A big factor leading to the increasing amount of over-medication is the rampant advertising of new drugs by the pharmaceutical companies.
- In addition to our desire for quick and easy solutions, America's preoccupation with youth and physical perfection is also to blame in the overflow of drug consumption in our society.

This last example is particularly good because it includes a **transition** ("**in addition to our desire for quick and easy solutions**") in the topic sentence. The topic of the preceding paragraph focuses on America's desire for quick and easy solutions, and the author used the topic sentence not only to advance her idea about youth and physical perfection, but she also reminded the reader of her previous topic, making her overall argument feel connected, part of a piece. Remember—make assertions in your topic sentences.

Once you have a clear, focused topic sentence, it is time to move on to the rest of your paragraph. For instance, say your topic sentence is: "The *Sensation* exhibit was an important test for American culture because First Amendment rights were at stake." What might be your next move? You should probably quote the First Amendment, or at least part of it. Then, explain how the *Sensation* exhibit was protected by the First Amendment. Give examples of specific pieces from the show that are pertinent to this discussion. This is also the right time to bring in quotes from other people that support your assertions. If you quote from another source, or if you quote from a primary text, be sure you explain how the passage you quote supports your thesis. (And, of course, cite the quote's origin.) The quote cannot explain itself—you must tell your audience why that quote is important, why and how the statistics you include are evidence the reader should pay attention to.

Finally, end your paragraphs well. The most common mistake students make when writing paragraphs is that they tend to trail off. Make that last sentence a kind of connector—make it tie everything in the paragraph back to the topic sentence. When possible, also reinforce the fact that your paragraphs are working together by writing transition sentences from one paragraph to the next. For example, a good transition in the essay on the *Sensation* exhibit would acknowledge the topic of the preceding paragraph and lead into the topic for the paragraph at hand. Such a sentence might look like this: "Not only did the *Sensation* exhibit reinforce First Amendment rights of the artists, it underscored the right of viewers and museum-goers to enjoy art their tax dollars helped support." Note how this sentence refers to the subject of the previous paragraph (artistic freedom) and also how it informs us of the topic we are about to engage (publicly funded art).

Start on your next paragraph with the same model. Keep doing this until you have built yourself a paper. Then go back and revise and edit, revise and edit, revise and edit. The key to building good paragraphs is using them to make arguments. The next section walks you through that process.

DRAFTING THE WHOLE ESSAY

Although we spend a great deal of energy explaining various strategies for composing a paper, it still comes down to the actual work of thinking about a topic, doing your own method of prewriting (outlining, brainstorming, etc.), and putting the words on paper. In other words, you still have to write that first draft.

Sentence by sentence, and paragraph by paragraph, you start building your paper. Remember to give as much detail as possible. Include examples from the text you are writing about, and try to avoid plot summary or unnecessary description. Remember: *Analyze, do not summarize.* In other words, do not simply provide information—make sense of information for us.

Once you finish your first draft, you may discover that buried somewhere in your closing paragraph is the very good articulation of the thesis you have been trying to prove for several pages. This happens because, as we have said, writing is a discovery process. So by working through your ideas, your arguments, your textual examples, you start to focus on what you have been trying to say all along.

Now that you have a better idea of what you want to say, it is time for the real work—editing and revising.

EDITING AND REVISING, EDITING AND REVISING, EDITING AND REVISING

The single biggest mistake student writers make is turning in their first draft. The first draft is often little more than a blueprint—it is merely an experiment. In the editing and revising stage, you convert the process of writing into the written product. Here, you turn a bad paper into a decent one, or a good paper into a great one. You can clear up confusing sentences, focus your argument, correct bad grammar, and, most important, make your paper clearer and more thorough. Students think that they are good writers if papers come easily. This is the biggest myth in writing. A good paper happens through several stabs at editing and revising.

There are a number of strategies for editing and revising, so we'll give you a couple of our favorites. First, when you are ready to edit and revise, read your paper through backward. Start at the very end, and read it backward, one sentence at a time. This forces you to slow down and see the sentence as its own entity. It is probably the most useful strategy for correcting your own writing. Even more helpful is getting a peer to read your paper. Another person can point out errors, inconsistencies, or vague statements that you may miss because you are too close to the process. An often painful but very effective way of editing is reading your paper out loud. The authors often do this, especially when presenting their work to other people.

Finally, we also recommend that although you may write hot, you should edit cold. What we mean by this is that you need to step back from your paper when you edit. Look at it objectively. Try not to get caught up in your prose or your argument. Work on being succinct and clear. Practically, this means not working on your paper for a period of time, even if that period is hours, not days. As professors, we are well aware that you may wait until the last minute to write a paper. Although we are not endorsing this way of composing, you still need to find a way to step away from the paper and come back to it to get some perspective on what you have written.

This is also the time go to back over the arguments you made. (Here we introduce some terms that you see again in the upcoming "A Guide for Building Arguments" section.) Look at your **logos** and **pathos**—are they appropriate? Have you made argumentative errors? Are you guilty of using fallacies? Do you supply enough good evidence to support your assertions? Do you end your paragraphs well?

It may take several drafts (in fact, it should) before you feel comfortable with your paper. So, we recommend at least three different passes at editing and revising before turning in your paper. We advocate going back over and looking at your language one last time. Do not use words that are not part of your vocabulary; try to avoid stating the obvious. Be original, be honest, and be engaged. We urge you, above all else, to think complexly, but write simply. A note here from one of the authors: In writing a recent book, he has, conservatively, rewritten his introduction to a chapter more than thirty times. Revising is often a great deal of work, and sometimes rewriting takes multiple drafts.

Finally, we want to reiterate here that writing is not easy or simple for anyone. Although you may think that you are not a strong writer, and that others write more easily and naturally, the truth is that all "good" writers spend a significant amount of time revising their work. In fact, most good writers enjoy this part of the composing process, because it is the time when they see their writing actually turn into something worth sharing with someone else.

TURNING IN THE FINISHED PRODUCT

The most enjoyable part of the process! Double check spelling and grammar issues. If you did a research paper, check your citations and go over your Bibliography or Works Cited pages. Confirm you did *not* plagiarize.

Turn in the paper and go celebrate!

SOME FINAL TIPS–A RECAP

- Distinguish between a topic and a thesis.
- Your thesis does not have to be one concise sentence; it can be several sentences, perhaps even an entire paragraph. It might even be helpful to think of your thesis as your focus, your idea that you are trying to support.
- "Thesis" comes from "hypothesis." A hypothesis is an educated guess. So is your thesis. It is an educated guess, an idea that you are trying to support. You do not have to develop an over-the-top airtight argument; you simply want your reader to consider your point of view.
- Writing is conversation; it is dialogue. Keep asking questions of yourself, your writing, and your topic. Ask yourself, "Why is this so?" Make sure you answer. Be specific; be thorough.
- Consider your audience. You should never assume they have read the text you are writing about, so do not toss around names or scenes without explaining them a little. It is called "giving context." There is a big difference between giving context (valuable information) and summarizing the plot (regurgitation).
- Make good arguments. Use logos, pathos, and ethos appropriately. Try to avoid fallacies.

PART IV. HOW DO I ARGUE ABOUT POPULAR CULTURE TEXTS? A GUIDE FOR BUILDING GOOD ARGUMENTS

KNOWING YOUR ARGUMENTS

As we suggest in the previous section, building a good paper is dependent on making good **arguments** and supporting them with solid evidence. In contemporary American culture, "argument" tends to carry negative connotations. Few like getting into arguments, and no one wants to be seen as an argumentative person. However, in writing, "argument" has a slightly different meaning. When we talk about arguments or argumentation, what we mean is staking out a position or taking a stance. In writing and rhetoric, "to argue" means to put forth an assertion or a proposition, and to support that position with evidence. If you are using this book, then most of the writing you do in your class involves making an argument and backing it up. So, in your regular, nonwriting life, feel free to go on avoiding arguments, but in your writing life, we urge you to think positively about the prospect of making a compelling argument.

Before we go into specific kinds of arguments, it might be useful to think about why we make arguments. In academic settings, it is important to be able to argue a specific point because almost all information is debatable, particularly in the arts, humanities, and social sciences. Should welfare be abolished? Is capital punishment moral? Is Picasso's *Guernica* transgressive? Is the Transamerica pyramid in San Francisco an ugly building? Is Tiger Woods a jerk? Is there a relationship between Christianity and Buddhism? Should we discount the poetry of Ezra Pound, T. S. Eliot, and e. e. cummings because of some anti-Semitic passages? These are important questions with no clear answers. Accordingly, you need to be able to justify or explain your opinions on these issues. Holding an opinion and backing up that opinion is argument, and we engage in this kind of argumentation all the time. What is the best album of the '90s? What is the best horror movie? What five books would you take to a desert island, and why? These are fun arguments, and perhaps mostly intellectual exercises, but down the road, being able to argue persuasively might be important in a job ("Here is why we should choose Bob's marketing strategy"), a relationship ("Honey, I know you think I should get an MBA, but let me tell you why an MFA in creative writing is better for me and the kids"), to making purchases ("Let me give you seven reasons why you do not need that Hawaiian shirt"). In fact, in putting this book together the co-authors had daily (but friendly and funny) arguments over what readings to publish, the tone of this very chapter, and what should go on the cover. Finally, knowing how arguments work also helps you discover more fully your own stance on a particular issue. Often, understanding how you feel about a topic is difficult if you do not write or talk about it.

The question is, *how* does one make an effective argument? There are two ways to look at this question. The first is to approach it from the perspective of the argument; the other is to approach it from the perspective of the audience. When we think of arguments, we tend to break them down into two types—logical and emotional. Arguments that appeal to our sense of logic are arguments of **logos** (Greek for "word" or "reason"); those that cater to our emotions are arguments of **pathos** (Greek for "suffering" and "feeling"). Both are effective forms of persuasion, but they function in different ways and sometimes serve different purposes. Although you should use both in your essays, your main focus should be on building an argument based on **logos.**

Arguments of logos appeal to our sense of reason and logic. They tend to rely on facts, statistics, specific examples, and authoritative statements. Your supporting evidence for these kinds of arguments is critical. It must be accurate, valid, and specific. For instance, while looking over essays we thought might be useful, we came across a study arguing that long-distance romantic relationships among college students generally did not last very long. Based on this description, what kinds of evidence do you think the authors of the study relied on? Rumor and innuendo? A survey of people who graduated from college in 1979? A close examination of TV shows about college students? A review of the film *Animal House?* Of course not. The authors were sociologists who surveyed hundreds of college students who were or had been involved in long-distance relationships. They provided almost six pages of statistics; they allowed for differences in age, race, gender, and location; and they did their survey over a respectable amount of time. In short, they relied on objective data, scientific reasoning, and sound survey practices to help make their argument that long distance relationships in college tend not to work out.

Think about what kinds of information would persuade you in certain situations. What would make you buy an iPod over some other MP3 player? Or, more importantly, what would convince you to buy a Volvo over a Hyundai for driving around your new-born twins? If you were going to write a paper on fire safety, would you rely on the expertise of a fire marshal or a medical doctor? If you were writing an essay on water pollution, would you consult scientific journals and EPA studies, or would you rely on the Webpages of chemical corporations? Readers are more likely to be moved by the soundness of your argument if your supporting evidence seems logical, objective, verifiable, and reasonable.

Having said that, it would be a mistake to dismiss arguments of pathos outright. In fact, we believe that many teachers and writers have too easily separated intellect and emotion when talking about arguments. Arguments of pathos can be unusually powerful and convincing because they appeal to our needs, desires, fears, values, and emotions. The statement, "You should get an iPhone because they are just plain cooler than anything else out there" is an appeal to pathos. Notice how this claim ignores any information about warranties, durability, price, or functionality. Rather, the statement plays on our desire to be cool—a most powerful appeal. If you are truthful with yourself, you might be surprised just how often such arguments actually work.

Most television commercials and advertisements in popular magazines play on our sense of pathos. If you have found yourself moved by those Michelin tire commercials in which nothing much happens except a cute little baby plays around in an empty Michelin tire, then the good folks in the marketing department at Michelin have been successful. If you have fought back a tear at an image of an elderly couple holding hands, or believed (if even for an instant) that drinking a certain lite beer might get you more dates, then you have been moved by an appeal to your sense of pathos. Now, appeals to pathos are not necessarily bad or manipulative; on the contrary, they can be effective when statistics or logic feels cold and inhuman.

The authors believe that the most effective arguments are those that combine logos and pathos, and, as we discuss next, ethos. Emotional appeals without facts feel sleazy, and scientific data without human appeal feel cold. We still maintain that your essays should make appeals to logos over pathos, but we encourage you to build arguments in which emotion supports or enhances logic. Arguments that feature good combinations of logos and pathos make you and your essay appear both smart and human—a good mix.

Not only do you need to create an appropriate mix of logos and pathos for your intended audience, but you must also create an appropriate ethos. Greek for "character" or "disposition," a writer's ethos is his or her sense of credibility. For most conservative Republicans, Michael Moore has little credibility; so for them, he would have a low ethos. However, someone like Colin Powell enjoys the respect of many Republicans and Democrats. Most Americans trust him; they find him credible. Therefore, Powell's ethos is high. The ethos of public figures like Powell and Moore are easier to talk about than relatively unknown personalities, so as a beginning writer, you should be mindful of how you want to establish credibility and authority. If you are going to argue that the Vietnam Veterans Memorial is the ideal example of public art, it might undermine your argument if your best friend is the architect (or if you conceal that your best friend is the architect). Alternatively, if you argue that the Washington Redskins should not change their mascot from the potentially offensive epithet "redskin" but fail to mention that you own stock in the Redskins, then your credibility might be in jeopardy, and people might not take your argument seriously. Ethos, pathos, and logos make up what we call the "rhetorical triangle," and most arguments are made up of some combination of the three. Based on your audience, you need to adjust your own rhetorical triangle so that your argument contains the right mixture of reason, emotion, and credibility.

A reading aside: It is also helpful in reading to understand whether or how a writer is effective by analyzing their argument on whether they are writing from logos, pathos, or ethos. For example, if Colin Powell writes about the need for international diplomacy in the Middle East, it would automatically carry more weight than one made by your local city councilwoman, even if she had her master's degree in international relations.

MAKING CLAIMS

A claim is a kind of assertion that you make based on evidence, logical and emotional appeal, and solid reasoning. Other words for claims are "thesis" or "assertion."

It is important to distinguish between a claim and a fact, and a claim and an opinion. The sentence "Pearl Jam is a band from Seattle" is a fact. It is a true statement, and as such would not make a good thesis or a good topic sentence. The sentence "I think I prefer Pearl Jam to Soundgarden" is an opinion and, again, would not make a particularly good thesis or topic sentence, in part because this is not a disprovable statement. Maybe someone who knows you well could argue that in your heart of hearts you prefer Soundgarden to Pearl Jam, but the topic is so personal and so narrow, it holds little interest for other readers. However, the sentence "Although most critics prefer Nirvana, Pearl Jam has emerged as the most socially conscious Seattle grunge band" is a claim because it is something you could spend an essay supporting. It emerges from the small world of personal opinion ("I prefer") to the world of more universal interest.

Generally, there are three different types of claims—policy, value, and fact—and these claims are frequently linked to the kinds of appeals you make (ethos, pathos, logos). **Policy claims** are those claims that the writer thinks should happen. Often, one sees policy claims made in terms of ought, and they usually advocate action. These claims must be supported by a justification, and it is usually a good idea to address potential opposing ideas. Essays that argue for more funding for public art or that demand harsher penalties for graffiti are examples of policy claims.

The **value claim** is among the most popular of all claims; in fact, the Pearl Jam thesis is a value claim. These claims assert worth and value. If you were to argue that *The Simpsons* carries positive messages or that a certain building embodies anti-human architecture, you would be advancing a value claim. For a good example of a value claim, see Garance Franke-Ruta's essay in which she argues that *Heroes* has more to offer than *24* (pp. 156–159). Note that in this essay, the author grounds her arguments on standards and values. Although emotion can go a long way in these kinds of claims, it is never advisable to hinge value claims on pathos or emotion.

For many beginning writers, the most common claim is a **fact claim** (sometimes called a **claim of truth**). These types of assertions focus on classification or definition, and they assert that *X* is or is not *Y*. In fact claims, the thesis is incredibly important, because you do not want to argue something that is unprovable, nor do you want to argue for the obvious. For example, making the claim that *Talladega Nights* is a parody of NASCAR is pointless, because it is so clearly a parody of NASCAR. One of the most common mistakes writers make is confusing truth with argument (see our section on thesis statements for more help here). Fact claims attempt to clarify. They assert that a thing or idea should be seen in a certain way or considered from a particular perspective.

The key to making supportable claims lies in framing your assertions with balance and reason. Students often feel as though their arguments must be extreme in their coverage. Those kinds of claims tend to be less convincing because so little in life is absolute. Instead of arguing that Pearl Jam is the "best" Seattle band (because concepts like "best" and "worst" are impossible to prove), make a claim that Pearl Jam is the most socially conscious band (citing their lyrics and political activism), or argue that they are the most influential Seattle band (citing other songs that mimic them, interviews with other bands that mention Pearl Jam, and the opinion of music critics). Also, make sure your claims are reasonable in scope. Do not be afraid to use qualifiers. Limiting the Pearl Jam argument to Seattle bands or grunge bands circumscribes your claim and makes it doable in a five- or six-page essay.

Finally, now that you have made a claim, you must support that claim. The most common types of support include

- *Expert Opinion:* Citing the opinion of top scholars in a field or established experts is one of the most persuasive forms of support.
- *Statistics:* Readers like numbers, facts, and percentages. Use credible statistics to lend objectivity and data to your claims.
- *Analysis:* Close readings of a text by an insightful person can be quite convincing. This is where being a savvy semiotician is useful.
- *Analogies and Comparisons:* One way of illustrating what something is, is to show what it is *not*. Comparing and contrasting can highlight the values you want to explore.

In the next section, we expand our discussion of support, claims, and evidence to discuss how one implements these strategies to build a comprehensive argument and actually *write* that essay.

USING CLAIMS AND SUPPORT TO MAKE ARGUMENTS: SOME HELPFUL TIPS

Honesty and trust come into play when you actually make your arguments. You do not want to mislead your potential audiences, you do not want to alienate them, and you do not want to manipulate them in an unethical way. Making up facts, inventing sources, and leaving out important details are not merely bad argumentation—they are often unethical acts. More positively, writing is all about engagement. We write to make connections with others; we read to learn more about the world and our place in it. Next we provide some basic tips for making solid, convincing, ethical arguments.

■ Do Not Be Afraid to Acknowledge Differing Opinions

Some students think that if they acknowledge any aspect of the other side of their argument that they poke a hole in their own. Actually, just the opposite is the case. Letting your readers know that you are well informed goes a long way toward establishing your credibility. What's more, if you are able not only to identify a differing opinion and then refute it or discount it, your argument could carry even more weight. For instance, if you want to argue that Mel Gibson's film *The Passion of the Christ* succeeds as a work of art, you would do well to acknowledge near the beginning of your essay that some critics have problems with the film. In fact, you may decide to use their complaints and their weaknesses to help you make your own assertions.

■ Use Credible, Detailed Information and Sources to Help Support Your Arguments

This is perhaps the most important tip we can provide. Think about what kind of information convinces you to do anything. Are you persuaded by vagueness, or by specificity? If we wanted to convince you to meet us for dinner at a specific restaurant, which of the following would be the most persuasive?

- We heard from someone that the food is really good.
- A restaurant critic we respect said this is some of the best food in town.
- A restaurant critic, two chefs, and a group of our friends all recommend this place.
- We have been there a number of times, and the food is great, the service is fantastic, the scene is relaxed but cool, and the prices are reasonable.
- The restaurant's website claims it is the city's favorite restaurant.
- Your grandparents raved about it.

In general, we are persuaded by thorough, objective data. Although we trust people whose tastes are similar to our own, we tend not to trust people we do not know or who might have a stake in a certain argument. The best kinds of evidence are expert opinions, statistics from a reliable source (such as a scientific study), facts from an objective source (such as a newspaper or peer-reviewed journal), personal experience, and the testimony of others. However, if your grandparents previously recommended good restaurants, their ethos could match the so-called experts who recommended the place. Then again, their tastes may be much different than yours. Understanding the criteria that one uses in judging restaurants, movies, and television shows is crucial. For example, Roger Ebert, the well-known critic, admits before some Adam Sandler movie reviews he writes that he is no fan of Adam Sandler, giving his readers a warning that his criteria may not match their own.[7]

■ Establish Your Own Credibility and Authority, But Try Not to Overdo It

There are two different ways to establish authority—explicitly and implicitly. In the explicit method, you say up front that you are a specialist in a certain area. For instance, if you are going to write about the influence of Tejano music in South Texas, you might say in the opening paragraph that you are a Latina from Texas who grew up listening to your dad play in Tejano bands around San Antonio. The audience then knows your background and is likely to give your arguments more weight than if a white guy from Boston was making the same argument—unless, of course, the white guy in question was a scholar of Tejano music (which lends a different kind of credibility). Establishing authority implicitly may have less to do with you and more to do with the research you have done. Implicit authority is revealed to the reader slowly, in pieces, so that you carefully fill in gaps over the course of your essay.

There are, of course, many ways to establish authority—by being an expert, by quoting experts, and by building a knowledge base as a result of research—but however you establish authority, do so within reason (see "Supporting Claims"). If the essay becomes more about how much you know and less about your topic, you will alienate your reader. You want to keep your reader engaged.

■ Try to Avoid Fallacies

Fallacies are, literally, falsities, gaps, and errors in judgment. Sometimes called **logical fallacies**, these missteps are mistakes of logic, and they have been around for centuries. We are all guilty of falling into the fallacy trap now and then, but avoid that trap if possible. Here are a few of the most common:

- *The Straw Man fallacy:* When the writer sets up a fake argument or a "straw man" (an argument that does not really exist), only to refute it later.
- *The ad hominem fallacy:* Latin for "to the man," this occurs when a writer attacks a person and not an argument. When a politician accuses his detractors of personal attacks in an attempt to avoid the real issues, he is claiming that his opponents are making *ad hominem* assertions.
- *The hasty generalization:* When a writer jumps to a quick and easy conclusion without thinking through the leap logically. A hasty generalization would occur if one made an argument that Parker Posey appeared in *every* independent movie in the 1990s.
- *The post hoc ergo propter hoc fallacy:* Latin for "after the fact therefore because of the fact," this fallacy is a favorite among beginning writers. Literally, it means that because *X* comes after *Y*, *Y* must have caused *X*. In other words, it is a faulty cause-and-

[7]Jim Emerson, "Ebert on Sandler: All Thumbs," *Roger Ebert's Journal*, 22 June 2006 <http://rogerebert.suntimes.com/apps/pbcs.dll/article?AID=/20060622/COMMENTARY/60622001>.

effect relationship. Let us say someone observes that teen violence seems to be on the rise. This person also is beginning to notice more video games at the local video store. The *post hoc* fallacy would occur when this person concluded that the rise in teen violence was *because* of the increased video games.

- **The vague generality:** Also a favorite among college students, the fallacy of generalization takes place when a writer makes sweeping claims about a group but provides no specific detail or evidence to back up his claim. This can happen on a micro level with an overuse of the passive voice ("It is agreed that . . ." or "It is assumed that . . .") that does not attribute responsibility. It happens on a macro level when a writer makes a broad generalization about a group of people, like immigrants, lesbians, Republicans, Jews, professors, or students. In some ways, this fallacy is the cause of racism, as it assumes that behavior (or imagined behavior) of one person is shared or mimicked by an entire group. This is a dangerous strategy.

- **The non sequitur fallacy:** This is not a particularly common fallacy, but it is still useful to know. Latin for "it does not follow," a non sequitur is a fallacy of conclusion, like a faulty assumption. An example would be, "No woman I know talks about wanting a baby, therefore, there cannot be very many women in the world who want babies."

■ Use Inductive and/or Deductive Reasoning When Appropriate

As you write your paper, as you make your arguments and present your evidence, your reader must think through your arguments. However, before that happens, you must also think through your arguments so that you can develop them in the most cogent way. The two types of argument organization are **inductive** and **deductive**. Deductive reasoning begins big and moves to small; or, in other terms, deductive reasoning starts with the macro and moves to the micro. In classic rhetoric, this is called a **syllogism**. A classic syllogism might go something like this: Most Hollywood movies have a happy ending. *Forrest Gump* is a Hollywood movie. Therefore, it is likely that *Forrest Gump* has a happy ending. A typical syllogism begins with two broad statements and arrives at a narrower proposition based on those statements.

Inductive reasoning resembles detective work. You start with many small observations or bits of evidence, and then based on that conglomeration, you make a generalization. For instance, let us say you noticed that Parker Posey starred in *Party Girl, Best in Show, The House of Yes, Short Cuts, Broken English*, and *A Mighty Wind*. You also then realize that all of these movies are independent films. Therefore, based on all of this information, you make an argument about Parker Posey's contribution to independent film. Both approaches are valid, but each has its own pitfalls. Be sure you do not make big leaps in logic (see **hasty generalization**) that you cannot support.

Papers that use deductive reasoning almost always begin with a thesis or main argument. Most professors prefer this type of reasoning because it indicates that the author has thought about his or her argument in advance. However, the inductive approach can also be effective in certain situations, particularly those where the writer has established credibility. Typically, essays that follow the inductive model build an argument over the course of the essay and position the thesis near the end. Although this strategy is valid, it can be more difficult for beginning writers to execute. Writing instructors tend to favor essays written in the deductive model because the formula is simpler—the writer places the thesis near the beginning of the essay and spends the rest of the paper unpacking, proving, and supporting that thesis.

■ Consider Thinking Like a Lawyer When Building an Argument—Make a Case and Prove It

One of the best ways of making and proving an assertion with insight, clarity, and thoroughness is through what rhetoricians have come to call the **Toulmin system**. This term was derived from Stephen Toulmin, a British philosopher, who argued that the best way to win an argument is by making a strong case.[8] This may sound like stating the obvious, but it really is not. Rather than relying on airtight data to make an argument, Toulmin argued that in real-life situations, you can never be 100 percent certain of something. Someone always has a comeback or an opposing view to counter yours. So, for Toulmin (and many writing teachers), you make an argument by building a case, like a lawyer would in a trial. And, in essence, Toulmin's system resembles legal reasoning in that it makes a case and lays down evidence rather than pretending you have achieved complete certainty. Toulmin's system is useful because it does not insist on absolutes, which is important when writing about texts as subjective as those in popular culture. It is next to impossible to be "right" about what a movie like *Office Space* means, but it is possible to be convincing about your particular interpretation. You cannot say with complete certainty why someone liked *Office Space,* but it is possible to make a strong case about why students like *Office Space.*

According to Toulmin, one makes a convincing case by first making a **claim** (see "Making Claims," page 46) then by citing a "datum," or evidence, that would prompt someone to make a claim in the first place; then, one offers support for that datum via what he calls a "warrant." A warrant is a statement that underscores the logical connection between the claim and evidence. For instance, if you park your car outside a store, go inside, and return and it is gone, and say, "My car has been stolen," you are relying on the warrant that a car that is missing from a place one has left it must be stolen. Your claim: "My car has been stolen." Your datum: The car is missing. The warrant: Cars that are missing must have been stolen. But of course, another warrant could be argued—"A car that is missing might have been towed." The warrant is legitimized by what Toulmin calls "backing," or additional evidence.

How would this system work when arguing about popular culture? Let us use another film example. Say that you notice something about recent gangster movies. You observe that since *Reservoir Dogs* and *Pulp Fiction* were released, the gangster genre has become increasingly popular. Based on this observation, one could make an argument that Quentin Tarantino, the director for both movies, has had a rather significant impact on gangster films. In doing some research, we discovered that a number of recent directors cited either *Reservoir Dogs* or *Pulp Fiction* when asked about their films.[9] In the car example, the backing might be that you have parked in a high-crime area or in a tow-away zone, depending on the warrant you use. According to Toulmin, we have here all the necessary information to make a convincing case:

> *Claim:* Quentin Tarantino has had a significant impact on the gangster movie genre.
>
> *Datum:* Two popular gangster movies, *Reservoir Dogs* and *Pulp Fiction,* were directed by Tarantino.

---

[8]See Stephen Toulmin, *The Uses of Argument* (Cambridge, UK: Cambridge University Press, 1964).

[9]A simple Google search of "influenced by Quentin Tarantino" and "interview" brings up a few dozen references.

Warrant: Several directors cite either *Reservoir Dogs* or *Pulp Fiction* when talking about their own movies.

Backing: These comments appeared in respectable, reviewed publications.

Of course, if you were to build a paper out of this system, you would need one to two more pieces of data (what we called **points** or **reasons** earlier) and additional warrants; in this case, perhaps discussing how recent movies or television shows resemble specific scenes from the Tarantino movies.

The Toulmin system is not foolproof, but it does provide a model for argumentation, and it is particularly useful for making claims about popular-culture texts, or any text for which there is no clear "right" or "wrong" answer.

SYNTHESIS: PULLING IT ALL TOGETHER

Writing is about synthesis—combining differing elements—so learning to synthesize makes you a much better writer (and a better thinker). In the world of composition, **synthesis** refers to a couple of different things. First, a writer must synthesize her ideas; that is, she must pull together the various half-baked premises, vague notions, and uncompleted thoughts into one cohesive, central concept. Usually, this concept becomes your thesis, but sometimes it may take a draft or two of writing and condensing and collapsing before you arrive at what you want to say.

Another form of synthesis involves combining all of the secondary sources you amass into the body of your essay. This is one of the hardest things to master—weaving other voices into the tapestry of your own. How much of another quote do you include? Should you paraphrase or quote precisely? How does one lead into a quote succinctly and elegantly? We would love to provide some sure-fire tricks here, but, alas, that is impossible, as integrating secondary quotes, paraphrases, and ideas into your own work remains a kind of art that gets easier only with practice.

However, do not fear, because you engage in synthesis every day. Whenever you relate to your roommate what each person in your group thought about a concert or a movie, you synthesize. Take the process of deciding what movie to see. The entire process is one big act of synthesis—from seeing what's playing, to locating the best theater, to juggling the various reviews, to deciding whether you trust the opinion of your friends and family who have either seen the movie or talked to someone who has. You synthesize when you take all of the disparate material in your head, combine it, and from that whorl of data, arrive at a kind of personal claim: *I am going to see the new Harry Potter movie at the Balboa Theater at 9:15.*

Because synthesis is so important to becoming an inclusive, informed writer, increasingly more instructors require a **synthesis essay**. A synthesis essay is an essay that asks the writer to synthesize various kinds of information into one unified document. Typically, this means researching, paraphrasing, and presenting differing forms of data. That data could be opinions about a piece of art, quotations from experts on a new CD, or data from surveys on television use. How a writer delivers that information, however, is critical. A writer must either **paraphrase** (restate an idea in his or her own words) or **quote** (reprint the phrase or sentence exactly, using quotation marks) the material; in both cases, the writer must **cite** the passage by indicating where the material comes from. *The writer cannot pass this information off as his or her own work.* Most instances of plagiarism occur in the synthesizing process—because students do not know how to cite, do not know how to paraphrase, or think they do not need to do either one.

To illustrate synthesis in action, we use synthesis itself as an example. To do this, we consulted the Drew University On-Line Resources for Writers and the Bellevue College Online Writing Lab. The Drew site offers a full definition of synthesis writing:

> Although at its most basic level a synthesis involves combining two or more summaries, synthesis writing is more difficult than it might at first appear because this combining must be done in a meaningful way and the final essay must generally be thesis-driven. In composition courses, "synthesis" commonly refers to writing about printed texts, drawing together particular themes or traits that you observe in those texts and organizing the material from each text according to those themes or traits. Sometimes you may be asked to synthesize your own ideas, theory, or research with those of the texts you have been assigned. In your other college classes you'll probably find yourself synthesizing information from graphs and tables, pieces of music, and art works as well. The key to any kind of synthesis is the same.

It also enumerates these three features of synthesis:

1. It accurately reports information from the sources using different phrases and sentences;
2. It is organized in such a way that readers can immediately see where the information from the sources overlap;
3. It makes sense of the sources and helps the reader understand them in greater depth.

Our decision to cut and paste the definition and the three features exactly as they appear on the Drew site is a form of quotation or citation. Acknowledging Drew lets the reader know that the features come from a reliable source and that they are not the products of Silverman and Rader.[10]

However, the Bellevue site includes this explanation of synthesis:

WHAT IS A SYNTHESIS?

A synthesis paper is a certain kind of essay.

> According to the *Little, Brown Handbook* (Aaron & Fowler, 2001, p. 133), a synthesis is a way to "make connections among parts or among wholes. You can create a new whole by drawing conclusions about relationships and implications." What this means is, in order to write a successful synthesis paper, you must conduct research on your chosen topic, contemplate what this unique collection of knowledge may mean to you and the world, and develop an argument about it. Specifically, this means discussing the implications of the knowledge you have gathered. You have amassed a collection of information on a certain topic, and now you must say something unique and interesting about it.
>
> **A synthesis is not:** A summary
>
> **A synthesis is:** An opportunity for you to create new knowledge out of already existing knowledge, i.e., other sources. You develop an argument, or perhaps a unique perspective on something in the world (a political issue, how something works, etc.), and use your sources as evidence, in order to make your claim (thesis statement) more believable.

Thus, at the risk of confusion, here is how one might synthesize two different takes on synthesis in college writing.

---

[10]Sandra Jamieson, "Synthesis Writing," *Sandra Jamieson* 1999 <http://users.drew.edu/~sjamieso/Synthesis.htm, 3 April 2010>

Though the Drew Online Resources for Writers Lab and the Bellevue Online Writing Lab approach the concept of synthesis differently, they ultimately have more similarities than differences. What connects the two sites is an emphasis on combining information from various sources in order to make connections. Drew tends to focus on synthesis as it applies to written texts and as a means of presenting and collating sources so that readers can better understand varying information. In addition to a generous definition of synthesis, the Drew site lists three key features of synthesis, all of which focus on accurate presentation of source material. Despite the fact that Bellevue distinguishes between summary and synthesis (something Drew does not), their site underscores Drew's argument that synthesis can perform important work by taking existing information and combining it in a way that makes it rounder, more comprehensive, and more fresh.[11]

At its core, synthesis is about interpretation. In order to write this paragraph, we had to interpret what both sites had to say about synthesis. Notice how we did not just regurgitate the two sites. We made connections between the two (synthesized), and we unpacked the data from each so that we could 1) make it our own, and 2) distill it so that we could better explain it to you.

Synthesis takes work; one must be conscientious and careful while doing it. Do not take shortcuts and simply cut and paste—that's plagiarism. Consider each source separately, unpack each source, then present the theme of each source in your synthesis. This helps you avoid the traps of plagiarism and summary, and it enables you to connect with your audience.

KNOW YOUR AUDIENCE

An outspoken advocate of the Internet's capacity to share vast amounts of information has been invited to speak at a gathering of music company executives who are nervous about the thousands of people downloading free music. What kind of tone should she take when addressing this potentially hostile audience? Next, that person is going to speak to a gathering of college students, who are among the most avid downloaders of music. How would her presentation differ? Would she give the same presentation to both audiences? What strategies would she use with the hostile audience that she would not need for the sympathetic one? Keeping the assumptions, education, political leanings, and culture of your audience in mind helps you write a more appropriate essay than if you ignored these issues altogether.

When we were writing this introduction for the third edition, Michael Moore's controversial movie *Sicko* had just been released nationwide. A scathing indictment of America's health-care industry, Moore's film polarized viewers and critics. There is no doubt that the film makes a powerful argument, but one might ask who the audience of the movie is. Is Moore making the movie for Republicans, Democrats, or those in the middle? Many believe that because the movie is so one-sided it will change few people's minds, whereas others contend that it could move people to actually do something about this nation's health-care shortcomings. We would argue that Moore's audience is mainstream America; people who are most affected by nonexistent or poor insurance. Moore knows that his movie will probably be seen by those on the Right as propaganda, but his persistent arguments in the movie seem aimed at those who defend the status quo. If Moore was

---

[11]"What is a Synthesis?" *Bellevue College Writing Lab* http://bellevuecollege.edu/WritingLab/Synthesis. html, 3 April 2010

interested in a broader audience, there are any number of ways he might have kept his message but changed his method of delivering it—including interviewing sympathetic and thoughtful defenders of HMOs, insurance companies, and the health-care lobby, toning down some of his own antics, and most importantly, editing the film differently.

These examples reflect the three types of audiences you should consider when writing your papers—a sympathetic audience, an undecided audience, and an antagonistic audience. You would likely not write the same paper for the three kinds of audiences, but tailor your arguments based on who would be reading your essay. We do this kind of tailoring all the time. For instance, when you tell the story of a fabulous date you had the previous night to your mother, your best friend, and your ex, you probably tell three radically different stories. The potentially hostile audience (the ex) gets one version, the undecided audience (mother) gets another, and the sympathetic audience (roommate) gets yet another. All your stories might be accurate, but shaded and delivered differently based on what you know about each listener.

When writing for a sympathetic audience, you already have them on your side, so you do not need to try to win them over. In this case, an argument grounded in pathos may be the most effective. Chances are, they already know the information that might make them think a certain way, so giving them facts, statistics, and details they are familiar with is ineffective because it could come across as overstating the obvious or simply appearing repetitive. However, an emotionally powerful appeal supported by a strong ethos could be incredibly successful. Let us say you are going to write an essay on Kurt Cobain's contribution to American music for *Rolling Stone* or *Spin*. Most readers of these magazines are predisposed to agree with the facts you may present, so you do not need to list the number of records Nirvana sold or the awards they won. Instead, you may want to focus on how the music has affected you and your friends.

Alternatively, if you have been asked to write an article on Cobain for *Country Music Today,* the audience is less sympathetic to your topic. In this instance, you need to adjust your ethos and your approach. First, you could establish credibility by informing your readers that you are a fan of country music, perhaps even mention the important contributions of various artists you know these readers appreciate. When addressing a potentially antagonistic or skeptical audience, it is best to avoid an overly pathos-driven argument. You may come across as ill-informed and even irrational. Instead, you might want to point to specific Nirvana songs or chords that resemble country songs. A good strategy might be to make connections thematically, arguing that even though the music is different, Cobain, Willie Nelson, Lyle Lovett, Merle Haggard, and Waylon Jennings all write smart, catchy songs about disaffected, blue-collar Americans. Look for instances of overlap. If you have time to research, you might find out that Cobain listened to country music or that the people in the area he grew up in have a strong affinity for country music. With these kinds of audiences, the best way to establish credibility is to let your audience know that you have done your homework, and that you know their world as well as you know your own.

In some ways, writing for an antagonistic audience is easier than writing for an uncertain one, because you know what you are getting into. Writing for the vast middle can be truly challenging. When writing for an undecided audience, the best strategy is to establish strong ethos and logos. How much you rely on ethos or logos depends on you and your topic. If you are arguing that advertisements featuring skinny, near-naked female models are empowering to women, you might need to adjust your argument based on your gender or age. If you want to argue that the Names quilt should be taken seriously as art, focus not simply on the formal or artistic qualities of the quilt, but mention how the quilt affected you, that it fostered an interest in folk art and a love for art that inspires social change. Your audience responds more favorably to your claims if they trust you and your evidence. Be honest. Do not try to manipulate. Write in your own voice.

USE COMMON SENSE

You know what arguments are likely to persuade you. You have examples of documents in this book and elsewhere of compelling, sound, reasonable arguments. Use them as your models. The best argument is one that comes from a position of reasonableness.

Overall, making an argument is a key element of writing successful papers, perhaps more important than any other. For one, knowing what you are arguing often leads to clearer writing; it allows you to separate to some degree the processes of thinking and actually putting those thoughts onto paper. In an attempt to impress professors, students use big words and write in what they imagine a "scholarly" voice to be. Do not worry so much about tone. Write in your own voice. Remember: The best writing is complex ideas rendered in simple language—not the other way around.

PART V. HOW DO I RESEARCH POPULAR CULTURE TEXTS?

Thus far we have focused on the process of making arguments largely from processing and elaborating on one's observations. However, nontraditional texts can also be fruitful entering points for researching questions, both large and small, about culture.

For one, nontraditional texts often raise questions about the medium from which they come. When you watch a sitcom, it might make you think about other sitcoms. When you see a painting, it might make you think of other paintings. When you walk through another university's student union, you might think about how the two student unions are related—maybe a similar type of student goes to each university, or perhaps the student unions were built in different times. You might also notice that your student union has university-owned food and drink places, but your friend's union has chain restaurants. Researching the history of student unions would produce one type of paper, probably one more historical in nature, whereas researching the presence of corporations on campus would produce a paper that explored more explicitly political issues (the presence of corporations on campus is a highly sensitive issue for many associated with higher education). In either case, your walk through a public space might suggest to you some avenues for research.

Nontraditional texts can also raise issues about gender, race, and class, among other things. When observing stereotyped behavior on sitcoms, it can make you think about how other television shows present the same behavior, and perhaps how other creative genres do as well.

Nontraditional texts can also be places where one might explore how abstract concepts play out in practice, through portrayals of popular culture, as Katherine Gantz does with *Seinfeld* and the lens of queer theory. Gantz uses the concept of queerness (which is different than homosexuality) to demonstrate how *Seinfeld*'s characters have complicated relationships that test traditional definitions of masculinity. Queerness does not have to be the only lens—one could certainly use *Seinfeld* to explore issues of feminism, racism, and regionalism in current society. *Seinfeld* is ideal for this task because 1) it was for a number of years the most popular show in the country, and 2) it remains an active presence on television through syndication (reruns). That said, exploring such concepts in other, less popular media also has its value.

There are other ways of using nontraditional texts to engage research, but these methods are worth talking about further, because they offer relatively straightforward ways of using research to enhance understanding of both the texts at hand and the culture at large. In the first method of researching popular culture, the one used in student unions, the text is a window to further exploration of such issues as the corporatization of universities or the function of the environment in student lives.

In the second approach, examining the text and stereotypes in it, the text itself is the focus. In the third approach, the lens used to look at the nontraditional text is the focus; the nontraditional text is more a means to further discussion and elaboration of the concepts. In other words, queerness is the focus of Gantz's essay more than *Seinfeld.* All three approaches share the idea that these texts matter—that they reflect larger concerns in society.

There are other reasons why researching nontraditional texts might seem daunting. You may ask yourself who could have possibly written about Barbie dolls or *The Matrix.* Or you may not have written a paper that engages popular culture as a research topic. After all, is not research about "serious" topics? Traditionally, you have probably written research papers about historical events or movements, or about the author of a literary work, or perhaps literary movements. Although research of nontraditional texts may seem more difficult, students writing research papers about popular culture have a lot of resources at their disposal. There is a large and ever-increasing amount of work written on popular culture, such as music, the movies, technology, art, found objects, and television. There is even more work done on the more political elements of this textbook, such as gender and the media.

Because researching popular culture topics seems daunting, you might be tempted to amass as much information as possible before beginning your writing. However, we believe that one of the best ways of researching a paper about popular culture is to make sure you have already preliminarily interpreted whatever text you are analyzing before researching. That way, you have your ideas to use as a sounding board for others that might come your way. Finding out what you think about the text also allows you to research more effectively and probably more efficiently.

Generally, the trick to researching papers about popular culture is not only to find work that engages your specific topic, but something general or *contextual* about your topic. In the case of *The Matrix* (2000), a film popular with both viewers and critics, science fiction movies might be a good general subject to look up, but so might computers and culture. Broadly defined, *The Matrix* is a science fiction movie, but it is also a movie about the roles of computers in society. One of the movie's primary arguments is that our culture is quickly moving toward one that is run by computers with decreasing human control. That is the subject of more than a few movies, including *2001: A Space Odyssey* and *I, Robot,* but its message is even more crucial given the remarkable growth of the Internet since the mid-1990s. One could research the philosophical argument the movie is making, that humans and computers are somewhat at odds. One could research how other movies or books treat this subject, both within the science fiction genre and outside it. The movie also has a political bent, about the nature of not only computers but also about corporations, who seem to run Neo's life before he realizes what the Matrix is. It is also about the culture of computers, which Neo is immersed in before his transformation. In addition, it engages the idea of the future as well as the present, a temporal argument (about time). All these contexts—philosophical, genre-based, cultural, political, temporal—have strong research possibilities. You could write compelling papers on each of these topics, and each would be very different from the others. You can also see why understanding what you are arguing affects how you research a topic.

Another possibility for research is music CDs or even the iTunes store itself. Instead of thinking of particular contexts right away, you might begin by asking some questions of the text. For example, take as a text Johnny Cash's album *Solitary Man: American Recordings III*, which he released in 1999. Johnny Cash was a musician who recorded music for almost 50 years; he received his start about the same time and in the same place as Elvis Presley but had the same record producer as the Beastie Boys, a popular rap group. Such biographical constructions may shape your paper's direction, or they may not. In either case, in writing this paper, you might listen to the album and note some of the themes, symbols, and ideas. You might ask yourself: Was Johnny Cash writing about issues he had written about before? You could find this out by listening to other albums or seeking research materials about his recording career. You could also ask: What is it about the life of Cash that made him write songs like this? Material contained either in biographies of Cash himself or in general histories of country music could help this paper. Another question: Is Johnny Cash part of the recognizable genre of country music or a different genre altogether? Again, a general work about country music enables you to answer this question. Any of these questions can be the beginning of a good research paper. If you decided to focus only on the album, you could also read other reviews, and after you have staked out your own position, argue against other readings of this album.

Movies and music are good choices for research because they are texts that in some ways mirror traditional texts—movies have narratives like novels, and songs have lyrics that resemble poetry. But even found objects have strong possibilities for research. Objects like cars or dolls are not only easily described but have long traditions of scholarship, especially within cultural contexts. In the case of dolls, histories of dolls in American culture or the role of toys would provide historical contexts for your arguments; the same would be true for cars. As you get closer to the present, your methods of research may change. In the case of cars, current writers may not be writing about the context of a new model, but they certainly review them, and examining the criteria of car reviews may give you insight into the cultural context of a car. So might advertisements. Researching popular culture can include placing different primary sources (the source itself, like *Solitary Man* or *The Matrix* or advertisements for either of these texts) in context with one another, or using secondary sources—sources about the primary text, such as reviews, or scholarly articles, ones that are peer reviewed, reviewed by experts, and often have footnotes.

The most difficult thing about doing this research, somewhat ironically, is its flexibility; once you decide on researching popular culture, many different avenues, sometimes an overwhelming number, open to you. The authors have encountered students who enjoy this type of work but are overwhelmed by the possibilities in approaching popular culture texts as researchable topics. Most students eventually come away with not only a better understanding of their particular text but of researching generally.

RESEARCHING NONTRADITIONAL TEXTS: ONE METHOD

There are any number of ways to undertake the research process with nontraditional texts, given the complexities of the intersections among texts, issues, and culture. At Virginia Commonwealth University, where Dr. Silverman once taught, the department used the same approach in the university's required sophomore researched-writing class. Each student focused on what instructors called a "cultural text," which, for their purposes, meant nonliterary texts.

For the class, students were required in a four-step process to 1) identify and explore a particular cultural text and write about it; 2) choose research angles or avenues and write about the arguments between sources they encountered; 3) reread and write about the text through the research; and 4) merge the first three assignments (a kind of synthesis). The approach mimics to some extent the way many academics work, with a focus on text and context. This may involve doing a close reading of a text. A close reading examines the text details by paying attention to all of its inner workings, its colors, shapes, sounds, and symbols. When combined with research and larger cultural insight, a close reading can become a comprehensive paper.

The advantages of this approach are many. For one, you get a sense of how to do in-depth research that's not done for its own end but to provide better understanding of a particular topic. It also makes you as a writer learn how to incorporate others' ideas into your essay—which is what you have to do in school and long after you leave, when you have to complete market research and prepare reports.

From a purely academic perspective, this approach also demonstrates the diversity and depth of research being done on nontraditional texts and the even deeper well of information for issues of cultural significance (such as race, gender, and class). When faced with the prospect of doing in-depth college research, not to mention research on popular culture topics, students often believe there is not enough information for their topic. Sometimes this is true, but most times the process requires some cleverness and ingenuity.

NUTS AND BOLTS RESEARCH

Clearly, your university library is the place to start. Books have a much more comprehensive perspective on any possible text than most Websites. Think broadly when approaching what books you might look at; think about what category the books you are looking for might fall into. One of the best ways of doing this is through a keyword search involving "the perfect book." For a book about Johnny Cash, a simple keyword search on "Johnny Cash" might yield some useful sources. If not, a keyword search with "history," "country," and "music" might provide some results. If it does, write down a call number, the physical address of the book in the library, and head for the stacks; most libraries have separate floors or sections for their collection of books. When you get there, find the book number you have written down, but also be careful to look around on the shelves for other possibilities. Both authors have found that some of their best sources have come from browsing on the shelves of libraries.

Then it is on to periodicals.

Use an electronic database your university subscribes to; search engines like Google, Google Scholar, or Yahoo! are limited in what they come up with and may lead users to sources that are not reliable. The authors both like electronic databases like Infotrac (or

Academic Search Premier), JSTOR, Proquest, Omnifile, and LexisNexis, which many universities subscribe to (usually you can access these indexes through your library's Web site). The overall difference between Infotrac and LexisNexis and standard Internet searching is that Infotrac and LexisNexis, for the most part, have articles that appear in print form—generally, although not always—making them more reliable sources. Infotrac is an index to periodicals that tend to be scholarly, with footnotes, although some more-popular magazines are there as well. Some of the articles on Infotrac are full-text articles, which means the full version appears on the screen; some you have to head to the library to find. LexisNexis contains full-text articles from most large American and European newspapers as well as many magazines. It has a database geared toward general news and opinion and other databases geared toward sports, arts, science, and law.[12] If you are working with popular culture sources, the arts index, which contains reviews, may be helpful. Speaking of computers, you may also find the Library of Congress Web site, http://www.loc.gov, or WorldCat, a database of the holdings in major libraries, helpful to find if there are any books on the subject; you can then use your library's interlibrary loan to request a needed book. Be aware, however, that some books may take some time to arrive from another library to yours. The Library of Congress site also has an excellent collection of images. Overall, in doing research, be creative and thorough.

GUERILLA RESEARCH

Okay, if you have exhausted your library options and you *still* cannot find what you need, try a bookstore like Borders or Barnes & Noble. Bring some index cards and a notebook, and take notes on the books you want. And if you want an alternative, look at Amazon.com, where you can research books, movies, and albums; sometimes you can see what you need, especially bibliographic information, in Amazon's "look inside the book" feature.

PART VI. HOW DO I KNOW WHAT A GOOD PAPER LOOKS LIKE? AN ANNOTATED STUDENT ESSAY

Sometimes, students have the ability to write good papers; they just cannot visualize them. They simply do not know what a good paper looks like, what its components are.

An annotated student paper appears on the following pages. You see that we have highlighted the positive aspects of the essay and also some elements that need work. (Careful readers might notice additional stylistic and formatting inconsistencies.) One thing we like about this piece is a good move from general information to specific. The best papers are those with a clear, narrow focus. This student's thesis is also clear and well developed.

Sample student papers appear throughout *The World Is a Text*.

---

[12]The *Reader's Guide to Periodicals* is a complete non-electronic guide to periodicals such as newspapers and major magazines. You may be tempted to skip anything not online, but electronic sources generally go back only a decade, so for any type of historical research, you should probably hit the *Reader's Guide*.

Matt Compton

Professor Silverman

English 101

9 December 2001

"Smells Like Teen Spirit"

In 1991 a song burst forth onto the music scene that articulated so perfectly the emotions of America's youth that the song's writer was later labeled the voice of a generation (Moon). That song was Nirvana's "Smells Like Teen Spirit," and the writer was Kurt Cobain; one of the most common complaints of the song's critics was that the lyrics were unintelligible (Rawlins). But while some considered the song to be unintelligible, to many youth in the early 90s, it was exactly what they needed to hear. Had the song been presented differently, then the raw emotions that it presented would have been tamed. If the lyrics had been perfectly articulated, then the feelings that the lyrics express would have been less articulate, because the feelings that he was getting across were not clear in themselves. One would know exactly what Kurt Cobain was saying, but not exactly what he was feeling. The perfect articulation of those raw emotions, shared by so many of America's youth, was conveyed with perfect inarticulation.

1991 was a year when the music scene had become a dilute, lukewarm concoction being spoon-fed to the masses by corporations (Cohen). The charts and the radio were being dominated by "hair bands" and pop ballads; popular music at the time was making a lot of noise without saying anything (Cohen). Behind the scenes "underground" music had been thriving since the early eighties. Much of this underground music was making a meaningful statement, but these musicians shied away from the public eye. The general public knew little about them, because they had adopted the ideology that going public was selling out (Dettmar). Nirvana was a part of this "underground" music scene.

In 1991 Nirvana broke the credo, signing with a major label, DGC, under which they released the chart-smashing *Nevermind*.

The title appears in quotes because it represents a song title.

Good beginning—the "burst forth" is passive, but here it seems to work.

Good clarification, although he almost moves too quickly into unintelligibility.

This is a strong explanation, although it probably could have been condensed a bit.

The thesis is great—it is argumentative and clever. We know here what the rest of the paper is about. However, the passive "was conveyed" could be turned into the active "Cobain conveyed."

The writer gives a good background of the atmosphere before the song. Those more familiar with the era might raise objections to the definitiveness of the conclusion, but he uses a source to back up his opinion. We may not agree, but have to respect this research.

The topic sentence is weak here—there's a lot going on in this

"Smells Like Teen Spirit" was the first single from the record, and it became a huge hit quickly (Cohen). Nirvana stepped up and spoke for the twenty something generation, which wasn't exactly sure what it wanted to say (Azerrad 223–233). A huge part of America's youth felt exactly what Cobain was able to convey through not just "Smells Like Teen Spirit" but all of his music. Nirvana shot into superstar status and paved the way for an entire "grunge" movement (Moon). No one complained that they could not hear Cobain, but many did complain that they could not understand what he was saying.

paragraph, and the first sentence and even the second do not adequately prepare the reader for the information.

The information itself is good—he's revisiting the ideas he talked about in his thesis, which in some ways makes up for the lack of organization in this paragraph.

Kurt Cobain did not want his music to just be heard and appreciated; he wanted it to be "felt" (Moon). His music often showed a contrast of emotions; it would change from a soft lull, to a screaming rage suddenly. And few could scream with rage as could Cobain (Cohen). There is a Gaelic word, "yarrrrragh," which " . . . refers to that rare quality that some voices have, an edge, an ability to say something about the human condition that goes far beyond merely singing the right lyrics and hitting the right notes." This word was once used to describe Cobain's voice by Ralph J. Gleason, *Rolling Stone* critic (Azerrad 231). It was that voice, that uncanny ability to show emotions that Cobain demonstrated in "Smells Like Teen Spirit."

Good move to the songwriter, Kurt Cobain, although the transition might have been stronger. Good topic sentence.

Cool Gaelic reference. Excellent research (although he could have cited a little more elegantly).

Cobain's raging performance spoke to young Americans in a way that no one had in a long while (Moon). Michael Azerrad wrote in his 1993 book, *Come as You Are: The Story of Nirvana,* "Ultimately it wasn't so much that Nirvana was saying anything new about growing up in America; it was the way they said it" (Azerrad 226). Cobain's music was conveying a feeling through the way that he performed. It was a feeling shared by many of America's youth, but it was also a feeling that could not have been articulated any other way than the way that Cobain did it (Cohen).

Another good topic sentence.

Again, a good use of research, although the repetition of *Azerrad* is unnecessary in parentheses.

The strong final sentence supports not only the topic sentence of the paragraph, but also the thesis of the paper.

"Smells Like Teen Spirit" starts out with one of the most well-known guitar riffs of the 90s. The four chord progression was certainly nothing new, nothing uncommon. The chords are played with a single guitar with no distortion, and then suddenly the bass and

This topic sentence is a bit on the narrative side and does not connect well with the previous paragraph.

drums come in. When the drums and bass come in the guitar is suddenly distorted, and the pace and sound of the song changes. The song's introduction, with its sudden change, forms a rhythmic "poppy" chord progression to a raging, thrashing of the band's instruments (Moon), sets the pace for the rest of the song.

The chaos from the introduction fades, and it leads in to the first verse, which gives the listener a confused feeling (Azerrad 213). In the first verse the tune of the song is carried by the drums and bass alone, and a seemingly lonely two-note guitar part that fades in and out of the song. The bass, drums and eerie guitar give the listener a "hazy" feeling. Here Cobain's lack of articulation aids in the confused feeling, because as he sings, one can catch articulate phrases here and there. The words that the listener can discern allow them to draw their own connections. Cobain's lyrics do in fact carry a confused message, "It is fun to lose, and to pretend" (Azerrad 213).

The pre-chorus offers up clear articulation of a single word, but this articulation is the perfect precursor to the coming chorus. As the first verse ends, the pre-chorus comes in; Cobain repeats the word "Hello" fifteen times. The repetition of the word Hello draws the confusion that he implicates in the first verse to a close, and in a way reflects on it. As the tone and inflection of his voice changes each time he quotes "Hello," one is not sure whether he is asking a question or making a statement, or both. It is like he is saying, "Hello? Is anybody at home?" while at the same time he exclaims, "Wake up and answer the door!"

The reflection that he implicates in the pre-chorus builds to the raw raging emotions that he expresses in the chorus, as the guitar suddenly becomes distorted, and he begins to scream (Azerrad 214, 226). In the chorus he screams, but somehow the words in the chorus are actually more articulate than those in the verse. As Cobain sings, "I feel stupid, and contagious," anyone who has ever felt like a social outcast understands exactly what Cobain is saying (Cohen), and they understand exactly why he must scream it.

I remember the first time that I heard that line and thinking about it; I was about thirteen, and I thought that there was no better

The description does an excellent job of describing how the song sounds. It is a very difficult task to do this well.

This is a very good topic sentence—it not only leads us from the last paragraph, but also sums up the current one.

Good quote from the song. (He might have cited the song itself, but wanted to include Azerrad's ideas.)

Another good topic sentence, and here the transition is much better implied than in those mentioned earlier.

An insightful analysis of what seems to be a pretty simple lyric. This is excellent work—complicating the simple is a staple of good work in reading culture. The writer also makes a good analogy here.

Omit unnecessary "actually." Again, good reading of the song. So far the writer has done a lot of strong work in (1) contextualizing the song, (2) studying its music, and (3) analyzing its lyrics. It is almost a formula for doing this type of work.

This personal aside adds to the paper, in our opinion—but you word than *"contagious"* to describe the way it feels being in a social situation and not being accepted. Because no one wants to be around that person, they will look at the person with disgust, as if they have some highly *contagious* disease. There is certainly a lot of anger and confusion surrounding those feelings. People needed to hear Cobain scream; they knew how he felt, because they knew how they felt.

People who were experiencing what Cobain was expressing understood what he was saying, because they understood how he felt. In much the same way when someone hits their hand with a hammer that person does not lay down the hammer and calmly say, "Ouch, man that really hurt." They throw the hammer down, and simultaneously yell an obscenity, or make an inarticulate roar, and one knows that they are going to lose a fingernail. Anyone who has smashed their finger with a hammer understands why that person is yelling; in the same way anyone who has felt "contagious" or confused about society knows why Cobain is screaming about feeling "stupid and contagious." Cobain is not examining society. He is experiencing the same things as his audience (Moon); he is "going to lose a fingernail." As the chorus draws to a close, the music still rages, but it changes tempo and rhythm slightly.

The chorus is the most moving part of the song; it is a display of pure emotion. In the chorus Cobain demonstrates what it was that connected with so many; his lyrics said what he meant (Moon). But what he said had been said before, and whether he was articulate or not, people felt what he meant. It was the articulation of that feeling that gained the song such high praise (Moon).

The chorus ends with the phrase, "A mulatto, an albino, a mosquito, my libido"; this line is a reference to social conformity. Cobain is referring to things, or the ideas associated with them that are "outside" of social conformity, and then relating those things back to himself with the phrase "my libido" (Azerrad 210–215). This end to the chorus again goes back to reflect on the feelings expressed in the chorus, and ties them together with a return to the confusion expressed in the verses.

should check with your teacher before including it.

Another analogy—comparison, done in reasonable doses, is an effective technique in doing analysis, particularly if one does it thoughtfully.

The move back to narrative is jarring.

Good topic sentence, although it could be condensed into one sentence.

See previous comment—the topic sentence is doing excellent work but not doing it as "writerly" as it could be done.

The articulation of the lyrics in the second verse gives the confusion more focus than in the first verse. He begins the second verse with the lyric, "I'm worse at what I do best, and for this gift I feel blessed." Although the lyrics are more articulate in the second verse, the feelings of confusion are still there, due to the tempo and rhythm of the music. After Cobain has sung the second verse he returns to the pre-chorus, the repetition of the word Hello. The cycle begins anew.

"Smells Like Teen Spirit" in its entirety gives the listener a complete feeling after listening to it, especially if that listener is feeling confused and frustrated. The song carries one through an entire cycle of emotions, from confusion, to reflection, to frustration. Tom Moon, a Knight-Ridder Newspaper writer, described Nirvana's music as having moments of "tension and release." Being carried through those emotions allows the listener to "vent" their own feelings of confusion and frustration, and at the same time know that someone else feels the same way (Azerrad 226–227). Despite the connection that Cobain made with many there were still many who did not "get" the song; these people often complained about the inarticulation of the lyrics (Azerrad 210).

Weird Al Yankovic utilized the common criticism of the song in his parody "Smells Like Nirvana"; Yankovic parodied "Smells Like Teen Spirit," based entirely on Cobain's obscure articulation. Yankovic is known for parodying popular music, and with lines such as, "And I'm yellin' and I'm screamin', but I do not know what I'm saying," Yankovic stated exactly what so many of the song's critiques had, though he did it with a genuine respect for the song, and its impact (Rawlins).

Weird Al Yankovic's version struck a note with many who liked Cobain's music but could not understand his lyrics (Rawlins). There were many people who did not understand the feelings of confusion, frustration, and apathy that Cobain was getting across. In 1991 when "Smells Like Teen Spirit" first came out I was only 9, and I did not like that kind of music at all. I remember my brother, who is nine years older than me, and who listened to a lot of "heavy metal," bought

We like the way the writer connects ideas, music, and lyrics together again.

Good summary of the song's meaning/content. The writer does a good job of making sure the reader is following his argument.

Now, he switches to other voices. Because the choice is both surprising and apt, the use of Weird Al is a good choice for a source/comparison.

Again, we like the personal reference. It is not as relevant as the other one, but it somehow gives the argument more weight if we know where the writer is "coming from."

Yankovic's *Off the Deep End,* with his parody "Smells Like Nirvana" on it. He thought it was funny because he did not like Nirvana. He never really connected with Cobain's message; even though he did not get what Cobain was saying, he could still enjoy the music. When I became older I did connect with Cobain's music, and Nirvana was one of my favorite bands. My brother never did understand, like many people who never did understand what it was that Cobain was saying (Azerrad 210).

Nirvana made the generation gap clear. It was Nirvana that spoke for a large part of that generation (Moon), where no one else had ever really addressed the confusion and frustration about growing up in America at that time, or at least no one had expressed it in the same way that Nirvana did. They were not the first to vocalize a problem with corporate America, but they were the first *popular* band to convey the feelings that many were feeling *because* of growing up in corporate America, in the way that they did. Cobain did not just show that he has experienced those feelings, but that he was still *experiencing* them, and many young people connected with that (Moon).

In 1992 singer-songwriter Tori Amos illustrated why Cobain's "Smells Like Teen Spirit" had connected with so many by making a cover of the song that was a clear contrast to the original. She rendered the song with a piano, and a clear articulate voice. Her cover of the song became fairly popular, because it was different, and because many people could now understand the lyrics that Cobain had already popularized (Rawlins). The cover was interesting, to say the least; however, it would have been impossible for her version ever to have had the same impact as Cobain's (Rawlins). The lyrics to the song have meaning, and depth, but the emotions that the song conveyed were in and of themselves abstract.

Amos's version of the song articulated each word clearly, her clear voice hit each note on key; her song was comparable to a ballad. Cobain's "Smells Like Teen Spirit" could be described as "sloppy," his guitar distorted through much of the song; he either screamed or mumbled most of the song (Azerrad 214). The two versions of the song illus-

The transition is not strong here, but the topic sentence is good. It again summarizes—this time the band, not the song.

The "corporate America" reference is not clear here. As readers, we know vaguely what he is talking about, but he does not use sources in the same way he has previously when making similar points.

Again, the writer puts comparison to good use. Some writers make the mistake of doing multiple comparisons that all make the same point. Here, the writer uses Tori Amos, whose work is very different from that of both Nirvana and Weird Al, to useful effect—reinforcing his argument.

The writer does a good job of extending the comparison as a way of bringing his own argument to a close.

trate a clear contrast: it is as if Cobain is "angry about being confused" (Azerrad 213), while Amos sings the song to lament Cobain's feelings.

Amos's version of the song became popular for the same reason that it could never have paved the way as Cobain's version did. It was like a ballad, and after everyone heard what Cobain was saying, about society, about America, about growing up, there is one clear emotion that follows the confusion and frustration: sadness. Her "ballad-like" cover of "Smells Like Teen Spirit" exemplified that sadness. But at the same time, people had written ballads about being confused or frustrated, and performed them as Amos performed "Smells Like Teen Spirit"; that was nothing new. However, no one had yet demonstrated such clear and yet abstract confused, frustrated emotions as Cobain did, and at that moment in time that was exactly what America needed to hear (Azerrad 224–225).

Cobain had written and performed a song about his own confusion, and in the process he had connected with young people all over the United States (Moon). He had helped those people to understand their own confusion better. The problem with "Smells Like Teen Spirit" was not that Cobain was not articulate; he could not have articulated his point more clearly than he did. The problem was that not everyone knew what he was talking about, just like not everyone knows what it is like to strike their finger with a hammer. And in the same way, if someone does not know what it is like they might say something foolish like, "That couldn't *hurt* that bad," or "What's *his* problem?" when someone else hits their finger with a hammer, and they make an inarticulate roar. That roar expresses exactly what that person is feeling, but only those who know that feeling, can really understand it. As Michael Azerrad, author of *Come as You Are: The Story of Nirvana,* put it, "you either get it, or you do not" (Azerrad 227). Thus was the case with Cobain's music. "Smells Like Teen Spirit" was his inarticulate roar; it was articulate in that it expressed exactly what he was trying to point out; however, not everyone could grasp what that was.

The conclusion approaches, with the writer putting the work into final context.

The conclusion could be a little stronger—the writer might have taken this argument beyond Nirvana, or put it in a little greater context. He chose instead to close the work by restating the thesis, which is an acceptable way to end the paper.

Overall, the work this paper does is outstanding—it approaches a "cultural text"—a famous song and brings the reader multiple perspectives on it, using comparison, literary and sound analysis, and analogy. It is a good model for doing this type of work.

Works Cited

Azerrad, Michael. *Come as You Are.* New York: Doubleday, 1993.

Cohen, Howard, and Leonard Pitts. "Kurt Cobain Made Rock for Everyone but Kurt Cobain." *Knight Ridder/Tribune* 8 Apr. 1994. Infotrac.

Dettmar, Kevin. "Uneasy Listening, Uneasy Commerce." *The Chronicle of Higher Education.* 14 Sept. 2001: 18. LexisNexis.

Moon, Tom. "Reluctant Spokesman for Generation Became the Rock Star He Abhorred." *Knight Ridder/Tribune* 9 Apr. 1994. Infotrac.

Nirvana. *Nevermind.* David Geffen Company, 1991.

Rawlins, Melissa. "From Bad to Verse." *Entertainment Weekly* 5 June 1992: 57. Infotrac.

PART VII. HOW DO I CITE THIS CAR? GUIDELINES FOR CITING POPULAR CULTURE TEXTS

As you probably know, you must cite or acknowledge any kind of text (written or otherwise) that you use in an academic or professional essay. Most students think that citing work has mostly to do with avoiding plagiarism—and that is certainly an important part of it—but there are other reasons why citing work is important.

As a researcher, your job is often to make sense of a particular phenomenon and in doing so, make sense of the work done before you on the same subject. When you do that, you perform a valuable service for your reader, who now not only has your perspective on this phenomenon, but also has an entry into the subject through the sources you cite. For this very reason, professional researchers and academics often find the works cited pages and footnotes as interesting as the text itself.

As writers in the humanities, you typically use MLA (Modern Language Association) formatting in your papers. There are two other major forms of citing—APA (American Psychological Association), often used in the social sciences and science, and "Chicago" (named for its association with the University of Chicago Press) or "Turabian," often used in history and political science.

All three ways of citing are part of a system of citation. How you *cite* (say where information comes from) is directly related to the bibliography or, in the case of MLA, the works cited page. You indicate in the text who wrote the article or book, and at the end of the paper, the sources are listed in alphabetical order, so the reader can see the whole work, but without the intrusion of listing that whole work within the text; seeing (Alvarez 99) is much easier than seeing (Alvarez, Julia. *How the Garcia Girls Lost Their Accents*, New York: Plume, 1992, 99.) in an essay.

USING PARENTHETICAL REFERENCES

In MLA, you cite using parenthetical references within the body of your essay. The format for the parenthetical reference is easy. If you know the author's name, you include the author's last name and the page number(s) in parentheses before the punctuation mark. For instance, if you are quoting from LeAnne Howe's novel *Shell Shaker*, your parenthetical reference would look like this:

> The novel *Shell Shaker* does a great job of conveying Choctaw pride: "I decide that as a final gesture I will show the people my true self. After all, I am a descendent of two powerful ancestors, Grandmother of Birds and Tuscalusa" (Howe 15).

If the author's name has already been used in the text in a particular reference (not earlier in the essay), then you simply provide the page number (15). If there are two or three authors, then list the authors' last names and the page number (Silverman and Rader 23). For more than three authors, use et al. (Baym et al. 234).

The same holds true for citing an article. Simply list the last name of the author of the article or story or poem, followed by the page number (Wright 7). You do not need to list the title of the book or magazine.

If you use works from the Internet, the system of citing is the same, except you sometimes do not have page numbers, and you often cannot find authors (although you should look hard—sometimes the authorship appears at the end of the text, rather than the beginning). In citing an article from the Internet, use if you can the page's title, rather than the home page. For example, if you are looking at admissions policies at Virginia Commonwealth University, you come to the page and it says "Admissions" at the top. You would then in the text, after your information, type: ("Admissions")—not "Virginia Commonwealth University" and definitely not the webpage address: http://www.vcu.edu/admissions. This form of citing also applies to non-Internet articles without authors. Some of your professors may ask you to tell them from which paragraph the information comes. If that is the case, your in-text citation might look like this: ("Admissions" par. 2).

BUILDING THE WORKS CITED PAGE

A works cited page consists of an alphabetized list of the texts that you cite in your paper. This list goes at the end of an essay in MLA format. This list tells your readers all of the pertinent publication information for each source. It is alphabetized by the last name of the author or, if there is no author, by the title or name of the text. Generally, works cited pages start on a new page and bear the heading "Works Cited." For books, you use the following format, not indenting the first line but indenting the remaining lines.

Clements, Brian. *Essays Against Ruin.* Huntsville: Texas Review Press, 1997.

Notice the crucial aspects in this citation—the author's name, the title of the work, the date it was published, and who was responsible for publishing it. The general rule of citing work is to find all four of these elements in order to help a fellow researcher (or your teacher) find the source and to give appropriate credit to both those who wrote the book and those who brought the book to the attention of the general public. Of course, citing a magazine requires a different format, but with the same idea, as does citing a webpage or a song or a movie. We provide examples of many different sources later.

PLAGIARISM

Citing your work is critical. If you quote from a text in your paper, or if you use information in any way but do not cite this source, the use of this material is plagiarism. At most institutions, plagiarism is grounds for failing the assignment and even the class. At many universities and colleges, students can be dismissed from the institution entirely if plagiarism can be proved.

A student can commit plagiarism in several different ways. One is the deliberate misrepresentation of someone else's work as your own—if you buy a paper off the Internet, get a friend's paper and turn it in as your own, or pay someone to write the paper, you are committing the most serious form of plagiarism.

Then there is the previous example of using someone's work in your text but without citing it, which is also a serious offense. Some students do this inadvertently—they forget where their ideas came from, or mean to find out where the information came from later but do not. Still others want their teacher to think they are intelligent and think that using someone else's work may help. The irony of the last way of thinking is that teachers often are more impressed by the student who has taken the time to do research and incorporate those ideas thoughtfully into a paper—that is what real researchers do.

It is also possible to commit plagiarism without such intent. If you do not paraphrase a source's work completely—even if you cite the source—that is also plagiarism.

Besides the general ethical problem of using someone else's work as your own, the more practical issue with plagiarizing is that you are likely to get caught. As teachers, we become so familiar with the student voice in writing, and a particular student's voice, that it is often not very difficult to catch a cheating student.

WORKS CITED EXAMPLES

The examples shown here cover most citation contingencies; however, if you have trouble deciding how to cite a source, there are a number of options, the best of which is to consult the *MLA Handbook for Writers of Research Papers,* which your library owns, if you do not. Otherwise, you can find any number of Web pages that provide examples of MLA documentation. We recommend the Purdue Writing Center site (http://owl.english.purdue.edu) and the award-winning "Guide for Writing Research Papers" site at Capitol Community College (http://webster.commnet.edu/mla.htm).

Citing Books

Book entries include the following information:

Author's last name, Author's first name. *Title.* City of publication: Publisher, year of publication.

A Book by a Single Author

Clements, Brian. *Essays Against Ruin.* Huntsville: Texas Review Press, 1997.

A Book by Two or Three Authors

After the first author, list subsequent authors' names in published (*not* alphabetical) order.

Levitt, Steven D., and Stephen J. Dubner. *Freakonomics: A Rogue Economist Explores the Hidden Side of Everything.* New York: William Morrow, 2005.

Two or More Books by the Same Author

Arrange entries alphabetically by title. After the first entry, use three hyphens instead of the author's name.

Garber, Frederick. *Thoreau's Fable of Inscribing.* Princeton: Princeton UP, 1991.

---. *Thoreau's Redemptive Imagination.* New York: New York UP, 1977.

An Anthology or Compilation

Silverman, Jonathan, and Dean Rader, eds. *The World Is a Text: Writing, Reading, and Thinking about Culture and Its Contexts.* 4th Edition. Upper Saddle River: Pearson, 2010.

A Book by a Corporate Author

Bay Area AIDS Foundation. *Report on Diversity: 2001.* San Francisco: City Lights Books, 2001.

A Book with No Author

A History of Weatherford, Oklahoma. Hinton: Southwest Publishers, 1998.

A Government Publication

If no author is known, begin with the government's name, and then add the department or agency and any subdivision. For the U.S. government, the Government Printing Office (GPO) is usually the publisher.

United States. Forest Service. *Alaska Region. Skipping Cow Timber Sale, Tongass National Forest: Final EIS Environmental Impact Statement and Record of Decision.* Wrangell: USDA Forest Service, 2000.

The Published Proceedings of a Conference

Ward, Scott, Tom Robertson, and Ray Brown, eds. *Commercial Television and European Children: an International Research Digest. Proceedings of the Research Conference, "International Perspectives on Television Advertising and Children: The Role of Research for Policy Issues in Europe," Held in Provence, France, July 1–3 1984.* Brookfield: Gower, 1986.

An Edition Other Than the First

Gibaldi, Joseph. *MLA Handbook for Writers of Research Papers.* 5th ed. New York: Modern Language Association, 1999.

Citing Articles

Articles use a similar format as books; however, you must include information for the article and the source of its publication. They follow the following format:

Author(s). "Title of Article." *Title of source* day month year: pages.

For newspapers and magazines, the month or the day and the month appear before the year, and no parentheses are used. When quoting from a scholarly journal, the year of publication is in parentheses. When citing articles from periodicals, the month (except May, June, and July) is abbreviated.

An Article from a Reference Book

Deignan, Hebert G. "Dodo." *Collier's Encyclopedia.* 1997 ed.

Voigt, David G. "America's Game: A Brief History of Baseball." *Encyclopedia of Baseball.* 9th ed. New York: Macmillan, 1993. 3–13.

An Article in a Scholarly Journal

Crawford, Rachel. "English Georgic and British Nationhood." *ELH* 65.1 (1998): 23–59.

Ingrassia, Catherine. "Writing the West: Iconic and Literal Truth in *Unforgiven.*" *Literature/Film Quarterly* 26.1 (1998): 53–60.

A Work in an Anthology

Begin with the author of the poem, article, or story. That title goes in quotation marks. Then, cite the anthology, as before. Include the page numbers of the text you use at the end of the citation.

Haven, Chris. "Assisted Living." *The World Is a Text: Writing, Reading, and Thinking about Culture and Its Contexts.* Eds. Jonathan Silverman and Dean Rader. Upper Saddle River: Prentice Hall, 2003. 89–99.

An Article in a Monthly Magazine

Sweany, Brian D. "Mark Cuban Is Not Just a Rich Jerk." *Texas Monthly* Mar. 2002: 74–77.

An Article in a Weekly Magazine

If the article does not continue on consecutive pages, denote this with a plus sign (+).

Gladwell, Malcolm. "The Coolhunt." *The New Yorker* 17 Mar. 1997: 78+.

An Article in a Newspaper

Hax, Carolyn. "Tell Me about It." *The Washington Post* 29 Mar. 2002: C8.

An Article with No Author

"Yankees Net Bosox." *The Richmond Times–Dispatch* 1 Sept. 2001: D5.

A Letter to the Editor

McCrimmon, Miles. "Let Community Colleges Do Their Jobs." Letter. *The Richmond Times–Dispatch* 9 Mar. 1999: F7.

Silverman, Melvin J. "We Must Restore Higher Tax on Top Incomes." Letter. *The New York Times* 8 Mar. 1992: E14.

A Review

Smith, Mark C. Rev. of *America First! Its History, Culture, and Politics*, by Bill Kauffman. Journal of Church and State 39 (1997): 374–375.

A Cartoon

Jim. Cartoon. *I Went to College and It Was Okay.* Kansas City: Andrews and McNeel, 1991. N. pag.

Electronic Sources

A Book Published Online

If known, the author's name goes first, followed by the title of the document or page in quotation marks. If the document/page is part of a larger work, like a book or a journal, then that title is italicized. Include the date of publication, the date of access if known, and the address or URL (uniform resource locator) in angle brackets.

Savage, Elizabeth. "Art Comes on Laundry Day." *Housekeeping—A Chapbook. The Pittsburgh Quarterly Online.* Ed. Michael Simms. Dec. 1997. 20 Mar. 2002 <http://trfn. clpgh.org/tpq/hkeep.html>.

An Article from a Web site

Silverman, Jason. "*2001:* A Re-Release Odyssey." *Wired News* 13 Oct. 2001. 20 Mar. 2002 <http://www.wired.com/news/digiwood/0,1412,47432,00.html>.

A Review

Svalina, Mathias. Rev. of *I Won't Tell a Soul Except the World,* by Ran Away to Sea. *Lost at Sea* July 2001. 2 Mar. 2002 <http://lostatsea.net/LAS/archives/reviews/records/ranaway-tosea.htm>.

A Mailing List, Newsgroup, or E-Mail Citation

If known, the author's name goes first, followed by the subject line in quotations, the date of the posting, the name of the forum, the date of access and, in angle brackets, the online address of the list's Internet site. If no Internet site is known, provide the e-mail address of the list's moderator or supervisor.

An E-Mail to You

Brennan, Brian. "GLTCs." E-mail to the author. 21 Mar. 2002.

An Electronic Encyclopedia

"Play." *Encyclopædia Britannica.* 2007. Encyclopædia Britannica Online. 27 July 2007 <http://www.britannica.com/eb/article-9060375>.

An Article from a Periodically Published Database on Infotrac

Gordon, Meryl. "Truly Deeply Maggie." *Marie Claire* 1 Sept. 2006. 31 July 2007. *LexisNexis Academic.*
   (Some of your professors will ask for a more complete version of this, which includes the place you found it and the original page number.)
Gordon, Meryl. "Truly Deeply Maggie." *Marie Claire* 1 Sept. 2006: 208+. *LexisNexis Academic.* Henry Birnbaum Library, Pace University. 31 July 2007 <http://www.lexis-nexis.com.rlib.pace.edu/universe>.

Other Sources

A Television or Radio Program

List the title of the episode or segment, followed by the title of the program italicized. Then identify the network, followed by the local station, city, and the broadcast date.

"Stirred." *The West Wing.* NBC. WWBT, Richmond, VA. 3 Apr. 2002.

A Published Interview

Morrison, Toni. Interview with Elissa Schnappell. *Women Writers at Work:* The Paris Review *Interviews.* Ed. George Plimpton. New York: Modern Library, 1998: 338–375.

A Personal Interview

Heinemann, Alan. Personal interview. 14 Feb. 2001.

A Film

Olympia. Dir. Bob Byington. King Pictures, 1998.
  Or (depending on emphasis in your paper)
Byington, Bob, dir. *Olympia.* Perf. Jason Andrews, Carmen Nogales, and Damien Young. King Pictures, 1998.

A Sound Recording from a Compact Disc, Tape, or Record

The Asylum Street Spankers. *Spanks for the Memories.* Spanks-a-Lot Records, 1996.

A Performance

R.E.M. Walnut Creek Auditorium, Raleigh, NC. 27 Aug. 1999.

A Work of Art in a Museum

Klee, Paul. *A Page from the Golden Book.* Kunstmuseum, Bern.

A Photograph by You

United States Post Office. Bedford, NY. Personal photograph by author. 15 Aug. 2001.

An Advertisement

Absolut. Advertisement. *Time* 17 Dec. 2002: 12.

Cars, Buildings, Outdoor Sculptures, and Other Odd Texts

Although many of your teachers would not require you to cite a primary text like a car or a building, if you have to do so (or want to), we suggest you follow the guidelines for a text like a movie, which has a flexible citing format, but always includes the title and the date, and hopefully an author of some kind. For example, if you were going to cite something like a Frank Lloyd Wright building, you might do something like this:

Wright, Lloyd Frank, arch. *Robert P. Parker House.* Oak Park, IL: 1892. ("arch." stands for *architect,* like "dir." stands for *director.*)

If, for some reason, you were to cite a car, you might do something like this:

Toyota Motor Company. *Camry.* 1992.

Or, if you knew where the car was built:

Toyota Motor Company. *Camry.* Georgetown, KY: 1992.

But if you knew the designer of the car, you could use that person as an author, similar to the way you can use a screenwriter or a director or an actor for the "author" of a movie.

PART VIII. HOW AM I A TEXT? ON WRITING PERSONAL ESSAYS

We think the best papers come from one's own viewpoint—after all, writing is thinking, and for the most part, the thinking you do is your own. The texts you have been writing about, however, were texts you read from a more general perspective.

But say your professor wants a personal essay, as many freshman composition instructors do. Is it possible to write one using the ideas and techniques of reading texts? Indeed—you are a text, and so are your experiences, feelings, ideas, friends, and relatives. What's more, your experiences and emotions are not culture neutral—they have in some ways been influenced by the expectations living in our culture has generated. Take, for example, one of four ideas often used as personal essay topics in freshmen classes: the prom, the class trip to the beach, the loss of a loved one, or coming to college.

Just so you know, these are the topics we instructors often brace ourselves for, because students often have so little new to say about them. The essays are often laden with description of familiar landscapes, emotions, and events at the expense of any real reflection—they do not tell us anything new about the prom or grief.

Yet, in some way, even going to the beach should be a rich textual experience. Here's why: Not only are you going to the beach, but also you are going to the beach with ideas of the beach in mind, with cultural expectations of what beaches are like, what people do at beaches, and so on. For example, how do we know to wear bathing suits, wear sunscreen, and play volleyball at the beach? Not only because we have done it before, but because we have seen others do it before and have incorporated their ideas about beachgoing into our beachgoing.

So if you write about the prom or a loved one getting ill or dying, try to focus not only on the emotions attached to such an event, but your emotional expectations as well. Did you "not know how to feel"? Why? Was it because you had expected to feel a certain way? How did you know how to act? Were there cultural clues? Did you see a movie about a prom or about death? Proms are a particularly American phenomenon, and have been featured in any number of movies, usually teen romances. Use that knowledge about the prom (or any other subject) in your own writing.

Take another common example. Dying in America has any number of traditions attached to it, depending on what American subculture you belong to. Foreign cultures have very different ways of looking at death. How you view death or illness also may have to do with religious beliefs, the closeness of your family, and so on. But even these ideas about illness and death come from somewhere, and you owe your reader your best guess at how you came to them. So do ideas about what brothers, mothers, fathers, and grandmothers should be if you choose to write about them.

What we are talking about here is what personal essayists often call *reflection*—the idea that we are not only describing our lives but also contemplating them at the same time. Entering college is a particularly ripe time for contemplation; at a minimum, you have a new learning environment, but for most of you, there is a change in friendships and social environments as well. For some of you, it is time for even more upheaval—you may change your career path or your worldview. You probably will not know all this if you decide to write about entering college, but you have some ideas about what your expectations for college are and where you received them. The university setting is a rich cultural text; reading it may provide you additional insight into your own experiences there.

There are more subjects that are worthy of personal reflection than we can count here (the ones we already named are some of the hardest). The idea is to take an experience or event, put it in your own perspective, and reflect on how your perspective may fit in with others. Anything from a trip to the grocery store to a road trip to a phone call to a visit can be the subject of a reflective essay; so can relationships with other people. But what you have to do in these essays is to make sure they matter not only to you but to others as well—that is why focusing on putting your experiences in a cultural perspective can make your writing worth reading (not just worth writing).

Some of you might object to this sort of self-analysis and wonder why you cannot just simply describe your experiences in a paper. For some papers and some teachers, that might be acceptable. But if writing is thinking and writing about oneself is thinking and self-discovery, you owe your reader—and yourself—your best shot at unearthing cultural expectations.

One last note about personal essays: Students often misunderstand their purpose. Although the topic of the personal essay might be your experience, the personal essay is not written for you but for your audience. The story that you tell about the beach or the prom or the death of a loved one is not as important as what you learned from the event. Simply recounting your trip to the beach is not nearly as interesting as what you saw, observed, and learned from your trip to the beach. Even more important is to consider what your audience can learn from what you learned. How can your experiences help the reader? The two great advantages you have as a personal essayist are recognition and discovery. In the best personal essay about a prom, the reader recognizes something familiar (an awkward moment, a romantic dance, the smell of hairspray), but also discovers something new about the text that is a prom because of your essay. So, as you sit down to draft a personal essay, think about how you might use this opportunity to help your reader learn something new about a topic they think they already know.

ONE LAST WORD ON MAKING THE WORLD YOUR OWN TEXT

The authors are readers, which is why this book keeps changing. For every article that makes it in, we have often read anywhere from a half dozen to a dozen or more. We say this only to encourage you to read on your own. Some of our favorite periodicals include (many of which we drew from for this and previous editions): *The New Yorker*, *Slate*, *Salon.com*, *The New York Times*, *Mental Floss*, *Good*, *Harper's*, *Wired*, *Vanity Fair*, *Mother Jones*, *Utne Reader*, *The Washington Post*, *The Village Voice*, *Talking Points Memo*, *FiveThirtyEight.com*, *MediaShift*, *Sports Illustrated*, *Mashable!*, *Rolling Stone*, and so on. We have placed a list of links on our Website to many of these and other periodicals.

The World Is a Text

READING

1 Reading and Writing about the World Around You

"There was a time when meanings were focused and reality could be fixed; when that sort of belief disappeared, things became uncertain and open to interpretation." This observation, from British painter Bridget Riley, serves as a way into the second part of *The World Is a Text*, and, in particular, to this first chapter. Here and elsewhere we emphasize the possibility and importance of "reading" and interpreting the world around you by paying attention to the arguments texts make.

In the introduction, we gave you a theoretical basis for reading the world as a text; here we show you how writers might perform such a task. We asked colleagues and students to undertake analyses of topics of their choosing, using an approach that focused both on how to read such a text and that performed a reading of said text. In making their choices, they show us how diverse both the topics and the approaches might be.

The idea behind this chapter is to introduce you to the act of thinking about common texts as thought-out constructions designed to enable some kind of effect or reaction. Or, put in the language of rhetoric—we want you to learn to recognize how texts—even seemingly small texts—make arguments. For example, Elisabeth Piedmont-Marton unpacks numerous arguments various clothes can make by identifying our associations with jeans or shirts or sweaters. Catherine Zimmer writes about what YouTube might mean. Of course, paying attention to how other texts make arguments helps you when it comes time to make arguments of your own in your papers.

The essays in this chapter have two main purposes: to help model reading and writing about nontraditional texts. The writers walk readers through the interpretation of nontraditional texts in a sophisticated but accessible voice, putting the theory behind semiotics to work. Our hope is that these help you approach your own papers, and one way of making the transition to writing your own papers is by noticing how other writers are doing their work. As you read these essays, pay attention to the details the authors use to make their points. Do they have a thesis? Do they use specific examples? Do they back up their arguments with evidence? What processes do they use to "read" and "interpret" the various texts? If you recall the section on lenses from the Introduction, you might also ask yourself what lenses the authors use to interpret their texts. Our hope here is that you begin to notice the way other writers make connections, ground their observations in concrete examples, and take informal readings and make them formal. In other words, we want you to see how these writers decode the rhetoric of nontraditional texts and use this to make their own rhetorical constructions. A few writers in this section have also reflected on their own processes of writing their essays. We want you to see how different writers approach the idea of writing.

Thirsty? See the essay "Reading and Writing about the Road" later in the chapter (p. 103).

As we mention in the Introduction, this chapter is composed entirely of original, commissioned essays written especially for this issue of *The World Is a Text*. Jonathan Silverman, the co-author of this book, has published in a number of fields, including literary studies, American studies, and music. He also recently completed a book on Johnny Cash. Similar to Rader, Silverman looks at signs and signifiers along American highways. Elisabeth Piedmont-Marton is a professor at Southwestern University, where she directs the writing center. She, too, has published widely, including a number of essays on art, culture, and politics. Jonathan Hunt, a professor in the highly regarded Program in Writing and Reading (PWR) at Stanford, contributes a reading of the "fixie" bicycle—a phenomenon that reaches beyond San Francisco. Peter Hartlaub has one of the best jobs on the planet—he is the pop culture critic and video game reviewer for the *San Francisco Chronicle*. His essay "reads" video games. Catherine Zimmer is an assistant professor of English and film studies at Pace University. Lee Transue is a recent graduate of Pace University who is now working for a start-up publishing house in New York. His essay reads *Family Guy* through the lens of a stream-of-consciousness. Cristina DeLuca, the former editor-in-chief of *The Pace Press* and a recent graduate of Pace University, now works for the New York City Parks and Recreation Department. Her essay addresses the question: What do those Facebook photographs really mean? Brandon Brown is a physicist and the associate dean for science at the University of San Francisco. Brown recently won first prize in *Seed Magazine's* science essay contest. His contribution examines a science lab as a complicated text. Dean Rader, the co-author of this book, and Silverman collaborate on a how-to essay for reading an advertisement. Phil West is a writer, arts organizer, public relations professional, and educator based in Austin, Texas. And he is three degrees from Kevin Bacon. (He was in *SlamNation* (1998) with Saul Williams, who was in *K-PAX* (2001) with Alfre Woodard, who was in *Beauty Shop* (2005) with Kevin Bacon.)

Reading and Writing about Fashion

Elisabeth Piedmont-Marton

MOST HIGH SCHOOL STUDENTS would be surprised to learn that they are highly skilled semioticians, or readers of signs. Able to recognize a complex array of signs and symbols at twenty paces or more, they can form remarkably reliable conclusions about the person heading toward them in the hall outside the cafeteria or dawdling in front of the kiosk in the mall. The guy with the oversized pants and the faux-hawk? Skate punk. A guy with short-sleeved white shirt and ill-fitting blue pleated chinos? Science teacher. Depending on geographic region, size, and the populations they serve, high schools have different categories into which fashion texts can be divided, but the reason most students are such skilled readers of these texts is that high school has a relatively fixed number of subject positions, or selves, that fashion can indicate. Even the girl with blue hair slumped against her locker signifies that she rejects the constraints of high school fashion by signifying that she belongs to the group of kids who wish to signal that They Don't Belong. Once free from the fixed taxonomy of high school, however, these skilled semioticians must broaden their symbolic lexicon and sharpen their skills at both reading and composing fashion texts.

Fashion, or more broadly, dress, is the outer text of the body, signifying basic information such as gender, class, age, and status and occupation. In high school, these categories are relatively stable: everyone is about the same age, and has neither a professional identity nor independent means. The terms that are variable communicate status, economic and otherwise; values, such as religion and politics; avocation, such as sports, art, computers, and other interests; and affiliation, such as what kind of music one listens to. Fashion can say a lot of things. It cannot, however, say nothing. In other words, if you want to dress in such a way to signify that you care nothing about fashion, then you must nevertheless use the language of fashion in order to construct that text. The dream of creating a meaning-neutral mode of dress is a powerful one: it's the rationale for both school uniforms and for the imaginary unisex jumpsuits of science fiction. If there is any doubt that the uniform cannot diffuse fashion's signifying charge, consider the rich variations schoolchildren and professional athletes display in their uniforms.

Even when we roll out of bed and pull on the first thing we can find, we are authoring a text. That text can say, "I just got out of bed and don't care what I look like at the moment." Or can also say, "I don't choose to participate in the textual exchange of fashion." What we cannot say with our haphazard and apparently artless dress is "Fashion is not a text," because we would have to use the language of fashion in order to send that message.

Although the text of fashion is incapable of refusing signification, it does not follow that what it signifies is narrowly determined. As many theorists have argued in recent decades, all sign systems are always indeterminate and unanchored, and fashion is no exception. From this perspective, the richness and the pleasure of the text is in the endless possibilities for play, for destabilizing fixed categories, subverting expectations, up-ending categories, and generally messing with people's heads. This play is perhaps most visible when women dress like men and vice versa, but also takes more subtle forms, such as when a young hipster wears pants that once apparently belonged to a professional golfer in 1970. The surprise and delight we experience when we read a text like that derives from the unexpected contrast between register of the wearer and the signifying charge of the plaid polyester pants. The same pleasure is not obtained if the hipster also dons a matching shirt and shoes. Then it's just a costume, which doesn't invite readers into the same level of engagement.

Like texts of all kinds, fashions won't yield immediately to our critical strategies. Encountering a fashion text that we don't quite "get" is one of the great pleasures of becoming attuned to the semiotics of dress. I'll close with a story of an encounter with an enigmatic fashion text that refused to yield to my exegetical powers. Several years ago, a young and quite successful fiction writer and screenwriter visited the campus where I work. He very much looked the part of the young literary star: long haired and rumpled clothing made from quality fabrics, punctuated with stylish and expensive shoes. At the dinner with invited faculty, however, he added a piece to his ensemble, as if to recognize the formality of the occasion where professors wear their once-a-year suits and dresses. He had added an ugly brown cardigan sweater made from acrylic fiber, a sweater only Mr. Rogers could have loved. At the end of the evening and after investigating at close range, I concluded that it was a hilarious ironic commentary on the mannered tweediness and trying-too-hard hipness of the professoriate. But then he also wore it the next night when he delivered his reading and lecture to a large audience. Far away on the stage the sweater just slumped there on his slight shoulders, not looking at all ironic. It may have been contemptuous ("I don't care enough about your little college to dress for the occasion, so I'm wearing this crappy sweater"), or reassuring ("I'm terribly insecure in these situations, and this sweater I got from my grandfather's closet after he died comforts me"), or hyper-cool ("What?! You don't know that brown polyester cardigans are featured in everyone's runway shows this season?").

Another important lesson from this experience is that there is often a potential gap between the *intention* of the wearer and the *reception* of the viewer. That is, this guy may have wanted to send one message by wearing the sweater, but, for whatever reason, I received a different message. Who knows what message other people received? Wearing Chuck Taylor sneakers with a suit could be interpreted a number of different ways—that the wearer is hip, that the wearer is homeless or out of pocket, or that the wearer has a long walk to public transportation. So, although we may obsess over the messages sent by the clothes our friends, boyfriends, girlfriends, teachers, parents, and idols wear, we must always keep in mind that fashion is a fluid text, contingent on interpretation. As any reader of a poem or short story knows, the key to accurate interpretation is context. So, what the guest writer may have been suggesting with the combination of hip clothes but ratty sweater is something like, "Even though I'm now a cool Hollywood writer, I'm also, really, at my core, a lot like you academic types." Of course, he also may have been mocking us academic types.

I could never decide what the sweater signified, but I'm sure it was trying to tell me something. If I ever run into the writer again, I'm going to ask him what the sweater meant, but who knows if he will tell the truth!

How I Wrote This Essay Elizabeth Piedmont-Marton

Why did you write this piece—what was the assignment or motivation for writing?

I wrote this because the editors asked me to contribute. I think I came up with the idea of writing about fashion.

How did you begin?

I think I started with the idea of the famous author's (Michael Chabon's) cardigan sweater. He had been here for a visit, and I couldn't get that thing out of my mind.

Describe the process of writing the first draft.

Just sat down at the computer and wrote it pretty quickly.

Did you write a draft all the way through?

Yes.

How much editing did you do as you wrote?

Probably not much, but certainly some.

How long would you say the process took?

A couple of hours all told.

How did you edit the draft?

As usual, I really need to print out and look at a hard copy before I get a full sense of the necessary revisions and corrections. Then I go back to the computer.

What was the response when you turned in your essay?

I think Dean liked it, but made a minor few suggestions. I also seem to recall that he just went ahead—with my permission—and rewrote one sentence.

Are you satisfied now with what you wrote? Would you make any changes?

I'm pretty satisfied with it. Looking back at it, I wish I had pushed back a little harder and written a better last sentence myself. Not that Dean's isn't fine—it's just not what I would have written, and I was too busy to do much about it at the time.

Reading and Writing about a Bicycle

Jonathan Hunt

NOT LONG AGO, and quite suddenly, it seemed, my neighborhood was overrun by bicyclists on a new kind of bike—a sort of *reduced* bike, with no brakes or gears. Or let me put it more precisely: *I* was nearly overrun. The culprit was a young person who sped through an intersection against the light and without slowing, leaving consternation and resentment behind her among the pedestrians and motorists who—naively, it now seemed—allowed their movements to be guided by illuminated signals. As she flew away down the street, I could see that she was on a track bike, a special kind of racing

Fixie graffiti, downtown San Francisco (2007). © Jonathan Hunt. Some rights reserved.

Racers at Hellyer Park Velodrome (2007). © Steven Ryan. Some rights reserved.

Sylvester Stallone as Judge Dredd.

bicycle built for indoor competition, characterized by a single fixed gear; hence its more popular name, the "fixie."

But the fixie subculture in my neighborhood had nothing to do with track racing, which shares most of the visual features of the professional road racing. If you have cable, you can watch it on *Versus* (the rodeo, kickboxing, deer-hunting, and cycling channel): brightly colored bicycles matching the tight Lycra outfits of their athletic riders, bicycles and cyclists alike splashed all over with the names and logos of corporate sponsors, all shaved legs and huge lungs topped with Judge Dredd helmets, chasing each other around and around according to complicated and opaque rules.

The skinny kids congregating in front of the coffee shop down the street or in certain corners of the local park didn't look like that. They had unruly hair and tattooed arms, and their astonishingly tight pants were scuffed black denim, not shiny Lycra.

"Sweet Pink Fixie in SF" (2006). © Jean Davis. All rights reserved. Used by permission.

Their gleaming, matchy bicycles at first seemed a contrast to their scruffy appearance: I saw an orange bike with an orange seat, orange wheels, orange tires, orange pedals and orange handlebar tape, its few chrome bits polished to a gleam. Another bike, flawlessly powder blue, featured white handlebar tape with red hearts on it, and an ace of hearts playing card to match, stuck jauntily in the spokes of the rear wheel. Among these pristine steeds, some bikes seemed to have the same careful carelessness as their owner's hairstyle: an old, chipped steel frame seemed to take pride in the worn decal with the name of a long-dead Italian frame-builder; a low-end ten-speed crusted with grease and dirt, converted to a fixie by removal of the brakes and replacement of the back wheel.

In fixie subculture, then, the bikes themselves vary widely, but two properties are invariably prized. The first of these is minimalism. None of the fixed-gear bikes I've spotted have racks, baskets, fenders, chain guards, cushy seats, bells, or other common bicycle accessories in the style of Pee-Wee Herman's beloved cruiser. The second property is a related lack of safety features: very few have reflectors or brakes (in fact, a T-shirt in circulation proclaims "If it's fixed, don't brake it")—in a related sartorial code, few fixie riders I've seen wear helmets, favoring faded cycling caps with Italian brand names: *Campagnolo, Cinelli, Bottecchia*. In one sense, the values of a subculture are conveyed quite clearly in the choice of display objects (bikes, in this case, but hairstyles, handbags, or hot rods would do equally well). The fixie rider values sleek minimalism tinged with rebellious nostalgia, a reaction against the gadgetry-driven "newer-is-better" ethos that dominates the bicycle industry and American consumer culture more broadly. Against

Trackstars (2007). © Randy Reddig. All rights reserved. Used by permission.

Still from *The Impossible Hour* (1974).

the ever-more-complicated gearing, braking, and suspension systems of mountain and road bikes, the fixie recalls a lost golden age of European cycling, an age before Lycra shorts, neon colors, and Styrofoam helmets (a sacred text is *The Impossible Hour*, Danish director Jørgen Leth's 1974 homage to cycling on the track). Against the square practicality of conventional bicycle advocates, the fixie rider values a stylish recklessness, an affiliation with outlaw bike messenger culture (which pioneered the fixed-gear trend decades ago). Steve Carell's character in *The 40-Year-Old Virgin* is the antithesis of fixie cool.

Yet the meaning of a display-oriented subculture goes beyond the conscious messages associated with choices of accessories, clothing, hairstyles, or music. The fixie cyclist (or fixist? fixster?) announces her or his difference or departure from the "parent" culture (and other bicycle subcultures), but in doing so, remains entwined in systems of sameness and difference that constitute all cultural affiliations. In short, fixie variation takes place within an overarching sameness: the fixie enthusiast seems free to choose colors (generally eschewing patterns) and certain limited accessories (the playing card in the spokes, the saddle), and in fact, the act of making these choices is strongly encouraged. The oohs and ahs down at the coffee shop are exclusively reserved for unique bikes, such as the one with mismatched wheels but perfect color coordination, a combination of components displaying the owner's creativity and design sense. Fixie cool has its boundaries, just as any kind of design or fashion statement: *cool* involves breaking certain sets of rules (and, in some cases, laws), but at the same time, it requires adherence to a strict new set of conventions.

The fixed-gear bike is thus not just a vehicle for transport (although it is that), but it is also a vehicle for communicating the values and characteristics of its owner. Many of

"Off-the-rack Masi" (2007). © Jonathan Hunt. Some rights reserved.

these values and characteristics are transmitted intentionally, such as design sense, mechanical aptitude, and riding skills; the fixster values these traits in her- or himself and in fixie "colleagues." In selecting components, in assembling the bicycle, and in surviving urban traffic on a bicycle with no brakes, the fixist broadcasts these desirable traits—traits that, to those not attached to the subculture, seem annoying or irresponsible.

The fixie bicycle, then, is a marker of opposition to mainstream culture, with its sensible values and readily available consumer choices. Trapped in a world where people are defined by the objects they buy at the mall, the fixist aspires to be different by assembling a unique machine—because of this aspiration, an off-the-rack Bianchi or Masi fixie from the bike shop is practically a badge of shame (note, however, that even corporate manufacture of fixies adheres to the style code: the dreaded Bianchi is all chrome, with minimalist decals). Like any consumers, fixsters seek to map out their individualities with a constellation of purchases, but as with purchasers of Levi's and Mini Coopers, their individuality is commodified by the very gesture (the purchase) that seeks to establish it.

The meaning of the fixed-gear bike—like the meaning of any object—depends on a play of sameness and difference: it is like other bikes, yet not like them; its rider is like other consumers, yet different. Like other texts, the fixie can be read in isolation or in relation to related systems of meaning (e.g., the fashion system, the gender system). Some of its meanings are explicit and intentional; others, less flattering to the rider, cannot be outrun no matter how fast they pedal.

"Your Fixie Makes You Look Fat" (2006). © Franco Follini. Some rights reserved.

Reading and Writing about Video Games

Peter Hartlaub

WE ARE AT THE BEGINNING, and there is only Pong.

Like a single-celled organism crawling out of the primordial ooze, it appears as an outhouse-size arcade game in a few bars and pizza parlors in 1972, before a much smaller take-home version starts selling at Sears. Both are as simple looking as a block of cheese.

Reading the game takes a split second, if you're slow. Two long rectangles moving on a vertical axis try to block a small square block traveling horizontally or diagonally, with numbers in the upper left and right corners of the screen that represent the score. Instructions aren't necessary—if you can operate a thermostat, you can play Pong. Two round dials control the paddles. A switch in the back turns the machine on and off.

The first mainstream video game says almost nothing about the people who enjoy it, or even its creator. What are his artistic influences? Is he an optimistic person, or filled with darkness and doubt? Does he have a humorous or whimsical side? You won't learn these things from playing Pong.

The Dragon's Lair arcade game is, in the words of a 10-year-old in 1983, "Totally rad." The front and sides have ornate and colorful drawings of knights and fire-spitting dragons, not unlike the ones that are appearing on the sides of conversion vans and the covers of heavy metal albums at this time in American popular culture.

The creator of the game, Don Bluth, has worked with Disney, but you knew that when you walk up to the monitor—which for the first time uses a laserdisc to simulate animation that is as good as anything you'll find in the theaters. The presentation is grand and musical and a bit funny, like a trip through the Pirates of the Caribbean ride at Disneyland.

Just a few years earlier, people in video games were basically stick figures. But your character, Dirk the Daring, looks and acts like a real person, whose body language alone tells the story of a man who is brave, foolish, and uncomfortable in his own skin. His lanky body and clumsy stride make you wonder how he got to be a knight in the first place. Did his father have connections in the royal guard?

There's a joystick and four buttons on the front of the game, with a few instructions written underneath the monitor in a medieval font. The only words on-screen are the "Credits = 0" text in the bottom right corner. Presumably, the creator of this game wanted nothing to clutter his artistic statement.

On-screen text in video games was like an arms race in the 1990s, and by the turn of the century there's enough readable information to tell a fairly complete story with a single image. The following is gathered from one screenshot, a pause in action from the 2001 Xbox video game *Halo:*

A ship hovers overhead, but the ornate writing on the side doesn't come from the world of Master Chief, the Earth-born commando whose movements you control from the first-person perspective. The ship's hostile intentions are confirmed from the frozen-in-time pink laser blasts in the space soldier's direction.

Master Chief is carrying a big gun, but it will soon be useless. The bulky blaster rifle carries sixty shots, but a counter on the gun that faces the player reveals that only four rounds are left—with no remaining clips.

Another counter at the top left part of the screen displays some more bad news: Master Chief's grenade reserve is down to three, and a gauge on the top right reveals that his shields have taken a hit.

In the lower left-hand corner of the screen a circular radar sensor shows that six heavily armed insect creatures are on foot, fifteen meters away, and closing ground fast. The space bugs are about to win.

The boxer trading punches with Muhammad Ali is you, assuming you chose to bother with the create-your-own-character mode in the 2007 video game *Fight Night Round 3.*

Read the Xbox 360 title like a text, and you can discover something about its creators, the real-life boxers whose likenesses are included in the game and the executives who make the marketing and business decisions for the company.

Unlike *Halo,* the game has no letters, numbers, or shaded meters to let players know the status of their fighter. (The boxer's heart rate can be felt on the controller, which rumbles heavily when he's about to fall.) But the background is filled with writing, including banners advertising an athletic clothing line that are visible at every angle, and background music that is carefully chosen to launch a hot new artist. Text displays the band's name and album information as each new song is played.

The game also says something about the person playing it. Do you attack your opponent, or lay back to parry blows? Is your boxer wearing simple clothing, or the sequined trunks of a modern-day Apollo Creed, with your name boldly emblazoned across the wasteline?

And if you chose to make the fighter on screen in your own image, does the character on-screen look like you, or the person you want to be? Do you give your video game doppelgänger love handles, a receding hairline, and that bad tattoo you got in Mexico on spring break thirteen years ago, or will he be a new improved version of whatever really looks back at you in the mirror every morning?

Video games have evolved quickly since the early 1970s, beginning as toys and developing into an art form that is exceptionally participatory. With each new advance, the act of reading them becomes more dynamic.

Audiences influence many art forms, especially theater and music. Even a television show such as *American Idol* gives the viewer multiple chances to become part of the show. But with avatars, online cooperative play, and the *Grand Theft Auto* "digital sandbox" model of cities that players can freely explore, games are becoming less about the creators and more about the imaginations of whoever is playing.

As we move forward into an age of photorealism, accurate simulations, and controllers that are sensitive to the motions of the human body, is a walk down the street in a video game that much different than a walk down the street in your neighborhood?

During the Pong era, reading a video game wasn't much different than reading a hula hoop (or, perhaps more accurately, a game of catch between two robots). Years later, the process has become almost as complicated and nuanced as real life.

Reading and Writing about Social Networking Sites: Making Friends and Getting "Poked"

Cristina DeLuca

SO, HOW MANY FRIENDS DO YOU HAVE?

If this question immediately makes you think of the last time you logged on to your Facebook or MySpace page, then you already have the skills to "read" a social networking website (and all this time you thought you were procrastinating on the Internet). As you probably know firsthand, perfecting a Facebook or MySpace profile is an activity on which college students spend inordinate amounts of their time. This might be because between high school and college, students experience the freedom to shift away from their constraining high school identities toward something completely new. Once you arrive on campus, no one knows the "jock," "alpha girl," "nerd," or "drama queen" you may have been categorized as in high school, and for many students, this newfound anonymity can be quite liberating. In fact, the innumerable opportunities to remake identity are the main draws of these sites and the reason young people—the very demographic struggling toward identity—are turning to virtual sites instead of traditional social groups.

For many students, the transition from high school to college life is stressful because they are met with the arduous task of finding a new circle of friends. Because browsing their peers' Facebook or MySpace profiles online requires no personal contact, social networking sites allow students the liberty to look for potential friends without having to utter a single (potentially embarrassing) word or feel self-conscious about proper body language. Similar to how certain clothes or hairstyle make a first impression, social networking sites can provide a flattering first look into a student's personality. What type of music they listen to, books they've read, Internet video clips that make them laugh, and what their friends have to say about them all converge into a webpage that is their own unique cyber fingerprint. These pages are thoughtfully constructed and continuously managed—entirely not-random text. A profile page on a social networking site is the result of a series of careful choices based on information we want to reveal about ourselves.

The profile photo on the top of the page is the key component of all social networking websites and sets the tone for the entire profile. A site user's interests in books, movies, and music all seem secondary to this feature. Exploring this all-important feature semiotically can not only make you a savvier site user but may also provide some insight into the presentation of your own profile page. Although there are minor exceptions, the profile photo exists in three varying forms: the photo of the user surrounded by friends or in a social situation, the artsy self-portrait, and the irreverent photo. All three types of images represent the first impression of the profile page, summing up the site user in one single frame.

For instance, a person would most likely want to be viewed as "social" if his profile photo displays him holding a plastic red cup with his arms around a bunch of equally happy guys and girls. This type of photo conforms to a popular category of users among friends, and it is a natural choice. Humans instinctively find comfort in groups of other people and showing to the world that we "fit in." This photo tells viewers, *I am well liked, and I am with other people who think I am friendly and fun too.* The red plastic cup probably contains beer, and that shows that the user isn't uptight and likes to have a good time. However, some users may see the photo and dismiss this person as a shallow frat brother. Users with social profile photos also risk looking insecure. If a person has to be surrounded by people to prove his self-worth, perhaps he doesn't know himself very well.

Attempting to present the opposite appearance that the social photograph does is the artsy self-portrait. A typical example of this picture includes a photo of a girl or guy in a dimly lit room, looking away from the camera very seriously. This common pose adds an element of mystery and intrigue to the profile. The darkness and stylized aspects of the photograph reveal characteristics that say, *I'm too deep for this website.* Perhaps the artsy self-portrait is the user's way of proclaiming his or her reluctance to join the social networking craze. Taking the picture themselves, and thereby controlling every aspect of the photograph, those who choose the self-portrait may be less interested in being perceived as well liked and more interested in creating a profile page that displays their unique perspective of the world. A viewer of this photo could be either intrigued by the user's resistance to prove his or her popularity, or possibly turned off by the user's potentially self-righteous (*It's all about me!*) attitude.

Of course, both of these photos can pigeonhole the user into a very specific category (such as "party animal" and "dramatic," respectively) before the viewer even reads the rest of the profile. That's where the irreverent, completely out of context, photo comes in. An irreverent photo is any one (animal, vegetable, or mineral) that is not actually a picture of the user himself. This may show that the user has a sense of humor, either about himself or the website. "Identifying" yourself as some physical person or object other than you goes against conventional wisdom. For example, if someone has a photo of a panda bear on his profile page, you are forced to think, *This person is obviously not a panda bear*, and read further into it to devise some kind of meaning. Perhaps he is mocking the predictable structure of the site, or the mores we follow to express ourselves in the "correct" way. Or, he doesn't want to have his photo plastered on a website for millions to see. Or, of course, he just might really like panda bears. The viewer of this photo may laugh along at its absurdity or dismiss it as plain confusing. Viewers of the irreverent photo might also be disappointed that they cannot see what the individual actually looks like.

Whatever the photo, the site user's intended meaning will not always come across successfully to every viewer. As with face-to-face encounters, site users cannot completely control every aspect of how their profile pages will be received. These variables aside, social networking websites allow users to fashion an online identity that enables them to meet others that can appreciate their profile choices (and weed out those who don't). So I say, treat these next few years as an opportunity to remake yourself by logging on and discovering who is online. Not just another Web page in cyberspace, each profile on a social networking site is a cultural text brimming with meaning, and waiting to be examined.

PS: Facebook me, won't you?

How I Wrote This Essay Cristina DeLuca

Why did you write this piece—what was the assignment or motivation for writing?

I chose to write about the social networking site Facebook because I have always been interested in how people (myself included) use the website as an extension of their "selves." Since Facebook has become a top pastime among college students, I thought it would be worthwhile to explore how they use this technology to express identity. Because every aspect of the Facebook profile can be individually customized, the user makes dozens of deliberate choices via Facebook as to how best present himself to the rest of the world. I loved the idea of thinking critically about a website that is not necessarily viewed in such an "academic" way.

What did you do when you got the assignment/decided to write your essay?

When I first received the assignment to write my essay, I was fortunate to finally have the opportunity to justify my compulsive Facebook usage for "academic purposes." I spent a lot of time studying the profile photos of my friends; in particular I examined the composition of each photo and tried to make meaning from each of its elements: is the person facing the camera? Is the entire body visible? Is the person photographed in a group? Etc.

How did you begin?

I began by typing. Normally I hand write an outline before I begin an academic paper, but I was really excited about this subject. I just started typing my ideas, and those sketches of ideas later served as blueprints for topic sentences, from which I could further flesh out my essay.

Describe the process of writing the first draft.

As I wrote the first draft, I was careful to write straight through and not second guess what I was writing, even if I did not know where a particular idea would lead. I find that stopping and starting frequently disrupts my thought process. I also like to listen to music when I write and type along freely to the rhythm, getting into a groove without stopping. Whatever I do, I try my hardest to just keep writing.

In my first draft I wrote about all aspects of the Facebook profile page, including the "interests and activities" sections and "wall." As I began the editing process, I realized that my strongest ideas were in the sections where I discussed the profile picture, so I decided to cut the rest and stick with that.

Did you write a draft all the way through?

Yes, I wrote a draft all the way through and then edited it significantly afterwards.

How much editing did you do as you wrote?

I tried to not edit as I wrote because I tend to lose good ideas when I edit too quickly. Even if I think I have spelled a name or word incorrectly, I don't stop.

Did you do research as you wrote or before you started writing? What databases did you use?

The only research I did for this essay was the "reading" of Facebook profile pages.

How long would you say the process took?

The entire writing process, from concept to final product, took about a month.

How did you edit the draft?

I edited the draft by first printing it out and editing the hard copy. My editing process consists of first shifting around sentences and paragraphs, then further developing ideas, then rewriting sentences for clarity, and finally improving transitions between paragraphs, grammatical issues and word choice.

What was the response when you turned in your essay?

I wrote this essay two years after I graduated from college and a year before I entered graduate school, so to say the least, I felt my writing was pretty rusty. The response to my ideas was positive, but the essay was sorely lacking in effective transitions. Fortunately I was able to work on improving them in the second draft.

Are you satisfied now with what you wrote? Would you make any changes?

I am very satisfied with what I wrote; however, the problem with writing an essay about technology is that it soon feels dated. For example, when I first created the title for the essay, "poking" was much more of a poplar feature on Facebook, whereas now it isn't used as often, if at all. If I could change anything, I would probably change the title.

Reading and Writing about *Family Guy:* The Semiotics of Stream of Consciousness

Lee Transue

IT IS THE CERTIFICATION OF TRUE TALENT when a storyteller can write that which he or she feels *can* be written, and not what *should* be written by typical literary standards, while the audience remains unaware of his or her sleight of hand. There are many words and phrases to describe the technique, foremost amongst them *stream of consciousness;* however, such qualifications fail to embrace the varied and complex forms this type of writing takes for simple reasons: There are simply too many pieces of literature so vastly incomparable to the next that to call one piece a work written in stream of consciousness acts only to cyclically render other works of totally different execution, but also written in stream of consciousness, a different "style" of the form. Of course this creates a fundamental problem with stream of consciousness. The form becomes much like the color blue. Yes, the sky is often blue. Your parents may have once owned a blue Volkswagen Beetle. You may feel "blue" during the winter months, and you just might be reading this with Blue Öyster Cult's Donald Roeser singing "Ooooooh, Godzilla!" through your buds. So what is *blue*? And what is *stream of consciousness*? The easy answer is that they're both vague concepts with a great number of examples to define them. Typically, the form is written quickly, sometimes rabidly, by an author who is free-associating each word or concept with the next with no real concern for the immediate structure of the text. Rather, he or she is concerned with the work as a whole, representing the mass of competing ideas all masterfully packed into one story, somehow all coming together in the end through bits and pieces by way of the conscience splayed out in some poetic collage. And there is one example of a work of stream of consciousness that millions of both Americans and Europeans ingest happily and with ease on a weekly basis. That work being, of course, Seth MacFarlane's perennially successful animated television series, *Family Guy*.

Stream of consciousness is not an unfamiliar concept to sitcom viewers; however, *Family Guy's* brand of the form is alien to the free-association style of humor that, say, *Seinfeld* gained massive popularity with (often touted as "the show about nothing"). Unlike the famously loose plots of *Seinfeld*, the premise of *Family Guy* is the convention for most television sitcoms, live action or animated, present or past, in that it follows the Griffins, a standard nuclear American family (in its case a father, Peter; mother, Lois; two adolescent siblings, Chris and Meg; an infant, Stewie; and their dog, Brian) through their blue-collared existence in the fictional town of Quahog, Rhode Island. But unlike most typical sitcom families, there are certain exceptions that set the Griffins apart from the lot. Peter is an unapologetic drunk with the attention span and sense of humor of a seven-year-old; Lois is an articulate, strong woman from an exceedingly wealthy family; Meg is unpopular and unattractive (and is constantly reminded of both); Chris is simply dumb (but held a stint as a professional artist for one episode); Stewie, the infant (and a star of the series), continuously tries to kill Lois and obtain world domination (a bit more drastic than the occasional, "How rude!"); and Brian, the dog, can talk, drives a hybrid, and loves martinis. And Quahog beyond the Griffin household is just as colorful: The mayor is a delusional Adam West of *Batman* fame (voiced by Mr. West himself); Peter's neighbors and friends consist of a sexual deviant, a paraplegic police officer, and a gentle deli owner who is one of the few black characters on the show. Many other characters appear infrequently on the show, including a soft-voiced, elderly ephebophile, a giant chicken that battles Peter each time they come across one another, an evil monkey that lives in Chris's closet, and the Grim Reaper (who still lives with his mother and can't get dates). So, as Jerry Seinfeld and Co. all-too-perfectly present a stream-of-consciousness representation of life in New York City for the upper-middle class using loose, unpredictable plots, the Griffins take the audience through stories that are quite grounded in convention, but with unpredictable halts in the action that separate it from other styles of the form that television viewers are more familiar with. But what exactly are these halts in action that define it as a stream-of-consciousness text?

Despite its unique take on the sitcom formula, it isn't the absurd foundations on which *Family Guy* is built that makes it a *stream-of-consciousness* text. To understand that argument, one must look further than the barmy cast of characters because it's not the people (or animals) that define the form of a particular work; it's the way in which their story is told. And for those familiar with the show, and therefore with Seth MacFarlane's writing style, this argument comes easy. But for those who are outsiders in the *Family Guy* universe, its "stream of consciousness"-ness, and the many levels therein, might not become obvious until you familiarize yourself with the text, and with examples of the form.

An easy way to read *Family Guy* through the stream-of-consciousness filter is by examining the show's structure on a whole before getting down into the nitty-gritty of the characters' contribution to the form. The same can be said for nearly any work written in this way. Take, briefly, James Joyce's watershed novel *Ulysses* as an example. For their part, the characters in this stream-of-consciousness masterpiece are relatively identifiable and, I daresay, normal. Yes, Joyce's protagonist Leopold Bloom does have his quirks (the bar of soap he carries in his pocket, his enjoyment of flatulence, and the occasional bit of public masturbation), but on the whole he and the rest of the work's characters are *honest*, in that, like most characters in sitcoms, they are composed of both negative and positive characteristics that help the audience identify with them.

But just like *Family Guy's* Peter Griffin, *Ulysses'* Leopold Bloom is not what defines the form of the novel (or in Peter's case, the show). That definition is all to do with the structure. With *Ulysses*, the story is presented in a way that was truly revolutionary at its time of full publication in 1922. Joyce's cast of strangely unique and believable characters simply existed inside of a story told like no other. Broken into eighteen "episodes," *Ulysses* ends with one of the most impenetrable examples of stream of consciousness ever printed. The eighteenth episode, "Penelope," is recited by Leopold's wife, Molly, in a roughly fifty-page soliloquy that consists of only eight sentences (each many pages long) with almost no punctuation to speak of for its entirety. Molly, like Leopold, is a character that could easily be found in most forms of literature. But it is how she and her words appear that define the work. It is why *Ulysses* stands apart, acting as a true archetype of the genre. And similarly, the manner in which episodes of *Family Guy* are built does the same for animated sitcoms.

The structure of each very seldom changes. There is a distinct style MacFarlane relies on, and it is what makes the show unique and successful. Dispersed throughout each episode are brief, tangential jokes that are present for no purpose other than to entertain with their idiosyncratic deviations from the plot, (which they never act to advance). The majority of these defining sight gags are introduced by Peter by way of what I'll call a trigger. For example, there is a scene in the episode "North by North Quahog" (original air date, May 1, 2005), during which Peter and Lois are involved in a car chase after stealing the film reel for a sequel to *The Passion of the Christ* from Mel Gibson's hotel room. During the chase, Peter states: "Oh man, this is even more intense than that time I forgot how to sit down." The scene immediately cuts to Peter at home walking up to an armchair in the family's living room, staring at it blankly for a few moments, then leaping into it with a humorously violent result. In this case, the "Oh man . . ." statement is the trigger.

Nearly every one of *Family Guy*'s characteristic vignettes is introduced in a similar fashion. Although likely well thought out in advance by MacFarlane and his staff of writers, this joke and all of those like it are presented bundled within the main story; therefore, they appear to the viewer as full stops in the action for the sole purpose of inserting this sort of comical ADD into an otherwise linear plot. That, too, raises interesting implications about *Family Guy* being read as a stream-of-consciousness text. The development of the show's script is arguably not stream of consciousness, because one can assume that the show's writers spend many hours carefully constructing the jokes in the show. This is antithetical to the style itself; however, when the show is viewed at once by an audience, it then becomes stream of consciousness in a way that is unique to film and television. It is a visual representation of the form, not a literary one, and that is how it must be *read*. The human thought process is an erratic one. It jumps from idea to idea, and although these ideas may seem random, even unrelated, they all contribute to one cogent flow that somehow remains linear, or at least travels meanderingly to a clear end. It was an unprecedented achievement for authors like Joyce to translate that process into a work of literature, and so is it an achievement for *Family Guy* to do the same in the form of an animated television series. A text doesn't need to be written in the form to be perceived that way, and *Family Guy* pioneered that idea in its genre. And just as *Ulysses* should be read for its undeniable contribution to literature, so too should *Family Guy* for its similar invention.

In addition to the vignettes, most of the characters in the show have mannerisms that perpetuate the form. It should be remembered, however, that just because a character is quite strange indeed doesn't make for a stream-of-consciousness text; it is their actions that do so. I mentioned a few extraneous characters previously, including the evil monkey and the giant chicken. Yes, it's strange to have an evil monkey and a giant chicken as characters. But that's just silliness not stream of consciousness. The line there is crossed, however, when those characters act as triggers for the non-plot-advancing-full-stop sight gags. The evil monkey is the weaker of these two examples because he appears more frequently than the giant chicken. Although quite real, the evil monkey has been seen only by Chris (who is always met with ridicule when he suggests that the evil monkey, in fact, exists). Such mentions of the pernicious primate generally begin with a simple discourse between family members, but end with Chris making a comment such as, "I don't want to go to my room—there's an evil monkey that lives in my closet!" Predictably, the family laughs, but then it happens: Chris looks down a hallway, or to the top of the stairs, and there, accompanied by a jolt of ominous music, is a small monkey revealing a threatening set of fangs, his brow furrowed, an accusatory finger pointed in Chris's direction. Interestingly, but of little consequence to my argument, the episode "Ready, Willing, and Disable" (original air date, December 20, 2001) revealed that the evil monkey wasn't always evil, but was made that way when he returned from work one day to find his wife in bed with another monkey.

An even stronger example of stream of consciousness through character appearances is that of the giant chicken, who has been featured in just four episodes. In three of those four appearances, Peter and the giant chicken have randomly come across one another on the street, and on seeing one another, begin fighting incredibly violent battles that last for several minutes and take the two characters to dramatic locales across the city. These segments, which look a lot like modern action films, aren't properly explained in any way (aside from the chicken's first appearance, where he hands Peter an expired coupon on the street) until the fourth episode, in which a flashback shows Peter bumping into the chicken (whose name is revealed to be Ernie) at a country club while dancing with Lois. The chicken becomes enraged, but this friend calms him down, saying, "You'll probably never see him again" ("Meet the Quagmires," original air date, May 20, 2007). These epic battles always end with Peter as the victor. Bloodied and bruised, his clothing hanging in shreds, Peter walks off thinking that Ernie the giant chicken is finally dead, but at the last moment the camera pans to his lifeless body to show an eye dramatically cracking open, or the movement of a limb. To solidify these cut scenes as stream-of-consciousness meditations (or lack thereof), Peter always rejoins whatever conversation he was holding when he encountered Ernie, often in mid-sentence, acting as if the entire battle never happened. This, again, is a perfect example of how the form works by flowing naturally with the erratic patterns of the human thought process, and a perfect example of why reading *Family Guy* in this way is important. Yes, the fight with the giant chicken seems arbitrary. And it is. But arbitrariness is a staple of sitcoms, live action or animated. We typically don't realize the arbitrary nature of the sitcom until we are forced to see it (television is, after all, an escape for most of us). The giant chicken battles do just that. Once the battle is over and Peter returns to a scene mid-sentence, we must acknowledge that the story is unchanged by the absurd halt in action.

Perhaps it is the fact that *Family Guy* works so naturally with the human thought process that we find these vignettes to be so humorous. Critics might say that such comedy is forced, but, actually, the opposite is true. It is more difficult for our brains to follow the standard, unfalteringly linear structure of other sitcoms because they never allow our thought processes to occasionally derail, as they do naturally. *Family Guy* does allow that, and that makes it unique and very important. It, just like other sitcoms, follows a fairly linear path to a conclusion (and then the credits, of course). But for the benefit of our collective firing synapses, it meanders just like our brains do, and just like all great stream-of-consciousness works do.

These are but a few examples of how both *Family Guy*'s structure and its characters act to bring to life a text that can easily be read as stream of consciousness, even if it was originally written otherwise. And although unique to the medium, it is but one of the most recent works to use the ever-nebulous and in some ways ancient form of storytelling. Much like *Ulysses, Anna Karenina, The Garden of Cyrus, Metamorphosis,* and others that are quite different but tied with the stream-of-consciousness twine, *Family Guy* tells stories that are not obscure, but are rather quite grounded, or at least fundamentally and generally understood. It just does so in a way that breaks it from the traditional sitcom, animated or otherwise, much like M. C. Escher can take a flight of stairs and bend it on an impossible angle. It is still recognizable as a stair, but now it is quite obviously a stair through the eyes of the famous artist. In the case of *Family Guy*, the linear storylines are the stairs, and the artist—Seth MacFarlane—twists them with his wonderful vignettes.

The show remains a recognizable sitcom, but with a somewhat surreal and certainly eccentric study on stream of consciousness. It is almost like an experiment in which the audience is the object: Will the millions of viewers walk this broken stair? Fortunately for the series, they have, and have done so with much enthusiasm, making *Family Guy* one of the most successful animated television programs (and stream-of-consciousness texts) ever. And MacFarlane, like Faulkner or Woolf, continues to deliver a text that he has painstakingly crafted to an audience of millions to receive as a natural-flowing story with the occasional (although not unexpected) ninety-degree turn in the form of stream of consciousness. We, as the audience, make it what it is, and are therefore partially responsible for *Family Guy* being such an achievement artistically. And because the show adheres successfully to the "*can*, not *should*" ideal of storytelling while venturing into previously untapped territory with its audience interactivity, MacFarlane's *Family Guy* truly is one of the great modern texts.

How I Wrote This Essay Lee Transue

Why did you write this piece—what was the assignment or motivation for writing?

After being invited to participate by Dr. Jonathan Silverman, a co-editor of the book, I began thinking of the concept of writing about non-literary, cultural phenomena as if they were traditional texts. Because there were limitless topics to choose from, I decided on writing about *Family Guy* because of its popularity, its complexity in terms of writing options, and because I am a fan. The one thing that always stood out to me about this particular show was its undeniably ridiculous A.D.D. approach to gag humor. As I watched a few episodes I began to realize that many of the storylines in *Family Guy* followed a pattern ("pattern" being used very loosely here), and that was that they had a structure that was perpetually interrupted by vignettes of absurdity that I thought were fitted well to the idea of stream of consciousness in literature. From there, it was only a matter of watching episodes and documenting this absurdity to prove my thesis.

What did you do when you got the assignment/decided to write your essay?

When I got the idea to write about stream of consciousness in *Family Guy*, I did what anyone does when writing academically – I sat down and did research. After watching several episodes from several seasons (I was fortunate to have them on DVD already), and after several take-out orders and six-packs of German beer, I was confident that I had enough examples from the source material to begin writing my piece with a sound argument. I read over my notes, I re-watched some specific scenes (the Peter vs. Chicken fight scene was overplayed to near-schizophrenic levels), and got to writing.

How did you begin?

As I mentioned, my preparation included quite a bit of source material viewing; however, that was not my only preparation. I also breezed over some of my favorite stream-of-consciousness texts and writers, particularly James Joyce. I wanted to reacquaint myself with the literary epitomes of the style to avoid a common mistake in academic writing:

pretending like you know what you're talking about with the unavoidable consequence of sounding like an idiot and embarrassing yourself. Once I was confident I had enough of a grasp of the more well-known historical literary examples of stream of consciousness, I was ready to apply it to the unlikely topic I had chosen to write about. To my surprise, and to the delight of my chronic "eh, that's good enough-edness" it was easier to draw parallels and show *Family Guy* to be the stream of consciousness that I thought it would be.

Describe the process of writing the first draft.

Once I felt I'd done enough research to at least begin, I started writing and quickly grew comfortable with the flow the essay had taken on. I drew up a simple outline that included a brief description of stream of consciousness, along with various examples from the show and their relation to examples in literature. I also wanted to set the show apart as a "new" form of the style, and why that made *Family Guy* stand out as somewhat of an innovator of it. I believe I also drew a T-Rex with a shoulder-mounted laser canon somewhere in the margins; however, that proved to distract from the writing more than it did aid it. Once the outline was finished and I had a solid idea of how to progress through each section, the writing came naturally and quickly.

Did you write a draft all the way through?

Yes. Once I began to write, I finished in one sitting and I believe the first draft was completed in about three hours.

How much editing did you do as you wrote?

I didn't do too much editing as I wrote, but I went back and added/subtracted some material and cleaned up the transitions once the first draft was knocked out.

How long would you say the process took?

With combined research and writing time, I estimate the whole process took me approximately 10 hours.

How did you edit the draft?

I edited my draft in a boringly standard way. That is, I reread it several times and cleaned up my transitions, fixed long, awkward sentences, and added to some sections after rewatching particular *Family Guy* scenes I was focusing on to prove my thesis. And in my typical fashion I labored over the introductory and concluding paragraphs, convincing myself they were terrible and would turn my essay into a pretty solid and entertaining academic sandwich on crappy nutrient-devoid white bread bookends. After some serious tweaking, I changed my mind and was happy with the entirety of the essay. Very few editorial changes were made after I had handed my piece over, which I tried to stay modest about and failed, at least when talking to friends about it.

What was the response when you turned in your essay?

Co-editor Jonathan Silverman was my main contact through the process, and he was the one who contacted me about contributing in the first place. His feedback to my essay was really positive, which I was happy about. It was really an honor to be a part of the book, along with such great writers with really entertaining and insightful contributions. I believe my mother is still trying to find a magnet large enough to hang the book on her refrigerator.

Are you satisfied now with what you wrote? Would you make any changes?

I am satisfied with what I wrote. I think, by-and-large, it stands up to most of what is in *The World is a Text*. Obviously there are some huge, impressive names contributing, but it's such a novel concept for a book, and as a read it's so wide-ranging, fun, and at the same time intellectual and important, especially in the current state in which we as a society ingest information. I'm sure I could go back and add and add to what I wrote, and in the meantime I've thought of so many other ideas that I would love to write similarly about. I'm very much looking forward to new editions, and in the meantime I'll be wondering who is going to write the first Twitter novel, and just how Edward Cullen is going to become the first vampire president.

Reading and Writing about a Laboratory

Brandon Brown

ENTER A SCIENTIFIC RESEARCH LABORATORY, and confront three levels of text: the linguistics, the success, and the humanity of specific science. All send coded messages to the studied reader.

Like any space inhabited by humans and technology, a science laboratory is a complicated place in which there are many levels of communication and grammar. By *scientific linguistics,* I simply mean the exact type of science conducted in that laboratory space. Organic or inorganic chemistry? Laser physics or condensed matter? Yeast genetics or mammalian cell cultures? These questions are akin to asking the language of a printed book. Italian or Spanish? Japanese or Korean? That's not a very interesting question—one could create a translation dictionary full of equipment types, fume-hood widths, pungent smells, and safety requirements. With a long enough compendium, any visitor could eventually learn to name the exact type of science at work. That kind of factual reading is useful, but is ultimately more limiting than looking beyond the superficial cues to interpret the interplay of work and accomplishment.

Reading success presents a subtler task. Is this research team bringing in grants? Are they publishing results at a good clip? Are they working intensely? On topics they believe to be important?

Key factors include activity, reading material, and the state of equipment. In a successful lab, people hustle more than lounge. Even if they crack wise with their lab mates, they do so while mixing solutions, labeling sample tubes, or recording numbers from recent measurements. The lab members sometimes ignore cell-phone rings. The laboratory hums—centrifuges, pumps, or agitators whir even when people are absent. When vacant, there is a tangible, "Oh, they just stepped out" feeling in the space. Several haphazard stacks of recent research articles should dot the horizontal surfaces, with notes and question marks scrawled in the margins. Equipment in the lab shines as if it was just removed from packaging. Stainless steel tubes gleam free of finger grease. Tiny red and green lights blink regularly.

Similarly, certain signs underline a stagnant lab culture, with scientists who are less than captivated by the questions they ask of nature. Although some ask the universe about its childhood or its sex life, others shrug, clear their throats and avoid eye contact with the divine. The room itself may smell strongly—mold from an untreated water leak, or a nose-twisting vapor from an organic solvent improperly contained. Lab notebooks lie open on a desk but look as though the pages haven't turned in months. People in the lab surf the Web or play computer games. Other than the computers, chitchat, and perhaps music, there is little sound. On the walls and bulletin boards, data plots are rare in a sea of snowboarding or camping photos. Most of the equipment lies asleep, electronic eyes long closed, and a few cables snake unattached across the floor.

These readings are straightforward and should consume less than an hour. With more patience, a visitor can begin to read the humanity of a laboratory. Only an intensely curious and intrusive reader can hope to find this last text. The reader must be willing to linger and watch the inhabitants.

In approximately 400 years, the scientific enterprise has made little progress on recognizing the humanity of its practitioners. An unspoken veneer remains: the good scientist becomes a cold, objective robot when she conducts her experiments. Her facial expression and irrational thoughts disappear when she enters her laboratory. So forgive the space if only the most superficial elements of personal history and drama appear on your first inspection of a laboratory. You will always encounter a few photos of family and friends, an obligatory drawing from a child. In the less familial graduate students, workspaces include sub-pop-culture images and references—ironically bad television series or some such. But start poking around. Laboratories possess rich narratives of both competition and also awkward scientific adolescence.

The waters of intellectual ownership run murky and turbulent through a lab's culture. Not only does one lab member rush an experiment, hoping to complete and publish the work before rival scientists in other labs, but the boundaries of discovery can also smear within a single laboratory. Two geneticists start on separate problems but quickly find themselves examining the same gene—it happens to control two completely different things. Because an entire career rests on owning specific ideas and breakthroughs, emotions can flare far beyond the robotic scientific ideal. An observer may notice two people who intentionally turn away from one another, even in groups. One lab member may close her notebook quickly when the rival enters the lab. The process is entirely human. Identical situations could create a fast friendship and collaboration for one set of personalities, whereas other versions fester and swell until a new company and a university do legal battle over what once sat in a petri dish, between two sets of eyes.

Although tensions among equals can involve enormous stakes, the most poignant drama in a research lab replays parent–child separation. A graduate student moves steadily from admiration and respect for an advisor, through a realization that the advisor is imperfect, to eventually craving solo flight from the nest and an unfurling of her science wings. Each student–advisor relationship evolves uniquely, but for the students, their experience is more about their biological parents than their new intellectual parent. Was the student a wild child in high school? Watch to see if she deviates from her advisor's instructions for the next experiments. Or perhaps the student had a more obedient stance for his parents, oozing passive resentment. This young scientist complains openly in the lab when the advisor is absent, questioning the advisor's work habits, focus, or even wardrobe. Yet there are those who enjoyed famous friendships with mom and dad growing up. These students still call their parents regularly and enjoy a breezy open dialogue with their advisors in most cases.

In the end, a laboratory presents several major elements of a written text. Science sets the story in fluorescent lighting, with the humming of equipment, and inevitable clutter. Plastic wrap, notebooks, glass vials, cables, and computer disks coat the laboratory. An observer can quickly learn to recognize the language of the place. By turning a few pages in the first chapter, an experienced reader gets a sense of whether the narrative has quality, whether the writing is exceptional or amateur. And by carefully spending some time with the text, the reader enjoys character development. Dramatic scenes come to life, full of humor, remorse, and romance.

The omnipresent theme of obsession fills a lab. The obsession can spring from intense curiosity or desperation, appearing romantic or creepy. It can gaze serenely at a scientific problem with an adoration tempered by experience, or it can stare with foolish and feverish puppy love, destined for heartbreak. The obsession can be rewarded with discovery or rejected with inconclusive data and failed experiments. But it unifies the laboratories, drawing the characters from one chapter to the next.

How I Wrote This Essay Brandon Brown

Why did you write this piece—what was the assignment or motivation for writing?

I wrote this on assignment, you could say, after being invited by the editors.

What did you do when you decided to write?

First I made a few notes on a pad of paper, trying to list out some possible strands or focal points. Next, I actually went to a few laboratories to help me think about the topic and get some of the details in my toolbox.

How did you begin?

The beginning for me is always leaving a few days of baking in the back of my head. So after the initial notes and visual stimuli (e.g., the labs themselves in this case), I leave a few days with no writing at all, if the deadline allows for this. I honestly try to think about whatever little bit I'm writing before I go to sleep for those few nights, since I believe our dream lives chew on our waking topics, given the chance.

Describe the process of writing the first draft.

I write with abandon, trying to write a first draft for something of this length in 30 minutes or so. This clearly doesn't work for a longer piece, and it may be why I've never written a book. I often then throw the first draft away, and that was true in this case. I deleted the file. But I claim this is very helpful.

Did you write a draft all the way through?

Yes, in this case I did.

How much editing did you do as you wrote?

Very little, given the goal of getting a more or less full draft on paper (or into the computer.)

How did you edit the draft?

As mentioned above, I deleted it outright. The second draft was typed more slowly, with a rough outline in place, and that took a couple of hours.

What was the response when you turned in your essay?

The response was positive. I received a couple of concrete suggestions for making the piece fit better in the overall compilation, and those suggestions made sense to me. I was happy to make the changes.

Are you satisfied now with what you wrote? Would you make any changes?

I think it's just fine, but I'm sure it would be very different if I wrote it today. What's odd is to write this for a college reader and to never get student feedback. Is the piece thought-provoking? Did it make any of them consider a lab in a different light than before? Does it seem like a bunch of made-up crap? Would they play the video-game version? That kind of thing.

Reading and Writing about the Road

Jonathan Silverman

AMERICAN POPULAR CULTURE IS OBSESSED with the road, as witnessed by the enormous output of writers and movie-makers across time and place. Such works range from the Jack Kerouac classic *On the Road* to Cormac McCarthy's Pulitzer-Prize winning novel *The Road* to movies like *Thelma and Louise* and *Easy Rider* and the Bob Hope–Bing Crosby road movies (e.g., *The Road to Rio, The Road to Morocco*), not to mention John Ford's adaptation of John Steinbeck's *The Grapes of Wrath*. Earlier works that focus on movement could also be classified as road narratives; they include diaries by those crossing the Oregon Trail, letters by African American migrants from the South to North, and accounts by Native Americans regarding the Trail of Tears; even many narratives by the Puritans have elements of later conceptions of the road in them. When reading these accounts, we often get a sense of both identity and continuity that mark movement in the United States.

As these examples illustrate, the road in American culture is well traveled. Accordingly, in writing about such a familiar and mythic place, one might feel insecure about the ability to say anything new—such a feeling applies not only to the road but also to other familiar topics as well. One way to approach such a subject is to simply discuss what we see; taking what we observe and analyzing it rather than worrying about trying to understand all of a subject is a way around this issue. It does not mean ignoring context, but it does mean relying on one's power of observation as the *primary* source of content. In other words, we can write our own road stories.

With this in mind, I photographed a recent trip across the country. In the summer of 2007, I drove from Connecticut, where my parents live, to Santa Fe, New Mexico, making several stops along the way. I took photographs at every stop I made in an attempt to document what kinds of messages we encounter as we drive across the country. Following are some examples of photographs that make some statements about the road, my encounter with it, and perhaps some larger truths associated with travel as well. I should note here that these photos are just a few of the hundred or so I took, and that my goal in writing about the Road was to combine my photography with analysis; such an approach requires *choosing*. Had I been required to write about all my photos and all my stops, there is no guarantee that I would have been able to come up with a coherent narrative. In writing about other nontraditional texts, you too will have to choose, in much the same way you might have to choose passages of a traditional text, like a poem or short story, to bolster an argument.

My approach also reflects a particular way of traveling across the country. Some like to move slowly, stopping at tourist destinations along the way, or pacing themselves by traveling only a short way each day. Some like to motor down the interstate in RVs, whereas others stick to the "Blue Highways," the national and state highways that preceded the Interstate, as termed by William Least Heat-Moon. And some like to travel like I did this time, in a hectic pace, marked by stops to visit friends, but with very little interaction with the culture beyond the road itself. Regardless of whether one stops to get to know a people or a place, signs, buildings, towns, people, and even the landscape seem to want to be looked at. Indeed, why would anything constructed near or along a road want to be *ignored*? Because traveling along a road presents a myriad of semiotic moments, traveling by road is always accompanied by a perpetual act of reading. In making this journey I found that I was reminded how much consumption was part of travel, how variable and dominant the landscape is on the road, and how signs marked the landscape in a variety of ways. But I also found that my interpretations seem unstable in that they seemed to come from this particular trip (and reading of such).

Consumption

Food is an essential part of travel. Westward travelers used to have to pack supplies in order to make the journey, though very quickly markets were created to cater to travelers. Now, we have convenience stores and travel stops (Fig. 1). For many travelers, the accessibility of food of both good nutrition or less so (Fig. 2) is an enjoyable part of venturing across the country. Consider the Moon Pie. It is not a national brand; you can find it mostly in the Midwest and the South, and so a hardy traveler venturing forth is buoyed by the find of this delectable mix of banana-flavor coating, cakelike filling, and marshmallow. (It is funny, too, that it bills itself as "The Only One On The Planet!" given the fact that one chooses one Moon Pie among a display of many.) I also like the universality of the moon in the Moon Pie—the sky is one constant in traveling, and often a way of marking one's progress across the country is by the different views we have of the sky and the horizon.

Although it is often home to the delectable Moon Pie, the travel center itself (Fig. 1) goes beyond the convenience and corner store in that it is also a center of symbolic consumption. Until recently, most were associated with one gasoline brand and that's

Fig. 1 This rest stop is just outside of Albuquerque, New Mexico, on I-40.

it. But here we see the trend of collaborating with other national brands, in this case, Dairy Queen. This particular center is devoted to nostalgia—note the Route 66 sign, which refers to the most romantic of former roads that was consonant with the first wave of pleasure road trips out West, as well as the path for migrants from Oklahoma to California during the Dust Bowl. Originally cutting a path from Chicago to Los Angeles, Route 66 has been replaced by I-40. You can not see it well, but Phillips 66 is behind the '50s inspired sign. This particular sign intentionally evokes the romanticized image of Route 66 that Lisa Mahar documents. (Note, too, the faux space-age arrow seemingly straight out of the 1950s, an arrow that was supposed to signify progress. Now it points back to itself; it's a symbol of the future that harks back to the past.)

The travel stop is also a monument to American commercialism (Fig. 3). Here, more than 100 bottles of electrolyte drink are displayed in a scene that seems a form of deliberately constructed commercial beauty. My own view here is mediated by the photographs of Andres Gursky, particularly his *99 Cent*, a photograph of a convenience store in Los Angeles. The bigger question is: can anyone be *that* thirsty? But the prominence of these drinks also might signal the transition to the Desert Southwest, where people worry about dehydration.

To me, the Moon Pie, Route 66, and Gatorade drinks form a triptych of road consumption, symbolizing the plenty one can find on the road, as well as the way images speak to us in unexpected—and sometimes unexpectedly beautiful—ways.

Fig. 2 The Moon Pie (nestled on top of GoogleMaps). Purchased in a rest stop off I-70 in Ohio.

Fig. 3 America might be thirsty.

Landscape

Roads frame landscapes by guiding travelers through a particular area; they then become part of what they frame, as the associated parts—guardrails, medians, exit signs, and others, not to mention the podlike businesses that surround the exits—become part of the landscape itself. In other words, the discussion about landscape actually began in the previous section. The road's landscape is also framed, however, by the response of its travelers. For some, highways are anonymous, empty routes that exist only as means of travel to one's destination. For others, seeing unfamiliar landscapes, even if they bracket a long, relatively unchanged road, is part of the exploration of travel.

A familiar landscape to one traveler might be exotic to another. Witness my own traveling through the mid-section of the country. For those who grow up on the coasts, the sheer flatness and vision of the land can be both breathtaking and in the case of weather, a little frightening. Shown are two shots taken from the road—the first (Fig. 4) driving North in Arkansas, and the second (Fig. 5) on I-70 in Kansas.

For me, someone who grew up in Connecticut, where the horizon is hidden by trees, the big sky and flat plains are fascinating and beautiful. They suggest the openness so commonly associated with the West and westward expansion, a hypnosis-inducing means of crossing the country. But to others, they are just the background of daily living. When I was in graduate school in Texas, I took my first journey across West Texas on my way to Colorado to visit a friend. I was buoyed by the beauty of the landscape

Fig. 4 On I-55 in Arkansas.

Fig. 5 On I-70 in Kansas.

throughout my travel, but I thought the cotton fields outside of Lubbock were particularly beautiful. I expressed this thought to a clerk at a convenience store, who demanded to know where I was from.

"Connecticut," I said.

She responded by saying something to the effect of "It's beautiful there. This is ugly."

Signs

Signs are literal markers on a highway, telling its travelers what to do (drive a speed limit, slow down, change lanes) or where to go (St. Louis, Exit 287, north). But signs are also signs of a different sort—they can be unpacked to show some of the idiosyncrasies of road travel. Figure 6, taken off I-70 in Utah, illustrates the many possibilities one might choose to view the landscape. Standing in the rest area, an arbitrary location carved out in this case to view the scenery, there is no possibility that one will go the wrong way. So when looking backward, I was struck by the repetition of a sign that seems superfluous in contrast to a "beautiful landscape."

For those who find direct religious expression difficult to process, landscape combined with religious signage sends several coded messages. Is the sign in Figure 7 referring to the afterlife, or this particular place? Is Hell an emotional state, or a destination? Maybe this sign is also about travel of a different sort.

And then we have signs that reveal much about the country we live in, such as the Homeland Security sign taken in a rest stop in Richfield, Utah (Fig. 8). Such a sign could reveal the political leanings of the owner—not necessarily a statement of risk.

Fig. 6 Utah rest stop.

Fig. 7 On I-71 in Ohio.

Fig. 8 Off I-70 in Utah.

The signs in Figure 9 suggest a great deal of options traveling across the country, a mix of various routes, subroutes, and in the case of Route 66, historic or even nostalgic routes. When approaching this intersection, knowing how (and not only where) one is going seems imperative.

And then we have these signs (Fig. 10) marking a bathroom in Utah, signaling the sort of universality of highway travel—bathrooms where distinction is both signified by inclusion of all three possible restroom symbols (and certainly a throwback—the symbol for the women does not reflect any sort of standard of female dress in the twenty-first century).

Although this is not actually a street sign (Fig. 11), the bear and the hedges do reveal through a close reading some of the concerns of this rest stop in Grand Junction, Colorado. The bear is native to the area, but also a symbol of wildness and, more important, of nature itself. In a way, so are the hedges next to the bear, on top of a constructed stone wall, in front of manicured grass. But taken together, they suggest a manicured nature, perhaps the nature that travelers prefer to encounter. Taken as a whole, this photograph also reminds the traveler of his or her own home as well as the pull of nature.

Another trip down another road might engender an entirely different semiotic experience and a different interpretation. The cultural and visual rhetoric of the road is always active, although because it is stationary, it may feel passive. However, we are the ones for whom the road and its many texts are designed. Paying attention to the various associations bears and signs and products carry may help us understand how the road tries to determine its own interpretation.

Fig. 9 In Flagstaff, Arizona.

Fig. 10 In a rest stop off I-70 in Utah.

Fig. 11 Off I-70 in Grand Junction, Colorado.

Reading and Writing about YouTube: The You in YouTube

Catherine Zimmer

WHEN *TIME* MAGAZINE CHOSE TO DECLARE "You" their Person of the Year for 2006, their cover presented this choice with a square reflective material intended to offer the reader back to him- or herself at the same time that it indicated a computer screen.

Of course, the Person of the Year was not, in fact, *me* (or *you*, for that matter). What *Time* referred to was the rise of YouTube, the Internet video-sharing site that revolutionized the dispersal, and thus, in many ways production, of digital moving images. *Time* chose YouTube as not only representative of that particular website (and apparently, you), but also the larger arena of "peer production" or "consumer-generated content" characteristic of websites from YouTube to Wikipedia to MySpace.[1] Implicit in *Time*'s selection of You/YouTube/etc. as "person" of the year is the question of how much Internet users are themselves present in YouTube versus how much that site and the culture surrounding the Internet have already defined the persona of the "you" in YouTube (as well as other related sites). In other words, to what degree is our self-presentation via this website influenced or even determined by the technological, economic, and cultural milieux of YouTube? Arguably, despite the fact that a peer-produced website such as this provides a platform for "anybody" to share or view a diversity of video works, YouTube ultimately reflects the possibilities and limitations of the Internet market as much as, if not more than, it reflects "you."

[1]Lev Grossman, "*Time*'s Person of the Year: You," *Time* December 13, 2006, http://www.time.com/time/magazine/article/0,9171,1569514,00.html (accessed July 2, 2007).

The site's very name indicates the manner in which we must begin to consider the history and stakes of YouTube as a media environment. The "tube" seems to be a clear reference to one of the core televisual technologies: the cathode ray tube.[2] This tube was the primary element in the display, but not production, of both television and video images.[3] In other words, the cathode ray tube was the central technology literally behind the screen of your television monitor; "the tube" eventually became common slang for television. This did not, however, carry a particularly positive connotation. The added designation of "boob tube" to the term suggested a moronic dependence on television, an attitude that was in large part a result of the kinds of media critics that arose with the television era—most significantly, Marshall McLuhan. McLuhan's famous quote that "the medium is the message" has gained renewed attention in the digital era, when the content of our media seems increasingly informed by the manners in which that content can be produced and delivered technologically.[4] In other words, what we might find on the Internet is at times only marginally as important as the fact that we might be able to get that information on the new Apple iPhone.

Thus, YouTube, by virtue of its very name, as well as its base in a highly technologized media culture, seems to want to cast itself as both in the tradition of television entertainment, "the tube," and as a departure—this departure apparently constituted by the "you" in YouTube. So who, and what, is the "you"? If the tube is the form, is the "you" the content? Not exactly. Quite simply, the idea is that one can find virtually anything on YouTube. Anything, everything, and conceivably, nothing people might want to see is available on

---

[2]Although if YouTube had not emerged the year before Senator Ted Stevens infamously declared the Internet to be a "series of tubes," we might also read the site's name as an ironic commentary on the (mis)characterization of the Internet by legislative bodies.

[3]The distinction between television and video technologies is a vague one at best, because they are interrelated, but suffice it to say for now that the specificity of television has to do with the transmission of the television signal, whereas video seems to refer more to the magnetic tape technology on which video images were recorded in the era before they were immediately converted to digital information.

[4]McLuhan began to elaborate this concept in his book *Understanding Media: The Extensions of Man*, originally published in 1964 by McGraw-Hill, New York.

YouTube—crucially, this content is entirely uploaded by users. YouTube thus markets itself as user-generated media, as truly democratic entertainment, information, and artistry. But, to what degree is this possible? Home videos are indeed a staple, particularly humorous videos, music, or stunts. In addition, you can find snippets of previously broadcast/published materials, such as clips of television shows that have become topics of conversation, or materials that are re-edited/digitally manipulated (these manipulations of existing material are a mainstay of digital audiovisual culture). Where else can one go to find a video of a housecat nursing an orphaned chipmunk, followed by a Duran Duran video from 1984, followed by a clandestine recording of Lindsay Lohan falling down drunk? It is also a simple matter to either "embed" the video stored on YouTube into an alternate website, or to link to YouTube from other sites. This is all to say that the premier site for video on the Internet *produces no content* itself—it is simply the platform for storage and dispersal.

It is this element that seems to suggest a you-ness to the system. In a television era in which, despite the proliferation of channels, media outlets are increasingly controlled by very few multinational media conglomerates, a democratizing resource such as YouTube and the other sites championed by *Time* in their cover story would seem to suggest that the peer-produced quality of the Internet is the most significant site of resistance to the kinds of entertainment and information control that have tended to characterize television, the original tube. Certainly, there is a kind of "wild" element to both YouTube and the Internet at large—an "anything is possible" attitude that contrasts starkly with the sense of entrenchment, repetitiveness, and powerlessness that seems to reign broadly over other American media and political arenas. But despite the characterization of Internet media intervention as an uncontained organic force, I think we are still hard pressed to determine where the "you" is that has some sort of power in this environment.

A casual survey of the YouTube site reveals a mixture of self-produced video and material captured from already produced work. Any small video produced can catch hold of a wide Internet audience. Your video could gain international notoriety within a couple of days if your YouTube contribution gets taken up by any number of popular referring sites, such as Digg or BoingBoing. These videos are then forwarded between individuals ("Check out the video of this drummer I found on YouTube!"). Literally millions of people could see your video of your talented skateboarding dog. And despite the fact that I am using the more amusement-based, inconsequential examples of YouTube possibilities, there is the theoretical implication here that a talented filmmaker could gain a foothold in the popular imagination and eventually in the media industry without necessarily operating within the traditional power structures of the entertainment industry. Political interventions could be made on this site, as they have been on others, by providing alternative sources of news and a wider reach for activism and organizing. Thus, YouTube would seem, as a neutral web platform for video, to have endless possibilities for the democratization of media and the leveling of the information playing field.

A notable example of the kind of intervention possible via YouTube is the (in)famous video of former Senator George Allen from the 2006 election (dubbed "The YouTube Election" by *The New York Times*).[5] The video shows Allen during his reelection campaign, at a small speaking engagement, twice using the word *macaca*, a racial slur (http://youtube.com/watch?v=r90z0PmnKwI). The video was posted on YouTube, where it

---

[5]Ryan Lizza, "The YouTube Election," *The New York Times* (August 20, 2006).

"rocketed to the top of the site's most viewed list."[6] It was then picked up by larger print and broadcast media; Allen eventually lost the election, despite having been favored to win. Obviously, the exposure of the Virginia senator's racism was a coup for the opponent's campaign, and it was, in fact, no accident: The video was recorded by a student working for Allen's opponent. Even more remarkable was the fact the racial slur was not just recorded by, but directed at the student recording the video. This student thus produced (through both his presence at and his recording of the event) and distributed an amateur video that constituted him as a very potent "you" on YouTube.

The form of the video itself suggests ways that we can understand the action and power of this "you." After a straightforward introductory title providing the senator's name, the name of the event, and the date and location, the video is simply an approximately one-minute recording of a moment from the event in which Allen points directly at the camera and refers to the man recording him as *macaca*, later repeating the word and saying, "Welcome to America." There is no commentary, editing, or anyone else visible within the frame of the video, seeming to allow the material to speak for itself and suggesting a lack of manipulation of the image and thus of the viewer. The camera is clearly hand-held, shaking somewhat and zooming rather inexpertly. Positioned slightly below the eye line of Allen, the video is presented to us as recorded by an "average person," a "you," a spectator at the Allen event. As viewers of the video, we are thus looking from the position of that student (through his "eyes" as it were), and when George Allen points at the young man holding the camera and demeans him racially, he is also pointing at *us*, putting us in a position to perhaps feel personally attacked by his comments, whatever our racial background might be. Thus, beyond simply providing a record of the senator's racism, we might see that the amateur structuring of the video itself encourages political action by creating a community of "yous."

And yet, it also seems reasonable to suggest at this point, despite this moment of apparent intervention, and despite *Time*'s cover story, that the democratization of media via the Internet, and the accompanying political possibilities, has not undermined the power of the larger media machine; despite the proliferation of "you" on the Internet, there does not seem to be any threat to the existing and overarching structures in place in both media and politics.[7] The Allen video, after all, only became what is considered "news" after it was picked up by newspapers and broadcast news shows—the established media outlets. Furthermore, it is not inconsequential that the student was working for the democratic opponent of George Allen, and even if the video did influence the outcome of the election, that election was still defined by the *de facto* two-party system in place in the United States.

The fact is that we are living with what would seem to be a striking contradiction: the unparalleled democratizing power of information exchange on the Internet and the unprecedented centralization of media corporations. How can we explain why these two

---

[6] *Ibid.*

[7] Even the intensive restructuring of music distribution forced by Napster, Limewire, and other file-sharing sites has been relatively reabsorbed into a corporate economy via Apple iTunes, Verizon VCAST, and others that take advantage of the new possibilities of digital music sales. This is not to deny that the digitally aided rebellion did, indeed, lower music prices and allow independent artists increased possibility for distribution; merely that although some of the players have changed and positions have shifted, the game remains the same in many significant ways.

seemingly opposite situations co-exist fairly easily? One primary thing we must recognize is that YouTube and the Internet at large, although radical in their seeming existence as pure space that anyone might occupy with whatever they like, do not exist outside of an already present global economy. Despite the frequent characterization of the Internet as a free non-space of endless possibility for everyone, it is in fact a very real material space composed of technologies to which access is limited by social circumstances and a market economy. The Internet is *not* an alternate universe where all may play freely—it is part of the material world in which we live, and both the problems and the pleasures of that world find their place there. After all, when you go to YouTube you are as much surrounded by paid advertisements as you are by democratic content. And although the videos might be user-generated, everything from the software that makes them viewable to the established categories of video on the site are out of your hands. The idealism surrounding the Internet on the part of both the public and some media theorists thus comes up against a wall when we encounter the realities of the way technologies are deployed. Although it is certainly—and thankfully—true that the Internet has dispersed the control of information, and the possibility for creative distribution has thus greatly increased, to suggest that the Internet is entirely free of the economic and ideological constraints of the rest of media culture would be naive.

Beyond this general point that we cannot entirely separate the functioning of YouTube from other media outlets, it is instructive to return to some of the terminology with which we began in discussing the "tube" and the "you," and in that way to return to our initial investigation of what and who is presented/represented on YouTube. For instance, when a video (or, in fact, any item) takes hold and achieves a certain reach on the Internet, it is said to have "gone viral." Some websites even have a category for "viral videos." This is certainly not the first time that the idea of the "virus" has been used in relation to computer culture—obviously, it is the term most frequently used to describe computer code that makes its way into your computer system and breaks down certain elements of its functionality. The rhetoric of virus, infection, bugs, and so on, is prevalent here. What the notion of the viral video has done is reframe the thinking about infection in terms of the positive possibility of the Internet. Used to connote the infectious quality of certain Internet items that come and go like a brief hysteria, a viral video is generally very short, and usually has an immediate effect of great hilarity, amazement, or shock. In this way, viral videos, in both their short length and generally nonnarrative nature, can be broadly compared to the earliest forms of motion pictures, what Tom Gunning famously dubbed "the cinema of attractions."[8] In many ways, this is not a new form of entertainment, but a very old one, in which motion pictures were initially enjoyed in the same way as a brief circus attraction or magic trick, rather than immersed as one would be in a novel and later a narrative film (not that these need to be considered necessarily mutually exclusive). A recent example, "Dramatic Chipmunk" (http://youtube.com/watch?v=a1Y73sPHKxw), first picked up by Digg and then Gigglesugar, swept the Internet in days, and within a week had undergone at least five video incarnations as it made its rounds.[9]

---

[8] I am indebted to my student, Tucker Dyer, at Pace University for initially pointing out the similarity between YouTube and the cinema of attractions to me.

[9] Accessed July 3, 2007.

But it is the characterization of the distribution of these works as "viral" that can be our best indicator of both their possibilities and limitations. As I note earlier, Internet media have the strength of an organic force, but what does it mean if that force is one characterized as microbial and infectious, rather than as that of a thinking, speaking, human subject? What I would like to suggest is that the organizing models of digital culture is both organic and dehumanizing at the same time. The "you" in YouTube begins as the human subject who places a video online, but only emerges as an Internet entity in the form of an infectious agent. Within traditional thinking, we might be asked to mourn this loss of the originary "human" subject in the rise of an Internet presence, but perhaps we should instead ask what we might gain by embracing both YouTube's and our own status as carriers of infection. If a virus is, arguably, the most powerful organism on Earth, we might look into what is to be gained by infecting certain systems (cultural, computer, political, and otherwise) with ourselves—and our creative productions—as viruses.

However, this characterization of the individual dispersal of media on the Internet as viral also carries with it a notion of a thoughtless, instinctive, parasitic, and thus wholly unethical existence. If we are again to ask why there has not been a media overhaul given the incredible possibility of YouTube and its like, I argue that it is partly because despite the great power inherent in the metaphor of the virus, the virus seems unable to have a political or social conscience. Its purpose is merely to reproduce itself—thus, the elements that "go viral" tend to be things that we consider relatively innocuous and without an agenda: kittens, songs, jokes. Indeed, one video, significantly to be found on an *alternate* video site, glumbert, parodizes the rise and fall of a viral Internet sensation: Mustard Face Dancing Guy (http://www.glumbert.com/media/internetsens).[10] As this video aptly points out, those things that go viral are often so completely arbitrary that they defy any reasonable explanation for their appeal beyond that very randomness. Thus, it seems reasonable to suggest that these are things that both we and the Internet are happy to serve as carriers because they seemingly propose no threat to the system at large. What seems clear is that if the ambiguous "you" in YouTube is to become the pivotal player in Internet culture in a way that truly has effects on systems of media, one must consider the ways in which one's participation in that system is being offered and characterized, and how that characterization to a certain degree already positions your place in that system and your contributions to it. Viruses, after all, must mutate if they are going to progress.

Reading and Writing about Advertising: Two Case Studies

Dean Rader and Jonathan Silverman

YOU PROBABLY ENCOUNTER ADVERTISEMENTS on a daily basis. On television, on the radio, in magazines, on the Web, and now even at the movies, we confront advertisements in almost every aspect of our lives. Researchers suggest we see between 100 and 300 advertisements per day, whereas it would be unusual if you were to read 100 poems in an entire year. What's more, most experts agree that the American public believes or is open to at least one advertisement out of every eight that it sees. That may not sound like much, but if you see 100 ads per day for 365 days, that's 36,500 ads per year. If

---

[10]Accessed July 2, 2007.

researchers are correct, then you probably believe or consider at least 4,562 commercials per year. Think that is a lot? Consider this: The average nineteen-year-old has probably been paying attention to advertisements for about thirteen years. So, if these estimates are correct, most nineteen-year-old Americans have taken into their consciousness and devoted some aspect of their reasoning ability to more than 59,000 ads over the course of their lifetime. If you are nineteen, then you have likely seen more than 450,000 ads. By the time you are thirty, it is probable that more than one million ads have made their way into your brain.

By now, it is a cliché to claim that ads sell an image, but . . . ads sell an image. They not only sell images of us and their products but also of a culture. In advertiser's lingo, this is called the "promise." Ads make promises to people all the time, but they tend to be implied or suggested promises. When you read an advertisement, ask yourself what kind of promise the ad is making to you. In addition, ads also work to cultivate another image—their own. This is why so many companies are very protective of their names, trademarks, and product use. For instance, you may be familiar with the court case in which Mattel toys sued the rock band Aqua over a critical song about "Barbie." And, in an example closer to home, we were denied permission from Tommy Hilfiger to reprint the advertisement we describe later—even after personal letters from the authors. We suspect Tommy was worried about what our reading might do to their branding. So, keep in mind that although ads may be funny, informative, and persuasive, they also help promote the company's image.

Thus, reading the image that a company tries to cultivate is all part of the larger experience of reading an advertising text. It would appear that many advertisers worry about how we might *use* their ads. Understandably, they are concerned about how their ad, their product, their image might look out of context. So, because so much of advertising is about branding, where an ad appears is as important as the ad itself. Sadly, that means we must *describe* the ad, rather than provide it.

We have chosen a widely published Tommy Hilfiger ad that features six young, handsome/beautiful, smiley people (two white men, two black men, a white woman, and a black woman) lounging around in red, white, and blue Hilfiger clothes on the expansive front lawn of a country home. The large house stands in the right corner of the photo, and in the upper left corner of the photo, a big American flag waves just over the left shoulder of one of the models. Advertising Tommy cologne, the ad's tagline reads in large white letters along the bottom, "tommy: the real american fragrance."

When we began to read this ad so that we could write about it (the same process you will engage in), we asked ourselves, *What textual cues are in the ad?* Here is what we saw: In this ad for Tommy Hilfiger cologne, all the people in the photograph are young, well-scrubbed, and attractive. And they are happy! Now, what about the setting of the photograph? Where does it take place? It appears to be a rural area, perhaps a country club or a farmhouse in New England. What other textual cues or signs do you see? In this ad, we see a large American flag waving in the upper left corner of the ad. The text, "tommy: the real american fragrance," runs along the bottom fourth of the image, while a picture of the featured cologne balances the flag in the bottom right corner. Smaller than the American flag but similar to it, the Tommy Hilfiger logo hovers above the writing, but seems to be affixed to the White woman's body.

Then we asked ourselves, *How do we describe the appearance of the people in the ad?* How are they dressed? Well, for one thing, they are all wearing Tommy Hilfiger clothes.

This tells us a lot. What is the demographic for Tommy Hilfiger clothes? Who buys them? Who hangs out in large, well-kept farmhouses in New England? Who spends time at a country club? The answer to all of these questions seems to be middle-class or upper middle-class White Americans, although the ad suggests that Tommy Hilfiger clothes and cologne appeal to a plurality of people—perhaps even that Tommy clothes and cologne promise racial harmony, an upper middle-class lifestyle, *and* a good time.

But is this so? We decided to make a list of who or what is missing—what is *not* in this picture. Off the top of our heads, we came up with quite a list: people who look poor, anyone over 30, any sign of work (a briefcase, a shovel, a computer, a uniform), anyone who is even remotely overweight, a Mexican flag, a tenement building, any sign of anger, Native Americans, anything having to do with a city, any reference to a blue-collar or working-class situation, clothing other than Tommy Hilfiger, people who are unattractive, reading material such as books or a newspaper, and finally, any clue as to what these people are doing dressed in Tommy Hilfiger clothes out in the country. What message does the absence of these things send? Is this ad suggesting something about the role of these things in the "real America"? We don't know exactly, but by asking these questions we might come closer to understanding not only the ad, but also the culture from which it comes and the culture it tries to sell. Advertisers use various techniques to get us to respond to their ads, most of which involve making the viewer feel desired, accepted, important, or exclusive. What individual techniques does this ad use to make us feel these things? The flag? The pretty, happy people sitting close together? The sense of affluence suggested by the large house out in the country? The sense of racial harmony evoked by the people of various ethnicities laughing together? Now, when you combine all of these cues, what is the overall argument or promise of the ad? Take this one step further: What does this text suggest about how Tommy Hilfiger, the company, sees itself? And, what does this text suggest about how Tommy Hilfiger, the company, sees America? Does this version of America mesh with your own? Does this version of America reflect mainstream American values?

Although we ended up with more questions than answers here, finding what questions to ask helps us understand the text we are looking at. In more general terms, learning how to read advertisements not only makes you more aware about companies and how they market their products and themselves but also how mainstream advertising and media outlets create a vision or even a myth of our culture. What's more (and perhaps at this moment, most important to you), learning how to read advertisements, poems, and public spaces helps you write better papers, as the reading process is fundamentally linked to the writing process.

While preparing the manuscript for this new edition, we were tempted to take out the previous reading of the Tommy ad, but we like the ad so much—we still do not know why we were denied permission—we thought we would keep it and augment this section with a shorter semiotic reading of an ad that we could actually get permission to print. But we were denied permission here, too. The ad is part of the Soft-N-Dri "Strong and Beautiful" campaign.

Chances are, you would have noticed the same things we did. An attractive white woman (blonde), dressed in skimpy tight pink clothes, work gloves, and a pink gimme cap stands rather defiantly in front of a big, black (and rather menacing) semi-truck. Over the windshield, again in pink, are the words, "PRINCESS OF THE OPEN ROAD," and lower, in the middle of the page, where her legs would begin to show, her body is cut off by the black page. Over the line separating the text from the image are the words "STRONG & BEAUTIFUL," with the "strong" in white and the "beautiful" in pink.

Rather than walk you through this ad, we'll give you the questions we asked:

- Why did the ad folks put the model in pink? What does pink suggest?
- Why a semi-truck?
- Why a black semi-truck?
- Why is she wearing work gloves (leather) and a hat? Why aren't the gloves pink?
- Look closely at the model's body. What is different about her body from the body of a woman or girl you might see in a Calvin Klein or Victoria's Secret ad?
- Also, what do you notice about her features? Her facial expression?
- Given the fact that this deodorant features a "power stripe," why are her gloves and the truck important?
- Is it *clear* which is strong and which is beautiful—the truck or the model?
- How about the text copy at the bottom—what do you make of the use of the phrase "long haul"?
- This is a more delicate question, but how would the ad be different with an Asian model? An African-American model? A man dressed in pink?
- Do you think there is any relation between the whiteness of the model and the fact that the word "strong" is also in white? Why wouldn't it be the same color as the truck?
- Is this an effective ad? Is it sexist? What makes it effective or sexist? Could it be both?

Now it is time to read an ad yourself. Open any magazine and see how advertisers try to "sell" anything.

Based on our answers to these questions, we can then move on to the work of writing the essay. Remember that it is okay if you don't know what a text means right away, or if you don't know what you want to argue about that text. Persistent, careful, and insightful semiotic observations eventually lead you to the door of writing.

Reading the Puffy Taco

Phil West

IN THE YEAR 2000—technically, the end of the millennium, though try telling that to everyone who saw 2000 as a bright new beginning—the San Antonio Missions debuted its new official mascot, awesomely named Ballapeño.

Riding out in the middle of the first inning of home games on a motorized scooter, Ballapeño indulges in the sort of fun, wacky antics you'd expect of a mascot playing to 4,400 a night who've come to watch Double A players with big league aspirations. He rides in the back of a truck around the perimeter of Nelson Wolff Stadium and shoots rolled-up T-shirts into the crowd as the truck loops its way past the infield seats. He dances on top of the dugout. He wanders into the crowd, pulls caps off children's heads playfully, and slaps hands with adults who cannot resist the pull of a giant jalapeño pepper with googly eyes.

But at the end of the sixth inning, another, more mysterious mascot heads to second base, to the instant recognition and obvious delight of the crowd. This is the unofficial mascot, who has been with the team since a local restaurant sponsored him to come out to the Missions' former home stadium back in 1988 for a series of promotional appearances. In 2003, *Newsweek* named him the minor league mascot of the year, even though Ballapeño had been the official Missions' mascot three years running. This seems unfair to Ballapeño, until you feast your eyes—pun totally intended, by the way—on The Other Mascot.

The Puffy Taco is a beloved San Antonio institution.

Ladies and gentlemen, I present to you: Henry the Puffy Taco.

The Puffy Taco very nearly defies conventional mascot wisdom. Typically, mascots are cartoonish depictions of people or animals or even objects, yet they wear distinctive human features like eyes and a mouth. It's for the same reasons that babies and baby animals come into the world cute—to start the process of attachment, to allow the parents to want to care for it.

But the Puffy Taco doesn't even try for recognizable facial features. It is, simply, magnificently, without pretense, a taco. More precisely, the costume is an open shell facing forward and standing on its end, covering the head and torso, with holes for the arms and legs to protrude from the shell. Because there's no better way to describe this, vulva-like folds of lettuce and cheese protrude slightly from behind the open folds of the shell, all but enveloping the dark-red cylinder at the center of the taco, which is clearly where the actor's head and torso fit, and which has to be meant to represent the meat at the center of the taco, although this would make the costume more of a hot-dog taco than a ground beef taco. "Henry the Puffy Taco" is stitched along the back of the taco shell at its bottom edge, for the four or five people in the audience on any given night who need clarification on who this is.

The Puffy Taco's act is simple yet effective and is a thirty-second case study in everything that is glorious yet low-rent about minor league baseball—that, indeed, is glorious precisely because it is so low-rent. The Puffy Taco starts at second base, and runs for home plate by way of third. A child is selected from the audience; it is his or her job to tackle the Puffy Taco before he reaches home. There's a Roadrunner and Wile E. Coyote certainty to the act; it always concludes with the child tackling the Taco, and the show has evolved to incorporate an additional moment of triumph in which the child is allowed to clamber on top of the Taco and lift his or her hands skyward to make the "raise the roof" gesture. I think you can probably figure out what the crowd does in response.

Then, the Taco gets up and does a dance. He circulates through the stands for another half-inning or so, slapping hands and greeting the kids who flock around him, before giving the stage over to the Ballapeño for the rest of the evening. It is interesting to note that the same Missions' employee plays both roles during a typical game.

The Taco's act has evolved on its own over time. Initially, there was no tackling—as Missions' Assistant General Manager Mickey Holt explains, the first tackle was actually an overzealous kid bumping into the Taco during a race. What was ordained from the beginning was that the kid was always supposed to win. Holt recalls that on the one occasion the Taco won the race, when the Taco's act was still in its early stages of development, the crowd reacted with enough booing and general displeasure to assure that *that* wouldn't ever be happening again. Over time, the two concepts—kid always triumphs, kid triumphs by tackling the Taco before he reaches home plate—merged into what is now the standard nightly ritual.

As mascot theater goes, the Taco's act is simple and slapstick and interactive and allows a child to emerge triumphant in a situation that is not quite man v. beast but is similar enough to evoke feelings of top-of-the-food-chain superiority and the resultant joy that comes with that. For San Antonians, there's an additional level to why the victory over the Puffy Taco works as a gimmick, and that has a lot to do with the fact that people in San Antonio really like their food.

Every April, to cite the most obvious example of San Antonio's rampant food lust, the city essentially shuts down for a 10-day conglomeration of festivals and parades called Fiesta. At the heart of the 100-plus Fiesta events are two major parades which draw as many as half a million spectators and are serviced by a staggering number of makeshift festival food stands. The Night in Old San Antonio event, which runs four days in the city's La Villita and is another major Fiesta draw, allows its thousands upon thousands of annual attendees a chance to eat and drink with abandon. There's music and dancing and street festival frivolity to be had here, but ask any attendee, and they're more likely than not to tell you they are there for the variegated meats on a stick or the gorditas or the fresh handmade tortillas or the bratwurst or crepes or frog legs or potato skins or any number of other foods. This is a city, to drive the point about San Antonio and food home further, in which people will sit at restaurants and talk about food they've eaten at other restaurants.

The Puffy Taco mascot gets its name from a Tex-Mex innovation that has been adopted by a number of the city's vast array of Mexican restaurants. Specifically, it was Jamie Lopez, the son of the Henry's Puffy Tacos owner, who came up with the idea for the Puffy Taco mascot in 1988 as a way to further associate the puffy taco dish with his dad's restaurant. Henry's Puffy Tacos, a Westside restaurant which opened in 1978 and relocated to a former Luby's cafeteria around the corner in 1996, naturally lays claim to its title dish despite having many other offerings on the menu.

The puffy taco is a crispy taco with a shell that puffs up in the deep-frying process, filled to bursting with meat, lettuce, tomatoes, and cheese. An arcane yet timeless Citysearch review of Henry's noted, "The shell of Henry's signature dish is what newly fallen snow would feel like in your mouth—if it was fried."

Essentially, this is a love story; an equation of slapstick + kids + food, as if "America's Funniest Home Videos" and the Food Network birthed a low-rent theater piece. For a minor league team trying to ensure that its product is a Fun Family Experience, the familiarity and longevity of the Puffy Taco (and, to a lesser degree, not to bum him out or anything, Ballapeño) is maybe a more salient selling point than any of the players themselves. Because players at the Double-A level are either aspiring to the majors or trying to prolong fading careers, they're generally more transitory than players at the highest levels, adding some credence to the "rooting for laundry" theory forwarded by comedian Jerry Seinfeld. Though the Missions' lineups change from year-to-year, and fluctuate even during the season with the promotion or demotion of certain players, the team in black and gold is harder to get to know than, say, the city's NBA franchise, the San Antonio Spurs, who have a core of players much-beloved by fans who are signed to long-term deals and referred to by first name (Tim, Tony, Manu) in thousands of South Texas living rooms.

Even the parent club of the Missions has changed over the years. Currently, the Missions are tied to the San Diego Padres. Before that, the Missions were tied to the Seattle Mariners (leading to at least one end-of-season treat for Mariners fans in which the Puffy Taco and Ballapeño gallivanted with the Mariners' official mascot, which is the admittedly not-so-nautically-themed Moose). At one point, the Los Angeles Dodgers were the Missions' parent club.

But as the Missions soldier on, thankfully, the mascots will soldier on with them. It's a safe bet that years from now, between the sixth and seventh innings of future Missions' games, the Puffy Taco will take his place at second base, and a child currently not yet born will take his or her place alongside the Taco. They will run around the bases. The Taco will not make it to home plate, being tackled along the way. And as the Taco lies on the ground, to the cheers of the crowd for another in a chain of consecutive nights, the Taco will know his place is secure. In a city where traditions rule all, and in which the Taco has become a quirky and enduring tradition, no one will let the Taco escape this mortal coil. Even today, if you listen closely between the sixth and seventh inning as the Taco makes his entrance, underneath the cheers, you can hear a handful of people quickly explaining to those who don't yet know—the children, the visitors, the neophytes—the answer to the inevitable question, the variations on the theme of What the Hell Is That.

READING WRITING

This Text: Reading

1. What approach unifies these essays? In what ways are these pieces consistent, despite very different topics?
2. Pick three or four of the essays in this chapter and try to identify the "lens" each of the authors uses to read their particular text.
3. Each of these essays is relatively *persuasive*; that is, each is an argumentative essay that asserts a thesis. Look at the essays by Peter Hartlaub, Catherine Zimmer, and Cristina DeLuca—all three read video-based texts. How are their theses similar? Different?
4. What is Elisabeth Piedmont-Marton's main argument in her essay on fashion?
5. Brandon Brown's essay on reading a science lab is not really like any other piece in this chapter. Traditionally, such spaces are not particularly concerned with décor, but Brown argues that such spaces are rich texts. Is his argument compelling? Why or why not?

6. Think of a few nontraditional texts. Now imagine these authors tackling the subjects. How would these various essays be different under these authors? How would they be different from the way you would want to approach these subjects?

Your Text: Writing

1. Find a readable text that is part of the world around you. Ask a series of questions about it the way Rader and Silverman do toward the end of their co-authored essay on advertising. Based on the questions and the answers to them, build a thesis and write a persuasive paper on your text.

2. Write a comparison paper on two of the essays in this chapter. Pick essays that differ either in style (Brown and Transue; Hartlaub and Zimmer) or in subject matter (Hartlaub and Brown; Piedmont-Marton and Silverman) and argue for a similar way of unpacking a text.

3. Gather photos you have taken in a day or on a trip or even in a family scrapbook. Now try to write a paper that ties them together.

4. Find a text you want to explore. Instead of beginning writing right away, list at least five ways you might approach the text. Then, choose one approach to the text and begin drafting or freewriting!

READING BETWEEN THE LINES

Classroom Activities

1. Spend 10–15 minutes "reading" your classroom. Pay attention to details you might not normally notice—paint color, décor, windows, ceiling height, flooring, even the size and comfort of your desk or table. What visual cues about the classroom help the room "make an argument?"

2. A good homework assignment is for everyone to come to class having read someone else's dorm room. Why do we personalize our space? It's pretty easy to get an idea of someone's personality by intentional cues (Barack Obama posters, Dave Matthews Band cds, lots of philosophy books, posters of women in bikinis on Porsches), but what about *unintentional* cues?

3. One of the author's favorite classroom activities is to take his class outside and have them read the semiotics of the Lone Mountain gate and stairway at the University of San Francisco (see chapter three). Go outside and read various constructed spaces on your campus. What arguments do those spaces make?

4. Read the logo and team mascot of your college or university.

5. Do some research and see if your college has done any local or national advertising on radio, television or the Internet. Do a semiotic reading of the ads. Or look at the college's recruiting materials and read those. What sorts of arguments is the college making about itself?

6. Next time you drive to campus or from campus, read the road. Look at normally ignored details—billboards, landscaping, guardrails, streetlights, fences, and signs. What feeling do you get? In what way are the areas along roads constructed texts? Is there disagreement in class about such spaces' "beauty" or "utility"?

7. Does your town or city have an official logo? Does it have official branding? If so, track it down and do a collaborative in-class reading of your city's visual branding. Does the message it sends mesh with your reading of the city?

8. Watch a YouTube video in class. Talk about the video as a constructed text. Does watching a video on YouTube differ from watching the same clip on TV? How? Why?

9. Locate an old map of your town/city and a new one. Read them side-by-side. What do you see? What information do the maps have? Or, find old and new postcards of your town. What has changed besides the obvious?

Essay Ideas

When reading the world around you, literally, the entire globe is your textbook, so feel free to look at things you never have before in ways that are totally new. Here are just a fraction of the options available to you.

1. Write an essay on any of the topics above. Do some research and be sure to use a lot of specific detail.

2. Write a comparison/contrast essay in which you read a science lab and an art studio. What are the similarities? Differences? How do the regular users of the spaces "brand" their rooms?

3. If you can, revisit one of your high school classrooms. Take some photos of it. Now, write an essay comparing your high school classroom with a typical college classroom. What stays the same? What changes? Are there semiotic texts that scream "high school" or "college?" If so, what and how?

4. Write a paper on the various forms of transportation in a college parking lot. Look at cars, SUVs, bikes, motorcycles, and scooters. What does the aggregate tell you about the demographic of your school? Do we tend to associate certain types of people with specific modes of transportation? If so, why? And what are the associations?

5. Write an essay on what you think are three new or interesting fashion trends: tattoos, a haircut, a kind of jean, a hip T-shirt, or the popularity of flip-flops. Give a semiotic reading of each fashion trend and explain what message the wearer intends to send by donning that accessory.

6. Write a comparison/contrast paper in which you read your university's dining hall and your favorite local restaurant. What is similar? What's different? Does your dining hall do anything to try to approximate a restaurant?

7. Give a semiotic reading of some space in your dorm/residence hall. Maybe you read all of the material on dorm room doors on your hall; maybe you read all of the notices and ads on a bulletin board; maybe you read the main entryway; or, maybe you give a semiotic reading of a bathroom on your floor.

2 Reading and Writing about Television

WRITING ABOUT TELEVISION

You may be surprised by how much you already know about *reading* television as opposed to *watching* television (and reading television is important since you are *writing* about television). For example, you undoubtedly know the structure of sitcoms, talk shows, and sporting events. You know about the probable audiences of these particular shows, and you probably know something about plot devices and laugh tracks, and the way television networks spread out and time commercials.

The fact that you are familiar with television programming is more help than hindrance when writing about them. But watching television is different than reading television. Watching is passive; reading is active. Take, for example, the act of reading a traditional text such as a poem or a short story. These texts force us to confront and unlock their meanings. We read complex passages over and over and think about the way writers arrange words as well as more general concerns such as theme and plot. Plus, we are also taught to think about what literature means—we assume it has a larger significance beyond mere plot. Yet when we watch television, we rarely attend to these concerns. We have been watching television since we were small children with little or no guidance. Our parents, our friends, and newspapers and magazines may tell us what we can and should watch, but once we get in front of the television we tend to let the show dictate our response without our interaction. To understand television, we have to learn to question the structure and content of television shows as well as the presence and absence of ideas, people, and places. And so when watching and writing about television, we should consider a number of things.

THE STRUCTURE OF TELEVISION ENCOURAGES PASSIVE VIEWING.

When we read a book or magazine or newspaper, the text is in our hands. We can start and stop reading whenever we want to; we can reread at our convenience. We can underline these texts and make notes on them. We can, of course, take this particular text with us on the bus, to the bathroom, or to the coffee shop. However, when we watch television, we are already physically disconnected from the text. Unless we have an iPod or some small, portable television, we cannot pick it up, and worse, we cannot mark it up. Only recently have we been able to control its flow with a remote control and Tivo. But even when we watch with the remote control, there is a laugh track telling us not only when but how to laugh, commercial interruptions telling us to wait, and familiar plot conventions telling us to respond in predictable ways.

America's Top Model is one of the country's favorite reality shows. But is it important? See our suite on reality television beginning on page 167.

Various aspects of modern life also contribute to a consumption of television that is not particularly critical. For instance, it's likely that your home lends itself to passive television watching. Most people arrange their dens or family rooms so that the TV is center stage, the main focal point of the room. And, after a long day of work (or school), there is often something comforting about settling down in front of the television for an episode of *Lost*, a baseball game, or a movie. Our architecture, our work, and our home lives facilitate watching television as an act of disengagement.

Are networks and television producers conspiring to have us watch this way? Some of television's harsher critics would say yes, but others might view television as a form of escape from the realities of modern life or a form of education. In either case, we can better understand television by watching with critical engagement, taking notes, and if possible, replaying the program before sitting down to write about it.

UNLIKE WORKS OF LITERATURE, TELEVISION SHOWS HAVE NO RECOGNIZABLE AUTHOR.

When we pick up a book, we know who has written it—the name of the author is usually displayed as prominently as the title. Once we know who has authored a book, we can use this information accordingly. Traditionally, when scholars study written texts, they often focus on the words on the page, the symbols, the themes, and the plot contained within, but many also use the life of the author, and the author's other texts, to gain deeper understanding. Though modern scholars have diminished the power of authorial reputation, the author, even if less important to scholars, still exists and may exist profoundly for readers.

Who authors less traditional texts is not always clear. In movies, for example, we have two, and sometimes three people, to whom to attach authorship: the screenwriter, the director, and sometimes either the producer or cinematographer; in architecture, sometimes an entire firm serves as the author of a building.

In television, even more so than movies, there is no discernable author. We might consider the show's writers the authors, but as you well know, writing is only a small part of a visual text. There are the various settings, the clothing the actors wear, and the angles cameras use. In addition, we never know quite who has composed a particular show. There are writers listed, but we also hear stories about actors writing their own lines, as well as the presence of ad-libbed material. In addition, unlike authors of their own works who are responsible for virtually all of the production of the text (except of course for the book itself), the producers of a television show do not have the same direct connection to the texts they construct. They often play defining roles in shaping elements of the text that we can also make use of—the casting, the setting, the themes, even who technically writes the show—but do not do the writing, the set construction, or the casting themselves.

So the question is, how do we or can we refer to a show's author when writing about TV? One way is to refer to the show's *authors,* and use as a possibility for discussion what the presence of group authorship means to a particular text as opposed to discussing a single author. In any case, the question of authorship is one large difference between television and more traditional texts. What's important to consider when writing about television is that even reality shows and basketball games are *made* events. They are *directed, edited*, and *produced*. They don't just exist on their own. They have been created, essentially, by a conglomerate for you to consume. Your job as a writer is to look beyond, behind, under, and around television production to get at the real cultural work TV programming does.

TELEVISION SHOWS ARE CHARACTER DRIVEN, GENRE BASED, AND PLOT ORIENTED.

Television shows are much more genre driven than the traditional texts we read. While literature contains a number of different types of forms, many of which do not fit into a particular genre, television shows operate almost exclusively within genres. A genre is a type of a medium with established and expected formulas and devices. Romances and Westerns are prime examples of novel genres. Most works of fiction that critics consider as literary do not fit into a particular category of novel such as romances, Westerns, and science fiction, and it is rare that a literature class will discuss works from these categories since scholars and professors often consider them to be formulaic, with easily predicted plots. In recent years, critics have begun to study these works more carefully, but their interest in these texts has probably not often made it into your classroom.

Television, on the other hand, is all about genre. Dramas, comedies, action shows, reality shows, or various hybrids like "dramedies," all have recognizable components. Traditional texts have these components as well, but in television shows, they are often omnipresent. We know what to expect from sitcoms, gritty police dramas, and shows about families. The fact that shows about hospitals, lawyers, and the police comprise almost 80 percent of the hour-long dramas on prime-time network television speaks to the ubiquity of genre. One reason innovative programs like *Arrested Development, Northern Exposure, Twin Peaks, Freaks and Geeks* and *Wonderfalls* had short lives on television was because they could not be placed in any particular genre. Viewers did not know how to watch them because they didn't know what to expect from them. Television shows tend to be neglected as a field of study in the college classroom because they are genre oriented; if television shows were novels, we would be less likely to write about them.

So in writing about television, we have to understand that in large part shows fall into a particular category. We may want to ask whether an individual program "transcends" the normal fare of that genre, as well as what conventions of that genre a particular show follows. Once we start thinking about genre, we might also think about how this might affect the audience's viewing experience.

THE AUDIENCE PAYS FOR ITS FREE TELEVISION.

On its surface, network television would appear to be free; however, upon closer scrutiny, it turns out that we do pay for TV in a number of ways. First of all, we buy (and keep buying) more and more expensive television sets. Secondly, most Americans get their programming through monthly cable or satellite subscriptions that add up to between $300 and $800 per year. More and more people are subscribing to services like TiVo, which costs additional money. Contrast the price of a TV set and cable with the fee of a library card, which is free, and TV may not seem like such a bargain.

These are direct costs that we remain aware of for the most part. What we may not consider, though, are the indirect ways we pay for television. Instead of charging viewers to watch, television networks present commercials, paid for by advertisers. Advertisers, in turn, choose shows in which to advertise. Then, the price for those ads likely gets passed onto you in the purchase price of the items you buy.

But we pay for television in another way as well, and that is with our time and attention. If you watch a commercial, then you are essentially paying for that program with your time. Advertisers know this and plan accordingly. You can often tell what audience an advertiser thinks it is getting by watching its commercials. Because they in part are responsible for paying for a show, advertisers do play a role in what makes it to television, although the networks play a much larger role. If a show's content is considered controversial, advertisers may shy away, with the idea that it may lose potential customers who attach the advertisers to the show's content. If advertisers do not want to advertise with a show, the show may not survive.

The size of an audience may also play a factor in how we view a particular program. We might think about how a show geared toward appealing to millions differs from a novel, which often has (and can have) a more limited appeal. Television is entertainment for the masses, and its direct connection to commerce is another factor we have to look at when writing about it.

WHAT IS NOT THERE IS OFTEN AS IMPORTANT AS WHAT IS.

What is not in a show is often as important as what is in it. For example, as Oprah Winfrey pointed out when the cast of *Friends* came on *Oprah*, there is no black "friend." Winfrey's observation raises another: What does the absence of minorities of any kind in a city of incredible diversity say about the creators of a show? (We can make the same comments about any number of sitcoms: see *Two and a Half Men, Will and Grace, How I Met Your Mother*, and *Seinfeld* [although *Seinfeld* is smart enough to talk about its relative whiteness]). The ethnicity of the casts may send a message about the target audience for the show but also what kind of family, relationship, or group is considered "normal" or "cool." Unlike 30 years ago, there are now a number of programs that feature people of color that are, in fact, written and perhaps even directed by people of color, which was usually *not* the case even 20 years ago. Despite this notable improvement, many American groups get little or no representation on TV. For instance, as this book goes to press, there is no show that looks at Asian American, Arab American, or Native American families, relationships, or culture on prime-time television. Whether it is people of a certain age, particular areas of the country or world, or specific jobs, many aspects of modern life do not appear on television.

When writing about sitcoms or other television shows, also note the presence or absence of traditional gender roles, realistic dialogue, and typical, real-time events. Looking for absence rather than presence is difficult but rewarding; trying to understand what is missing often helps us understand the flaws of a show (or any text for that matter). It relates to the idea of writing about text through a lens, which we discuss in the introduction.

VISUAL MEDIA HAVE SPECIFIC CONCERNS.

Television is a decidedly more visual medium than traditional texts such as short stories and poems. Thus, we have to take into account how a show looks as well as sounds. The visual presence comes most obviously in its setting. In some shows, the setting is crucial. In *Seinfeld*, for example, New York City drives a great deal of the plot. In *The Simpsons*, the midwestern averageness of Springfield often determines the issues the show addresses, sometimes explaining a character's actions. *Grey's Anatomy* is set in Seattle, but how much really is Seattle a "character" in the show (as opposed to in *Seinfeld*, for example)? We also might look at three other settings. In the case of *Friends*, the coffee shop, Rachel and Monica's apartment, and Joey and Chandler's apartment. Are they appropriate for people of their age and wealth? Are they particularly male or female? What does the coffee shop represent to these characters and the audience? And how come that sofa is *never* occupied by anyone else?

You might also ask how the clothing of each cast member contributes to the audience member's idea of who and what the character is supposed to represent. On shows like *Jersey Shore, The Wire, The Sopranos, The Bachelor,* and even *Oprah,* clothing plays a crucial role in what the audience is supposed to understand about the show's characters, or in the case of *Oprah,* the host. Finally, you might ask how cameras are used and the colors that dominate the broadcast. A show like *CSI* uses handheld cameras, ostensibly for a more realistic look. A soap opera uses close-ups held for a number of seconds before cutting away to another scene or commercial.

Because settings and clothing are visual and present in every show, and are a result of choices the show's authors make, they are often useful subjects for writing. Papers about the relationships between the characters and the places they live or work can be the basis of a paper about the implicit values of a show. What do these techniques say about the shows in which they are used? Overall, the visual elements are crucial to understanding some of the show's intended and unintended messages, and its distinction from more traditional texts.

FINDING THEMES IS EASY, BUT FINDING MEANINGFUL ONES IS DIFFICULT.

Themes are often the intended meanings that authors give their works. For example, a theme of Harper Lee's *To Kill a Mockingbird* would be that racism can interfere with justice, and this interference is highly destructive to a society's fabric. *CSI* essentially has the same theme in every episode—criminals always leave traces, and smart, attractive people will find you. *Modern Family's* theme changes from episode to episode, but the message remains consistent—contemporary families have new rules and have to be their own models. Every text has a theme, and whether we know it or not, we pick up on a text's thematics.

Of all the elements involved with watching television, the theme is the most easily discerned and often the least interesting. Most often, any television theme revolves around tolerance and patience and above all, the problematic nature of jumping to conclusions. Although many critics sometimes justifiably complain about the violence of television shows, most shows favor right over wrong, happiness over sadness, lessons learned over lessons forgotten. Shows like *The Sopranos, Seinfeld,* and even *Modern Family* play with these traditions, which is one reason critics tend to praise them. All in all, looking for a theme is often the easiest task a television reader has.

What's more difficult is trying to understand whether the television author(s) handled these lessons too simplistically or offensively, or at the expense of the quality of the show. In other words, does the theme take away from the show's other elements? In watching sitcoms, finding the theme is easy, but one must be careful. *The Simpsons,* for example, has a traditional television sitcom theme in many of its shows but often brutally satirizes American culture. So which message is more important? Clearly, what happens during the show matters more than what happens at its end, which the authors of *The Simpsons* often use to criticize the conventions of television itself.

Overall, the medium of television has a number of general concerns that play into our enjoyment as well as our critical stance. As a writer, you do not have to take into account all of the above, but thinking about them is a good way of breaking free of your traditional relationship to television. There are also more specific ways of analyzing a television show. Following this introduction we give a list of questions you can ask of a television show when you are getting ready to write about it.

THIS TEXT

1. How does the background of the authors influence their ideas about television?
2. Do the authors have different ideas about class, race, and gender and their place in television? In what ways?
3. While it will be impossible for you to know this fully, try to figure out the writing situation of each author. Who is the audience? What does the author have at stake?
4. What is his or her agenda? *Why* is she or he writing this piece?
5. What social, political, and cultural forces affect the author's text? What is going on in the world as he or she is writing?
6. What are the main points of the essay? Can you find a thesis statement anywhere?
7. How does the author support his or her argument? What evidence does he or she use to back up any claims he or she might make?
8. Is the author's argument valid and/or reasonable?
9. Do you find yourself in agreement with the author? Why or why not?
10. Does the author help you *read* television better (or differently) than you did before reading the essay? If so, why?
11. How is the reading process different if you are reading an essay as opposed to a short story or poem?
12. What is the agenda of the author? Why does she or he want us to think a certain way?
13. Did you like this? Why or why not?
14. Do you think the author likes television?

BEYOND THIS TEXT: READING TELEVISION

Genre: What genre are we watching? How do the writers let us know this? (Visually, orally, etc.)

Characters: Who are the characters? Do they represent something beyond actors in a plot? How do the writers want us to perceive them, and why? How would changing the characters change the show?

Setting: What are the settings? What do they say about the show? What do the writers want us to think about the setting? Could the show take place somewhere else and remain the same?

Plot: What happens? Is the plot important to understanding/enjoying the show?

Themes: What do the show's writers think about the issues/ideas/subjects they present? (Themes are what writers believe about issues, ideas, and subjects, *not* the ideas and issues themselves.)

Figurative language: What symbols, metaphors, and motifs present themselves in the show? What effect does their repetition have?

Visual constructions: How do the writers make us see (or hear) the show?

Absences: What is missing? What real-world notions are not represented in the show?

Conventional/nonconventional: In what ways is the show typical of its genre? Atypical?

Race/ethnicity/gender/class: How do the writers talk (or not talk about) these issues? How do these issues show up in other categories we have mentioned, such as character, setting, plot, and theme?

Reality: In what way does what is depicted in a particular television show or in general reflect the world as you normally experience it? What is different? Does this matter?

QUICK GUIDE FOR WRITING ABOUT TELEVISION

Keep a remote control handy when writing about television. You need to make what is a passive activity, active.

Ask a question about your subject before beginning your viewing. Writing about and watching a show becomes more focused if you have a question you are trying to answer.

Take notes extensively. One reason is to remember the text better, but the more important reason is to gather information.

Brainstorm for a thesis. Even if you do not use your original thesis, it helps when writing a draft.

Organize ideas by paragraph. If you have a first draft with definable paragraphs, the draft will be stronger and easier to revise.

"Not That There's Anything Wrong With That": Reading the Queer in *Seinfeld*

Katherine Gantz

Katherine Gantz uses the lens of "queer theory" in her 2000 discussion of Seinfeld. *Notice how Gantz strictly defines not only the term "queer" but the particular questions she intends to ask of her text using "queer." Here we are taking her work and examining it as a scholarly work.*

Scholarly articles are sometimes a mystery to students. They are long, often spend a lot of time talking about subjects that seem related but not specifically about the subject or text at hand, and most importantly, use a lot of language that students may not understand. While some scholars do write for a general audience, they most often are writing to a very specific audience—their scholarly peers. Both these terms and some additional related terms need a little explanation. A scholar is someone who studies and conducts studies within a discipline or field of study (sometimes abbreviated as "the field"). A peer is a fellow scholar in a field of study.

Fields of study or disciplines are the way scholars organize themselves in order to study similar or related questions. For example, scholars who are interested in studying literature written in English usually are in English departments; scholars who interested in studying life forms are usually in biology departments. Of course, as you may have encountered at your university, disciplines are becoming more complex. There are biochemists (people who study the chemistry involved in biology), and people in cultural or American studies (people who study the United States or culture using multiple disciplines). So when writing a scholarly article for a journal or collection, or writing a book, a scholar's work is reviewed and read by other people in the same discipline and often people who study the same subject in the same discipline.

In terms of language, writing for an audience in a particular language is something with which you are already familiar; you may use terms like "lol" or "brb" in texting or chatting, but you would not (or should not) use them in a paper for class (and probably not an e-mail to your professor). The scholar uses language that other scholars understand but that may not be completely understandable to a reader outside the field. What we are going to do here is discuss one of our favorite essays in the book and the work the writer is doing and how you might read it.

The first sentence indicates that this will be an academic essay because of phrases like "the world mass culture" and words like "homophobic." When writing this term, Gantz assumed that an audience familiar with these terms would be reading it—this article appeared in an academic collection—so she used phrases that they would be sure to understand, even though more general readers might not.

THE WORLD OF MASS CULTURE, especially that which includes American television, remains overwhelmingly homophobic. Queer theory offers a useful perspective from which to examine the heterosexism at the core of contemporary television and also provides a powerful tool of subversion. The aim of this article is twofold: first, it will outline and explain the notion of a queer reading; second, it will apply a queer reading to the narrative texts that comprise the situation comedy *Seinfeld*. The concept of the queer reading, currently en vogue in literary analysis, has evolved from a handful of distinct but connected sources, beginning with the popularization of the term "queer." In 1989, the AIDS activist group ACT UP created Queer Nation, an offshoot organization comprised of lesbians and gays dedicated to the political reclaiming of gay identity under the positively recoded term "queer."[1] The group was initially formed as a New York City street patrol organized to help counteract escalating hate crimes against gays. As Queer Nation gained visibility in the public eye, the use of "queer," historically a derogatory slur for homosexuals, entered into standard parlance in the gay and lesbian press.[2] Eve Kosofsky Sedgwick's *Epistemology of the Closet*[3] appropriated the term with a broadened interpretation of "queer," suggesting not that literature be read with the author's possible homosexuality in mind but instead with an openness to the queer (homoerotic and/or homosexual) contexts, nuances, connections, and potential already available within the text. The concept of "queerness" was elaborated once more in 1991, with the publication of *Inside/Out: Lesbian Theories, Gay Theories;*[4] within this assemblage of political, pedagogical, and literary essays, the term was collectively applied to a larger category of sexual non-straightness, as will be further explained.

As the political construction of "queer" became increasingly disciplinized in academia, the emerging body of "queer theory" lost its specifically homosexual connotation and was replaced by a diffuse set of diverse sexual identities. Like the path of feminism, the concept of queerness had been largely stripped of its political roots and transformed into a methodological approach accessible to manipulation by the world of predominantly heterosexual, white, middle-class intellectuals. It is with this problematic universalization of queer theory in mind that I undertake an application of queer reading.

In what could be deemed a reinsertion of the subversive into a "straightened" discipline, Alexander Doty's book *Making Things Perfectly Queer: Reading Mass Culture*[5] has taken the queer reading out of the realm of the purely literary and applied it to analyses of film and television texts. From this ever-transforming history of the queer reading, the popular situation comedy *Seinfeld* lends itself well to a contemporary application.

In the summer of 1989, NBC debuted a tepidly received pilot entitled *The Seinfeld Chronicles,* a situation comedy revolving around the mundane, urbane Manhattan existence of stand-up comic Jerry Seinfeld. Despite its initially unimpressive ratings, the show evolved into the five-episode series *Seinfeld* and established its regular cast of Jerry's three fictional friends:

culture, the language is still academic; the reference to the
Möbius strip is an indication
that the writer is appealing to a
scholarly reader. Yet for many
scholarly readers, who often
wade through journal articles
and books about more
traditional texts, reading such a
paragraph is a joy. Indeed, this
book is a tribute to such notions,
because we think scholarly work
can be done about ANYTHING.

George Costanza (Jason Alexander), ex-girlfriend Elaine Benes (Julia Louis-Dreyfus), and the enigmatic neighbor Kramer (Michael Richards). By its return in January 1991, *Seinfeld* had established a following among Wednesday-night television viewers; over the next two years, the show became a cultural phenomenon, claiming both a faithful viewership and a confident position in the Nielsen ratings' top ten. The premise was to write a show about the details, minor disturbances, and nonevents of Jerry's life as they occurred before becoming fodder for the stand-up monologues that bookend each episode. From the start, *Seinfeld*'s audience has been comprised of a devoted group of "TV-literate, demographically desirable urbanites, for the most part—who look forward to each weekly episode in the Life of Jerry with a baby-boomer generation's self-involved eagerness," notes Bruce Fretts, author of *The "Entertainment Weekly" "Seinfeld" Companion.*[6] Such obsessive identification and selfreflexive fascination seems to be thematic in both the inter- and extradiegetic worlds of *Seinfeld*. The show's characters are modeled on real-life acquaintances: George is based on Seinfeld's best friend (and series cocreator) Larry David; Elaine is an exaggeration of Seinfeld's ex-girlfriend, writer Carol Leifer; Kramer's prototype lived across the hall from one of David's first Manhattan apartments.[7] To further complicate this narcissistic mirroring, in the 1993 season premiere entitled "The Pilot" (see videography for episodic citations), Jerry and George finally launch their new NBC sitcom *Jerry* by casting four actors to portray themselves, Kramer, and Elaine. This multilayered Möbius strip of person/actor/character relationships seems to be part of the show's complex appeal. Whereas situation comedies often dilute their cast, adding and removing characters in search of new plot possibilities, *Seinfeld* instead interiorizes; the narrative creates new configurations of the same limited cast to keep the viewer and the characters intimately linked. In fact, it is precisely this concentration on the nuclear set of four personalities that creates the *Seinfeld* community.

If it seems hyperbolic to suggest that the participants in the *Seinfeld* phenomenon (both spectators and characters included) have entered into a certain delineated "lifestyle," consider the significant lexicon of Seinfeldian code words and recurring phrases that go unnoticed and unappreciated by the infrequent or "unknowing" viewer. Catch phrases such as Snapple, the Bubble Boy, Cuban cigars, Master of My Domain, Junior Mints, Mulva, Crazy Joe Davola, Pez, and Vandelay Industries all serve as parts of the group-specific language that a family shares; these are the kinds of self-referential in-jokes that help one *Seinfeld* watcher identify another.[8] This sort of tightly conscribed universe of meaning is reflected not only by the decidedly small cast but also by the narrative's consistent efforts to maintain its intimacy. As this article will discuss, much of *Seinfeld*'s plot and humor (and, consequently, the viewer's pleasure) hinge on outside personalities threatening—and ultimately failing—to invade the foursome. Especially where Jerry and George are concerned, episodes are mostly resolved by expelling the intruder and restoring the exclusive nature of their relationship. The show's camera work, which at times takes awkward measures to ensure that Jerry and George remain grouped together within a scene, reinforces the privileged dynamic of their relationship within the narrative.

Superficially speaking, *Seinfeld* appears to be a testament to heterosexuality: in its nine-year run, Jerry sported a new girlfriend in almost every episode; his friendship with Elaine is predicated on their previous sexual relationship; and all four characters share in the discussion and navigation of the (straight) dating scene. However, with a viewership united by a common coded discourse and an interest in the cohesive (and indeed almost claustrophobic) exclusivity of its predominantly male cast, clearly *Seinfeld* is rife with possibilities for homoerotic interpretation. As will be demonstrated, the construction, the coding, and the framing of the show readily conform to a queer reading of the *Seinfeld* text.

Here I wish to develop and define my meanings of the word "queer" as a set of signifying practices and a category distinct from that of gay literature. Inspired by Doty's work, I will use "queer"—as its current literary usages suggest—as relating to a wide-ranging spectrum of "nonnormative" sexual notions, including not only constructions of gayness and lesbianism but also of transsexualism, transvestism, same-sex affinity, and other ambisexual behaviors and sensibilities. Queerness at times may act merely as a space in which heterosexual personalities interact, in the same ways that a queer personality may operate within an otherwise heterosexual sphere. In this system, "queer" does not stand in opposition to "heterosexual" but instead to "straight," a term that by contrast, suggests all that is restrictive about "normative" sexuality, a category that excludes what is deemed undesirable, deviant, dangerous, unnatural, unproductive. "Queer," then, should be understood not so much as an intrinsic property but more as the outcome of both productive and receptive behaviors—a pluralized, inclusive term that may be employed by and applied to both gay and nongay characters and spectators.[9]

The second point I wish to clarify about the use of the term "queer" as it relates to my own textual analysis of a mass culture text is the indirect, nonexplicit nature of the queer relationships represented in *Seinfeld*. Explicit references to homosexuality subvert the possibility of a queer reading; by identifying a character as "gay," such overt difference serves to mark the other characters as "not gay." Sexual perimeters become limited, fixed, rooted in traditional definitions and connotations that work contrary to the fluidity and subtle ambiguity of a queer interpretation. It is precisely the unspokenness ("the love that dare not speak its name") of homoeroticism between seemingly straight men that allows the insinuation of a queer reading. As Doty rightly notes, queer positionings are generated more often through the same-sex tensions evident in "straight films" than in gay ones:

Traditional narrative films [such as *Gentlemen Prefer Blondes* and *Thelma and Louise*], which are ostensibly addressed to straight audiences, often have greater potential for encouraging a wider range of queer responses than [such] clearly lesbian- and gay-addressed films [as *Women I Love* and *Scorpio Rising*]. The intense tensions and pleasures generated

This paragraph serves as a transition back from textual description to the lens. A more detailed description of the word queer follows. The reader may rightly ask why another go through the use of queer. Two things I think are going on here. One is that the first go through is a conversation, letting the reader know the evolution of the term. This one is a more careful explanation of the term itself and how it's going to be used. The two sections might have been combined, but I think Gantz rightly splits it up because she wants to keep the reader engaged through a discussion of *Seinfeld*.

This is the crucial point of the essay, and one most of my students have missed in reading this article. They often say, the writer is saying Seinfeld is gay. Gantz is not. She is actually pointing out that sexuality is ambiguous and subtle. And thus another point about scholarly articles, particularly in the humanities; subtlety is a crucial element of the joyful scholarly read. Readers want to be in on the joke.

by the woman-woman and man-man aspects within the narratives of the former group of films create a space of sexual instability that already queerly positioned viewers can connect in various ways, and within which straights might be likely to recognize and express their queer impulses. (8)

Of course, there is a multitude of possibilities for the perception and reception of queer pleasures, but, to generalize from Doty's argument, the implications in the case of the *Seinfeld* phenomenon suggest that while queer-identified viewers may recognize the domesticity between Jerry and George as that of a gay couple, straight viewers may simply take pleasure in the characters' intimate bond left unbroken by outside (heterosexual) romantic interruptions.

This more directly addresses the idea of homosexuality. You might have noticed that Gantz seems to be anticipating arguments in her text. That is part of the goal in participating in a scholarly conversation.

This is not to say that *Seinfeld* ignores the explicit category of homosexuality; on the contrary, the show is laden with references and plot twists involving gay characters and themes. In separate episodes, Elaine is selected as the "best man" in a lesbian wedding ("The Subway"); George accidentally causes the exposure of his girlfriend Susan's father's affair with novelist John Cheever ("The Cheever Letters"); and, after their breakup, George runs into Susan with her new lesbian lover ("The Smelly Car"). At its most playful, *Seinfeld* smugly calls attention to its own homosexual undercurrents in an episode in which Jerry and George are falsely identified as a gay couple by a female journalist ("The Outing").[10] Due to the direct nature of such references to homosexuality, these are episodes that slyly deflect queer reading, serving as a sort of lightning rod by displacing homoerotic undercurrents onto a more obvious target.

Such smoke-screen tactics seem to be in conflict with the multitude of queer-identified semiotics and gay icons and symbols at play within the *Seinfeld* text. Most notably, no "queer-receptive" viewer can look at the *Seinfeld* graphic logo (at the episode's beginning and before commercials) without noticing the inverted triangle—hot pink during the earliest seasons—dotting the "i" in "Seinfeld."[11] Although the symbol dates back to the Holocaust (used to mark homosexuals for persecution), the pink triangle has recently been recuperated by gay activists during ACT UP's widely publicized AIDS education campaign, "Silence Equals Death," and has consequently become a broadly recognized symbol of gayness.

Even if the pink triangle's proactive gay recoding remains obscure to the "unknowing" viewership (i.e., unfamiliar with or resistant to queerness), *Seinfeld* also offers a multitude of discursive referents chosen from a popular lexicon of more common gay signifiers that are often slurs in use by a homophobic public. In an episode revolving around Jerry and Kramer's discussion of where to find *fruit*—longstanding slang for a gay man—Jerry makes a very rare break from his standard wardrobe of well-ironed button-up oxfords, instead sporting a T-shirt with the word "QUEENS" across it. Although outwardly in reference to Queens College, the word's semiotic juxtaposition with the theme of fruit evokes its slang connotation for effeminate gay men.

You might be thrown by this sentence, which speaks in an academic voice. But you probably can figure out what Gantz means by thinking about the sentence in relationship to the rest of the paragraph, which talks about setting.

Narrative space is also queerly coded. Positioned as Jerry and George's "place" (or "male space"), the restaurant where they most often meet is "Monk's," a name that conjures up images of an exclusively male religious society, a "brotherhood" predicated on the maintenance of masculine presence/feminine absence, in both spiritual and physical terms.

Jerry's puffy shirt challenges traditional notions of masculinity. But Kramer loves it!

Recurring plot twists also reveal a persistent interest in the theme of hidden or falsified identities. As early as *Seinfeld*'s second episode ("The Stakeout"), George insists on creating an imaginary biography for himself as a successful architect before meeting Jerry's new girl-friend. Throughout the *Seinfeld* texts, the foursome adopts a number of different names and careers in hopes of persuading outsiders (most often potential romantic interests) that they lead a more interesting, more superficially acceptable, or more immediately favorable exis-tence than what their real lives have to offer: George has assumed the identity of neo-Nazi organizer Colin O'Brian ("The Limo"); Elaine has recruited both Jerry and Kramer as sub-stitute boyfriends to dissuade unwanted suitors ("The Junior Mint" and "The Watch"); Kramer has posed as a policeman ("The Statue") and has even auditioned under a pseudo-nym to play himself in the pilot of *Jerry* ("The Pilot"). Pretense and fabrication often occur among the foursome as well. In "The Apartment," Jerry is troubled by Elaine's imminent move into the apartment above him. Worried that her presence will "cramp his style," he schemes to convince her that she will be financially unable to take the apartment. In private, Jerry warns George that he will be witness to some "heavy acting" to persuade Elaine that he is genuinely sympathetic. Unshaken, George answers: "Are you kidding? I lie every second of the day; my whole life is a sham." This deliberate "closeting" of one's lifestyle has obvious connections to the gay theme of "passing,"[12] the politically discouraged practice of hiding one's homosexuality behind a façade of straight respectability. One might argue that *Seinfeld* is simply a text about passing—socially as well as sexually—in a repressive and judgmental society. It must be noted, however, that George and Jerry are the only two char-acters who do not lie to each other; they are in fact engaged in maintaining each other's secrets and duplicities by "covering" for one another, thus distancing themselves somewhat from Kramer and Elaine from within an even more exclusive rapport.[13]

Another thematic site of queerness is the mystification of and resulting detachment from female culture and discourse. While Jerry glorifies such male-identified personalities as Superman, the Three Stooges, and Mickey Mantle, he prides himself in never having seen a single episode of *I Love Lucy* ("The Phone Message"). Even Elaine is often presented as incomprehensible to her familiar male counterparts. In "The Shoes," Jerry and George have no problem creating a story line for their situation comedy, *Jerry,* around male characters; however, when they try to "write in" Elaine's character, they find themselves stumped:

> JERRY: [In the process of writing the script.] "Elaine enters." . . . What does she say . . . ?
> GEORGE: [Pause.] What *do* they [women] say?
> JERRY: [Mystified.] I *don't know.*

We're now in the middle of the exploration of *Seinfeld.* So to recount: Gantz identified her lens, her text of choice, defined the lens further, and is now examining the text. Not all humanities scholarly papers are organized in precisely this fashion but many are. And these papers perform many functions, with a few that stand out— understanding both the lens and the text better.

After a brief deliberation, they opt to omit the female character completely. As Jerry explains with a queerly loaded rationale: "You, me, Kramer, the butler. . . . Elaine is too much." Later, at Monk's, Elaine complains about her exclusion from the pilot. Jerry confesses: "We couldn't write for a woman." "You have *no idea?*" asks Elaine, disgusted. Jerry looks at George for substantiation and replies: "None." Clearly, the privileged bond between men excludes room for an understanding of and an interest in women; like Elaine in the pilot, the feminine presence is often simply deleted for the sake of maintaining a stronger, more coherent male narrative.

Jerry seems especially ill at ease with notions of female sexuality, perhaps suggesting that they impinge on his own. In "The Red Dot," Jerry convinces the resistant George that he should buy Elaine a thank-you gift after she procures him a job at her office. Despite George's tightfisted unwillingness to invest money in such social graces as gift giving, he acquiesces. The duo go to a department store in search of an appropriate gift for Elaine. Jerry confesses: "I never feel comfortable in the women's department; I feel like I'm just a *little* too close to trying on a dress." While browsing through the women's clothing, George describes his erotic attraction to the cleaning woman in his new office:

> GEORGE: . . . she was swaying back and forth, back and forth, her hips swiveling and her breasts—uh . . .
> JERRY: . . . convulsing?

George reacts with disdain at the odd word choice, recognizing that Jerry's depiction of female physicality and eroticism is both inappropriate and unappealing. (It should be noted that the ensuing sexual encounter between George and the cleaning woman ultimately results in the loss of both their jobs; true to the pattern, George's foray into heterosex creates chaos.)

Although sites of queerness occur extensively throughout the *Seinfeld* oeuvre, the most useful elucidation of its queer potential comes from a closer, more methodical textual analysis. To provide a contextualized view of the many overlapping sites of queerness—symbolic, discursive, thematic, and visual—the following is a critique of three episodes especially conducive to a queer reading of *Seinfeld*'s male homoerotic relationships.

"The Boyfriend" explores the ambiguous valences of male friendships. Celebrated baseball player Keith Hernandez stars as himself (as does Jerry Seinfeld among the cast of otherwise fictional characters), becoming the focal point of both Jerry's and, later, Elaine's attentions. Despite Elaine's brief romantic involvement with Keith, the central narrative concerns Jerry's interactions with the baseball player. Although never explicitly discussed, Jerry's attachment to Keith is represented as romantic in nature.

The episode begins in a men's locker room, prefiguring the homoerotic overtones of the coming plot. The locker room is clearly delineated as "male space"; its connection to the athletic field posits it as a locale of physicality, where men gather to prepare for or to disengage from the privileged (and predominantly homophobic) world of male sports. The locker room, as a site of potential heterosexual vulnerability as men expose their bodies to other men, is socially safe only when established as sexually neutral—or, better still, heterosexually charged with the machismo of athleticism. This "safe" coding occurs almost immediately in this setting, accomplished through a postgame comparison of Jerry's, George's, and Kramer's basketball prowess. As they finish dressing together after their game, it is the voracious, ambisexual Kramer who immediately upsets the precarious sexual neutrality, violating the unspoken code of locker-room decorum:

> KRAMER: Hey, you know this is the first time we've ever seen each other naked?
> JERRY: Believe me, *I* didn't see anything.
> KRAMER: [With disbelief.] Oh, you didn't sneak a peek?
> JERRY: No—did you?
> KRAMER: Yeah, I snuck a peek.
> JERRY: Why?
> KRAMER: Why not? What about you, George?
> GEORGE: [Hesitating] Yeah, I—snuck a peek. But it was so fast that I didn't see anything; it was just a blur.
> JERRY: I made a conscious effort *not* to look; there's certain information I just don't want to have.

Jerry displays his usual disdain for all things corporeal or carnal. Such unwillingness to participate in Kramer's curiosity about men's bodies also secures Jerry firmly on heterosexual ground, a necessary pretext to make his intense feelings for Keith "safe." The humor of these building circumstances depends on the assumption that Jerry is straight; although this episode showcases *Seinfeld*'s characteristic playfulness with queer subject matter, great pains are taken to prevent the viewer from ever believing (or realizing) that Jerry is gay.

After Kramer leaves, Jerry and George spot Hernandez stretching out in the locker room. With Kramer no longer threatening to introduce direct discussion of overtly homoerotic matters, the queer is permitted to enter into the narrative space between Jerry and George. Both baseball aficionados, they are bordering on giddy, immediately starstruck by Hernandez. Possessing prior knowledge of Keith's personal life, Jerry remarks that Hernandez is not only a talented athlete but intelligent as well, being an American Civil War buff. "I wish *I* were a Civil War buff," George replies longingly. Chronically socially inept, George is left to appropriate the interests of a man he admires without being able to relate to him more directly.[14]

Keith introduces himself to Jerry as a big fan of his comedy; Jerry is instantly flattered and returns the compliment. As the jealous and excluded George looks on (one of the rare times that Jerry and George break rank and appear distinctly physically separated within a scene), Keith and Jerry exchange phone numbers and plan to meet for coffee in the future. Thus, in the strictly homosocial, theoretically nonromantic masculine world of the locker room, two men have initiated an interaction that becomes transformed into a relationship, consistently mirroring traditional television representations of heterosexual dating rituals. The homoerotic stage is set.

Later, at Monk's, Jerry complains to Elaine that three days have passed without a call from Keith. When Elaine asks why Jerry doesn't initiate the first call, he responds that he doesn't want to seem overanxious: "If he wants to see me, he has my number; he should call. I can't stand these guys—you give your number to them, and then they don't call."

Here, in his attempts not to seem overly aggressive, Jerry identifies with the traditionally receptive and passive role posited as appropriate female behavior. By employing such categorization as "these guys," Jerry brackets himself off from the rest of the heterosexual, male dating population, reinforcing his identification with Elaine not as Same (i.e., straight male) but as Other (Elaine as Not Male, Jerry as Not Straight). Elaine responds sympathetically:

ELAINE: I'm sorry, honey.
JERRY: I mean, I thought he liked me, I really thought he liked me—we were getting along. He came over to *me,* I didn't go over to *him.*
ELAINE: [Commiserating.] I know.
JERRY: Here I meet this guy, this *great* guy, ballplayer, best guy I ever met in my life...well, that's it. I'm *never* giving my number out to another guy again.

Jerry is clearly expressing romantic disillusionment in reaction to Keith's withdrawal from their social economy. Elaine further links her identity—as sexually experienced with men—to Jerry's own situation:

ELAINE: Sometimes I give my number out to a guy, and it takes him a *month* to call me.
JERRY: [Outraged.] A *month?* Ha! Have him call *me* after a month—let's see if *he* has a prayer!

Thus, Jerry's construction of his relationship with Keith is one bound by the rules of heterosexual dating protocol and appropriate exchange; the intensity of his feelings and expectations for his relationship with Keith have long surpassed normative (that is, conventional, expected, tolerable), straight male friendship. By stating that Keith's violation of protocol will result in Jerry's withdrawal, it is clear that Jerry is only willing to consider any interactions with Keith in terms of a romantic model—one that, as suggested by Keith's relative indifference, is based in fantasy.

Elaine suggests that he simply put an end to the waiting and call Keith to arrange an evening out. Jerry ponders the possibility of dinner but then has doubts:

JERRY: But don't you think that dinner might be coming on too strong? Kind of a turnoff?
ELAINE: [Incredulous.] Jerry, it's a *guy.*
JERRY: [Covering his eyes.] It's all very confusing.

Throughout the episode, Jerry is content to succumb to the excitement of his newfound relationship, until the moment when someone inevitably refers to its homoerotic nature (terms such as "gay" and "homosexual" are certainly implied but never explicitly invoked). Elaine's reminder that Jerry's fears about a "turnoff" are addressed to a man quickly ends his swooning; he covers his eyes as if to suggest a groggy return from a dream-like state.

To interrupt and divert the narrative attention away from Jerry's increasingly queer leanings, the scene abruptly changes to George at the unemployment office, where he is hoping to maneuver a thirteen-week extension on his unemployment benefits.[15] There, George evades the questions of his no-nonsense interviewer Mrs. Sokol until she forces him to provide one name of a company with which he had recently sought employment. Having in truth interviewed nowhere, he quickly concocts "Vandelay Industries," a company, he assures her, he had thoroughly pursued to no avail. Further pressed, he tells Mrs. Sokol that they are "makers of latex products." His blurting-out of the word "latex" must not be overlooked here as a queer signifier directly associated with the gay safe-sex campaigns throughout the last decade. Whereas "condoms" as a signifier would have perhaps been a more mainstream (straight) sexual symbol, latex evokes a larger category of products—condoms, gloves, dental dams—linked closely with the eroticization of gay safe-sex practices. When Mrs. Sokol insists on information to verify his claim, it is telling that George provides Jerry's address and phone number as the home of Vandelay latex. George's lie necessitates a race back to Jerry's to warn him of the impending phone call; once again, he will depend on Jerry's willingness to maintain a duplicity and to adopt a false identity as the head of Vandelay Industries.

As if to await the panicked arrival of George, the scene changes to Jerry's apartment, where he is himself anxiety ridden over his impending night out with Keith. In a noticeable departure from his usual range of conservative color and style, he steps out of his bedroom, modeling a bright orange and red shirt, colors so shocking that they might best be described as "flaming." Pivoting slightly with arms outstretched in a style suggesting a fashion model, he asks Elaine's opinion. Again, she reminds him: "Jerry, he's a guy." Agitated (but never denying her implication of homoerotic attraction), he drops his arms, attempting to hide his nervous discomfort.

Jerry's actual evening out with Keith remains unseen (closeted) until the end of the "date"; the men sit alone in the front seat of Keith's car outside of Jerry's apartment. In the setup that prefigures the close of Elaine's date with Keith later in the episode, Jerry sits in the passenger seat next to him; a familiar heterosexual power dynamic is at play. Keith, as both the car owner and driver, acts and reacts in his appropriate masculine role. Jerry, within the increasingly queer context of an intimate social interaction with another man, is left to identify with what we recognize as the woman's position in the car. As the passenger and not the driver, he has relinquished both the mechanical and social control that defines the dominance of the male role. In a symbolic interpretation of power relations, Jerry's jump into the feminized gender role is characterized by the absence of the steering wheel:

JERRY: [Aloud to Keith.] Well, thanks a lot, that was really fun. [Thinking to himself.] Should I shake his hand?

This anxiety and expectation over appropriate and mutually appealing physical contact expresses the same kind of desire—that is, sexual—that Keith will express with Elaine later on; whereas Keith will long for a kiss, Jerry's desires have been translated into a more acceptable form of physical contact between men. It would seem that part of Jerry's frustration in this situation comes from the multiplicity of gender roles that he plays. Whereas in his interactions with George, Jerry occupies the dominant role (controlling the discourse and the action), he is suddenly relegated to a more passive (feminine) position in his relationship with the hypermasculine Keith Hernandez. Part of the tension that comprises the handshake scene stems not only from Jerry's desire to interact physically *and* appropriately but also from wanting to initiate such an action from the disadvantaged, less powerful position of the (feminine) passenger's seat. I would suggest that the confusion arising out of his relationship with Keith is not strictly due to its potentially homosexual valences but is also the result of the unclear position (passive/dominant, feminine/masculine, nelly/butch) that Jerry holds within the homoerotic/homosexual coupling.

Once again, the humor of this scene is based on the presupposition that Jerry is straight and that this very familiar scene is not a homosexual recreation of heterosexual dating etiquette but simply a parody of it. Nonetheless, Jerry's discomfort over initiating a handshake betrays the nature of his desire for Keith. From behind the steering wheel (the seat of masculine power), Keith invites Jerry to a movie over the coming weekend. Jerry is elated, and they shake hands: a consummation of their successful social interaction. However, Keith follows up by telling Jerry that he would like to call Elaine for a date; the spell broken, Jerry responds with reluctance and thinly veiled disappointment.

Back in Jerry's apartment, George jealously asks for a recounting of Jerry's evening with Keith. Again, the handshake is reinforced as the symbol of a successful male-to-male social encounter:

> GEORGE: Did you shake his hand?
> JERRY: Yeah.
> GEORGE: What kind of a handshake does he have?
> JERRY: Good shake, perfect shake. Single pump, not too hard. He didn't have to prove anything, but firm enough to know he's there.

George and Jerry share a discourse, laden with masturbatory overtones, in which quantifying and qualifying the description of a handshake expresses information about the nature of men's relationships. This implicit connection between male intimacy and the presence and quality of physical contact clearly transcends the interpretation of the handshake in a heterosexual context. Upon hearing that Jerry had in fact shaken hands with Keith, George follows with the highly charged question: "You gonna see him again?" Here, the use of the verb "to see," implying organized social interaction between two people, is typically in reference to romantic situations; George has thus come to accept Jerry in a dating relationship with Keith.

Elaine enters and immediately teases Jerry: "So, how was your date?" Not only has she invaded Jerry and George's male habitat, but she has once again made explicit the romantic nature of Jerry's connection to Keith that he can only enjoy when unspoken. Jerry is forced to respond (with obvious agitation): "He's a guy." Elaine quickly reveals that she and Keith have made a date for the coming Friday, perhaps expressing an implicit understanding of a rivalry with Jerry. Realizing that such plans will interfere with his own "date" with Keith, Jerry protests with disappointment and resentment. Elaine mistakes his anger as being in response to some lingering romantic attachment to her:

> ELAINE: I've never seen you jealous.
> JERRY: You weren't even *at* Game Six—you're not even a fan!
> ELAINE: Wait a second . . . are you jealous of *him* or are you jealous of *me*?

Flustered and confused, Jerry walks away without responding, allowing the insinuation of a queer interpretation to be implied by his silence.

Jerry steps outside of the apartment just as Kramer enters; he sits alone with Elaine as George disappears into the bathroom. Predictably, it is just as Kramer finds himself next to the phone that the call from the unemployment bureau arrives; Kramer, the only one uninformed about George's scheme, answers the phone and responds with confusion, assuring the caller that she has reached a residential number, not Vandelay Industries. Having overheard, George bursts from the bathroom in a panic, his pants around his ankles. Despite his frantic pleading with Kramer to pass him the phone, Kramer is already hanging up; the defeated George collapses on the floor. Precisely at this moment, Jerry reenters the apartment. In a highly unusual aerial shot, the camera shows us Jerry's perspective of George, face down, boxer shorts exposed, and prone, lying before him on the floor in an obvious position of sexual receptivity. Jerry quips: "And you want to be my latex salesman." Once again, Jerry's reinvocation of latex has powerful queer connotations in response to seeing George seminude before him.

The next scenes juxtapose Elaine and Keith's date with Jerry's alternate Friday night activity, a visit to see his friends' new baby. Elaine, the focal point of a crowded sports bar discussing Game Six of the World Series with Keith, has occupied the very place (physically and romantically) that Jerry had longed for. In the accompanying parallel scene of Jerry, he seems both out of place and uncomfortable amid the domestic and overwhelmingly heterosexual atmosphere of the baby's nursery. The misery over losing his night on the town to Elaine is amplified by his obvious distaste for the nuclear family, the ultimate signifier of "straightness."

The scene again changes to Keith and Elaine alone in his car, this time with Elaine in the passenger seat that Jerry had previously occupied. Elaine, comfortable in her familiar and appropriate role as passive/feminine, waits patiently as Keith (in the privileged masculine driver's seat) silently wonders whether or not he should kiss her, mirroring Jerry's earlier internal debate over suitable intimate physical contact. Although they kiss, Elaine is unimpressed. Later, just as George had done, Jerry pumps Elaine for information about her date. When Elaine admits that she and Keith had kissed, Jerry pushes further: "What *kind* of kiss was it?" Incredulous at Jerry's tactlessness, Elaine does not respond. Jerry at last answers her standing question: "I'm jealous of everybody."

Keith calls, interrupting one of the few moments in the episode when Jerry and George share the scene alone. After hanging up, he explains with discomfort that he has agreed to help Keith in his move to a new apartment. George seems to recognize and identify with Jerry's apprehension over this sudden escalation in their rapport. "This is a big step in the male relationship," Jerry observes, "the biggest. That's like going all the way." Never has Jerry made such a direct reference to the potential for sexual contact with Keith. Of course, Keith has by no means propositioned Jerry, which makes the queer desire on Jerry's part all the more obvious in contrast with the seemingly asexual nature of Keith's request. However, Jerry has made clear his own willingness to homoeroticize his friendship with another man. By likening "going all the way" to moving furniture, Jerry is able to fantasize that Keith shares Jerry's homosexual desire. Ingeniously, he has crafted an imaginary set of circumstances that allow him to ignore Keith's preference for Elaine as a sexual object while tidily completing his fantasy: Keith has expressed desire for Jerry, but now Jerry has the luxury of refusing his advance on the moral ground that he will not rush sexual intimacy. Once Keith arrives, Jerry tells him that he cannot help him move, explaining that it is still too soon in their relationship. Again, by positing Keith in the masculine role of sexual aggressor, Jerry in turn occupies the stereotypically feminine role of sexual regulator/withholder.

Kramer and Newman arrive just as Jerry declines Keith's request; not surprisingly, Kramer jumps at the opportunity to take Jerry's place. As he and Newman disappear out the door to help Keith move his furniture, Jerry commiserates with Elaine over the phone: "You broke up with him? Me too!" Even as Jerry's homoerotic adventure has drawn to a close, Kramer's last-minute appearance lends an air of sexual unpredictability to end the episode on a resoundingly queer note.

In contrast to "The Boyfriend," in which the queer subtext is exploited as the source of the humor, "The Virgin" and its companion episode "The Contest" present an equally queer narrative expressed in subtler and more indirect ways. Within these interwoven episodes, the "knowing" spectator—one familiar with gay culture and receptive to potentially homoerotic situations—is essentially bombarded by queer catchphrases and code words, gay themes, and gay male behavior, while the "unknowing" spectator would most likely only recognize a traditionally "straight" plot about heterosexual dating frustrations. "The Virgin" drops its first "hair-pins" almost immediately;[16] Jerry and George are drinking together in a bar when Jerry spots Marla, a beautiful woman whom he recognizes across the room. "She's in the closet business—reorganizes your closet and shows you how to maximize your closet space. She's looked into my closet." In the same instant that we are introduced to a potential female love object for Jerry, she is immediately identified with the closet, a widely recognized metaphor referring to a gay person's secret sexual identity. Queerly read, Marla could be interpreted as (and will in fact become) a nonthreatening, nonsexual female object. Having "looked into his closet," Marla functions as a woman who is aware of Jerry's homosexuality and will be willing to interact with him in ways that will permit him to pass while still maintaining the homoerotic connections to the men around him. By allowing him this duplicity, she will indeed maximize Jerry's "closet space."

While at the bar, George bemoans the fact that he is miserable in his relationship with television executive Susan, his first girlfriend in some time. He is instead more interested in the new partnership that he has developed with Jerry, writing his new situation comedy pilot for NBC. The ostensibly platonic nature of such privileged male–male relations becomes further queered by Jerry's insistence that George "maintain appearances" with Susan until she has persuaded the network to pick up their pilot. The Seinfeldian recurring theme of hidden identities and guarded appearances puts into place the knowing viewer's suspicions about the homosexual potential between George and Jerry.

In the following scene, the spectator is given a rare view of Jerry's bedroom, made even more rare by the presence of a woman with him. Although the scene employs the standard formula for a possible sexual encounter (a man and woman alone in his bedroom), the couple remains perpetually framed inside Jerry's open closet; Jerry's coded homosexuality, symbolically surrounding the couple as they speak, prevents the sex scene from occurring.

To further complicate Jerry's interaction with Marla, his friends start to invade the apartment, interrupting the potential for intimacy. First, Kramer intrudes, taking over the television in the living room. (He is desperate to see *The Bold and the Beautiful*, a show whose soap opera genre is largely identified with a female viewership.) Jerry kicks Kramer out only to have Elaine buzz over the intercom a moment later. In the few private moments left, Marla confesses that the reason for her breakup with her ex-boyfriend was his impatience with her virginity. Elaine arrives before they can discuss it.

Marla and Elaine, Jerry's current and past romantic interests, stand in stark contrast to one another. The timid, traditional, and virginal Marla is further desexualized in the presence of the heterosexually active Elaine; this contrast is intensified by Elaine's crass description of her embarrassment at a recent party when she accidentally let her diaphragm slip out of her purse. As she laughs knowingly, Jerry winces, sensing Marla's shock at Elaine's casual remark: "You never know when you might need it." This exaggerated reference to female sexuality makes Marla's virginity even more pronounced; she is unable to hide her discomfort any longer and excuses herself in haste. It seems that Jerry, socially and romantically attached to a woman horrified by even the discussion of sex, could himself not be further from heterosexual activity.

Upon hearing that her indiscretion has lost Jerry a potential girlfriend, Elaine chases after Marla in hopes of repairing the damage. Over coffee at Monk's (clearly a female invasion of Jerry and George's male space), Elaine tries to dissuade Marla from her horror of sex with men. However, her lecture quickly dissolves into a listing of male failings: their thoughtlessness, manipulations, and fear of emotional attachment after sex. Despite Elaine's outward intentions to reunite Jerry and Marla, she has instead instilled an intensified mistrust of men. Once again, Jerry's friends have been the cause of his distancing from women; he remains insulated in the homoerotic network of his male friends and is ushered through acceptable straight society by his platonic female friend.

In a strange reversal of roles, George is still engaged in a romantic relationship with a woman (even if he is unwillingly "maintaining appearances" with Susan). At the crucial meeting with the NBC executives, George greets Susan with a kiss, an appropriate and public gesture of straightness. However, by exposing Susan as his girlfriend, George compromises her professional standing with the network. Not only is she fired, but she also breaks off her relationship with George (and consequently later "becomes" a lesbian).[17] Despite George's delight at having inadvertently rid himself of Susan, the overall message is clear: straying out of his queer context sparks destructive results in the straight world.

Juxtaposed with George's ultimately disastrous straight kiss is one of Jerry's own; he and Marla, back in his bedroom, are finally embracing passionately. The (hetero)sexual potential suggested in this scene is diffused, however, by the viewer's instant recognition that the couple is not only framed by Jerry's closet but in fact that they are embracing inside of it. Marla, as a nonsexualized female object with knowledge and access to Jerry's closet(edness), poses no threat of engaging in "real" sexual intimacy with Jerry. Their embrace is made comically awkward by the clutter of Jerry's hanging clothes around them; the encounter is again cut short as Marla recalls Elaine's unflattering depiction of typical male behavior after sex. Even in absentia, Jerry's friends precipitate the woman's departure and his own separation from the possibility of (hetero)sex.

"The Contest" follows up on this storyline; Jerry is still patiently dating the virginal Marla while, as usual, spending the bulk of his social time with George, Kramer, and Elaine. As George arrives to join them for lunch at Monk's, he announces sheepishly (yet voluntarily) that he had been "caught" by his mother. Although never explicitly mentioned, George is clearly making reference to masturbation. Believing himself to be alone in his mother's house, he was using her copy of *Glamour* magazine[18] as erotic material when his mother entered and discovered him masturbating. In her shock, Mrs. Costanza had fainted, hurt herself in the fall, and ultimately wound up in traction. It is essential to note the homosexual underpinnings of masturbation as a sexual act; the fetishization of one's (and in this case, George's) own genitalia is often closely linked in psychoanalytic theory to the narcissism and reflexive fixation associated with same-sex desire. Mrs. Costanza was not reacting so much to her recognition of her son as sexual but instead to his inappropriate sexual object choice, the (his) penis. George has paid dearly for being exposed to straight eyes while practicing queer pleasure.

Traumatized by his experience, George announces that he is swearing off such activity for good. Jerry and Kramer are skeptical of the claim, and the three men find themselves in a contest—regulated by the "honor system"—to see which of them can abstain the longest from masturbating. The wager is steeped in homoerotic potential; in fact, the three *Seinfeld* men have entered into a kind of sanitized "circle jerk" in which they monitor (and consequently augment) each other's sexual tension, voyeuristically waiting to see who will be the first to "relieve" himself. When Elaine, who has been listening to their conversation from the periphery of their queer circle, wants to enter the contest as well, the men protest that she would have an unfair advantage. As Kramer explains: "It's easier for women—it's part of *our lifestyle.*" By creating a stiff binary opposition between women and "our lifestyle," he not only employs a phrase closely associated with the "alternative lifestyle" of homosexuality, but he also demonstrates an obvious ignorance and detachment from female sexuality, perpetuating myths about the limited appetite and imagination of the female sexual drive. Despite her protests, Elaine is forced to stake fifty dollars extra to even the odds before entering into the contest.

In the next scene, the foursome returns to Jerry's apartment, where Kramer immediately spots a naked woman in the window across the street.[19] The sexually ravenous Kramer is unable to control himself; he excuses himself immediately and returns to announce what we had been led to predict: "I'm out." Of the three male characters, Kramer takes on the most ambisexual valence, moving freely from the homoerotic circle shared with Jerry and George to the distinctly heterosexual desire he expressed for the naked woman. While highly sexualized, neither Kramer's intimate and often seductive relationship with Jerry and George nor his frequent erotic encounters with women serve to posit him in clear homo- or heterosexual territory. Functioning as a sort of sexual fulcrum depending on the social context, Kramer may well be acting as *Seinfeld*'s embodiment of queerness.

The three remaining contestants are left to their own frustrations. In her aerobics class, Elaine finds herself positioned behind John F. Kennedy Jr., the popular object of white, privileged heterosexual female desire. George is disturbed and aroused by his discovery that the privacy curtain separating his mother's hospital bed from her beautiful roommate's creates an erotic silhouette of the stranger's nightly sponge bath.[20] Locked in a passionate embrace in the front seat of Jerry's car, Marla pulls back and asks Jerry to "slow down"; he politely acquiesces, assuring Marla that her virginity is not hindering his enjoyment of their relationship.

On the surface, Marla's virginity is posited as an intensifying factor of her attractiveness; the withholding of not only sex but also of her sexuality seems to make the possibility of physical intimacy even more inaccessible—and thus desirable. In fact, Marla's virginity is a crucial element to balance (and perhaps camouflage) the more important discussions and representations of masturbation. Marla's introduction to the periphery of Jerry's bet with Kramer, George, and Elaine serves a twofold purpose. First, her virginity becomes both a presence and an obstacle between Jerry and Marla, impeding any progress toward a heterosexual encounter. Second, without Marla as Jerry's ostensible love object, the "masturbation episode" would take on a glaringly homosexual tone. Marla's presence serves to divert attention away from what is more or less a circle jerk among homosexualized men: a collective and voyeuristic study of each other's (auto)erotic activity, focusing—if we may momentarily exclude Elaine's participation—on the male orgasm brought on reflexively by the male participants. As a virgin, Marla serves to deflect the queerness of the contest away from Jerry while never threatening the homoerotic trinity of Jerry, George, and Kramer.

Elaine, by comparison, is indeed a heterosexually active female. Why is Elaine allowed to participate in the otherwise queerly coded masturbatory abstinence contest? In effect, she never truly is cast as an equal participant. Throughout the episode, she is consistently figured as the "odd man out"; at the restaurant table where the triangulated male bodies of Jerry, George, and Kramer construct the terms of the bet, Elaine is seated in the corner of the booth. Within the frames, she appears either alone or with her back partially turned to the camera, surrounded by the men who look toward her, clearly separated from the intimate boy talk of the others who share the booth with her. As mentioned before, the men's misconception that women are naturally predisposed to such masturbatory abstinence works to further distance female sexuality—and thus females—from their own collective experience of (same-sex) desire. Perhaps most importantly, Elaine's strongest connection to the trio is through her relationship with Jerry, a friendship that is predicated on their previous failure as (hetero)sexual partners. Her potentially menacing role as Straight Female is mitigated by her position as Not Love Object. Elaine may participate in the contest from the sidelines without truly interrupting its homosexual valence.

Despite the remaining contestants' boasts of being "queen of the castle" and "master of my domain," their sexual frustrations are evident in the four juxtaposed scenes of their private bedrooms: Jerry appears restless in his bed of white linens; George thrashes beneath his sheets printed with cartoon dinosaurs;[21] Elaine is sleepless in her darkened room; Kramer, however, long having satisfied his desire, snores peacefully.

Grumpy from his sleepless night, Jerry tells Kramer that he can no longer tolerate the view of the naked neighbor across the street. As he prepares to go over and ask the woman to draw her shades, the infuriated Kramer tries to stop him, doubting Jerry's sanity for wanting to block their view of a beautiful nude woman. Kramer has called into question Jerry's priorities, which seem to be clear: Jerry privileges his participation in the queerly coded contest over the visual pleasure Kramer experiences from the nude woman.

In the next series of juxtaposed bedroom shots, the viewer discovers from Elaine's restful sleep that she has given in. The next morning, as she sheepishly relinquishes her money, she explains that rumors of JFK Jr.'s interest in her had prompted her moment of weakness. Jerry marvels that "the queen is dead," thereby leaving only himself and George to compete for the pot.

In the following scene, two embracing figures are stretched out on the couch in Jerry's dark apartment. In the close-up shot, we see that Marla is on top of Jerry; not only does this physicality suggest a heightened potential for sexual intimacy between the ordinarily distant couple, but Jerry's positioning on the bottom of the embrace casts him in the stereotypically feminine, passive role of a woman in a straight couple (a role evocative of the one he occupied in his relationship with Keith Hernandez). In keeping with the episode's (and indeed the show's) pattern, such menacing circumstances should surely create chaotic results.

Taking her cue from Jerry's receptive position, the previously hesitant Marla becomes the aggressor, initiating a (masculine) invitation to have sex: "Let's go in the bedroom." From beneath her, Jerry's somewhat timid voice sounds unsure: "*Really?*" Now too close for comfort, Jerry must find a way to disengage from the heterosexual situation in which he is now entangled; Marla's virginity is no longer a sufficient buffer. When Marla asks why he looks so tense, he thoughtlessly (or so it would appear) recounts the details of the contest to explain his (ostensible) relief at the chance to have sex with her. Marla reacts with horror and disgust and quickly exits, leaving Jerry alone.

On the street, Marla bumps into Elaine, who is eagerly awaiting the arrival of JFK Jr. for their first arranged meeting. Marla pulls away from Elaine in revulsion: "I don't want to have anything to do with you or your perverted friends. Get away from me, you're horrible!" Having clearly identified Jerry, George, and Kramer as sexually deviant (i.e., not "straight"), Marla leaves, removing the safe, female heterosexual anchor that her presence provided to the otherwise transparently queer contest.

Believing that JFK Jr. stood her up, Elaine complains to Jerry only to hear from George that Kennedy had just driven away with Marla. As they look out the window, Jerry spots Kramer in the arms of the beautiful woman across the street.

In the final series of four bedroom shots, Jerry and George are at last also enjoying a restful sleep; Kramer snores next to his new lover, and Marla compliments "John" on his sexual prowess. Whereas the two latter scenes depict the postorgasmic satisfaction of the two heterosexual partners that share it, the two former scenes are ambiguous by contrast: no explanation is provided for how or why Jerry and George relieved their pent-up sexual energies at the same time. With no female love object available (no recent viewings of the erotic sponge bath for George, and Jerry's potential lover has left him) to dehomosexualize Jerry and George's two-member circle jerk, the viewer is left with the suggestion that they have satisfied their sexual frustrations together. Intensified by the "success" of the hypervirile JFK Jr. in the face of Jerry's sexual failure with Marla, the narrative closes with individual shots of George and Jerry—alone and yet paired off. Quite apart from the strong homoerotic sensibility of The Contest's construction, the simple and familiar plot resolution—the duo's inability to sustain a romantic relationship with a woman leaves them again alone with each other—marks the episode as incontrovertibly queer.

Seinfeld's narrative design would, at first glance, seem to lack the depth necessary in character and plot to facilitate a discussion of the complexities of homoerotic male relationships. The sort of nonspecific, scattered quality of the *Seinfeld* text, however, makes it well suited to the fluid nature of a queer reading, whose project is more concerned with context than fixity, more with potential than evidence. Nonetheless, *Seinfeld* is full of both context and evidence that lead the text's critics toward a well-developed queer reading. *Seinfeld* enjoys a kind of subculture defined by a discursive code that unites its members in a common lexicon of meaning. The narrative restricts its focus to the foursome, containing and maintaining the intimate bonds between the show's three men and its one woman (the latter being clearly positioned as sexually incompatible and socially separate from the others). Directly related to this intense interconnection, the foursome often causes each member's inability to foster outside heterosexual romantic interests.

Jerry and George share the most intimate relationship of them all; they aid each other in perpetuating duplicities while remaining truthful only with one another. They are the two characters who most frequently share a frame and who create and occupy male-coded narrative spaces, whether in the domestic sphere of Jerry's apartment or in the public sphere at Monk's.

All of these relationships are in motion amid a steady stream of other discursive and iconic gay referents. Their visibility admits the "knowing" viewer into a queerly constructed *Seinfeld* universe while never being so explicit as to cause the "unknowing" viewer to suspect the outwardly "normal" appearance of the show.

Reading the queer in *Seinfeld* sheds a revealing light on the show's "not that there's anything wrong with that" approach to representations of male homoeroticism. While sustaining a steadfast denial of its gay under-currents, the text playfully takes advantage of provocative semiotic juxtapositions that not only allow but also encourage the "knowing" spectator to ignore the show's heterosexual exterior and instead to explore the queerness of *Seinfeld*.

The conclusion does not push much beyond the interpretation offered in the rest of the essay. That's deliberate; Gantz was clear up front about how the conclusions she was going to draw. As readings of academic writing, most professors are as interested in the how as much as the what (the journey as much as the destination).

Selected *Seinfeld* Videography
(Seinfeld. Created by Jerry Seinfeld and Larry David. NBC-TV, 1989–98.)

"The Apartment." Writ. Peter Mehlman. 4 Apr. 1991.
"The Boyfriend." Writ. Larry David and Larry Levin. 12 Feb. 1992.
"The Café." Writ. Tom Leopold. 6 Nov. 1991.
"The Cheever Letters." Writ. Larry David. 28 Oct. 1992.
"The Contest." Writ. Larry David. 13 Nov. 1992.
"The Dog." Writ. Larry David. 9 Oct. 1991.
"The Junior Mint." Writ. Andy Robin. 18 Mar. 1993.
"The Limo." Writ. Larry Charles. 26 Feb. 1992.
"The Outing." Writ. Larry Charles. 11 Feb. 1993.
"The Phone Message." Writ. Larry David and Jerry Seinfeld. 13 Feb. 1991.
"The Pilot." Writ. Larry David. 20 May 1993.
"The Red Dot." Writ. Larry David. 11 Dec. 1991.
"The Shoes." Writ. Larry David and Jerry Seinfeld. 4 Feb. 1993.
"The Smelly Car." Writ. Larry David and Peter Mehlman. 15 Apr. 1993.
"The Stakeout." Writ. Larry David and Jerry Seinfeld. 31 May 1990.
"The Statue." Writ. Larry Charles. 11 Apr. 1991.
"The Subway." Writ. Larry Charles. 8 Jan. 1992.
"The Virgin." Writ. Larry David. 11 Nov. 1992.
"The Watch." Writ. Larry David. 30 Sept. 1992.

Notes

All dialogue quoted in this essay, unless otherwise indicated, comes from my own transcriptions of the television programs in question.

1. Dave Walter, "Does Civil Disobedience Still Work?" *Advocate*, 20 Nov. 1990, 34–38.
2. For further discussion of the political and semiotic history of the word "queer," see Ernesto Laclau, *New Reflections on the Revolution of Our Time* (London: Verso, 1990); Teresa de Lauretis, "Queer Theory: Lesbian and Gay Sexualities," *differences* 3:2 (1991): iii–xviii; Michelangelo Signorile, "Absolutely Queer: Reading, Writing, and Rioting," *Advocate*, 6 Oct. 1992, 17.
3. Eve Kosofsky Sedgwick, *Epistemology of the Closet* (Berkeley: University of California Press, 1990).
4. Diana Fuss, ed. *Inside/Out: Lesbian Theories, Gay Theories* (New York: Routledge, 1991).
5. Alexander Doty, *Making Things Perfectly Queer: Reading Mass Culture* (Minnesota: University of Minnesota Press, 1993).
6. Bruce Fretts, *The Entertainment Weekly "Seinfeld" Companion* (New York: Warner Books, 1993), 12.
7. Bill Zehme, "Jerry and George and Kramer and Elaine: Exposing the Secrets of *Seinfeld*'s Success," *Rolling Stone* 660–61 (6–22 July 1993): 40–45, 130–31.

8. As evidence of this Seinfeldian shared vocabulary, I offer one of my primary resources for this paper, *The Entertainment Weekly "Seinfeld" Companion*. Author Bruce Fretts creates a partial glossary of these terms, situating them in their episodic contexts, cross-referencing them with the episodes in which the term recurs, and finally providing a chronological plot synopsis of episodes 1–61, ending with the 1993 season premiere, "The Pilot."

9. Doty outlines the political and semiotic complexities of the term "queer" in his insightful introduction to *Making Things Perfectly Queer*.

10. My essay takes its title from this episode; while combating the rumor of their homosexuality, the phrase "not that there's anything wrong with that" serves as Jerry and George's knee-jerk addendum to their denials. The catchphrase becomes a running joke through the episode, being echoed in turn by Jerry's and George's mothers and, later, by Kramer as well.

11. During the 1994 season, the *Seinfeld* triangle suddenly switched to blue. Might this suggest that the show's creators wished to distance themselves from an overly gay-identified icon, or does a queer interpretation suggest that Jerry is simply attempting to be more butch during that period? The 1995 season was marked with an ambiguous green triangle; the icon continued to change in each following season. One can only speculate that the shift away from the pink triangle is meant to mirror the shift away from the queerness of the early seasons—as evidenced by Susan's abrupt renunciation of lesbianism and subsequent return to George (my thanks to colleagues Melinda Kanner and Steve Bishop for their insightful ideas on this subject).

12. A particularly useful example of this theme occurs in "The Café," in which George, terrified of his girlfriend Monica's request that he take an IQ test, fears that he will not be able to pass. Out of desperation, he arranges for the more intelligent Elaine to take the test for him by passing it out to her through an open window. Jerry too has approved their secret plan to pass George off as an intelligent, appropriate partner for Monica: "Hey, I love a good caper!" Despite their best efforts to dupe Monica by presenting George in a false light, she discovers their duplicity and breaks up with him.

13. When questioned, Jerry makes no secret about the intensity of his "friendship" with George; in "The Dog," he confesses that they talk on the phone six times a day—coincidentally, the same number of times a day that he gargles.

14. A queer reading of the social differences between Jerry and George reveals a substratum of conflict: within the homoerotic dynamic that groups them together as a couple, George is constantly portrayed as crude, unrefined, and in need of direction. When George is paired with Jerry in the intimate, caretaking relationship they share, their connection suggests a domestic partnership in which Jerry, the more successful and refined of the duo, acts as their public voice, correcting George's social missteps allowing them to "pass" less noticeably through acceptable, urban, upper-middle-class society.

15. It should be noted that George's presentation as both unemployed and desperate accentuate the clear class differences between him and Jerry, the successful stand-up comic being courted by a celebrity athlete.

16. In *Gay Talk* (New York: Paragon Books, 1972), Bruce Rodgers defines the expression "drop hairpins" (also "drop beads" or "drop pearls") as "to let out broad hints of one's sexuality" (69). Historically rooted in gay male culture, this expression is useful here to express the texts' many links to gay icons and lexicon. It should be noted, however, that the intentionality suggested by the phrase "drop hairpins" is problematic in the context of this paper, as I am not entering into an analysis of whether or not the creators of *Seinfeld* have knowingly or inadvertently produced a heavily queer text.

17. In "The Smelly Car," George runs into Susan for the first time since their breakup and is shocked to see her with Mona, her new lover. Although Susan alludes to her longstanding attraction to women, George makes multiple references to how he "drove her" to lesbianism. After Mona is inexplicably seduced by Kramer's mystique, Susan makes a new romantic contact in Allison,

another of George's ex-girlfriends. The implication is not only that George is a failure as a heterosexual but also that, even in his attempts to connect romantically with women, he is attracted to inappropriate (or equally conflicted) female object choices.

18. George's use of *Glamour,* a women's fashion magazine, is a notably odd choice for visual sexual stimulation. In contrast to such heterosexual pornography as *Playboy,* in which nude women are presented in ways to elicit sexual responses from men, George has instead found sexual pleasure from a magazine whose focus is women's beauty culture—fashion, health, cosmetics—and not women themselves. It is essential to recognize that George's masturbatory activity was not in response to heterosexual desire for women's bodies but instead connected to something only indirectly related to their appearances.

19. In contrast to George's interest in *Glamour,* Kramer provides us with a more familiar example of an "appropriate" erotic stimulus for the heterosexual male; the sight of a nude woman directly and immediately enacts Kramer's sexual response.

20. This visual joke is revived in "The Outing": having been falsely identified in the newspaper as Jerry's lover. George attempts to set his shocked and still-hospitalized mother "straight." However, the tempting silhouette of the beautiful patient and her nurse has been replaced by the erotic shapes of a muscular male attendant sponge-bathing a brawny male patient.

21. Again, the spectator is privy to a subtle material reference to the class distinctions apparent within the coupling of Jerry and George; the contrast in their choices of bed linens—Jerry's tasteful white and George's childish, colorful pattern—provide a point of reference from which to understand the power dynamic between them as middle- to upper-middle-class (Jerry) and lower-middle- to working-class (George) gay men.

READING WRITING

This Text: Reading

1. Gantz indicates to an extent her writing situation when she labels American television as homophobic. How does this play out in her essay?
2. Gantz focuses on "queer theory" in this essay, which she essentially uses as a lens to view her text. Are there other lenses we might use in discussing popular culture? Using another lens (such as gender, race, or class), examine *Seinfeld* or some other popular text.
3. What other works might yield the same type of results with examination by queer theory?
4. Why might *Seinfeld* be a particularly good show to examine? Does Gantz indicate this in her essay?
5. In what ways might queer theory apply in your daily experiences of reading?
6. What is the difference between "queer" and "homosexual"? Does Gantz make the distinction clear?

Your Text: Writing

1. Using the same lens of queer theory as Gantz, examine another popular television show.
2. Using another lens (such as race, gender, class), examine *Seinfeld* or another popular show. How does reading through a particular theory affect the writing process?
3. Write a short response paper to the essay itself. What did you like about it? What, if anything, disturbed you about it?

Why did you write this piece–what was the assignment or motivation for writing?

Initially, the piece began as the final paper for a graduate school course in Women Studies that looked at gendered relationships in the media.

What did you do when you got the assignment?

I was working on my PhD in French, and at that point in my life, I'd only ever undertaken literary analysis. While I knew what to do with books, I didn't have an entirely clear idea of how to "do television." As a *Seinfeld* fan, I had long known that there was plenty of queer content that I wanted to talk about, but I needed a more thorough way of organizing my evidence and thinking through my ideas than what my own casual viewing of the show had permitted to that point.

How did you begin?

Because the moment I was writing in (1997) predated any printed, anthologized collections (much less any online search) of *Seinfeld* scripts, it felt imperative to begin with a clear question of what I'd be looking for before I began reviewing and transcribing videos of all the seasons of the show currently available at that time. I started by setting up some parameters in my argument of how I would define queerness for the purposes of the piece. I already had an idea before I began writing of what I thought would be the most compelling examples or the most useful arguments, but it wasn't until I'd written out how I intended my reader to understand the constellation of queer signifiers in the *Seinfeld* universe that the process became more fluid, both in collecting the rest of my "textual" evidence and in paring away the extraneous parts.

Describe the process of writing the first draft.

The first draft was written, I think, with perhaps an overly specific sense of my audience—that is, my graduate school classmates. While nearly everyone was fluent in the composition and content of *Seinfeld,* queer theory was largely *terra incognita* in those days. Consequently, as I struggled to fuse those two elements in the first draft, I felt steadily conflicted between a desire to lapse into shorthand (based on the assumption that all readers would be equally familiar with the show) and the need to over-explain and over-justify the nuances of a theoretical lens toward which my peers were expressing some degree of suspicion. In retrospect, it made for very tense, schizophrenic writing: casual and conversational in some places, labored and defensive in others.

Did you write a draft all the way through?

I wrote the draft in chunks as I assembled enough material from the transcripts to start to see which episodes, which quotes, etc, made the most compelling argument.

How much editing did you do as you wrote?

Although it's been quite a while since I wrote the initial paper, I think I worked up an extensive outline first. Once my roadmap was clear, I only edited moderately once the full draft was complete.

Did you do research as you wrote or before you started writing? What databases did you use?

As mentioned, my research was based on my own transcription of the sitcom episodes.

How long would you say the process took?

The graduate school paper took nearly three weeks to complete. The transformation of that paper into a piece for publication in a scholarly work took considerably more revision. I worked intermittently for a year before submitting the piece to an editor.

How did you edit the draft?

The editing of the course paper into a scholarly article took a substantial amount of time and labor, beginning by re-envisioning its readership. I had hoped to place it in a journal or anthology with a focus on queer theory, so I recalibrated the tone of the piece to reflect a different kind of familiarity with the reading I was applying. Conversely, I had to situate *Seinfeld* in some larger cultural context in the introduction to accommodate for the fact that, by the time my revised piece was being sent out for consideration (1998), the show was at its height in pop culture.

What was the response when you turned in your essay?

Strangely, I've had completely separate and contradictory responses to my essay. I got very positive feedback from the grad school professor, which is what encouraged me to prepare the piece for scholarly submission.

When it first appeared in an edited collection on the theme of straightness and queer theory, I didn't get any response at all; as is so often the case, the piece faded into relative academic obscurity.

However, when it was first reprinted in *The World is a Text,* I suddenly had a new audience: college students were reading the piece, and a good bit of angry feedback showed up in my e-mail and on blogs. It turned out that the 18–22-year-old demographic had a lot invested in their sitcom heroes, and some of them were unhappy with my interpretation of the show. (That hasn't happened in some time, however. I'm not sure to what I attribute this fact, whether it's an increasing familiarity with gay themes in mainstream media or the public's slow disengagement from *Seinfeld* now that the show has been off the air since 1999).

The most unusual response, however, was the e-mail I received in 2005 from the producers of the "E! True Hollywood Story" who were planning on doing an episode on *Seinfeld* and asked if I'd care to grant them an interview on some of the more "scandalous subjects" the show addressed. It was clear that no one from E! had actually read my piece; more likely, some research assistant had done an Internet search on *Seinfeld* and had found links to my article—the word "queer" came up, and they thought they'd hit on something salacious. I explained that I'd done a scholarly reading of the show through the critical lens of queer theory, that there was no implication that Jerry Seinfeld the actor was gay, and they immediately lost interest (thank heavens).

Are you satisfied now with what you wrote? Would you make any changes?

I occasionally long for the chance to update the piece, to reconsider the implications of both *Seinfeld* and the queer reading from a twenty-first century perspective. Sometimes, the ways in which the piece stakes out the terrain of queerness seems a bit antiquated, but I struggle to remind myself that this was written a good bit more than a decade ago. Theory and television are sure to outpace you. Still, I'm happy with much of the writing, and that element—the act of articulating the idea—was the most satisfying part of the job.

Beyond Fear: Heroes vs. 24

Garance Franke-Ruta

Garance Franke-Ruta is a senior editor at The American Prospect, *in which this essay was originally published in 2007. Although she grew up in Mexico, she has lived in New Mexico, New York City, and Washington, D.C. In this essay, Franke-Ruta argues that* Heroes *has surpassed* 24 *as the favorite action-adventure drama on American television. She links this shift to changing American values. Do you agree with the way she describes the connections between politics and television content? If not, what are some other theories about the relationship between politics and television?*

WHEN PETITE, BLONDE DIXIE CHICKS lead singer Natalie Maines told a British audience ten days before the 2003 American invasion of Iraq: "Just so you know, we're on the good side with y'all. We do not want this war, this violence, and we're ashamed that the president of the United States is from Texas," the political climate was such that she rapidly found herself the subject of international controversy. War supporters burned the group's CDs, and the three-woman alternative country rock band lost half its audience, which at the time was more partial to Toby Keith's *Shock'n Y'all*-style bluster than to the Chicks' anti-war doubts, at concerts over the next year.

Go back to that moment in your mind. Imagine what would have happened if a television show had dared to suggest that the anniversary of September 11 was anything less than a sacred moment for national reflection and mourning, or that the president was a jingoistic impostor using the specter of terrorism for evil, selfish, and ultimately un-American ends. Most likely such a show would have sparked national outrage, advertisers would have fled, and the writers and actors would have been forced to grovel in apology on the national stage in order to keep working.

But, oh, how times have changed. The misguided invasion of Iraq has gone sour, and so, too, has the American public, among whom Bush supporters now number roughly 30 percent. In June, more than four years after the Chicks were bashed for opposing the president's war, Maines' husband, the actor Adrian Pasdar, portrayed on a prime-time network series a terrorism-era American president who is the living embodiment of evil—and won the best audience numbers in his time slot.

The hit show is NBC's *Heroes,* a meandering sci-fi epic about a band of normal looking men and women whose genetic anomalies grant them extraordinary powers and link them in a shared struggle to prevent a nuclear explosion in New York City. With the penultimate episode of its first season, which aired in May, the show moved from the realm of fantasy into biting political commentary, filled with ripped-from-the-headlines scenes unimaginable during the peak years of the Bush administration. In that episode, the show flashed forward to a post-attack future whose fifth-anniversary memorial service visually echoed the first September 11 commemoration, and was presided over by a platitudinous president who has used the terrorism attack to suspend laws and persecute those who disagree with him.

Middle East scholar Juan Cole has compared *Heroes* to FOX's anti-terrorism hit *24;* the affection of the lead character in that show, Jack Bauer, for "enhanced interrogation" techniques has become such a cultural touchstone that it cropped up during a Republican presidential primary debate. "I'm looking for Jack Bauer at that time, let me tell you," Colorado Rep. Tom Tancredo declared at the second GOP presidential debate, after being

24: Enhanced interrogation or torture?

conveniently presented with a *24*-style ticking-nuclear-timebomb scenario by FOX's news division, which was hosting the debate.

"But while *24* skews to the right politically, *Heroes* seems like a left-wing response" to September 11 and the rise of international terrorism, Cole wrote. More than that, the show represents the passing of the moment in which fear of terrorists and fear of the president ruled, and both were used to justify actions that undermined America's values, legal traditions, and citizens' ability to freely criticize their leaders. While *24*, which airs Monday nights on FOX against *Heroes*, makes heroes of its torturing CIA agents, *Heroes*' heroes are everyday men and women called to greatness by the necessity of their times: a cheerleader, a Japanese salaryman, a bumbling cop who can never quite get that promotion. They are civilians hunted by the FBI—portrayed in the show's pre-attack moments as a feckless organization that fails to grasp what's truly going on, and that doesn't listen to whistle-blowers and warnings, to boot—and forced to fend off the storm troopers of the post-attack Department of Homeland Security with *Matrix*-like superpowers and samurai swords. To be sure, they sometimes go awry when using their powers, over which they have imperfect control, injuring innocents or endangering themselves. Trapped in a world they don't quite understand, with fresh betrayals and revelations in every episode, the heroes slowly recognize their destiny: to learn to control their powers, and through this self-restraint and self-mastery, to "save the world."

As such, they are descendents of an older tradition in American television, which pits heroic individuals against the corrupt political sphere or government forces. Where *24* makes heroes of its state agents, *Heroes* sharply questions their actions.

The plot of *Heroes* is complicated, going back and forth between time periods, with the narrative thread of past and future constantly evolving from episode to episode in

According to Franke-Ruta, *Heroes* is more about family and protection than *24*.

response to the characters' interventions, and new mutants being revealed as old ones are captured or killed off. Even the characters rely on comic books that tell the future to help guide them through the plot twists and turns.

In the penultimate episode, the camera shows us one possible future in a Las Vegas club, where Niki, one of the ensemble show's many recurring characters, is working as a stripper in the wake of the heroes' inability to stop the nuclear bomb from exploding in New York, an attack that claimed her son and husband. In this episode, as the caption "America Remembers" flashes across a TV screen, overlaid on the image of fires licking the ruins of New York, Niki sighs, "Today's just another day." Her reaction to the anniversary of this fictional attack seems apposite given the real world, where the current mayor of New York, Michael Bloomberg, can tell reporters in the wake of a recent bomb scare: "There are lots of threats to you in the world. There's the threat of a heart attack for genetic reasons. You can't sit there and worry about everything. Get a life."

Later in the show, Niki sees President Nathan Petrelli (Adrian Pasdar)—a fellow mutant—on the TV screen at the fifth-anniversary memorial service, a huge American flag in the background, the stars of the presidential seal on his podium before him. Niki, earlier restrained in her grief, throws a glass at the screen as Petrelli launches into a speech filled with platitudes that should be recognizable to us all. He praises the "sacrifices" that the population has made and "the laws that we have had to pass to keep our citizens safe . . . We've all lost. We've all mourned. And we've all had to become soldiers, heroes. This is a battle that we've entered knowing that the enemy is ourselves," he intones, before declaring a false victory against the mutants in the form of a "cure" that is really a poison. "We've been vigilant. We have been uncompromising, and our efforts have paid off. The nightmare is finally over. The world is safe."

In fact, as the show continues, it is soon clear that the world has never been less safe, for that talking head is not Nathan Petrelli at all, but the evil Sylar, a man who kills the mutants to steal their powers. He's the show's vicious anti-hero, who, in the flash-forward, is believed to have caused the explosion, having stolen the powers of a radioactive man. At the time of his presidential impersonation, he has added shapeshifting to his repertoire of skills, and has dragooned the entire apparatus of the U.S. state into his quest for new mutants whose powers he can steal.

Sylar, in his own way, is a victim of the same lack of self-control as Nathan's brother Peter Petrelli, a former nurse who innocently absorbs other mutant's powers and who is revealed in an earlier episode to be the actual exploding man—a "human bomb"—who cannot control the radioactive powers he absorbed involuntarily from another character. Sylar, too, cannot control his urge to destroy. It's up to the others to stop him.

In the final episode of the first season, which jumps back to the main, pre-explosion plot five years earlier, Nathan, who can fly, saves Peter and the world by grabbing his brother and flying him up into space as his hands pulse orange, mere moments before he explodes (shades of Superman). Peter, who has absorbed the power of regeneration, will be back next season. But Nathan may well have made a real sacrifice, laying bare the ultimate lesson of this antidote to 24. It is not in torture and the frantic tossing off of our legal standards that we find freedom and safety, but in learning to control our vast and growing power in response to the threats we know we face. And, should any individual fail to do so, we have a responsibility to rein that person in.

READING WRITING

This Text: Reading

1. The author opens her piece with a reference to the Dixie Chicks and September 11. In what way does this opening gambit influence how you read her arguments about 24 and *Heroes*?

2. The author argues that 24 feels like a right-wing show (conservative) and *Heroes* like a left-wing show (progressive). What is her rationale for this? Do you agree?

3. Franke-Ruta buries her thesis deep in the essay. Locate her main argument. Is it easy to see what her main points are? Does she support her assertions?

Your Text: Writing

1. Write a comparison/contrast essay about two television shows you think occupy opposite points of the spectrum. *Heroes* and 24 are vaguely located in the same genre—adventure/thriller—but are much different shows in a number of different ways. Make sure you pick shows of the same genre to support your case. Arguing that *That 70s Show* and *CSI* are radically different is not too compelling; however, a paper contrasting *Oz* and *Prison Break* might be interesting.

2. Take a different tack than Franke-Ruta—argue that 24 is a more appropriate response to 9/11. How will you support this assertion?

3. Many have compared *Lost* and *Heroes* to one another—the supernatural, ordinary people put in extraordinary circumstances, the interplay of past and present. Write a paper in which you explain the phenomenon of these two shows at *this* moment in history.

Sex Sells: A Marxist Criticism of *Sex and the City*

Dave Rinehart

Student Essay

Dave Rinehart wrote this essay in 2006 while a student at the University of San Francisco (USF). Rinehart's essay stands as a good example of reading a television text through a lens—in this case, the lens of Marxism. Rinehart recently graduated from USF and is teaching English in Japan.

Introduction

ARTHUR ASA BERGER, in his book *Media Analysis Techniques,* writes: "The bourgeoisie try to convince everyone that capitalism is natural and therefore eternal, but this idea, say the Marxists, is patently false, and it is the duty of Marxist analysts to demonstrate this" (51). It will be my duty over the course of this paper to expose and explicate the capitalist, consumerist, and classist aspects of the TV show *Sex and the City* using Marxist criticism.

Sex and the City aired its final episode in spring 2004, concluding a massively successful six-season run on the HBO network. The series, created by Darren Star, is based on the sex advice columns of Candace Bushnell. The fictionalized TV version re-imagines Bushnell as Carrie Bradshaw (Sarah Jessica Parker), a young, single New York woman who narrates the show and serves as its primary focus. Each episode is based around her weekly column, with the topic typically regarding relationship dynamics between men and women. Over the course of an episode, Carrie will write on her laptop

Carrie Bradshaw: Feminist hero? Bourgeois hero? or Capitalist hero?

(with accompanying narrative voiceover), wine and dine with her group of closest friends Charlotte, Samantha, and Miranda, and carouse with her boyfriends, who come and go in and out of her life through various episode arcs. This essay will analyze, using Marxist techniques, Carrie's role as the "bourgeois hero," the show's capitalist and consumerist aspects, the ways in which its characters and viewers may engage in commodity fetishism, and the show's representation of classism.

Carrie Bradshaw as the "Bourgeois Hero"

Karl Marx wrote, "The ideas of the ruling class are, in every age, the ruling ideas; i.e., the class which is the dominant material force in society is at the same time its dominant intellectual force" (78). Throughout history, the ruling class has been responsible for the production of the most popular culture industry texts. It makes sense, then, that the ruling class would utilize the media to glorify and promote themselves, producing texts that celebrate the bourgeoisie lifestyle. The main characters that populate these texts, then, often function as "bourgeois heroes," who "maintain the status quo by 'peddling' capitalist ideology in disguised form and by helping keep consumer lust at a high pitch" (60). (To clarify, Berger separates "bourgeois heroes" and "bourgeois heroines," but I have made the term gender-neutral.)

As the show's main character and narrator, Carrie functions as *Sex and the City's* bourgeois hero. The series details her many travails through high society New York, mingling with wealthy socialites and dating powerful investment bankers and corporate executives—and then getting paid well to detail said interactions in her newspaper column. In a typical episode, Carrie will shop at upscale boutiques, dine in fancy restaurants, sip expensive wines, and/or receive dazzling gifts. While in the first two seasons she is seen wearing rather generic (though good-looking) clothing and flat-soled shoes, from season three on she seemingly only wears designer clothing and stilettos.

The show's producers, however, do attempt to portray Carrie as down-to-earth: she chain-smokes cigarettes, gets hangovers, cries, and ends up in many embarrassing situations. These situations make her relatable to the show's majority female viewership, while simultaneously placing her on a pedestal of bourgeois taste and lifestyle. While many female viewers might see themselves in Carrie's various character nuances, they will also be envious of her abundance of expensive possessions. To use an example from the opposite gender: male comic book readers see a little or a lot of themselves in gawky teen Peter Parker, but dream of rising beyond their real-life state and taking to the skyscrapers as Spider-Man.

Capitalism and Consumerism

In pretty much any episode, it is difficult to find scenes where characters are interacting without simultaneously consuming. Carrie is nearly always smoking a cigarette while writing, she talks to her friends over meals at nice restaurants, and she goes to bars and clubs with her beaus. Even while walking and talking, the friends will also be sipping lattes or have the obnoxious neon ads of Times Square as a backdrop.

One could argue that these types of scene setup are merely a reflection of the kind of interactions people have on a daily basis. I would argue, however, like Berger did in his quotation that introduced this paper, that this is just an example of the bourgeoisie trying "to convince everyone that capitalism is natural and therefore eternal" (51). *Sex and the*

City is a celebration of capitalism, as its characters drift in and out of various capitalist outposts, finding new and exciting ways to consume. It is amazing, then, how rarely we see them actually in the act of spending money; but this is, again, Berger's argument of natural capitalism. Drinks are poured, food served, and pedicures administered as if this was the way of the world.

This style of episode structure fosters in its audience a false consciousness, "in leading people to believe that 'whatever is, is right' " (Berger 49). After being beaten over the head with images of the program's characters interacting and consuming, viewers may be led to believe that the one cannot happen without the other. In order to talk with friends about serious, thought-provoking matters, the characters must do it over drinks or dinner.

Commodity Fetishism

Operating at peak popularity with virtually no slowdown for the past several years, *Sex and the City* has, therefore, been a prominent trendsetter in the world of fashion. Many of the main characters' clothing, shoes, and various accessories have exploded in real-life as hot commodities among upper-class women. Specific examples include Carrie's "Carrie" necklace, which inspired women to get their own personalized necklace, and her distinctive Manolo Blahnik and Jimmy Choo stilettos. The show has functioned as a go-to source for fashion tips among the viewers who can afford to, both financially and physically, wear the same items.

But the commodity fetishism *Sex and the City* inspires in its audience would be nothing if not practiced by its own characters. Indeed, characters will often spend an entire episode wanting a particular commodity, and the majority of their dialogue will even focus around it. As a grand example of irony, one of the last episodes in season six had Charlotte, the naïve do-gooder of the group, indulging a salesman's shoe fetish in return for free high heels, so long as she let him fit her. She returns again and again, unwilling to let her personal shoe fetish go and simultaneously satiating his, far more sexual one.

Regarding Samantha, the group's vixen, it is important to bring in the concept of hegemony. The basest definition of the word is provided by Berger as "that which goes without saying," and in television it regards the different standards of conduct between the genders, races, ages, etc. that are taken for granted. John Fiske, in his essay "British Cultural Studies," writes: "women, so the hegemonic reading would go, are rewarded for their ability to use their beauty and talents to give pleasure to men" (303).

Sex and the City can easily be typified as antithetical to typical TV gender hegemony. While regular programming may portray men going through a series of female partners, *Sex* reverses this notion by portraying a group of independent, freethinking women who keep men at their mercy. But ultimately, the show's progressive feminism is canceled out by commodity fetishism, a condition which makes the women vulnerable and willing to lower their typically high standards.

For example, Samantha uses sex as a way to satisfy her expensive tastes. Until the final season, she exclusively dates exceedingly wealthy men who pay for her every indulgence. In season two, she even leads on a mid-70s executive-type man, remaining in bed with him so long as he whispers fantasies of dream vacations in her ear. Although Carrie chastises her for this decision, Samantha remains on, dreaming of happiness based on material wealth.

Classism

Class is an issue that is addressed on both latent and manifest levels in *Sex and the City*. Latently, differences can be shown with the four main women interacting with a dichotomy of workers: newspaper or hot dog vendors are usually always Hispanic males and beauty salon workers Asian females, while employees of the upscale restaurants and shops are usually always white men and women. Carrie, Samantha, Charlotte, and Miranda live life in a vacuum, staying on a narrow track that leads them from event to event with similar working, acting, and looking people.

Class differences are made manifest in episodes like one from season two where Miranda, a self-made millionaire, struggles with dating a blue-collar bartender, Steve, who in subsequent seasons becomes her husband and the father of her child. Unlike other TV programs, class is certainly not ignored or overlooked in *Sex and the City* but, as Berger states, it acts as an apologist "for the ruling class in an effort to avert class conflict and prevent changes in the political order" (51). *Sex and the City* portrays ethnic men and women doing the "dirty work" and white people enjoying the comforts of the bourgeois lifestyle as the natural, unbreakable order of the American class system.

Marxist Criticism

Marxist criticism seems to be the most heavily criticized of the five primary media analysis techniques. Berger has qualms with Marxists in that they are "prisoners of the categories of their thought, and the questions they ask of a work of popular art carried by the media are often rather limited" (66). Similarly, Theodor Adorno writes: "[T]he very intelligentsia that pretends to float freely is fundamentally rooted in the very being that must be changed and which it merely pretends to criticize" (Jay 116). Since the analysts are so firmly imbedded in the culture they are attempting to critique, their results cannot be trusted for objectivity and truth. I think that Mimi White says it best, however, in her essay "Ideological Analysis and Television." She writes:

> [T]he classical Marxist approach is limited by its inability to account for the fact that . . . most people watch television, most of the time, because they find it enjoyable. In this sense, classical Marxism does not provide sufficiently subtle critical and theoretical perspectives for dealing with the pleasures of contemporary culture, including watching TV. (166)

My Marxist criticism of *Sex and the City* is perhaps marred by my personal enjoyment of the show. It is difficult for me to abandon my appreciation of the show's sharp writing and clever scenarios to systematically tear down its capitalist overtones. Like White says, my critiques fail to take in the aforementioned ways in which fellow viewers could also enjoy the show, even ignoring its consumerist celebration and commodity fetishism. (For instance, fetishisms for expensive high heels and personalized necklaces are completely lost on me, a straight male viewer.)

Methods such as content analysis and semiotic analysis are more conducive to studying television. A content analysis of *Sex and the City* could count the frequency of scenes where characters are interacting and simultaneously consuming, and compare it to the amount of times they converse without the burden of consumerism. Semioticians could have a field day with the series, analyzing the signs and signifiers in its main title sequence, analyzing its characters' evolution over the six seasons using a diachronic perspective, and even applying Propp's dramatis personae to the main characters and revolving door of supporting characters. These are merely methods of analysis, however. In my opinion, Marxist criticism is best suited as a method for breaking down the series' most contemptible elements; those rooted in capitalism and consumerism.

Works Cited

Berger, Arthur Asa. *Media Analysis Techniques*. 3rd ed. Thousand Oaks: Sage, 2005.

Fiske, John. "British Cultural Studies." *Channels of Discourse, Reassembled*. 2nd ed. Ed. Robert C. Allen. Chapel Hill: Univ. of North Carolina Press, 1992.

Jay, Martin. *Adorno*. Cambridge: Harvard Univ. Press, 1984.

Marx, Karl. *Selected Writings in Sociology and Social Philosophy*. Ed. T. B. Bottomore, M. Rubel. New York: McGraw-Hill, 1964.

White, Mimi. "Ideological Analysis and Television." *Channels of Discourse, Reassembled*. 2nd ed. Ed. Robert C. Allen. Chapel Hill: Univ. of North Carolina Press, 1992.

READING **WRITING**

This Text: Reading

1. Rinehart does a nice job of using Marxism as a lens for reading *Sex and the City*. How does he explain how he will use the concepts of Marxism?

2. Does this essay make you see *Sex and the City* through a different light? Why or why not?

3. Although both authors like *Sex and the City*, it tends to be a show that appeals primarily to women. Do you think Rinehart's opinion of the show is affected by his gender? Is there evidence in his essay that he reads the show from a male perspective?

Your Text: Writing

1. Using a major concept as a lens for reading a text is a classic approach to an essay. Write an essay in which you read a television program through a particular ideological lens, like democracy, Christianity, capitalism, or feminism.

2. Write an essay in which you compare the major themes of *Sex and the City* with *The L-Word*. How are they similar? Different? Or, write an essay comparing *Sex and the City* with *Entourage* (what some have called men's *Sex and the City*).

Media Journal: *The Rosie O'Donnell Show*

Hillary West

Student Essay

Hillary West was a student at Virgina Commonwealth when she wrote this for an English 200 course.

Week of February 14, 1999

ROSIE JUST MIGHT BE A CONTROL FREAK. She controls her audience. She controls her guests and she controls her production.

The very young Olympic gold medalist, Tara Lapinski appeared as Rosie's first guest on Wednesday February 17. Rosie fired questions and comments at her left and right. Tara seemed to be ok with it. What else was she to do? She was trying to plug her special that was to air that night. Maybe Rosie knew ahead that Tara would need a lot of prodding. After the interview I noticed that I was standing in the middle of my kitchen staring at the television. There was nothing relaxing or restful about watching that bit. Now that I think about it I am always standing up when I watch the show. Rosie is quick witted and clever. It is part of her charm. But, maybe it is a little intense as well.

Rosie's next guest was fellow talk show host, Matt Lauer. Her demeanor was dramatically different. She immediately opens with the statement, "Matt, you threatened me." Evidently, earlier that morning Matt was hosting *The Today Show* and two young ladies appeared at his outside gate where the crowds gather for the show and on the air expressed their concern that they could not get on the Rosie show for that afternoon. Matt, on live TV, gave Rosie an ultimatum, put the girls on the show or he would not come on as a guest that afternoon. That afternoon Rosie accused Matt of threatening her. He agreed. Perhaps he realized he had stepped over a line. He had stepped over Rosie's line. It is Rosie's show and she is definitely in control. But we should never underestimate the innate goodness of Rosie. Not only did the girls get into the Rosie show, they were invited on stage to sit with Matt Lauer during his interview. Rosie played it very cool. Was she kidding or was she genuinely irritated that she had been pushed into an awkward position? Throughout the interview with Matt, Rosie was very subdued, so unlike her encounter with Tara. But, by inviting the girls to come on stage, it certainly made Rosie look like the hero, even though she may not have appreciated having been manipulated. Or, the entire episode could have been a joke.

Rosie may feel a great need to control all that she can because she extends herself so much to others. We are always learning of how she is helping someone, family, friends, neighbors, or just fans who want to meet her or one of her guests. She is very friendly with her audience. It is as if they have all come over for a drink and she is the hostess. But she has control over the audience. She is in the limelight and they are under the darker lights. She decides if members of the audience will be mentioned or not. It can be very spontaneous and at random. This Wednesday, while in the middle of a conversation with her band leader, John, she calls out, "Oh, I just realized it is Ash Wednesday!" Several people in the audience still had their ashes on their foreheads and she was trying to make out what it was that made them look so different from the others. She was friendly, amusing and made everyone feel at ease. But Rosie was the one in charge. The cameras then shot to those in the audience to whom Rosie was referring.

Maybe this brief encounter with Matt Lauer has revealed a different Rosie. Or, it could be that she has a weakness: the need to control. She can control whether or not she wants to be overweight, funny, successful, or a good mom. It is interesting that there is no man in her life to share with the raising of her children. Maybe she doesn't want to share the opportunity because she will have to relinquish some of her control. To be as successful as Rosie has become, she must have some drive that pushes her along. If it is the need to control all that surrounds her, then fine. As long as she doesn't hurt anyone.

Week of March 15, 1999

It might be fake, but I don't think it is. Rosie is an honest, real life role model. She probably has some idea of the impact she makes, but maybe not. Everyone loves her and she seems to appear to be genuinely grateful when people are kind to her. As a role model she is generous, sincere, sensitive and moral.

Barbara Walters was a guest this week on Rosie. Rosie has mentioned many times that she would not and did not watch the Monica Lewinsky interview. Yet, Rosie is all too happy to have Barbara on her show and they are obviously very close. Rosie speaks her mind, though. She immediately reminds Barbara that she did not watch the interview and she doesn't want to talk about it because it upsets her so. Then Rosie launches into a two to three minute discourse about the fate of Hillary Clinton. Seldom does Rosie give a candid opinion about an issue. Perhaps it is because she is so adamant about things. Whatever the reason, the world listened and Rosie's opinion was duly noted. Tens of thousands of middle class moms heard her and have been influenced by what she had to say.

Rosie is believable because she is one of them. She cheats on her exercise and diet regime because she has had "a stressful week." What woman, what person could not relate to that? We crave her words, her thoughts, her opinions because she makes a difference and she is like us so maybe we could make a difference too even with all our faults. Rosie's stressful week began at an event, in her honor, whereby a celebrity friend was singing a song as a tribute to her and fell off the stage. The friend was all right but Rosie was not. She cried uncontrollably and all week she couldn't stop thinking about her friend. Each time she would mention the incident tears would well up in her eyes. Rosie was definitely not herself this week.

Her sensitivity makes her an emotional wreck and by some that may be perceived as a weakness. But her general audience relates to her sympathetic nature because they see themselves in the same light. For Rosie it means another session in therapy. For her viewers it probably means three more donuts and more exercise in the famous Rosie Chub Club.

What you don't want to do with Rosie is get on her list! Once the word is down, this stubborn Irish woman is not budging. If she doesn't like you, she doesn't like you. She has been very vocal about how she feels about Monica Lewinsky and consequently Bill Clinton. Although she loves the actors on *Party of Five,* her favorite TV show, she is very critical of their moral behavior. She is the last of the do gooders and does not allow R rated language on the show as she once again reminded Barbara Walters. Barbara, in mentioning the film *When Harry Met Sally* refrained, at Rosie's request from using the word orgasm. It's not even a swear word! Her strict Catholic upbringing must be the basis for her high moral fiber.

Every day members of the audience receive gifts. They are sponsor promotional pieces and the audience loves them. But Rosie's generosity stems far beyond that. She always pumps her celebrity guests for donations to E-bay to be auctioned off so that the proceeds will help needy children. And because she interacts so much with her audience, she learns quickly of a need. One visiting family lost their home and pets to a devasting fire. Rosie, sympathetic to the sorrow of the children, made arrangements for the family to receive a new cat and dog. Another elderly woman had not seen her sister in nine years and Rosie gifted her with a plane trip, car and driver and hotel room to visit her sister. Rosie confesses that giving things away makes her feel better and after all, she has had a "stressful week."

She isn't perfect, we all know that. But she is a positive role model for a sea of viewers who probably don't feel very good about themselves and spend too much time watching television and yelling at their kids. Rosie helps viewers see the good in themselves despite their faults because she is open about her own weaknesses. It is easy to look up to someone who is honest about who she is. I hope I don't discover one day that Rosie is a total hoax and I have been tricked into thinking she is a decent human being.

The Reality TV Suite

The authors of *The World Is a Text* live on opposite coasts, so they agreed to meet in the desert Southwest to work on the second and third editions of this book, and in particular, to write this new suite on reality TV. In a bizarre coincidence, as one of the authors was about to fly back to the West Coast, he found himself in an airport restaurant with the cast of *The Real World.* Cameras were everywhere; MTV handlers circled the restaurant and were staged at various places in the airport. Dozens of travelers peeked over into where the cast (and the author) were eating. It is entirely possible that one of the authors was in the background of an episode of *The Real World* long before you read this mini-introduction. The entire scene was profoundly unreal, and yet . . . not.

This suite explores the phenomenon of reality television. Reality TV first arrived in the United States in 1992, when MTV broadcast *The Real World,* a surprise hit. However, reality TV truly became a phenomenon in 2000, when *Survivor* appeared on CBS and completely entranced the American public. Since then, a plethora of reality shows have reached American viewers. Although the fact that so many shows are successful (and so many are given chances to be successful) indicates that the American public loves them, many are critical of a genre that promises "reality" but delivers something else.

We begin with Laurie Ouellette and Susan Murray's piece from the introduction to their 2004 book, *Reality TV: Remaking Television Culture.* Ouelette and Murray place reality TV in context and provide some useful terms for making sense of reality TV genres. Maribeth Theroux wrote her essay on *NEXT* for Dr. Patricia Pender's class at Pace University in 2007. For more information about the assignment, please see the "Third-Wave Feminism Suite" in Chapter 6, "Reading and Writing about Gender." Finally, we are adding to this edition a piece that explores the implications of only having white contestants on *The Bachelor* by Thea Lim, the deputy editor of the wonderful blog *Racialious.*

For the most part, media critics and conservative commentators lambaste reality TV as bad entertainment that has no basis in reality. Others contend that it is going to become the new soap opera and that it makes celebrities out of ordinary people. Television studios love reality TV because the shows are cheap to produce but bring in a great deal of money, suggesting the fad is not going away any time soon.

Consider, as you work your way through these essays, how reality TV has changed television, your own ideas about the world, and how we see the entire concept of "entertainment." Also, for those of you who have become hooked on *Survivor,* or like one of the authors, the first *Bachelor* series, think about where your overt interest in these shows comes from. Why is it we watch these shows? What do they give us that the everyday world does not?

Americans seem to idolize *American Idol*

Reality TV: Remaking Television Culture

Laurie Ouelette and Susan Murray

IN FALL 2002, THE CHARACTERS ON *The Simpsons* appeared as contestants on a fictional reality TV program. Donning nineteenth-century clothing and giving up all modern conveniences, they agreed to be filmed around the clock by the Reality Channel while living in a nineteenth-century-style home complete with TV cameras and a video "confessional" room. When their show fails to generate high ratings, the producers move the house to a remote location in the Amazon, forcing the cartoon family to navigate the ravages of nature as well as the hardships of premodern life and the surreal process of living their lives in front of millions of TV viewers. When the Simpsons encounter a disillusioned "tribe" of North Americans assembled for another reality show, they join forces to overthrow the production team, escape the house, and return to the comforts of their suburban life, which—most important to the family—includes television viewing.

The episode pokes fun at the recombinant nature and ratings-driven sensationalism of much reality TV in scenes where producers copy the format of successful European shows and frenetically scan U.S. channels for ideas about attention-grabbing plot twists. Taking the conventions of programs like *Survivor, Big Brother,* and *1900 House* as a shared cultural reference point, it satirizes viewer fascination with the televisual display of "real" people, the agreed-on surveillance inherent to reality TV, and the commercial pressures that have coalesced to create simultaneously "authentic," dramatic, popular, and profitable nonfictional television programming. The parody suggests that reality TV is a pervasive and provocative phenomenon that is remaking television culture and our understandings of it.

Situating Reality TV

What is reality TV? The classification of generic labels is always contextual and historical. While there are certain characteristics (such as minimal writing and the use of nonactors) that cut across many reality programs, we are ultimately more concerned with the cultural and "branding" discourses that have coalesced to differentiate a particular moment in television culture. We define reality TV as an unabashedly commercial genre united less by aesthetic rules or certainties than by the fusion of popular entertainment with a self-conscious claim to the discourse of the real. This coupling, we contend, is what has made reality TV an important generic forum for a range of institutional and cultural developments that include the merger of marketing and "real-life" entertainment, the convergence of new technologies with programs and their promotion, and an acknowledgment of the manufactured artifice that coexists with truth claims.

We have seen the rapid proliferation of television programming that promises to provide nonscripted access to "real" people in ordinary and extraordinary situations. This access to the real is presented in the name of dramatic uncertainty, voyeurism, and popular pleasure, and it is for this reason that reality TV is unlike news, documentaries, and other sanctioned information formats whose truth claims are explicitly tied to the residual goals and understandings of the classic public service tradition. Although the current wave of reality TV circulates ideologies, myths, and templates for living that might be called educational in nature, it eschews the twin expectations of unpopularity and unprofitability that have historically differentiated "serious" factual formats from popular entertainment. If the reality programming that we examine here celebrates the real as a selling point, it also distances itself from the deliberation of veracity and the ethical concerns over human subjects that characterize documentary programming in its idealized modernist form.

While the convergence of commercialism, popularity, and nonscripted television has clearly accelerated, much of what we call popular reality TV can be traced to existing formats and prior moments in U.S. television history. The quiz formats of the late 1950s represent an early incarnation of highly profitable TV programming that hinged on the popular appeal of real people placed in dramatic situations with unpredictable outcomes. Other precursors include the staged pranks pioneered by *Candid Camera*, celebrations of ordinary people in unusual or unusually contrived situations (examples include *Queen for a Day, It Could Happen to You, That's Incredible,* and *Real People*), and the amateur talent contest first brought to television by *Star Search*. The landmark cinema verité series *An American Family*, which is often cited as the first reality TV program, also provides an important reference point, as does low-budget, nonprofessionally produced television, from the activist and amateur programming shown on cable access stations to the everyday home video excerpted on *America's Funniest Home Videos*. Daytime talk shows, the favored reality format of the late 1980s and early 1990s, anticipated the confessional ethos and cultivation of everyday drama that permeate contemporary reality TV. Yet it wasn't until the premiere of *The Real World* on MTV in 1991 that we began to witness the emergence of many of the textual characteristics that would come to define the genre's current form. By casting young adults in a manner intended to ignite conflict and dramatic narrative development, placing the cast in a house filled with cameras and microphones, and employing rapid editing techniques in an overall serial structure, the producers created a text that would prefigure programs such as *Survivor* and *Big Brother*. It could also be argued that *The Real World* trained a generation of young viewers in the language of reality TV.

Today, reality TV encompasses a variety of specialized formats or subgenres, including most prominently the gamedoc (*Survivor, Big Brother, Fear Factor*), the dating program (*Joe Millionaire, Mr. Personality, Blind Date*), the makeover/lifestyle program (*What Not to Wear, A Wedding Story, Extreme Makeover*), and the docusoap (*The Real World, High School Reunion, Sorority Life*). Other examples include the talent contest (*American Idol*), popular court programs (*Judge Judy, Court TV*), reality sitcoms (*The Osbournes, My Life as a Sitcom*), and celebrity variations that tap into many of the conventions for presenting "ordinary" people on television (*Celebrity Boxing*). What ties together all the various formats of the reality TV genre is their professed abilities to more fully provide viewers an unmediated, voyeuristic, yet often playful look into what might be called the "entertaining real." This fixation with "authentic" personalities, situations, and narratives is considered to be reality TV's primary distinction from fictional television and also its primary selling point.

Beyond the textual characteristics and appearance of new subgenres, what differentiates today's cultural moment is a heightened promotion of the entertaining real that cuts across prime time and daytime, network and cable programming. For a variety of complex reasons that the authors explore, reality TV has moved from the fringes of television culture to its lucrative core as networks adopt reality formats to recapture audiences and cable channels formulate their own versions of reality formats geared to niche audiences. Consequently, not since the quiz show craze of the 1950s have nonfictional entertainment programs so dominated the network prime-time schedule. Talk shows and game shows have historically been relegated to daytime or late-night hours, while networks have relied on dramas and sitcoms to secure their evening audience base. While cable stations were the first to begin airing reality programs during prime time, the success of CBS's *Survivor* eventually led the networks to follow suit. By early 2003, the staying power of the genre, along with the success of new shows like *American Idol, The Bachelorette,* and *Joe Millionaire,* convinced networks to make long-term plans for reality TV and its accompanying business strategies. In a front-page story on the topic in the *New York Times*, Leslie Moonves, president of CBS Television, proclaimed that "the world as we knew it is over."[1] The networks plan to stagger the release of new reality programs throughout the year instead of debuting them en masse in September. They also plan to jettison repeats of the programs altogether. These additional scheduling shifts will help networks compete more aggressively with cable channels and, they hope, retain reality TV's young, upscale audience base. By January 2003, one-seventh of all programming on ABC was reality based. ABC executives, along with NBC, Fox, and CBS, promised to bring even more reality to their schedule in the coming season and cut back on scripted fictional drama series and sitcoms.[2] A few months later, the first "reality movie," *The Real Cancun,* was released in

---

[1] Bill Carter, "Reality Shows Alter the Way TV Does Business," *New York Times*, 25 January 2003, A1.
[2] Lynn Elber, "ABC Defends Increased Use of Reality TV," *Associated Press*, 15 January 2003.

theaters just as development plans for Reality Central, an all-reality cable channel scheduled to debut in 2004, were announced. While some industry insiders remain skeptical about the long-term viability of the reality craze, the spread and success of the genre has already exceeded expectations.

Is Reality TV Real?

Reality TV's staying power renders an investigation of its relationship to truth and authenticity even more urgent. Many reality formats maintain noticeable connections to the documentary tradition. In particular, the use of handheld cameras and lack of narration found in many reality programs is reminiscent of observational documentaries, and carries with it an implicit reference to the form's original promise to provide direct access to the experience of the observed subject. This has the effect of bolstering some of reality TV's claims to the real. Scholarly discussions of documentaries have tended to turn on issues of the ethics of representation and the responsibilities associated with truth telling and mediation. In *New Documentary: A Critical Introduction*, Stella Bruzzi points out that at the root of these discussions is a naive utopian belief in a future in which "documentaries will be able to collapse reality and fiction" by "bypass[ing] its own representational tools" with the help of particular techniques such as those commonly associated with cinema verité.[3] The reception of reality TV programming evokes similar questions and concerns as critics (but not necessarily audiences) wring their hands over the impact that editing, reconstruction, producer mediation, and prefab settings have on the audience's access to the real. Despite such similarities in claims and critical concerns, however, reality TV also establishes new relationships between "reality" and its representation.

Although reality TV whets our desire for the authentic, much of our engagement with such texts paradoxically hinges on our awareness that what we are watching is constructed and contains "fictional" elements. In a highly provocative and influential article in the *Television and New Media* special issue on *Big Brother*, John Corner claims that the commingling of performance with naturalism is a defining element of what he calls television's "postdocumentary context."[4] In this contradictory cultural environment, critics like Corner contend that viewers, participants, and producers are less invested in absolute truth and representational ethics and more interested in the space that exists between reality and fiction. Reality TV promises its audience revelatory insight into the lives of others as it withholds and subverts full access to it. What results is an unstable text that encourages viewers to test out their own notions of the real, the ordinary, and the intimate against the representation before them. Far from being the mind-numbing, deceitful, and simplistic genre that some critics claim it to be, reality TV supplies a multilayered viewing experience that hinges on culturally and politically complex notions of what is real, and what is not.

Central to what is "true" and "real" for reality TV is its connection to the increase in governmental and private surveillance of "ordinary" individuals. In an era in which a

---

[3]Stella Bruzzi, *New Documentary: A Critical Introduction* (New York: Routledge, 2000), 255-59.
[4]John Corner, "Performing the Real: Documentary Diversions," *Television and New Media* 3, no. 3 (August 2002): 255-60.

THE REALITY TV SUITE

"total information awareness" of all U.S. citizens has been made a top governmental priority, the recording and watching of others—and ourselves—has become a naturalized component of our everyday lives. Surveillance cameras are everywhere in the United States. In fact, the American Civil Liberties Union found in 1998 that in New York City alone, 2,397 cameras (both privately and governmentally operated) were fixed on public places such as parks, sidewalks, and stores.[5] By 2001, a company providing security services, CCS International, reported that the average New Yorker was recorded seventy-three to seventy-five times a day.[6] Since the events of 11 September 2001, even more cameras have been installed. Reality TV mitigates our resistance to such surveillance tactics. More and more programs rely on the willingness of "ordinary" people to live their lives in front of television cameras. We, as audience members, witness this openness to surveillance, normalize it, and in turn, open ourselves up to such a possibility. We are also encouraged to participate in self-surveillance. Part of what reality TV teaches us in the early years of the new millennium is that in order to be good citizens, we must allow ourselves to be watched as we watch those around us. Our promised reward for our compliance within and support of such a panoptic vision of society is protection from both outer and inner social threats. Surveillance is just one of the promises of "public service" that reality TV makes. Reality TV is cheap, common, and entertaining—the antithesis of public service television and a threat to the well-informed citizenry that it promises to cultivate, according to conventional wisdom. And yet, a closer look at reality TV forces us to rethink the meaning and cultural politics of public service, democracy, and citizenship in the age of neoliberalism, deregulation, conglomeration, and technological convergence.

The Commercialization of the Real

If reality TV raises cultural and ethical questions, it also points to the medium's changing industrial context. In the late 1980s, a shifting regulatory climate, network financial troubles, and labor unrest forced the television industry to reconsider its programming strategies. Finding reality formats cheap to produce, easy to sell abroad, and not dependent on the hiring of unionized acting and writing talent, the industry began to develop more programs like *Unsolved Mysteries, Rescue 311*, and *America's Most Wanted*. In Europe, public television stations also embraced reality programming, mainly as a financial survival mechanism. Faced with deregulatory policies and heightened pressures to compete with commercial channels that aired popular (and often U.S.-produced) programs, public stations in the United Kingdom, the Netherlands, and other European locales developed the reality genre.

The explosion of reality programming in the 1990s was also the product of a changing industrial environment—both in the United States and abroad. Feeling threatened by new recording devices such as TiVo and ReplayTV (which contained commercial-skipping

---

[5]Dean E. Murphy, "As Security Cameras Sprout, Someone's Always Watching," *New York Times*, 29 September 2002, A1.
[6]Ibid.

features) and an ever increasing number of cable stations, U.S. television networks were open to the possibility of new production and financing models, including the purchasing and selling of formats rather than completed programs, the expansion of merchandising techniques, an increased emphasis on audience interactivity, and the insertion of commercial messages within programs. (This last strategy isn't entirely new, of course, but is a variation on the indirect-sponsorship model used in the 1950s and revived within the deregulated policy milieu of the 1990s.)

If reality TV is at the center of major shifts within the television industry, its proliferation has also corresponded with the rapid development of new media technologies. Much of reality TV in the late 1980s and early 1990s, such as *Cops* and *America's Funniest Home Videos*, depended on the availability and portability of handheld video cameras. The most recent wave of reality programs has relied on small microphones and hidden cameras to capture private moments such as those that occur on *Big Brother* and *The Real World*. Yet the marketing and distribution of reality TV has also developed in particular ways in its use of the Internet, streaming video, cell phone technology, radio, and digital television. Viewers are no longer limited to just watching the completed text of a show, but can keep in touch through short message service (SMS) updates sent to their cell phones, by accessing live twenty-four-hour footage on websites, and by calling to cast their votes. New technologies have also facilitated new advertising strategies that enable sponsors to cut through the clutter of traditional television advertising.

One of the most compelling aspects of reality TV is the extent to which its use of real people or nonactors contributes to the diversification of television culture. *Survivor,* for example, has made it a point to use people from diverse age, racial, geographic, class, and sexual backgrounds. Reality TV opens up new possibilities and limitations for representational politics, as the authors in this volume demonstrate. The fifteen minutes of fame that is the principal material reward for participating on the programs limits the selection of "real people" to those who make good copy for newspaper and magazine articles as well as desirable guests on synergistic talk shows and news specials. Indeed, many of the participants on *Survivor* and other successful reality programs have gone on to star in Hollywood films, host television shows like MTV's *Spring Break*, and appear as contestants on new reality programs. While participation in reality TV doesn't seem to lead to an acting career, it does appear to provide a continuation of the observed life, as former participant/players' offscreen behaviors are tracked by the media even after their show airs. The celebrification of "average" folk further complicates the contours of television fame and the way that its star personas have been constructed as existing in a space between the ordinary and the extraordinary.

For some critics, reality TV's commercial orientation has co-opted its democratic potential. The dream of "the people" participating directly in television culture can be traced to the alternative video movements of the 1960s and 1970s, which sought to collapse the hierarchy between producers and receivers, and to empower everyone to participate in electronic image making. Influenced by the writings of Hans Magnus Enzensberger and Bertolt Brecht, video pioneers sought to "remake" television as a democratic endeavor, bypassing one-way transmission for a participatory model that allowed a full range of people to tell their stories and document their struggles, "unfiltered" by the demands of convention, stereotyping, and commercial sponsorship.[7] While this philosophy lives on in the alternative productions of Paper Tiger TV, Deep Dish TV, and Free Speech TV, it is now more commonly associated with the television industry itself, which emphasizes the democratic potential of reality TV by promising unscripted programs filled with (and sometimes made by) real people from all walks of life. Even advertisers have jumped on the trend, as the Gap uses real people to sell jeans and the Subway sandwich chain claims that a recent television commercial was "shot by real teenagers."

However opportunistic, the commercial embrace of popular reality programming does signal representational shifts, and with them, openings that warrant special consideration. The reality boom has spawned an opportunity to wrest control of television images and discourses away from the culture industries.

The theoretical assumptions and methodological principles on which we have come to depend are no longer sufficient tools to analyze an increasingly complex televisual environment. Television has become more sophisticated, not just in the presentation of reality programming that simultaneously claims authenticity yet rewards savvy viewers for recognizing constructed or fictional elements but in its reliance on interactive technologies, novel commercial strategies, and an intertextual environment in which real people slip in and out of the roles of celebrities, and vice versa. The global context in which reality programs are produced and shared is changing too: as media conglomerates become international entities, and as television formats are exchanged and revamped across national boundaries, we need to revise our political–economic frameworks and ways to understand how meaning can be both culturally specific and globally relevant.

The NEXT Plague: MTV's Sexual Objectification of Girls and Why It Must Be Stopped

Maribeth Theroux

Student Essay

Maribeth Theroux wrote this essay for Dr. Patricia Pender's class at Pace University in 2007. For more information about the assignment, please see the "Third-Wave Feminism Suite" in Chapter 6, "Reading and Writing about Gender."

[7]See Bertolt Brecht, *Brecht on Theatre*, ed./trans. John Willett (New York: Hill and Wang, 1964), and Hans Magnus Enzensberger, "Constituents of a Theory of the Media," in *Video Culture*, ed. John Hanhardt (New York: Visual Studies Workshop Press, 1986), 96-123. For an overview of the history and goals of alternative television, see Dee Dee Halleck, "Towards a Popular Electronic Sphere, or Options for Authentic Media Expression beyond *America's Funniest Home Videos*," in *A Tool, a Weapon, a Witness: The New Video News Crews*, ed. Mindy Faber (Chicago: Randolph Street Gallery, 1990), n.p.; Deirdre Boyle, "From Portapack to Camcorder: A Brief History of Guerilla Television," *Journal of Film and Video* 44, nos. 1-2 (1992): 67-79; William Boddy, "Alternative Television in the United States," *Screen* 31, no. 1 (1991): 91-101; and Laurie Ouellette, "Will the Revolution Be Television? Camcorders, Activism, and Alternative Television in the 1990s," in *Transmission: Toward a Post-Television Culture*, ed. Peter d'Agostino and David Tafler (Newbury Park, Calif.: Sage, 1995), 165-87.

REALITY-BASED TELEVISION HAS become both a phenomenon and a plague in recent years. Each network broadcasts shows in this genre, one that can no longer be called simply a trend since it shows no signs of going away. MTV's reality shows are a huge part of their weekly schedule. The craze began with their *The Real World,* and today the network broadcasts such reality shows as *Road Rules, Date My Mom, Exposed, Room Raiders, Parental Control, True Life, Made, The Hills,* and *NEXT.* MTV is ranked the number one cable network for the 12- to 24-year-old demographic, with viewers in 342 million homes worldwide (Stern 1). In addition, girls between the ages of 12 and 19 comprise 30% of MTV's audience (Eads 5). On a network that broadcasts not only reality shows, but reality *dating* shows, it is crucial to analyze the messages that these shows send to viewers, especially girls. Eads explains, "Girls look to TV programming to decipher what it means to be a woman, to try out different roles, and to learn sexual expectations and behaviors" (14). It is my argument that in looking to these shows girls are taught to be sexual objects through seeing other girls forced into that role. In addition, the shows police female appearance and behavior in specific, harmful ways that rob girls not only of their control and power but also of their worth as individuals.

The third wave of the feminist movement and the reality television movement are both influencing American culture, but their messages are primarily in conflict with one another. In her article, "The Third Wave's Final Girl," Irene Karras writes, "Third wave feminists . . . are struggling to define their femaleness in a world where the naming is often done by the media and pop culture" (3). This is why cultural production is so important to third wave feminism. Positive female representations are necessary in movies, television, and music because otherwise stereotypes and societal expectations that restrict girls will be perpetuated. A 1998 *Time* article asks, "Is Feminism Dead?" If reality-based dating shows such as MTV's *NEXT* and the way they portray and treat girls continues, the answer to that question will ultimately be a resounding "yes." The article asks, "For the next generation, feminism is being sold as glitz and image. But what do the girls really want?" (60). Do girls want to be paraded off of a bus as a male contestant chooses between them based on their appearances, as *NEXT* does? Do they want to pose suggestively in front of a camera and make sexually explicit comments for the viewing pleasure of over 342 million homes worldwide? MTV turns girls into hypersexual objects for men and boys to look at and for other girls to emulate, and this needs to not only be analyzed and critiqued, but also put to an end.

NEXT and other television dating shows rely on the sexuality of contestants to attract viewers. In order to understand why this is so harmful to girl participants and viewers, the word "sexuality" itself must be understood. As feminist theorist Catharine MacKinnon writes, "What is sexual is what gives a man an erection" (480). By this definition, there is no possibility for empowerment that girls can gain through being made into sexual spectacles on shows like *NEXT.* This relates to the arguments of Laura Mulvey who has theorized that film intrinsically sets up females to be sexually objectified solely for male pleasure. She writes, "The way film reflects, reveals and even plays on the straight, socially established interpretation of sexual difference . . . controls images, erotic ways of looking and spectacle" (297). Mulvey is relating this idea to film during Hollywood's "Golden Age" in the 1930s and 40s, but unfortunately her theories lend themselves just as well to the television dating show genre of recent years. Mulvey explains that when sexual pleasure can only be gained from "watching, in an active controlling sense, an objectified other" this is an extreme perversion (298). There is no doubt that contestants on *NEXT* are in a controlled setting in which they are objectified. And if this is the case, is *NEXT* not trying to make all of its viewers throughout its 342 million homes worldwide into female objectifying perverts? MTV has a long tradition of producing reality-based shows such as *The Real World* in which "women partake in their own degradation, learning to make the male gaze their own" (Stern 3). That being said, if females are given no other choice but to gain pleasure through watching other females being objectified, when will sexual objectification stop? Additionally, when a show like *NEXT* is as antifeminist and problematic as it is, how will girls even *know* that they are being sent dangerous messages that they should not accept, and more importantly, should not emulate?

The basis of *NEXT* is that there is one contestant who has the opportunity to go on five separate dates. To avoid confusion, I will call the person choosing between the five people the "contestant," and the people who she/he must choose between will be called the "dater/s." The majority of the episodes of *NEXT* feature dating under hetero-normative conditions in which the contestant is choosing between five dates of the opposite sex. There are also episodes featuring homosexual contestants and daters, but these are not aired regularly. The daters are concealed on a bus and leave the bus individually for their date with the contestant. This leaves the contestant in suspense of who else is on the bus throughout the episode. One of the most disturbing and revealing aspects of *NEXT* is the fact that daters receive $1 for each minute that they last before the contestant "nexts" them, sending them back to the bus. The title of the show comes from "nexting," in which the contestant tells their date "Next!," the date is forced to return to the bus with however much money they "earned," and the next date gets her/his turn with the contestant. In turn, if a contestant likes one of their dates enough to ask them on a *second* date, the dater must choose between however much money she/he has accumulated and a second date, forfeiting any money she/he has "earned" should she/he accept the second date. Shows like *NEXT* further normalize male objectification of females in a world where this kind of behavior is ever-present. MacKinnon writes, "Women cope with objectification through trying to meet the male standard, and measure their self-worth by the degree to which they succeed" (484). In terms of *NEXT*, the ultimate success for a female dater is being asked on a second date by the male contestant. Under these circumstances, the girl daters' only options are to decline the second date and receive their payment for each minute they were objectified, or to accept the second date. By forgoing all money they earned the male contestant can thus sexually objectify the girls free of charge, which is more realistic in regards to a world in which "all women live in sexual objectification like fish live in water" (MacKinnon 484). One female dater responds to being sent back to the bus with $1 by flashing the male contestant. Immediately after, she stands in front of the camera, waving her dollar, and says, "Usually on Spring Break I show my boobs for free." Girls have been so normalized to their sexual objectification that it has become not only something they are subjected to, but something they actively participate in. Shows like *NEXT* play a role is this normalization that cannot be ignored.

A spoof of *NEXT*, entitled *Jesus on NEXT*, makes light of the fact that female daters are nothing more than objects to the male contestant. The male contestant judges them solely on their appearances. The mere fact that a spoof of this kind exists is proof in itself of the impact and influence that MTV's reality dating programs have on young viewers. *Jesus on*

NEXT features a male contestant, a representation of Jesus, who goes on dates with five females. At one point in the film that is featured on YouTube.com, Jesus "nexts" a girl who he has been getting along with very well for no other reason except, as he reasons, "I just have to see what else is on that bus" (*Jesus*). The use of the word "what" instead of "who" exemplifies the blatant objectification that occurs on actual episodes of *NEXT*. The people who produced this spoof realize the horrible messages that *NEXT* sends, but do all viewers? And more importantly, does realizing these messages do anything to prevent them from influencing viewers' perceptions?

The sad reality of actual episodes of *NEXT* is that they are in many cases more disgusting than any spoof. This is especially true of a special "Spring Break 2007" episode of *NEXT* in which a male contestant, Lorenzo, 25, goes on dates with five girls in the following order: Amaris, 19, Rachel, 21, Jenn, 25, Alysha, 18, and Catherine, 18. A particularly revealing moment on this episode is when one of the girls asks the others if they would ever consider appearing on a *Girls Gone Wild* video. Alysha, an 18-year-old aspiring go-go dancer who works at Hooters, replies, "Yeah, why not?" and the four other girls look at her, jaws dropped in disbelief. It is my argument, however, that *NEXT* objectifies girls in the same way that the *Girls Gone Wild* videos, which are notorious for showing girls flashing their breasts, kissing other girls, and dancing suggestively, do. While *Girls Gone Wild* is specifically marketed towards a male audience, *NEXT* has a wider and younger audience but provides the same basic, implied message that it is natural to sexually objectify girls, therefore proving *NEXT* more harmful.

When I first began researching *NEXT* I knew that it was far from anything even resembling third wave feminism, but I thought it might reflect some ideals of girlie feminism. Irene Karras states, "Girlie feminists claim their femininity as a source of power. . . . By embracing the feminine—make-up, clothing, and even Barbies—third wave feminists are sending the message to society that women are powerful on their own terms" (7). While the girls on *NEXT* embrace make-up and revealing clothing, they are in turn objectified and demeaned by boys. There is nothing empowering about girls dressing this way or wearing a lot of makeup because if they *do not* present themselves this way then they are most often "nexted" and sent back to the bus. This is an obvious form of policing female appearance and behavior.

Perhaps the most disturbing aspect of *NEXT* is that not only does the male contestant police female behavior, the female daters and a female narrator whose voice is heard throughout the episodes polices and demeans girls, as well. When Rachel exits the bus for her date with Lorenzo one of the four remaining girls on the bus asks the others if they think Rachel will "win." Jenn replies, "Maybe if she went on the salad diet like six months ago." Lorenzo instantly sends Rachel back to the bus. Their date would have consisted of them racing dune buggies on the beach, and as Rachel walks back to the bus the female narrator says, "When Rachel's clothes were a bit too snug, she didn't get to drive the dune bug." The input from this narrator is similar to a device used on the dating show, *Blind Date,* in which text pops up on the screen accompanying the action of the show. In the article, "Pop (Up) Goes the Blind Date: Supertextual Constraints on 'Reality' Television," the authors critique the show's "supertext," which they say "serves to maintain the social order and punish deviance from behavior traditionally regarded as normal" (185). The narrator on *NEXT* serves the same purpose, reinforcing insulting comments from contestants and daters. This further naturalizes the show's message to girls that there is an ideal image they must embody to "win" boys' approval and in turn their own self-worth.

Proponents of *NEXT* may claim that the show is empowering to girls because it allows one girl to choose between five male dates on some episodes. Although this gives the female contestant some agency, it does not reverse the objectified role that she is still forced into. Despite having the control to choose between five dates, these boys compensate for their lack of control by objectifying and bad-mouthing the girl even more when/if she decides to "next" them. This rejection in one episode led a boy to return back to the bus and declare to the other four boys, "The girl is flat. She's got stretch marks on her legs." In addition to these hetero-normative episodes, on rare occasions MTV airs episodes of *NEXT* featuring homosexual contestants and daters. Rather than showing positive representations of gay girls and boys, however, *NEXT* makes spectacles of them by exaggerating gay stereotypes such as hyper-sexuality and flamboyancy. These episodes are even more laden with sexual innuendos and objectify homosexuality in the same way that female sexuality is on other episodes.

MTV is watched worldwide by millions of young viewers. The network therefore has a responsibility to send positive messages to this audience, instead of messages that perpetuate and further normalize the sexual objectification of females. Univision, as one of the only Spanish-speaking networks broadcast on American television, has its own responsibilities to its viewers. In February 2007 Univision was punished for filling up slots meant for children's educational programming with *telenovelas*, or soap operas. Univision agreed to pay the Federal Communications Commission (FCC) $24 million (Abrams). Univision failed to meet government rules for children's educational programming, instead showing racy, sexually explicit *telenovelas*. Univision failed its young viewers in the same way that MTV continues to fail its own. As Jennifer Eads states, "Girls look to TV programming to decipher what it means to be a woman, to try out different roles, and to learn sexual expectations and behaviors" (14). If MTV's programming is a source of education to girls and boys alike then they should be held just as responsible as the Univision network. Just because MTV may not be subject to government rules about children's educational programming does not mean that their programming is not used by children for educational purposes. The media is used for sexual and gender role education by young viewers and therefore must be held responsible for the messages it sends and the consequences of those messages. It is wrong for MTV to promote the sexual objectification of girls, and just as Univision was punished for its offences, as should MTV.

MTV promotes the expendability of people through its dating shows, turning daters into objects that can easily be thrown away. On its website, potential contestants are instructed, "The minute you get annoyed, angry, or just plain bored, simply kick 'em to the curb saying 'NEXT' and start over with someone new" (*NEXT* summary). The way *NEXT* was designed works to rob daters of their dignity. A comment that dater, Jenn, makes to contestant, Lorenzo, exemplifies this point. She says, "Get me naked before you next me, idiot." Her words reveal that Jenn is basing her own worth solely on her physical appearance, and is offended that her looks were not enough to secure her a second date. The message that being "nexted" by a male contestant sends and that the narrated voice reinforces is that the girls are worthless. Girls' appearances and behaviors are thus policed when they realize how easily they can be replaced by a different girl whose appearance and behavior is more valued. Danielle Stern discusses the commodification of female sexuality in *The Real World,* and this commodification is even more clearly present in *NEXT* where girls are immediately given the money they "earned" after being "nexted." MTV, however, is earning far more for these girls' appearances on *NEXT*. Stern reports, "Advertisers are willing to spend anywhere from $10,000 to $20,000 for a 30-second slot to target MTV's young viewers" (2). Not only is MTV making money by sexually objectifying girls, the companies that advertise during *NEXT* are also capitalizing on the show's sexual displays, and it is girls who ultimately pay the very high price.

Shows like *NEXT* cannot be written off as simply innocent, silly television dating programs. Catharine MacKinnon writes, "only 7.8 percent of women in the United States are not sexually assaulted or harassed in their lifetimes" (476). Reality-based television cannot be disassociated from the role it plays in creating such alarming statistics. 92.2% of United States women have been sexually assaulted or harassed in their lifetimes, and the fact that 100% of women are sexually objectified on *NEXT* should be no less of an alarming statistic. The harsh realities of reality-based television dating shows must be realized before the harmful and dangerous roles that girls are forced into can or will ever change. MTV should not be allowed to define femaleness and it should not be allowed to turn girls into sexual, disposable objects. Sexual objectification is something that is even more prevalent than reality-based dating shows. Reality-based dating shows feed off of female sexual objectification, and this plague needs to be eradicated if girls will ever have the opportunity to base their worth on something other than male approval and subsequently gain the empowerment and agency they so deserve but are so rarely given the chance to claim.

Works Cited

Abrams, Jim. "Univision Agrees to Record $24M Fine From FCC Over Lack of Children's Programming." *Yahoo! Finance* 24 Feb. 2007. 27 Apr. 2007 http://biz.yahoo.com/ap/070224/univision_fine.html?.v=4.

Baumgardner, Jennifer and Amy Richards. "Third Wave Manifesta." *Feminist Theory: A Reader.* Comp. Wendy K. Kolmar and Frances Bartkowski. New York: McGraw-Hill, 2005. 568–569.

Derose, Justin, Elfriede Fursich, and Ekaterina Haskins. "Pop (Up) Goes the Blind Date: Supertextual Constraints on "Reality" Television." *Journal of Communication Inquiry* 27.2 (2003): 171–189. 20 Feb. 2007.

Eads, Jessica. *Construction of Adolescent Girls' Identity in the Age of Reality Television.* Diss. The Univ. of North Carolina at Greensboro, 2004.

Ferris, Amber. *Playing the Dating Game: the Relationship Between Viewing Reality Dating Programs on Television and College Students' Perceptions of Dating.* Diss. Michigan State Univ., 2004.

Jesus on NEXT. 7 Jan. 2007. *YouTube.* 23 Feb. 2007 http://www.youtube.com/watch?v=f0ulGU19sP4.

Labi, Nadya. "Is Feminism Dead?" 29 June 1998. *Time.*

Mulvey, Laura. "Visual Pleasure and Narrative Cinema." *Feminist Theory: A Reader.* Comp. Wendy K. Kolmar and Frances Bartkowski. New York: McGraw-Hill, 2005. 296–301.

"*NEXT* Summary." *MTV.* 18 Feb. 2007 http://www.mtv.com/#/ontv/dyn/next/summary.jhtml.

NEXT. MTV. 19 Mar. 2007.

Phillips, Lynn. "Sexuality." *The Girls Report.* New York: National Council for Research on Women, 1998. 33–43.

Stern, Danielle M. "MTV, Reality Television and the Commodification of Female Sexuality in the Real World." *Media Report to Women* 33 (2005): 13–22. 22 Feb. 2007.

Syvertsen, Trine. "Ordinary People in Extraordinary Circumstances: A Study of Paricipants in Television Dating Games." *Media, Culture & Society* 23 (2001): 319–337. 19 Apr. 2007.

The Bachelor/ Bachelorette's White Elephant

By Thea Lim

OVER AT *FEMONOMICS* COCA COLO asks why everyone on *The Bachelor* and *The Bachelorette* is white:

> *The Bachelor* and *The Bachelorette* are two of the whitest shows on television. Not only is the star always white, but so is the host, and so, by nature of our society's continued discomfort with interracial dating, are almost all of the suitors.

The all-white star phenomenon then becomes a self-perpetuating cycle, because the newest star is usually picked from one of the nearly rejected contestants, who are all themselves white . . .

Now, simply choosing a black (or Hispanic, or Middle Eastern, or Asian, or South Asian, or mixed race) star would certainly not remedy the problem. In fact, it would likely only highlight it, since naturally ABC would never reverse the formula and stock this cast with all people the same race as the star (that would make *The Bachelor* a "niche" show, they would say). Nonetheless, at least we would have taken a small, token step toward inclusiveness. I know *The Bachelor* is ridiculous, that the formula of trying to find love in a couple months with 25 strangers is nonsense, and that we have bigger representation problems than television. You can tell me all that, and yet it still enrages me how white this show is. So ABC, you're on notice.

I get Femonomics' exasperation on this—as a race and pop culture blog, one of Racialicious' biggest problems actually is poor representations of people of colour on TV. But the *Bachelor/Bachelorette's* myriad problems aside (like the heteronormativity and the bizarre power dynamics), the consequences of a bachelorette/bachelor of colour could equally be heartily positive, or completely negative. Indulge me in some baseless what-if-ing—colouring the *Bachelorette/Bachelor*: what could go right (or wrong)?

Let's imagine a *Bachelorette/Bachelor* of colour. It would be just lovely to see people of colour pursuing love in their own way and taking charge of their sexuality, especially when you consider that people of colour are usually portrayed as asexual (Eddie Murphy in *Beverly Hills Cop*), comically hypersexual (Donna on *Parks and Recreation* or Long Duk Dong in *Sixteen Candles*), sexual vessels for someone else's fantasy (any number of East Asian women playing bit roles in white vehicles), or the perpetual wingperson (any number of black women playing sassy black best friend roles in white vehicles). It could be our (sexy) time to shine!

Then again, there are just as many things that could go wrong. Imagine if we had, say, a Korean bachelorette. I doubt we would make it through a single episode without references to said bachelorette's exotic beauty and delicate hands. Or what if we had a bachelor of colour pick a white suitor? We'd have another disastrous portrayal of white beauty being selected over nonwhite.

Before you accuse me of hating on interracial lovers and their offspring, let me just say that it is not individual interracial white/nonwhite couples that trouble me. It is rather the constant movie/televisual representations of mixed race couples and their corollary that tires me out: which is that white folks are always portrayed as more loveable and desireable than people of colour. Whatever the actual context of a mixed race white/POC bachelor(/ette) pairing, the mere optics would simply reinforce a demoralising message that people of colour are sick of hearing: we are never as dateable as white folks, or if we are dateable it is in a weird-ass creepy fetish way that we'd rather go without, thankyou.

Ok, so let's imagine there are (more) suitors of colour on the casts of the *Bachelor/Bachelorette*. That would be nice for representation figures alone, and breaking up the wall of whiteness Femonomics identified. It would do wonders for the dating self-esteem of men and women of colour all over North America (even though vying for white folks' approval ain't that healthy). Yet what are the odds we'd just see our brethren getting rejected? I don't know, but they might not be good, and that could be mighty demoralising.

More positives and negatives accompany a scenario whereby a white bachelor(ette) chooses a suitor of colour. It could be portrayed as just your run-of-the-mill miracle of love thing. Which would be good. But it could also turn into something nauseatingly post-racial, with the couple getting back-pats for being so brave and courageous; missing the point that you should date someone just because you like them, and not out of some twisted desire to end racism by humping someone of another race.

A potential positive that has few potential negatives—at least from an anti-racist point of view? The casting changing on the *Bachelorette/Bachelor* to the point that we get to see a POC/POC couple on the *Bachelor/Bachelorette*. But it may be a while before we see some-thing like that. What do you think? Would you like to see a bachelor/bachelorette of colour no matter who they choose? Would you be happy to see more suitors of colour, or does the risk of seeing yet another man/woman of colour get rejected on international television outweigh the positives of modifying the love demographic?

Or should we just continue whittling sailboats out of twigs and shooting marbles until there's better POC programming on TV?

READING **WRITING**

This Text: Reading

1. Can you detect a bias in Ouelette and Murray's piece? Do they have a stance on the usefulness or importance of reality TV?
2. Theroux's essay is a classic persuasive piece. She argues that *NEXT* is sexist and manip-ulative. That is not a unique argument, but her take is compelling. How successful is her argument?
3. Thea Lim's piece on *The Bachelor* franchise of reality shows is provocative and subtle at the same time. Is she making a specific argument? Why or why not does the piece work?
4. When taken as a whole, what do these five pieces reveal about reality TV and American culture?

Your Text: Writing

1. Write a comparison/contrast essay in which you examine the pro/con arguments regarding reality TV.
2. Track down some of the old episodes of *TV Nation.* Is this show reality TV? How about Sunday morning political talk shows? All of those home-makeover shows? Are these reality TV? Write a paper in which you define reality TV and give examples of what is and is not reality TV.
3. Write an essay in which you read American culture and tastes through the popularity (and unpopularity) of certain reality TV programs.
4. Write an essay in which you explain exactly why and how reality TV programs are *not* "real."
5. Write an essay in which you explain why reality TV is so popular in the United States and Europe. Why has it caught on *now?* If it does die, what will be the cause of its death?

READING BETWEEN THE LINES

Classroom Activities

Realistic?

Watch a show in class taking notes on what is realistic about the show. Do you find its setting realistic? Its dialogue? The characters—both in the way they act and their gender, ethnic, and class make-up? In what ways do the show's creators try to be realistic? In what ways are they admitting that television shows are not realistic? Do you think whether a show is realistic an important consideration in whether you watch it? What are the differences between television shows and "real life"?

Advertising

Watch the commercials in a particular television show. Can you tell from them who its target audience is? Do you think advertisers are reaching their intended audience?

Is This a Good Show?

What are your criteria for saying a show is "good"? Are they similar or different than the ones you might use for literature and/or movies?

Casting

Who would play you in a sitcom about your life? Why would you make this choice?

Genre

What is your favorite type of television show? Why? Do you feel you have something in common with others who like these types of shows?

Show Loss

Talk about a show that went off the air that you miss. What emotions did you feel when this show ended its run? Do you think the run ended too early? What do you think makes a successful television show?

Essay Ideas

The General Television Assignment

1. In this paper, read an episode of a television show and write a paper analyzing some aspect of it. What do we mean by "read" and "analyze"? You might start by describing the text at hand, performing an inventory of sorts. Then think about what these elements say about the text. What conclusions can you draw about the work from the observations you have made? A television show has traditional elements of texts such as a narrative and symbolic language of one sort or another, as well as visual elements that contribute to the show's meaning.

Look at the Fashion

2. For this paper, notice the way the characters dress on a particular television show. From what you know about fashion, what are the creators of the show trying to convey with their choices of fashion for their characters? Are they hoping to tie into prevailing

opinions about the way certain groups (e.g., those of color, class, gender, and age) dress in providing clues on how we're supposed to understand these characters? Taken together, what conclusions can we draw from the fashion choices of the creators?

Analyze the Theme

3. In most sitcoms and many dramas, there is an explicit "moral of the story" that those who script the episode attach to the ending. Taking one such show, a night of shows on a particular network, or an accumulation of the same shows, what sorts of morals are presented to the audience? Do you think the creators think these morals are important? If so, do they present an honest attempt to educate the audience, or are they a vehicle for laughs? Do you know any shows that do not have "a moral of the story"? How would you compare them to the shows that do have morals?

The Unintended vs. the Intended

4. Sometimes television shows are explicit about what they are trying to convey. Sometimes, however, what is not present in a show says as much about the show as what is there. For example: Oprah Winfrey made a comment to the cast of *Friends* on her show: "Why isn't there a black 'friend' on your show?" Look at a popular sitcom and try to determine what may or may not be missing on a show. You might focus on the racial make-up of the characters or their gender, class, or age.

Real vs. Unreal

5. Many people may say that they watch television "to escape reality." In what ways do the producers of shows try to be "real"? In what ways do they ignore reality? You may already have noticed that we tend to watch characters in action with other characters, and that basic human functions like bathing, eating, sleeping, and going to the bathroom are ignored. On a more philosophical level, you may also notice that the problems these characters face are resolved relatively quickly, and the communication between characters is highly evolved. For this paper, you might discuss what overall effect the inclusion of "reality" might have on the audience.

Understand the Audience

6. Creators of television shows often target their shows to particular audiences—or their advertisers do, in order to see a greater return on their investment. Watch a television show, or several, and see if you can determine what demographic they are appealing to or what show their advertisers feel they are. Are the two audiences different? Is one more broad than the next? What do you think are some of the problems inherent in targeting a particular demographic?

Race and Ethnicity

7. For a long time, race and ethnicity has been an issue on television. Watch a show and see what they say and do not say about questions of race and ethnicity. Do members of a particular race play a particular role on the show? Do these roles embrace or reject previous stereotypes?

Honor the Show

8. Write an essay on why you feel a show is "good." Your first step, of course, is defining what you mean by "good." Does "good" mean writing that is funny, realistic, philosophical, or a combination of these factors or others? Is good defined by the quality

of the actors? Can you define what a good television show is without constructing the criteria from the show you like? What other shows fit into the definition you constructed?

Disparage the Show

9. Write an essay on why you feel a show is "bad," going through the same process as you did when you defined what "good" meant. A useful exercise is to write both positive and negative reviews.

Follow the Character

10. What single character on a television show do you most identify with? Why? Does this identification make you at all uncomfortable? What does this identification say about you and the television character?

Media Journal

Using the worksheet at the front of the book as a guide, we want you to follow a phenomenon for the length of the course. It could be a television show, a continuing story in the newspaper (make sure you choose one that will continue), or a continuing event (such as a sport). Each journal entry should provide some sort of commentary on the phenomenon, moving beyond general plot concerns. A brief (two- or three-sentence) summary is fine but should not dominate the entry. See "Media Journal, *The Rosie O'Donnell Show*," by Hillary West, for an example.

Visualizing Writing

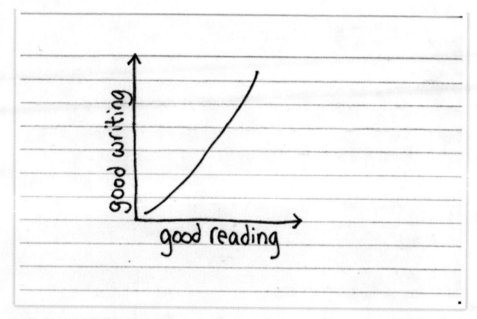

Credit: Jessica Hagy from *Indexed*

3 Reading and Writing about Public and Private Space

Whether we are in bedrooms, bathrooms, coffeehouses, classrooms, stadiums, or record stores, we are always someplace, and understanding our relationship to these places and spaces helps us better understand the world. How? By providing us tools to recognize the way the physical world influences our inner world, the way those constructing spaces might shape us, or attempt to.

In this introduction, we will talk about public and private space, architecture, and design as constructed texts as an entrée into writing about those spaces. What we mean by space is the environment created by human-made activities, including built areas, such as classrooms, stadiums, shopping malls, and dorm rooms. Architecture and design are forces that help construct these places and spaces and give them their particular personality.

In a sense, architects and designers are the authors of buildings and public spaces; they construct these texts through a series of decisions. And if you look around you, not only will you see patterns of decisions made by architects and designers but you will also see the influence of those who pay the designers and the people who use or live in that particular space.

For example, architects may have had some leeway in designing your classroom, but their decisions about certain aspects of appearance or comfort might have been affected by construction cost, local building codes, and state educational requirements. The kind of institution you attend, whether it is a private or public university or college, probably had some impact on these decisions. The designers and architects were limited by function—putting a fireplace or a wet bar in a classroom would be inappropriate. And the designers were undoubtedly influenced by the period in which they lived; if you think about it, you can pinpoint the date within twenty years of construction based on colors, materials, and lighting. For instance, rectangular buildings built with brick or cinder blocks reflect the architectural style of the '60s and '70s, whereas a wooden Victorian house was probably built as much as 100 years earlier.

Such decisions also exist in corporate and retail venues. If you walk into a Starbucks, for example, you will see the results of a series of carefully made judgments: the color scheme, the décor and the lighting, the font type of the signs that describe coffee products, and where all of this is placed. It is not hard to gather from these aspects of design that Starbucks is going for both "cool" and familiar in its space. They want customers to feel they are not only purchasing coffee but that they are having some unexpressed secondary experience as well. Stores like Anthropologie, restaurants like Rain Forest Café, and cafes like Panera Bread all use décor, design, and detail to send a message and to create an aura.

◄ This probably is not your idea of college; for more discussion about why, see our college suite and college photo essay starting on page 239.

Is it one element that creates this aura? No—it is a series of details taken together. Drawing conclusions from architectural decisions and public space is not much different than making these conclusions from reading literature; each has its own "grammar," symbols, and themes that we interpret to get a picture of the work as a whole. Here are some other things to think about when writing about public space and architecture.

COLORS AND SHAPES OFTEN HAVE SYMBOLIC VALUE.

Part of the grammar we wrote about in the last paragraph (color and shape) helps architects and designers speak to the public in a language they understand, either consciously or subconsciously. Psychologists have shown that particular shapes and colors have psychological effects on their viewers. Designers and architects also draw on traditional uses of color and shape, again, as a sort of grammar of construction. Of course, homeowners may think they choose certain shapes or shades because they look "pretty," or "nice," but what they mean by "pretty" is arbitrary as well. Still, it is very unlikely that the walls in your classrooms are red or black. They are probably also not adobe, wood, or steel. We venture that they are not painted in a checkerboard style or with stripes. Rather, they are probably white or off-white, neutral in some way so as not to distract you from the process of listening and learning.

Combinations of these colors and shapes often form recognizable designs that are imitated repeatedly, especially in regard to public structures that want to suggest something beyond mere functionality. For example, arches, columns, and white picket fences often symbolize ideas that transcend their simple presence—arches and columns have often stood for power and tradition, and the white picket fence stands for tradition as well, but perhaps a different kind of tradition. The Washington Monument on the National Mall in Washington, D.C., is, from a functional perspective, a poor use of space. You can't do anything in there. Its significance is symbolic; accordingly, a great deal of thought went in to selecting a design that would signify the values the government wanted. As important as the structures themselves are the spaces surrounding the structures. A house with a white picket fence around it is a much different text than a house with a high metal security gate enclosing it.

We associate certain kinds of structures with economic and social class—brick versus mobile homes, skyscrapers versus corrugated tin buildings, strip malls versus warehouses. Buildings and spaces are rarely *just* buildings and spaces. When it comes to public space, almost nothing is random. So, when you begin constructing your own papers about architecture or space, we recommend that you begin by jotting down notes in your journal about your topic. If you are writing about your campus, try to get at the associations of things like "ivy," "columns," and even the word "campus." What do these connote? From there, you can begin to unpack the packed world of space and design.

COST AND COMMUNITY PREFERENCES OFTEN CONTRIBUTE TO THE DESIGN OF A PUBLIC OR PRIVATE SPACE.

Although most designers seek to make buildings and spaces both beautiful and useful, there are other factors that often interfere with stated goals. Cost is always an issue—people can only build what they can afford, and some materials are prohibitively expensive for a given function. Design help can also cost money, as does land, construction, and so on.

The surrounding community also plays a role in design. Community standards, often in the form of zoning laws, will have an effect on what something looks like. Zoning regulations determine the use of a particular piece of property and, depending on the locale, can also determine the size and function of what is built on that property. Even politics can help determine how something is designed. For example, at the University of Texas at Austin in the 1970s, a prominent student meeting-place was significantly altered when the administration built large planters to restrict student gatherings protesting administration policies. Similarly, at the State University of New York at Binghamton, a beloved and locally famous open space in the center of campus called the "Peace Quad," where students gathered to read, protest, talk, eat, and listen to music, was paved over so that a large new building could be erected in its place. Issues of class and race can also affect public and private spaces. For example, there are very few upper class communities near industrial plants, nor does one often find a poor neighborhood that has easy access to the attractive elements of a city. Think about where Mercedes dealerships are located. In the same place you might find the best auto repair spots? Or, think about country clubs versus public golf courses. Wine bars and dive bars?

In some cases entire communities determine how a city can look. Santa Fe, New Mexico, has a city ordinance that requires new buildings to have an adobe look. Hilton Head, South Carolina, prohibits certain kinds of signs. San Francisco, California, has some prohibitions on large chains and franchises. Houston, Texas, has no zoning, which makes it wildly inconsistent from block to block. These communities are particularly aware that how a space looks can affect how we feel in that space.

SPACE CAN BE MANIPULATIVE, COMFORTING, OR BOTH.

Designers have conscious ideas about the world they construct, and they often think about how and where they want people involved with their work. If you have ever found yourself frustrated in a poorly designed building, you may have wondered what idiots designed the place. The design of casinos, for instance, is most interesting. Casinos have no windows, usually only one or two exits, and you almost always have to walk through the slot machines to get to either of them. Why might this be the case?

In your life, how do elements of design work? Think about sidewalks. Do they always take you where you want to go? What about doorways? Are they always at the most convenient place? In your own room, think about where you put your desk, your chairs, and your bed: What is your main concern in placing them—your convenience or someone else's? All of those decisions influence those who enter your room. Think too about most classrooms at your institution. What do they resemble? Do they create a certain mood? For example, is talking about a movie or a story different in a large classroom than in a café? Why or why not? Sometimes places are friendly to their visitors or inhabitants; others are less so, either through oversight by designers, or more deliberately, as in the case of the Peace Quad or student protest space at the universities mentioned before.

What is important to know is that your emotional reaction to certain spaces is *intended*. If you have been to a court, then you know that the heightened judicial bench inspires a bit of trepidation; if you have walked in a particularly beautiful cathedral, the sense of awe you feel is not arbitrary; if you enter the library of an old or prestigious university, you probably experienced a hushed sense of tradition that was designed to be elicited in you when it was still in blueprints. Thus, writing about these issues means that you also need to understand the cultural work architectural and design elements do.

USERS HAVE WAYS OF ALTERING LANDSCAPES THAT CAN HAVE PERSONAL AND POLITICAL IMPLICATIONS.

One of these ways is through decoration. Humans love to personalize their spaces, whether it is a cubicle, an office, a dorm room, their computer desktop, or their cars. How we inhabit space is a means of establishing identity; space is a text we are always making and re-making. Think about your own spaces. Posters lining a room, particularly in the dorm rooms and bedrooms of your contemporaries, are usually there to send a message—that the inhabitant is a man or a woman, or someone concerned with music, art, beer, and/or cars. Some rooms scream that the inhabitants are trying to be cool, while others ooze sophistication.

When one gets older, it is usually time to say goodbye to the rock posters, M.C. Escher prints, and the beer ads, but what to replace them with becomes a question all of us grapple with for the rest of our lives. Some people decide they have a style they feel comfortable with and make their decisions based on that; others feel their way through the process; still others delegate their design choices to someone else. However, there are effects from these decisions, whether they are intended or unintended. The space you live in—how you decorate it, your traces within it—is a kind of text that people can (and do) read to understand something about you.

Entities as large as cities can try to influence the way its inhabitants and visitors feel. If you have visited Santa Fe, for example, you know that art is everywhere—in front of the state capitol, in parks, outside buildings, in restaurants, in courtyards, in and outside of private homes. The message this sends is not simply that Santa Fe and its residents like to decorate their landscape, but that it is a place that values art, how things look, and how art makes you feel. Salem, Massachusetts, with its gabled houses, restored wooden buildings, and American colonial feel strives for what we might call New England charm. The abundance of art sends a message of sophistication, worldliness, and a progressiveness that is welcoming. You may not always be conscious of it, but spaces that pay close attention to design and beauty probably make you feel quite good.

Of course, there can also be a gap between what the occupant of the space wants to suggest and what is actually suggested—in this way, spaces can be revealing texts. Knowing about space will help you not only be better readers of someone else's space, but may also help you avoid pitfalls of constructing unwelcoming space yourself. You may think that posters of near-naked women reclining on cars are cool, or you may think black mammy figurines are quaint, but there will be a sizeable audience out there who might wonder about you and your values based on how you arrange and decorate your space.

OTHER ELEMENTS CAN CHANGE THE LANDSCAPE IN WAYS NOT IMAGINED BY DESIGNERS.

Graffiti alters the public landscape, and so does public art. Neglect can change public space, as well as new construction surrounding a previous design. How we use and design space gives some indication of our personality, among other things. Walking into someone's dorm room, office, or living room gives us a clue of who they are (and who they think they are). When you walk into a business, you also receive some indication of how they view themselves. For example, compare the interior at McDonald's to a fancy restaurant, or to a TGI Fridays, Applebee's, or Chili's; the interiors and exteriors are littered with clues about what these places think they are about. Similarly, how do Mexican restaurants tell us that they serve Mexican food? How do Chinese restaurants create an "Asian" setting? Think too about the way movies and television shows set scenes; often the settings of movies give us an indication of how we're supposed to view the characters. In *Modern Family* or *Friends,* for example, we see the presence of couches, bright lighting, the expensive, clean homes (in the case of *Friends,* far too expensive for New Yorkers their age) as clues to how we are supposed to relate to them. If you ever watched *Roseanne* or *The King of Queens* you see an entirely different aesthetic.

Public spaces are especially curious in this way. Dams completely alter natural environments, flooding entire valleys. Roads paved through forests bring cars and tourists and pollution. In urban areas, for example, some public parks have become centers for both drug use and needle exchange programs—no doubt a *very* different use of public space than was intended. We leave our imprint everywhere. And, just as we make our rooms or cubicles our own, so, too, do we make public space our own—for better or worse.

Ultimately, the space that surrounds us says a number of things about that particular location—who inhabits that space, what the space is used for, and how we are to read that space. Additionally, we can discern a great deal about what kinds of spaces or buildings are important given the amount and kind of space devoted to them. As you read this chapter, think about how certain spaces force you to interpret the world in a certain way, and as you write your papers, work on combining your own observations about spaces with solid research so that your arguments are strengthened by two kinds of authority—subjective experience and objective data.

THIS TEXT

1. How does the background of the authors influence their ideas about public space?
2. Do they define public space differently? In what ways?
3. Do the authors have different ideas about class, race, and gender? In what ways?
4. Try to figure out the writing situation of each author. Who is the audience? What does the author have at stake? What is the agenda of the author? Why does she or he want me to think a certain way?
5. What is his or her agenda? Why is she or he writing this piece?
6. What social, political, and cultural forces affect the author's text? What is going on in the world as he or she is writing?
7. What are the main points of the essay? Is there a specific thesis statement? Remember that it doesn't have to be one sentence—it could be several sentences or a whole paragraph.
8. What type of evidence does the author use to back up any claims he or she might make?
9. Is the author's argument reasonable?

Worksheet

10. Do you find yourself in agreement with the author? Why or why not?

11. Does the author help you *read* public space better than you did before reading the essay? If so, how?

12. How is the reading process different if you are reading an essay as opposed to a short story or poem?

13. Did you like this? Why or why not?

BEYOND THIS TEXT

Shapes: What are some of the dominant shapes you see in a public space or building? Do they symbolize anything to you? Are they supposed to? Do they remind you of other shapes in other spaces? How do the shapes relate to the space's use?

Colors: What are the dominant colors? What emotions do they evoke? Why? How would the space or architecture change if the color changed? How does the color relate to the space's use?

Size: How big is this place? How does this affect the way you view it, and the feelings it inspires? Is there a way to change the size to evoke different feelings? In what ways do the space's or architecture's size relate to its use?

Use: What is the use of this particular space or architecture? How do we know from the elements you see? Do you see unintended uses that might result from this construction? Do you see an emphasis on practicality or ornament in this space?

Interaction between architecture and space: How do the two work together? What elements in the architecture affect the way the space is constructed? Are there ways of changing this interaction?

Overall beauty: What is your general view of the place's beauty? What standards or criteria do you find yourself relying on?

Emotional response: What is your overall emotional response to this place? Why? What elements contribute to this response? What elements could you change that might provoke a different response?

Overall statement: What do you think this space or architecture says? What is it trying to say? How might this gap between what it says and is trying to say be changed?

A QUICK GUIDE TO WRITING ABOUT PUBLIC SPACE:

1. **Define your space.** Figure out exactly where you are writing about.

2. **Note materials and colors.** Writing about public space is often focused on the details, and these details often give some insight on the intentions of the designers.

3. **Observe how people use the space.** Observing and thinking about the ways people use a space—perhaps in unintended ways—can help us to understand whether the space works or in what ways it works.

4. **Brainstorm/freewrite about the space either at the space or soon after visiting.** Getting your impressions down early makes it easier to write.

5. **Think of a thesis and paragraph ideas before starting to write.** It will make the first draft easier.

Architecture, Experience and Meaning

Liz Swanson

Liz Swanson is an award-winning architect, designer, and artist. She is an associate professor of architecture at the University of Kentucky. Her research focuses on the relationship between landscape and identity. She currently directs the first-year program for beginning design students. Immediately after Hurricane Katrina, Swanson and her husband Mike McKay, a native of New Orleans, worked with their students in New Orleans helping to rebuild and redesign areas of the city. This essay, written especially for this edition of The World Is A Text, *is an introduction to reading architecture.*

THINK BACK TO A PLACE YOU LOVED AS A CHILD—a favorite spot where you instinctively felt free or safe, excited, or at ease. Now think of the physical characteristics of that place: was it open or enclosed? Dark or bright? How did you get there and what was the view once you arrived? For me, this place existed under the sagging canopy of a willow tree. Its droopy branches formed a shady circle of dappled light within which I could hide, barely visible to others through the dense screen of its leaves. While not literally a building, my experience of this space was nonetheless architectural: it was a cozy room, just my size, with windows and skylights that shifted in the breeze.

As children, we seek out places that inspire our imagination and in doing so begin to understand the connection between architecture and experience. Like landscapes, buildings guide how we use and move through space; we see and feel the impact of the physical world long before we have the vocabulary to describe it. This understanding evolves as we grow to include more sophisticated aspects of meaning, such as culturally specific associations and learned behaviors that further affect how we occupy any area. Consciously or not, each time we interpret the possibilities of a place, we engage in an ongoing dialogue with our surroundings.

But perhaps because buildings are everywhere and this dialogue so constant, it is easy to overlook the specificity of how our surroundings frame and inform our activities. Indeed, the entirety of the built environment may be read as series of semiotic patterns that reveal the intricacies of human relationships. Take a stroll down the main street of your hometown, and ask: what do the buildings say about my community? How does the architecture guide my actions? In answering these questions, we begin to read the physical environment as something that shapes social interaction.

Likewise, we begin to understand the impact of architectural design: that the places we inhabit are planned on purpose, the result of an architect's desire to express a specific intention. Just as an author of a great novel carefully plans the way a plot will develop and how each of the characters will contribute to the overall story, architects plan how buildings and landscapes contribute to the overall quality and identity of a place. For example, Washington D.C. was planned specifically to communicate the ideals of our nation, and therefore many of the buildings are designed using monumental styles that symbolize democracy. Additionally, the city streets are organized to orient travel toward significant landmarks, such as the White House, while zoning stipulates that no structure can be built taller than the Capitol. In contrast, the stylistic diversity of Chicago's soaring skyline and the unrelenting grid of its city streets can be read as a result of the city's position as a hub

Fig. 1 This streetscape, for example, is clearly a constructed text. If we were to read it, we might begin with the "message" the environment tries to convey. How do we use these spaces, and how are we supposed to feel here? In what kind of place might such a scene exist? How can you tell? Notice the details: the doggie dish, the planted divider, the detail of the fleur de lys on the building—when taken together, what do they suggest?

of industry and architectural innovation, a quality that Chicagoans claim as a source of pride. The physical characteristics of the city—as with all places—indicate not only how it functions, but part of the identity of its inhabitants.

In this essay, we will unpack and explore a few of the fundamental elements of architecture—space, form, and material—to examine the various ways these can be used to create specific experiences, and therefore, meaning. Throughout, we will focus on the relationship between the action and consequence of design: we will read how places are made in order to draw some conclusions as to why.

Space
Defining space

When thinking of "space," one might imagine something similar to the outer limits of the atmosphere: an infinite and unbounded expanse of air in which tangible objects are located. The architect, however, conceives of space differently. When designing anything—from a large park to single room—the architect's job is to consider the shape of the space between things, the void in which people dwell.

Is the space large and voluminous, like a grand auditorium? Is it tight and narrow, like a back alley or secret hiding place? Is a room small or big, and how does this make one feel? When we start to pay attention to the proportion, distance, and degree of enclosure between the solid stuff (floors, walls, ceilings, etc.), we can begin to read

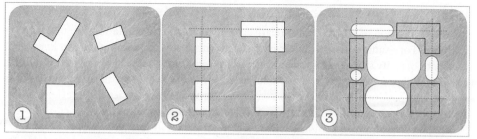

Fig. 2 Whether designing a single room or an entire community, the architect's job is to design the space that exists between things. The objects in this diagram can be read at any scale—as four separate buildings or as four building components, such as walls, roof, etc.—as the principle remains the same.

1. Objects located randomly, with little relationship to each other. The space between them is 'left-over,' i.e., not specifically considered.

2. The same objects, this time designed in relationship to each other, with edges and center-points that align.

3. This alignment results in the creation of specific spaces that are perceived as strongly as the objects themselves.

space as something that's sculpted to create specific sensations. For example, a survey of residential design from the past century reveals a change in family values, and consequently, a shift in how we experience space. Homes built in the 1900s included formal dining rooms, kitchens, and public parlors that were designed to separate and compartmentalize activities according to gender and privacy. Each room had a distinct purpose, and therefore a distinct boundary of enclosure that cued inhabitants on how the room was to be occupied. By contrast, many contemporary homes remove these boundaries altogether, featuring bar-seating within kitchens that open to family rooms and dens that are used for all types of gathering, thus encouraging a greater sense of informal communality.

Space can be read as a sign; interpretation depends on cultural knowledge

Unlike conventional signs and symbols, the impact of space is not visual as much as it is physical. We perceive space with our bodies, using all five senses. A closed door prohibits passage; our voices echo when speaking in a cavernous room. These are physical facts that do not require any architectural training to understand; however the way we interpret these facts depends on our cultural knowledge of what such qualities might mean. A young child might enter a movie theater and continue to talk loudly, but those who understand the function of this room know why the space is large and the lights are low, and respond accordingly. Hence, when evaluating the purpose and meaning of any place, it is important to ask: how much of my interpretation stems from the actual physical design of the space itself? How much is influenced by my individual lens of perception, i.e., my personal experience, education, and cultural background?

Interpretation of space is relative, depends on context

Our interpretation of a space is also relative: we read its impact in relationship to what surrounds it. For example, if you have ever traveled within a major metropolis you know that the width of a city street seems increasingly more constricted as the height of the buildings grow on each side; the street has not changed, but the proportion of the space has. In this way, our perception of space shifts as we move through it as a series of experiences that unfold over time, a phenomenon that architects use to accentuate the impact of design. For instance, the towering volume within a cathedral, and in turn, its spiritual resonance, is exaggerated by the contrast of the low ceilings of the entry vestibule that precedes it. By taking us through a relatively compressed space first, the sensation of openness (and perhaps awe) is emphasized. Like a well-written story, we experience architecture as a sequence of related events.

Form
Definition of form

Yet, we can also read buildings as objects. In fact doing so might be the most common way people perceive buildings. What does a building look like? What shape does it take, and what might we read from its appearance? Take, for instance, a long, linear structure with few windows, smoke stacks and a series of loading docks; what might it suggest that a small building with two stories, a bay window, and front porch does not? Indeed, almost as a matter of habit, we regularly encounter buildings and draw conclusions about their function or message, often without ever experiencing the spaces within. A large building with arches, a spire and walls predominated by stain-glass windows, for instance, tends to communicate "church" because these elements have come to identify that type of building— even if the interior space has been appropriated for another use. For better or worse, one of the most accessible aspects of architecture and our reading of its meaning relies heavily on what we can see: the solid stuff, or what architects refer to as form: the shape, size, orientation, and visual movement of a building as a figure in space.

Form can be read as a sign; interpretation depends on cultural knowledge

Whether looking at the shape of a doorknob or the contour of an entire landscape, we can begin to read form as the result of two related considerations: the function it must perform and the message the designer wishes to convey. For example: in practical terms, columns allow a building to stand while simultaneously allowing for passage. But ornately carved, classical columns communicate an association with Greek or Roman ideals, while sleek, slender columns that move asymmetrically across the building's exterior may speak of a more contemporary fascination with pure, visual rhythm.

Similarly, steel beams may be necessary to carry the massive load of a building's weight, but the choice to expose them as a prominent design feature expresses them as a value.

Consequently, all built form may be read as a sign of some kind. A pharmacy shaped like a mortar-and-pestle is a symbol that indicates the building purpose; a large big box store that camouflages its nature as a one-stop shop by decorating its exterior like Main Street U.S.A. is a sign of the company's desire to project the image of a personable community (Fig. 5).

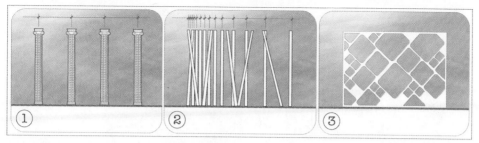

Fig. 3 The shape and visual movement of building elements can convey different messages.

1. Columns with Classical decorative carving, spaced at regular intervals convey an association with Greek or Roman ideals.

2. Columns with no ornamentation, spaced asymmetrically, may convey a more current architectural interest relating to contemporary culture.

3. Here, a wall system that doesn't use columns at all. What might this design communicate?

Fig. 4 A Gothic cathedral, The Eiffel Tower, and Pompidou Center in France are all examples of buildings whose forms emphasize a reading of structure. Each was considered "cutting edge" in its day, using the most innovative materials and construction techniques available at the time, allowing the architect to achieve new heights and forms. Rather than hide the structure, a choice was made to expose and highlight its prominence (with color and light), expressing it as a value.

Fig. 5

Fig. 6 Think of the definition of form: the shape, size, orientation, and visual movement of a building. What makes the tower in the middle of this skyline unique from its surroundings? What makes it similar to its surroundings?

Still, other forms may be signs of the times. Buildings that use innovative or more abstract shapes that do not rely on recognizable images from the past are examples of how architects design as a way of speaking about contemporary culture. The design of a curvilinear skyscraper with undulating surfaces, for example, may be the result of the architect's search for environmentally-sensitive forms: shapes that maximize ventilation and natural light, and minimize the threat to migrating birds who cannot perceive the depth of traditionally-designed rectilinear towers with flat facades.

The design of Frank Lloyd Wright's famous house, *Falling Water*, features stone walls that resemble the surrounding terrain and cantilevered, horizontal roof planes that relate to the lines of the existing landscape. The building typifies Wright's attempt to create a new American architecture based on indigenous materials and free-flowing spaces that integrate with nature. The form of the building moves asymmetrically across the site to create a visual rhythm of shifting elements, connoting the organic topography and tectonics of the earth.

Interpretation of form is relative; it depends on context

This brings up yet another consideration of form: how it responds to context. For instance, the example outlined in Figure 6 can be read in one of two ways: separate from its setting (because it is curvilinear); or particularly site-specific (inspired by the local climate and ecology). The important thing is that we recognize that all forms can be read in terms of the dialogue they create with their surroundings—a conversation that goes well beyond looks. Size, height, and distance from the street, for example, all contribute to how buildings either blend in or distinguish themselves from their environment. A residence that mimics the ornamental style of adjacent historic homes but dwarfs them in terms of size may be less contextual than a modern design that carefully considers the scale of the neighborhood.

Fig. 7 *Falling Water*, designed by Frank Lloyd Wright, is a building that seeks to express nature as a value. How is this accomplished?

Conversely, other forms may be designed specifically to contrast their surroundings in order to achieve a goal, such as increasing tourism by creating a unique, modern icon within an otherwise traditional setting.

Material
Definition of material

Of course, one's understanding of space and form would not be complete without a corresponding conversation about materials. After all, as children we learn early on that different materials have distinct strengths and capacities. The fable of the Three Little Pigs teaches us that unlike straw and sticks, a house made of bricks can withstand even the strongest winds. Similarly, we understand immediately that a room devoid of windows and light has an entirely different effect on one's psyche than one enclosed with lots of glass. Materials—meaning the actual physical matter that comprises individual building components—affect the qualities of a place as well as one's perception, and therefore our sense of what any architectural design might mean.

Material can be read as a sign; interpretation depends on cultural knowledge

Take, for instance, the various messages embodied within the simple construction of a fence. Spatially, its purpose is to divide while formally it acts like a wall: a long, thin vertical plane that marks the length of a boundary. But now imagine the divergent messages communicated by the choice of chain-link fence topped with barbed wire versus one made

Fig. 8 1. While the house on the right shares the same kind of traditional details as other houses on the block, its height and size is out of scale with the neighborhood.

2. In contrast, the scale of the white 'modern' house seen here is in keeping with its neighbors.

Which house do you think fits its context more appropriately?

of wooden white pickets. What does the one say that the other does not? While both effectively delineate territory, the meaning of the message varies—in part because of their contrasting physical characteristics (barbed wire causes pain) but also because of the cultural associations attached to each.

Indeed, the power of cultural associations can influence the development of entire communities and thus reveal our position within the world (Figure 10). While one subdivision may consider vinyl siding a convenient, durable material that is easy to clean, another may eschew it as tacky and cheap, prohibiting its use altogether. In other places, the legacy of a material's use—once chosen for its physical properties—can come to signify the character and identity of its inhabitants. Modern technology makes it possible for any building to exist in Santa Fe, but residents have codified the use of adobe for its long-standing historic and cultural significance.

Conversely, in contemporary architecture, materials may be chosen specifically for their ability to communicate outside of conventionally established connotations—again, a sign of the times. An architect might choose a raw material for its intrinsic properties, but

Fig. 9 Symbolism in names and material choices

1. The entrance gate to Equestrian View, a neighborhood in Lexington, Kentucky that seeks to reinforce its connection to the region: by choosing the name "Equestrian View" (Lexington is known as the 'Horse Capital of the World'); and by choosing stone as its material (Lexington has a rich collection of stone walls throughout its countryside).

2. The entrance gate to Tuscany, another neighborhood in Lexington, Kentucky that seeks to distance itself from the region: by choosing the name "Tuscany," a region in Northern, Italy; and by choosing Venetian plaster as its material (a finish associated with old Europe and not common to Kentucky).

   What might the designers of these two communities be trying to communicate by these name and material choices?

   What connotations might a prospective buyer associate with each?

work with it in a way that expressly resists any kind of symbolic meaning, instead opting to highlight the phenomenal qualities—i.e., the patterns, light, and sensory affects—that the material offers. For example, wood might be chosen because the rhythmic pattern of its grain enlivens the reading of a surface or its capacity to be milled in standard lengths increases the efficiency of construction. The material itself does not represent or symbolize anything; it simply is what it is, a visual affect or tectonic quality indicative of current architectural interests.

Fig. 10 Pictured here are two very different single-family homes. What does the material choice of each one communicate? What might you read from the design of the space or form of each building? Where, when and for whom do you think these homes were built?

Fig. 11 Many buildings are designed with concepts that are not symbolic. In these buildings, materials are not chosen for their connotations, but for their capacities and sensorial affects.

1. Surface patterns: Some materials, such as this marble, are chosen for their ability to enliven a surface via patterns and color.

2. Adaptability; light qualities: Some materials, such as this sheet aluminum, are chosen for their adaptability (easily manipulated) or their reflective qualities.

3. Efficiency: Some materials, such as wood and steel, are chosen for their capacity to be milled, fabricated, or constructed with high degrees of efficiency.

Conclusion

This brings us finally to an important point when reading the built environment. Architecture, like literature, the arts and so many things, ultimately exists as a reflection of its time (Figure 12). We can take the pulse of a society by examining the qualities and concepts of its places, which over time create a rich palimpsest that locates our position in history. Symbol or not, every building is a sign. Their form, space, and materials—in conversation with numerous other elements of architecture, such as scale, light, and accessibility—are the result of an architect's desire, the inhabitant's values, or even a lack of intention at all, all of which reflect the interests and concerns of a specific era. Collectively, we can read buildings as texts and ask: what do the buildings of our towns and cities say about us? And what are we saying to each other through the kinds of places we build? For one of the greatest strengths of architecture remains its ability to inspire greater consciousness: of who we are, and who we wish to be.

Fig. 12 Cloud Gate, designed by Anish Kapoor for Chicago's Millennium Park, against the backdrop of the city's historic skyline. What might you read from the space, form, and material depicted in this scene?

READING WRITING

This Text: Reading

1. When studying literature, the vocabulary of reading is particularly important. Terms like plot, protagonist, setting, and conflict help explain what a story does. How does Swanson use design vocabulary to help us "read" buildings and spaces?
2. In what way is reading a building similar to reading a painting or a poem? Or, put another way, how can design convey meaning?
3. How does Swanson connect architecture and emotion?

Your Text: Writing

1. Write an essay on your favorite (or least favorite) building in the town where you live. What "values" does the building have—good or bad?
2. Write a paper in which you compare an older building (built before 1920) with a building built more recently (after 1960). How do the two buildings create values? How do they send messages about their contexts?
3. Write a paper in which you examine two very different spaces, like a town square and a college campus, or a playground and a bar. How do the spaces compare? How do they differ?
4. Read Dean Rader's essay on college campuses in the campus suite in this chapter. Using the terms Swanson lays out in this essay, write your own essay on a building or space on your campus. Show how your text makes an argument.

Reading the Rural

Dean Rader

Dean Rader is one of the authors of this book. He is a professor at the University of San Francisco, but he spent the first eighteen years of his life in a small town in Western Oklahoma. In this short essay new to this edition, he attempts to interpret representations of rural America.

"THE ONLY PROPER WAY TO LEARN ABOUT AND UNDERSTAND THE LANDSCAPE," writes John Fraser Hart in *The Rural Landscape*, "is to live in it, look at it, think about it, explore it, ask questions about it, contemplate it, and speculate about it. Reading about it," Hart continues, "is a sorry substitute" (1). But, unless you are, at this moment, in the middle of a rural area, *reading* about a rural landscape is probably what's on the agenda for you for the next few minutes. This book, these words, your imagination.

Imagination, as it happens, is important when reading a rural landscape—in part because visual representations of "the rural" are both romanticized and sentimentalized in American culture. Picturesque drawings of farm life, photographs of wide-open spaces, and sketches of tiny towns are part and parcel of the historical idea of America. Cornfields and mountain valleys, long prairies and unfolding deserts, steamy bayous and snowy mountain villages. It's hard to guess how many images like this you have seen either in books or on television. Even if you've never wandered through a wheat field in Kansas or coasted through the Florida everglades, you have, no doubt, imagined what places like this feel and look like.

Understanding America is difficult without understanding rural areas. Between the importance of agriculture, the history of exploration, and the significance of natural landmarks, almost every chapter of American history casts rural land and landscape as either protagonist or antagonist. However, few texts of contemporary popular culture engage rural America. There are no current television shows set in the country, and fewer and fewer movies take place outside of cities. Advertising embraces the urban, as do video games. And, you can forget hip-hop. Unfortunately, country music is pretty much the lone devotee to the rural, but the lyrics tend to celebrate country culture rather than the countryside. Even this book, with its essays on street art, urban spaces, and suburban design foregrounds city semiotics. But, here, I would like to pile this discussion into a pickup and drive it out to the country in order to do two things—explore the semiotics of representations of rural America and call for a reconsideration of rural spaces as public spaces.

Reading a landscape or a representation of a landscape (a photo, a painting, an illustration) is never an objective experience. We "read into" everything whether we want to or not. For some, a painting of a barn, a windmill, and some horses and chickens embodies a strong work ethic, a lovely pastoral scene, and a depiction of a genuine, innocent live/work relationship with the land. For others, the same painting evokes more negative associations: hillbilly, backward, simple, laborious, and primitive. So, how do you see America's rural roots and America's rural routes?

My own interest in reading the rural stems from my experiences growing up in a small town but living in a large city. For the past ten years, I have been a proud resident of San Francisco, one of the most densely populated cities in the country, but I grew up in an Oklahoma farm town, sixty miles from any approximation of a metropolitan area. My hometown, Weatherford, boasted a population of fewer than 10,000—between 3,000 and 8,000 for most of my life. Until I was six or seven, we lived "out in the country" (at least that's how we referred to it). We kept horses, goats, dogs, and a random cat. I didn't love the horses, but I used to strap on my Dallas Cowboys football helmet and butt heads with Sunshine O'Malley, my favorite goat. [Does that seem weird?] One of our regular outings was a trip to the family farm just outside Hinton, Oklahoma, a pint-sized version of Weatherford, where we would drive the perimeter of the farm and size up the wheat. I'm always startled when I return home how different notions of space are in San Francisco and in rural Oklahoma. It's a similar feeling to the one I had as a kid when we would drive from Weatherford to Oklahoma City; after sixty minutes of lolling farmland, the abrupt entry into the industrial and truck-stop dotted backdrop of Oklahoma City was particularly jarring. Now, when I go back I can't get over how far apart buildings are, how much open space there is, and how thoroughly saturated the landscape is with the accoutrement of rural life. I was back in Oklahoma in early 2010, just as we began working on the fourth edition of this book, and I was struck by how common it was for icons of ruralness—wagon wheels, windmills, tractors, silos, barns, and livestock—to appear in ads, on buildings, in logos, on flags, and on t-shirts. Even the cities are rural.

Part of what makes that shift from rural to urban disruptive is the associations we have with both kinds of landscapes. Urban sites we tend to see as sophisticated, cultured, exciting, and affluent. Industrial or factory sites we think of as productive, busy, and, well, *industrious*. Rural landscapes, on the other hand, get assigned adjectives like *lonely*, *isolated*, *backward*, *quaint*, *hick*, *dull*, and *bucolic*. We tend to think of the urban as complex and the rural as simple, but that might be because it is harder to imagine rural life and rural interactions behind the scenes. In the pasture outside our farm (Fig. 1), for example,

Fig. 1

even this low quality photo reveals a great deal if you know how to look at it. What might appear at first a sleepy scene, is to me, a contact zone of various forces. The first thing I notice is how dry the brush is and how beat down it looks. Brown and brittle, the natural grasses are in need of a good shower. The cloudless sky at least three colors of blue suggests that there is a better chance of a convertible Mini cruising by here than any trace of rain. I also see a big white llama hanging out with both black and brown cows. That tells me the rancher probably needs some money and is experimenting with another income source. The worn tire tracks are an indication of a fastidious, present owner who circles his property regularly to check on his livestock. Perhaps what jumps out at me most of all is the fence. I've always been intrigued by how people divide and signify property. In rural areas, property lines are critical, since what occupies your property is probably your main income source. The fence here is a mixture of new and old. Steel posts in the right foreground give way as your eye moves left to an old wooden H-post and to the left of it a crooked wooden pole that looks like it could give way any day. In total, this shot dramatizes the interplay of animal and human, natural and man-made. At one time, nothing is happening, and everything is happening.

One thing that's happening in the photograph in Figure 2 is, again, the division of property. I took this photo on an ill-advised trip through the former Yugoslavia back in the early 1990s. I was amazed by how similar it was to the farmland in Western Oklahoma. So windy are the American plains that early farmers would often demarcate property lines by a series of tall trees—windbreaks—that would not only cordon off farms and pastures but also provide protection from animals and the elements. If

Fig. 2

Fig. 3

you've been to Europe, you know how common it is for shrubbery, as is the case here, to section off property. In Wales, Scotland, and Ireland, farmers rely on fabulous stone walls. In both cases, these dividers serve as signifiers for human labor and a devotion to the land. I was struck by how fully the landscape here is vegetation: there are no animals, no irrigation equipment, a few bales of hay, and only one or two houses. A similar landscape (Fig 3.) features a few of things missing from Figure 2, namely fall foliage, maintained roads, and telephone poles. Telephone poles are, in this case, a classic example of a sign. They tell us a great deal simply by existing, mostly that this area is not off the grid. If you are a savvy reader of rural landscape, then you might also deduce from the poles, the combination of paved and gravel roads, and the speckles of structures off in the distance, that this is a photograph of someplace in the United States, probably the upper Midwest or the Northeast. My point, of course, is that seemingly "empty" rural scenes are probably rich texts with many signs of the cultural work they perform embedded in them.

The stunning leaves, all aflame against the blue and green, raise another provocative question about the rural—to what extent can rural landscapes be scenic landscapes? Traditionally, "rural" is defined as having to do with the country and in particular with an agrarian lifestyle. In fact, "rural" and "rustic" come from the same root. My theory is that we attach meaning and value to what we might call "rural settings" that we do not attach to what we might call "scenic vistas." Take a look at the following three images and ask yourself if these are *rural* or *scenic*:

Fig. 4

Fig. 5

Fig. 6

Figures 4, 5, and 6 are "out in the country;" a city is nowhere around, but I'm not sure we would think of any of these as "rustic" or "rural," unlike the scenes in figures 7, 8, and 9.

Part of what may make the former set "scenic" and not rural is the absence of an overt agrarian presence. But other things at work are the "beauty" of the shots and their recognizability. Figure 4 is a full moon over Half-Dome, a recreation of a famous photograph at Yosemite National Park by Ansel Adams. Figure 5 is of the famous Monument Valley in Arizona, which makes a cameo in a number of commercials. Though Figure 6 is not any notable landmark, it is an iconic scene we have come to link with concepts like "wintry beauty."

It would be a tough sell to make that claim for the subsequent set. Ducks making a break for the open road through a rickety fence, a cowboy saddling up a giant bunny, and

Fig. 7

Fig. 8

Fig. 9

a lone graveyard in a stubblefield might be *charming* or *quaint* or *precious*, but none of these are particularly "beautiful." In an earlier draft of this essay, I wanted to argue that for Americans "rural" equals "ugly," but Jonathan made the argument that for folks raised in New England (like him), ruralness is small New England towns and lovely winding roads.

A locale's beauty is important because we tend to apply the physical attributes of a place to the people who inhabit it. In other words, it is not just about landscape, though that is part of it. It is also about people—the kind of people who choose to live and work in rural locations. For example, even though the photograph in Figure 10 is not set on a farm, everything about it connotes rurality (I know this isn't a word, but it should be).

Fig. 10

Like Dorothea Lange's photographs of migrant workers in Oklahoma, North Carolina, and California, this shot of my mother with her grandparents tells a story. The barn in the background, the sad struggling little plant behind the fence, the stern visage of my great grandmother, and the seeming discomfort in their Sunday clothes are of a piece. One doesn't need a caption to read this photograph. Within it are the subtlest codes of its context: the subjects are posing outside a farmhouse because it is what they know and where their home is. They probably have neither the time nor the money to go somewhere to get this photo taken. Their lack of comfort in front of the camera probably reveals how rarely they pose for photos in fancy clothes. When I look at this photo, I see people who want to get back to work.

Also part of my theory about the rural is that it cannot be empty. The other author of this book, Jonathan Silverman, took the photograph below (Figure 11) at a rest stop in Kansas.

Fig. 11

I would ask you if you think this scene is rural. If so, why? If not, why not?

For me, this open field cannot be rural because it is landscape and landscape only. Landscape is a value-free concept—it is neither good nor bad. Rural, on the other hand, can have dramatically different values linked to it depending on who you are.

Consider the following two images:

Fig. 12

Fig. 13

CHAPTER 3 • Reading and Writing about Public and Private Space

The first, Joshua Tree in California and the second, Walden Pond in Massachusetts, are both protected parks, which denotes human involvement but not human cultivation. The overt presence of desert in Joshua Tree and water at Walden keeps these from being rural locales, despite their relative seclusion. I like thinking of rural areas as public spaces in part because of this human component. Solitary spaces are not particularly inviting, but locales that seem lived in, that contain traces of human activity and engagement are an ancient form of public space. They have a public function through their utility and also through their interactive design.

On the other hand, though, too much human signification can de-ruralize. For example, the photograph below (fig. 14) is of Main Street in my hometown, Weatherford, Oklahoma on Christmas Day in the mid-1990s. It is a small town, but it's not particularly rural. There is a sports bar, for instance, and a state university. It's now easy to get wireless Internet, good coffee, and designer shirts. Can such a place *really* be rural? Similarly, Jonathan's photo of the Dyess, Arkansas town center (fig. 15) is probably not rural but the subsequent shot just outside Dyess (fig. 16) is.

Fig. 14

Fig. 15

Fig. 16

Fig. 17

Why? Because the rural cannot be too cosmopolitan. It cannot be too *developed*. It cannot have too many structures, too many cars, too much *commerce*. Some balance has to be struck between the human and the non-human. There must be evidence that people have chosen not just to live but to make a living on and with the land surrounding them. Look again at Figure 16. What do you see? A plowed field in the foreground? The rusted tin roof on the small shack? Cars in the yard? Two large trees probably planted when the house was built? A dirt road, telephone poles, and if you look very close, you might make out a yellow disc plow to the right of the white truck. The lack of fences here actually enhances the degree to which this is a public space, as the distinction between public and private, personal and professional, is particularly blurry.

One might be tempted to over-simplify this scene, but as in the photo in Fig. 1, a deep interplay exists—not just in the landscape but also in the representation of the landscape. Signifiers and codes, signs and symbols. Whether you like it or not, rural symbology is a rich text. For example, when my first book of poems was published, I wanted the cover of that book to play with these very issues. The opening poem is about Oklahoma, and several other poems in the book deal with Oklahoma, the Dust Bowl, and the plains.

But, they also deal with art, philosophy, language, and God. Originally, I wanted a cool photo of a wheat field on the cover, but I understood that *that* visual iconography of landscape would not do the kind of work I wanted. When I found the photo of the vintage desk alone in a harvested field, it was an interesting juxtaposition of the agrarian and the bookish. The two symbols (wheat field and desk) could connote abandonment, studious devotion, some sort of creepy wheat field monster (a la *Children of the Corn*), or anticipation. When I showed the cover to a colleague, that person expressed surprise: "It's so rural," my friend exclaimed. I didn't know if that was a compliment or a critique, but one thing I did know is that decoding the semiotics of the rural can be a tricky proposition.

The stories we tell ourselves about what is rural and what is urban are often done visually. Many of you live in rural areas—your parents are farmers, ranchers, miners, and gardeners—and perhaps you have very strong ideas about the role your family and your community plays in the ongoing drama that is America. To be sure, there is a distinction between the stereotype of "rural America" that pundits and politicians like to refer to and actual rural landscapes where complex people live. Both are texts, but one is an invention

Fig. 18

while the other is a reality. Figure 18, taken in Turkey, Texas might be a little bit of both—but that doesn't make it any less layered. Learning to read the rural involves becoming aware of loaded signifiers that carry connotations of race, class, privilege, and history, as well as learning how to decode presences rather than absences. It is those presences that make it possible to rethink the rural as public space.

Works Cited

Hart, John Fraser, *The Rural Landscape*. Baltimore: The Johns Hopkins University Press, 1998.

READING WRITING

This Text: Reading

1. What is Rader's thesis here? He claims to be advancing two different but related issues. Does he succeed?
2. Re-read the author's interpretations of the various photos. Do you agree with his distinction between "landscape" and "rural"?
3. Does Rader define "rural" too narrowly? How would you define "the rural"?

Your Text: Writing

1. Take some photographs of areas you think are particularly rural. Now give close readings of the photos in which you demonstrate how and why these images evince ruralness.
2. Write a comparison/contrast essay in which you decode some of the images from this essay with some of the images of street art and urban landscapes. How are urban and rural vistas different? Are there any similarities?
3. Find some old representations of rural landscapes—paintings, drawings, photographs—and write an essay in which you unpack the associations you have with the iconography of rural areas.

Spatial Segregation and Gender Stratification in the Workplace

Daphne Spain

Daphne Spain wrote this essay as part of a larger work, Gendered Spaces *(1992). In this work, she writes about the way a specific type of public space—the workplace—and gender interact, an argument that you might find has implications beyond the workplace.*

TO WHAT EXTENT DO WOMEN AND MEN who work in different occupations also work in different spaces? Baran and Teegarden (1987, 206) propose that occupational segregation in the insurance industry is "tantamount to spatial segregation by gender" since managers are overwhelmingly male and clerical staff are predominantly female. This essay examines the spatial conditions of women's work and men's work and proposes that working women and men come into daily contact with one another very infrequently. Further, women's jobs can be classified as "open floor," but men's jobs are more likely to be "closed door." That is, women work in a more public environment with less control of their space than men. This lack of spatial control both reflects and contributes to women's lower occupational status by limiting opportunities for the transfer of knowledge from men to women.

It bears repeating that my argument concerning space and status deals with structural workplace arrangements of women as a group and men as a group, *not* with occupational mobility for individual men and women. Extraordinary people always escape the statistical norm and experience upward mobility under a variety of circumstances. The emphasis here is on the ways in which workplaces are structured to provide different spatial arrangements for the typical working woman and the typical working man and how those arrangements contribute to gender stratification. . . .

Typical Women's Work: "Open-Floor Jobs"

A significant proportion of women are employed in just three occupations: teaching, nursing, and secretarial work. In 1990 these three categories alone accounted for 16.5 million women, or 31 percent of all women in the labor force (U.S. Department of Labor 1991, 163, 183). Aside from being concentrated in occupations that bring them primarily into contact with other women, women are also concentrated spatially in jobs that limit their access to knowledge. The work of elementary schoolteachers, for example, brings them into daily contact with children, but with few other adults. When not dealing with patients, nurses spend their time in a lounge separate from the doctors' lounge. Nursing and teaching share common spatial characteristics with the third major "women's job"— that of secretary.

Secretarial/clerical work is the single largest job category for American women. In 1990, 14.9 million women, or more than one of every four employed women, were classified as "administrative support, including clerical"; 98 percent of all secretaries are female (U.S. Department of Labor 1991, 163, 183). Secretarial and clerical occupations account for over three-quarters of this category and epitomize the typical "woman's job." It is similar to teaching and nursing in terms of the spatial context in which it occurs.

Two spatial aspects of secretarial work operate to reduce women's status. One is the concentration of many women together in one place (the secretarial "pool") that removes them from observation of and/or input into the decision-making processes of the organization. Those decisions occur behind the "closed doors" of the managers' offices. Second, paradoxically, is the very public nature of the space in which secretaries work. The lack of privacy, repeated interruptions, and potential for surveillance contribute to an inability to turn valuable knowledge into human capital that might advance careers or improve women's salaries relative to men's.

Like teachers and nurses, secretaries process knowledge, but seldom in a way beneficial to their own status. In fact, secretaries may wield considerable informal power in an organization, because they control the information flow. Management, however, has very clear expectations about how secretaries are to handle office information. Drawing from their successful experience with grid theory, business consultants Robert Blake, Jane Mouton, and Artie Stockton have outlined the ideal boss–secretary relationship for effective office teamwork. In the first chapter of *The Secretary Grid,* an American Management Association publication, the following advice is offered:

> The secretary's position at the center of the information network raises the issue of privileged communications and how best to handle it. Privileged communication is information the secretary is not free to divulge, no matter how helpful it might be to others. And the key to handling it is the answer to the question. "Who owns the information?" The answer is, "The boss does." . . . The secretary's position with regard to this information is that of the hotel desk clerk to the contents of the safety deposit box that stores the guest's valuables. She doesn't own it, but she knows what it is and what is in it. The root of the word *secretary* is, after all, *secret:* something kept from the knowledge of others. (Blake, Mouton, and Stockton 1983, 4–5; emphasis in original)

In other words, secretaries are paid *not* to use their knowledge for personal gain, but only for their employers' gain. The workplace arrangements that separate secretaries from managers within the same office reinforce status differences by exposing the secretary mainly to other secretaries bound by the same rules of confidentiality. Lack of access to and interaction with managers inherently limits the status women can achieve within the organization.

The executive secretary is an exception to the rule of gendered spatial segregation in the workplace. The executive secretary may have her own office, and she has access to more aspects of the managerial process than other secretaries. According to another American Management Association publication titled *The Successful Secretary:* "Probably no person gets to observe and see management principles in operation on a more practical basis than an executive secretary. She is privy to nearly every decision the executive makes. She has the opportunity to witness the gathering of information and the elements that are considered before major decisions are made and implemented" (Belker 1981, 191).

Yet instructions to the successful executive secretary suggest that those with the closest access to power are subject to the strictest guidelines regarding confidentiality. When physical barriers are breached and secretaries spend a great deal of time with the managers, rules governing the secretary's use of information become more important. The executive secretary is cautioned to hide shorthand notes, remove partially typed letters from the typewriter, lock files, and personally deliver interoffice memos to prevent unauthorized persons from gaining confidential information from the boss's office (Belker 1981, 66).

The executive secretary has access to substantial information about the company, but the highest compliment that can be paid her is that she does not divulge it to anyone or use it for personal gain. Comparing the importance of confidentiality to the seal of the con-fessional, Belker counsels secretaries that "the importance of confidentiality can't be overemphasized. Your company can be involved in some delicate business matters or negotiations, and the wrong thing leaked to the wrong person could have an adverse effect on the result. . . . Years ago, executive secretaries were sometimes referred to as confiden-tial secretaries. It's a shame that title fell out of popular usage, because it's an accurate description of the job" (Belker 1981, 73–74).

Typical Men's Work: "Closed-Door Jobs"

The largest occupational category for men is that of manager. In 1990, 8.9 million men were classified as "executive, administrative, and managerial." This group constituted 14 percent of all employed men (U.S. Department of Labor 1991, 163, 183). Thus, more than one in ten men works in a supervisory position.

Spatial arrangements in the workplace reinforce these status distinctions, partially by providing more "closed door" potential to managers than to those they supervise. Although sales and production supervisors may circulate among their employees, their higher status within the organization is reflected by the private offices to which they can withdraw. The expectation is that privacy is required for making decisions that affect the organization. Rather than sharing this privacy, the secretary is often in charge of "gate-keeping"—protecting the boss from interruptions.

Just as there are professional manuals for the successful secretary, there are also numer-ous guidelines for the aspiring manager. Harry Levinson's widely read *Executive* (1981) (a revision of his 1968 *The Exceptional Executive*) stresses the importance of managerial knowledge of the entire organization. A survey of large American companies asking presi-dents about suitable qualities in their successors revealed the following profile: "A desirable successor is a person with a general knowledge and an understanding of the whole organi-zation, capable of fitting specialized contributions into profitable patterns. . . . The person needs a wide range of liberal arts knowledge together with a fundamental knowledge of business. . . . A leader will be able to view the business in global, historical and technical per-spective. Such a perspective is itself the basis for the most important requisite, what one might call 'feel'—a certain intuitive sensitivity for the right action and for handling rela-tionships with people" (Levinson 1981, 136).

The importance of knowledge is stressed repeatedly in this description. The successful manager needs knowledge of the organization, of liberal arts, and of business in general. But equally important is the intuitive ability to carry out actions. This "feel" is not truly intuitive, of course, but is developed through observation and emulation of successful executives. Levinson identifies managerial leadership as "an art to be cultivated and devel-oped," which is why it cannot be learned by the book; rather, "it must be learned in a rela-tionship, through identification with a teacher" (Levinson 1981, 145).

Because the transfer of knowledge and the ability to use it are so crucial to leader-ship, Levinson devotes a chapter to "The Executive as Teacher." He advises that there is no prescription an executive can follow in acting as a teacher. The best strategy is the "shine and show them" approach—the manager carries out the duties of office as effectively as possible and thereby demonstrates to subordinates how decisions are made. There are no formal conditions under which teaching takes place; it is incorpo-rated as part of the routine of the business day. In Levinson's words, "The process of example-setting goes on all the time. Executives behave in certain ways, sizing up problems, considering the resources . . . that can be utilized to meet them, and making decisions about procedure. Subordinates, likewise, watch what they are doing and how they do it" (Levinson 1981, 154).

Just as in the ceremonial men's huts of nonindustrial societies, constant contact between elders and initiates is necessary for the transmission of knowledge. Levinson implies that it should be frequent contact to transfer most effectively formal and informal knowledge. Such frequent and significant contact is missing from the interaction between managers and secretaries. Given the spatial distance between the closed doors of managers and the open floors of secretaries, it is highly unlikely that sufficient contact between the two groups could occur for secretaries to alter their positions within the organization.

In addition to giving subordinates an opportunity to learn from the boss, spatial proximity provides opportunities for subordinates to be seen by the boss. This opportunity has been labeled "visiposure" by the author of *Routes to the Executive Suite* (Jennings 1971, 113). A combination of "visibility" and "exposure," visiposure refers to the opportunity to "see and be seen by the right people" (Jennings 1971, 113). Jennings counsels the rising executive that "the abilities to see and copy those who can influence his career and to keep himself in view of those who might promote him are all-important to success." The ultimate form of visiposure is for the subordinate's manager to be seen by the right managers as well. Such "serial visiposure" is the "sine qua non of fast upward mobility" and is facilitated by face-to-face interaction among several levels of managers and subordinates (Jennings 1971, 113–14).

Both Levinson and Jennings acknowledge the importance of physical proximity to achieving power within an organization, yet neither pursues the assumptions underlying the transactions they discuss—that is, the spatial context within which such interactions occur. To the extent women are segregated from men, the transfer of knowledge—with the potential for improving women's status—is limited.

Office Design and Gender Stratification

Contemporary office design clearly reflects the spatial segregation separating women and men. Secretaries (almost all of whom are women) and managers (nearly two-thirds of whom are men) have designated areas assigned within the organization. . . .

Privacy can be a scarce resource in the modern office. Empirical studies have shown that privacy in the office involves "the ability to control access to one's self or group, particularly the ability to *limit others' access to one's workspace*" (Sundstrom 1986, 178; emphasis added). Business executives commonly define privacy as the ability to control information and space. In other words, privacy is connected in people's minds with the spatial reinforcement of secrecy. Studies of executives, managers, technicians, and clerical employees have found a high correlation between enclosure of the work space (walls and doors) and perceptions of privacy; the greater the privacy, the greater the satisfaction with work. Employees perceive spatial control as a resource in the workplace that affects their job satisfaction and performance (Sundstrom, Burt, and Kemp 1980; Sundstrom 1986).

Not surprisingly, higher status within an organization is accompanied by greater control of space. In the Sundstrom study, most secretaries (75 percent) reported sharing an office; about one-half (55 percent) of book-keepers and accountants shared an office; and only 18 percent of managers and administrators shared space. Secretaries had the least physical separation from other workers, while executives had the most (Sundstrom 1986, 184).

Two aspects of the work environment are striking when the spatial features of the workplaces for secretaries and executives are compared: the low number of walls or partitions surrounding secretaries (an average of 2.1), compared with executives (an average of 3.5), and the greater surveillance that accompanies the public space of secretaries. Three-quarters of all secretaries were visible to their supervisors, compared with only one-tenth of executives. As one would expect given the physical description of their respective offices, executives report the greatest sense of privacy and secretaries the least (Sundstrom 1986, 185). Doors do not necessarily have to be closed or locked in order to convey the message of differential power; they merely have to be available for closing and be seen as controlled at the executive's discretion (Steele 1986, 46).

The spatial distribution of employees in an office highlights the complex ways in which spatial segregation contributes to gender stratification. Workers obviously are not assigned space on the basis of sex, but on the basis of their positions within the organization. Theoretically, managers have the most complex jobs and secretaries have the least complex, yet research on secretaries and managers with equal degrees of office enclosure suggests that women's space is still considered more public than men's space. Sundstrom found that "in the workspaces with equivalent enclosure—private offices—[respondents] showed differential ratings of privacy, with lowest ratings by secretaries. This could reflect social norms. Secretaries have low ranks, and co-workers or visitors may feel free to walk unannounced into their workspaces. However, they may knock respectfully at the entrance of the workspaces of managers. . . . *Perhaps a private office is more private when occupied by a manager than when occupied by a secretary*" (Sundstrom 1986, 191; emphasis added). This passage suggests that even walls and a door do not insure privacy for the typical working woman in the same way they do for the typical working man. Features that should allow control of workspace do not operate for secretaries as they do for managers.

Works Cited

Baran, Barbara, and Suzanne Teegarden. 1987. "Women's Labor in the Office of the Future: A Case Study of the Insurance Industry." In *Women, Households, and the Economy,* edited by Lourdes Beneria and Catharine R. Stimpson, pp. 201–24. New Brunswick, N.J.: Rutgers University Press.

Belker, Loren. 1981. *The Successful Secretary.* New York: American Management Association.

Blake, Robert, Jane S. Mouton, and Artie Stockton. 1983. *The Secretary Grid.* New York: American Management Association.

Jennings, Eugene Emerson. 1971. *Routes to the Executive Suite.* New York: McGraw-Hill.

Levinson, Harry. 1981. *Executive.* Cambridge: Harvard University Press.

Steele, Fritz. 1986. "The Dynamics of Power and Influence in Workplace Design and Management." In *Behavioral Issues in Office Design,* edited by Jean D. Wineman, pp. 43–64. New York: Van Nostrand Reinhold.

Sundstrom, Eric. 1986. "Privacy in the Office." In *Behavioral Issues in Office Design,* edited by Jean Wineman, pp. 177–202. New York: Van Nostrand Reinhold.

Sundstrom, Eric, Robert Burt, and Douglas Kemp. 1980. "Privacy at Work: Architectural Correlates of Job Satisfaction and Job Performance." *Academy of Management Journal* 23 (March): 101–17.

U.S. Department of Labor. 1991. *Employment and Earnings* 38 (January). Washington, D.C.: Bureau of Labor Statistics.

READING WRITING

This Text: Reading

1. Do you think such constructions of public space matter? Are symbolic values of space crucial in our world?
2. Do you think genders have different ways of looking at public space? If so, where does this difference come from? Why does it persist?
3. What do you think Spain's "writing situation" is? Is she writing from experience or observation? Can you tell by reading her essay? Why does this distinction matter?

Your Text: Writing

1. Find another environment where gender and space interact. What about the space you describe makes it connect to the particular gender?
2. Think about other public spaces or buildings where separation of people into genders, races, or classes is built into the design. (*Hint:* Think of places where people spend more or less money to sit in different places.) Are those spaces considered problematic in the same way Spain thinks about the workplace? Write a paper that addresses this question.
3. Look at several dorm rooms or apartments of friends both male and female. Write a short paper that discusses which elements in particular define these spaces as particularly male or female.
4. Look at other things that are "gendered," such as advertisements, clothing, and cars. How do these gendered texts compare to the gendered spaces you described earlier? What elements do designers of any text use to designate gender? Write a paper that ties gendered space to another gendered text.

Making Space on the Side of the Road: Towards a Cultural Study of Roadside Car Crash Memorials

Bob Bednar has long been fascinated with the way we interact with public space. Here he writes about roadside shrines and the complex relationship that he has with documenting them. He is a professor of communication studies at Southwestern University in Georgetown, Texas. He previously wrote about tourist spaces for this collection's first and second volumes.

Bob Bednar

Road/Work

IT'S MY FIRST DAY OF INTENSE FIELDWORK while I am based in Santa Fe. I'm at the second of many stops on US-84/285, a four-lane divided highway north of Santa Fe that is under heavy construction. I'm running a fever, and the pace of my work is making it worse.

I have just finished photographing a set of three separate crosses near a busy intersection just north of Tesuque. The three crosses are all lined up in a row just on the outside of the guardrail on the east side of the road facing northbound drivers. The first displays a Harley insignia and the name Jerry Gurule (Fig. 1). About 30 feet ahead of that

Fig. 1

one is a five-foot-tall cross that says, "MOM." Fifteen feet farther up is a cross with a bear but no name.

Standing there taking the pictures with cars buzzing by and nothing but a guardrail between them and me, I can begin to visualize why there are so many crosses here.

After filling up with gas, I take a U-turn to photograph a white cross I had seen a few hundred yards from the other three and on the other side of the road. Like the other three across the road, this memorial is just on the edge of the right of way. Unlike them, this cross is engulfed by road construction and blends into the collection of construction signs, surveyor's stakes, and recently-cleared brush. I miss it and have to circle back.

After I locate the cross again, I park in the only partially safe place I find: a wide shoulder where a group of trucks and cars belonging to the road crew are parked. I pop on the hazards and grab my cameras, hop out of the car, and run across the field of freshly graded dirt and gravel, dodging a water truck, a grader, and two front-end loaders in the process.

The cross is old, dedicated to Herman Padilla, Age 18, October 59 to February 78 (Fig. 2). The road crew seems to have left it undisturbed, but its space is entirely circumscribed.

The dash back to the car is even more daunting than the way there. "What the hell am I doing?" I'm telling myself as I approach the car. Out of the corner of my eye, I notice a white highway department truck driving up behind me on the shoulder. Its flashing lights are on. "Maybe he is going somewhere else?" I think.

I have enough time to make it back to my car and drop off my cameras before he is out of the truck and walking towards me. I meet him at the back of my car. He is wearing a hardhat and inscrutable wrap-around sunglasses. His face is sunburned. The traffic is buzzing by. His face is more than sunburned: it is angry.

"You having some kind of car trouble here?"

"No. Just taking some pictures."

"Well, buddy, this is no place to take pictures. There's a nice spot up there at Camel Rock where there's a parking lot and an overlook. Try that. But we can't have you out here like this. You're gonna get yourself killed."

The rest of the day, the rest of the trip, I feel more personally involved in a research project than I ever have before. I'm beginning to see that the connection is thematic. Early on in the project, I had wondered what was at stake in the practice of roadside memorials. Now I knew what was at stake for me, at least in the field. Roadside memorials speak in different voices simultaneously, functioning as testaments to lives lived and violently lost, but also as cautionary tales.

At each stop, I'm there on the side of the road taking pictures, thinking about the memorials, thinking about the horrible scene that must have taken place, thinking about the terrible but also often beautifully indifferent scene that now sits before me, trying to read between the spaces of silence and exuberance. And at each stop—especially the ones with narrow shoulders or blind curves, or the ones buzzing with traffic—I begin to think: Someone died right here. Right here! And here I am taking a picture of it. What if I die taking a picture of the place where someone else died?

Overlooking Violence

> In looking there is always something that is not seen, not because it is perceived as missing—as in the case of fetishism—but because it does not belong to the visible.
> Victor Burgin, In/Different Spaces: Place and Memory in Visual Culture (1996)

When I am driving doing mobile fieldwork, my eyes are peeled—on the lookout for anything resembling a cross. Some scream out to be noticed even at highway speeds.

Others blend into their surroundings, easily overlooked among other, more institutional road signs (Figs. 3 and 4).

I find a lot, but I know from recursive traveling that I miss a lot as well (and see ones once that I cannot find later). I also get a little jumpy about it: often mistaking fire hydrants for crosses, for instance. When you are looking for something, you find it—and you find other things that you can't recognize at all because your head is spinning with one command: "find the shrine."

It's an odd space to inhabit. Part of you hopes that you will see no sites at all, that no one else has died, that everything is going to be OK for just a moment or a mile longer. Part of you hopes there are more—for "research purposes." And unfortunately, on the roads of Northern New Mexico, there are lots of opportunities to feel the conflict in your gut.

■ ■ ■

The first few times I stopped at memorials, I felt horribly self-conscious, almost shameful. If you have ever stopped at a stranger's memorial, you know what I mean. If you haven't, I hope some day you will. You feel as though you have been suddenly transported into a stranger's bedroom, and there are people watching you look through other people's stuff (Fig. 5).

There I am on the side of the road looking at, photographing, and sometimes touching the intimately symbolic objects of a person's life, and I don't know who they are or how they lived or how they died (Fig. 6).

And yet, these are not bedrooms—or even living rooms—but spaces on the side of the road visible to all who drive by (Fig. 7).

Fig. 2

Fig. 3

Fig. 4

Fig. 5

Fig. 6

Fig. 7

Whatever else we might see communicated by the memorials, one thing rings through clearly: that the people who attach crosses and flowers to fences and trees and guardrails and build grottoes and shrines along the right of way think that they have the right to do so—think that there is room for them (or at least should be room for them) in public space (Figs. 8 and 9).

The memorials say, "I want to carve out a space in the landscape, and thus the culture." As folklorist Alberto Barrera says, "roadside crosses are a way of saying to the departed loved one, 'I will remember you always, but I also want for the community to remember you as they come face-to-face with the cross on the roadside.'"

This is particularly the case in New Mexico. In some states—Texas, for instance—it is illegal to construct and maintain a roadside memorial, but in New Mexico the state has embraced the practice, using it in billboards and other official public media DWI messages. There is even a descanso at the edge of the parking lot at the State Police headquarters in Taos (Fig. 10).

Even here, though, the state has followed other states in offering an official DOT roadsign to memorialize drunk driving victims (Fig. 11).

The personal sites mark space in a different way, creating a space for private grief to be memorialized in an already circumscribed public landscape, but what do they "say" to those who drive by? What actually is there at the site and what/how does it communicate and to whom? There are so many things there at some of the sites that it is overwhelming. Are the sites themselves so "multiplicitous" that they are rendered mute? Or is it that they are so personal that they are illegible to those of us "outside the code"? You know the objects are meaningful to someone, but what do they mean to you the visitor? These are texts open to public consumption, but not necessarily constructed for it. The content of the message—especially the story of how the person died—is an absent presence, sometimes simply an absence (Fig. 12).

On the other hand, when you find yourself face-to-face with a cross emblazoned with silk flowers spelling the word "MOM," you can't help but notice the subjectivity of it: it pulls you in and pushes you away at the same time, saying, "This looks familiar and intimate, but it really isn't (Fig. 13)." This is no objective statement about a person with a name you and I could say and be talking about the same person. This is no historical marker put up by the state to tell public history. This is constructed by someone who is radically situated and located—a person who defines themselves in relation to the person who has died. This is the place where someone's Mom died.

And yet, the flower arrangements themselves are standardized. Any person with a mom can go into the store and see the exact same Mom arrangement and think it will provide a fitting tribute to their own Mom.

And that is exactly where my mind is now on the side of the road, where I see the distinction between the two main functions of the memorials—to remember and to caution—collapse. As much as I know my own mom is alive and well, I see the Mom cross and see it as my own mom. Or I see it as a memorial my daughter Anika and I might put up for Danielle if she were to die on the road.

And this last association is not at all random. You see, I am not alone on this fieldwork trip. Except for a day and a half while we are based in Santa Fe—when I am out working and they are playing in town—Danielle and Anika are right there with me the whole time, a barely absent presence always at least metaphorically and sometimes literally at the edge of the frame of my photographs (Fig. 14).

Fig. 8

Fig. 9

Fig. 10

Fig. 11

Fig. 12

Fig. 13

Fig. 14

CHAPTER 3 • Reading and Writing about Public and Private Space

Fig. 15

Fig. 16

Mobile fieldwork is always intense and surreal, but it is particularly surreal while you are also doing a family vacation with a two-year-old: Each site we see generates an instant cost-benefit analysis based on a quick glance at the memorial: what impact would stopping have on everyone else? Is it too soon for another stop? Is everyone maxed out on memorials for a while? Is this site really worth a stop?

When we are moving, we trade off driving and playing with Anika in the backseat. When Danielle is driving, I am in the backseat playing with Anika. I hate to admit that it takes me a while to learn to trust Danielle to see memorials and tell me about them.

When we stop, we say something like, "Anika, Daddy is going to stop to take some pictures." And Anika responds, "CHEESE!"

When I am driving and Anika is napping, Danielle is usually reading, creating a space for herself within the car, enjoying the moment of silence between bursts of toddler energy. I am doing something similar. I try to make mental notes of milemarkers in case we reach critical mass and the conditions are right for turning around at the end of the nap. Mostly I just talk to myself about letting go, or about what I've gained instead.

The car looks a little like our back room at home, and so do our activities: Living out of our car, dwelling in motion, we have taken our home on the road and made a home on the road. Distinctions between what we are researching and what we are playing and what we are thinking and what we are saying and what we are dreaming—they all bleed together.

Danielle and I have begun to call the trip "Winnie the Pooh and Descansos Too."

■ ■ ■

Anika is awake after a rare long nap.
"I thought you had him."
"I did, until Anika fell asleep."
"Oh, shit."
Winnie the Pooh is missing.

We finally figure out that we left him at a place fifty miles on the other side of Taos from where we are now. Driving the route again, I notice a memorial I missed the other two times I drove by that day. When I see it, I forget about my frustration with Pooh and am yet again happy that Anika is with me. It is about fifty yards up the road from a massive three-cross site I had stopped to photograph (Figs. 15 and 16).

The site I missed is unique, though: instead of crosses, this one features a Star of David. The wood on the Star is weathered and gray, which makes it blend into its surroundings. But this is only one reason I missed it. I was so busy looking for roadside crosses that I looked right past it—not just once but twice. What else have I not seen? What else do I not understand?

■ ■ ■

"In the Blink of an Eye"

Performance, for me, functions as an episteme, a way of knowing, not simply an object of analysis.
Diana Taylor, The Archive and the Repertoire: Performing Cultural Memory in the Americas (*2003*).

Back at home, I continually watch the paper for new deathsites to contemplate and photograph. In October, as I am finishing my paper for ASA, two separate groups of high school students in small towns south of Austin are involved in car crashes seven days apart. In the first, five kids die near Lockhart as the driver of the car overcorrects while steering around an Igloo Cooler sitting in the middle of the highway. In the second, a car plows into a high school cross-country team kneeling and praying on the roadside before their regular Saturday morning run. One runner is killed. Both stories run on the front page of the Austin paper. The second runs just above a story about how a disproportionate number of troops dying in Iraq are from small towns.

As with the space of fieldwork, here also I feel torn between the pain of imagining the actual losses for the families pictured in the paper and the excitement that I will have another site to explore. It's getting ghoulish, really.

The paper quotes Dale Guzman, one of the cross-country team members who was injured:

Guzman said he feels lucky to be alive, though sad that one of his teammates didn't survive. "He was one of our better runners and he was a good friend. I remember yesterday being in class with him . . . and the next day, in the blink of an eye, he's gone," he said.

In the blink of an eye. It seems an apt metaphor: Car crashes are so sudden that the victims and those who grieve the victims don't have time to process them. My guess is that no one who dies accidentally—not even a drunk driver—thinks it is going to happen to them until it is too late. Maybe that's why people construct roadside memorials: for those left to live and live with the story to have a place to physically embody their grief over time. But why on the roadside, and not in the home, or at the cemetery? Such a site could be (and often is) constructed in the homes of the survivors and at cemeteries, but the existence of ostensibly private memorials in public space shows that the people who made it want to remember publicly. A roadside memorial not only says "I remember you, and I will remember you," but also "I want the community to remember you."

■ ■ ■

A final moment . . .

I'm in New Mexico. I'm photographing another MOM site. This one is just a few miles from where we were camping for a couple of days, taking a break from the road. Part of the memorial is attached to the guardrail, and part is set just outside it (Fig. 17).

The cross carries the name, "Martha Martinez." The guardrail has a nasty dent in it. Is that from the crash?

I'm moving around the site when something catches my eye: a child's handprint in the concrete holding up the memorial. The handprint is surrounded by several names. I assume that they are her children, the people for whom "Mom" means "My Mom." I move closer, feeling compelled to place my hand near it—for scale and for connection (Fig. 18).

I glance back at the car, which is idling on the shoulder up the road at the next safest pullout spot. Anika is napping and Danielle is sitting in the backseat next to her. I had to slip out of the window of the driver's side door to avoid waking Anika up with a beeping door.

I frame a photograph with the cross and the car together. Would I want Danielle and Anika to put up a memorial if I died taking this picture? What would I hope it "said" about me? What would it look like? How would their site be related to the existing one in the same exact place? What if they were hit in our parked car and died while I was out of the car taking pictures? Would I create a memorial? How would I mark the space? What would it look like? Would I answer these questions differently if it happened closer to home, where I could visit more often? What if we all died?

Standing there on the side of the road, witnessing yet another deathsite, I see that these are not idle questions . . .

Fig. 17

Fig. 18

CHAPTER 3 • Reading and Writing about Public and Private Space

Why did you write this piece—what was the assignment or motivation for writing?

The piece here is based on a website I first developed to share my research on roadside shrines in 2004. It takes the central argument and narrative approach from the original conference paper—titled "Contested Sites of Violence and Belonging: Roadside Crosses in Contemporary Material and Visual Culture"—but focuses more on the process of doing the research than the research and analysis itself.

I began the "Making Space on the Side of the Road" project in January 2003, when I was working on a panel proposal for the American Studies Association conference later that year. I tell part of that story in the piece itself. I had been working with my colleague Renee Bergland on the theme of "Visuality and Violence" as an answer to the call for panels addressing the conference theme of "Violence and Belonging," and seized on roadside memorials as a cultural practice that was similar to my previous work on public uses of landscape and on media studies, but new enough to represent an exciting new direction for me.

As I look back on it now, I see that the project was indeed shaped a lot by its original historical moment. I think a lot of us were feeling that we needed a way to respond to the violence we all witnessed in the first few years of the decade—not only violence of September 11, but also the palpable violence throughout the country in the buildup to the invasion of Iraq in 2003. I wasn't fully conscious of it then, but my work on roadside shrines, which has since evolved into a much larger study of automobility, cultural memory, and trauma, was a way for me to make sense of the dispersed yet palpable everyday violence that runs throughout the contemporary U.S—and do so in a way that showed how I was implicated in it.

What did you do when you got the assignment?

This is part of the story I tell in the piece as well. The first thing I did when I came up with the idea to pursue the project was to search for other work done on roadside memorials. Searching on Amazon, I found only one scholarly book specifically on the topic; searching on EBSCO, I found only a few scholarly articles; searching on Google, I found thousands of links. Right then I decided that this would be the perfect project for me: what better project could there be for a scholar of popular cultural discourses than a prolific, diffused, and fascinating popular conversation as yet under-theorized and under-researched by academics . . .

How did you begin?

My first step was to do a lot of Internet research to scan the range of materials that mentioned roadside memorials. I printed most of the stuff out and put it in a file folder that in just a few months became a pile of file folders. As a photographer who had been developing a model of mobile fieldwork, I began planning my methodology for photographing a set of memorials I knew about in and around Austin, Texas, where I live. I read scholarly articles and the one scholarly book on the subject. Reading that book changed the direction of my project considerably: because I had originally seen this as a small side project,

I had planned to stay close to Austin in doing my fieldwork, but as soon as I saw that the book I read was also based entirely on memorials and memorial builders in the Austin area, I applied for funding to do fieldwork in the other site I knew would be fruitful for my analysis, northern New Mexico. Therefore, while I did a lot of background work on the project and had to produce initial rationales and descriptions of the project as early as January of 2003, my work on the project really didn't start until May of 2003, after I had received notification of acceptance of the abstract of my paper for the ASA conference and I had received notification of my grant for research funds to pay for my fieldwork in New Mexico.

Describe the process of writing the first draft.

I began writing my first draft about a month before I needed to present the paper at the conference. I had been keeping field notes and taking photographs of shrines for several months by then, and my first step was to select the photographs I wanted to feature and then develop a way of organizing them into a set of key themes to analyze. As I did this, I noticed that I was sorting through not only pictures of shrines but also of a family vacation. While I was in New Mexico photographing shrines, my wife and young daughter accompanied me for most of the work. Something about having them there with me while I was photographing deathsites struck me as ironic and poignant at the same time. Before long, I decided to include that dimension of my experience of the project into the paper itself, but was confused about how to proceed. My scholarly writing up to that point had been focused on analyzing specific places, texts, and discourses, and while I had worked hard to find my own voice as a scholar, I had always written in an academic format. In the classroom, I had been teaching students how to write both scholarly analysis and nonfiction narrative, but in separate courses. When I began writing about my family's presence in the car beside me, I recognized that I needed to develop a form that would present a scholarly analysis of the memorials while not only making space for that story but also taking the form *of* a story. Once I got there, the writing went very quickly. Indeed, before long, I realized that the parallels between car crash memorials and my research into them were part of my argument: just as car crash memorials represent an interlacing of public and private spheres, so too did my research practice, which interlaced my private life as a father and husband into my public life as a scholar and writer.

Did you write a draft all the way through?

I generally write first and edit later; I also generally write in spurts, where I can be working on a draft a little a day for a while and then get a blast of energy around a new conceptualization of my work that usually keeps me working through the night as I follow out an idea. With this piece and almost everything else I have written, the last week before it was due for presentation, I worked on it every chance I got, sleeping very little and setting other commitments aside so that I could focus my full attention on bringing coherence to the work.

How much editing did you do as you wrote?

I can't help myself from editing as I write (I even did it when I was writing this sentence!), but I generally try to write out my ideas before I edit them. That usually means that I end up with a lot more writing in early drafts than I end up using in a final draft. For this piece,

I wrote nearly 50 pages of field notes before I ever tried to write the essay, and then produced a first draft that was 30 pages long for a 10-page assignment.

Did you do research as you wrote or before you started writing? What databases did you use?

With this particular piece, I researched other people's work on roadside memorials before and after, but not during my writing process for the first few drafts. Usually, when I do scholarly writing, I sit down to write a first draft with a big stack of journal articles and books open in front of me and work my way through my ideas and others' ideas at the same time. With this piece, which only refers to other scholarly work generally and demanded more attention to building the narrative instead of critically engaging a critical conversation, I gave myself the challenge of not having anything in front of me while I wrote the first draft except my photographs and my fieldnotes. Therefore, I did most of my reading first, based on research I had done on Academic Search Premier on EBSCO, then sat down to write a full draft before looking out at other people's ideas to make sure I was telling the story as fully as possible.

How long would you say the process took?

I spent about a month writing my first full draft of this piece. I then shared it with my colleagues on the panel I was doing at ASA before continuing on to revise it for the final two weeks before I was due to present it. True to my regular writing/revision process, I was revising it up until the morning of my presentation, printing out my final copy about an hour before I was scheduled to present it.

How did you edit the draft?

My first draft was thirty pages long, but my presentation needed to be ten, so my first revisions were all about cutting. It was then that I solidified my commitment to the recursive and elliptical narrative structure I ended up using in the version here: seeing that I could not hope to tell the full story in ten pages, I chose to emphasize both the most vivid scenes and call attention to the gaps between them as a way of suggesting that there was more I could say if I had the time and space.

I began drafting this piece as a set of separate scenes, trying not to decide how they would be sequenced. I don't do detailed outlines. The closest I get to an outline is when I write out the names of sections of the paper in an order, but something like this is hardly more than 5 or 6 lines long. Instead, I name my separate sections and write each name on a note card so I can physically move the cards around as I imaginatively visualize the sequence of the paper. You can see the residue of that approach in the final draft in the form of subheadings. For example, as soon as I had my first relatively full draft of the piece included here, I wrote down subheadings on 3 × 5 note cards and spread them out on the floor, arranging and re-arranging the sequence until the trajectory felt right. Ordinarily, once I set up a basic pathway like that, I set the cards aside and only bring them back out if I cannot work my way through re-sequencing within the word-processing screen environment or printed drafts of the overall document.

What was the response when you turned in your essay?

When I read my essay at the conference, I was blown away by the extensive and energetic response of the audience. In the Q & A at the end of the panel, audience members responded to my photographs, my argument, and my narrative form, making connections to my topic that showed that they were personally affected by my work in addition to seeing its value as a scholarly argument. Their response confirmed for me not only that the topic was interesting to other people but that my way of writing about it was as well. Based on the audience's response that day, I decided to extend my work on roadside memorials even further, first developing it into the essay printed here, which has been posted online since 2004 and generated hundreds of responses from readers, and finally transforming that one essay into the beginning of a larger book project that has culminated in my current book project, *Road Scars: Trauma, Memory, and Automobility.*

Are you satisfied now with what you wrote? Would you make any changes?

I still like this piece a lot. I like its sense of integrity about the challenge of using narrative to show a scholarly argument about the connection between home and work and between researcher and researched in the context of a study of expressions of private grief in public landscapes. Reading the essay again six years later, I am amazed at how many of the ideas that I have now developed much more widely and deeply in the rest of the book I am writing on roadside shrines are there in condensed form in "Making Space." Indeed, that is the thing I value most about the piece: that it manages to show and tell a lot with very few words. I like the interplay of words and pictures as they both lead the reader through the story, and I like that the piece works with a strong range of ideas while always staying true to its narrative form. The problem of the piece is that while it can contain all sorts of different scenes and story elements, it cannot easily contain sustained analysis without bending the narrative backwards, which is why in later work I have re-worked it pretty extensively as I have incorporated it into my book manuscript. Still, I have kept this particular version in circulation. I periodically change a few words here and there when I look at the online version of the essay, but overall I think it does a good job at what it sets out to do.

READING WRITING

This Text: Reading

1. How much of this is storytelling and how much of it is analysis? Does it work?
2. Why do you think Bednar tells the reader how he feels when doing his work?
3. What other type of documentation might bring on the same mixed feelings that Bednar shares?

Your Text: Writing

1. Take some photographs, but as you are doing so, document what you are thinking about while you take them. Write about this experience.
2. Write a paper comparing this essay to one of the essays in the first chapter.
3. Write a paper researching the public displays of mourning. Where does Bednar's essay fit in this tradition?

The College Campus Suite

If you are a full-time student, a college campus is probably the place where you spend most of your time—especially if you live on campus. But even if you reside in a house or an apartment off-campus, you still probably spend more time on a college campus than in any other public space. The essays in this chapter each consider a college campus as a constructed text that can (and should) be read as a text.

Campuses are odd places, particularly college campuses. They often try to feel both natural and intellectual at the same time. Many campuses spend hundreds and thousands of dollars on landscaping, signage, and design. And, to be sure, a *genre* of campuses has emerged. Many have a mall—a large open grassy place at the center of the campus—or a quad. Most feature sculptures and perhaps a clock tower. If your campus is linked to a specific religious denomination it might even have a church located right on campus. You expect to see trees, maybe a fountain, places for students to gather. These details are not random. They connote sophistication and try to facilitate interaction.

But with the advent of distance learning and for-profit colleges like the University of Phoenix, campuses are playing a less vital role (at least for some institutions) in the learning process. The Academy of Art University in San Francisco, for instance, has 17 buildings across various parts of the city with no main campus whatsoever. Yet, for more traditional undergraduate colleges and universities, campuses remain a vital part of institutional identity. Consider, for example, how many university logos feature a signature building. Utah State, Palm Beach Atlantic University, Acorn State, Georgia College and State University, Belhaven University, Temple University, and Southeastern Oklahoma State University are just a few examples that include buildings in their official university logo or seal (you can see these all online). So, the built environment of a college can have an indirect effect on the learning environment.

This suite is comprised of three written essays and one visual essay, all of which explore how a college campus can suggest something beyond mere "education." In his reading of three San Francisco campuses, Dean Rader, a co-author of this book, argues that decisions about campus signage can reveal a college's priorities. Frances Halsband has worked on and in campuses for many years—as part of the New York architectural firm R. M. Kliment & Frances Halsband, as a professor at various universities, and as a former dean at Pratt Institute. Her firm has designed or renovated buildings as well as completed master plans on a number of campuses including Arcadia University, Brown University, Columbia University, Dartmouth College, New York University, Princeton University, Smith College, and Yale University. Here, Halsband examines the increasingly complex text that is the modern college campus. For a student's reaction to campus design and the learning environment, we have included Matthew King's essay "Reading the Nautical Star" that he wrote for his English 101 course when he was a student at Virginia Commonwealth University. In this fine piece, King offers a semiotic reading of a major piece of public art at VCU—the Nautical Star. In addition to these written pieces, we are also happy to include an entirely new visual essay. Compiled by the authors of this book and colleagues from various universities, these photographs of college campuses from around the world offer unique perspectives on what other campuses look like and how they use space and semiotics.

Reading and Writing about Your Campus

Dean Rader

INSTITUTIONS OF HIGHER LEARNING INVEST A GREAT DEAL IN THEIR IMAGE. Like companies and corporations, colleges maintain a profound interest in branding and market recognition. To be sure, "Harvard," is a kind of brand, as is "University of Florida," but for different reasons and to different demographics. How institutions of higher learning brand themselves—how they create identity—varies, of course, but one of the most important sources of college image-building is its campus. It is rare to hear of a potential employee turning down a job at Google or GM because she found the buildings ugly, but how often do we hear students talk about the role a campus played in their decision about where to apply and attend college? Have you ever seen a college admissions brochure that did not feature its most attractive lawns and buildings?

Campus aesthetics are not confined to current and prospective students. Administrators obsess about their physical plant because its main components like fountains, lawns, buildings, sculptures, statues, foliage (think: ivy), and signs all send messages about the institution. For example, why are so many buildings on campuses modeled on Greek and Roman structures? An initial response might be: Because Greek and Roman buildings look "important" or "imposing" or "learned" or "fancy" or "classical." But, then, the next step is to inquire into why a college might want to embody any of these ideals. What messages do columns, spires, fountains, gardens, gates, and walls send? How are these connected to the liberating power of education? Would a campus send a different message if its buildings resembled a Western mining town from the 1800s? Would Duke or Stanford have the reputations they do if their classes were held in strip malls? Most major universities and many small colleges in the United States feel a lot like parks or museums, but it is worth asking why that might be. What purpose does green space serve on a campus? Why have lawns and fields? Why not construct as many tall buildings as possible? Why plant flowers? Why not build more labs?

One answer might be that campuses want to feel inviting both to students and to the surrounding community. However, for better or worse, colleges in the United States have not always been the most welcoming places; in fact, for many years, many older, private institutions cultivated a reputation based on exclusion—how difficult it was to be admitted or how rigorous its classes were. With the rise of public universities and the community college system, college has become more accessible; accordingly, campus architecture and design have taken on a more welcoming posture. In fact, how a campus fronts the public—how it *welcomes*—can often say quite a bit about how a college wants to be seen. Consider campus signage. Signs on campus may seem utterly insignificant, but, in truth, they reveal a great deal—even among campuses just a few miles from each other. The University of San Francisco (USF), The City College of San Francisco (CCSF), and San Francisco State University (SFSU) are all first-rate institutions in the same city, yet their signs and points of campus entry differ dramatically. In the case of these colleges, region has less to do with their signage than institutional history, mission, and audience, all of which get encoded in their signage.

San Francisco State University is the only four-year public university in the city of San Francisco, and it enjoys a rich history of quality education, ethnic diversity, and open, progressive policies. The campus is located in the southwest part of the city, next door to one of the more popular shopping malls in the area. Although the neighborhood is largely

Fig. 1 A view of SFSU along 19th Avenue and its coffee and food kiosks.

residential and almost suburban, the campus fronts a major north–south artery in San Francisco and a major train route on the San Francisco Municipal Transportation line, situating the university at a crossroads of train, car, and foot traffic. The main access to the university (Fig. 1) is notable for its lack of pretense.

The modern sign, a basic gray monolith, blends in well with the clean modern lines of the building behind it to the left. Both the sign and the building are free of flourish and are almost understated in their muted colors, rectangular shapes, and unobtrusive design.

Notice how the sign refrains from boasting a date, a motto, or a mascot. To the right of the sign is an open sidewalk that runs along 19th Avenue, a busy street. You can see both cars and the train within a few feet of the campus entrance. At many institutions, one would expect a large wall or imposing shrubbery delineating the campus from the fray of the street, but at SFSU, no such barrier exists. In fact, Figure 2 reveals the openness of this part of campus. If you look closely to the right of the sign, you can make out the square umbrella-like tops of coffee and food kiosks. Here, the campus opens on to the sidewalk, the street, and the train stop, creating a sort of commons that is in concert with the university's image of an open, accessible, *public* university.

This sign seems consonant with SFSU's mission. Because San Francisco State enjoys a large enrollment of around 25,000 students of all ages and ethnicities, it's important that the institution send a message through its design that the campus is open, friendly, easily accessible, and familiar. The City College of San Francisco, one of the premiere community college systems in the country, makes similar arguments through its campus plan. Like San Francisco State, CCSF is a public institution, whose students are likely drawn to it not simply because of its quality but also because of its affordability and convenience (in fact, CCSF has eleven different sites around San Francisco). Its main campus, also in the southern part of the city, features a number of elements that stand as metaphors for the college's mission. Like State, City College's signs (Figs. 3 and 4) at its main campus are functional and free of pompous gesture. The

Fig. 2 The main access, San Francisco State University.

Fig. 3 Sign at the front entrance of the main campus of the City College of San Francisco.

Fig. 4 Signs fronting the main parking area at CCSF.

scrolling LED sign serves a practical purpose by disseminating valuable information to busy students, all of whom live off campus. This sign, like the ones in Figure 4, are helpful without being intimidating. In fact, that the second sign might resemble those found at many high schools may make students who are insecure about college feel like CCSF is a less scary transition. In addition, for the many commuting students at CCSF who also hold jobs and have families, easy parking is more important than stone walls or flower beds, so this aspect of the campus's physical plant sends the important message that the college meets student needs.

Like those at San Francisco State, the signage and entry points encourage the public to the campus. As you can see in Figure 5, the campus features an easy ingress from the street to the stairs leading to the main building. Although it is not an official sign, the small sculpture of the woman with open arms, as if welcoming visitors, accentuates the campus's many inviting indicators. The main building at the University of San Francisco, a private university at the Northeast corner of Golden Gate Park, is also at the top of a hill, with stairs leading up to it, but, as you will see, USF's campus planners made different decisions about how the hill and the stairs should be adorned.

Students (or their parents) who are willing to pay more than $30,000 dollars per year for a private college education likely expect more in terms of campus design than students who opt to attend a state-funded institution. The University of San Francisco, my home institution, has won awards for urban campus design

Fig. 5 Stairway and sculpture in front of the main building at CCSF.

and beauty, and it is a stunning place, especially from atop Lone Mountain, but some aspects of USF's campus design may reveal more about its past ambitions than its present vision. Like SFSU and CCSF, USF has many points of entry, but the main sites of ingress run along Golden Gate Street, separating "lower campus" from the gate, walls, and stairs that lead to "upper campus" (Figs. 6 and 7). The upper campus, or Lone Mountain campus, used to be a Catholic women's college, which may explain the design choices here—gates, walls, and stairs constructed to keep nice girls in and bad boys out. But, these choices serve other purposes. Consider all the architectural elements at work in the grand entrance to Lone Mountain. There are the Italian- and Spanish-influenced stairs (which, perhaps not coincidentally, resemble a goblet). Then, one notices the sculpted archways and the fountain (difficult to see in the photograph, but just below the opening in the arch, a stream of water pours out of the mouth of a lion). Beyond all this, the stately palm trees seem to frame the arch, and behind them, the faint outline of a cross. Every detail here is intentional, from the finely wrought light on the column, to the decision to display the institution's founding date (1855), to the font of the school name. The totality of these elements sends a clear message: This place is palatial, this place is imposing, this place is fancy, this is a place to be taken seriously. Interestingly, USF makes its sign part of the architecture of the space, advancing the argument that USF's education is as impressive as its design.

Fig. 6 The University of San Francisco's entrance to its Lone Mountain Campus off of Golden Gate Street.

THE COLLEGE CAMPUS SUITE

Fig. 7 USF's shrubbery sign on the Lone Mountain hill. Note the shrubbery wall on the far right of the photo.

However, USF, a Jesuit university, also advances an overt mission of civic engagement and social justice, so one might argue that despite its beauty, the intimidating stairs, the walls, the columns, and the gates (that suggest separation) are at odds with key components of USF's identity as an institution of justice, engagement, and inclusion.

There is much more one could say about these signs. You can see here that even so humble an object as a sign can reveal a great deal about a university. It would be easy to devote an entire essay to decoding the semiotics of the USF stairway or the bustling, open point of entry at San Francisco State. Similar work could be done either comparatively or individually on many aspects of these campuses —and your campus too. To that end, you might ask big questions like, what are the connections between architecture, public space, and human need? Or, why doesn't my institution devote some of the money it spends on flowers, gardens, and trees to scholarships? If you don't know the answer to these questions, it may be best to start smaller. Begin with a semiotic reading of your campus and pay attention to the symbols, cues, and icons you see every day. Why do all of the buildings on my campus look alike (or different)? Does my campus combine architecture, plants, and signage to create a specific image? If so, what is it?

Without question, your campus is a rich text. Learning to look at that text through a semiotic lens enables you to see your campus and your education with a renewed interest and an informed clarity those admissions brochures can never replicate.

Campuses in Place

Frances Halsband

Websites, View Books, and finally, campus visits.

Lost downtown.

No place to park.

"Mom, Dad, this is The Place. This is where I
want to be."

THE BEST UNIVERSITY CAMPUSES are places that
have been carefully designed over decades, even centuries. They are places that speak
to us of continuing care, thoughtful decision-making, reverence for tradition and ritual, and a harmony of nature, landscape, and architectural design. They are places that
invite us to participate in the thoughtful creation of our communal environment.
They are familiar, inviting, alluring, mysterious. Richard Brodhead has defined the
university as home: "a defensive structure," and a "world of belongingness thrown up
against a larger world of exposure and strangeness"—but also, essentially and fundamentally, a "terra incognita," a place of "disorientation, defamiliarization."[1] Walking
through the gates, we walk into the world of our future.

These qualities raise important questions for designers of new campus buildings and
open spaces. Many American university campuses began on open land outside developed
areas, but our cities have now grown to envelop them, complicating the distinction
between "town" and "gown." Today, many American universities are called upon to be
simultaneously inward-focused learning communities and outward-oriented providers of
service and amenity. Embedded in urban settings, their greens may be, in some sense,
public parks; their libraries, theaters and athletic facilities invite outsiders; and students
and nonstudents mingle in adjacent residential neighborhoods and commercial streets—
spaces whose rhythms are defined by the campus calendar, but which are fully open to the
outside world.

Many of the most difficult issues faced by universities are apparent at their perceived
edges. It is here that the characteristic tension between the university's desire to be both
included and separated from the larger *polis* becomes most apparent. On campus, pressure
to increase the density and scale of buildings often threatens the very qualities of space and
social interaction which make campuses memorable. But when universities try to push
outward, surrounding neighborhoods are likely to push back—and often with good reason, since these neighborhoods themselves have evolved into historic districts, with their
own memorable and distinctive qualities of space and architecture. As a result, campus
edges are frequently flashpoints of bitter controversy.

Faced with such strong opposition to external growth, university planners have recently
begun to look for new ways to coexist. One consequence is that the original design paradigm of academic life around a campus green, so carefully considered and nurtured
through the last century, is everywhere giving way to new informal places which hide their
academic roots. Starbucks is now at the center—and at the edge. Off-campus housing is the
new solution to on-campus life. Remotely located biotechnology laboratories are the new
norm.

Are these new university spaces "campuses"? Or are they something else entirely?
Have we lost the clarity of the original idea of "collegial" life to a blurring of domains; or

---

[1]Richard H. Brodhead. *The Good of This Place: Values and Challenges in College Education* (New Haven,
CT: Yale University Press, 2004), pp. 3–4, 53–54.

are dynamic new typologies of mixed-use places for research and learning emerging? Will the next generation of children get out of the car in the middle of this new melange of university and city and announce *"Mom, Dad, this is The Place. This is where I want to be!"*

An American Ideal

In the United States, the early twentieth century was a period of intense focus on campus design. The Olmsted Brothers, Warren Powers Laird, Paul Cret, Ralph Adams Cram, Frank Day, Charles Klauder, and others provided campus plans for numerous universities. These places continue to serve as cultural paradigms. Early Olmsted plans showed individual buildings gathered around green lawns with curving boundaries and paths. Typical were the oval lawns of Smith College, shaded with (now) enormous trees, ringed with energetically Victorian buildings, and affording tantalizing glimpses of Paradise Pond. Later designs by Laird, Cret and Klauder kept the sanctity of campus greens, but interpreted them as formal rectangles, bounded by connected ranges of buildings, "where one building serve[d] to enhance, because of proximity, the value of another."[2]

The shape and style of these places was not merely scenographic. Woodrow Wilson, president of Princeton from 1902 to 1910, envisioned a collegiate system of educating the whole man, in and out of the classroom. To him, the college experience required "a certain seclusion of mind preceding the struggle of life, a certain period of withdrawal and abstraction." He described Princeton as "this little world, this little state, this little commonwealth of our own."[3]

Wilson himself sketched a physical reconstruction of the Princeton campus which joined the buildings into quadrangles, or separate colleges, such as he had seen at Oxford and Cambridge. Wilson's Quad Plan was realized in Klauder's romantic design for dormitories that recalled Gothic precedents. The success of such plans at Princeton later influenced Cret, Day, and James Gamble Rogers to make drawings of the Gothic quads which would become the signature elements of Yale in the 1920s.

But the idea of designing a series of quads to define an inner campus space was also not limited to Oxbridge styles. Klauder designed infill buildings at Brown University based on its colonial precedents. He also invented a Tuscan Country style to frame the quads of the rapidly growing Boulder campus of the University of Colorado. These campuses have since been admired, copied, and identified as special places.

Qualities of Space and Building

As Barbara Stanton explains in this issue, the essential ingredients of campus are greensward and trees, in a ratio favoring green over buildings. But a campus is also a place that expresses a complex mix of privacy and public purpose. The territories of many older campuses are today defined by iron fences and gates—though the gates are always open and the spaces inside welcome outside participation and use.

Campus landscapes are also furnished with signs, maps and information kiosks; artwork and commemorative plaques (free of commercial advertising) reward visitors' attention; and

---

[2]Charles Z. Klauder and Herbert C. Wise. *College Architecture in America* (New York: Charles Scribner's Sons, 1920), p 40.

[3]August Heckscher. *Woodrow Wilson: A Biography* (New York: Charles Scribner's Sons, 1991), pp. 145–53.

amenities such as benches, night lighting, and bicycle racks make them safe, convenient, and pleasant to use. Some of the great university campuses also include broad flights of steps which still invite us to sit and watch the passing scene.

In addition, the elimination of much vehicle traffic on campuses creates an oasis of safety and quiet. With fewer cars, there is no need for wide road beds, harsh street lights, or clearly defined sidewalks. A simple lane, wide enough for a fire truck, edged with granite, speaks of a great freedom of pedestrian activities—walking, meandering, contemplating, even sitting down. It is no wonder that rituals such as "chalking the walk" have become much loved traditions in such settings.

Memorable university campuses may also be distinguished by a prevailing architectural style. However, uniformity is less an end in itself than a means to provide the sense of continuity, background and identity against which distinctive individual buildings may stand out. In design terms it is a question of establishing a "ground" against which a "figure" may become visible. An identifiable building style may also inspire a sense of belonging. Thus one may think of Princeton and Duke as Gothic, Harvard as Georgian, and University of Virginia as Classical—even when closer inspection reveals far more diversity among individual buildings.

The sense of a planned building ensemble is clearly important to the sense of a campus. Even on campuses where relatively little effort is made to arrive at a uniformity of style, a sense of appropriate scale still emerges. Often in such cases the landscape is made to do the principal work of tying the whole together. Thus, the intense green leafy canopy of Amherst College unites two hundred years of building design; the University of Oregon is distinguished by a finely woven tapestry of tiny inhabited spaces; and, the bold new master plan for the University of Cincinnati creates a unified setting for a variety of contemporary buildings.

Still other campuses, such at that of Brown University, find their identity as places with deliberately contrasting styles. Brown's buildings are diverse, quirky, often brilliant, always individualistic—all qualities that embody the character of the place. At Brown one has to ask which came first, the diversity of thought characteristic of its intellectual atmosphere, or the diversity of its buildings?

While campuses are distinctive as ensembles, their best individual buildings also proclaim a certain public orientation. Signs tell you their names and what you may expect to find inside. Grand front doors welcome entry. Public buildings are located in many other places in our cities, but rarely do we find the same quality of invitation.

Qualities of Campus Life

In the city, informal interaction is rare, sometimes dangerous, and requires extraordinary circumstances. But on a campus a sense of containment and common purpose, the coordination of schedules, and the existence of shared spaces for dining and living increase everyone's chances of encountering others with common interests, goals and desires. Add to this the social vitality of young adults, and one can see how a high level of informal interaction is typical of campus environments. On campuses there are people moving about at all times of the day and night: outdoor furnishings will be used.

Creativity blossoms in such free-flowing nonhierarchical environments, and college leaders have long defined their mission as going beyond mere classroom learning. The founders of Pembroke College sought to create "a new academic atmosphere with that inner quietness which only spacious and dignified surroundings permit."[4] Likewise, the trustees of Brown in 1925 recognized that even dormitory rooms were integral to the college experience: "A student's room is not only an effect, but a cause of his character, and a worthy and dignified environment is felt at once in the student's intellectual and moral life."[5]

Well-designed outdoor spaces, and plenty of them; in-door spaces like libraries and student centers; numerous and diverse places where people feel welcome: these are all ultimately essential settings for the nurture of informed citizens.

Campuses Today

Many of the qualities described above have characterized American campuses for more than two hundred years. But the campus of the twenty-first century is also a very different place than it was fifty, or even fifteen, years ago.

As noted earlier, the most obvious change has to do with physical growth. Maps of Brown clearly illustrate this exponential increase of size. Such growth reflects the reality of increasing numbers of students, faculty and staff. Students need classrooms and places to live; professors need offices and laboratories; and library collections will continue to expand and require more space.

Along with growth in the number of buildings has come an increasing differentiation and specialization of building types. Yesterday's multipurpose gym has given way to today's indoor track, basketball and hockey arena, fitness center, swim center, and squash courts. Laboratory space has become similarly specialized. And to support the growing number of employees and students living off campus, parking garages are now needed, despite the best efforts at demand management.

The size and scale of individual buildings also continues to increase. The footprint of a research laboratory is now about 60,000 sq. ft., and a width of 130 ft. is deemed desirable. Such a behemoth will not fit easily on a carefully crafted historic campus. If located in an existing neighborhood, its associated impacts, including increased traffic congestion, will often be fiercely resisted by nearby residents.

As the old campus becomes a revered historic artifact—a "garden of delights" in which to enact historic rituals—it also becomes, ironically, less amenable to changes that might keep it vital in everyday use. Campus design guidelines, historic designations, tradition, nostalgia, and the force of alumni sentiment all combine to limit needed flexibility and change. Yet simultaneously, the desire to constantly reinvent and regenerate the institution requires expression in new forms, new styles, creating a parallel demand for associated places where new things are welcome.

Of course, there are very few, if any, old campuses which are so perfect that they cannot tolerate positive change. Architecture magazines and websites show infill projects of subtlety and charm: new buildings, additions, and renovations which transform worthy old containers into exciting spaces for new programs. Indeed, the opportunity to work in a context rich with association, with a client group willing to take intellectual risks, makes campus commissions among the most highly desired by architects. Similarly, the best current campus plans manage to identify new building sites and

---

[4]From *Bulletin of Brown University. Report of the President to the Corporation.* Vol. IV, No. 4 (October 1907), p. 31.

[5]From *Bulletin of Brown University. Report of the President to the Corporation.* Vol. 1, No. 4 (October 1904), p. 9.

THE COLLEGE CAMPUS SUITE

craft design guidelines for them that reflect awareness of both contemporary and historical values.

A Question of Boundaries

Even so, the reality is that as universities face pressures for growth they have been trying to expand beyond their traditional edges. Examined collectively, such efforts seem to indicate that different types of campuses exhibit different potentials for development. In particular, some edges seem to invite incremental expansion, while others seem to demand a more radical leapfrogging to distant sites.

Campuses with clearly defined edges are more likely to expand by taking the form of the adjacent city. These extensions are likely to be commercial in character and made up of large-scale buildings which hug the street line. In such buildings, public uses are allowed to occupy the ground floor, and little attempt is made to continue patterns of associated open space or landscaping that might tie them to older campus traditions. Their style may express an overt rejection of historical campus precedents (even if the real choice was dictated by the necessity of making peace with the neighbors).

Designing new campus buildings to look like a part of the adjacent city, and including services, commercial and office space in them, are clearly strategies of camouflage and disguise. To appeal further to residents of surrounding communities, such "stealth" expansion may even involve inviting private developers to construct the buildings. Thus commercial housing developers are increasingly being called on to build and operate university housing, and Barnes & Noble may now be the university bookstore of choice.

Following this paradigm, Columbia's new student dormitory on Broadway includes a public library and a video store on the ground floor. Access to these spaces is from Broadway, while the students must enter their residence from a side street. In this case, the local community board indicated that its approval of the project was contingent on it being clad in Upper West Side yellow brick, not Columbia red brick.

The story of Ohio State's High Street development, described in this issue by David Dixon, shows the lengths to which campus planners have gone to address community concerns.

> Here is the key to the whole matter: The object of the college, as we have known and used and loved it in America, is not scholarship (except for the few, and for them only by way of introduction and first orientation), but the intellectual and spiritual life. What we should seek to impart in our college, therefore, is not so much learning itself as the spirit of learning. This spirit, however, they cannot get from the classroom unless the spirit of the classroom is the spirit of the place as well, and of its life, and that will never be until the teacher comes out of the class-room and makes himself a part of that life. Contact, companionship, familiar intercourse, is the law of life for the mind. The comradeships of undergraduates will never breed the spirit of learning. The circle must be widened. It must include the older men, the teachers, the men for whom life has grown more serious and to whom it has revealed more its meanings. So long as what the undergraduates do and what they are taught occupy two separate, air tight compartments in their consciousness, so long will the college be ineffectual.
>
> **—Woodrow Wilson**
>
> 1905 Phi Beta Kappa oration at Harvard University[6]

[6]As reported by President Faunce of Brown in the *Bulletin of Brown University. Report of the President to the Corporation.* Vol. II, No. 4 (October 1905), pp. 21–23.

Fuzzy vs. Hard Boundaries

Criteria for expansion are not as clear-cut at campuses whose edges are less well defined. Here opportunities may exist for expansion following a more gentle continuum, easing the tensions of the visible and fixed boundary, and paving the way for closer interconnection and interaction between town and gown.

Brown is one such place with fuzzier boundaries. Shared streets have provided an opportunity for limited expansion of its campus within the surrounding College Hill neighborhood. Such conditions have recently made it possible to plan for an extension of the campus walkway system to link the cores of the old Pembroke and Brown campuses across two city streets. The centerpiece of this plan is a new Walk, whose furnished green spaces are bounded by new academic buildings that open both internally to the greens and externally to neighboring streets. Among other things, the plan envisions retaining and reconfiguring significant historic buildings for new uses, while it also proposes moving one old house whose location conflicts with the new open areas to fill a gap elsewhere in the historic district.[7]

Another less obvious example of a university with fuzzy boundaries is New York University. Indeed, its edges are nearly impossible to identify. Over the years NYU has managed to expand largely by buying and renovating commercial loft buildings, transforming them into offices, classrooms, laboratories and housing, while maintaining commercial tenancies on the ground floor. While it has faced major battles in constructing new space, such gradual inhabitation of existing buildings continues without comment. In technical terms, New York zoning limits classroom uses to the area west of Broadway, but this boundary is visible only to university planners. On the street, the principal visual clue to the presence of NYU are the purple flags flown on all its buildings.

Moving Off Campus

In some cases, the edges of a university may ultimately prove immovable, and it may be essential to start anew in a distant place. This has long been the policy of the University of California, which has developed new campuses around the state rather than centralize its operations in a few locations. Today this process continues with the design and construction of a tenth UC campus in the town of Merced in the fast-urbanizing Central Valley. However, even in such situations, they point out, important questions surround the location and design of campus spaces, especially as they may be used to create new poles of growth or stabilize older patterns of development.

Smaller institutions can also employ a leapfrog strategy, especially when it comes to siting large new buildings. Brown is choosing to locate several large departments in buildings away from its existing campus on historic College Hill in areas of Providence dominated by abandoned manufacturing buildings and underutilized commercial properties. Eventually, it hopes to join the city in a broader redevelopment of one of these areas.

To maintain an identification with Brown, a new campus will need to have a physical connection through a clearly defined circulation infrastructure involving such elements as bicycle lanes, shuttle routes, and signage. The new satellite campus will also need many

---

[7]As cited in Robin Pogrebin, "A Man About Town, In Glass and Steel." *The New York Times*, Jan. 5, 2005, p. E1.

essential elements of the old campus: inviting furnished open spaces separated from traffic and surrounding commercial life, recognizable and permeable boundaries relevant to campus functions and the life of nearby communities, and buildings of public character and related scale.

Columbia University, long confined to an extremely hard-edged campus, is also planning a major expansion. Its new ensemble of buildings at Manhattanville will leapfrog geographic barriers and nearby neighborhoods and provide a link to their medical school campus further north. The redevelopment of Manhattanville is planned as a simultaneously urban and academic environment.

Literally and figuratively, this mixed-use precinct is being conceived as a "sandwich." It will be built on a "factory" of below-grade infrastructure and services provided by Columbia. But the three floors closest to street level will be devoted to public use. Above that, spaces will be occupied by university laboratories and other academic spaces. Renzo Piano has described this new effort as follows:

> The idea is not to make a citadel. One century ago, the only way to design a campus was monumental architecture, giving a sense of security. Today the university is in communication with life, so the story to tell today is completely different. It's more about permeability, more about participation. The model of the university today is more related to reality.[8]

Such a stratification of public urban space with academic space may well provide a new prototype for accommodating the variety of desires at the edges of the most urban university campuses. It allows local communities to maintain their identity, local governments to maintain the social fabric of the city, and deeply embedded urban universities to expand their facilities to compete with their peers.

The Future

There are some who would question the need for a "bricks and mortar" campus in our time. Stuart Strother recently described his experience teaching in a strip mall. Such "satellite campuses" offer the possibility for classes taught almost anywhere, books delivered by mail, and unlimited free parking. But he points out that students miss campus life, "the sidewalk culture of protest, music, art, free-love groups, and even hate groups that encourages students to think about life in new ways . . . the expansive common areas and green space of traditional universities [that] nurture expansive thinking and lively debate."[9]

The models for the future, then, include campuses disguised as extensions of the adjacent city, pieces of campuses constructed by commercial builders, satellite campuses of rented space, and Starbucks everywhere. Amidst such a collision of new ideas, however, it is important to continue to ask about the obligation, and the opportunity, that only an academic institution can bring to the city.

---

[8]Stuart C. Strother. "The Stripped-Down College Experience." *The Chronicle of Higher Education*, February 4, 2005, p. B5.

[9]R. M. Kliment & Frances Halsband Architects/Todd Rader & Amy Crews Landscape Architecture LLC. "The Walk: A Proposed Design for the Extension of the Brown University Campus Joining Lincoln Field and Pembroke Green," May 27, 2004.

Is this not to continue to construct and maintain those very qualities of open space, architecture, and social structure that invite free participation and dialogue, the informal mixing places that nurture creativity, and the public spaces that offer a forum for learning in a free society?

Reading the Nautical Star

Matthew King

Student Essay

HUMAN BEINGS ARE EXTREMELY SUSCEPTIBLE to becoming creatures of habit. We go about our day without taking much notice of the people around us. We follow the beaten path on a kind of autopilot. One of the most traveled pathways near us is Schafer Court, and especially the newly installed Nautical Star (I have determined this title, for that is what it appears to be). Sitting and watching how people use the Star is a study in human behavior and habit. After a few hours of unintentionally voyeuristic "people-watching" I have found that the populace has turned an intended pathway into a place of congregation.

The Nautical Star is located directly in front of Virginia Commonwealth University's Branch-Cabell Library, a hub of student activity. Constructed out of tan and slate grey brick and bronze metal, it is inlaid into the burnt orange brick of the surrounding pathways. Four points around the Star illustrate the directions orientating the star, with North being slightly to the right of the library. The Star is surrounded also by the Hibbs Building, Schafer Court, and a pathway to VCU's Life Sciences Building. Given the immense traffic these respective locations draw, the Nautical Star becomes a hub for students and faculty who pass through it on the way to classes or meetings.

The first trend I noticed while studying the diurnal flux of VCU's student body was that the Nautical Star, seemingly intended as a centerpiece for Schafer Court, had succeeded in that regard. The heaviest flow of traffic was always on or around the Star, given that it has four main entrances and exits leading to some of VCU's busiest buildings. Viewing the people milling about the circular brick decoration reminded me of looking down at the flow of people going through New York's Grand Central Station. The determined, tight-lipped looks seen in New York were the same I saw at the Star, as well. These looks were evidence to me that most people used the Star as a pathway, focused only on their respective destinations and not on the newly built brickwork that they were treading upon.

Despite the mass amounts of people going their various ways, there is a sense of calm amidst the chaos. There are no collisions between human and bike, no traffic flow issues, and no heated run-ins. There seems to be a pervasive flow or path that all participants in the journey seem to subconsciously follow. In fact, it appears as if this circular star fed by four outlets of traffic maintains a strange, unexplainable sense of efficiency, upholding the Star's intent as a way to move people through a complex courtyard to the buildings and classrooms where they need to be.

And yet, despite the seeming success of the Star's purpose (moving people and providing direction), I noticed that the people have quietly, perhaps unintentionally, changed the use of the Star. While the majority of the people follow the motion flow and move through the Star to their destination, a small faction have decided to buck the trend and instead use the Star as a meeting place, a destination as opposed to a gateway to a destination.

Given this fact, it is ironic that the designers of the Star saw no need to install sitting anywhere near the Star. They did not think to allow a structure in which to facilitate people's lollygagging. The Star remains a directional guide, pushing the people through it, around it, anywhere but onto it. That said, the desire for people to congregate there and remain there seems at once unnatural and yet completely logical, despite the obvious irony of a directional device being used as a destination in itself.

Perhaps the explanation for the student body's decision to remain on the Star can be found in the layout and flow of the rest of the university. Being an extremely far-flung university, there are few main areas where mass amounts of the students congregate. In addition to the Schafer Court area, only the Student Commons (located approximately 3/4 of a block away) serves as a communal "meet market" and congregational area. That being said, however, the various designers that have toiled away at the university over the years have usually included ample seating around the veins of transportation. Benches, tables, unusually wide stairs and the like have been included to make student R&R an easily afforded benefit of campus life. Even walls near walkways have historically been constructed so as to facilitate easy seating and gathering, as evidenced by the Schafer Court/Cabell Library shared spaces. So it seems odd that VCU's latest addition to its conduit system would lack simple elements such as seating and gathering space. And yet, the students have created these things in a non-material way, simply sitting when the mood strikes and consistently meeting with friends at the Star's center or edges.

In a way, the whole system is reminiscent of Fiske's comment in "Shopping for Pleasure" of the weak unseating the powerful. The intent of the designers was for the Star to be a place for mobility and information-giving, not a place to meet fellow students or friends. So why has the Star turned into something seemingly not intended when it was built? Perhaps the designers were too successful in constructing an attractive yet functional centerpiece for Schafer Court.

One main purpose of the Star, besides the ones mentioned above, was for it to be an attractive centerpiece for the university. Perhaps it was just that—an attractive centerpiece that people found so magnetic that they congregated there, drawn by the uniqueness and symmetry. Numerous groups of people gather on all points of the Star, engaging in conversation and gossip, scanning the hordes of passing students for friends and acquaintances. Meanwhile, solitary students dot points on the outside perimeter of the Star, waiting to meet friends and significant others for shared classes or a quick bite to eat at Hibbs. Some talk on cell phones, giving directions to the Star or encouraging the other party to hurry up. Whatever reason has drawn these people here, their behavior has turned the Nautical Star on its ear, so to speak. They have made a decision, though not necessarily a conscious one, to mold the Star to fit their needs and to make its seeming unfaithfulness to previous university constructs a seemingly meaningless issue in regards to seating and gathering.

Surprisingly, what I learned from this experiment was that taking a small slice of a person's day (their passage through Schafer Court and the Star) can actually tell one a tremendous amount about human behavior in general. People are often so set in their routine (or so tired or hung over) that they seem to blur out everything but their destination. In fact the zombie-like look of some members of the student body are almost frightening in their one-dimensionality. People seem bound to a sense of flow, almost unable to break free of a predetermined path. However unconscious these movements may be, a few of them tend to shatter the paradigm with outright force, neglecting the intent or focus of architects and work-a-day construction workers in favor of simple convenience. All of these observations prove that habit is a powerful force in our lives, and even if we don't realize it, we can subconsciously shift the intent of the powerful.

The Campus Photography Essay

IN THIS SUITE OF PHOTOGRAPHS, we examine the architectural idea of "collegeness." If you have seen *Animal House*, *Van Wilder*, or even *Community* (NBC's current show about college) or visited a number of different colleges or universities, you might know what we are talking about. Without question, the college is a constructed text that makes arguments about itself through architecture and public space. Student unions, quads, big libraries, and classic architectural forms like columns or porticos are all examples of how a university tries to cultivate a reputation or create an aura. But perhaps some of you go to a community college or an urban campus that has no room for spacious lawns or neo-classical architecture. Or perhaps your university was built in the 1950s at the height of what historians call modernist architecture (which often means less flourishes like columns and porticos, what architectural historians often call ornamentation).

Nonetheless, colleges are almost a perfect semiotic text because both signifiers (the physical part of a sign) and the signified (its meaning) are unstable. By this we mean that sometimes a campus could look like a traditional college but is not, and other times universities do not look like our imagined idea of a university but function very traditionally. In this series of photos, we offer different ideas of collegeness. Most of these photos we have taken ourselves, as we are particularly interested in how colleges are themselves texts.

This is also a call to send us your own photos of your campus—perhaps we will feature it on our Facebook page or even in the next edition of *The World Is a Text*. E-mail us at WorldIsAText@gmail.com.

Here we have four separate sections of the photo essay. The first one is devoted to the prototypical aspect of the university: **the quad** (short for quadrangle). But as you will see, not every university has a quad. We also have some photographs for what is considered **classic** architecture, a staple at many universities. But also a staple is **modern** architecture, mostly from the period when campuses grew at an astounding rate—in the 1950s and 1960s when more and more young people went to college. Finally, we have three pictures of the University of Cork's entrance in Cork. Each seems to say something different about the university—but what?

Quad:

In order, the University of Cork in Ireland; Virginia Commonwealth University in Richmond, VA; the University of Oslo in Norway; Trinity College in Dublin, Ireland; Pace University in New York City (courtesy of Tom Henthrorne and Kristen Di Gennaro; University of Bergen in Norway; Frances King School of English in London, England.

CHAPTER 3 • Reading and Writing about Public and Private Space

Classic:

In order, University of Copenhagen; University of Virginia; Dartmouth College; Trinity University.

Modern:

In order, Bielefeld University (Germany); University of Bergen; University of Oslo; University of London; Dartmouth College.

Cork: Three entrances

READING WRITING

This Text: Reading

1. Rader is on the faculty at the University of San Francisco; yet he writes about USF and two other San Francisco universities. Is he biased? Does he give a fair reading of his own campus and the other local institutions?

2. Through what kind of lens does Halsband read college campuses? If this is a difficult question, think about what kinds of universities she mentions and how that colors her analysis. Are there community colleges here? Small state colleges? Would her reading of campus space work for your institution?

3. Toward the end of the piece, Halsband brings up the need for brick and mortar campuses. What function do actual campuses serve? How might taking a class on a traditional college campus be different than taking one online or in a strip mall?

4. Do you live in a college town? What makes it so? If not, what would make it a college town?

5. How does King show that the Nautical Star is part of the VCU built environment? How does his micro reading of the star contribute to the macro reading of VCU?

6. Read Liz Swanson's opening essay in this chapter on architecture, then go back and take another look at these three in the suite. How do the authors use the terms and ideas Swanson talks about to make his points?

Your Text: Writing

1. Give a semiotic reading of your campus. You can either read the campus as a whole—making an argument that it sends a specific kind of message—or, you can read a specific part as a microscope (a small thing that functions as a symbol of something larger).

2. Write an essay on how the commercial and the educational merge at your institution. Does your campus have commercial enterprises run by outside vendors? Are there advertisements in rooms, in dorms or on campus elsewhere? In what ways does that affect the campus atmosphere, if at all? Does it detract from the stated mission of your university?

3. Find some aspect of your campus that seems nontraditional in its construction or use and give a reading of that space. You might consider off-campus housing, a virtual classroom, a space that merges with the community, or even a new dorm. What makes this place nontraditional?

4. Write about the college campus as a public place. What makes a campus public? Should a private university be a public place?

READING BETWEEN THE LINES

Classroom Activities

1. Look around your classroom. How do you know it's a classroom? Of course, there are the chalkboard and the desks, but what other qualities does this room have that make it a classroom? How is it designed? Does it facilitate learning, alertness, and discussion?
2. Walk outside the classroom. What elements identify the walk as a college campus? What emotions does the walk evoke? Could it be improved?
3. What does the public space outside the classroom building say? Does it identify the campus as any particular type of school—private, public, urban, rural, suburban? What would a potential student read into this particular space? Would they be inclined to come to school or not because of this reading? Why or why not?
4. What particular place makes you feel the most comfortable? Least? Frightened? What is it about the spaces themselves that evoke these emotions? Are they human driven or architecturally or design driven? Can you think of a space that has bad or good memories driven mostly by the space itself?
5. Design the perfect classroom. What would it look like? What would it have in it? Where would everyone sit? What tools would everyone have? How would being in this classroom change your learning experience?
6. Design the perfect building at college. What would it look like? What would it have in it?

Essay Ideas

Building as Analogy

Find a building you want to write about. Does it remind you of something besides a building in 1) its physical construction; 2) the emotional response it encourages; 3) its purpose; or 4) its structure? In what way are these disparate elements alike? Different? What does the analogy in general say about commonalities of texts generally?

Emotional Response

Walk around a building or a public area such as a mall or your school's common area. What do you "feel"? What about the place makes you feel such an emotion? Are these effects intended or unintended?

Commercial versus Artistic

What dominates this particular building or space—its artistic aspects or commercial ones? Or do the two work together?

My Favorite Place

If possible, analyze a place you feel close to and figure out why you feel that way. Is there a theme attached to this place? How would you describe the décor? The architecture? Do you feel your attachment to this place—or places like it—is unique?

Does this Building or Space "Work"?

Find a place—do you think it succeeds on its own terms? What are its "terms"—what criteria is it trying to fulfill? Does is succeed? Why or why not?

The Person from the Space

Go to an office or a dorm room or car, or some place that "belongs" to someone. What can you tell about this person from the space? How did you arrive at your judgments? Are there other ways to interpret the information?

The Common Element

Compare similar spaces. What makes them similar? What are their differences? What do their differences or similarities say about this type of space?

Visualizing Writing

Taken by Barrett Torkheim, curated by Bethany Keeley of *The Blog of Unnecessary Quotations:* http://www.unnecessaryquotes. com.

4 Reading and Writing about Race and Ethnicity

SESQUICENTENNIAL - 150 YEARS

PRESIDENT OBAMA

The *dream* has arrived.

Of all the introductions we have written, this one made us feel the most uncomfortable. Writing about people, skin color, and the relationship between appearance and attributed behavior is a minefield for any prospective author. We wanted to put our anxiety on the table right away because we believe that this anxiety mirrors the way you might feel when you are talking about race and ethnicity whether you are Hispanic, African American, Asian American, American Indian, white, or, most likely, some combination of ethnicities.

As you will notice in this introduction, we are constantly hedging—saying "to a degree" or "to some extent." And there is a reason for this hesitation. When it comes to race or ethnicity, there are few if any absolutes; yet, unfortunately, racism seems to operate within a system of ignorant absolutes. Assumptions about individuals because of skin color and perceptions about ethnicities based on unexamined stereotypes lump individuals into groups where it is easy to make sweeping generalizations that never take into account individual nuances, abilities, and personalities. When these experiences occur because of perceived common characteristics, an individual experience becomes a community one. Prejudice, then, projects perceived or assumed racial characteristics on a single person or groups of people. Again, saying a group of people is not qualified to do particular work because of how they look or the ethnicity they belong to is a clear example of prejudice.

To an overwhelming degree, these experiences are socially constructed. Indeed, most scientists believe that race is a social, not a biological, determination. In other words, race as it was commonly perceived in the past—as a means of attributing characteristics to individuals of a common group—is not scientifically or biologically defensible. Scientists believe that perceived traits of races are a product of social experiences, despite the way we often visually identify someone of a particular race. To put it a different way, one's skin color does *not* determine race; factors contributing to one's race are far more complex.

We are *not* saying that biology does not determine the color of one's skin; clearly, biology determines skin pigmentation, as it does the color of our eyes and our hair. What we are saying (and what most scientists also argue) is that the idea that biological traits are associated with a particular skin color is false. As humans of different shades of color, we are much more alike biologically than we are different. Even if some groups do have a higher incidence of disease (African Americans with sickle-cell anemia, Jews with Tay-Sachs disease), environmental factors largely shape their existence. For example, Americans are much more likely to have heart conditions compared to the French. The characteristics of Americans are more alike than characteristics of people from Tibet,

◀ Some observers have made explicit links between various leaders and President Barack Obama. For more on this, see our Obama suite starting on page 310.

which is to say that our biology and our cultural community connect us in more ways than our perceptions of race might suggest.[1]

Self-perception is even more of a factor in racial or ethnic identity, as people often "switch" ethnicities or at least change their affiliation with a certain group. For instance, a recent study shows that more than one-third of respondents in a census identified themselves as a different ethnicity than when they responded to the same census only two years later. This is not to say that race is not important—it is. Race and ethnicity, even if socially constructed, guide much of our public life. By putting the burden on social constructions of race, we have to think about the way we construct race more completely rather than accept that things like skin color and racial traits are simply the way things are.

In the past, people from various groups had a tendency to impose a set of values onto certain groups based simply on skin color, a tendency that has certainly diminished in the last 50 years (though we would be the last people to claim that this type of behavior is gone, and the first to acknowledge that prejudice is still very much a part of too many people's lives). Our goal in this chapter is to help you become more sensitive readers of race and ethnicity by becoming more aware of the social forces that construct the volatile texts of race and racism.

THE DETERMINATION THAT RACE, ETHNICITY, AND CLASS ARE SOCIALLY CONSTRUCTED HAS LED TO NEW WAYS OF THINKING ABOUT OUR IDENTITY THAT CARRY POLITICAL AND SOCIAL IMPLICATIONS.

Not too long ago, and for most of the history of the Western world, people made assumptions about other people based on their appearance, most notably their skin color. White people wrongly, and often tragically, assumed blacks were inferior or that American Indians were "savages." For centuries, groups have enslaved other groups based on that group's race or ethnicity. In the last few decades, we have gone from the biological construction of race—one based on parentage—to one based more on social groups and associations. "Hispanic" means something different than it did twenty years ago, as does "Native American." For example, there has been a persuasive shift in identification. We tend to view Native Americans by tribe or nation, and those from Central and South America, the Caribbean, and Mexico by country of origin and nationality, rather than the catchall of ethnicity. We talk of Choctaw, Zuni, and Osage rather than "Indian." We identify folks as Cuban, Columbian, or Mexican, rather than "Hispanic." At the University of San Francisco, there is a resistance to Pan–Asianism among students. There are, for example, a number of different Filipino student organizations, each more or less political than the others. Precise linguistic markers more accurately articulate identity, as anyone familiar with racial and cultural history can tell you.

---

[1] One such source is Audrey Smedley and Brian D. Smedley, "Race as Biology is Fiction, Racism as a Social Problem Is Real: Anthropological and Historical Perspectives of the Social Construction of Race," *American Psychologist* 60.1 (2005): 16–26.

TO A DEGREE, RACE AND ETHNICITY ARE VISUALLY CONSTRUCTED, BUT THOSE VISUAL CONSTRUCTIONS ARE HARDLY WITHOUT CONTROVERSY.

We tend to categorize people by their appearance, not by their biological background, for the most obvious reason: We have no other way of reading people. We do construct race, ethnicity, and gender, and its multiplicity of meanings and ideas visually, not only through a person's skin but also through what they wear, how they walk, how tall or short they are. We are not trying to demonize this process as much as we are trying to draw attention to it. Like other visual constructions, it must be slowed down and digested more actively. Thus, every time we see someone and register that person's skin color, we are doing a reading of his or her ethnicity. We pick up on external codes that we think cue us into that person's racial background, but what, really, do those cues tell us? For one, even if we can determine if someone is Chinese or Russian or Kenyan or Navajo, that tells us very little about who she is as a person, what he likes to eat, what she is good at, how smart he is, what sports she plays, or what his values are.

As we indicate earlier, for centuries people in power (mostly white but not always) used skin color as a means of identifying both ethnicity and character. One of the worst and most tragic fallacies one can commit is to conflate external and internal in regard to race; to see "Asian" or "African American" and think _____. There is a funny scene in the movie *Carbon Copy*, when George Segal (anglo) assumes his black son (Denzel Washington), a grown man who he has just met, is good at basketball simply because he is black. In an attempt to make money, Segal challenges a father and son who are shooting hoops to a pickup basketball game for cash. Segal's expectations, those of the other father and son, and those of the viewers, are undermined when the Denzel Washington character is terrible at basketball. Here Segal engages in a classic misreading of race. In this instance, he only lost money; however, in the case of slavery, Japanese internment, and Native removal, the consequences of racial misreading were much more significant.

TO SOME EXTENT, READING THE "OTHERNESS" IN SOMEONE'S APPEARANCE MAKES US UNCOMFORTABLE BECAUSE OF REASONS BOTH POLITICAL AND PERSONAL.

We want to be—and are explicitly trained to be—democratic in the way we view others, by the way they act toward us, not the way they look. "Don't judge a book by its cover," we say, but we are always judging books by their covers and people by their appearance, and this makes many of us *very* uncomfortable. This discomfort is magnified when it comes to race, ethnicity, gender, and class because we know our constructions have political, cultural, social, and personal consequences for us and for the people we are trying to read. Our democratic nature wants us to read neutrally, but our less controllable side does not, because we have been conditioned through decades and even centuries of reading values into otherness. Perhaps you have noticed or even commented on someone's ethnicity, then felt strange about it. In one classic episode of *Seinfeld*, George and Elaine muse over the ethnicity of Elaine's new boyfriend, an endeavor that makes George extremely uncomfortable.

Throughout the episode, he keeps saying, "I don't think we're supposed to be talking about this." This is because we want things that seem to be mutually exclusive—to acknowledge someone's difference but not be affected by it. Yet, how can we *not* be affected by something we notice and then think about?

The simple act of noticing that someone's ethnicity is different from your own creates an immediate otherness for both of you. Moreover, with this perception of otherness comes, perhaps, assumptions about that person and about yourself—that you are scarier or smarter or wealthier or poorer. In fact, in the history of America, the fact that we can and do see otherness in our fellow Americans has caused more hardship, violence, and death than we can even imagine.

DEFINITIONS OF RACE ARE ALWAYS CHANGING.

In the late nineteenth and early twentieth centuries and to some extent afterwards, race and ethnicity were often conflated. For instance, at the turn of the century, Jews and Italians were considered racial groups (not ethnic groups). Similarly, fewer than fifty years ago, many places in the South considered anyone to be African American if they had an African American ancestor; this was called the "one-drop" rule. Because the vast majority of Americans do not think this way now, it may seem difficult to believe that this past existed, but understanding it is crucial in understanding contemporary notions of race and race theory.

As casinos bring more money, power, and prestige to American Indian reservations and communities, Indian identity has become an increasingly sensitive issue. For some tribes, one must have a certain "blood quantum" level and/or be an enrolled member of a tribe. A hundred years ago, someone with any amount of Indian blood could be imprisoned or killed, but now the same level of "Indianness" that could have gotten you killed in the 1800s might not be enough to enable you to become a member of a tribe.

Race, like gender and class, are fluid texts, so it is important *not* to assume too much about individuals or groups based on what they appear to be.

ALTHOUGH WE CLAIM TO BE NONDISCRIMINATORY NOW, DISCRIMINATORY PRACTICES IN THE PAST HAVE INFLUENCED THE PRESENT SOCIAL, POLITICAL, ECONOMIC, AND CULTURAL STRUCTURE OF OUR COUNTRY.

This may seem like a highly political statement, and it is. However, the authors believe that discrimination in the past gave the white male majority a head start in this generation; race theorists call this phenomenon "white privilege." As you know, blacks, Asians, Hispanics, and Native Americans were frequently, if not regularly, denied admission to colleges, job interviews, loans, and access to restaurants and hotels and even basic medical service. Affirmative action, the idea that employers and schools should actively seek historically underrepresented individuals to fill their slots, is a response to this phenomenon by ensuring that minorities get fair consideration by employers and admission offices (for the most part, affirmative action does *not* involve a quota system, despite misconceptions popularly

articulated). But the theory behind affirmative action, looking for ways to engage the past while living in the future in making decisions about schools and employment, is not only a government program but also a factor in admitting legacies to colleges, incorporating one's progeny into a family business, and so on. While preferential treatment may be decried as un-American in some quarters—after all, the Bill of Rights says all men are created equal—the fact is the past has always shaped how people are treated in the present.

What's more, generations of broken promises, abuses of power, and institutional discrimination and oppression have left some members of minority communities bitter toward institutions of power and law. People are smart. They know that history repeats itself; they know that the past is always present in some form or another. Thus, the reality of slavery, the history of American Indian genocide and removal, and the memory of Asian internment constitute a legacy that still affects how members of these groups see America and its institutions, and it is a legacy that contemporary America must take seriously.

RACE, ETHNICITY, AND GENDER ARE POLITICAL CONSTRUCTIONS AS WELL AS SOCIAL ONES.

We now think of members of so-called races as political groups as well as social ones. If you read about politics, you will notice commentators talking about how a candidate was trying to "appeal to African Americans" or "appeal to women" (or more specific groupings like "soccer moms" or "the Catholic Latino vote"). The recognition that these groups have political power in one sense has empowered members of these groups and given them political power in ways they may not have had. However, of course, some people within these groups do not want to be identified as group members; it too easily reminds them of the way society constructs their identity negatively. For example, Toni Morrison, the Nobel Prize-winning author, has said that she does not want to be thought of as an African American writer but merely as a writer. The tendency, the need, in America to preface any such statement with the racial descriptor, goes to show how completely we see race and, perhaps, how often we cannot see past it.

Even more important, the goals of an ethnicity as a whole may not be those of the individual. In fact, it may be impossible to state, with any certainty, what the goals of any one ethnicity may be, as all people are complex and in the process of change. Supreme Court Judge Clarence Thomas will have very different ideas about what African Americans need than will the Reverend Jesse Jackson or Minister Louis Farrakhan, even though all are intelligent, upper class African American men. Which of the three best represents black Americans? That may depend on what group of black Americans you poll.

STEREOTYPING OCCURS AS A RESULT OF OUR PERCEIVED VIEW OF RACIAL OR ETHNIC CHARACTERISTICS.

Unless you are the rare completely neutral human being, someone the authors feel does not exist, you attach stereotypes to groups—even if they seem like stereotypes that are positive, such as all professors are smart, nuns are nice, textbook authors are cool, and so on.

You may also, without knowing it, hold negative stereotypes. The problem, of course, with all stereotypes is their propensity to attribute group characteristics to individuals. Believing all Jews are smart or all African Americans are athletic can have subsequent negative effects that balance out any positives.

How do we acquire our stereotypes? Some believe stereotypes are based on a grain of truth. That sort of thought makes the authors and others nervous, because the next logical step is thinking that traits or behaviors are inherent or natural. Researchers believe we pick up stereotypes in a variety of ways, including through popular culture and our upbringing. That is why we have stressed throughout this book the importance of looking for treatments of race and ethnicity as they appear—or do not appear—in texts.

There is also disturbing evidence that people mirror stereotyped expectations. As we discuss in the chapter on gender, mainstream American society has a tendency to punish those individuals who operate outside of the perceived norms of a certain group. Thus, stereotypes keep getting reinforced generation after generation, despite efforts from all groups to eradicate them. As the suite in this chapter suggests, many American Indian groups are frustrated by their inability to do much about the sanctioned stereotyping of Native Americans through sports mascots and nicknames. One wonders and worries about what messages these stereotypes send to both Native and non-Native communities—especially children. Similarly since 9/11 Arab Americans have had to face unfair suspicion and discrimination based on the radical behavior of a *very, very* small number of extremists.

YOUR VIEW OF THESE ISSUES PROBABLY DEPENDS ON YOUR PERSONAL RELATIONSHIPS AS WELL AS POLITICAL AFFILIATION.

When surveying the landscape of these issues, we are likely to take our personal experiences and make them universal. If we are white and have African American friends or relatives, not only are we more likely to be more sympathetic to black causes, we are probably going to take the part of the whole for better or worse. If we have no friends of color, and our only exposure is through popular culture and our political affiliations, that too will shape the way we look at race and ethnicity. It is an overgeneralization to be sure, but the authors believe that proximity brings understanding in ways that reading about race and ethnicity can never bring. So does, we believe, actively thinking about the ways we construct race and ethnicity.

Sadly, in the United States, views on race are often influenced by financial concerns. We wonder about the number of people who are critical of immigrants from Latin American countries but whose standard of living relies on illegal immigrant labor. Similarly, in the 1800s, Asians suffered horrible forms of racism, but investors were eager to have them build railroads for almost no money.

Every bit of evidence suggests that racism is a learned behavior, which means that we are taught to *read* ethnicity. There is a famous scene on an episode of the television show *Montel*, when the children of black guests and white extremists are shown playing together in the Green Room. Despite such harmful lessons, personal relationships can often overcome flawed teaching and empty stereotyping.

CLASS IS A MORE CRUCIAL ELEMENT IN AMERICAN LIFE THAN MANY PEOPLE THINK.

Class also has similar connections to both self-identity and outside reality. Studies show most Americans believe they are middle class. And because there is no set way of determining what someone's class is, a person making $200,000 a year can call himself middle class; so can someone earning $20,000 a year. Are their lives different? Absolutely. However, they may not see that. Of course, class issues run through issues of race and ethnicity, in ways both simple and complex. Some researchers believe that race and ethnicity are mostly a class problem, with the members of ethnic groups disproportionately represented among the nation's poor. There probably is some validity to this claim. However, because the nation has had a long bloody history of clashes between ethnicities of the same class, it is hard to see class as the primary issue in racial or ethnic discrimination.

On the other hand, perceptions of reality can be as strong or stronger than reality itself, and in a capitalist country that tends to link economic prosperity with personal worth, the prevailing perceptions of which groups have more can shape how we see certain people. Thus, although class may not be the primary factor in racial discrimination, it is difficult when talking about race to separate it from issues of class. When the third edition of this book went to press, the website *Stuff White People Like* was a cultural phenomenon. But as many argue (including one of the authors of this book), the site is more about what left-leaning yuppies like than, say, what blue collar whites from the Deep South like. In other words, the site pretends to be about race, but it is really about class, and the assumptions Americans make about how class and race manifest.

WRITING ABOUT RACE, ETHNICITY, OR CLASS CAN BE DONE IN A VARIETY OF WAYS.

In the introduction, we discuss writing about popular culture through various lenses, including race and ethnicity. Practically that means noticing how race and ethnicity manifest themselves in a television show or movie. As Michael Omi notes, writers, producers, and directors often use stereotypes when employing actors who are different from/than them. It is also true that characters of particular backgrounds can be used as symbols rather than as fully-drawn characters.

ABSENCE OF RACES IS OFTEN A STATEMENT.

So far there have been no seasons of *The Bachelor* or *Bachelorette* involving someone other than whites.[2] The number one sitcom in the country, *Two and a Half Men*, has no prominent characters of race and ethnicity. What does the absence of characters of diverse backgrounds say about these television shows? Does it reflect perceptions of the show's creators about the preferences of audiences? Or something to do more with the creators' own preferences?

---

[2]Thea Lin, "The *Bachelor/Bachelorette*'s White Elephant," *Racialicious* 16 Mar. 2010 <http://www.racialicious.com/2010/03/16/the-bachelorbachelorettes-white-elephant/>.

The complicated nature of race and ethnicity is reflected here in the selections, which include a variety of perspectives and methodologies to consider.

THIS TEXT

1. While it will be impossible for you to know this fully, try to figure out the writing situation of each author. Who is the audience? What does the author have at stake? What is his or her agenda? *Why* is she or he writing this piece?

2. What social, political, and cultural forces affect the author's text? What is going on in the world as he or she is writing?

3. How does the author define race and ethnicity? Is the definition stated or unstated?

4. When taken as a whole, what do these texts tell you about how we construct race and ethnicity?

5. How do stories and essays differ in their arguments about race and ethnicity?

6. Is the author's argument valid and reasonable?

7. Ideas and beliefs about race and ethnicity tend to be very sensitive, deeply held convictions. Do you find yourself in agreement with the author? Why or why not? Do you agree with the editors' introduction?

8. Does the author help you *read* race and ethnicity better than you did before reading the essay? If so, why? How do we learn to read race and ethnicity?

9. Did you like this? Why or why not?

10. What role does science play in the selected essay?

BEYOND THIS TEXT: READING RACE AND ETHNICITY

Media: How are different ethnicities portrayed in news or magazine articles? Is the author taking the "part for the whole" (talking to one member of a group as representative of all members of the group)?

Advertising: How are different ethnicities portrayed in print or broadcast ads? Is there anything that "signals" their ethnicity—is clothing used as a "sign" of their color or identity? Is the advertiser using a "rainbow effect" in the ad, appearing to be inclusive by including multiple ethnicities? Does this effect seem forced or genuine?

Television: How are different ethnicities portrayed in a particular television show? Do they conform to predictable stereotypes? Are the people of color more than merely representative? Is there a lone African American or Hispanic American on a mostly white show? One white person on an African American dominated show? Are the members of different races allowed to date? Does their dating engage the idea of intergroup dating or ignore it?

Movies: How are different ethnicities portrayed in the movie? Do they conform to predictable stereotypes? Are the people of color the first to be targeted for death (if it's an action movie)? Are the people of color more than merely representative? Is there a lone African American or Hispanic American in a mostly white movie? One white person in an African American dominated movie? Are the members of different races allowed to date? Does their dating engage the idea of intergroup dating or ignore it?

The Campus Photography Essay   **261**

A QUICK GUIDE TO WRITING ABOUT RACE, CLASS, AND ETHNICITY

1. **Think about the question you might be trying to answer by watching the show or movie.** It could be as simple as "How are people of various racial, ethnic, or class backgrounds being portrayed in the movie?" Or it could be, "What messages does the lack of diversity in a television show send to viewers?" But even more complex ideas about race, ethnicity, class, and nationality should be articulated as questions before watching, if possible.

2. **Make sure you write down scenes you think might serve as evidence for the points you make.** Using examples always helps illustrate a point you are trying to make. And often they serve as good introductions to the questions you are trying to answer.

3. **You might also talk to friends about the show or movie you watched.** Sometimes particularly controversial or complex texts benefit from deep discussion.

Why Are All the Black Kids Sitting Together in the Cafeteria?

Beverly Daniel Tatum

Beverly Tatum is a psychologist who writes about race and race relations in America. This essay is taken in part from her book, Why Are All the Black Kids Sitting Together in the Cafeteria? And Other Conversations About Race *(1999). Here she argues that both teachers and students need to talk actively about race, especially in the teenage years when identity is being formed.*

WALK INTO ANY RACIALLY MIXED high school cafeteria at lunch time and you will instantly notice an identifiable group of black students sitting together. Conversely, there are many white students sitting together, though we rarely comment about that. The question is "Why are the black kids sitting together?"

It doesn't start out that way. In racially mixed elementary schools, you often see children of diverse racial boundaries playing with one another, sitting at the snack table together, crossing racial boundaries with an ease uncommon in adolescence.

Moving from elementary school to middle school means interacting with new children from different neighborhoods than before, and a certain degree of clustering by race might therefore be expected, presuming that children who are familiar with one another would form groups. But even in schools where the same children stay together from kindergarten through eighth grade, racial grouping begins by the sixth or seventh grade. What happens?

One thing that happens is puberty. As children enter adolescence, they begin to explore the question of identity, asking "Who am I? Who can I be?" in ways they have not done before. For black youths, asking "Who am I?" includes thinking about "Who am I ethnically? What does it mean to be black?"

Why do black youths, in particular, think about themselves in terms of race? Because that is how the rest of the world thinks of them. Our self-perceptions are shaped by the messages we receive from those around us, and when young black men and women reach adolescence, the racial content of those messages intensifies.

Here is a case in point. If you were to ask my 10-year-old son, David, to describe himself, he would tell you many things: that he is smart, that he likes to play computer games, that he has an older brother. Near the top of his list, he would likely mention that he is tall for his age. He would probably not mention that he is black, though he certainly knows that he is. Why would he mention his height and not his racial group membership?

When David meets new adults, one of the first questions they ask is "How old are you?" When David states his age, the inevitable reply is, "Gee, you're tall for your age!"

It happens so frequently that I once overheard David say to someone, "Don't say it, I know. I'm tall for my age." Height is salient for David because it's salient for others.

When David meets new adults, they don't say, "Gee, you're black for your age!" Or do they?

Imagine David at 15, six-foot-two, wearing the adolescent attire of the day, passing adults he doesn't know on the sidewalk. Do the women hold their purses a little tighter, maybe even cross the street to avoid him? Does he hear the sound of automatic door locks on cars as he passes by? Is he being followed around by the security guards at the local mall? Do strangers assume he plays basketball? Each of these experiences conveys a racial message.

At 10, race is not yet salient for David, because it's not yet salient for society. But it will be.

Understanding Racial Identity Development

Psychologist William Cross, author of *Shades of Black: Diversity in African American Identity*, has offered a theory of racial identity development that I have found to be a very useful framework for understanding what is happening with those black students in the cafeteria. In the first stage of Cross's five-stage model, the black child absorbs many of the beliefs and values of the dominant white culture, including the idea that it's better to be white.

Simply as a function of being socialized in a Eurocentric culture, some black children may begin to value the role models, lifestyles and images of beauty represented by the dominant group more highly than those of their own cultural group. But the personal and social significance of one's racial group membership has not yet been realized, and racial identity is not yet under examination.

The Encounter Stage

Transition to the next stage, the encounter stage, is typically precipitated by an event—or series of events—that forces the young person to acknowledge the personal impact of racism.

For example, in racially mixed schools, black children are much more likely to be in a lower track than in an honors track. Such apparent sorting along racial lines sends a message about what it means to be black. One young honors student said, "It was really a very paradoxical existence, here I am in a school that's 35 percent black, you know, and I'm the only black in my class. That always struck me as odd. I guess I felt that I was different from the other blacks because of that."

There are also changes in the social dynamics outside the school. In racially mixed communities, you begin to see what I call the "birthday party effect." The parties of elementary school children may be segregated by gender, but not by race. At puberty, when the parties become sleepovers or boy–girl events, they become less and less racially diverse.

Black girls who live in predominantly white neighborhoods see their white friends start to date before they do. One young woman from a Philadelphia suburb described herself as "pursuing white guys throughout high school" to no avail. Because there were no black boys in her class, she had little choice. She would feel "really pissed off" that those same white boys would date her white friends.

Another young black woman attending a desegregated school to which she was bussed was encouraged by a teacher to attend the upcoming school dance. Most of the black students did not live in the neighborhood and seldom attended the extracurricular activities. The young woman indicated that she wasn't planning to come. Finally the well-intentioned teacher said, "Oh come on, I know you people love to dance." This young woman got the message.

Coping with Encounter

What do these encounters have to do with the cafeteria? Do experiences with racism inevitably result in so-called self-segregation?

While a desire to protect oneself from further offense is understandable, it's not the only factor at work. Imagine the young eighth-grade girl who experienced the teacher's use of "you people" and the dancing stereotype as a racial affront. Upset and struggling with adolescent embarrassment, she bumps into a white friend who can see that something is wrong. She explains. Her white friend responds—perhaps in an effort to make her feel better—and says, "Oh, Mr. Smith is such a nice guy, I'm sure he didn't mean it like that. Don't be so sensitive."

Perhaps the white friend is right, but imagine your own response when you are upset, and your partner brushes off your complaint, attributing it to your being oversensitive. What happens to your emotional thermostat? It escalates. When feelings, rational or irrational, are invalidated, most people disengage. They not only choose to discontinue the conversation but are more likely to turn to someone who will understand their perspective.

In much the same way that the eighth-grade girl's white friend doesn't get it, the girls at the "black table" do. Not only are black adolescents encountering racism and reflecting on their identity, but their white peers—even if not racist—are unprepared to respond in supportive ways.

The black students turn to each other for the much needed support they are not likely to find anywhere else.

We need to understand that in racially mixed settings, racial grouping is a developmental process in response to an environmental stressor, racism. Joining with one's peers for support in the face of stress is a positive coping strategy. The problem is that our young people are operating with a very limited definition of what it means to be black, based largely on cultural stereotypes.

READING WRITING

This Text: Reading

1. Do you find yourself personally involved (or implicated) in Tatum's analysis? How do you think she would respond to your response?
2. In what ways is Tatum performing a semiotic analysis of the idea of race? In what ways have race and ethnicity contributed to "semiotic situations" in your own life?
3. Where does her analysis fit into what we traditionally think of as the American Dream?
4. Why is the cafeteria such an important location for a discussion like this? What happens in a cafeteria that might not happen in a classroom?

Your Text: Writing

1. Using your own experiences, write an essay about the role race and ethnicity have played—or didn't play—in your experiences growing up.
2. Tatum's essay balances personal experience with research; do you think this method of writing is effective? Why or why not? Do you think this is important for this type of topic? Why or why not?
3. Can you think of a personal topic that would benefit from a combined research/personal approach?

Mother Tongue

Amy Tan

Amy Tan is the well-known author of The Joy Luck Club *and other novels. In this 1991 piece, she writes about her experiences with her mother and her mother's use of language.*

I AM NOT A SCHOLAR OF ENGLISH OR LITERA-TURE. I cannot give you much more than personal opinions on the English language and its variations in this country or others.

I am a writer. And by that definition, I am someone who has always loved language. I am fascinated by language in daily life. I spend a great deal of my time thinking about the power of language—the way it can evoke an emotion, a visual image, a complex idea, or a simple truth. Language is the tool of my trade. And I use them all—all the Englishes I grew up with.

Recently, I was made keenly aware of the different Englishes I do use. I was giving a talk to a large group of people, the same talk I had already given to half a dozen other groups. The nature of the talk was about my writing, my life, and my book, *The Joy Luck Club.* The talk was going along well enough, until I remembered one major difference that made the whole talk sound wrong. My mother was in the room. And it was perhaps the first time she had heard me give a lengthy speech, using the kind of English I have never used with her. I was saying things like, "The intersection of memory upon imagination" and "There is an aspect of my fiction that relates to thus-and-thus"—a speech filled with carefully wrought grammatical phrases, burdened, it suddenly seemed to me, with nomi-nalized forms, past perfect tenses, conditional phrases, all the forms of standard English that I had learned in school and through books, the forms of English I did not use at home with my mother.

Just last week, I was walking down the street with my mother, and I again found myself conscious of the English I was using, the English I do use with her. We were talking about the price of new and used furniture and I heard myself saying this: "Not waste money that way." My husband was with us as well, and he didn't notice any switch in my English. And then I realized why. It's because over the twenty years we've been together I've often used that same kind of English with him, and sometimes he even uses it with me. It has become our language of intimacy, a different sort of English that relates to family talk, the language I grew up with.

So you'll have some idea of what this family talk I heard sounds like, I'll quote what my mother said during a recent conversation which I videotaped and then transcribed. During this conversation, my mother was talking about a political gangster in Shanghai who had the same last name as her family's, Du, and how the gangster in his early years wanted to be adopted by her family, which was rich by comparison. Later, the gangster became more powerful, far richer than my mother's family, and one day showed up at my mother's wedding to pay his respects. Here's what she said in part: "Du Yusong having business like fruit stand. Like off the street kind. He is Du like Du Zong—but not Tsung-ming Island people. The local people call putong, the river east side, he belong to that side local people. That man want to ask Du Zong father take him in like become own family. Du Zong father wasn't look down on him, but didn't take seriously, until that man big like become a mafia. Now important person, very hard to inviting him. Chinese way, came only to show respect, don't stay for dinner. Respect for making big celebration, he shows up. Mean gives lots of respect. Chinese custom. Chinese social life that way. If too important won't have to stay too long. He come to my wedding. I didn't see, I heard it. I gone to boy's side, they have YMCA dinner. Chinese age I was nineteen."

You should know that my mother's expressive command of English belies how much she actually understands. She reads the *Forbes* report, listens to *Wall Street Week,* converses daily with her stockbroker, reads all of Shirley MacLaine's books with ease—all kinds of things I can't begin to understand. Yet some of my friends tell me they understand 50 percent of what my mother says. Some say they understand 80 to 90 percent. Some say they understand none of it, as if she were speaking pure Chinese. But to me, my mother's English is perfectly clear, perfectly natural. It's my mother tongue. Her language, as I hear it, is vivid, direct, full of observation and imagery. That was the language that helped shape the way I saw things, expressed things, made sense of the world.

Lately, I've been giving more thought to the kind of English my mother speaks. Like others, I have described it to people as "broken" or "fractured" English. But I wince when I say that. It has always bothered me that I can think of no way to describe it other than "broken," as if it were damaged and needed to be fixed, as if it lacked a certain wholeness and soundness. I've heard other terms used, "limited English," for example. But they seem just as bad, as if everything is limited, including people's perceptions of the limited English speaker.

I know this for a fact, because when I was growing up, my mother's "limited" English limited my perception of her. I was ashamed of her English. I believed that her English reflected the quality of what she had to say. That is, because she expressed them imperfectly her thoughts were imperfect. And I had plenty of empirical evidence to support me: the fact that people in department stores, at banks, and at restaurants did not take her seriously, did not give her good service, pretended not to understand her, or even acted as if they did not hear her.

My mother has long realized the limitations of her English as well. When I was fifteen, she used to have me call people on the phone to pretend I was she. In this guise, I was forced to ask for information or even to complain and yell at people who had been rude to her. One time it was a call to her stockbroker in New York. She had cashed out her small portfolio and it just so happened we were going to go to New York the next week, our very first trip outside California. I had to get on the phone and say in an adolescent voice that was not very convincing, "This is Mrs. Tan."

And my mother was standing in the back whispering loudly, "Why he don't send me check, already two weeks late. So mad he lie to me, losing me money."

And then I said in perfect English, "Yes, I'm getting rather concerned. You had agreed to send the check two weeks ago, but it hasn't arrived."

Then she began to talk more loudly. "What he want, I come to New York tell him front of his boss, you cheating me?" And I was trying to calm her down, make her be quiet, while telling the stockbroker, "I can't tolerate any more excuses. If I don't receive the check immediately, I am going to have to speak to your manager when I'm in New York next week." And sure enough, the following week there we were in front of this astonished stockbroker, and I was sitting there red-faced and quiet, and my mother, the real Mrs. Tan, was shouting at his boss in her impeccable broken English.

We used a similar routine just five days ago, for a situation that was far less humorous. My mother had gone to the hospital for an appointment, to find out about a benign brain tumor a CAT scan had revealed a month ago. She said she had spoken very good English, her best English, no mistakes. Still, she said, the hospital did not apologize when they said they had lost the CAT scan and she had come for nothing. She said they did not seem to have any sympathy when she told them she was anxious to know the exact diagnosis, since her husband and son had both died of brain tumors. She said they would not give her any more information until the next time and she would have to make another appointment for that. So she said she would not leave until the doctor called her daughter. She wouldn't budge. And when the doctor finally called her daughter, me, who spoke in perfect English—lo and behold—we had assurances the CAT scan would be found, promises that a conference call on Monday would be held, and apologies for any suffering my mother had gone through for a most regrettable mistake.

I think my mother's English almost had an effect on limiting my possibilities in life as well. Sociologists and linguists probably will tell you that a person's developing language skills are more influenced by peers. But I do think that the language spoken in the family, especially in immigrant families which are more insular, plays a large role in shaping the language of the child. And I believe that it affected my results on achievement tests, IQ tests, and the SAT. While my English skills were never judged as poor, compared to math, English could not be considered my strong suit. In grade school I did moderately well, getting perhaps B's, sometimes B-pluses, in English and scoring perhaps in the sixtieth or seventieth percentile on achievement tests. But those scores were not good enough to override the opinion that my true abilities lay in math and science, because in those areas I achieved A's and scored in the ninetieth percentile or higher.

This was understandable. Math is precise; there is only one correct answer. Whereas, for me at least, the answers on English tests were always a judgment call, a matter of opinion and personal experience. Those tests were constructed around items like fill-in-the-blank sentence completion, such as, "Even though Tom was _____, Mary thought he was _____." And the correct answer always seemed to be the most bland combinations of thoughts, for example, "Even though Tom was shy, Mary thought he was charming," with the grammatical structure "even though" limiting the correct answer to some sort of semantic opposites, so you wouldn't get answers like, "Even though Tom was foolish, Mary thought he was ridiculous." Well, according to my mother, there were very few limitations as to what Tom could have been and what Mary might have thought of him. So I never did well on tests like that.

The same was true with word analogies, pairs of words in which you were supposed to find some sort of logical, semantic relationship—for example, "Sunset is to nightfall as _____ is to _____." And here you would be presented with a list of four possible pairs, one of which showed the same kind of relationship: red is to stoplight, bus is to arrival, chills is to fever, yawn is to boring. Well, I could never think that way. I knew what the tests were asking, but I could not block out of my mind the images already created by the first pair, "sunset is to nightfall"—and I would see a burst of colors against a darkening sky, the moon rising, the lowering of a curtain of stars. And all the other pairs of words—red, bus, stoplight, boring—just threw up a mass of confusing images, making it impossible for me to sort out something as logical as saying: "A sunset precedes nightfall" is the same as "a chill precedes a fever." The only way I would have gotten that answer right would have been to imagine an associative situation, for example, my being disobedient and staying out past sunset, catching a chill at night, which turns into feverish pneumonia as punishment, which indeed did happen to me.

I have been thinking about all this lately, about my mother's English, about achievement tests. Because lately I've been asked, as a writer, why there are not more Asian Americans represented in American literature. Why are there few Asian Americans enrolled in creative writing programs? Why do so many Chinese students go into engineering? Well, these are broad sociological questions I can't begin to answer. But I have noticed in surveys—in fact, just last week—that Asian students, as a whole, always do significantly better on math achievement tests than in English. And this makes me think that there are other Asian-American students whose English spoken in the home might also be described as "broken" or "limited." And perhaps they also have teachers who are steering them away from writing and into math and science, which is what happened to me.

Fortunately, I happen to be rebellious in nature and enjoy the challenge of disproving assumptions made about me. I became an English major my first year in college, after being enrolled as pre-med. I started writing nonfiction as a freelancer the week after I was told by my former boss that writing was my worst skill and I should hone my talents toward account management.

But it wasn't until 1985 that I finally began to write fiction. And at first I wrote using what I thought to be wittily crafted sentences, sentences that would finally prove I had mastery over the English language. Here's an example from the first draft of a story that later made its way into *The Joy Luck Club*, but without this line: "That was my mental quandary in its nascent state." A terrible line, which I can barely pronounce.

Fortunately, for reasons I won't get into today, I later decided I should envision a reader for the stories I would write. And the reader I decided upon was my mother, because these were stories about mothers. So with this reader in mind—and in fact she did read my early drafts—I began to write stories using all the Englishes I grew up with: the English I spoke to my mother, which for lack of a better term might be described as "simple"; the English she used with me, which for lack of a better term might be described as "broken"; my translation of her Chinese, which could certainly be described as "watered down"; and what I imagined to be her translation of her Chinese if she could speak in perfect English, her internal language, and for that I sought to preserve the essence, but neither an English nor a Chinese structure. I wanted to capture what language ability tests can never reveal: her intent, her passion, her imagery, the rhythms of her speech and the nature of her thoughts.

Apart from what any critic had to say about my writing, I knew I had succeeded where it counted when my mother finished reading my book and gave me her verdict: "So easy to read."

READING **WRITING**

This Text: Reading

1. Tan points out that language is a sign for others trying to read her mother. What other nonvisual elements might be signs? How do we normally read them?
2. Talk about the way we discuss or react to people with accents. Why do accents mark, or set off as different, people? Is there any established non-marked way of speaking? Who speaks this way?
3. How do you think Tan feels about the situation in which she is placed by having to serve as her mother's "agent"? Is there a way around it?

Your Text: Writing

1. Write an essay talking about ways we mark people as different through non-visual means through popular culture. What forms of popular culture are especially guilty of this?
2. One of the things that Tan's essay brings up is the idea of Americanness. How should we define such a concept? Are there degrees of Americanness? Research and see what others say about this.
3. In what way is this piece an argument? What is Tan arguing? In your own work, use a story to argue a particular point.

True Tales of Amerikkkan History Part II: The True Thanksgiving

Jim Mahfood is a comic artist who often takes on stereotypes and race in his work. Here is his 1998 response to popular ideas about Thanksgiving.

Jim Mahfood

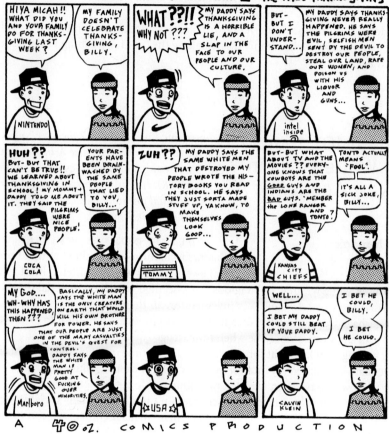

Source: *Stupid Comics* © 1998 by Jim Mahfood

READING WRITING

This Text: Reading

1. Compare Mahfood's approach to ethnicity to those taken in this chapter's suite.
2. What other subtext does Mahfood address with the boy's T-shirt? With the girl's Native American garb? Are these relevant to the main storyline? Why or why not?

3. What perspective do you think Mahfood is writing/drawing from? What do you think is motivating his writing?
4. Who do you think is Mahfood's audience? Does your answer depend on consideration of the medium he's using?

Your Text: Writing

1. Find a political cartoon and analyze it in terms of signs.
2. Write a short essay discussing why visual texts can communicate ideas effectively. You might compare a visual text and written text that have similar ideas but present them differently.
3. How does your previous experience with comics affect your ability to take political cartoons seriously? Write a short essay making the case for teaching visual culture at an early age.

Qallunaat 101: Inuits Study White Folks in This New Academic Field

Zebedee Nungak

A long-time Inuit activist, Zebedee Nungak is also the co-author with Eugene Arima of Inuit-Stories: Povungnauk-Légendes inuic Povung-nituk *(1988). In this wry piece, Nungak turns the traditional anthropologist subject-observer relationship on its head.*

LIKE MANY INUIT BOYS OF MY GENERATION, I had a fascination with Qallunaat that bordered on awe. The few we encountered lived in warm wooden houses, while we grew up in igloos. They seemed to lack no material thing. Their food was what the word *delicious* was invented for, all their women were beautiful, and even their garbage was impressive! As a boy, I had an innocent ambition to be like them. The measure of my success would be when my garbage equaled theirs.

I lived among the Qallunaat for seven years. In my time in their land, my discoveries of their peculiarities sparked my interest in what could be called Qallunology.

Many of us who have been exposed to Qallunaat-dom through deep immersion in their world could write some credible discourses on the subject. Their social mores and standards of etiquette could fill several volumes. Their language contains all sorts of weirdness. Their sameness and distinctness can be utterly baffling. An Irishman from Northern Ireland looks exactly the same as one from the Irish Republic. A close look at Albanians and Serbs has them all looking like bona fide Qallunaat. Why such savage conflict among such same-looking civilized people?

Look, Look! See Sally Run! Oh Dick, Oh Jane! Why do your parents have no name? Are all dogs in Qallunaat-dom Spot, all cats Puff? There was absolutely no Fun with Dick and Jane as we Inuit children crashed head-on into the English language. The cultural shocks and tremors have never completely worn off those of us who were zapped with such literature.

The Qallunaat custom of abbreviating first names does not seem to follow a standard formula. Robert can be Rob, Robbie, Bob, Bobby or Bert. Joseph is Joe, James/Jim, Sidney/Sid, Arthur/Art, and Peter/Pete. Charles is Charlie but can be Chuck. What sleight of hand makes a Henry a Hank? And how does Richard become a Dick, if not a Rich or a Rick? Do you see a B in William on its way to be a Bill? Don't ever say *Seen* for Sean (sh-AWN) or *John* for Jean, if the person is a francophone male.

Qallunaat women can have very masculine names clicked feminine by ending them with an A: Roberta, Edwina, Phillippa. Shortened names are mostly chopped versions—Katherine/Kate, Deborah/Debbie—except for some ready-made like Wendy and Kay. Liz is drawn from the midsection of Elizabeth, unlike in Inuit use, where these names are entirely separate as Elisapi and Lisi. Many names can fit both sexes: Pat, Jan, Leslie, Kit.

One of the most distinctive features of life among Qallunaat, the one most markedly different from Inuit life, can be summed up in this expression of theirs: keeping up with the Joneses. Not much is communal and few essentials are shared. Life is based on competition, going to great lengths to "get ahead," and amassing what you gain for yourself. People around you may be in want, but that is their problem.

We know Qallunaat, of course, by the way they eat: with a fork and a dull knife known by Inuit as *nuvuittuq* (without point). There is a whole etiquette to eating too cumbersome to describe in detail. But, if one has the misfortune to burp, belch, or fart during the meal, one has to be civil and say "Excuse me!" in a sincere enough demeanor. Never forget to say "please" in asking for the salt or potatoes to be passed. Don't ever just up and walk away from the table.

Having visitors over (company) is mostly attached to some ritual or activity, such as a bridge game. If alcohol is served to guests, it is amazingly incidental, and not the main item of attention. Nobody gets drunk, but there is a lot of talking! Then there seems to be an obligation to talk even more at the door before leaving. Guests and hosts lingering forever at the entrance to talk about nothing in particular is one of the surest trademarks of being in Qallunaat-dom.

There is a ritual called dating, which is hard to describe in Inuit terms. It can't really be described as husband- or wife-hunting. Maturing people of opposite sexes mutually agree to "go out" to some form of enjoyable activity. Sometimes it is to test their compatibility as a possible couple, sometimes simply to genuinely enjoy each other's company. It seems to be a permanent occupation of some, whom Inuit might call *uinitsuituq* or *nulianitsuituq*, meaning "un-attachable to a husband or wife."

I don't proclaim to be an expert on Qallunaat and what makes them tick. But my commentaries on Qallunology are based on having eaten, slept, and breathed their life for some years, learning their language, and tumbling along in their tidy-square thought processes. The resulting recollections are no more superficial than those of the first Qallunaat to encounter the Inuit, who unwittingly illustrated their educated ignorance when they tried to describe us. That has changed. Today, even Qallunaat with strings of academic degrees attached to their names are more often seeking guidance from the reservoir of traditional Inuit knowledge.

Eskimology has long been a serious field of study by Qallunaat. Scores of museums and universities all over the world have great departments and sections devoted solely to the subject. Serious Qallunologists, on the other hand, are likely to sweat and toil in unrewarding anonymity until the academic currency of their field of study attains the respectability of being labeled officially with an "-ology."

Eskimologists have carted off traditional clothing, artifacts, hunting implements, tools, ancient stories and legends, and human remains for display in museums, bartering these for very little. Qallunologists will find nothing worth carting away for display. All Qallunaat stuff is for immediate use, much of it disposable, easily replaceable, and now available in mass quantities to Inuit as well. It all costs quite a lot, and one will be prosecuted for stealing any of it.

Eskimology was triggered by others' curiosity about who we are and how we live. It has flourished to the point that we Inuit have in some ways benefited from it by reclaiming some essences of our identity from various collections in others' possession. Qallunaat, meanwhile, are not in any danger of having to go to museums to pick up remnants of who they once were.

READING WRITING

This Text: Reading

1. Do you think this piece is funny? Why or why not?
2. What points is Nungak making about the relationships between Inuits and whites? Have you heard these issues before? Is Nungak treating these ideas differently?
3. Does anyone study white people as an anthropological study? If not, should they? If so, who does?

This Text: Writing

1. Do your own anthropological study of a group or phenomenon that seems familiar but can still be studied (cafeteria, gym, supermarket, etc.).
2. Find a traditional anthropological study and write a compare and contrast piece.

Race Is a Four-Letter Word

Teja Arboleda

In this piece, taken from his 1998 book, In the Shadow of Race, *Arboleda explores what it means to be multiracial. A producer and performer, Arboleda wrote and directed* Got Race, *his first feature-length movie, which premiered in October 2003.*

I'VE BEEN CALLED *nigger* and a neighbor set the dogs on us in Queens, New York.
I've been called *spic* and was frisked in a plush neighborhood of Los Angeles.
I've been called *Jap* and was blamed for America's weaknesses.
I've been called *Nazi* and the neighborhood G.I. Joes had me every time.
I've been called *Turk* and was sneered at in Germany.
I've been called *Stupid Yankee* and was threatened in Japan.
I've been called *Afghanistani* and was spit on by a Boston cab driver.
I've been called *Iraqi* and Desert Storm was America's pride.
I've been called *mulatto, criollo, mestizo, simarron, Hapahaoli, masala, exotic, alternative, mixed-up, messed-up, half-breed,* and *in between.* I've been mistaken for Moroccan, Algerian, Egyptian, Lebanese, Iranian, Turkish, Brazilian, Argentinean, Puerto Rican, Cuban, Mexican, Indonesian, Nepalese, Greek, Italian, Pakistani, Indian, Black, White, Hispanic, Asian, and being a Brooklynite. I've been mistaken for Michael Jackson and Billy Crystal on the same day.

I've been ordered to get glasses of water for neighboring restaurant patrons. I've been told to be careful mopping the floors at the television station where I was directing a show. Even with my U.S. passport, I've been escorted to the "aliens only" line at Kennedy International Airport. I've been told I'm not dark enough. I've been told I'm not White enough. I've been told I talk American real good. I've been told, "Take your hummus and your pita bread and go back to Mexico!" I've been ordered to "Go back to where you belong, we don't like *your* kind here!"

I spent too much time and energy as a budding adult abbreviating my identity and rehearsing its explanation. I would practice quietly by myself, reciting what my father always told me: "Filipino-German." He never smiled when he said this.

My father's dark skin told many stories that his stern face and anger-filled tension couldn't translate. My mother's light skin could never spell empathy—even suntanning only made her turn bright red. My brother Miguel and I became curiosity factors when we appeared in public with her. During the past 34 years, my skin has lightened, somewhat, but then in the summers (even in New England where summers happen suddenly, and disappear just as quickly), I can darken several degrees in a matter of hours. This phenomenon seems a peculiar paradigm to which people's perceptions of my culture or race alter with the waning and waxing of my skin tone. I can almost design others' perceptions by counting my minutes in the sun. My years in Japan, the United States, Germany, and the numerous countries, cities, and towns through which I've traveled, have proven that my flesh is irrelevant to the language I speak, to the way I walk and talk, or the way I jog or mow my lawn or to the fact that I often use chopsticks to eat. It is irrelevant to *who* or *what* I married, my political viewpoints, my career, my hopes, desires and fears.

I don't remember being taught by my parents never to *question* skin color, yet when I compare the back of my hand to these pages, I cannot help myself—I must know. Like a sickness coursing through my veins with the very blood that makes me who I am, I ask: What color am I? And, what color was I yesterday? Tomorrow? There is also that pesky, familiar feeling I get when, in the corner of my eye, I catch passing strangers with judgments written on their brows. Maybe paranoia, maybe vanity, but the experiences and memories of too often being "different" or "undefinable" have left me with a weary sense of instant verdict on my part. And sometimes I study their thousands of faces, hoping somehow to connect. I know that they ask themselves the same questions, as they are plagued by the same epidemic, asking and reasking themselves, ourselves, "Who and what are we?"

Overadapting to new environments has become second nature to me, as my father and my mother eagerly fed me culture. As a child I felt like I was being dragged to different corners of the planet with my parents, filling their need for exploration and contact, and teaching us the value and beauty of difference. Between packing suitcases and wandering through unfamiliar territory, all I had ever wanted was to be "the same."

They were successful in some respects—I do believe I am liberal in my thinking—but inevitably there was a price to pay. With each step, each move, each landing through the thick and tenuous atmosphere of a new culture, my feet searched for solid ground, for something familiar. The concept of home, identity, and place become ethereal, like a swirl of gases circling in orbit, waiting for gravity to define their position.

In a sense, I have been relegated to ethnic benchwarmer, on a hunt for simplicity in a world of confusing words that deeply divide us all. In response, I learned to overcompensate. New places and new faces have rarely threatened me, but I have a desperate need to belong to whatever group I'm with at any particular moment. I soak in the surrounding elements to cope with what my instincts oblige, and deliver a new temporary self. I am out of bounds, transcending people and places. I carry within my blood the memories of my heritage connected in the web of my mind, the marriage of history and biology. I breathe the air of my ancestors as if it were fresh from the sunrises of their past. I am illogical, providing argument to traditional categories of race, culture, and ethnicity. I am a cultural chameleon, adapting out of necessity only to discover, yet again, a new Darwinism at the frontiers of identity.

"What are you, anyway?" sometimes demandingly curious Americans like to ask. "I'm Filipino-German," I used to say. I have never been satisfied with abbreviating my identity to the exclusion of all the other puzzle pieces that would then be lost forever in shadowy corners where no one ever looks.

Do I throw a nod at a Black brother who passes me on the street? And if I did so, would he understand why I did? Do I even call him "brother?" Does *he* call *me* "brother?" If not, should he call me a "half-brother," or throw me a half nod? In the United States do I nod or bow to Japanese nationals in a Japanese restaurant? Would they know to bow with me? In Jamaica Plain, Massachusetts, if a Hispanic male gestures hello to me, is it a simple greeting, or a gesture of camaraderie because I might be Hispanic? Do I dress up to go to a country club because, in the eyes of its rich White men, I would otherwise live up to their idea of the stereotypical minority? Should I dance well, shaking and driving my body like Papa's family afforded me, or should I remain appropriately conservative to preserve the integrity of a long-gone Puritan New England? Do I shave for the silver hallways of white-collar high-rises so as not to look too "ethnic?" Do I agree to an audition for a commercial when I know the reason I'm there is just to fill in with some skin color for an industry quota?

"I know you're *something*," someone once said. "You have some Black in you," another offered. "He must be ethnic or something," I've overheard. "I've got such a boring family compared to yours," another confided. "You're messed-up," an elementary school girl decided. "Do you love your race?" her classmate wondered. "*What* did you marry?" I've been asked. "*Who* did you marry?" I've been asked. "Is she just like you?" I've been asked. "You are the quintessential American," someone decided.

■ ■ ■

America continues to struggle through its identity crisis, and the simple, lazy, bureaucratic checklist we use only serves to satisfy an outdated four-letter word—*race*. Like the basic food groups, it is overconsumed and digested, forming a hemorrhoid in the backside of the same old power struggle. I am only one of many millions of Americans, from this "League of Outsiders," demanding a change in the way we are designated, routed, cattle-called, herded, and shackled into these simplified classifications.

The United States is going through growing pains. The immigrants coming to the United States and becoming citizens are no longer primarily of European origin. But let's not fool ourselves into thinking that America is only now becoming multicultural.

In 1992, *Time* magazine produced a special issue entitled, "The New Face of America" with the subtitle, "How immigrants are shaping the world's first multicultural society." The cover featured a picture of a woman's face. Next to the face was a paragraph that suggested her image was the result of a computerized average of faces of people of several different races.

The operative words on the cover are "races," "culture," and "first." Race and culture are very different words. Race in America is predominantly determined by skin color. Culture is determined by our experiences and our interactions within a society, large or small.

Then there is this idea of being "first." Are we to say that this continent was never populated by a mix of people? Are we to say that the Lacota and Iroquois were of exactly the same culture? What about the different Europeans who settled here later on? Of course, African slaves were not all from the same tribe, and they certainly were not of the same culture as the slave traders.

In the middle of the magazine, there was a compilation, more like a chart of photographs of people from all over the world. The editor and computer artist scanned all the pictures into a computer. Then, by having the computer average the faces together, they produced a variety of facial combinations. Remember, however, they said on the cover, "People from different *races* . . . to form the world's first *multicultural* society." But in the body of the article and its accompanying pictures, many people were not identified by their *race*, but rather by their *nationalities*—such as Italian and Chinese—in other words *citizenship*, a very different word.

Through it all, *Time* was trying to educate us, but at the same time, we're miseducated. The world—not just this country—has always been and always will be a multicultural environment. So what is it about the words *multicultural* or *diversity* that is confusing or overwhelming?

In the next 20 years, the average American will no longer be technically White. This will have to be reflected in the media, in the workplace, and in the schools, not out of charitable interest, but out of necessity. More people are designating themselves as multiracial or multicultural. People continue to marry across religious, cultural, and ethnic barriers. A definition for "mainstream society" is harder to find.

■ ■ ■

My mother's father, Opa, died a year after Oma passed away. The day after the funeral in Germany, my mother's relatives told her, for the first time, that her father was not really her father (i.e., biologically). All the people who knew the true identity of her father have long since passed away. So, if my mother's biological father was, let's say, Italian or Russian, does that make her German-Italian or German-Russian? She says no. German, only German, because that's how she was raised.

My brother, Miguel, married a Brazilian. (*Pause.*) Do you have an image in your head of what she looks like? I did when he first told me about her over the phone. Well, she is Brazilian by culture and citizenship, but her parents are Japanese nationals who moved to Brazil in their early 20s to escape poverty in Japan after World War II. So she *looks stereotypically* Japanese. But she speaks Portuguese and doesn't interact socially like most Japanese do.

■ ■ ■

I offer myself as a case study in transcending the complex maze of barriers, pedestals, doors, and traps that form the boundaries that confine human beings to dominant and minority groups.

I am tired. I am exhausted. I am always looking for new and improved definitions for my identity. My very-mixed heritage, culture, and international experiences seem like a blur sometimes, and I long for a resting place. A place where I can breathe like I did in my mother's womb: without having to open my mouth.

READING WRITING

This Text: Reading

1. In what ways does Arboleda present himself as a text? In what ways do people "misread" him?
2. The author writes in a vivid first person style; in what ways would this story be different if it were in the third person?
3. How does Arboleda describe his identity? How is his idea of identity different from the identity he finds in others' reactions to him?

Your Text: Writing

1. Write about a time when you were mistaken for another group, whether enthnicity, gender, class, or age. What assumptions did the people mistaking you for someone else make?
2. Do research on multiracial identity and determine what issues are "in the air." *Hint:* Both the recent census and Tiger Woods's statements about his identity have made this issue more prominent. Then re-read this text or another one that involves this issue, such as the movie *The Human Stain.* In what ways do the text and research speak to one another?

Censoring Myself

Betty Shamieh

Betty Shamieh, an Arab American, is a highly regarded writer and performer. Her play Chocolate in the Heat—Growing Up Arab in America *was staged in 2001 in New York. A graduate of Harvard and the Yale School of Drama, Shamieh's essay (2003) is about being read as a certain kind of text—an Arab American—in the wake of 9/11.*

I AM A PALESTINIAN-AMERICAN PLAYWRIGHT—and I'm Christian. Significant numbers of Arabs are Christian, which is something many Americans do not know; Arab society is not by any means homogeneous.

I was born in San Francisco, so I'm a citizen of this country. I went to Harvard and Yale and what attending institutions like that provides is access to people in positions of power.

Yet, part of me is terrified to be writing these words singling myself out as an Arab-American at this stage in American history, because I don't know what the ramifications of that are or will be. Part of me wants to heed President Bush when he lets it be known on national television that he thinks citizens better "watch what they say," but part of me is extremely cognizant of the fact that over a thousand Arab- and Muslim-Americans were picked up and held for months without trials and without our government releasing their names following the attacks of Sept. 11; that it was 18 months after Pearl Harbor that Japanese Americans were sent to internment camps; and that this country does not have a history of showing tolerance toward any racial minority whose members are easy to pick out of a crowd.

There are certainly acts of intolerance short of internment of which governments are capable. I have been censored in many ways. But I think the most overt example of censorship I have yet faced is my experience with a project called the Brave New World Festival.

The Brave New World Festival at New York City's Town Hall was—as its Web site declared—designed for artists to explore "the alternate roots of terrorism." For the most part, only very well-established playwrights were asked to participate, but I—who had just finished Yale School of Drama a year before—was invited partly because of my work at the "Imagine: Iraq" reading, which drew 900 people to Cooper Union in New York City in November 2001, to hear plays about the Middle East. I am an actress as well as a playwright, and, at the "Imagine: Iraq" reading, I performed a monologue I wrote about the sister of a suicide bomber who mourns not knowing what her brother planned to do and not being able to stop him. The piece is very clearly a plea for non-violence.

When the organizers of the Brave New World Festival asked me to perform the same monologue for them, my first thought was that I did not want to be in Town Hall on the first anniversary of Sept. 11 presenting a play that deals with such potent subject matter. Then I realized that it was especially important at that time and in that place to present precisely such work. So, despite all my fears and concerns, I agreed to their request—but asked the organizers to get Marisa Tomei (who was already involved in the project) or an actress of that caliber to play the role. I felt that if there was going to be a backlash, I didn't want to be dealing with it alone.

I got a call from an organizer a few weeks later. She told me she loved the piece and that—at my request—she had given it to Marisa Tomei. But she also said that some of her colleagues had objected to the content of my piece. She informed me that I was welcome to write something different but that they were rescinding their offer to present my monologue.

At this time, I did not know that they were also censoring people like Eduardo Machado, who is the head of the playwriting MFA program at Columbia and one of the best-known playwrights of his generation.

So, in an Uncle Tom–like manner, instead of holding my ground, I wrote another piece. I did so because I was the only Arab-American playwright in the lineup. Arab-American artists are largely faceless in this country and I felt that, by dropping out, I would be helping those who are trying to keep it that way.

The new piece I wrote for them was a very mild and humorous short play. The narrator, an Arab-American girl, tells the audience of a fantasy she has about ending up on a hijacked plane and talking the hijackers out of their plans. The people on the plane listen to the hijackers' grievances and actually refuse to get off the flight until all people have a right to live in safety and freedom. Then, in her fantasy, the narrator ends up on "Oprah," and has a movie made about her starring Julia Roberts.

Harmless, right? Especially for a forum designed to present theater that asked real questions.

But when I got into rehearsal on the day of the performance with the director, Billy Hopkins, and actresses including Rosie Perez, I realized someone had censored the text, deleting chunks of my work that deal with the main character talking to the hijackers and making them see the error of their ways.

Of course, I had my own original copy with me. I had just begun to distribute it when the stage manager stepped into the rehearsal. She announced that because the performance schedule had grown overlong, my piece, the token Arab-American playwright's play, had been cut, along with a number of others.

What made the experience particularly disturbing was that the organizers had touted this event as a venue for alternative ideas and voices. To censor voices that present exactly those perspectives made it seem as though those voices don't exist.

Many people ask me if I—as a Palestinian-American playwright living in New York in a post–Sept. 11 world—have been facing more censorship in the wake of that horrific event that changed all of our lives. The answer—which might surprise many—is no.

The reason is that there was such as astounding level of censorship in American theater when it comes to the Palestinian perspective before Sept. 11, that I really haven't felt a difference in the past two years.

Indeed, the last time there was a serious attempt to bring a play written by a Palestinian to a major New York stage was in 1989. Joe Papp, artistic director of the Joseph Papp Public Theatre, asked a Palestinian theater troupe that had toured throughout Europe to bring its highly acclaimed show, *The Story of Kufur Shamma,* to his theater.

Joe Papp was a theatrical visionary. In other words, he wasn't going to stick a piece of mindless propaganda on his theater's stage. But his board objected to his decision to bring the show to New York.

Papp, arguably the most powerful man in the history of American theater, did not feel he could stand up to his board members. He rescinded his offer because, as the *Philadelphia Inquirer* reported, "he had come under a great deal of pressure and that he could not jeopardize his theater."

I'm telling this story only because I think its relationship with my work is intriguing. For the three years I was a graduate student at the Yale School of Drama, I, in effect, censored myself. I did not produce a single play about the Palestinian experience, which is an enormous part of who I am as a person and an artist.

I wanted to avoid confronting the kind of censorship anybody faces when portraying the Palestinians as human beings. I wanted to avoid that kind of controversy until I had a bit of a name for myself, a bit of a following.

Unfortunately, what happened as a result of my self-censorship was my work was eviscerated. Now, I write about the Palestinian experience not only just because it deserves—as all stories deserve—to be heard, but also because if I hope to make vital theater I can only write about what I care deeply about. And vital theater is the only kind of theater I'm interested in making.

It came down to a very clear choice for me. I either had to give up writing for the stage or decide to write about what I knew and cared about and, therefore, face what it meant to be a Palestinian-American playwright working in New York at this time. I, either wisely or unwisely, have chosen the latter.

When you think of all the ethnic minorities in this country who have had their story told multiple times in the theater, you wonder—would it do such harm to add to that mosaic one story about the Palestinian perspective?

Are the people involved in the incidents I mentioned being rational when they try so hard to keep a Palestinian perspective out of the public eye, which they unfortunately and—in my opinion—unnecessarily see as contrary to their own?

Aren't they overreacting a little bit? I mean, really. Is theater that powerful?

The answer is yes. A good play, a play that makes you feel, allows you to see its characters as fully human, if only for two hours.

If more people actually saw Palestinians as human beings, our foreign policy could not and would not be the same.

READING **WRITING**

This Text: Reading

1. What are some of the problems Shamieh has had to face as an Arab American?
2. Shamieh refers to a decision as being Uncle Tom-esque. What does she mean by this?
3. How is this essay about identity? Does Shamieh have a thesis? If so, what is it?

Your Text: Writing

1. Write a first-person essay, like Shamieh's, in which you talk about your own identity as a text. How have people read and misread you?
2. Write an essay in which you respond to Shamieh's. What did you learn from her piece?
3. Write a comparison/contrast paper on Shamieh's essay and Amy Tan's "Mother Tongue." How are they similar? How does gender figure in to issues of race?

Gender Expectations and Familial Roles Within Asian American Culture

Amy Truong

Student Essay

Amy Truong wrote this essay for Professor Brian Komei Dempster's Asian American Literature survey course at the University of San Francisco. Here, she reads the texts of gender, race, and family alongside Lan Samantha Chang's novella The Unforgetting. *Dempster says of Truong's essay, "I admire the synthesis of literary analysis and family history." To achieve this effect, Truong shifts back and forth between readings of Chang and Truong.*

> In Mercy Lake he started his new job as a photocopy machine repairman . . . He maintained the new Chevrolet sedan—changed the oil, followed the tune-up dates, and kept good records of all repairs . . . He labored on the yard. (Chang, 135–136, 140)
>
> She laundered Ming's new work clothes: permanent-press shirts with plastic tabs inserted in the stiff, pointed collars; bright, wide ties . . . In the kitchen, Sansan learned to cook with canned and frozen foods. She made cream of tomato soup for lunch, and stored envelopes of onion soup mix for meat loaf or quick onion dip. More often . . . Sansan consulted the Betty Crocker cookbook. (138–139)

Are these from an episode of *Leave It to Beaver*? No. These are excerpts from Lan Samantha Chang's, "The Unforgetting." Ask yourself what these excerpts mean to you. They may just simply remind some of you of an episode of *Leave It to Beaver* because these were the characteristic roles of men and women some decades ago when television sets only came in black and white—men were the breadwinners while women were the caretakers. For others, including myself, they are reminders of the life that still exists; a life that is representative of many Asian American families today.

In many Asian cultures, gender plays a role in dictating what you do. Certain members of the family are designated specific responsibilities that complement their respective gender roles much like the characters in *Leave It to Beaver*. The males support the family financially and control the household, and the women take care of the family and household chores. Lan Samantha Chang's novella, "Hunger," parallels the events in my life and shows how gender roles are still very apparent in today's Asian American families. This essay seeks to capture that parallel experience of interpreting Chang's text and the texts of my own experiences.

Within Asian culture, women are raised and taught to be silent and obedient. I am a first generation Vietnamese American and growing up, I was told, "Do not comment or speak up," whenever I wanted to voice my opinion. My opinion was considered unimportant. And for many years of my life I believed that this was true. I never spoke a word unless I was asked to speak or spoken to; until I finally became tired of being mute. As a young teenager, my parents were going through difficult times with their marriage. One night, my mother, father, grandmother, brother and I sat down to have a family meeting about the issues between my parents. My dad did all the talking while my mom sat in silence like she always did. "Your mother has committed terrible sins and has destroyed our family," he said to us sternly in our native language. Not once during the entire family meeting did anyone in the family speak other than my father. Before the meeting ended, I finally worked up the nerve to defend my mother since she refused to defend herself. "Daddy, you shouldn't speak about Mommy like that in front of us," I declared. As soon as I said it, my father slapped me hard on the back of my head and told me, "Do not ever speak unless you have been instructed to." I immediately received a scolding from my mother and grandmother as well. Ironically, it was my mind that they thought was poisoned, and they blamed America for my "rebellious" breaking of silence.

The characters in Lan Samantha Chang's "Hunger" also suffer from silence. Min, the wife, very rarely speaks a word when she does not agree with her husband. Instead, she lets him do as he pleases and remains quiet as a good Asian wife. For instance, her husband treats their youngest daughter in ways that she does not particularly agree with. Her husband places a lot of pressure on their daughter and that is not how she wants their children to grow up. Yet she remains silent, because she believes that it is her place to let her husband control their family and their daughter in the way that he wants. For example, the mother's silence is demonstrated on one occasion when her daughter and husband are screaming:

> Baba, let me stop! You go ahead and cry! . . . You cry all you want! . . . You cry! But—play! . . .
> As I ironed I watched Anna fiddle with the frayed towels that had once been pink but now were faded to a creamy white . . . I opened my mouth but my throat was dry. (59)

She wishes to protect her daughter and attempts to speak, but chooses to refrain from doing so due to her respective roles as a woman and wife. Ironically, it is only after her death that she is able to voice her thoughts. In essence, the novella's point-of-view is symbolic and emphasizes how a woman's voice can be silenced due to her gender role.

Ruth, the youngest daughter, is also silenced and lets her father live vicariously through her. Though she hates it, she does not speak against his wishes. For example, her father makes her play the violin and has her practice for hours on end. She practices so much everyday that it brings her to tears and causes her to resent her father, because she cannot do or say anything that will prevent him from forcing her to play. For instance, when she and her father are locked in the practice room, he tells her,

> Do you understand? From now on, you work. You practice everyday . . . No no no no—
> Her voice rose to a shriek. There was a slam as he closed the door, and they were trapped inside the room together. . . . He clapped and counted. She played and cried. (60)

Though she cries and screams, she continues to play because this is her father's desire. Irony once again occurs. Just as Tian leaves his family to pursue his passion for music, Ruth's passionate hate for that same music drives her to leave her family as well. As a woman, she is put in an impossible position: her breaking of silence and fighting back is a form of defiance and shows a lack of respect towards the male figure, causing the destruction of this family.

In Vietnamese culture, the oldest daughter is also expected to play a major role in the house—she is expected to handle household chores and responsibilities in the absence of a mother. My mother is the oldest daughter and was only fourteen when she arrived in the United States after the Vietnam War. My mother came to this country with her older brother, Nihn (age 18), her two younger brothers, Can (10) and Toan (4), and her younger sister, Ngoc (5). "Life was very hard and unbearable sometimes," she said. My mother had to take on the difficult responsibility of taking care of all her siblings. At the tender age of fourteen, she assisted her siblings with their schoolwork, put food on the table and clothes on their backs, attended school, worked a part-time job, and attempted to learn the English language. My grandparents finally arrived in the United States (along with two more children) when my mother was 22 years old. "I thought it was over," she told me. But this was not the case. My grandparents expected more from my mother because after eight years in the United States she spoke the English language, understood how the system worked, and already seemed to have things under control. My grandparents soon developed a bad gambling habit and left my mother to take on the burden of caring for her six siblings. I ask my mother why she continued to put up with it. She responded only by saying, "I am obligated, Amy." Till this day my mother is the one who holds her family together, and one day she expects me (the oldest and only daughter) to do the same for my siblings and our family.

In "Hunger," Anna is the oldest daughter who, like my mother, has the responsibility of taking care of the home in the absence of her mother. She hires men to work on the home, decorates it so that it will be more presentable, and even gives tours to interested buyers. Strangely, she denies bids on the house and does not move out into a beautiful loft, a comfy townhouse or spacious condominium. As much as Anna longs to sell the house in order to rid of all their unhappy memories, a part of her feels obligated to stay there. For instance, Anna's mother watches her as she lays in bed and notices, "through all this, Anna sleeps; but on some nights, as the melodies fade away, she shudders and sits up in bed . . . Perhaps she has been dreaming of her greatest hope and fear—that the house is gone, that it is destroyed, and nothing more remains of it" (114). Anna's personal desire to forget her family's past conflicts with her duty to her family to keep their home. Anna stays loyal to her gender and familial role by remaining in that home, resulting in restless nights due to her split conscience.

On the other hand, men play a very different role in an Asian family. They are the primary (and often only) breadwinner in the family. My father came to the United States when he was 23. Because of his limited knowledge of English, he found it difficult to obtain good work or even go back to school. "No one would hire me because my English was very hard to understand," he explains. This affected him ten years later when he and my mother married. Because my father did not know the language well, my mother was the breadwinner in their relationship. This made my father "lose face." Not being able to contribute to the household as much as your wife was a shameful thing and made him lose a lot of his pride. "I was very embarrassed that your mother made more than me. I was too ashamed to even go out because I worried that others would see me and speak badly of me," my father states, no longer embarrassed. Not being able to provide for the family financially, my father expressed his "manliness" in other ways. Though my mother made most of the money, he decided where that money would go and how it would be distributed. He was also very strict, held strongly to Vietnamese traditions, and made sure we knew that he still wore the pants. He made sure that I was never out late, because traditionally it was not appropriate for a young lady to be out past dark. Even to this day, I am expected to be home and in bed at 10 P.M. He made sure that we never spoke English in the house so that we would remember where we came from and so that others would know that we were still very Vietnamese even though we were born American. When we spoke English, he either ignored what we said or scorned us for doing so. "You must remember your origins. This house is not a white man's house," he droned in our native language. He also made sure of this by having my mother cook traditional Vietnamese meals every day and restricted us from having things such as burgers, fries and sodas. He told us, "Vietnamese food is healthier than American food . . . tastes better too. All Americans know how to do is fry their food. The Vietnamese, on the other hand, are real chefs." My father is now trying to regain his respect and honor by taking night courses and practicing his English with my mother and his children. He hopes that by doing this he will earn a better job with better money so that he can fulfill his duty as a man and father.

Tian, the father in "Hunger," is the breadwinner and the head of his household, much like my father. He provides the only source of income and does so by first working as a music professor, then in a restaurant. He also calls all the shots and makes all the decisions for each member of his family. For example, he decides that Ruth is going to play the violin and that she is going to play it well by forcing her to practice whenever she has free time. According to the novella, "All morning during summer vacations, plus two evenings a week, he sat in the tiny room for hours and helped her practice" (62). Though the text indicates that he is helping Ruth, no normal teenager wants to be locked in a room practicing a craft that he/she has no interest in. Therefore, force is used on Tian's part to get her to do so. He also decides that she is not going to attend the university where he once taught even after they offer her a scholarship. They have an argument and he demands,

> You're staying here. Let go of my arm! You're hurting me! You are not leaving this house as long as you are still a child. Do you hear me? I'm not a child! You're my daughter and I'm your father! (72)

It is not traditional among Asian families for a child to leave the home to attend school. His refusal to succumb to this American tradition represents his need to control the family.

Tian also tells his wife Min what to do. One such incident occurs after his recital. Tian's colleagues want him to stay and have some drinks. He tells them that Min is tired, but it is she who insists that they stay. He hushes her quickly and tells her that they are going to go home. Min urges him,

> It is okay. My [Min's] voice cracked against the words . . . Come on, said Tian. He took my arm and pulled me around the corner, to the coatrack. I'm not that tired; I could have gone out with them . . . Why did you want to leave so much? . . . I want to go home. (22)

Though Min is persistent that her husband mingle with his American friends, his desire is apparently more important than hers, displaying both his power and her silence. Tian, like many other Asian men, including my father, is the money-earner and controller of the family. They both support the family financially and make all the decisions pertaining to each member of the family whether or not protest occurs.

Male sons also have a respected role in the Asian family. They are expected to bring in income and help with the household expenses as well. My younger brother, Tim (19), lives with my parents and has paid rent every month since he was seventeen and received his first job. My parents do not like to call it rent. They prefer to term it "duty" or "obligation." Tim is still young and would prefer to spend his money to go out and have fun with his friends. He and my parents constantly argue about this topic but my parents do not budge. "Tim, it is your responsibility to contribute to the needs of the family. This is only preparing you so that one day you can handle the responsibility of being a father, the man of the house, when it is your time," they continually insist to him in Vietnamese. Likewise, they tell Tim that American traditions have made him ungrateful and lazy. In due time, they will be lecturing the same thing to my other younger brother, Will (5), as well.

In "Hunger," all of the characters, like my brother, struggle between achieving their individual desires and observing their respective gender and familial roles. Min wishes to speak her thoughts, but her role as a wife prevents her from doing so. Min has other desires and yet after "Twenty-one years . . . I had never admitted my disappointment with him. I had not complained about a lack of money or time together. I had taken what he brought home and made it into our daily lives" (94). Min is very unhappy and though she yearns to express her disappointment and opinion, she can not because she has to maintain her role as dutiful wife.

Tian decides to pursue his love for music but at the cost of abandoning his family and his responsibilities to them. According to Tian,

> Everyone . . . has things they want to do in their lives. But sometimes there is only one thing— one thing that a person must do. More than what he is told to do, more than what he is trained to do. Even more than what his family wants him to do. It is what he hungers for. (28)

Unlike some members of his family, Tian chooses his own personal longing over his obligation to his respective gender and familial role, claiming that it is something that he must do, as though he has no choice.

Ruth challenges her prescribed role as a daughter so that she can live the life that she always wanted to, also at the cost of her family. She searches for freedom from her duties, saying, " 'I'm quitting! I'm never going to pick up a violin again for as long as I live.' And without a pause, he cried, 'Then I don't want you! You are not my daughter! You are nothing!' " (88). After this heated exchange, Ruth "walked to the door, opened it, and stepped outside" (90). Ruth and Tian have their differences, but they are very much alike. As stated earlier, they both leave their families to pursue their dreams, disregarding their responsibilities to their family.

Anna wishes to forget all her memories by selling their home. Instead, she is true to her respected role and remains in that home even against her own wishes. For example, "One day she opened the door to a brisk young couple full of plans, the woman's belly swollen with hope like freshly risen dough . . . They bid, and Anna refused to sell" (107). Anna has invested much money into fixing the house so that she can begin to forget the past it holds, but her obligation to stay in that house so that her family's story can be saved keeps her from doing so.

Like my brother, the characters of "Hunger" make sacrifices in order to fulfill their roles. Likewise, those who follow their desires make huge sacrifices as well. Their personal longings and respected gender and familial roles create internal conflicts that are a part of their everyday lives just as is so with members of today's Asian American families.

It has been thirty years since my parents first arrived in the United States. Most people would expect them to assimilate to the American culture by now but they are deep-rooted in their Asian traditions and way of thinking, just as Min and Tian from "Hunger" are. They raised my brothers and me by attempting to pass on their way of thinking, hoping that we honor our roots. We are Vietnamese and were raised to understand and adhere to Vietnamese values, meaning that we are to accept our gender and familial roles as many of

Chang's characters do. What my parents fail to understand is that we are also American and have been greatly immersed in and influenced by the American culture as well. My siblings and I believe that gender roles are a thing of the past . . . a thing that belongs to the generation, time, and country in which my parents grew up.

In essence, my siblings and I are Anna and Ruth in "Hunger" while my parents are Min and Tian. We are a great representation of an Asian American family torn apart by our prescribed gender and familial roles. Reminiscent of the family in "Hunger," my family is one of many Asian American families conflicted with such issues. These issues tear apart the family in Chang's story, but many Asian American families are learning to cope with these problems by finding a balance between familial responsibilities and personal desires instead of letting one or the other dictate their lives completely. For us, these issues have become an everyday part of our lives and our struggles seem to be far from over. There is much that my siblings and I need to understand about the immigrant generation and vice versa. Whether or not these conflicts will ever disappear is still a mystery and has yet to stand the test of time.

Works Cited

Chang, Lan Samantha. *Hunger: A Novella and Stories.* New York: Penguin Books, 1998.

The Native American Mascot Issue

The very day we sat down to write the introduction to this suite for the second edition, we read in the papers that Southeast Missouri State University had decided to drop their Native American mascots. The board of regents voted unanimously to cease using "Indians" for its men's athletic teams and "Otahkians" for the women's teams and instead use "Redhawks." This time around, the mascot issue making the news is Chief Illiniwek and the University of Illinois, where a close friend of one of the authors has taken over as director of the Native American House. Unrest over Chief Illiniwek has been percolating for some time, but a 2005 policy by the National Collegiate Athletic Association (NCAA) that prohibits institutions with Indian mascots and imagery from displaying either at NCAA events, thrust the Chief and the University into an uncomfortable spotlight. The issue polarized the campus, and some Native scholars at the university have had property vandalized and even received

death threats. However, in February 2007, the University officially announced that it would cease using Native imagery and that Chief Illiniwek would dance no more.

The move by Illinois is one of more than 300 mascot changes that have occurred since the early 1980s. Activists first began raising questions about the ethics of Native American mascots in 1968, when the National Congress of American Indians began a campaign to address issues of stereotypes in the media. The following year, students, faculty, and other interested parties protested Dartmouth College's "Indian" nickname. It was on April 17, 1970, however, that the dam burst. The University of Oklahoma, a sports powerhouse with a visible Native mascot, retired "Little Red," its disturbing mascot that it had used since the 1940s. Over the next few years, Marquette, Stanford, Dickinson State, Syracuse, St. Bonaventure, and Southern Oregon all got rid of their Indian mascots. Since then, a number of groups such as the United Methodist Church, the state of Minnesota, the American Jewish Committee, the State of Wisconsin Department of Public Instruction, the U.S. Patent and Trademark Office, the United States Commission on Civil Rights, and even the NCAA have taken official public stances against the use of American Indian stereotyping.

That said, there remains a strong enclave of support for Native American mascots. Fans of the Washington Redskins, Cleveland Indians, Chicago Blackhawks, Kansas City Chiefs, Illinois Illini, and Florida State Seminoles have repeatedly fought movements to do away

with Indian mascots. The issue at the University of Illinois is among the most public and the most hotly contested. Alumni, students, and administrators remain divided over the use of an Indian in full headdress as the university's mascot and in particular the "chiefing" (an invented ritualistic dance) of Chief Illiniwek. Supporters of the mascot and the chief claim that both honor the dignity, nobility, and bravery of Native peoples, whereas opponents claim the mascots and the dance engender and perpetuate stereotypes, racism, and bigotry.

The following images and texts explore the cultural, racial, aesthetic, historical, emotional, and political issues surrounding the Native American mascot issue. We included some fun pieces—a series of hilarious political cartoons and a cycle of funny prose poems by the Choctaw writer LeAnne Howe (known for her award-winning novel *Shell Shaker*). Howe's pieces come from her book of poems, *Evidence of Red*, which won the Oklahoma State Book award in 2006.

The mascot issue remains a critical topic of public debate because it hones in on the conflicts between freedom of expression and civil rights. It also marks an interesting overlap among politics, sports, and visual culture. Do images carry weight? To what degree are caricatures racist? Do these comical, infantilizing, and hostile images contribute—even subconsciously—to the way in which most Americans view American Indians? Finally, how do these images affect Native American identity?

A Suite of Mascot Poems

Leanne Howe

Noble Savage Confronts Indian Mascot

NOBLE SAVAGE: What are you doing in my closet?
INDIAN MASCOT: Sugar, can I wear your loin cloth to the big game tonight?
NOBLE SAVAGE: No, and don't call me sugar.
INDIAN MASCOT: C'mon. Besides, you've outgrown it.
NOBLE SAVAGE: No I haven't. Take off those feathers.
INDIAN MASCOT: You said you liked my ostrich boa.
NOBLE SAVAGE: Only that one time. I wish you'd forget it.
INDIAN MASCOT: I will never forget it.
NOBLE SAVAGE: I don't feel the same about you.
INDIAN MASCOT: Don't pull that colonizer shit with me, baby. First you say you love me, then you say you don't. I'm not your toy baby. Listen, I'm the better half of you six days of the week, and twice on Sunday. (He screams and goes a little crazy.) And don't you forget it!
(Long Pause)
NOBLE SAVAGE: (shrugs) Sorry.

Noble Savage Contemplates His Fate

Dear Diary;
I can't fall in love with anyone.
I'm here to make all men believe
They're just like me.

Indian Mascot Joins The Village People

At last,
I'm in step with Hollywood,
No longer a transitory subaltern
On center stage
I surpass Fred Astaire,
Michael Jackson,
his sister,
and,
(You can't touch this)
Beatboxer Alien Dee.

I'm masculine prowess
a male dancer in beads and skins,
See the stadium crowd
how they jump to their feet in a
Reverent,
Religious,
Fervent,
Fit.
"YMCA, YMCA, YMCA, YMCA"
an old chant—
Young Men's Christian Association
Young Men's Christian Association
Young Men's Christian Association
Young Men's Christian Association.
Yeah, some decades are more ironic than others.

Indian Mascot Encounters Prejudice (from real Indians)

My own people hate me.
When the Red woman and her child see me,
They weep.
And I weep, too.
"He's white," the Indians, cry. "He's a bestial impersonator."
I try to humor them with my beautiful smile,
My half-time fancy footwork,
but they throw rotten apples.
At moi.
"You're a fiction." They shout.
"A character, that much is certain." I reply.
"An invention?" They chant.
"No more than you!"
"A failure?" They charge.

"Not a chance. I have fans."
And the show must go on.

American Indians Attempt to Assassinate Indian Mascot

Now,
only the whites protect me.
Indians scream, "Monster."
"He inspires disgust," they cry.
Their words sting like bullets.
Where is my Noble Savage when I need him?
He always defends the weak.

In defiance, I mock my detractors,
"Not butch enough for you, *eh*?"
I pull out all the stops.
Listen,
"I fought beside Red Shoes against the British in 1720."
"I fought with Little Turtle at the 1794 Battle of Fallen Timbers."
"I fought at Horseshoe Bend in the 1814 Red Stick War."
"And, I *Killed* Custer at the Battle of Little Big Horn."

An Indian boy will not stand for my blasphemy.
He draws his revolver from a backpack,
Aims,
Fires,
Dead on,
Straight.
At the last possible moment my beloved
rides to the rescue on a white horse,
and
we take the bullet simultaneously.
Mortally wounded,
We sigh together.

Ah, my love.

What happened to Indian Mascot and Noble Savage—After the shooting?

Nothing.
They were never real.
This is Hollywood.

A Suite of Cartoons

Source: © 2002 Lalo Alcaraz/Universal Press Syndicate.

READING WRITING

This Text: Reading

1. Based on this chapter, do you think the authors of this book take a position regarding the mascot issue? What evidence is there that we make a particular argument here?
2. How do the comics and Howe's poems argue with one another?

Your Text: Writing

1. Write an essay in which you take a stand on the Native American mascot issue. What evidence will you use to help support your assertions?
2. Write an essay in which you analyze the rhetorical strategies of the comics and poems.
3. Write an essay in which you explore why there are still dozens of Native American mascots in the United States. Why is there resistance to changing them? Why do non-Indians have so much invested in holding on to Native American mascots?
4. Write an essay in which you look at the mascot issue through the lens of freedom of expression.
5. Write an essay on the mascot issue through the lens of hate speech and civil rights.
6. Are there other arguments for or against the mascot issue that these writers and artists have not provided? What are they?
7. Write a comparison and contrast essay in which you read the comics alongside the LeAnne Howe piece. How do the authors use humor to defuse the mascot tension?

The Obama Suite

The Obama Suite

Barack Obama is the first African American president. The simplicity of that fact belies the complexity behind it. Because he was the first non-white person even to be the standard-bearer for a major party, the 2008 election was historic. It was also symbolic.

People read the campaign and election in a way that went beyond mere history. Obama and his campaign had something to do with that, embracing slogans like "Yes We Can" and themes like "Change" that were meant to inspire beyond the mere fact of governing. They also use a campaign that combined a rising sun and a flag and employed modern-looking fonts.

Outside observers created their own symbols too, most prominently in the work of Shepard Fairey's famous "Hope" poster. But the symbolism also had to do with race. Supporters often tied Obama into the legacy of African American and other historic leaders, while some conservative detractors decried what they saw as a relative lack of experience and empty rhetoric that was built about his historic election. A lot of symbolic work was often created below mainstream media consciousness—racist imagery about Obama was shared by e-mail, as was information that seemed to place doubt on Obama's stated religion and national origin. Eventually this information became public and part of the meta-campaign—a campaign that talked about itself—that was a distinctive part of the 2008 election.

Our own interactions came into play in May 2008, when we began *SemiObama*, a blog about the semiotics of Barack Obama's candidacy. We wrote about all of the issues above, engaged the symbolic importance of the Obama campaign, and documented the public symbolism on display. Here we have included some of our favorite pieces, all of which we cited, solicited, or wrote ourselves. The first is by University of San Francisco political scientist James Taylor, who was one of the most active commentators on the issue of race in the 2008 presidential election. The piece below addresses the optics of the election and the actions and reactions of people who respond to the idea (and the image) of a black president. The next piece, by Katia Bachko of the *Columbia Journalism Review*, talks about the image of "professor" that media organizations are fond of using—an example of not only media criticism but how symbols manifest themselves over and over again. The last two are ones we wrote for the blog—the first about a citizen who "renamed" her small town in California after Obama, and the second is about the way Obama's love of fantasy football gets at a particular type of masculinity.

Target: Obama

James Taylor

"Kill him!" "Terrorist!" "Traitor!" "Sit down, boy!" "He is not one of us!" "He's an Arab," "Socialist," and "Bomb Obama!" are just a few of the audible rants of Americans, heard at McCain-Palin gatherings in recent weeks.

Wow, how we long for the good ol' days of feeling bombarded when William Horton (he was given the name "Willie" by Atwater, not his mother) was introduced to the

Republicans by Al Gore in 1988—providing Lee Atwater and Bush 41 the race-baiting, fear-mongering fodder that resulted in the defeat of Dukakis after having the lead entering the final weeks of the 1988 campaign.

This is not to suggest the Obama campaign has been innocent of smear tactics, such as linking McCain to the anti-immigrant demagoguery of Rush Limbaugh on Spanish-speaking TV. But this did not amount to all-Mexican and all-Black crowds calling for McCain's Mississippi Irish blood.

The Right's rage against Obama has bordered on fanatical, and the die may have been cast, regrettably, by Hillary Clinton's defeated campaign, which provided the blueprint that the McCain-Palin ticket is currently following. This tenor was stirred earlier this week by the Republicans' answer to Hillary Clinton—Sarah Palin. McCain should take note; it did not work effectively for Sen. Clinton.

This animus we are witnessing may be owned by the Republicans, but it was brought and brought first by the Democrats during the primary campaign. Pundits called it the "kitchen sink" strategy. Indeed once Sen. Clinton's campaign was on the verge of defeat in late May—just weeks before the 40th anniversary of Robert F. Kennedy's assassination—she reminded an editorial board in South Dakota, "My husband did not wrap up the nomination in 1992, until he won the California primary somewhere in the middle of June, right? We all remember Bobby Kennedy was assassinated in June in California. You know I just, I don't understand it," she said, dismissing the idea of abandoning the race at that time.

It was the fourth time which Clinton alluded to RFK's late June assassination as precedence for not suspending or ending her campaign (on March 6th she used the word "assassination" in a TIME magazine interview; on May 7th in Washington, D.C. and later in West Virginia she redacted the word, but mentioned the tragedy). After reasserting the word in late May amid much criticism, Sen. Clinton apologized.

In a January 8th interview with BET's Jeff Johnson (What's In It For Us? special), Barack Obama himself, conceded, that early reticence among older African Americans—who witnessed the murders of JFK, MLK, and RFK—centered on concern for his safety. It has been widely reported, but only whispered, that Barack Obama received Secret Service protection beginning in May 2007, earlier than any presidential candidate in recorded history of the Service; "I've got the best protection in the world," Obama said in a previous interview, "So stop worrying."

But Obama made the request for protection himself. On the eve of Obama's Democratic nomination acceptance speech on August 28, three "lone wolf" white supremacist meth addicts, Tharin R. Gartrell, 28; Shawn R. Adolf, 33; and Nathan D. Johnson, 32, were arrested for plotting to kill Obama. Initially, officials said there was no credible threat—despite their possession of two rifles, one with a scope, in the car, along with walkie-talkies, a bulletproof vest and licenses in the names of other people—but they now consider it a serious plot.

During this campaign, the world witnessed the tragic assassination of Pakistani opposition leader Benazir Bhutto, who like Obama, was a left-of-center political leader and equally an historic figure as the first woman to be elected head of an Islamic state.

In 1963, Texas oil tycoon Haroldson Lafayette (H.L.) Hunt publicly stated that JFK should be shot since "there was no way to get those traitors out of government except by shooting them out." His son, Nelson Bunker Hunt and others, took out a full-page advertisement in the Dallas Morning News on November 22nd accusing JFK of being a Communist sympathizer and a traitor to the nation—precisely the charges against Obama for his ties to Bill Ayers and Jeremiah Wright.

JFK, like Obama, was a "first" in being a serious Irish Catholic candidate (Al E. Smith lost in 1920) and his faith, like Obama's racial mix, was a perennial issue in the 1960 campaign. The Hunts also ran a propaganda machine called the International Committee for the Defense of Christian Culture and like the venomous Fox News demagogues, Sean Hannity and Bill O'Reilly, they used their radio programs Facts Forum and Life Line to spew hatred of the president before he was killed.

Martin Luther King, of course, lived with death threats every day of his public life until it was taken April 4, 1968. Like Malcolm X, it is depressingly true that in such an eerie atmosphere as the present, Barack Obama is safer abroad than he will be, should he win, in America, even as President of the United States.

Some might remember comedian Eddy Murphy's 1980s *Delirious* stand-up routine where he joked about whites voting for Jesse Jackson—after a night of drinking and pranks—only to discover the next morning, that Jackson had been elected; during his fictitious inaugural address, Jackson ran back and forth from left to right of the stage as the imagined assassins, in southern drawl, looked through a rifle scope saying, "He won't stand still, he won't stand still."

That was funny; the tenor of this political moment is not.

Politics has always been a "blood sport," and campaigns often bring out the lowest common denominator in people; the "us" against "them" trope. But there is something of a spiritual sickness in a nation where our political process has been reduced to calls of "Kill him," and something only slightly less troubling about Hillary Clinton saying, "Let's wait and see what happens."

Add the ingredient of the worst global economy since the Great Depression or the crash of 1877, and it makes for a combustible atmosphere. And in the end, if this is the course that our politics take—again, then what voice, pray tell, do you think many people might invoke? Does the Rev. Jeremiah Wright ring a bell?

Professor Obama: The Press Goes for Style Over Substance on the Press Conferences

Katia Bachko

In a remarkable show of consensus, news outlets from *The O'Reilly Factor* to NPR all landed on one word—professorial—to describe Barack Obama's demeanor at Tuesday's press conference. The sentiment initially lingered as *The New York Times* assessed Obama's performance at yesterday's town hall (emphasis mine throughout): "Mr. Obama, adopting the teacher-like tone he used during Tuesday's press conference, launched into a lengthy explanation . . ."

Wednesday, writing in the *Times*, Peter Baker and Adam Nagourney went for the surface assessment in their lede:

For just under an hour on Tuesday night, Americans saw not the fiery and inspirational speaker who riveted the nation in his address to Congress last month, or the conversational president who warmly engaged Americans in talks across the country, or even the jaunty and jokey president who turned up on Jay Leno.

Instead, in his second prime-time news conference from the White House, it was Barack Obama the lecturer, a familiar character from early in the campaign. Placid and unsmiling, he was the professor in chief, offering familiar arguments in long paragraphs—often introduced with the phrase, "as I said before"—sounding like the teacher speaking in the stillness of a classroom where students are restlessly waiting for the ring of the bell.

USA Today also paused to note Obama's bearing: "The president's tone was a mix of the populist—"I'm as angry as anybody about those bonuses," he said at one point, albeit with a calm demeanor—and the professor."

And, on CNN, Anderson Cooper also tried to assess the president's elusive nature: "We've seen one candidate Obama and two President Obamas . . . During the campaign sweetness, light and hope, and the first press conference very pessimistic, and last night taking the middle ground, sort of like the somewhat positive, but at the same time very cautious, trying to look like the steady hand in the tiller, almost sounding professorial at times."

The depiction of Obama as "the professor" is nothing new and, is based in, you know, fact, since he actually was a professor at University of Chicago.

But as written, or spoken, these references aren't designed to evoke Obama's years at the lectern. The references are derogatory. His professorial demeanor isn't meant to be interpreted as "that cool professor who said really interesting, stimulating things, who took an interest in his students," but rather as "that boring professor who goes on and on, without understanding his audience and what they care about."

Which may or may not be a fair assessment, but it's a hardly objective take. Given that only a certain percentage of people reading the next day's presser recap actually watched the event themselves, it seems wasteful to let policy details play second fiddle to subjective details like demeanor.

These articles' implicit assumption—that the president's (and his cabinet's) job is, primarily, to strike the right tone—offers a poor rubric by which to evaluate his success as a leader. Yes, his public persona is an important consideration, but shouldn't the focus be on the substance of his policies actions, not the aura that he projects or the content of his speeches?

One reason why post-presser reports are short on substantive analysis may be that press conferences rarely generate actual news. If the president says nothing new about his economic plans, then why treat his recycled sound bites as new, right?

But, looking at the substance of presser write-ups, it becomes clear that the White House press conference has become a see-and-be-seen event, rather than an actual news-gathering exercise. And if that's the case, then the answer is sort of obvious: if there's no news, there's no story. Press conferences might be good places to gather context quotes for later reporting, but if nothing new happens there and then, just don't write it.

Just to be clear, a press conference or a speech isn't a news event, and treating them as such is misguided. Actions speak louder than words. Not what he said. Not how he said it. What he did. That should be the story.

This isn't to say that speeches can't be significant, and that the press shouldn't cover what politicians say when it's new or newsworthy. But even if the press conference is devoid of actual news, I'm not convinced that Obama's tone is newsworthy enough to earn prominent mention in the headlines, "In a Volatile Time, Obama Strikes a New Tone," like the *Times* declared.

Yet, if the tone's the thing, if it is the only consummately newsy thing that happens in a press conference, ought it not be reported with a tad more objectivity and distance than the "professorial" labels evoke? Instead of labeling it with the press corps nom du jour, why not reach out to actual viewers for reactions? What was the people's response? How did they perceive the president's tone? Instead of telling people how they should feel, why not ask them? If tone matters, let's treat it with some dignity. But, since it doesn't, let's just stick to the issues.

In the end, the focus on tone demonstrates all over again how the press transforms politics into a blood sport with quantifiable winners and losers, which is disconnected from the significance of actual policy—roads built, hospitals staffed, schools renovated. The impulse to cover the horse race at the cost of the seriousness of governance persists. In this case, if Obama's the professor, then the press is a bunch of unruly kids who won't calm down after recess. The election is long behind us, get back to work.

Obama, CA

Dean Rader

We're grateful to Jan Davidson of Olema (or is that Obama), California for sending Semi-Obama the photo to the left.

The small town of 55 souls is positioned just about an hour north of San Francisco on the lovely Highway 1, just a Palin's throw from the Pacific Ocean. Though Olema has not officially changed its name to Obama, Kelly Emery's sign might lead passers-by to assume the opposite.

A Marin County code allows political signs on personal property, and Emery (below) installed this one on the site of her Bed and Breakfast. So far, residents seem to be both pleased and amused by the sign, perhaps because they expect to see the senator crossing the street.

One of the things we like about this text is its seamless merging of Obama iconography and the semiotics of normal traffic signs. It sends the message that an idea of an Obama presidency has already become part of the literal and cultural landscape.

Obama and Fantasy Football, or What Obama Has in Common with FiveThirtyEight.com

Jonathan Silverman

Barack Obama is a recognized sports fan. We know about his basketball, and then there was a recent article about Obama's fantasy football team, written by Rick Reilly, now of ESPN. The article itself, like most of Reilly's stuff, was really about Reilly—after all the column is called the Life of Reilly—but it also revealed another heretofore unseen aspect of Obama's personality.

The article revealed directly at least one part of Obama that only gets displayed indirectly most of the time—his inherent American masculinity. In this case, however, it's a particular kind of masculinity, the sports geek; his knowledge of fantasy football makes him part of the growing legion of American men who love both sports and numbers. Combine this with Obama's relationship with basketball, his appearance on the cover of *Men's Health*, his smoking habits, his hiring of a former sports player and academic as an aide, (not to mention his poker playing) and you have a man who can move in many different circles of masculinity, seemingly all very easily.

But back to fantasy football. It's a sport where people pretend to own teams; they draft players, often pretend to pay them, and then compete against other teams. It's becoming more and more popular, with almost every sports website sponsoring a game. There is also fantasy baseball, basketball, golf, horse racing, hockey, and NASCAR. Being successful depends on a laser focus on numbers and predictions based on numbers.

The link between masculinity and geekdom has only blossomed in the last few decades, with technology nerds becoming kings of the universe, and more specifically, to this post, geeky sports nerds being hired as the cool kids. That's why it's entirely appropriate that Nate Silver, the *Baseball Prospectus* writer, is this election's geek sensation; his FiveThirtyEight.com, a highly technical but eminently readable guide to election polling, is the go-to site for those of us who are geeked out on polls.

That somehow Obama's connection to fantasy football makes him cooler is of some consequence to those of us who have had to explain to friends and romantic partners why we are spending hundreds of dollars and hours on a game with little chance of making any of that back.

More importantly for this election, it probably means that Obama reads FiveThirtyEight.com, the website about political polling and statistics—the breakout blog of the political season—and other geeky blogs; this year, politics is the new fantasy sport . . .

READING WRITING

This Text: Reading

1. Describe the different approaches in the suite to President Obama. Which are the most analytical? Which focus on his behavior? Which are about a larger symbolism? Which one do you like the best?
2. Which two approaches fit together the best—which two are the easiest to compare?
3. The authors found it difficult to write about the president after the election. Why do you think that is?

Your Text: Writing

1. Find an old campaign ad or bumper sticker of the president—or any candidate for that matter—and do a semiotic analysis of it. What has changed about the ad or sticker since the election?
2. Write about the differences between the symbolic nature of campaigning versus the symbolic nature of governing.

READING BETWEEN THE LINES

Classroom Activities

1. Although most scientists believe that race is socially constructed, that still leaves open the question of how we construct our ideas of race. In class, discuss some of the ways you see this process working in culture attributed to particular ethnic groups, and in white America as well.

2. In his essay, "In Living Color: Race and American Culture," Michael Omi discusses the way race and ethnicity are portrayed on television. Using your own observations, discuss how popular culture treats race and ethnicity.

3. Discuss clothing and what pieces of clothing signify in general. Do you tend to characterize different groups by what clothes they wear?

4. After reading Beverly Tatum's piece, talk about the presence of race and ethnicity on campus. Do you notice patterns that can be inferred? Do you feel your campus is enlightened about race and ethnicity?

5. Some people still believe races and ethnicities have particular cultures, or cultures that are generated from groups from particular ethnicities. Discuss the phenomenon of people from different cultures participating in each other's culture.

6. Watch *Do the Right Thing* in class. What ideas about race does Spike Lee explore? What about his narrative makes you uncomfortable? What do you think his ideas about race are?

7. Watch *Mississippi Burning* with *Rosewood*. Compare how the two treat the idea of African American participation in remedying racism. What problems do you see in the narratives? What have the filmmakers emphasized in their narratives? Is it at the expense of more "real" or important issues?

8. Watch two television shows, one with an all white or largely white cast, and one with an all African American or largely African American cast. How does each treat the idea of race and ethnicity?

9. Using the same shows, notice the commercials playing—how do these construct a view of race and/or ethnicity?

10. Rent the movies *Smoke Signals*, and, if you can find it, *Naturally Native*—two of the more common films about Native American realities. How do the movies address the issue of Native American representation?

11. On the Web, look at paintings by Jaune Quick-To-See Smith, Michael Ray Charles, and Freddy Rodriguez. Give a semiotic reading of the work by these authors. How do they deal with the visual politics of race?

Essay Ideas

1. Trace the evolution of the portrayal of race and/or ethnicity in a particular medium—television, movies, art, public space. Has it changed in your lifetime? Why or why not?

2. Go to the library or the computer and do a keyword search on a particular ethnicity and a politician's name (example: "Cheney" and "African American"). What comes up when you do this? Is there a trend worth writing about?

3. Do some research on the nature of prejudice. What do researchers say about its nature?

4. Get stories or novels from 75 years ago; look and see how different authors, African American, white, Italian, Jewish, and so on, portrayed people of different skin color and ethnicity. How would you characterize the treatment as a whole?

5. What are the signs that are encoded in race and ethnicity? How are they portrayed in popular culture and the media? Do a sign analysis of a particular show or media phenomenon.

6. Watch two television shows, one with a largely white cast, one with a largely African American cast. Compare how each deals with the idea of race or ethnicity.

7. Using the same shows, notice the commercials playing—how do these construct a view of race and/or ethnicity?

8. Look at a film or films made by African American, Hispanic, or other ethnic directors. How do these directors deal with the idea of race and ethnicity, compared to white directors dealing with similar ideas?

9. Write an essay on racially questionable comments uttered by celebrities (e.g., Michael Richards, Fuzzy Zoeller, Joseph Biden, Frederic Rouzaud, Mel Gibson, and George Allen) and what these transgressions say about race, our culture, and the people who made them.

Visualizing Writing

For Better or For Worse®   by Lynn Johnston

The main character in this particular strip is a working journalist, not immune to the pressures of writing. . . .

5 Reading and Writing about Movies

The contemporary American poet Louis Simpson writes in one of his poems: "Every American is a film critic." He is probably right. Just about everyone we know loves movies, and as much as we love movies, we love talking about them. We freely disagree with movie reviewers and each other. Andre Maurois once quipped that in literature as in love, we are astonished by what others choose. That may be doubly so for movies. This makes writing about movies even more fun—you get to commit your good ideas and strong opinions to print.

Despite our familiarity with movies and our apparent willingness to serve as movie critics, we sometimes resist taking a more analytical approach to them. For many of us, movies are an escape from school or critical thinking. After a long day, most of us want to sit in front of a big screen and veg out for a couple of hours with *The Hangover* or *The Matrix* or *He's Just Not That Into You*. Your authors confess that we have been known to veg out too, so we are not knocking the idea of losing oneself in front of a seemingly mindless action flick. However, we do want you to be aware of the fact that movies are never *just* mindless action flicks. They are always some kind of cultural text, loaded with ideas about a particular culture, either consciously or unintentionally expressed.

For instance, some film and cultural critics have argued that despite the futuristic special effects, the *Star Wars* movies create a sense of nostalgia for the value systems of the 1950's; values that by today's standards may seem racist, sexist, and blindly patriotic. In fact, one of our students has written an essay along these lines, which we have included here. For others, the 90s favorite *Fatal Attraction* is more than a suspenseful movie about a crazed psycho-killer boiling a bunny. Some see the film as an allegory on AIDS, claiming the film reinforces the central fear of AIDS: If you sleep around, you risk death. Still others see the film as a document that confirms the backlash against women during the conservatism of the Reagan years. In a much different vein, cultural critics and film historians have argued that genre movies like comedies, family melodramas, and gangster flicks tell stories about and support mainstream American values—the centrality of parenting, traditional heterosexual marriage, the necessity of law enforcement, and the security of suburbia. In fact, some film and cultural critics like Thomas Schatz and Andre Bazin have argued that Westerns like *The Searchers, Red River,* and *Broken Arrow* reflect an era's views on race, justice, and "American values." Greg Barnhisel, a professor at Duquesne University, posted a review of *The Dark Knight* on the blog *The Weekly Rader* arguing that the film essentially supported the mass surveillance of Americans as practiced by the Bush Administration. You may disagree with these particular readings, but they show how movies can be a rich source for cultural exploration and debate.

Part of the culture of movies is the media and advertising blitz surrounding their promotion. Sometimes with popular movies, it is nearly impossible not to see them through the lens of their marketing schemes. For more about the world's most popular movie at the time of this printing, see our suite on *Avatar* beginning on page 343. (Photo of *RepoMen* advertisements courtesy of Judith Taylor)

However, there are obstacles when writing about movies from a purely cultural perspective. In some ways, our familiarity with movies becomes a liability when trying to analyze them. Because you have seen so many movies, you may believe that you already know how to read them. In some ways, you do. As informal movie critics, you are geared toward analyzing the plot of a movie or determining whether a film text is realistic or funny or appropriately sad. And if asked about music, fashion, setting, and dialogue, you would likely be able to talk about these aspects of filmmaking. But when reading literature, you prepare your brain for a more intense act of *analysis* than you do when you watch *Legally Blonde 2*. You probably have not been taught to look *through* the plot and dialogue of movies to see the film as a cultural text. Though at times difficult, the process is often rewarding.

For instance, pay attention to how many Asian or American Indians you see in contemporary movies. Watch for roles for strong, confident women. Look for movies in which poor or blue-collar people are treated not as a culture but as interesting individuals. See how many films are directed by women or minorities. Pay attention to product placements (that is, brand products such as soda cans, cereal, kinds of cars, or computers) in movies. Work on seeing cinematic texts as products, documents, and pieces of evidence from a culture. Rather than diminishing your enjoyment of movies, this added component of movie watching should enhance not only the actual film experience but also your understanding and appreciation of movies as produced, constructed texts. This approach is also absolutely critical when you begin to freewrite, outline, and construct your papers.

So, when writing about movies, try to keep a few of the following things in mind:

LIKE LITERATURE AND MUSIC, MOVIES ARE COMPRISED OF GENRES.

Movies, perhaps even more than literature and music, are comprised of genres, such as Westerns, science fiction, comedy, drama, adventure, horror, documentaries, and romance. You may not think about film genres that often, but you probably prepare yourself for certain movies depending on the genre of that particular film. You come to comedies prepared to laugh; you arrive at horror movies prepared to be scared; you go to "chick flicks" expecting romance, passion, a video montage, and a happy ending. If you don't get these things in your movie experience, you will likely feel disappointed, as though the film didn't hold up its end of the bargain. Notice, in reading the selections here and movie reviews generally, how critics do or do not pay attention to genre. Though they should be familiar with genre, many critics insist on reviewing all movies as if they are supposed to be as earnest and dramatic as *Casablanca* or *Titanic,* when movies like *Borat* or *Funny People* clearly try to do different things.

The idea of genre in movies is as old as film itself. In the early days of Hollywood, the studio system thrived on genre movies, and in fact, genre films were pretty much all that came out of Hollywood for several decades. Even today, blockbuster movies are most often genre pieces that adhere to the criteria of a particular genre. *Twilight* is not *Old School; The Notebook* is not *Saw.* Different genres evoke different emotions, and they comment on (and reinforce) different values.

Being aware of genres and their conventions will help you when it comes time to write a paper on movies. When you "read" a film, think about how it fits into a particular genre. Taking into account formal, thematic, and cultural forces (the Cold War, civil rights, Vietnam, feminism, the Great Depression, the economic pressure to turn a profit) will allow you to see movie production as a dynamic process of exchange between the movie industry and its audience. In your papers, be mindful of why we like certain genres and what these genres tell us about our culture and ourselves. The fact that some writers and critics distinguish between "movies" (cinema for popular consumption) and "films" (cinema that tries to transcend or explode popular genre formulations) suggests the degree to which genres influence how we write about movies.

MOVIES ARE A POWERFUL CULTURAL TOOL.

A hundred years ago, people satisfied their cravings for action, suspense, and character development by reading books and serials; today, we go to the movies, or, more and more frequently, avoid the communal experience of the theater for the private experience of renting DVDs. Innovations like TiVo, On Demand, and Netflix have made watching movies at home (and writing about them!) even easier. Still, we are living in a visual age. In America, video and visual cultures have become the dominant modes of expression and communication, and learning to "read" these media with the same care, creativity, and critical acumen with which we read written texts is crucial—both for being a savvy viewer and a savvy writer. To better understand the phenomenon of movies, we need to contextualize the movie experience within American culture, asking in particular how thoroughly American movies affect (and reflect) American culture.

In addition, movies are not just indicators for American culture—they determine culture itself. Fashion, songs, modes of behavior, social and political views and gender and racial values are all underscored by movies. For instance, *Wayne's World* made certain songs and phrases part of everyday American life. On a more complex level, many critics claim the movie *Guess Who's Coming to Dinner,* in which a wealthy white woman brings home her black fiancé, went a long way toward softening racial tensions in the 1960s. We even define eras, movements, and emotions by movies—the 1960s is often symbolized by *Easy Rider;* the 1970s by *Saturday Night Fever* and *Star Wars;* the 1980s by movies like *Fast Times at Ridgemont High* and *Do the Right Thing;* the 1990s by *Titanic* and *You've Got Mail;* the 2000s by *Lord of the Rings* and Judd Apatow movies. Because more people see movies than read books, one could argue that the best documents of American popular culture are movies. Thus, we tend to link the values and trends of certain eras with movies from those eras. Movies help us understand culture because they embody culture.

Movies also guide our behavior. In contemporary society, we often learn how to dress, how to talk, and even how to court and kiss someone, from the cinema. In fact, for many young people, their model for a date, a spouse, and a romantic moment all come from what they have seen in movies. In other words, influential models of behavior, aspects of their hopes and dreams, come not from life but from movies. So, as you read the following pieces, as you watch movies, and as you write your papers, ask yourself if the things you desire, you desire because movies have planted those seeds in your heads.

THE ADVERTISING AND MARKETING OF A MOVIE AFFECT HOW WE VIEW THE MOVIE AND HOW THE STUDIO VIEWS ITSELF AND US.

Next time you watch previews in a theatre or on a video or DVD you have rented, pay attention to how the film being advertised is presented to you. Be aware of how movies are packaged, how they are marketed, how actors talk about them in interviews. Whether you know it or not, you are being prepped for viewing the movie by all of these texts. Even independent films have become mainstream by marketing themselves as similar to other (popular) independent movies. Marketing is selling, and studios fund, market, and release movies not so much to make the world a better place but primarily to make money (though directors and actors may have different motivations). Also, unlike a book publisher, a studio has likely paid tens of millions of dollars to make a movie, so it needs a lot of us to go see it. We might ask ourselves how these considerations affect not only the advertising but also the movie itself.

In addition, Hollywood studios rarely have your best interest at heart. This is not to say that studios want to make you an evil person, but moviemakers have only rarely seen themselves as educators. For instance, few studios fund documentaries—and the controversy over Disney/Miramax refusing to distribute Michael Moore's incendiary documentary *Fahrenheit 9/11* is a testament to this fact. Few studios seem eager to make movies about poets, painters, composers, or philosophers because they know that not many people will go to see them. Movie studios began as a financial enterprise; studios and the film industry grew as America and American capitalist ideals grew. Nowadays, the topics and subjects of movies have been largely market tested just like any other consumer product such as toys, soft drinks, and shoes.

MOVIES USE VARIOUS TECHNIQUES TO MANIPULATE AUDIENCES.

Manipulation is not necessarily a negative term when we talk about the manipulation of everyday objects; but when we move into the realm of emotions, manipulative texts become problematic. Film is such a wonderful medium because directors have so many tools at their disposal; however, it is relatively easy to use those tools to manipulate audiences. Directors employ music, lighting, special effects, and clever editing to help make their movies more powerful. Music reinforces feelings of excitement (*Lord of the Rings*), fear (*Jaws*), romance (*Titanic*), or anger (*Do the Right Thing*). Lighting and filters can make people, especially women, appear more delicate or fragile. The famous film star from the 1930s and 1940s, Marlene Dietrich, would only be shot from one side and insisted on being illuminated with overhead lights. The first several minutes of *Citizen Kane,* widely considered the best American film ever made, are shot largely in the dark to help drive home the sense that the reporters are "in the dark" about media mogul Charles Foster Kane. In movies like *Avatar, The Matrix* trilogy, and *Lord of the Rings,* special effects make the story we are watching seem less like light and shadow and more like reality. Even how a filmmaker places a camera affects how we view the film. The close-up, spookily lit shots of Anthony Hopkins's face in *Silence of the Lambs* make us feel like Hannibal Lecter might eat *our* liver with some fava beans and a nice Chianti. Similarly, in many Westerns, the camera is placed at knee level, so that we are always looking up at the cowboy, reinforcing his stature as a hero. Director Orson Welles uses similar techniques in *Citizen Kane*. Alfred Hitchcock was a master of placing the camera in manipulative places. From *Psycho* to *Rear Window* to *Rope*, we see exactly what he wants us to see and how he wants us to see it. We see nothing more than what the camera shows us.

There are other forms of manipulation as well. Many people feel Steven Spielberg's movies end with overly manipulative scenes that pluck at the heartstrings of the audience, forcing overdetermined emotions and over-the-top melodrama. Such accusations are often leveled at teen romance flicks and so-called bio-pics because they make a person's life seem more maudlin, more heart wrenching than it could possibly be.

Costumes, colors, sounds and sound effects, editing, and set design all contribute to how the movie comes to us. Sound and music are particularly effective. In *Star Wars*, for instance, each character has a specific musical profile—a kind of theme song—whose tone mirrors how you are supposed to feel about that character. You probably all remember the dark, deep foreboding music that always accompanies Darth Vader. Like music, the clothes a character wears tell us how to feel about that person. The costumes worn by Ben Affleck and Will Smith in various movies probably reinforce gender expectations, as do the clothes of Kristin Stewart and Meryl Streep. How a spaceship or a dark scary warehouse looks puts us in the mood so that the plot and action can move us. Savvy viewers of movies will be aware of the ways in which films try to manipulate them because in so doing, they will be better able to read other forms of manipulation in their lives.

The best writers about movies—Anthony Lane, Roger Ebert, David Denby, Stephanie Zacharek, and David Edelstein—always pay attention to these issues in their reviews. Anthony Lane in particular always reads movies on his own terms. He sees them as he wants to—never as the studio or the director tries to present them. Great movie writing comes from great movie reading.

MOVIES ARE NOT JUST ABOUT IDEAS AND ACTION; THEY ARE ALSO ABOUT VALUES.

Next time you see a Hollywood movie, consider the value system the movie supports. By value system, we mean the values, priorities, and principles a movie advocates. For instance, although we liked the first *Legally Blonde* movie, we were shocked by how traditional the movie's ending was. While the entire movie demonstrates the ways in which the underappreciated female character gets the best of boys, law school colleagues, and professors—even her enemies in the courtroom—all of these very important successes take a back seat to the fact that, ultimately, she lands the hunky guy. It is as though all of her accomplishments were important *so* that she could win the cute boy in the end. The ultimate message, then, is that what women accomplish on their own is fine, if that is of interest, but the real victory, the real triumph, is snagging the cute guy.

Similarly, many Hollywood movies advocate the importance of social class, as Michael Parenti points out in his now famous essay "Class and Virtue." Movies like *Maid in Manhattan* and *Jerry Maguire* and classic romantic comedies such as *Pretty Woman*,

Trading Places, and *My Fair Lady* spend most of their energy figuring out ways for their characters to make a jump in social class. It is worth asking how many truly popular Hollywood movies are at the same time truly radical and how many reinforce traditional, mainstream middle-class values. We are not suggesting traditional middle-class values are *bad;* rather, we urge you to consider the value system advocated by the most powerful cultural machinery in the country. Our contention here is that this value system directly affects the movies you see, the stars acting in the movie, the plot structures, and the ultimate messages these movies send. They also affect how you see your own life, as you may find yourself, without knowing it, comparing your own life to that of Elle Woods. Again, paying attention to these issues will make you a smarter watcher of movies and a better writer about them as well.

THIS TEXT

1. While it will be impossible for you to know this fully, try to figure out the writing situation of each author. Who is the audience? What does the author have at stake? What is his or her agenda? Why is she or he writing this piece?
2. What are the main points of the essay? Can you find a thesis statement?
3. Do you think the authors "read into" movies too much? If so, why do you say this?
4. As you read the essays, pay attention to the language the critics use to read movies.
5. If you have not seen the movies the authors mention, rent and watch them—preferably with a group of people from your class.
6. Try to distinguish between a review and an argumentative or persuasive essay. You should also be aware of a distinction between a short capsule review, which is more of a summary, and a longer analytical review (like the ones printed here).

BEYOND THIS TEXT: FILM TECHNIQUE

Part of being a convincing writer about movies is being able to use the terminology of film. Being aware of these terms and knowing how to use them will make your papers more specific, more authoritative, and more professional.

Camera angles and positioning: How is the camera placed? Is it high, low, to the side? And how does it move? Is it a hand-held camera, or is it stationary? How does it determine how you *see* the movie?

Lighting: Light and shading are very important to movies. Are there shadows? Is the film shot during the day or mostly at night? How do shadows and light affect the movie and your experience of it?

Color and framing: Often, directors try to give certain scenes an artistic feel. Is the shot framed similar to a painting or photograph? Does the movie use color to elicit emotions? How does the movie frame or represent nature?

CONTENT

Theme: What are the themes of the movie? What point is the director or writer trying to get across?

Ideology: What ideas or political leanings does the movie convey? Are there particular philosophies or concepts that influence the message the movie sends?

THE WHOLE PACKAGE

Celebrities: What movie stars appear (or don't appear) in the movie? How do certain stars determine what kind of movie a film is? Do the actors ever look ugly or dirty or tired or sloppy?

Technology: What kind of technology is at work in the film? How do special effects or stunts or pyrotechnics affect the film viewing experience?

Genre: What genre does a particular movie fit into? Why? What are the expectations of that genre?

Culture: As a cultural document, a cultural text, what does this movie say about its culture? How does it transmit values? What kinds of ideas and values does it hold up or condemn?

Effectiveness: Does the movie "work" as a movie? Why or why not? What cultural forces might be influencing your criteria of effectiveness?

QUICK GUIDE TO WRITING ABOUT MOVIES

1. Before beginning to watch the movie, make sure you are trying to answer a question by watching the movie. For example, if you are watching *Twlight*, you might think not only about why vampires *are* but what they mean. In other words, the question you might be trying to answer is what do vampires say about American culture? Or what do they say about class, race, or gender in American culture?

2. If you are writing about a movie in a theater, make sure you bring a notepad and paper. Even if you take minimal notes in the screening, sit a few minutes, perhaps when the credits are rolling, and write down some ideas or images that struck you during the movie.

3. If you are writing by watching the movie through your computer or television, make sure you stop the DVD player every five or ten mintues, particularly if you have watched the movie before. For easier review, look at the controller time to see when key scenes take place.

4. Once you have watched the movie, quickly try to answer the question you posed. If you come up with a few answers, think about the scenes that best illustrate the points you are making.

Great Movies and Being a Great Moviegoer

Roger Ebert

Roger Ebert is probably the most famous movie reviewer in the country. A Pulitzer-prize winning columnist for the Chicago Sun-Times, *he became a household name through his participation in* Siskel and Ebert at the Movies, *a popular television show in which he and the late Gene Siskel argued (sometimes bitterly) about current movies. Ebert wrote this piece in 2000 to celebrate reaching the milestone of 100 "great movies" in his ongoing series. We like it because Ebert talks about why he likes certain movies and what it takes to be a good watcher of them. As you read, think about how movies are both public and private texts. Why do we love them, and what roles do they play in our lives? The entire Great Movies project can be found at http://rogerebert.suntimes.com/apps/pbcs.dll/section?category-greatmovies_first100.*

EVERY OTHER WEEK I VISIT a film classic from the past and write about it. My "Great Movies" series began in the autumn of 1996 and now reaches a landmark of 100 titles with today's review of Federico Fellini's *8 1/2,* which is, appropriately, a film about a film director. I love my job, and this is the part I love the most.

We have completed the first century of film. Too many moviegoers are stuck in the present and recent past. When people tell me that *Ferris Bueller's Day Off* or *Total Recall* are their favorite films, I wonder: Have they tasted the joys of Welles, Bunuel, Ford, Murnau, Keaton, Hitchcock, Wilder or Kurosawa? If they like Ferris Bueller, what would they think of Jacques Tati's *Mr. Hulot's Holiday,* also about a strange day of misadventures? If they like *Total Recall,* have they seen Fritz Lang's *Metropolis,* also about an artificial city ruled by fear?

I ask not because I am a film snob. I like to sit in the dark and enjoy movies. I think of old films as a resource of treasures. Movies have been made for 100 years, in color and black and white, in sound and silence, in wide-screen and the classic frame, in English and every other language. To limit yourself to popular hits and recent years is like being Ferris Bueller but staying home all day.

I believe we are born with our minds open to wonderful experiences, and only slowly learn to limit ourselves to narrow tastes. We are taught to lose our curiosity by the bludgeon-blows of mass marketing, which brainwash us to see "hits," and discourage exploration.

I know that many people dislike subtitled films, and that few people reading this article will have ever seen a film from Iran, for example. And yet a few weeks ago at my Overlooked Film Festival at the University of Illinois, the free kiddie matinee was *Children of Heaven,* from Iran. It was a story about a boy who loses his sister's sneakers through no fault of his own, and is afraid to tell his parents. So he and his sister secretly share the same pair of shoes. Then he learns of a footrace where third prize is . . . a pair of sneakers.

"Anyone who can read at the third-grade level can read these subtitles," I told the audience of 1,000 kids and some parents. "If you can't, it's OK for your parents or older kids to read them aloud—just not too loudly."

The lights went down and the movie began. I expected a lot of reading aloud. There was none. Not all of the kids were old enough to read, but apparently they were picking up the story just by watching and using their intelligence. The audience was spellbound. No noise, restlessness, punching, kicking, running down the aisles. Just eyes lifted up to a fascinating story. Afterward, we asked kids up on the stage to ask questions or talk about the film. What they said indicated how involved they had become.

Kids. And yet most adults will not go to a movie from Iran, Japan, France or Brazil. They will, however, go to any movie that has been plugged with a $30 million ad campaign and sanctified as a "box-office winner." Yes, some of these big hits are good, and a few of them are great. But what happens between the time we are 8 and the time we are 20 that robs us of our curiosity? What turns movie lovers into consumers? What does it say about you if you only want to see what everybody else is seeing?

I don't know. What I do know is that if you love horror movies, your life as a filmgoer is not complete until you see *Nosferatu.* I know that once you see Orson Welles appear in the doorway in *The Third Man,* you will never forget his curious little smile. And that the life and death of the old man in *Ikiru* will be an inspiration every time you remember it.

I have not written any of the 100 Great Movies reviews from memory. Every film has been seen fresh, right before writing. When I'm at home, I often watch them on Sunday mornings. It's a form of prayer: The greatest films are meditations on why we are here. When I'm on the road, there's no telling where I'll see them. I saw *Written on the Wind* on a cold January night at the Everyman Cinema in Hampstead, north of London. I saw *Last Year at Marienbad* on a DVD on my PowerBook while at the Cannes Film Festival. I saw *2001: A Space Odyssey* in 70mm at Cyberfest, the celebration of HAL 9000's birthday, at the University of Illinois. I saw *Battleship Potemkin* projected on a sheet on the outside wall of the Vickers Theater in Three Oaks, Mich., while three young musicians played the score they had written for it. And Ozu's *Floating Weeds* at the Hawaii Film Festival, as part of a shot-by-shot seminar that took four days.

When people asked me where they should begin in looking at classic films, I never knew what to say. Now I can say, "Plunge into these Great Movies, and go where they lead you."

There's a next step. If you're really serious about the movies, get together with two or three friends who care as much as you do. Watch the film all the way through on video. Then start again at the top. Whenever anyone sees anything they want to comment on, freeze the frame. Talk about what you're looking at. The story, the performances, the sets, the locations. The camera movement, the lighting, the composition, the special effects. The color, the shadows, the sound, the music. The themes, the tone, the mood, the style.

There are no right answers. The questions are the point. They make you an active movie watcher, not a passive one. You should not be a witness at a movie, but a collaborator. Directors cannot make the film without you. Together, you can accomplish amazing things. The more you learn, the quicker you'll know when the director is not doing his share of the job. That's the whole key to being a great moviegoer. There's nothing else to it.

READING WRITING

This Text: Reading

1. What makes a "great movie" for you? Do you think it would differ from Ebert's criteria? Based on his essay, what does it take for a movie to be "great" in Ebert's eyes?
2. What does Ebert mean when, in the final paragraph, he asks you to be a "collaborator"? How is this similar to being an active reader of texts?
3. What is Ebert's thesis in this essay? Does he have a clear argument, and if so, what is it? How would you describe his tone?

Your Text: Writing

1. Write an essay in which you argue that a certain movie is "great." This is a wonderful opportunity to write a definitional essay. Define what a great movie must be, then show how your movie is, in fact, great.
2. Take an oppositional stance to Ebert regarding one of the movies on the list. Make a compelling argument why a certain movie is *not* great. Be sure that your argument is more logos-based than pathos-based.
3. Write a paper about the entire process of labeling "great" movies. Why do we care if a movie is great or not? What is at stake in movie hierarchies like this?

Deciphering *I, Robot*: Random Thoughts from an Evolving Film Reviewer

Jason Silverman

Below are two different pieces by Jason Silverman, both written in 2004. The first is an original essay on the process of watching movies from the perspective of a movie reviewer, with specific examples from the recent movie I, Robot. *Following the essay is Silverman's actual review of* I, Robot *that he wrote for wired.com. A former artistic director for the Taos Moving Pictures Festival, Silverman is active in all facets of the independent movie scene. Currently, he is the director of the cinematheque at the Center for Contemporary Arts and the co-director with Samba Gadjigo of* SEMBENE!, *a documentary film about Ousmane Sembene, the legendary filmmaker and author.*

I'VE SPENT A GOOD CHUNK of the last 12 years watching and thinking about movies, and I still don't know what I'm doing. I'm not sure how to prepare or how to "watch" the movie once it starts. A kind of schizophrenia sets in when I'm in the theater, with voices in my head competing for attention: the (pseudo)-intellectual forcing me to take notes on sociopolitical–aesthetic issues; the eager-to-please freelance writer testing out witty phrases to use; and the little kid yanking on my sleeve, saying, "Loosen up! It's just a movie!"

It's not surprising that I'm conflicted while watching a movie. Movies are *complicated*. They rely on highly technical processes, and their mechanics remain a mystery to most viewers. Though the movies are mostly a form of amusement—a colossally expensive one—some film lovers insist that cinema is the ultimate form of art—a medium that incorporates all other media. Then there are the watchdogs, who are concerned that the movies have a variety of negative effects on our culture. They are right to worry; movies, after all, are persuasive transmitters of information, the favored medium of both propagandists and advertising firms.

For these and other reasons, cinema is a tricky medium to write about. The more I learn, the more I realize I don't know. But I have seized upon a few concepts to help me tackle the film reviews, articles, and essays I write. Here's how these concepts helped shape a review I wrote of *I, Robot* (reprinted below) for the online magazine *Wired News* (wired.com).

There are lots of pieces in this puzzle. Every second of a movie is packed with information, far too much to take in. But I try and get a sense of how the various elements—the writing, music, lighting, camera angles, performances, film stock, effects, editing—work together. Doing that helps me understand why the filmmakers made the choices they did.

- In Hollywood films, clumsy elements can jump out at me—an awkward edit, dialogue that feels staged, an especially bogus special effect. Studio films are generally supposed to be seamless. *I, Robot*'s team built a smooth-running film, and the cinematography, sets and performative, and editing style are well suited to the subject matter. From a technical standpoint, at least, *I, Robot* is highly proficient.

The most impressive element of *I, Robot* was the convincing interaction between the computer-generated (CG) characters (the CG imaging work is done long after the human actors have left the set). And, while I didn't think much of the screenplay as a whole (more on that below), the writers created a good part for the star, Will Smith. Like most Hollywood scores, the *I, Robot* music was overwrought and intrusive.

Story rules. Filmmakers say it again and again: good movies come from telling good stories. It's a cliché, maybe, but it's also true, especially if you expand your notion of what a story can be. Most feature films rely on conventional narratives—boy meets girl, alien attacks planet, detective hunts murderer, king grows paranoid, etc.—and unfold in specific three-act structure. Occasionally, artistic-minded filmmakers will experiment with more adventurous narrative forms. Experimental, non-narrative films (some have no characters, dialogue or plot) seek to tell stories of some kind. The form of the story is less important than its relevance—does it matter to me?—and the level of passion and ingenuity the film-makers use in transmitting it.

- The many loose ends and nonsensical scenes in *I, Robot* left me wondering how much the filmmakers cared about the integrity of the story. Give the plot a few lingering thoughts and it begins to disintegrate. More importantly, the filmmakers chose to take a highly relevant subject—our relationship to technology—and turn it into a relative caricature (robots bad, humans good).

It's more than entertainment. I think movies can influence behavior. Not that there is a one-to-one correlation—watching some dumb violent movie won't make every teen in the audience start knocking over convenience stores. But every movie, intentionally or not, can serve as a political and sociological text, transmitting information that can challenge or reinforce what we believe about ourselves and the world.

- I was initially excited at the prospect of an *I, Robot* movie—it's based on a 1950 Isaac Asi-mov book that explores the tension between humans and their increasingly sophisticated machines. The book feels a bit dated, but there's plenty of meaty, brainy stuff for an am-bitious film to delve into. Unfortunately, this *I, Robot* movie sends simplistic, technopho-bic messages: Smart machines are to be feared, but human ingenuity will save the day.

On the surface *I, Robot* takes an anti-corporate stance (the villain is a big robotics com-pany). Look a bit deeper, though: the film was made by 20th Century Fox—owned by the same multinational corporation that runs the business-friendly Fox News and scores of conservative newspapers—and it's filled with product placements (those mini-commercials for things like sneakers and soft drinks that Hollywood studios sneak onto the screen).

There are also interesting gender and race issues in the movie. Smith, playing the African-American policeman Del Spooner, is accused of being an anti-robot bigot, while oldfashioned, anti-black racism never becomes an issue. Nancy Calvin, the female protag-onist, is the latest in a long Hollywood line of lonely, frigid female professionals who have problems connecting with men. What does that stereotype tell us? That women who are successful in the workplace lead miserable personal lives.

✦**Movies are magic.** I try not to get *too* caught up in the politics of every single movie—a good one can be a mind-altering substance, transporting me to new, weird and/or wonderful places. I'm at my best when I can tune in intellectually to a film *and* experience it on a gut level.

- With special effects becoming more spectacular every month, it's easy to take for granted how great the new breed of sci-fi/fantasy films look. Five years ago, the visu-als in *I, Robot* would have been groundbreaking, but the computerized, futuristic landscapes somehow don't seem quite as startling in this age of digital wizardry, when any visual is possible. I found the robots to be remarkable, and genuinely frightening in a plastic, banal way. The lead robot, Sonny, was especially convincing.

Unfortunately, the magical moments weren't sustained for very long—*I, Robot*'s narrative gaps shook me out of any brief reverie.

Business rules. Entrepreneurs built the American film industry and, 100 years later, money still drives the movies. The average Hollywood film costs nearly $100 million to produce and market, so there's lots at stake with every release. Filmmakers are not immune to the profit motive—even Martin Scorsese and Woody Allen juggle financial considerations with artistic concerns.

- It's difficult to balance philosophical discourse and blockbuster action. When in doubt, Hollywood generally slugs it out—disposing of the brainy stuff and emphasizing fight and chase scenes. That's certainly true in *I, Robot,* which radically diverges from Asimov's edgy book. Did the producers worry that an idea-driven movie would scare off audiences? Perhaps. There are other signs of financial pressures here, including the movie's implausible happy ending, the casting of a beautiful young actress as Susan Calvin (she's something of an old bat in the book); and the inclusion of liberal amounts of product placements.

Beware the tricks. The so-called "moving image" is actually a physiological fluke: flash a series of images past the human eye and the human brain will read them as seamless motion. The idea that cinema exists thanks to a trick of the eye represents one level of movie manipulation. I'm also wary of the other tricks filmmakers have developed: the schmaltzy music to try and make me cry, the shrouding of a villain in sinister shadow, an explosion so fiery that I fear for my eyebrows. I admire a good cinematic trick as much as anyone, but also am aware that these tricks too often cover up inept storytelling.

- *I, Robot,* a film about the future, enjoyed showing off futuristic machinery. That's the advantage of sci-fi and other tech-oriented stories. I liked the filmmakers' relationship with gadgetry. It wasn't fetishistic; instead, they showed enough of the robots to give me an understanding of how they worked. The CG imagery was also used to good effect. Other standard-issue tricks—the button-pushing music, the sappy ending, the film noir–inspired lighting—were restrained, at least in terms of Hollywood blockbusters.

Don't be seduced by style. What passed for great filmmaking 50 years ago can today look stilted and clumsy. I've seen films made on laptops that have better effects than the original *Star Wars.* Styles that seem innovative and timeless right now will pass into obsolescence sometime soon (yes, that includes *The Matrix* and *The Lord of the Rings*). Style in itself does not qualify a film as a work of art. The stylistic choices in any good film reflect and deepen that film's intent. That's not to say I don't *ooh* and *aah* over eye-bending effects or stunning cinematography. I just try to avoid confusing them with artful filmmaking.

- *I, Robot* made some smart stylistic choices. The cinematographer shot the film, probably using filters, striving for a sci-fi/pulp fiction look, with shades of blue replacing the shades of gray familiar to fans of classic film noir. The result was relatively subtle and unified, and not especially memorable or innovative. But it was appropriate and served the story well.

Watch old stuff, too. The movies are only a century old—an infant compared to other forms of expression—and they continue to evolve at a fast pace. I don't claim a comprehensive knowledge of film history (there's just too many movies out there) but the more old movies I watch, the better I understand cinema's evolutionary path. That gives me more confidence when I critique a new film.

- What makes great science fiction, and why did *I, Robot* fall short? To me, the best sci-fi films do at least one of two things: they build a complete world and live within the rules that govern that world; or they use the future as a prism through which to investigate issues that affect our culture today. I love the first two *Terminator* films, both of which fulfill the first rule. You could think about them over and over and they still seemed to make sense. I remain one of the few defenders of *A.I: Artificial Intelligence*, which was as moving and troubling an examination of human–machine relationships as I've seen. Other sci-fi movies I've been impressed with: *A Clockwork Orange, Alphaville, Metropolis, Close Encounters, The Truman Show*. It's not a long list, partly because good sci-fi is hard to create. Special effects make these films expensive, and expensive movies usually don't have the luxury of exploring deep, philosophical issues. To me, that's *I, Robot's* central problem: Despite its potentially rich subject matter, it dedicated most of its resources to more conventional action sequences.

Read some books, too. My favorite film writers are able to put movies into the context of art, history, sociology, literature, theory, philosophy, geography, geology, theology . . . anything and everything. Good film writers do more than just compare one film to another. They offer a context in which to understand the movies as an artistic and cultural form, and as a window into the world.

- I re-read *I, Robot*, which I last picked up as a teenager, to prepare for this film. It's amazing how sharp and relevant Asimov's thoughts on artificial intelligence remain, given that the book predates the computer age. Reading the book, far more than seeing the movie, reinforced the urgency of considering our relationship to technology. Movies like *I, Robot* may not do all of the intellectual and philosophical work I want them to, but they do help push important issues into the pop-cultural slipstream.

■ ■ ■

I, Robot, No Deep Thinker

Near the beginning of his classic 1950 novel *I, Robot*, Isaac Asimov laid out the three commandments governing robot behavior: Thou shalt not allow harm to come to a human, thou shalt obey humans, thou shalt protect thyself.

Hollywood blockbusters have their own set of rules, too: Drop in little commercials for products whenever you can, replace meaningful dialogue with witty repartee, build lots of fight scenes, end happily (by saving the world, if budget permits) and dilute any brainy stuff.

In the movie version of *I, Robot*, Hollywood's rules rule. Asimov fans and others who like their sci-fi on the chewy side will probably revolt—the essence of the book is gone. But the average popcorn muncher will appreciate *I, Robot*—it's a good example of why the blockbuster formula works. It's funny, has a chilly, blue visual style (the robots look like the clamshell iBooks) and moves fast.

This *I, Robot* began life as a screenplay called *Hardwired*, about a robot alleged to have killed a human. The film's producers then acquired the rights to the Asimov book and decided to combine the two stories.

I, Robot; You, no deep thinker.

It's not clear how the novel influenced the finished film (the credits describe *I, Robot* as "suggested by," rather than "adapted from," Asimov). But this movie definitely has made the book's most sensational bit—the idea that robots could follow the three laws and take over the world—central to the plot.

Of course, if any alien group is plotting a hostile global takeover, best to cast Will Smith to stop them—he's a one-man Department of Homeland Security. In *I, Robot*, Smith plays Officer Del Spooner, a guy with a grudge against robots—he's even been accused of being an anti-tech bigot. Spooner also hates United States Robotics, the world's largest "mecha" manufacturer.

USR is preparing to roll out its new Automated Domestic Assistant, the almost-human NS-5, when one of the company's founders, Alfred Lanning, jumps to his death, leaving Spooner a cryptic message.

Convinced that Lanning's death is part of a bigger plot, Spooner sets out to investigate with help from USR scientist Susan Calvin (played by Bridget Moynahan as a distant relation, at best, to the Calvin of the book) and a robot named Sonny. His opponents include some pesky mecha assassins and Lawrence Robertson, USR's hard-edged CEO. *I, Robot* displays plenty of high-tech wizardry—cars rolling on balls instead of wheels; a slow-mo, airborne robot fight and, best of all, Sonny, who is one of the best movie robots yet. The film is set in 2035, and the NS-5s are still a few generations behind the Terminators and Steven Spielberg's A.I. mechas. Sonny is much more robot than human, a plastic, nearly affectless, truly creepy creature.

I've yet to see a convincing CG replication of human movement. Sonny, however, is supposed to move like a machine—like CG itself, Sonny is mechanical but aspires to be more lifelike.

Through Sonny, director Alex Proyas (*The Crow, Dark City*) takes a few stabs at exploring deeper man–machine questions. How will artificial intelligence parallel human thought processes? How can robots reconcile a complex world with their rigid rules of behavior? What happens when machines grow conflicted about the wisdom of their creators?

But Proyas' film never settles down long enough to dig deep. He's nodding in Asimov's general direction, not exploring his ideas.

Worse, Proyas' *I, Robot* stops making sense once you think about it. There are too many loose ends, too many plot-convenient moments and far from enough rigorous thought. To enjoy this *I, Robot,* you'll have to turn off your brain.

That may be what moviegoers expect to do over the summer, but it's the last thing Asimov, a master of clear, sharp logic, would have wanted.

How I Wrote This Essay Jason Silverman

Why did you write this piece—what was the assignment or motivation for writing?

Because my brother asked me (note: Jonathan Silverman *is* Jason Silverman's brother). Also, I thought it would be productive to compile my thoughts on movie writing.

What did you do when you got the assignment?

Freaked!

How did you begin?

I made notes about the various issues I hoped to explore and began thinking about an interesting way to organize them as a single essay.

Describe the process of writing the first draft.

This was for some reason a challenging piece for me to write. I experimented with different forms.

Did you write a draft all the way through?

No, I spent a lot of time working on the form and on the first section. Once I settled on that, which was probably five or six drafts, I wrote it all of the way through.

How much editing did you do as you wrote?

I edit a lot as I write. I usually write a section and then go back up to the top and edit down, and do that continually.

How long would you say the process took?

In hours, probably ten to twelve hours. That was over the course of a week.

How did you edit the draft?

The editing came relatively easily once I had the form and opening together. I just tightened and moved a few elements around, and made some clarifications.

What was the response when you turned in your essay?

Ecstasy. Celebration. Peace on earth.

Are you satisfied now with what you wrote? Would you make any changes?

The piece represents well where I was at that moment as a writer. I like the way it reads.

READING WRITING

This Text: Reading

1. What connections do you see between Silverman's observations in the first essay and his actual review?
2. In what ways does Silverman read movies as "texts"?
3. What is the most interesting (or unexpected) aspect of the way in which Silverman looks at movies? How is his system similar or different than your own?
4. Find Silverman's thesis (it's pretty clear). How does he try to "prove" his thesis throughout the essay?

Your Text: Writing

1. Write a rebuttal to Silverman's review of *I, Robot*. What don't you like about his review?
2. Find a more positive review of *I, Robot* and write a comparison/contrast paper on the two reviews. Which review is the more convincing? Why?

FILM AS CULTURAL COMMENTARY: TWO REVIEWS FROM *THE WEEKLY RADER*.

One of the authors of this book, Dean Rader, began an arts/culture/media/politics blog in 2008 in an attempt to do in the blogosphere what *The World is a Text* tries to do in the sphere of textbooks—look at events and objects in the world as constructed texts that can tell us about who we are and what's going on. We mention the blog to be forthcoming about the source of the following reviews, both of which appeared on *The Weekly Rader* (a not-so-funny reference to the famous *Weekly Reader* series you may have encountered in grade school). The first review by Greg Barnhisel reads *The Dark Knight* through the lens of politics, the Bush Administration, and surveillance. In addition to writing about modern poetry, he has authored his own writing textbook, *Media Matters*. Barnhisel is an associate professor at Duquesne University where he directs the writing program. Scott Andrews considers the *Twilight* series and all teen superhero movies as texts. He teaches American and American Indian literatures and classes on popular culture at California State University, Northridge. He has published book reviews, essays, poetry, and fiction.

The Dark Knight

Greg Barnhisel

I DON'T REALLY TALK about movies in my own blog because, well, I don't really see movies much anymore, what with two small children. My wife and I do have a Netflix subscription and use it frequently, but because of the multitasking way we watch our DVDs—both of us working/surfing on our laptops, going to the kitchen, going upstairs to help a restive child fall asleep—I don't feel like I've immersed myself in a film when I watch it at home. I really tried a few months ago, when I took out David Lynch's *Inland Empire*, but I just don't think I'm able to focus on a film unless I'm in a theater (and even then I have to be reminded not to use the iPhone). So I don't want to write about these films the way I write about books because in a sense it's not fair; unlike books, films don't receive my full attention when I see them on TV.

(Interestingly, this isn't the case with TV shows that I take out and watch—I give full attention to *The Wire, The Sopranos, Weeds*, whatever it is; or, rather, I find it much easier to give them full attention. There must be a series of cinematographic and screenwriting tricks that a TV director uses to focus a home audience's attention that a movie director doesn't need to use. I'll have to check out *Mad Men* and see if it's similarly engaging.)

But after seeing *The Dark Knight* this week I just can't resist talking about the movie: not because the film itself was great, or horrible, or anything—it's a summer blockbuster about a superhero, enough said—but because *Wall Street Journal* writer Andrew Klavan *argued* that this film is a 150-minute panegyric to George W., down to the similarity between the Batsymbol and the Current Occupant's middle initial. "*The Dark Knight*," Klavan argues, "is at some level a paean of praise to the fortitude and moral courage that has been shown by George W. Bush in this time of terror and war." Klavan points to how,

"like W., Batman is vilified and despised for confronting terrorists in the only terms they understand." He sees in *The Dark Knight* the Bushian argument that "that there is no moral equivalence between a free society—in which people sometimes make the wrong choices—and a criminal sect bent on destruction."

Predictably, liberal blogs screamed about this tortured reaching of the Bush dead-enders for cultural relevance and Hollywood validation. Isaac Chotiner in the *New Republic* almost choked with disbelief, and the generally shriller *Huffington Post* attempted to rebut the argument that Bush = Batman by arguing that because Batman willingly accepts that he *must* become an outlaw to save Gotham, this proves that Christopher Nolan and the film are arguing that Batman's "enhanced" tactics of crimefighting and civil-rights violations were wrong all along.

The problem is that the *Wall Street Journal* is right. In the film, Batman is confronted by the Joker, who is explicitly contrasted with the cartel of mafia gangs (ethnically stereotyped as sharp-dressed Italians, threatening African Americans, and swarthy lowbrowed Southeastern Europeans) that used to be the city's nemeses. The Joker represents an entirely new paradigm of villain: he is nihilistic, an "agent of chaos," pleased to bring evil for evil's sake and with no larger "goal" besides death. It's hard for me to see this as anything but an allegory for the post-Cold War period, when the "old" villains of Communism, dangerous but predictable and organized, have been supplanted by the

Is Batman's secret identity Bruce Wayne or George W. Bush?

"evildoers" of terrorism, whom conservatives consistently describe as being motivated simply by hate: "they hate our freedoms," "they love death." The Joker = Al Qaeda, and the Joker's ability to inspire the crazies of the city to join him and die in the process mirrors the Al Qaeda copycat phenomenon.

As with Al Qaeda, there is no negotiating with the Joker, for he doesn't want anything except the aftermath of the chaos he brings. (This notion, that Islamic terrorism is fundamentally autochthonous and self-perpetuating rather than a response to material conditions and a drive for particular goals, is most frequently advanced by those who use the term "Islamo-Fascism.") And because he is so unpredictable, so alien to the ordinary laws of human motivation, Batman and his allies (Gordon, the head of Major Crimes, and Harvey Dent, the paladin-like district attorney) must fight the war in new ways, using deception and the violation of civil liberties. As Dick Cheney said on September 16, 2001, "We also have to work, though, sort of the dark side, if you will."

The people, naturally, clamor for this. Terrified and stupid, the populace of Gotham needs to be directed and protected by a Strong Leader—or, rather, a leader-cadre divided up between the admirable figurehead of Harvey Dent (in whom the People Put Their Hopes) and Batman, the man who is willing to get his hands dirty, making the sausage, doing the things that have to be done but which can't be exposed. These leaders intend eventually to restore to the citizens their pre-Joker freedoms, but during the state of the emergency (Terror Alert Red?) they need to do things that they can't disclose. At one point, Batman figures out how to make every citizen's cellphone a kind of microphone and sonar imagery device all plugged into his central console, so that he—or his faithful lieutenant, Lucius Fox—can engage in simultaneous surveillance of every phone conversation and text message and have images of every point in the entire city. Fox is at first reluctant to wield this power, but Batman assures him that there is a safeguard against its irresponsible use: Fox's own conscience, and his trust in Fox to disable this useful but potentially dangerous technology as soon as the emergency ends.

I can't see how anyone, liberal or conservative, can see this as anything but a justification for the "Terrorist Surveillance Program" (warrantless wiretapping) and the "Total Information Awareness" initiative that sprung up in 2002. The Fourth Amendment safeguards that had been in place are no longer operational; we need this information NOW because there is a ticking bomb; you can trust us not to violate your liberties because we are good Americans.

The movie even sanctions torture. It's horribly violent, and although it doesn't engage in the stylization of violence typical of the Wachowski Brothers movies (*V is for Vendetta*) it makes it clear that even though the Joker desires violence and death (like "terrorists"), that can't stop us from using it for the greater good.

The final tentpole of this argument is the portrayal of Batman as a combination of Bush and Cheney. Like Batman in his muscled suit and "Wayne Enterprises," Bruce Wayne's military-contractor corporation, macho, martial, Bush on the aircraft carrier in his flight suit becomes an emblem of the irresistibility and sexiness of American military power and the military-industrial complex. Meanwhile Cheney, hidden in his undisclosed location, devises the strategies behind the scenes that will keep us safe. And while the population initially embraces, and even dresses as, Batman, as things get tougher the fickle public turns on their hero. Batman, though, knows that the fight must continue, that he must stick to his convictions even as the short-sighted citizens agitate for his arrest. In the end, after making clear to his team that he will be the scapegoat for the death of Dent, he is hounded from society. How satisfying Bush must find this! The hero, steadfast even when his fans turn against him, will never stop protecting us from evil, even when we are too foolish to understand that his extraordinary tactics are for our own good?

Or, as Klavan puts it,

> When our artistic community is ready to show that sometimes men must kill in order to preserve life; that sometimes they must violate their values in order to maintain those values; and that while movie stars may strut in the bright light of our adulation for pretending to be heroes, true heroes often must slink in the shadows, slump-shouldered and despised—then and only then will we be able to pay President Bush his due and make good and true films about the war on terror.

> Perhaps that's when Hollywood conservatives will be able to take off their masks and speak plainly in the light of day.

I think Nolan's been unmasked, and, to some degree, Klavan's been proven right.

In 2008, Barack Obama took advantage of Americans' repudiation of George W. Bush—whose approval ratings were among the lowest ever recorded as his second term ended—and swept into office on an emotional tide of "change" and "hope." The grubby realities of the War on Terror, the endless drip-drip-drip of revelations of torture and kidnapping and spying and murder, would be over, and we were going to restore the shine to our City on a Hill.

But the funny thing is that President Obama's been a lot more Harvey Dent than we thought. Prosecutions of those who ordered torture have been ruled out. Bush-era surveillance and detention policies have been reaffirmed, and in some cases even strengthened. Guantanamo endures, and the executive branch continues to do its best to avoid the Supreme Court's demand that prisoners and detainees receive legal rights. We've met the new boss, and I'm afraid that, at least when it comes to this, he looks a whole lot like the old boss.

Smells Like Teen Superheroes

Scott Andrews

When *New Moon* hit theaters in the United States in 2009, it made more than $290 million and set off another wave of vampire-mania. Perhaps I should not write "another," since the previous wave had not subsided. In fact, in 2009 it has swelled further, with EVEN MORE novel series and TV series about beautiful bloodsuckers.

It was a couple of years earlier, while watching previews for *Twilight*, that I began to wonder about possible connections between this tidal wave of hemophiles and other trends in popular culture that appealed to young Americans. There seemed to be something swirling in the collective American ectoplasm that had coalesced into some critical mass.

First there was *Harry Potter and the Philosopher's Stone*, published in the United States in 1998. The first X-Men film was released in 2000, though the comic book had been around for decades. *Twilight* was published in 2005, though Stephanie Meyers says the story came to her in 2003. *Heroes* arrived on NBC in 2006. *True Blood* appeared on HBO in 2008, though it doesn't clearly target a young audience. *The Vampire Diaries* debuted on the CW in 2009.

The new teen superheroes from *Twilight: New Moon*—different with a difference.

The life of an American teen is often times filled with anxiety, emotional turmoil, and alienation. This is true whether one is wealthy or poor, male or female. This is true regardless of race. There is something about being a teenager that makes one feel apart from the crowd, unusual. My generation (I am in my 40s) identified with our sense of being lovable but damaged goods—for instance, the short-lived TV series designed to appeal to my generation's sense of nostalgia, *Freaks and Geeks;* but the current batch of teenagers and college-goers seem to find it more pleasurable to imagine themselves to be different because they are special.

Misunderstood rather than misbegotten. Gifted and powerful rather than awkward and fearful and acne-plagued.

They have taken the leap from the John Hughesian question "Why can't I date a cheerleader?" to "Save the cheerleader. Save the world."

But I am not thinking of just wizards, mutants, and vampires. *American Idol* started rocking America's world in 2002. *America's Next Top Model* walked the runway in 2003. And before them, even before Harry Potter, came the grandfather of all Reality TV: *The Real World* on MTV in 1992. Young people, previously unknown, were instantly important and famous, though not necessarily talented. The emotional, social, and sexual problems of young people were no longer the subject of "After School Specials"—they were primetime, they were ratings hits. The American fascination with these young people was understood as a measure of their importance. Notoriety was understood as noteworthy.

For many decades, people were familiar with the American Dream. For the immigrant, this was the belief that one could come to the United States, work hard, and save money. Eventually one could obtain a comfortable lifestyle—and an even better lifestyle for one's children. For a long time, the American Dream for the immigrant was similar to the

American Dream for the citizen. You know the one: the dream of the happy family and the house with the white picket fence. Eventually the American Dream changed. You could say it got "super-sized." It became the belief that if one worked hard, saved money, and took advantage of opportunities for investing or starting one's own business, eventually one could obtain a more-than-comfortable lifestyle—one might even become rich. You know, that happy family and a house with the white picket fence, a deck in the backyard, a shiny Viking refrigerator, a sedan and an SUV in the garage, two Sea-Doos, and a time-share on the lake.

I think perhaps the American Dream has morphed again. I think it includes getting rich, but I think it has skipped the "work hard and save money" elements. In their place have been added "get famous" and "right now." The work ethic of my parents that was based on delayed gratification became the credit-card fueled consumer culture of my generation that wanted instant gratification. And the generation that has been raised by my generation has gone a step further into instant great-ification.

The advent of instant celebrity status is thanks largely to the Internet and its inbred cousin, reality television. Think Tila Tequila. Think that strange kid singing "Chocolate Rain." Perhaps we should thank Paris Hilton, the Queen of Instant and Talentless Celebrity Status, whose career was launched in 2003 with a sex video that went viral on the Internet and, later that year, with *The Simple Life*. She is the T-1000 to Puck's T-1.

I see a wave of narratives about young people who discover they are not just dorky and weird—they are different with a difference. They have special powers! And they have them right now! Not after years of training but now! Even Harry shows up at Hogwarts with abilities other students do not possess. Instant wealth has been symbolically replaced: They can fly! They can stop time! They are indestructible! Their powers, like wealth, allow them to go places and do things that other people (normal or middle class) cannot. Or in a more mundane setting, there is no need for years of apprenticeship—get up on stage, you 20-year-old, and sing so Simon can make you famous tomorrow!

It is easy to think of these changes as the product of young people being spoiled by the relative wealth of their parents' generation. I wonder, though, if it might speak also to a fear. Perhaps the world that lies ahead of these young people is so scary, so confusing, filled with so many choices as to be paralyzing, that imagining superpowers and immortality is reassuring.

I can totally relate.

READING WRITING

This Text: Reading

1. How would you characterize the tone of these reviews? Is it obvious they were written for a blog as opposed to a printed magazine or newspaper? Does Andrews have a different tone than Barnhisel? If so, how would you distinguish between the two?

2. One of the many things we like about these reviews is that they take an unusual approach to films. Rather than simply "evaluating" the movies, Andrews and Barnhisel read them through unique lenses; they use the films to make larger assumptions about culture. What do the authors ultimately say about American culture?

3. Which review is the most convincing? How does the author persuade you to come around to his point of view? Find specific examples of good argumentation and evidentiary support.

Your Text: Writing

1. Write a rebuttal to one of these reviews. You probably have strong opinions about one or both movies, and you likely disagree with one of the reviewers. So, set out to debunk either Barnhisel or Andrews. Pick apart their arguments in a respectful way, but also advance your own reading of the film in question.

2. Neither author pays much attention to the cinematic aspect of either movie, such as camera angles, lighting, special effects, dialogue, and editing. Write an essay in which you make an argument about how a film's formal qualities contribute to its themes.

3. One of the things the two reviews share is a claim that *The Dark Knight, Heroes,* and *Twilight* play off and/or exploit fears. Write a comparison/contrast essay in which you talk about the importance of "fear" in the Barnhisel and Andrews reviews. Be sure to include a section in your essay in which you give your own opinions about fear in these two films.

Star Wars and America

Whitney Black

Student Essay

WHITNEY BLACK WROTE THIS ESSAY WHILE A STUDENT at the University of San Francisco in 2003. In her short persuasive essay, she takes what is perhaps to most readers an unpopular stance. Black reads *Star Wars* through the lens of a classic American Western, arguing that the film essentially replicates the standard formula of Hollywood Westerns—even the good guys wear white and the bad guys, black. As you work through her essay, you might ask if Black reads too much into the film. Or, does she pick up on deep-seated American values that many people are reluctant to question? Finally, is it possible to identify problematic aspects of a movie but still love it?

THOUGH *STAR WARS* TAKES PLACE in the far off frontier of space, and is less concerned with recreating America's past than it is with imagining the future, the film is still a classic American Western, right down to the requisite good versus evil, us against them dualities. Like all formulaic Westerns, *Star Wars* is about opposition and the promotion of good old-fashioned American values. The environment is the unfamiliar galaxy, but the underlying message is pure Americana; *Star Wars* subverts patriotism within the rebel forces and religious "force," and establishes the rebellion's struggle against the tyrannical Empire as a pro-American ideological battle. The rebel forces, with their pared down attire and allegiance to the old "force" religiosity, are the antithesis to the techno-driven, machine heavy homogeneity of the Evil Empire; similar to how the American identity, with its commitment to traditional democratic values, differed from the oppressive threat of communism. Communism, during both the Red Scare and the Vietnam War, served as both a threat to American ideals as and a way to glorify those ideals by contrast. The un-American construct of the Empire, like the un-American Communist mentality, function as the perfect counterparts; both are outsider systems, whose differences illuminate America's "greatness," and generate a need to preserve that "greatness." The Rebellion is obligated to defend *a way of life,* a sense of individual freedom, from the Empire.

Like the Western's struggle between Cowboy and Indian, civilization and savagery, *Star Wars* simply modernizes the conflict, replacing cowboys with Jedi and Indians with evil empire affiliates. Though the characters have changed, the implicit Western message of expelling a threatening "other" remains. Both *Star Wars* and the classic Western are filmic homage to an American ideal; while the classic Western re-writes the past to stabilize and reassure the present, *Star Wars* acts as a cautionary tale against what an absence of those ideals means for the future. The "us against them" duality is less about racial differences than it is about America's ideological system. It is glorious democracy against a "bad" counter-government. Though *Star Wars* does not directly ally itself with America's geography, location is inconsequential; the rebels are as American as Indians killing cowboys, symbols of a filmic tradition advocating American values by setting them against an external threat.[30]

Star Wars succeeds at its "Western-ness" because of its dependence on opposition. Nothing solidifies the righteousness of "good" as much as the presence of a contrasting evil. The Evil Empire justifies the Rebellion (obviously a *force* is necessary to confront the manifestation of evil) while divulging the danger of sacrificing the rebel cause to the empire. The Empire is the ominous threat and represents everything opposing the rebel value system, persona, and way of life. The result is audience approval of the rebel cause; audiences, whether aware of it or not, identify with the rebels as individual heroes fighting against a different, and thus threatening, authority. While the rebellion, and its association to the Imperial Senate,

Luke, Leia, and Han: rebels or conservatives?

---

[30]For more information on *Star Wars* and American values, see Peter Lev's *American Films of the 70s: Conflicting Visions.*

most certainly symbolizes the people's voice, the Empire is ignorant of the wants of the common people, and is a realization of abused power, and a warning against forces opposed to American democracy. While America, with its own structured Senate, associates its ideals with a "power to the people" mentality, the Empire is in obvious contrast, determined to exploit technology (the Death Star) and become an ultimate power and oppressive regime.

Not only does *Star Wars* link technology to tyranny and oppression, but it also creates another opposition of technology versus nature, with nature encompassing the rural American identity of honor, duty, and goodness while technology embodies the age-old fear of change. Clearly, the death star is both an example of misused power, and a warning against change. The machine, because of its relation to the Evil Empire, is a digression away from humanity; technology threatens the existence of individual power and becomes an instrument for proliferating evil. The protagonist Luke Skywalker succeeds against the Empire by relying on the power of his subconscious, turning off his computerized tracking system to respond on instinct. He uses his faith in the force, a religion of nature, and old fashioned and unquestioned belief; the outcome of his success, his ability to defeat the Empire, perpetuates yet another American notion. Believe in its value systems and justice will be restored.

The film's message is clear: Hold fast to our present way of life and the future will be saved. Like any Western, *Star Wars* is a cinematic love letter to Americana, and the country's perpetual fear of confrontation. Westerns deal in oppositions, because the rebel in space or in the west is always sacrificing their own safety to salvage a community. Community salvation mirrors American salvation, and the protagonist's determination and commitment to deep-rooted American rightness serves as the best possible form of American patriotism and duty. The Western always needs a hero willing to die for the cause, ready to save America from the threat of change. Westerns contend that America is the "best and only way," oppositions are the worst imagined evil; both feared and destroyed and ultimately never tolerated.

Works Cited

Lev, Peter. *American Films of the 70s: Conflicting Visions.* Austin: University of Texas Press, 2000.

READING WRITING

This Text: Reading

1. What is Black's thesis here? Is it one sentence, or does it extend over several?
2. What do you make of her claim that *Star Wars* simply "modernizes" the cowboy vs. Indian motif of the American Western?
3. Do you agree with her reading of the movie's message ("Hold fast to our present way of life and the future will be saved")? Why or why not?

Your Text: Writing

1. *Star Wars* is an incredibly popular franchise. Write an essay in which you argue that *Star Wars* embodies the best American values. Be sure to explain what you think the "best American values" are.
2. Write a comparison/contrast essay in which you read *Star Wars* and *Avatar* alongside or against each other. How do they play out when compared to the other?

The *Avatar* Suite

As of April 1, 2010, *Avatar*, the much-hyped, much-praised, and much-hyperbolied film by James Cameron, had grossed over $2 billion dollars worldwide, making it the highest grossing film of all time, zooming past Cameron's other major project, *Titanic*. Though no one really knows for sure, the going assumption is that *Avatar* cost about $300 million dollars to bring to the big screen. So even though it was incredibly expensive to produce, it made a huge profit, and it made a lot of fans. It was nominated for nine Academy Awards and won Oscars for Best Art Direction, Best Cinematography, and Best Visual Effects. However, the Best Picture Oscar went to *The Hurt Locker*, directed by Cameron's ex-wife, Kathryn Bigelow, which made for some great Oscar night tension. One of the high points of the Oscar ceremony was when Ben Stiller appeared on stage dressed (and made up) to resemble one of the blue-skinned Na'vi from the movie. That the Na'vi-Stiller's job was to hand out the award for Best Makeup made the moment even funnier. Just a few months in and *Avatar* was already iconic.

Avatar's loss in the Best Picture race, but its nice showing in the production categories, might serve as an indictor of its priorities. For many, the flashy CGI and 3-D technology eclipsed the film's story, which even Cameron himself dubbed "an old-fashioned jungle adventure with an environmental conscience." But for others, *Avatar* exploded onto the screen in big blue strokes, painting its techno-canvas in the colors of biodiversity, futurism, and imperialism. In some ways, the film does recall classic American novels and films that foreground the issues when two utterly distinct cultures collide. The scholar Mary Louise Pratt coined the phrase "contact zone" to describe "social spaces where disparate cultures meet, clash, and grapple with each other." Pratt has identified

Are the Na'vi avatars for American Indians?

these places to be one of conflict, negotiation and oftentimes, colonialism. To be sure, Pandora, the mythical planet of *Avatar* is one enormous contact zone where the value systems of humans and the Na'vi crash into each other in alarming and redefining ways. Cameron has acknowledged the film's debt to the 1990 Kevin Costner Western *Dances with Wolves* in which a disaffected white soldier finds that he has more in common with the local Sioux than the American military. The contact zone of the Great Plains during the Civil War is, indeed, remarkable, and for all of its shortcomings, *Dances With Wolves* demonstrates the many ways America owes its Americanness to American Indians. *Avatar*, as *Salon* film critic Stephanie Zacharek notes, takes a page from the *Dances With Wolves* playbook, romanticizing the act of going Native. However, in Cameron's version, the act of going Native has environmental consequences in addition to social ones. It's a movie with a message.

How successful that message is communicated and how interesting of a message it actually is remains open for debate. We have assembled here four radically different reviews of *Avatar*, each of which reads the film through a different lens. Zacharek thinks *Avatar* is over the top and pokes fun at Cameron's earnest gadget-filled tale. What we like about Zacharek's take is not her personal stance on *Avatar* but her ability *not* to be immersed by the movie's big CGI hug. She takes a step back and reads the film from a distanced, critical perspective. This allows her to write some very funny lines and offer a smart take on some of the goofier parts of the film.

Three other reviewers offer different but complementary takes on *Avatar*. Slavoj Žižek is one of the most important living thinkers. A senior researcher at the Institute of Sociology, University of Ljubljana, Slovenia, Žižek writes about anything and everything. Sassy and highly theoretical, his review of *Avatar* takes the movie to task for being fundamentally racist. Mikhail Lyubansky also reads the movie through the lens of race, but he takes an opposite stance, arguing that all the special effects aside, *Avatar* makes important statements about race and race relations that span time, galaxies, and language. For him, *Avatar* does important cultural work in that it takes on sociopolitical issues in an entertaining and accessible way. Where Lyubansky watches *Avatar* through the lens of race, Ari Y. Kelman views it through the lens of technology. According to Kelman, the great irony of *Avatar* is that its pro-environmental/anti-technology message is delivered through the most high-tech cinematic system ever. For Kelman, *Avatar* engorges itself on technology; it celebrates it rather than celebrating a simpler return to reciprocal environmental values.

As authors, teachers, and editors, we do not endorse any of these reviews or approaches over another. We like all of these reviews for different reasons, and we like most of all how a conversation can emerge when we place them next to each other.

Avatar: Dances with Aliens

Stephanie Zacharek

THE PROBLEM WITH TAKING 15 YEARS to bring audiences the future of filmmaking is that someone else is bound to get to the future before you do. And while there are certain technical effects in James Cameron's *Avatar* that aren't quite like anything we've ever seen before, the movie is hardly a historical event, or even a grand achievement. It *is* a very expensive-looking, very flashy entertainment, albeit one that groans under the weight of clumsy storytelling in the second half and features some of the most godawful dialogue this side of *Attack of the Clones*. Sensitive viewers will also want to note that two characters engage in tasteful sex under a special tree that bears a close resemblance to a bachelor-pad fiber-optic lamp. Clearly, Cameron has looked everywhere for inspiration—nature, art, the Spencer's Gifts catalog—and this tree, in particular, isn't just any old plug-in prop. "There is something really interesting going on in there biologically," says the brainy scientist character played by Sigourney Weaver, and believe you me, she doesn't know the half of it. *Avatar* would be great fun, if only Cameron—the picture's writer, director, producer and editor—had a sense of humor about himself, which he clearly doesn't. Instead Cameron—who is no longer just King of the World but Emperor of the Universe—has to make it clear he's addressing grand themes: Characters must prove their bravery, their humility as human beings *and* their sensitivity to indigenous peoples. Like those "revolutionary" westerns directors kept making in the early '70s, or like the later *Dances With Wolves*, *Avatar* is Cameron's "Let's be fair to the Indians" movie. And while Cameron's political stand is solidly liberal—he takes a clear position, in particular, on the corporatization of military power—this isn't a picture fleshed out with deep, multifaceted ideas. Cameron is less a sage than a canny bonehead. Characters signal their motives and intentions with thundering dialogue, mouthed by the actors in ways that suggest the guy at the top has a tin ear, or at least some pretty strange ideas about punctuation. "It'd be a fresh start. In a new world. And the pay is good. Very good," says the movie's hero, Jake Sully (Sam Worthington), in an early scene, as he begins to explain his mission, and the movie's premise.

Jake is a wheelchair-bound Marine, injured in the line of duty, and because he happens to have the right DNA, he's been recruited to travel to a distant planet called Pandora, where a bunch of suits, along with the U.S. military and some scientist types, have set up shop. Their goal is to mine a special ore—its name, "unobtanium," is one of the movie's only truly witty jokes—that will allow them to solve the Earth's energy crisis. The big drag is that to get the magic rocks, they need to relocate, either by force or reason, the relatively peaceful Pandora natives, very tall blue people with pointed ears known as the Na'vi.

The atmosphere on Pandora is poisonous to humans, so the Earth bigwigs have developed something called the *Avatar* Program, in which human DNA is combined with Na'vi DNA to create remote-controlled half-human, half-Na'vi creatures who can safely breathe Pandora air. In his *Avatar* incarnation, Jake can walk, as well as run and hunt and generally enjoy all the physical freedom he'd been deprived of on Earth. He also meets, and falls in love with, a beautiful Na'vi named Neytiri. (Although the Na'vis are all animated via performance-capture techniques, Neytiri is played by, and even somewhat resembles, the lanky, graceful actress Zoe Saldana.) None of the other *Avatar*s have been accepted by the natives, but Neytiri recognizes something special in Jake, and before long he's been embraced, cautiously, by the local tribe. That also, of course, makes him instantly invaluable to his coarse, unobtanium-greedy fellow Earthlings, among them an obnoxious, wheeler-dealer business guy played by Giovanni Ribisi and a devious, gung-ho Marine played by Stephen Lang. "*Avatar*," as its press notes announce, is designed to "deliver a fully immersive cinematic experience of a new kind, where the revolutionary technology invented to make the film disappears into the emotion of the characters and the sweep of the story." That word "immersive" means that you're not just watching *Avatar*—you're soaking in it. The movie was made, and is designed to be seen, in 3-D, and no matter what anyone— particularly the movie's studio, 20th Century Fox—tries to tell you, the technology and not the story is the big selling point here: If a less famous and less nakedly self-promotional director had made the exact same story with a bunch of actors in blue latex, the Fandango ticket sales wouldn't be going through the roof. And if the technology is as revolutionary as Cameron has been claiming for years now, isn't it disingenuous for the publicity to turn around and suggest that we're really not supposed to notice it? In "*Avatar*," the technology is everything. And it does, at least, amount to *something*. Whatever the flaws of *Avatar* may be, Cameron does use performance-capture more effectively than any filmmaker has yet, and that includes el-creepo performance-capture high priest Robert Zemeckis, whose *Polar Express* has served as the basis for many of my recurring Santa-driven nightmares. While I hate to see an actress as charming as Saldana disappear into the skin of a technogimmick, looking at the graceful, stretched-out blue creature she's been transformed into, I could see traces of the same performer who so daintily stubbed out a cigarette with her pink toe shoe in the 2000 teen ballet drama *Center Stage*.

On the other hand, Worthington, whose character is duller and flatter than the one Saldana plays, isn't particularly improved by technology: Both as a human and as a faux-Na'vi, he repeats the same sullen performance he gave in *Terminator Salvation*. Although with all of these performance-capture characters—no matter how much they may resemble their real-life counterparts—it's hard to discern subtleties of expression. The Na'vis are intriguingly designed: Their faces, with their elongated almond eyes, resemble the faun in Guillermo del Toro's *Pan's Labyrinth*, although unlike that character, they also have shimmery skin and pale tiger stripes. They wear their hair in long braids that end in a cluster of tentacles with nerve endings; these anemones can be plugged into the tails of various forest creatures, forming a kind of natural circuit. When Jake, as he's being schooled in Na'vi hunting techniques by Neytiri, mounts a magnificent flying beastie, he's not just riding it, he's communing with it.

Cameron takes all this "We must be one with nature" business very seriously—so seriously that he doesn't seem to realize that one of the sacred Na'vi communal rituals, as he's dramatized it, looks an awful lot like a Beverly Hills yoga class. Still, Cameron and his team of designers and technicians (as well as the director of photography, Mauro Fiore) have managed to come up with some lovely, fanciful details. I was particularly taken with the delicacy of the movie's color palette, especially for such a flashy, big-budget crowd pleaser. At one point Jake, exploring the wonders of a Pandora rainforest, comes upon a stand of giant, funnel-like mushrooms that shrink away from his touch and disappear, shyly, into the earth. Their color is an earthy, translucent pinkish-red, in a tone that takes more thought and consideration than the bright, hothouse color another filmmaker might have automatically gone for.

The midsection of *Avatar*, in which Jake discovers Pandora's glorious flora and fauna, has some lyricism. But in the last third, when the tanks and helicopters start moving in, the picture begins to look no more innovative than a sophisticated computer game. Cameron's message may be strictly antiwar, but the second half of his movie relies on the brutalities of combat to whip up excitement:

War is wrong, but at least it's dynamic, and yet Cameron doesn't stage these sequences in a particularly compelling way. There's another problem with making a two-and-a-half-hour long 3-D feature, one that has nothing to do with pacing: 3-D movies aren't more realistic than 2-D movies; they're hyperrealistic, which means they're more physically demanding to watch, and eyestrain is no filmmaker's friend. Stiff, awkward performances don't help much, either. Weaver's character—her name is Dr. Augustine, and she's modeled, at least loosely, on Ripley from the "Alien" films—is most believable when, in her human incarnation, she's puffing on her nearly ever-present cigarettes. (A chain-smoking scientist: Now there's something you don't see in the movies every day. I wish Cameron would show us more of his naughtier side.) But like everyone else here, Weaver stumbles through the picture's cartoony dialogue. At one point Stephen Lang's toughie Marine, annoyed by the fact that the Na'vi won't just hand over their sacred turf, barks, "We will fight terror with terror." It's sub-comic-book prose made deadly earnest.

You can make dumb dialogue work if you're serving up a classic Saturday matinee-style entertainment. But if you're out to change the face of filmmaking, you have to work much harder at a lot of the things Cameron just shrugs off. You need well-rounded characters, and a great story that, even if it follows a familiar template, illuminates some angle of human experience in a fresh way. And you need to give your actors something to do. Looking at "*Avatar*," you can see why the thing took a thousand years to make—every frame has been fussed over. But the actors don't live in the movie so much as drift through it like zombies—they seem to know, subconsciously, that in Cameron's grand vision, they're beside the point, obsolete. *Avatar* isn't *about* actors or characters or even about story; it's about special effects, which is fine as far as it goes. But for a movie that stresses how important it is for us to stay connected with nature, to keep our ponytails plugged into the life force, *Avatar* is peculiarly bloodless. It's a remote-control movie experience, a high-tech "wish you were here" scribbled on a very expensive postcard. You don't have to be fully present to experience *Avatar*; all you have to do is show up.

Return of the Natives

Slavoj Žižek

Beneath the idealism and political correctness of *Avatar*, in the spotlight at the Oscars, lie brutal racist undertones.

JAMES CAMERON'S *AVATAR* TELLS the story of a disabled ex-marine, sent from earth to infiltrate a race of blue-skinned aboriginal people on a distant planet and persuade them to let his employer mine their homeland for natural resources. Through a complex biological manipulation, the hero's mind gains control of his "avatar," in the body of a young aborigine. These aborigines are deeply spiritual and live in harmony with nature (they can plug a cable that sticks out of their body into horses and trees to communicate with them). Predictably, the marine falls in love with a beautiful aboriginal princess and joins the aborigines in battle, helping them to throw out the human invaders and saving their planet. At the film's end, the hero transposes his soul from his damaged human body to his aboriginal avatar, thus becoming one of them.

Given the 3-D hyperreality of the film, with its combination of real actors and animated digital corrections, *Avatar* should be compared to films such as *Who Framed Roger Rabbit* (1988) or *The Matrix* (1999). In each, the hero is caught between our ordinary reality and an imagined universe—of cartoons in *Roger Rabbit*, of digital reality in *The Matrix*, or of the digitally enhanced everyday reality of the planet in *Avatar*. What one should thus bear in mind is that, although *Avatar's* narrative is supposed to take place in one and the same "real" reality, we are dealing—at the level of the underlying symbolic economy— with two realities: the ordinary world of imperialist colonialism on the one hand, and a fantasy world, populated by aborigines who live in an incestuous link with nature, on the other. (The latter should not be confused with the miserable reality of actual exploited peoples.) The end of the film should be read as the hero fully migrating from reality into the fantasy world—as if, in *The Matrix*, Neo were to decide to immerse himself again fully in the matrix.

This does not mean, however, that we should reject *Avatar* on behalf of a more "authentic" acceptance of the real world. If we subtract fantasy from reality, then reality itself loses its consistency and disintegrates. To choose between "either accepting reality or choosing fantasy" is wrong: if we really want to change or escape our social reality, the first thing to do is change our fantasies that make us fit this reality. Because the hero of *Avatar* doesn't do this, his subjective position is what Jacques Lacan, with regard to de Sade, called *le dupe de son fantasme*.

This is why it is interesting to imagine a sequel to *Avatar* in which, after a couple of years (or, rather, months) of bliss, the hero starts to feel a weird discontent and to miss the corrupted human universe. The source of this discontent is not only that every reality, no matter how perfect it is, sooner or later disappoints us. Such a perfect fantasy disappoints us precisely because of its perfection: what this perfection signals is that it holds no place for us, the subjects who imagine it.

The utopia imagined in *Avatar* follows the Hollywood formula for producing a couple—the long tradition of a resigned white hero who has to go among the savages to find a proper sexual partner (just recall *Dances With Wolves*). In a typical Hollywood product, everything, from the fate of the Knights of the Round Table to asteroids hitting the earth, is transposed into an Oedipal narrative. The ridiculous climax of this procedure of staging great historical events as the background to the formation of a couple is Warren Beatty's *Reds* (1981), in which Hollywood found a way to rehabilitate the October Revolution, arguably the most traumatic historical event of the 20th century. In *Reds*, the couple of John Reed and Louise Bryant are in deep emotional crisis; their love is reignited when Louise watches John deliver an impassioned revolutionary speech.

What follows is the couple's lovemaking, intersected with archetypal scenes from the revolution, some of which reverberate in an all too obvious way with the sex; say, when John penetrates Louise, the camera cuts to a street where a dark crowd of demonstrators envelops and stops a penetrating "phallic" tram—all this against the background of the singing of "The Internationale." When, at the orgasmic climax, Lenin himself appears, addressing a packed hall of delegates, he is more a wise teacher overseeing the couple's love-initiation than a cold revolutionary leader. Even the October Revolution is OK, according to Hollywood, if it serves the reconstitution of a couple.

In a similar way, is Cameron's previous blockbuster, *Titanic*, really about the catastrophe of the ship hitting the iceberg? One should be attentive to the precise moment of the catastrophe: it takes place when the young lovers (Leonardo DiCaprio and Kate Winslet), immediately after consummating their relationship, return to the ship's deck. Even more crucial is that, on deck, Winslet tells her lover that when the ship reaches New York the next morning, she will leave with him, preferring a life of poverty with her true love to a false, corrupted life among the rich.

At this moment the ship hits the iceberg, in order to prevent what would undoubtedly have been the true catastrophe, namely the couple's life in New York. One can safely guess that soon the misery of everyday life would have destroyed their love. The catastrophe thus occurs in order to save their love, to sustain the illusion that, if it had not happened, they would have lived "happily ever after." A further clue is provided by DiCaprio's final moments. He is freezing in the cold water, dying, while Winslet is safely floating on a large piece of wood. Aware that she is losing him, she cries "I'll never let you go!"—and as she says this, she pushes him away with her hands.

Why? Because he has done his job. Beneath the story of a love affair, *Titanic* tells another story, that of a spoiled high-society girl with an identity crisis: she is confused, doesn't know what to do with herself, and DiCaprio, much more than just her love partner, is a kind of "vanishing mediator" whose function is to restore her sense of identity and purpose in life. His last words before he disappears into the freezing North Atlantic are not the words of a departing lover, but the message of a preacher, telling her to be honest and faithful to herself. Cameron's superficial Hollywood Marxism (his crude privileging of the lower classes and caricatural depiction of the cruel egotism of the rich) should not deceive us. Beneath this sympathy for the poor lies a reactionary myth, first fully deployed by Rudyard Kipling's *Captains Courageous*. It concerns a young rich person in crisis who gets his (or her) vitality restored through brief intimate contact with the full-blooded life of the poor. What lurks behind the compassion for the poor is their vampiric exploitation.

But today, Hollywood increasingly seems to have abandoned this formula. The film of Dan Brown's *Angels and Demons* must surely be the first case of a Hollywood adaptation of a popular novel in which there is sex between the hero and the heroine in the book, but not in its film version—in clear contrast to the old tradition of adding a sex scene to a film based on a novel in which there is none. There is nothing liberating about this absence of sex; we are rather dealing with yet more proof of the phenomenon described by Alain Badiou in his *Éloge de l'amour*—today, in our pragmatic-narcissistic era, the very notion of falling in love, of a passionate attachment to a sexual partner, is considered obsolete and dangerous.

Avatar's fidelity to the old formula of creating a couple, its full trust in fantasy, and its story of a white man marrying the aboriginal princess and becoming king, make it ideologically a rather conservative, old-fashioned film. Its technical brilliance serves to cover up this basic conservatism. It is easy to discover, beneath the politically correct themes (an honest white guy siding with ecologically sound aborigines against the "military-industrial complex" of the imperialist invaders), an array of brutal racist motifs: a paraplegic outcast from earth is good enough to get the hand of a beautiful local princess, and to help the natives win the decisive battle. The film teaches us that the only choice the aborigines have is to be saved by the human beings or to be destroyed by them. In other words, they can choose either to be the victim of imperialist reality, or to play their allotted role in the white man's fantasy. At the same time as *Avatar* is making money all around the world (it generated $1bn after less than three weeks of release), something that strangely resembles its plot is taking place. The southern hills of the Indian state of Orissa, inhabited by the Dongria Kondh people, were sold to mining companies that plan to exploit their immense reserves of bauxite (the deposits are considered to be worth at least $4trn). In reaction to this project, a Maoist (Naxalite) armed rebellion exploded.

> Arundhati Roy, in *Outlook India* magazine, writes that the Maoist guerrilla army *is made up almost entirely of desperately poor tribal people living in conditions of such chronic hunger that it verges on famine of the kind we only associate with sub-Saharan Africa. They are people who, even after 60 years of India's so-called independence, have not had access to education, health care or legal redress. They are people who have been mercilessly exploited for decades, consistently cheated by small businessmen and moneylenders, the women raped as a matter of right by police and forest department personnel. Their journey back to a semblance of dignity is due in large part to the Maoist cadres who have lived and worked and fought by their sides for decades. If the tribals have taken up arms, they have done so because a government which has given them nothing but violence and neglect now wants to snatch away the last thing they have—their land . . . They believe that if they do not fight for their land, they will be annihilated . . . their ragged, malnutritioned army, the bulk of whose soldiers have never seen a train or a bus or even a small town, are fighting only for survival.*

The Indian prime minister characterised this rebellion as the "single largest internal security threat"; the big media, which present it as extremist resistance to progress, are full of stories about "red terrorism," replacing stories about "Islamist terrorism." No wonder the Indian state is responding with a big military operation against "Maoist strongholds" in the jungles of central India. And it is true that both sides are resorting to great violence in this brutal war, that the "people's justice" of the Maoists is harsh. However, no matter how unpalatable this violence is to our liberal taste, we have no right to condemn it. Why? Because their situation is precisely that of Hegel's rabble: the Naxalite rebels in India are starving tribal people, to whom the minimum of a dignified life is denied.

So where is Cameron's film here? Nowhere: in Orissa, there are no noble princesses waiting for white heroes to seduce them and help their people, just the Maoists organising the starving farmers. The film enables us to practise a typical ideological division: sympathising with the idealised aborigines while rejecting their actual struggle. The same people who enjoy the film and admire its aboriginal rebels would in all probability turn away in horror from the Naxalites, dismissing them as murderous terrorists. The true avatar is thus *Avatar* itself—the film substituting for reality.

The Racial Politics of *Avatar*

Mikhail Lyubansky

AVATAR IS SO VISUALLY STUNNING it seems almost a shame to break it down and analyze the micro components. I saw it in 3-D, and a day later, I still recall the sensation of being surrounded by grasses and ferns in the jungle and ducking my head during battle. This isn't just a movie you'll want to see again—Ebert wrote that "it is predestined to launch a cult"—it is a movie you'll want to see again in the theatre, especially if you had the misfortune to originally see it in 2-D. In between viewings, you might want to learn the Na'vi language. Seriously.

If you're already fluent in Klingon, it'll probably come easy, and it might help you kameie (please pardon the conjugation; I'm still learning) the Na'vi in an entirely different way. On the other hand, don't let your mono-lingualism stop you. The action scenes speak to geeks and non-geeks alike, and though the Na'vi do speak in their own language, their dialogue is considerably subtitled for those of us who have yet to master it. Point being: this film has something for everyone.

The Na'vi are a sight to behold.

All that said, *Avatar* is so heavily loaded with racial allegory that it's impossible, even for a casual viewer, to ignore its sociopolitical currents. On the surface, *Avatar* is an obvious, at times even heavy-handed, pro-environmental and anti-war missive. It's purpose (besides entertaining) is to hold a mirror up to humanity and show us the folly of our greed and disregard for human life, while at the same time showing us what our own planet could have been like if its indiginous peoples were allowed to retain their cultures rather than being overrun by European colonialization.

If this sounds a tad familiar, it should. Other films, most notably *Dances With Wolves*, had similar aims and the similarities are not lost on the critics, many of whom have compared the two films in ways that are not entirely favorable to either. More specifically to the context of racial politics, the buzz I heard about *Avatar* prior to seeing it was that it was a sci-fi version of *Dances With Wolves*: White men invade natives, one particular [and handsome] white man stays to learn the native ways, grows to like them, falls in love with beautiful native girl, and eventually winds up rescuing the tribe.

You can read *Avatar* that way, and, for good reason, many critics have, but to simply dismiss this film as yet another "white savior" film is, I think, to miss some very important points about both *Avatar* and contemporary racial politics. Below are five observations I think most critics have missed.

1. Jake Sully serves a vital role.

Some bloggers have asked why the Jake Sully character is even necessary: By the end of the film you're left wondering why the film needed the Jake Sully character at all. The film could have done just as well by focusing on an actual Na'vi native who comes into contact with crazy humans who have no respect for the environment. I can just see the explanation: "Well, we need someone (an *Avatar*) for the audience to connect with. A normal guy [read, a white male] will work better than these tall blue people."

I actually agree that Jake's main function is to serve as the connection between the audience and the Na'vi culture, but unlike the blogger above, I don't dismiss that as yet another manifestation of white privilege.

The *Avatar* allows Jake to see, hear, and otherwise "sense" the Na'vi culture, and the audience needs the same conduit to the Na'vi. Jake is OUR *Avatar*. He allows us (and by "us" I mean "humans") to experience what he experiences and, in that process, to appreciate the Na'vi the way he does.

Moreover, Jake offers moviegoers an opportunity for redemption. Just as Jake turns his back on corporate greed and exploitation, so can we all. Without Jake, all we have is the alien (or racial) Other. We might be able to enjoy THEIR triumph, but we (and I'm talking here about a multiracial "we") can't share it, not even vicariously. To the extent that this film might actually inspire personal growth and change and offer the possibility of redemption, Jake is necessary.

2. Jake is more than just a (white) outsider.

By far the most common critique of *Avatar* is that it patronizes the racial other. Will Heaven articulates this sentiment in his excellent review:

> As Left-wing conceits go, this one surely tops all the others: the ethnic Na'vi, the film suggests, need the white man to save them because, as a less developed race, they lack the intelligence and fortitude to overcome their adversaries by themselves. The poor helpless natives, in other words, must rely on the principled white man to lead them out of danger.

I don't disagree with this analysis. To the contrary, I think it's very much on target, but I also think it misses some important elements that at the very least make the relationship between Jake and the Na'vi more complex than described above and perhaps even give it some redeeming qualities: Jake may be human, but the *Avatar* whose consciousness he inhabits is, according to the film, a "genetically engineered hybrid of human DNA mixed with DNA from the natives of Pandora . . . the Na'vi." On the surface, this linking of consciousness may seem like a form of conquest, or even collonialization—the scientists even refer to the process as "driving," but Jake describes it as a rebirth, and I think that's exactly what it is from his perspective. In his *Avatar* form, Jake IS Na'vi, not just culturally (though by the end of the film he is clearly that too) but biologically, at the DNA level. Thus, if we are to read the film as a racial metaphor (and I think doing so is appropriate), the protagonist is not so much White as Biracial.

3. Jake embodies multiculturalism.

It has become fashionable to rail against white ethnocentrism, privilege, and lack of cultural sensitivity. Again, for good reason. But if there are poor and insensitive ways to interact with racial minority groups, isn't there an implication that there are also appropriate and positive ways? Multicultural scholars and activists suggest that the appropriate way is to approach another group hermeneutically. According to the principles of hermeneutics "it is only possible to grasp the meaning of an action or statement by relating it to the whole discourse or world-view from which it originates." In other words, one must approach a cultural group by trying to understand its various cultural practices and traditions from that group's own perspective, rather than from the perspective of an outsider.

This is precisely what Jake does, and not just because he is supposed to do that as part of the scientific team. Though he was supposedly spying for the Colonel and working with the scientists to learn about the Na'vi, Jake clearly establishes his disdain for both. He follows Neytiri, not because he is supposed to but because he is curious to learn about her and her people. He follows her because he wants to. It is this "wanting" that has been described as a manifestation of privilege. And it is privilege in the sense that Jake is leading a double life. If the "native thing" doesn't work out, he can always go back to being human.

The Na'vi (and, by extension, people of color) don't have the option of not being who they are. But Jake isn't approaching Neytiri from a privileged position. He is approaching her partly out of genuine curiosity and partly out of desperation. He had become separated from the other scientists and doesn't know how to survive in the Pandora jungle. Moreover, he takes to his Na'vi body from the start, and it is clear that he much prefers it to his original one. When a short time later, he tells the Na'vi chief that he is "empty" (meaning that he has let go of human ways and is ready to be filled up with the ways of the Na'vi), it has emotional truth. Jake isn't there as part of a job or as some exotic experience. He is there out of a sincere desire to not only understand but to learn the Na'vi ways. Isn't this the way we want outsiders to approach a cultural group?

4. Jake is an immigrant, not a tourist.

Extending the multicultural theme still further, I believe that, among other things, *Avatar* is a quintessential immigration story. At the start of the film, Jake was obviously human, but he felt betrayed by humanity, which withheld from him the technology to restore his legs. He came to Pandora for a new start, not knowing what he'd find but prepared to embrace something different. I think that when he arrived on Pandora, he was already "empty" or open. He didn't at first have any allegiance to the Na'vi, but nor did he have much loyalty to his country, certainly not to its corporate and military face. In many ways, he was like an immigrant arriving at a new shore, not knowing what future it will hold, but committed to building a life there, with no intention of ever returning to the old one.

5. The Na'vi rescue themselves.

It is true, of course, that Jake becomes a super-version of the Na'vi, taming and riding the red flying beast that is recognized as the most ferocious of the jungle. When he swoops down from above, he becomes not just a mythical hero, he practically becomes the messiah. This is problematic and entirely unnecessary to the story. But by this point (as I've argued all along), Jake is Na'vi, in every sense of the word, and the methods he and the other Na'vi use to fight off the humans are entirely Na'vi. Other than sounding the warning, Jake brings in no "outside" knowledge or expertise. He uses Na'vi methods to gain trust and unite the tribes, and communicates with the Pandora life-energy through a method accessible only to the Na'vi. And at the end of the day, Pandora isn't rescued by anyone. Ultimately, and appropriately, the planet saves itself.

Conclusion

Don't get me wrong. For all that it gets right (and I do think some of the criticism is misguided), *Avatar* is still sociopolitically flawed, and the flaws are not minor. Most of the characters are stereotypical caricatures, traditional gender roles are (mostly) reinforced, and there is that uncomfortable messiah undertone.

Avatar and the Gluttony of Technology

Ari Y Kelman

ANYONE WHO BUYS A TICKET to see *Avatar* is going to see technology on display. That's what all the press has been about, that's why the film has won awards, that's why it sold out my local IMAX ™ theater on Friday night (some two months after its original release). Despite its pseudo new-age lust for the natural, the film is a gluttonous celebration of technology.

Couched as a struggle between a money-hungry and heartless corporation and a peaceful tribe wholly in tune with nature, the film sells viewers the latter but delivers the former with more technological firepower than the mercenary (ex-)marines it features as bad guys. The thin script and the cast's paltry performances are literally no match for the fantastical animations and imaginary worlds brought to life by director James Cameron and his animation army. Any shred of humanity or trace of emotion, connection or affect is churned under the unrelenting barrage of computer-generated images (in 3D!) that seem to pile up, one after another, each trying to out-do the last without any sense of fun or excitement (indeed, rather than exploratory or curious, the film takes a rather triumphant, and, dare I say militaristic approach to showing just what technology can do).

That might be the film's act of hubris, but here's what I find even more troubling about my two-and-a-half hour journey on Pandora: Once you can do anything with computers and computer animation, I find it harder to be impressed. Once the door to imagination is thrown completely wide open, and computers are capable of rendering anything imaginable on screen, then what's the big deal of having 8-foot-tall blue characters or fiddle ferns the size of SUV's? Once you can make computers do anything, what's the big deal when they do anything, at all? Once anything is possible, who cares what happens? It's the cinematic equivalent of eternal life (lord knows, the film felt about that long)—it may last a long time, but why does it matter?

Avatar at once captures the gluttonous revelry of technology and its absolute failures. Cameron's attempt to critique technology in the film ultimately collapses beneath the film's bloated, burdensome reliance on technology to tell this story. Yet, at the same time, the film's meta-emphasis on its own story-telling technology so radically opened up the possibilities of animation that it diminished its own ability to highlight those very possibilities. In this way, the film fails twice and twice as hard.

But ultimately, for all its technophilia and bloated self-promotion, and notwithstanding the awards it has won and will win, the film's greatest failure seems to be not technological, but human. For all its armament and animation, the film's greatest failure was its absence of any real, human imagination at all. There is still no technology powerful enough to hide hackneyed plot points, recycled dialogue, and flat acting. By letting technology tell the story, *Avatar* obliterates its desire to tell a human story, leaving only a trail of computer-generated fantasy worlds in its wake.

READING **WRITING**

This Text: Reading

1. Describe the tone of each of the reviews in one word. Don't think about it; just jot down the first word that comes to mind for each of the reviews. If you've seen *Avatar*, think about how you would describe the movie in one word. Do you see any overlap in how you see *Avatar* and how you see the respective reviews?
2. Which of the reviews is the most convincing? Do you feel this way simply because the author shares your own opinion of *Avatar*? Or are there other aspects of the review that you find particularly compelling?
3. Why do you think Lubyansky was taken in by *Avatar's* statements on race but Žižek was not? What did he notice (or let slide) that he did not?
4. We find Lubyansky's review particularly interesting. For him, *Avatar* is a racial allegory, and its moral message trumps any other shortcomings the movie might have from an artistic or storytelling perspective. Do you agree? Does a text's political or social message take precedent over its artistry? Its composition?

Your Text: Writing

1. Write your own review of *Avatar*. Don't try on a "movie reviewer voice"—just use your own. Be sure not to engage in too much plot summary. Instead, talk about what you think the film is trying to do or what you think the film succeeds (or fails) at. The key to interpreting texts is simple: *analyze; don't summarize.*
2. Write a comparison/contrast essay in which you read two of the reviews against each other. Be sure you talk about what you think each of the reviews gets right.
3. See *Dances With Wolves* and write an essay on *Avatar* as seen through the lens of *Dances With Wolves*. That is, if you look at *Avatar* from the perspective of Kevin Costner's Western, does Cameron's movie become less or more interesting?
4. Watch a classic science fiction movie or television show about contact with another culture—*District 9, E.T., Planet of the Apes, Lost, Star Trek, V*—and write a comparison/contrast essay on *Avatar* and the text of your choosing.
5. Write a definitional essay on *Avatar* in which you demonstrate how *Avatar* is a good example of something. You could argue that the movie is a fine example of "socially responsible cinema" or a model of "biodiversity moviemaking." You could even argue that *Avatar* is the new standard for "21st Century Movies." Writing a definitional essay is not complicated, but you must state clearly *and define* the terms you use. For example, if you're claiming *Avatar* is socially responsible cinema, you need to define the term. Then, show how (using specific examples) *Avatar* embodies your definition.

READING BETWEEN THE LINES

Classroom Activities

1. As a class, watch one of the movies under review in this section. Write your own review of the movie without talking to anyone else in class about the movie. Then, after a class discussion, write yet another review of the movie. How does your own reading of the movie change after class discussion?
2. Watch a movie in class and write a group review. What are the major points of disagreement? On what was it easy to agree?
3. View any of the movies that you have read about in the previous texts. Do you agree with the writers? Why or why not?
4. Is watching a movie in class different than watching one at home or in a theater? Why? Have a class discussion on the space of watching movies.
5. Write a poem about the *experience* of watching a particular film. How does writing a poem about a movie differ from writing a journal entry or a formal paper? Is there a relationship between poems and film?
6. Bring advertisements or commercials about particular movies to class. Discuss the demographic the studio is targeting. Do the commercials and ads tell you how to read the movie?
7. As you watch a movie in class, write down every form of manipulation you notice (such as music, close-ups, special effects, camera angles, unusual editing, intense colors).
8. Watch a recent movie that was praised by critics but was seemingly ignored by the general public (these might include *The Lives of Others, Tully, The Fast Runner, Three Kings, Red, Simple Men, Fish Tank, The Straight Story, Rushmore, Secrets and Lies, You Can Count on Me, Boys Don't Cry, American Movie, The Winslow Boy, Ghost World*). Why do you think not many people saw these films? Why do you think critics loved these particular movies? Is there tension between critical and popular taste?
9. Talk about the criteria and expectations of different genres in class. What characteristics must a romantic comedy have? What is the purpose of a Western? What does an action–adventure movie need to do? What makes a good scary movie?
10. Find a copy of the American Film Institute's top 100 American movies. Talk about the list in class. Why did these movies make the list? What movies are missing? Why?

Essay Ideas

1. What is the "greatest" movie you've seen? Write an essay in which you argue why your choice is the greatest.
2. Chances are, you have seen *Avatar* or *Star Wars*. Write your own analytical review of one of these films. Feel free to reference one of the reviews you have read. Perhaps you will agree or disagree with one (or many) of the reviewers. Be sure to analyze the film; do not simply write a plot summary.
3. As we were working on this edition, *The Hurt Locker* won the academy award for Best Picture for 2009. If you have seen the film, write an essay comparing that movie to other war movies. What makes it outstanding?

4. Write an essay on a director's body of work. People like Steven Spielberg, Woody Allen, Quentin Tarantino, Penny Marshall, Stanley Kubrick, John Sayles, Spike Lee, Michael Bay, Paul Verhoven, or Howard Hawkes, who have directed a number of different movies, will make your essay more interesting. Is there an overarching theme to their movies? How have they contributed to film history? To American culture?

5. Write an essay in which you explore issues of gender in one or two recent movies. Perhaps you can pick a movie directed by a woman and one directed by a man. How are women represented? How are women's bodies presented or framed? Male bodies? Do the women have strong roles, or are they limited, stereotypical roles? Do the women date or love men their own age, or are the men much older? Do the women have good jobs and healthy lifestyles?

6. Write an essay in which you explore issues of race. As in gender, how are issues of race and power represented in the film? What kind of music runs through the film? Are minority characters filmed or framed differently than Anglo characters? There is an old joke that the one black character in a horror film is one of the first to die. Is this still the case? While there are a number of wonderful movies by people of color (*Do the Right Thing, Smoke Signals, The Joy Luck Club, Mississippi Masala, El Mariachi*), you might also consider how minorities are represented in movies made by Anglos.

7. Explore notions of class in American cinema. How often are poor people in movies? While there may be women and people of color in Hollywood and in the studio system, how well does Hollywood understand low-income America? Are there realistic film portrayals of working-class or low-income families? Some would say that America is more classist than racist: Is this theory proved or refuted by Hollywood?

8. Write an essay in which you offer a reading of a film based solely on the film techniques: sound, lighting, camera angles, music, framing, and editing. How can technique determine meaning?

9. *Star Wars* is beloved by millions. Do you agree with Whitney Black's critical reading of the film?

Reading and Writing about Images

With the proliferation of television, movies, video games, computers, and advertising, we have become a culture that tends to define itself through visual images. Even the act of reading these words on this page remains a visual activity. As we explain in the introduction, reading is nothing more than visual decoding of images so familiar that we do not even think of them as images. We don't imagine text on the page as pictures, but each word is a small picture of curved, slanted, and dotted marks that we call "letters." When we put certain combinations of these letters together, they conjure up a particular idea or image in our heads. While words are images themselves and reflect other images, we're more concerned here with the way we constantly decode (often with little conscious effort) the multiple images that we encounter each day—from people's faces to television shows to book covers to signs to architecture. One of this book's main ideas, in fact, is slowing down the reading process of visual images. As you may have noticed, almost all of the chapters in this book involve visual decoding of some sort.

Our book's insistence on this type of reading stands behind our idea to present some images as a way of focusing our attention on the visual. The kinds of images we offer need little introduction, but to this end, we've identified and reiterated a few points about reading visual images:

IMAGES ARE TEXTS THAT CAN AND SHOULD BE READ.

Again, as we point out in our discussion of semiotics in the introduction, we ask that you apply the vocabulary and attention you devote to reading written texts to reading visual texts. When we open a book or look at directions or scan a newspaper, we are conscious of the act of reading. We know that our eyes move across a page and process information, and most important, we are conscious of the information that this process of looking produces. That is, we know we are reading for information, for content—we know that there is a message to most written texts.

However, the title and the thesis of this book is that the world is a text; that means that all images are texts, and as such demand to be read as thoroughly as a poem or textbook. In fact, we would argue that visual images such as advertisements, television and movies, photographs, album covers, movie posters, and T-shirts should be read with particular care because images transmit many values and assumptions but do so quietly and subconsciously. Because images do not come in the language of analysis (words), we tend not to analyze them as closely, if at all. We urge you to analyze all images.

READING IMAGES IS USUALLY AN INFORMAL RATHER THAN A FORMAL PROCESS.

As we noted earlier, reading images tends to be an informal process—that is, we are not always aware of the process of reading images. We take them in and move on, giving very little thought to the thousands of visual cues we see every few seconds. To formalize the process, all we need to do is become conscious readers of images as constructed texts. For instance, this morning if you combed your hair, washed, shaved, put on makeup—if you thought about what to wear at all—then you did some work in constructing yourself as a text. You knew that today, like every other day, you were going to be read, on some level, and you wanted to send certain cues. Perhaps you wanted to suggest that you are alternative, conservative, athletic, bookish, or sophisticated. Depending on the image you wanted to project, you would don the appropriate signifiers.

When the other students look at you as you walk into class or when patrons in the coffee shop regard you as you order a latte, they do an informal reading of you—even if it is very brief and even if they don't know they are doing it at all. They might notice something has changed about you, but they would likely acquire even this information informally—virtually no one would actively ask the question, "How has X changed her appearance today? Let me take a thorough inventory of hairstyle, clothing, grooming." The same kind of quick informal reading usually goes into our appraisal of images. How often do we really stop to consider everything, all the details, that contribute to the overall message of the image? Here is where reading images mirrors reading visual arts—we must be aware of issues of composition, how the image is put together. As soon as you begin asking questions about what message a certain image is supposed to send, as soon as you read the image on your own terms—that is, when you begin to read the image not as the image wants to be read but as something to analyze—then you will formalize the reading process and begin to see the world in a more complex way.

THE READER/VIEWER ALWAYS PARTICIPATES IN THE CONSTRUCTION AND SIGNIFICANCE OF THE IMAGE.

The Confederate flag, the "Stars and Bars," has become one of the most controversial American images in the past 50 years. Perhaps more than any other American icon, the Stars and Bars reveals how deeply our own backgrounds, culture, and political beliefs determine how we "read" images. For some white Southerners, the flag stands as a symbol of rebellion and independence. For white Northerners or those not from the South, the Stars and Bars may reinforce negative stereotypes about Southern culture. For yet another population, African Americans, the Stars and Bars stands as a salient and prominent symbol of slavery and racism. Why do each of these groups have such different interpretations of a simple red rectangle, crossed by two blue bars and some white stripes? The answer is simple. We cannot "see" the flag (or any image) outside of our own ideas.

Whether the image under debate is a photo of Osama bin Laden, Bill Clinton talking with Monica Lewinsky, a topless supermodel, a multiracial couple, an electric chair, a fetus, a church, or a chemistry textbook, we each bring to the image our own set of assumptions and prejudices. This realization is important because it underscores the gap between intention and reception. By intention or intent, we mean the motivation behind producing or displaying the text, whereas reception is the reaction to the text—how the text is received. In many instances, intention and reception have nothing to do with each other. Not long ago, the chief justice of the Alabama Supreme Court, Roy Moore, was removed from office for placing a monument of the Ten Commandments in the rotunda of the courtroom. A number of people were outraged, claiming that hanging up the Ten Commandments was publicly stating that the judge would rule from a position that is sympathetic to an Old Testament Judeo–Christian perspective, thereby admitting *de facto* discrimination against non-Christians. Was the judge intending to send this message? Maybe, maybe not. Is this message a valid reception of the text? Probably.

In addition, the American flag means something different in Afghanistan than it does in Ireland. The logo for the Atlanta Braves sends one message to folks in Georgia and another to folks on the Rosebud Indian Reservation in South Dakota. The photograph of incoming First Lady Hillary Rodham Clinton holding hands with outgoing First Lady Barbara Bush incites very different reactions depending on your political leanings. Our point is that no reading of an image is ever value-free. We are active participants in the construction and reception of an image, and by extension, the world.

What follows is a series of images, without captions or explanations, that we feel make rich visual texts.

The below signs are from:

1. The University of Bergen in Norway
2. The Palace Grill in Oslo, Norway
3. Turkey, Texas
4. Oslo, Norway
5. Stockholm, Sweden
6. New Mexico (near Santa Fe)
7. Sunset Boulevard in Los Angeles
8. Saratoga Race Course in Saratoga Springs, N.Y.
9. Canyonlands, Utah
10. Aberystwyth, Wales
11. Cork, Ireland
12. Regional train, Norway
13. San Diego, CA
14. Napa, CA
15. Nashville, TN
16. Norsk Oljemuseum (Norwegian Petroleum Museum) Stavanger, Norway
17. Turkey, Texas
18. Museum of Modern Art, New York, NY
19. Montreal, Quebec, Canada
20. Thurles Race Course, Thurles, Ireland

Fig. 1

Fig. 2

Fig. 3

Fig. 4

INTERCHAPTER • Reading and Writing about Images

Fig. 5

Fig. 6

Fig. 7

Fig. 8

INTERCHAPTER • Reading and Writing about Images

Fig. 9

Fig. 10

Fig. 11

Fig. 12

Fig. 13

Fig. 14

Fig. 15

Fig. 16

INTERCHAPTER • Reading and Writing about Images

Fig. 17

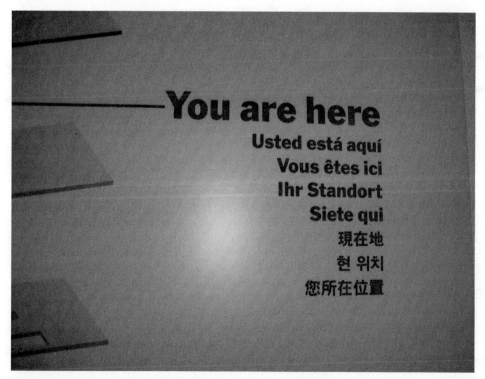

Fig. 18

Fig. 19

Fig. 20

INTERCHAPTER • Reading and Writing about Images

The American Signs on Route 66 Suite

In reading through dozens and dozens of books for the 2nd edition of this book, we came across what both of the authors think is one of the coolest books we have seen in years—*American Signs: Form and Meaning on Route 66,* by Lisa Mahar. One of the authors grew up in a small town in which Route 66 was the town's main street, and he is familiar with many of the signs featured, but even without that personal connection, the book is simply amazing.

Mahar begins with the premise that the roadside sign is not simply a symbol of the open road but a marker of economic, social, and cultural trends. Signs are larger-than-life clues to the values, images, icons, and traditions of the areas in which they exist. Examining motel signs on both a micro and macro level, Mahar traces their influences, shows their arguments, unpacks their conceptual framework, and explains their appeal.

We have reprinted here (with the gracious help of Mahar herself) the opening pages of Chapter 3. What we like about these images is not simply how Mahar notes the influences of popular signs, but the care and detail with which she reads them. The book is also a model of document design—it is itself a text as rich and provocative as the motel signs it features.

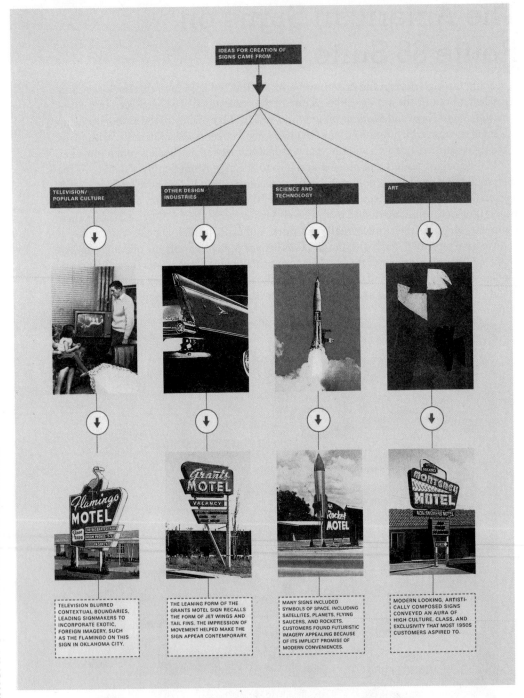

3

3.2 > FORMAL ETYMOLOGY

The Hacienda Holiday Motel sign in Oklahoma City is an example of how far signmakers went to create original compositions for their clients. Fearing that they might lose control over the design process to an emerging class of professional designers, signmakers looked for inspiration in other disciplines, especially art and science.

The use of abstract symbols common in art of the period, such as this detail from Joan Miro's *Woman in Front of the Sun* (1950), made signs appear up-to-date.

Script lettering was used to convey unique-ness and add visual drama to the sign.

Forms and structures were often angled to create more dynamic, and therefore notice-able, compositions, as seen in this late 1950s building.

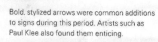

Bold, stylized arrows were common additions to signs during this period. Artists such as Paul Klee also found them enticing.

Abstracted figurative elements were also found in the design world, as seen in this mid-1950s engraved bowl designed by Ingeborg Lundin.

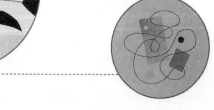

Irregular shapes were non-traditional and therefore appropriate forms for signmakers looking to create original signs. Artists also made use of them, as in this 1959 mobile, "Big Red," by Alexander Calder.

Asymmetrical compositions, as in this plate design by Florence Wainwright, conveyed individuality and uniqueness.

THE AMERICAN SIGNS ON ROUTE 66 SUITE

Nowhere was the break from tradition seen more dramatically than in a sign's form. Signmakers chose irregular, asymmetrical shapes over traditional ones, whether or not the business the sign identified was new. By the mid-1950s, many signmakers had begun creating their signs as fragmented compositions, a final abandonment of traditional form.

In the mid-1950s, the Wishing Well Motel in Springfield, Missouri, replaced its traditional sign, which was based on a 1:2 rectangular sign box, with an L-shaped composition of four elements. Though the L shape recalls earlier Main Street signs, the shape of the Wishing Well's sign box is irregular, more dramatic, and includes decorative elements. The words "Wishing Well" and "motel" are treated as separate elements through the use of different colors and type styles.

The asymmetrical form, large wrapping arrow, script type, and advertising panels of the Rest Haven Court's mid-1950s sign are characteristic features of motel signs from the period.

The only elements that remained the same on these two signs from the mid-1940s and the early 1950s were the name (although depersonalized with the removal of "Clark's") and the square, sans serif letters. The newer sign has no formal relationship to its context. The angled structure, palette-shaped sign box, and bright red paint all help to separate it from nearby buildings and natural elements.

THE AMERICAN SIGNS ON ROUTE 66 SUITE

The updated Tower Motel sign in Santa Rosa, New Mexico, formally distances itself from the traditional inverted T form of the mid-1940s sign. Each element on the new sign is perceived as a distinct component: the name "Tower" is spatially segregated from "motel," and the letters are treated as individually articulated elements.

The simple, symmetrical sign for the Skyline Motel in Flagstaff, Arizona, was replaced with a larger and bolder asymmetrical arrangement.

Early signs, like the one for the Conway Motel in El Reno, Oklahoma, were often composed of geometrically pure shapes. In this example, the form also reflected the circular motel office. The late-1950s replacement was designed with only contemporary stylistic trends in mind—it was no longer important to maintain a formal connection to the motel's architecture.

THE AMERICAN SIGNS ON ROUTE 66 SUITE

Although motel chains did not gain widespread popularity until the late 1950s, Holiday Inn had begun to expand nationwide much earlier. The most visible aspect of the first major chain's growth was the "great sign," as it was referred to. And like the older signs it took its aesthetic cues from, the Holiday Inn sign garnered recognition that attested to the skill with which independent motel owners and signmakers were able to define their businesses' identity. A sign functioned as the motel's logo; it appeared on stationery, ads, and other materials. While independent motel signs influenced the first Holiday Inn sign, as the chain expanded it was the Holiday Inn sign that began to influence the vernacular.

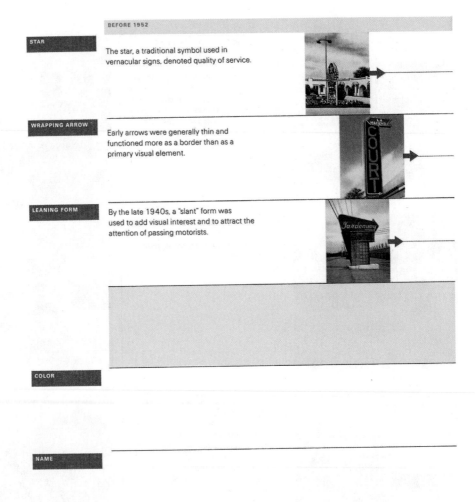

BEFORE 1952

STAR

The star, a traditional symbol used in vernacular signs, denoted quality of service.

WRAPPING ARROW

Early arrows were generally thin and functioned more as a border than as a primary visual element.

LEANING FORM

By the late 1940s, a "slant" form was used to add visual interest and to attract the attention of passing motorists.

COLOR

NAME

THE AMERICAN SIGNS ON ROUTE 66 SUITE

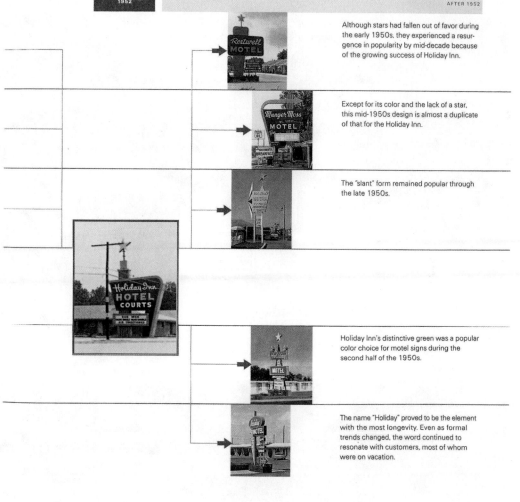

1952

Although stars had fallen out of favor during the early 1950s, they experienced a resurgence in popularity by mid-decade because of the growing success of Holiday Inn.

Except for its color and the lack of a star, this mid-1950s design is almost a duplicate of that for the Holiday Inn.

The "slant" form remained popular through the late 1950s.

Holiday Inn's distinctive green was a popular color choice for motel signs during the second half of the 1950s.

The name "Holiday" proved to be the element with the most longevity. Even as formal trends changed, the word continued to resonate with customers, most of whom were on vacation.

THE AMERICAN SIGNS ON ROUTE 66 SUITE

> STRUCTURE

As compositions became more complex, structure became an increasingly important element of the sign. Structure was used either as an abstract framework for organizing the sign's varied elements or as a conceptual and visual connection to a motel's architecture. Only rarely was it used as an overtly thematic component of the sign, as it had been during the late 1940s and early 1950s.

THE AMERICAN SIGNS ON ROUTE 66 SUITE

Early attempts to make structure an important aesthetic component were focused on creating a solid, relatively permanent visual barrier that contrasted with the natural context and related to the man-made one. This early-1950s structure for the Pine Tree Lodge in Gallup, New Mexico, was massive and therefore more noticeable. It was built from the same materials as the motel building, thus creating a visual connection between the sign and the architecture.

The sign box for the Tower Motel sign in Oklahoma City conveyed the visual weight of earlier, architectural structures like the Pine Tree Lodge's, but the structure consisted of easy-to-install metal poles. Unlike traditional pole structures, however, their placement was determined as much by aesthetic reasons as by functional ones. The gradual return to pole-based structures also made it possible to build taller signs—those constructed from architectural building materials had to remain relatively small.

Poles made it easy to arrange separate, irregular components such as those on the Flamingo Motel sign in Elk City, Oklahoma. They were readily available and did not require specialized labor, as did architectural materials like brick.

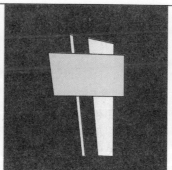

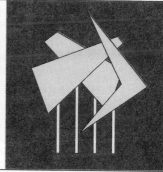

THE AMERICAN SIGNS ON ROUTE 66 SUITE

READING WRITING

This Text: Reading

1. What do you make of Mahar's connection between motel signs and rockets, cars, Miro paintings, and fish? Are her arguments solid?
2. Mahar argues that in the 1950s signs entered a kind of revolution, becoming irregular, asymmetrical, and original. What cultural and artistic forces might account for this shift in signs and sign making?
3. Look at the various arguments about art, such as Diana Mack's in Chapter 7: Reading and Writing About Art. Based on their criteria, are these signs art? Why or why not?
4. Why do you think Mahar chose motel signs? Why motel and not restaurant signs?

Your Text: Writing

1. Find some classic motel or restaurant signs in your town. Write a paper in which you read them in the same way as Mahar.
2. Write a paper in which you analyze two major signs, such as billboards or public signs, near your house. What kind of symbolism is at work?
3. Many of these signs appear in Oklahoma, New Mexico, and Arizona. Is there something about the Southwest that lends itself to these kinds of irregular images? Write a paper in which you examine the cultural influences on these signs.
4. Write a comparison/contrast paper in which you read the sign of a popular local chain hotel (Wyndham, Hyatt, Marriott, Hampton Inn, La Quinta) against one of the classic signs in the book. What "work" does each sign do? How does it do that work?

THIS TEXT

1. What is the semiotic situation of the image? What are its signifiers?
2. What social, political, and cultural forces affect the image?
3. What visual cues appear in the text?
4. What kinds of details, symbols, and codes send messages in the image?
5. What is the composition of the image?
6. Do you think there might be any tension between the image's intention and reception?
7. What kind of story does the image tell? How does it tell that story?
8. Does the image rely on patriotic or sentimental associations to manipulate the viewer?
9. Can you sum up the theme of the image?

BEYOND THIS TEXT

Media: How do news programs, magazines, and newspapers use images to tell stories or convey ideas?

Advertising: Advertising is perhaps the most notorious user of loaded images. How do magazine ads and billboards use images to help sell products? What values do we tend to see in ads? What kind of associations, people, and cultures tend to reappear over and over?

Worksheet

Television: To what degree does television rely on images? Would you sit in front of a TV if there were only words and no picture? How are characters in shows carefully constructed texts? And, what about commercials? How do commercials use images to manipulate viewers?

Movies: Do movies use images differently than television? If so, how?

Icons: The swastika. The peace symbol. The bald eagle. A cactus. A white cowboy hat. The McDonald golden arches. The American flag. The Mexican flag. High heels. All of these are icons. How do icons rely on strong values associated with visual images? How are icons constructed texts?

Public space: How do public and private areas rely on images to get us to feel a certain way? More specifically, what roles do billboards and murals play in public life? What about things like posters or framed art in a dorm room, bedroom, or house?

Music: How does what a band looks like, or what an album looks like, influence the way we look at a band?

6 Reading and Writing about Gender

"**How** in the world does someone *read* gender? Isn't gender obvious?" If you are looking at this introduction for the first time, we suspect this is what a lot of you are thinking right now. For many of you, details of gender are cut and dried, black and white, male and female. This book deals with gender as a text, and, as you will soon see, there are many other reasons why one might be interested in reading gender in a sophisticated way.

Without question, gender has become one of the most hotly contested subjects in recent American culture, but this issue is not new. On the contrary, it's been at the forefront of public debate for centuries. Ancient poets like Sappho and Greek plays like Aristophanes' *Lysistrata* explored issues of inequality between the genders long before Gloria Steinem (perhaps the most public feminist of the past four decades). More recently than Sappho or Aristophanes, an amazing Mexican nun named Sor Juana de la Cruz wrote poems and letters extolling the virtues of education for women, citing Biblical passages as examples for equality. And more than 200 years before Susan Faludi's *Backlash* (a controversial book appearing in 1992 that posited a backlash against American women), Mary Wollstonecraft wrote an important and influential essay entitled "A Vindication of the Rights of Women" in which she called for a recognition of women as "rational creatures" capable of the same intellectual and emotional proficiency as men. So while certain aspects of this chapter may feel new to you, in truth, people have been reading (and writing about) gender for centuries.

Still, perhaps it would be beneficial to talk about what we mean by the term "gender." When we use "gender" we refer to socially constructed behaviors and identity tags, such as "feminine" and "masculine." Gender should not be confused with "sex," which speaks only to biological differences between males and females. "Sex," then, refers to biology, whereas "gender" refers to culture and society.

If you have read the chapters on movies or television, then you know that having experience reading a certain text is not the same as reading it well. Similarly, many of you have significant experience reading genders, but you may not be very *probing* readers of gender. This chapter in particular (and college in general) is designed to remedy that. On one hand, reading gender implies a kind of superficial determination of another person's sex. In some cultures, that used to be easier than it is now; in fact, it can be somewhat difficult to tell if a person is a man, a woman, or neither. Those of you with a soft spot for classic rock may remember a similar line from the long-haired Bob Seger who, in his song "On the Road Again," adopts the persona of someone making a critical remark about his long hair: "Same old cliché / Is it a woman or a man?" This statement and the simple fact that we assume that we can tell if a person is male or female suggests that there are traits or cues that might tip us

What could Wonder Woman be thinking about? Saving the world? Why Superman gets all the props? Why her costume is so tight? What's really going on with Robin? Why she's pretty much the only female super hero? (*Pensive Wonder Woman*, Judith Taylor, c 2010)

off about gender. Using or reading these codes or behaviors is called "doing gender," and we all do gender at some point. "Doing gender" means participating in any behavior associated with a certain gender such as painting your nails, growing a beard, and wearing high heels, earrings, makeup, neckties, and sports jerseys. In each of the previous examples, every one of you associated a certain trait with a certain gender. Did you link painting nails with men or wearing neckties with women? Probably not, but it is likely that most of you have seen a man sport painted nails or a woman wear a necktie. These people are playing with typical expectations of gender, and to some degree, we all do that a little bit. In fact, if, like us, you have lived in New York or San Francisco, where gender diversity is more common and more accepted, then you have likely encountered women sporting facial hair and men donning heels.

If there are external traits in a culture, then it is probable that there are assumed internal gender traits in a culture as well. Although these external indicators may seem minor, ultimately, as you have probably noticed by now, doing gender often translates into men doing dominance and women doing submission. For instance, in America, most people tend to associate nurturing behavior with women and aggressive behavior with men. Similarly, women are "dainty" while men are "rough;" women are "refined," whereas men are "brutish." But is this always the case? As you read this, you are probably thinking of some dainty guys you know and some brutish women. What's more, you should be able to identify specific moments in your own lives and in the lives of your parents, siblings, and close friends when they have, even for an instant, done something that reminded you of another gender. The point is that we carry so many assumptions—many of them dangerous—about genders that we may discover that we have already *interpreted* gender before we have read and thought deeply about gender and genders.

Our goal in this chapter is to encourage you to rethink any preconceptions about and expectations of gender. Why do we expect women to be "emotional?" Why do we expect men to be "responsible?" Why is there societal pressure on women to be thin? Why are not men expected to wear makeup and shave their legs? Why is there no male equivalent for "slut"? Why are not women taught to see marriage as the end of a certain kind of independence the same way men are? Why do not boys get dressed up and play groom? Why are all of our presidents men? Why are most kindergarten teachers women? These are puzzling phenomena that raise more questions than answers; however, what we do know is that learning to read gender as a text will help you make sense of the world as roles become less black and white, less right and wrong, less male and female.

Social scientists remind us that gender is socially constructed, and therefore, in a way, we are recruited to gender. Consequently, society tends to punish those who don't conform to its gender roles. The goal of this chapter is to help you read the various means of recruitment; we want you to become savvy readers of the texts that encourage you to *do* gender.

WHILE ONE'S SEX MAY BE DETERMINED BY BIOLOGY, GENDER IS CONSTRUCTED.

What we mean by "constructed" is that gender is built, invented, created. Of course, while some gender traits might seem to be related to one's biological make-up, gender can still be constructed or "performed." We can think of these traits in both external and internal terms. For instance, our culture assigns certain behaviors or characteristics to maleness.

These may include strength, rationality, virility, affluence, and stability. To send out cues that he possesses all these things, a man may bulk up, he may wear designer clothes and drive a sports car, he may watch and play a lot of sports, he may date a lot of women or men. However, what if the values our culture assigned to maleness were grace, daintiness, refinement, monogamy, and nurturing? What if *these* traits were the most male traits? Would men still bulk up, watch football, go hunting, watch *Rambo* movies, and drive pick-ups? Some might, but most would not. Why? Because they would be ostracized and stigmatized, not seen as "real" men, according to society's expectations of masculine behavior. Men who adhere to socially constructed codes of gender behavior have read the texts of maleness and America well—they know how to fit in.

Just as external elements connote gender, so do internal elements. For instance, what if mainstream heterosexual female behavior were characterized by aggression, dominance, sexual assertiveness, and independence? Would women still wait for men to make the first move? Would women still link their sense of identity with men? Would women think of marriage in the same way? Would women feel differently about their bodies? Would women be afraid to beat their dates in bowling, or fear appearing smarter than their male partners? So, without even knowing it, you are probably performing or doing gender in various aspects of your lives. There is not necessarily anything wrong with this; however, you should be aware that there can be negative implications, and we would encourage you to read your own gender and the genders of others with increased care and sensitivity.

Though we have talked mostly about gender in heterosexual terms, doing gender is not reserved for straight folks. Chances are, you are familiar with terms like "butch," "femme," and "queen." That these terms exist suggests how important gender constructs are to our identities, and they reveal how, even in same-sex relationships, we do gender. What's more, as many gay and lesbians will confirm, gender has nothing to do with biology. Most gays and lesbians would argue that genders are, in fact, fluid. For many, having a penis does not prohibit someone from being or living as a woman, just as having breasts and a vagina does not prohibit many people from living or passing as a man. Here, the distinction between "sex" and "gender" is critical. You may have your own assumptions about how gay men and women do gender, just as you have expectations about how straight men and women do gender.

OUR PERCEPTIONS OF GENDER CAN BE INFLUENCED BY A NUMBER OF FACTORS, INCLUDING STEREOTYPES, TRADITION, POPULAR CULTURE, AND FAMILY.

We are all aware of stereotypes surrounding gender: Women are better communicators, men are stronger; men like power tools, women like chick flicks. Without realizing it, you may make gendered assumptions about traits of women all the time. For instance, if you are in a grocery store, and you want to know the ingredients for a cake, who are you most likely to ask: a woman or a man? If someone tells you they have a wonderful new doctor, are you more likely to assume it is a man or a woman? If you hear that someone went on a shooting spree in a school, are you most likely to assume that person was male or female? Stereotypes are amazingly powerful, and we may not realize the degree to which our thoughts, beliefs, and actions are shaped by them.

Similarly, cultural and family traditions continue to affect how we see ourselves and other genders. We have a number of female and male friends who complain about how, after every holiday dinner, the men adjourn to the living room to watch sports, while the women clear the tables and do the dishes. At that same dinner, it is likely that the father or grandfather carves the turkey or ham and even says the prayer. One might say that these are roles that both genders silently agree to, yet others might say that these behaviors reflect and inscribe a pattern suggesting that the important duties are reserved for men, while the menial tasks remain women's work. Thus, we grow up not merely ascribing values to genders but linking the importance of specific genders to the importance our society places on the kind of duties we think of as female and male.

Equally persuasive is popular culture. How many of our preconceptions about gender come from billboards, television shows, advertisements, movies, and commercials? Research indicates quite a bit. For instance, psychologists and advertisers suggest that the average viewer believes about one in eight commercials she or he watches. That may not seem like a great deal, but over the course of eighteen or nineteen years, you have seen (and probably internalized) a number of commercials, many of which have, no doubt, influenced your own views of gender. From rock and country music lyrics to commercials for cleaning products to NFL pregame shows to advertisements for jeans and tequila to television sitcoms to the infamous beer commercials, images of men and women doing gender flood us from all sides. Because of this, pop culture can fuse into stereotype, and tradition can meld into popular culture; at times, we may not know which comes from which. So many people conform to the expectations of gender roles, that gender roles appear natural or innate. We urge you to stop and think for a moment before assuming anything about gender.

Oddly, perhaps the most influential source for our gender roles comes from our own families. Before we are even aware of it, we see our mothers *be* women, and we see our fathers enact maleness. In fact, most agree that our early caretakers—whether it is our mothers, grandmothers, nannies, fathers, uncles, or siblings—provide for us the foundations of gender roles. What we see our fathers do, we think is what most men do, and more importantly, what men are supposed to do. As you get older, you will be shocked at how easily you slip into the same gender roles and gendered duties you observed your family engaging in for eighteen years. What's more, over time, these behaviors get coded, recoded, and coded again. Every time you see your father turn on the TV and not help clear the table, it sends messages about what men and women do and do not do. Similarly, every time you do see your father change a diaper or your mom fix a car, it sends other messages about what men and women can do. Most importantly, these behaviors can send subtle but powerful messages about what *you* can do. So, as you think about gender roles in your own life, consider how gender in your family is a complex but powerful text.

FEMINISM (OR FEMINISMS) CAN AND SHOULD BE SUPPORTED BY BOTH MEN AND WOMEN.

Often we ask our students if they believe that women should be paid the same as men. They say yes. We ask them if they think men are inherently smarter than women. They say no—usually an emphatic no. We ask them if they believe that women should be afforded the same opportunities for employment as men. They all say yes. We ask them if they think that there should be equality between men and women. All claim there should. Yet, when we ask how many are feminists, virtually none raise their hands. This reality continues to be perplexing and frustrating. The authors of this book are straight men, and both identify as feminists—so why the resistance among students?

One reason may be the text "feminism." There are any number of definitions of feminism, ranging from very open definitions (if you think men and women should be treated equally, then you are a feminist) to more forceful definitions, such as Barbara Smith's ("Feminism is the political theory and practice that struggles to free *all* women: women of color, working-class women, poor women, Jewish women, disabled women, lesbians, old women—as well as white, economically privileged, heterosexual women"). Some people think that a definition of feminism must be religiously conceived, since much discrimination has ties to religious conservatism (a feminist is a person who supports the theory that God the Mother is equal to God the Father). Though neither of the authors are women, both lean toward a definition of feminism that is broad enough to take in all interested parties. For us, feminism is the understanding that there has been an imbalance between how men and women have been treated, and that balance between genders must be restored. We also tend to believe that feminism implies more than a passing interest in bringing about this change; feminists must, on some level, act in a way that helps facilitate a more equitable balance. These actions might be as small as refraining from using sexist language or as large as protesting in front of the Capitol. Thus, we prefer the term "feminisms" because it acknowledges the fact that feminism is as individual as each individual.

For some reason, many students associate feminism with hating men, refusing to shave legs, being bitchy, being militant, being strident, and, in general, being unlikable. None of these traits has ever been part of the mission of feminism. Rather, feminism as an idea, as an ideology, has always been about equality. In fact, there remains no single feminism but, as we've suggested, inclusive and intriguing "feminisms." Instead of thinking of feminisms as exclusionary, it is more helpful and more accurate to think of feminisms as inclusive. And, like any text, feminism is always open to revision.

THERE IS A DOUBLE STANDARD IN AMERICA REGARDING MEN AND WOMEN.

You do not need a textbook to tell you this—most of you already know it. Many women would acknowledge that they feel a palpable pressure to be thin, virginal, and refined, whereas American culture not only allows but also encourages males to be physically comfortable, sexually adventurous, and crass. Similarly, women who work in the corporate world have argued for decades that female behavior characterized as bitchy, cold, and calculating when enacted by women, is praised and considered commanding, rational, and strategic when carried out by men. On the other hand, both men and women have suggested recently that cultural pressure on men to be in control, in charge, and emotionally cool leaves little room for personal growth and fulfillment.

Even though America has grown immensely in terms of gender equity, there remain dozens of unwritten or even unspoken codes that both men and women feel compelled to adhere to. Thus, how people of different genders act in the world has everything to do with cultural expectations placed on their genders. Moreover, when men and women do gender properly—that is, as society dictates they should—they make gender seem invariable and inevitable, which then seems to justify structural inequalities such as the pay gap, the lack of elected female politicians, or even good roles for women in theater, film, and television.

In short, issues of gender involve more than leaving the toilet seat up; they arise out of personal, public, private, and cultural worlds. We hope that this chapter will make you a more engaged reader of how gender gets enacted in each of these worlds.

THIS TEXT

1. While it will be impossible for you to know this fully, try to figure out the writing situation of each author. Who is the audience? What does the author have at stake? What is his or her agenda? Why is she or he writing this piece?

2. What social, political, and cultural forces affect the author's text? What is going on in the world as he or she is writing?

3. This is a chapter about gender, so, obviously, you should be aware of the gender of the author.

4. How does the author define "gender"? Does she or he confuse "gender" and "sex"?

5. When taken as a whole, what do these texts tell you about how we construct gender?

6. How do stories and essays differ in their arguments about gender?

7. Is the author's argument valid? Is it reasonable?

8. Ideas and beliefs about gender tend to be very sensitive, deeply held convictions. Do you find yourself in agreement with the author? Why or why not? Do you agree with the editors' introduction?

9. Does the author help you read gender better than you did before reading the essay? If so, why? How do we learn to read gender?

10. If you are reading a short story or poem, then where does the text take place? When is it set?

11. What are the main conflicts in the text? What issues are at stake?

12. What kinds of issues of identity is the author working with in the text?

13. Is there tension between the self and society in the text? How? Why?

14. How do gender codes and expectations differ among cultures?

15. Did you like this? Why or why not?

BEYOND THIS TEXT

Media: How are men and women portrayed in television shows, movies, video games, and music videos? Do the media try to set the criteria for what is "male" and what is "female"? How do they do this?

Advertising: How are women and men portrayed in magazine ads? Do advertisers tend to associate certain products or tasks with a specific gender? How do ads influence how we read gender roles?

Television: Is there much variance in how men are portrayed on television? What kinds of shows are geared toward men? What about women? What kinds of activities do we see women engage in on television? Are gender roles related to stereotypes about race, class, and geography?

Worksheet

Movies: Many actors and actresses bemoan the lack of good movie roles for women. Why is this the case? Can you think of many movies in which a younger man falls for an older woman? How often do women rescue men in movies? Why is male nudity so rare and female nudity so coveted?

Public space: How do we know that a place is geared toward men or women? What visual clues do we see?

QUICK GUIDE TO WRITING ABOUT GENDER

1. Before starting, think of a question related to gender—do not just use gender as your lens. Locate it in time or within a particular part of culture. For example, if you are writing about gender in *Avatar*, do not ask only "how is gender portrayed in *Avatar*?" Perhaps ask, "What does the way gender is portrayed in *Avatar* say about the way we visually contruct gender in movies?"—or—" How does the way gender is portrayed in *Avatar* reflect current attitudes about gender?"

2. If the paper is more observational or personal, think of how you are defining gender. Are you focusing on behavior? Attitudes? Is your paper more about biology or culture? Consider using a specialized dictionary or a textbook to define it further.

3. Do not be afraid to write about feminism if your teacher wants a persuasive essay. But feminism has both simple and complex definitions; so it's best to define what you mean by feminism when you are writing about it.

Marked Women, Unmarked Men

Deborah Tannen

Linguist Deborah Tannen uses a conference as a semiotic setting to read three other women. Based on textual cues (or signs) of the women's hair, clothes, and mannerisms, this 1993 essay gives a reading of each of these "texts," suggesting that women, more than men, are marked by cultural expectations.

SOME YEARS AGO I was at a small working conference of four women and eight men. Instead of concentrating on the discussion I found myself looking at the three other women at the table, thinking how each had a different style and how each style was coherent.

One woman had dark brown hair in a classic style, a cross between Cleopatra and Plain Jane. The severity of her straight hair was softened by wavy bangs and ends that turned under. Because she was beautiful, the effect was more Cleopatra than plain.

The second woman was older, full of dignity and composure. Her hair was cut in a fashionable style that left her with only one eye, thanks to a side part that let a curtain of hair fall across half her face. As she looked down to read her prepared paper, the hair robbed her of bifocal vision and created a barrier between her and the listeners.

The third woman's hair was wild, a frosted blond avalanche falling over and beyond her shoulders. When she spoke she frequently tossed her head, calling attention to her hair and away from her lecture.

Then there was makeup. The first woman wore facial cover that made her skin smooth and pale, a black line under each eye and mascara that darkened already dark lashes. The second wore only a light gloss on her lips and a hint of shadow on her eyes. The third had blue bands under her eyes, dark blue shadow, mascara, bright red lipstick and rouge; her fingernails flashed red.

I considered the clothes each woman had worn during the three days of the conference: In the first case, man-tailored suits in primary colors with solid-color blouses. In the second, casual but stylish black T-shirts, a floppy collarless jacket and baggy slacks or a skirt in neutral colors. The third wore a sexy jump suit; tight sleeveless jersey and tight yellow slacks; a dress with gaping armholes and an indulged tendency to fall off one shoulder.

Shoes? No. 1 wore string sandals with medium heels; No. 2, sensible, comfortable walking shoes; No. 3, pumps with spike heels. You can fill in the jewelry, scarves, shawls, sweaters—or lack of them.

As I amused myself finding coherence in these styles, I suddenly wondered why I was scrutinizing only the women. I scanned the eight men at the table. And then I knew why I wasn't studying them. The men's styles were unmarked.

The term "marked" is a staple of linguistic theory. It refers to the way language alters the base meaning of a word by adding a linguistic particle that has no meaning on its own. The unmarked form of a word carries the meaning that goes without saying—what you think of when you're not thinking anything special.

The unmarked tense of verbs in English is the present—for example, visit. To indicate past, you mark the verb by adding ed to yield visited. For future, you add a word: will visit. Nouns are presumed to be singular until marked for plural, typically by adding s or es, so visit becomes visits and dish becomes dishes.

The unmarked forms of most English words also convey "male." Being male is the unmarked case. Endings like ess and ette mark words as "female." Unfortunately, they also tend to mark them for frivolousness. Would you feel safe entrusting your life to a doctorette? Alfre Woodard, who was an Oscar nominee for best supporting actress, says she identifies herself as an actor because "actresses worry about eyelashes and cellulite, and women who are actors worry about the characters we are playing." Gender markers pick up extra meanings that reflect common associations with the female gender: not quite serious, often sexual.

Each of the women at the conference had to make decisions about hair, clothing, makeup and accessories, and each decision carried meaning. Every style available to us was marked. The men in our group had made decisions, too, but the range from which they chose was incomparably narrower. Men can choose styles that are marked, but they don't have to, and in this group none did. Unlike the women, they had the option of being unmarked.

Take the men's hair styles. There was no marine crew cut or oily longish hair falling into eyes, no asymmetrical, two-tiered construction to swirl over a bald top. One man was unabashedly bald; the others had hair of standard length, parted on one side, in natural shades of brown or gray or graying. Their hair obstructed no views, left little to toss or push back or run fingers through and, consequently, needed and attracted no attention. A few men had beards. In a business setting, beards might be marked. In this academic gathering, they weren't.

There could have been a cowboy shirt with string tie or a three-piece suit or a necklaced hippie in jeans. But there wasn't. All eight men wore brown or blue slacks and nondescript shirts of light colors. No man wore sandals or boots; their shoes were dark, closed, comfortable and flat. In short, unmarked.

Although no man wore makeup, you couldn't say the men didn't wear makeup in the sense that you could say a woman didn't wear makeup. For men, no makeup is unmarked.

I asked myself what style we women could have adopted that would have been unmarked, like the men's. The answer was none. There is no unmarked woman.

There is no woman's hair style that can be called standard, that says nothing about her. The range of women's hair styles is staggering, but a woman whose hair has no particular style is perceived as not caring about how she looks, which can disqualify her for many positions, and will subtly diminish her as a person in the eyes of some.

Women must choose between attractive shoes and comfortable shoes. When our group made an unexpected trek, the woman who wore flat, laced shoes arrived first. Last to arrive was the woman in spike heels, shoes in hand and a handful of men around her.

If a woman's clothing is tight or revealing (in other words, sexy), it sends a message—an intended one of wanting to be attractive, but also a possibly unintended one of availability. If her clothes are not sexy, that too sends a message, lent meaning by the knowledge that they could have been. There are thousands of cosmetic products from which women can choose and myriad ways of applying them. Yet no makeup at all is anything but unmarked. Some men see it as a hostile refusal to please them.

Women can't even fill out a form without telling stories about themselves. Most forms give four titles to choose from. "Mr." carries no meaning other than that the respondent is male. But a woman who checks "Mrs." or "Miss" communicates not only whether she has been married but also whether she has conservative tastes in forms of address—and probably other conservative values as well. Checking "Ms." declines to let on about marriage (checking "Mr." declines nothing since nothing was asked), but it also marks her as either liberated or rebellious, depending on the observer's attitudes and assumptions.

I sometimes try to duck these variously marked choices by giving my title as "Dr."—and in so doing risk marking myself as either uppity (hence sarcastic responses like "Excuse me!") or an overachiever (hence reactions of congratulatory surprise like "Good for you!").

All married women's surnames are marked. If a woman takes her husband's name, she announces to the world that she is married and has traditional values. To some it will indicate that she is less herself, more identified by her husband's identity. If she does not take her husband's name, this too is marked, seen as worthy of comment: she has done something; she has "kept her own name." A man is never said to have "kept his own name" because it never occurs to anyone that he might have given it up. For him using his own name is unmarked.

A married woman who wants to have her cake and eat it too may use her surname plus his, with or without a hyphen. But this too announces her marital status and often results in a tongue-tying string. In a list (Harvey O'Donovan, Jonathan Feldman, Stephanie Woodbury McGillicutty), the woman's multiple name stands out. It is marked.

I have never been inclined toward biological explanations of gender differences in language, but I was intrigued to see Ralph Fasold bring biological phenomena to bear on the question of linguistic marking in his book *The Sociolinguistics of Language*. Fasold stresses that language and culture are particularly unfair in treating women as the marked case because biologically it is the male that is marked. While two X chromosomes make a female, two Y chromosomes make nothing. Like the linguistic markers s, es or ess, the Y chromosome doesn't "mean" anything unless it is attached to a root form—an X chromosome.

Developing this idea elsewhere, Fasold points out that girls are born with fully female bodies, while boys are born with modified female bodies. He invites men who doubt this to lift up their shirts and contemplate why they have nipples.

In his book, Fasold notes "a wide range of facts which demonstrates that female is the unmarked sex." For example, he observes that there are a few species that produce only females, like the whiptail lizard. Thanks to parthenogenesis, they have no trouble having as many daughters as they like. There are no species, however, that produce only males. This is no surprise, since any such species would become extinct in its first generation.

Fasold is also intrigued by species that produce individuals not involved in reproduction, like honeybees and leaf-cutter ants. Reproduction is handled by the queen and a relatively few males; the workers are sterile females. "Since they do not reproduce," Fasold says, "there is no reason for them to be one sex or the other, so they default, so to speak, to female."

Fasold ends his discussion of these matters by pointing out that if language reflected biology, grammar books would direct us to use "she" to include males and females and "he" only for specifically male referents. But they don't. They tell us that "he" means "he or she," and that "she" is used only if the referent is specifically female. This use of "he" as the sex-indefinite pronoun is an innovation introduced into English by grammarians in the 18th and 19th centuries, according to Peter Muhlhausler and Rom Harre in "Pronouns and People." From at least about 1500, the correct sex-indefinite pronoun was "they," as it still is in casual spoken English. In other words, the female was declared by grammarians to be the marked case.

Writing this article may mark me not as a writer, not as a linguist, not as an analyst of human behavior, but as a feminist—which will have positive or negative, but in any case powerful, connotations for readers. Yet I doubt that anyone reading Ralph Fasold's book would put that label on him.

I discovered the markedness inherent in the very topic of gender after writing a book on differences in conversational style based on geographical region, ethnicity, class, age and gender. When I was interviewed, the vast majority of journalists wanted to talk about the differences between women and men. While I thought I was simply describing what I observed—something I had learned to do as a researcher—merely mentioning women and men marked me as a feminist for some.

When I wrote a book devoted to gender differences in ways of speaking, I sent the manuscript to five male colleagues, asking them to alert me to any interpretation, phrasing or wording that might seem unfairly negative toward men. Even so, when the book came out, I encountered responses like that of the television talk show host who, after interviewing me, turned to the audience and asked if they thought I was male-bashing.

Leaping upon a poor fellow who affably nodded in agreement, she made him stand and asked, "Did what she said accurately describe you?" "Oh, yes," he answered. "That's me exactly." "And what she said about women—does that sound like your wife?" "Oh yes," he responded. "That's her exactly." "Then why do you think she's male-bashing?" He answered, with disarming honesty, "Because she's a woman and she's saying things about men."

To say anything about women and men without marking oneself as either feminist or anti-feminist, male-basher or apologist for men seems as impossible for a woman as trying to get dressed in the morning without inviting interpretations of her character. Sitting at the conference table musing on these matters, I felt sad to think that we women didn't have the freedom to be unmarked that the men sitting next to us had. Some days you just want to get dressed and go about your business. But if you're a woman, you can't, because there is no unmarked woman.

READING WRITING

This Text: Reading

1. What do you make of Tannen's claim that women are "marked"? Is that an appropriate word?
2. Would you agree with her that men are not marked?
3. What is Tannen's evidence for her claims? Is it solid evidence? Do Tannen's arguments follow a logical progression?

Your Text: Writing

1. Go to a coffee shop or a restaurant and read a group of women sitting together. Are they marked? How? Then write an essay, similar to Tannen's, on your reading of the women. How do contemporary cultural expectations of women influence how you read other women?
2. Write an essay on how men are marked.
3. Are there other female markings that Tannen does not mention? Write an essay in which you give a reading of other kinds of female markings.
4. Read Maxine Hong Kingston's "No Name Woman," and write an essay in which you demonstrate how the aunt was marked.

Out of Style Thinking: Female Politicians and Fashion

Annette Fuentes

Hillary Clinton was one of the leading Democratic candidates for president for the 2008 presidential elections—the first time a woman has been in this position. Annette Fuentes, a journalist who covers health and policy issues for a number of American publications, is a contributing editor at In These Times *magazine. In her short 2007 piece for* USA Today, *Fuentes argues that many Americans—even journalists—look at female politicians through a lens of gender or a lens of fashion rather than seeing them first and foremost as politicians. Note Fuentes' thesis, and note how she backs up her thesis with specific examples and quotes.*

IF SOME THINGS HAVE CHANGED, the news media's take on female politicians has a tendency to recycle the same old clichés about them. Coverage of first female House Speaker Nancy Pelosi's fashion sensibility in the media is Exhibit A.

First there was a *Washington Post* article published shortly after the elections on the presumptive new House speaker, "Muted Tones of Quiet Authority: A Look Suited to the Speaker." It offered the information that "Pelosi's suit was by Giorgio Armani—the Italian master of neutral tones and modern power dressing—and she wore it well." The article at least appeared in the newspaper's Style section, but was chock-full of psychoanalytic forays into Pelosi's wardrobe choices, asserting that "an Armani suit, for a woman, is a tool for playing with the boys without pretending to be one." I would wager that Pelosi is one woman who doesn't play around with anyone.

A "Fashion Leader"

Then there was a *New York Times* article in January in its Thursday Styles section titled "Speaking Chic to Power." While noting that Pelosi, barely in her new job a month, had brought the House to votes on a minimum wage increase, stem cell research, and Medicare drug prices, the article said "she did it looking preternaturally fresh, with a wardrobe that, while still subdued and overreliant on suits, has seldom spruced the halls of Congress."

Similar articles appeared in the *Baltimore Sun* and *Chicago Tribune*. Mentioned were other women politicians and their fashion choices, such as Sen. Hillary Clinton's hair style and preference for black pantsuits or Florida Rep. Debbie Wasserman Schultz's haircut. The question is whether focusing on the clothing choices of serious female political players risks rendering them less than serious. Another question is whether such reports warrant precious space. After all, with rare exceptions, male politicians are seldom scrutinized for their choice of suits.

Some reporters and editors haven't figured out a way to cover female politicians that doesn't rely on the old stereotypes, says Gail Dines, sociology and women's studies professor at Wheelock College in Boston. "To be a woman politician, you have to strategize and work hard, and yet what matters is what designer you're wearing. It's a way to make women in power less scary." Dines notes, "it's putting women into a comfort zone for those who are still baffled by how to treat strong women."

Trivializing Women

The articles seem a throwback to a time when women were only spouses, not players, says Ruth Mandel, director of the Eagleton Institute of Politics at Rutgers University. "To focus on their attire, the cut of their clothes . . . is to be in danger of trivializing who they are, the important role they play and the meaning behind women's advancement to positions of power: That is, we're moving to a true democracy of shared leadership."

The problem is the media haven't quite caught up. "A woman who rises to a leadership position at any level is going to dress appropriately," says Kathleen Hall Jamieson, professor at the Annenberg School of Communications at the University of Pennsylvania. "It underscores her competence and is not a distraction. You take for granted that it would not be worthy of comment any more."

Jamieson thinks the underlying motivation for reporting on female politicians' style is "the natural news interest in talking about what changes, and men don't look different. There is a uniform for men in power and we all know what it looks like. The only thing to change is the color of the shirt or tie."

Because women have greater fashion options, changes they make are more obvious and invite analysis. Now that Pelosi's "uniform" has been established, that should be the end of it. Ditto for Clinton. "Clinton now has a range of what she wears," Jamieson says. "She hasn't been changing hairstyles or her pantsuits. That is our definition of what she wears, and that should end it."

Tom Rosenstiel, director of the Project for Excellence in Journalism, thinks reporting that describes women politicians' appearance is justified in profiles of them.

"Beyond that, there comes a point where it reflects badly on the press," he says. "The only way the appearance of a politician is really politically relevant is if they are so dazzlingly charismatic or strange looking that people can't look at them. Whether it's Condoleezza Rice, Madeleine Albright or Nancy Pelosi, they all fall into the same zone as their male counterparts. They all look like regular people, none is a runway model or the elephant man."

Female politicians will certainly survive such silly coverage, and, some argue the stories are harmless. But these women are role models for young women and offer an alternative to the fashion model and celebrity in setting the standard for female beauty and worth.

Dines worries that when the media emphasize the appearance of women, it perpetuates attitudes in the larger world that devalue and limit women. "These are fortunate, privileged women," Dines notes of politicians, "but for young women trying to make it in the world, how they look can affect their opportunities."

READING WRITING

This Text: Reading

1. What is Fuentes' thesis here? Can you locate it?
2. Do you agree that the articles she cites "trivialize" women? Why or why not?
3. What do you make of the argument that there is a "uniform" for men in power?

Your Text: Writing

1. Write a comparison/contrast essay in which you look at the pieces by Fuentes and the previous essay by Tannen. How do they make similar arguments?
2. Most of us watched Hillary Clinton run for president. Be honest with youself—did you expect specific "female" behavior from her? If so, what was it? Write an essay on Hillary Clinton's run for president. How did you, men, the media *read* her?

Dispatches from *Girls Gone Wild*: Girls Get Naked for T-Shirts and Trucker Hats

Ariel Levy

Ariel Levy is a staff writer for the New Yorker *and the author of* Female Chauvinist Pigs: Women and the Rise of Raunch Culture. *As part of her research for the book, Levy was "embedded" with the* Girls Gone Wild *crew as they filmed on the beaches of South Beach, Florida during spring break of 2004. We were intrigued by Levy's project when we first read her reports in* Slate. *Part journalism, part travel writing, and part personal essay, her dispatches are an interesting genre. In these pieces, Levy does something a lot of men and women would probably like to do—go behind the scenes of* Girls Gone Wild *and see what really happens both when the cameras are on and off. We'd like you to pay particular attention to two different but related aspects of her essays. First, see if you can find her thesis statement or statements. What is it? How does she advance and support her thesis? Second, look closely at the moment she engages in a meta-discussion in the third dispatch. What is the effect of this move? Is it successful?*

From: Ariel Levy
Subject: Spanking on the Beach

Posted Monday, March 22, 2004, at 4:17 PM ET

SOUTH BEACH, Fla., Friday, March 18, 2004. If you ever watch television when you have insomnia, then you are already familiar with *Girls Gone Wild*. Late at night, infomercials show bleeped-out snippets of the brand's wildly popular, utterly plotless videos, composed entirely from footage of young women flashing their breasts, their tushes, or occasionally their genitals at the camera, and usually shrieking "Whoo!" while they do it. The videos range slightly in theme, from *Girls Gone Wild on Campus* to *Girls Gone Wild Doggy Style* (hosted by Snoop Dogg), but the formula is steady and strong: Bring cameras to amped-up places across the country, Mardi Gras, hard-partying colleges, sports bars, and, of course, spring break destinations, where young people are drinking themselves batty, and offer T-shirts and trucker hats to the girls who flash or to the guys who induce them to do so. I am in just such a place.

It's 11 on a Friday night in never sedate but usually upscale South Beach, and the area has been taken over by sunburned spring-breakers in tight, synthetic clothing. An SUV passes by and two blond heads pop out of the sunroof like prairie dogs, whooping into the night sky. On the front porch of the Chesterfield Hotel on Collins Avenue, a GGW crew is assembling for a night of filming. They were out last night, too, and they made a new friend, a local who has offered to take them to a club in nearby Coconut Grove. "That's Crazy Debbie," says Mia Leist, GGW's 25-year-old tour manager. "I love her. She's like a *Girls Gone Wild* groupie. She gets so many girls for us."

Crazy Debbie is a 19-year-old personal trainer by day. She wears body glitter, white stilettos that lace up to her knees, and a rhinestone Playboy bunny ring. "I did a scene for them last night," she says proudly, which is to say she masturbated for the GGW cameras in the back of a bar. "People watch the videos and think the girls in them are real slutty, but I'm a virgin! I just think this is fun. Miami is one of the few places where people aren't ashamed of their bodies. And yeah*, Girls Gone Wild* is for guys to get off on, but the women are beautiful and it's fun!" A song Crazy Debbie likes is blaring from the bar inside, and she starts doing that dance that you sometimes see in music videos, the one where women shake their butts so fast they seem to blur.

"She calls that vibrating," says Sam, a shaggy-haired cameraman who's here from L.A. "She told me, 'I can vibrate.'"

Another cameraman, Puck, a very handsome, surprisingly polite 24-year-old, is loading equipment into the car when two stunning young women who are already very close to naked approach him. They notice his *Girls Gone Wild* T-shirt and hat and ask him if they can come along with him if they promise to make out with each other later, possibly even in a shower. Alas, there is no room for them in the car, but the crew is unfazed: This happens all the time. "It's amazing," says Leist. "People flash for the brand. Debbie got naked for a hat."

The brand is so popular they will soon launch an apparel line, a compilation CD with Jive Records of GGW-approved club hits, and a restaurant chain. "It'll be like Hooters with better food," says Bill Horn, a 32-year-old in Pumas who is GGW's vice president of communications and marketing. Justin Timberlake has been photographed in their hats, and Brad Pitt gave out GGW videos to his Troy cast-mates as wrap presents. Horn won't tell me how much GGW is worth (he doesn't have to; it's privately owned), but a few years ago founder Joe Francis told *Variety* that he pulled in $4.5 million in 2001.

The company's success doesn't surprise me much. For the past year, I have been working on a book for the Free Press about how all the things that feminism once reviled, *Playboy*, strippers, wet T-shirt contests, are currently being embraced by young women as supposed symbols of personal empowerment and sexual liberation. To most of the girls I've met (at CardioStripTease classes in Los Angeles, at CAKE parties in Manhattan, at shopping malls outside of Chicago), bawdy and liberated are synonymous. *Girls Gone Wild* is only an extreme example of what's happening in our culture all the time in more subtle ways. Think about the popularity of Britney and Christina and their porn-y aesthetic (and poor Janet's desperate halftime attempt to catch up). Think about the ubiquity of thongs (in this country, the tiny garment's sales rose from $570 million in the period between August 2001 and July 2002, to $610 million for the same period the following year according to the market research firm NPD Group). Bimbos are back. But this time, women, like Mia Leist, are behind the scenes as well as in front of the cameras.

"It's not like we're creating this," Leist tells me once we get to Crazy Debbie's dance club in Coconut Grove. "This is happening whether we're here or not. Our founder was just smart enough to capitalize on it." As if to emphasize her point, two girls at the table next to us start giving a double lap dance to a young man who seems pleased by his good luck.

Bill Horn doesn't even notice them. He is staring across the room at a phalanx of blondes in tops tenuously fastened by lots of string ties. "Now those are some girls who should go wild," he says. "Jesus, listen to me; this job is turning me into a straight guy."

Puck and Sam pass by with three young women who have volunteered to do a "private" out on the balcony. "Here we go," says Bill. "There's some part of me that always wants to shriek, 'Don't do it!'" But he doesn't, and they definitely do. The trio starts making out in a sort of ravenous lump. It all looks very much like interpretive dance. Ultimately, one girl falls over and lands giggling on the floor, a characteristic endpoint for a GGW scene. On their way back inside, I ask one of them, a blonde in a turquoise miniskirt and now, of course, a hard-earned GGW hat, what they do when they are not on spring break. "We're grad students," she says, with only a slight slur. "It's sad. We'll have Ph.D.s in three years."

In what, I ask.

"Anthropology."

From: Ariel Levy
Subject: The View From the Sidelines of the "Sexy Positions Contest"
Updated Tuesday, March 23, 2004, at 3:52 PM ET

Saturday, March 20. It is 3 a.m., and I am with the *Girls Gone Wild* crew at a bar in Miami Beach called Senior Frog's. We're within walking distance of the Delano Hotel, but in here, watching the "Sexy Positions Contest," minimalism and snobbery feel very far away. Two chunky women with the familiar spring break combination of hair that's been bleached to a yellow white and skin that's been charred to a brownish coral are pretending to hump each other on a raised platform. A circle of maybe 90 men and 30 women has formed around them, and a rhythmic chant of "TAKE IT OFF! TAKE IT OFF!" rises from the crowd, followed by a hearty chorus of boos when the women decline to do so. As a consolation prize, the taller one pours beer over the shorter one's head and breasts.

"Girls! This is not a wet T-shirt contest!" The MC bellows over the mike. "Pretend you're fucking! Let me emphasize, pretend you are really fucking! I want you to pretend like you're fucking the shit out of her doggy style." But the women are too inebriated to achieve sufficient verisimilitude, and the crowd hollers them off the stage. Next up, a cheery, muscular African-American guy in extremely baggy jeans somehow manages to hoist his partner up so that her legs straddle his face while the rest of her body flies Superman-like into the air, supported by his hands under her breasts. The crowd is duly impressed by this unusual show of brute strength and lewd creativity. They may have found a winner.

This is all well and good, but Mia Leist, *Girls Gone Wild*'s tour manager, is more excited by what she's just heard from the bartender: Later in the week, there will be a "girl on girl box-eating" contest in Fort Lauderdale. This will no doubt yield excellent footage for the tapes sold to GGW subscribers, the people who get three raunchy videos every month for $9.99 each, as opposed to the occasional buyers who pay $19.99 to order a single tape of milder content, girls flashing and making out, from a GGW infomercial. "We never shoot guys," says Bill Horn, GGW's vice president of communications and marketing, who today is dressed in jeans and a vintage T-shirt. "That's not what Joe wants. And no pros. It has to be real."

The Joe he is referring to is GGW founder Joe Francis, and reality has always been Francis' beat, specifically, those realities that appeal to people's darkest impulses: voyeurism, violence, and eroto-mania. On the GGW Web site, you can still purchase Francis' debut effort, *Banned From Television*: A hideous compilation featuring "a public execution, a great white shark attack, a horrifying train accident and an explicit under-cover video from a sex club bust!" as the video is described on the site. "That's how Joe made his first million," says Horn. Horn recently pitched Francis for an MTV *Cribs* episode, and last week ABC shot a segment on him for a show called *Life of Luxury*. (Based on what little Francis has said about his finances, it's safe to assume he makes in the neighborhood of $5 million a year off GGW.)

But GGW hasn't exactly bought respectability for Francis, the former reality snuff filmmaker; he still has charges pending against him for racketeering, although he was recently acquitted by a judge of charges that he offered a girl $50 to touch his penis. ("As if!" Horn shrieks. "As my boyfriend said, when has Joe ever had to pay for a hand job?") But GGW has made Francis rich and fairly famous and certainly a particular kind of L.A. celebrity: His ex-girlfriends include such prize *Girls Gone Wild* as Paris Hilton and Tara Reid.

Francis is not here right now, but his presence is felt. The cameramen receive bonuses if they can capture a hot girl, instead of just a regular girl, flashing on camera. "Joe's looking for 10s," says Leist. "You know, 100 to 110 pounds, big boobs, blond, blue eyes, ideally no piercing or tattoos." Leist herself is short and has brown hair and recently graduated from Emerson in Boston. One of her professors (who knew the last GGW tour manager) got her this job. "I've had discussions with friends who were like, 'This is so degrading to females,'" she says. "I feel that if you walk up to someone all sly and say, 'Come on, get naked, show me your box,' that's one thing. But if you have women coming up to you, begging to get on camera, and they're having fun and being sexy, then that's another story." I ask Leist if she would ever appear in a GGW video. She says, "Definitely not."

She's right that the crew doesn't need to do any sly entreating. Girl after girl approaches Puck, the cute cameraman. He is dressed in a GGW hat and T-shirt and carrying a camera, and that seems to be enough to draw women to him as if by ensorcellment while he makes his way around Senior Frog's. Usually the girls start out joking, they plead with him to give them a GGW hat, and then they pretend to peel up their shirts or lift their skirts, but little by little the tease becomes the truth, and they are taking off their clothes as he records them for later viewing by God knows who.

Out on the balcony, a group of 10 men gather to watch a very pretty 19-year-old girl named Jennifer Cafferty from Jupiter, Fla., lift up her pink tube top for the camera. "OK now show me your thong," says Puck. She giggles and twirls her honey-colored hair around her forefinger. "Just show me your thong," he says again. "Just really quick. Show me your thong. Show me your thong now." She whips around and lifts her skirt.

"Yeah!" One of the guys in the crowd hollers, elated. "Yeah! Yeah!" Jennifer Cafferty turns to Puck with her hands on her hips. "Now where's my hat?"

From: Ariel Levy
Subject: Spanking on the Beach
Posted Wednesday, March 24, 2004, at 3:38 PM ET

Sunday, March 21. It is my third morning here in South Beach reporting on *Girls Gone Wild* for a book I am writing about why young women today are embracing raunchy aspects of our culture that would likely have caused their feminist foremothers to vomit. I have been embedded with a GGW camera crew for the last 72 hours and am starting to experience the aversion to sunlight common to spring breakers and vampires. But I'm also having another problem, one that's come up many times before throughout the course of this project: a nagging feeling that I have no idea what I'm talking about.

My argument is that women have forgotten that sexual power is only one, very limited, version of power and that this spring-break variety of thongs-and-implants exhibitionism is just one, very limited version of sexuality. Is it the one that arouses us, or, even, men, the most? To find out we would have to stop using the same unimaginative erotic shorthand, Strippers! Hooters! *Playboy! Maxim!* Brazilian Waxes! Boobies!! to signify sexiness. But what if I'm just uptight? What if this is actually fun and these girls get a genuine kick out of being porn stars for 15 minutes? What makes me so sure that all this is subtly insidious and not just a giant national keg party? Who do I think I am?

I ask GGW's tour manager, Mia Leist, and VP Bill Horn what they think. Do they have any ambivalence about what they do? Do they ever feel there's something vaguely ugly about watching drunk, attention-hungry girls expose themselves to video cameras for a living?

"Well, if it gets guys off," says Horn, over a plate of French toast.

"If it gets girls off!" Leist interrupts.

"At the end of the day it turns people on," Horn says democratically.

"We know the formula," says Leist. "We know how it works. In a perfect world, maybe we'd stop and change things. But it's a business."

After breakfast, we cross Ocean Avenue and meet up with the cameramen, Puck, Matt, and Sam, on the beach. We parted ways with Matt late last night before we went to the "Sexy Positions Contest" at Senior Frog's, and he went roaming the streets of South Beach to look for filmable action. "I got," he says proudly, "a shower scene."

Matt has long dreadlocks and wacky teeth, and he is wearing a black T-shirt with a decal of a devil Vargas girl gone wrong on it. Puck and Sam are in their usual GGW T-shirts and hats; and pretty soon the throngs of hungover tanners notice that there's a camera crew on the beach.

"We want our picture with you!" says a blonde in a bikini shaking her digital camera in the air.

"We don't want pictures," Leist yells back at her. "We want boobs!"

"I think I'm going to have that embroidered on a pillow," says Horn.

A small pack of guys are drinking beer out of a funnel, and they decide they want GGW hats. Badly.

"Show them your tits," one yells at the two girls splayed on towels who are with them. "What's your problem? Just show them your tits."

Puck sets up the shot and waits with his camera poised for the female response.

"No way!" The girl in the black bikini says and giggles.

"You know you want to," the funnel-wielder taunts. People are starting to circle around, like seagulls sensing a family is about to abandon their lunch.

"Do it," the guy says. "Yeah, do it!" yells a spectator.

"Show your tits!" screams another. "Show your ass!"

There are maybe 40 people now gathered in a circle that is both tightening inward and expanding outward around Puck and the girls and their "friends" with every passing second. The noise is rising in volume and pitch. I catch myself hoping that the crowd will not start throwing rocks at the girls if they decide to keep their clothes on.

We'll never know, because after a few more minutes pass, and a few more dozen dudes join the now massive amoeba of people hollering and standing on top of beach chairs and climbing up on each other's shoulders to get a good view of what might happen, it happens. The brunette pulls down her black bathing suit bottoms. She is rewarded with an echoing round of shrieks and applause that slices through the air.

"More!" Someone yells.

Other people have pulled out their cameras. The spectators who have cameras built into their cell phones have flipped them open and are jumping up to try and get a shot over the human wall.

The second girl gets up off her towel and spanks her friend several times.

"Yo, this is the best beach day yet!" A guy says into his phone.

My faith in the validity of my project (if not in humanity) is restored, so when the bikini bottoms are back on and the throng disperses, I tell Puck and Bill and Mia that I'm going home. Puck gives me the soft, handsome smile that has melted the clothing off of hundreds of breasts over the course of this weekend.

He holds up his camera. "Can I get a picture with you before you go?" he asks.

"Yeah, um, I'm really not taking my clothes off," I say.

His face crumples and then he looks at me as though I'm mean and insane. "Do you really think I would ask you to do that?"

READING WRITING

This Text: Reading

1. Levy acknowledges that she goes into this experience with the predetermined belief that programs like *Girls Gone Wild* are bad for women. Does this bias undermine her observations or her argument?

2. How would you describe Levy's tone in this essay? Angry? Playful? Comic? Critical? Ironic? Bemused? Resigned? Optimistic? Pessimistic?

3. Are you surprised that one of the main characters in the GGW crew is a woman? Does her participation in the GGW project support or call into question Levy's thesis?
4. How does the format of these dispatches affect how you read and interpret them?

Your Text: Writing

1. Read some of the essays in the following suite on Third Wave Feminism, then go back an re-read Levy's dispatches. Then, write an essay in which you talk about feminism and the state of women's issues in the present day. Why does Levy think the women who participate in *Girls Gone Wild* videos are taking a step backward in terms of women's issues?
2. Levy is perplexed by why women are so eager to get naked for a GGW hat and be naked on film for thousands of men to see. Write an essay in which you explain why posing for GGW is *not* degrading but rather a freeing, celebratory, comic act that embraces female sexuality.
3. In Levy's eyes, many of the women who strip for GGW don't come off looking so great. But, what about the men? How are they implicated in this? Write about GGW not in terms of what it tells us about women but in terms of what it tells us about men.

¡"Vaya, Vaya, Machismo!: Almodóvar and Spanish Masculinity"

Pjeter Dushku

Student essay

IN THIS ESSAY FOR ENGLISH 201, A SOPHOMORE-LEVEL research and writing class at Pace University, Pjeter Dushku looks at the films of Pedro Almodóvar through the lens of machismo, which he suggests is a more specific type of masculinity.

SPANISH CINEMA IN the first half of the twentieth century was primarily restricted to the nation of Spain. Unlike films of the United States, France, and Italy, which are successful examples of exported cinema, Spanish films had little international presence outside of the Iberian Peninsula and Latin and South America; the themes, issues, and culture of Spain were widely restricted to these Spanish speaking countries. All this changed in 1975 when the nationalist despot General Francisco Franco died after nearly 40 years of iron-fist politics (Esenwein). With the nation on the road to democracy, art, and in particular cinema, began to express the uniquely Spanish experience. If we were to choose one director, writer, or producer that exemplifies this movement, it would be Pedro Almodóvar. Widely considered to contemporary face of Spanish expressionism who is to cinema what Picasso was to art, Almodóvar has created a reputation as a free-spirited, controversial Spanish artist of the latter half of the twentieth century. In his works, particularly *¿Qué He Hecho Yo Para Merecer Esto!*, *¡Átame!*, and many more, Almodóvar unapologetically shows Spain and Spanish culture on an international stage.

Almodóvar once claimed in an interview that his success has been remarkable and unexpected: "I was not born in the right place in the right family in the right town in the right language or in the right moment to make movies" (D'Lugo 1). In fact, compared to his contemporaries of the 1980s, Almodóvar was an outcast; he was of humble Manchegan upbringing while the others were well-off, middle-class professionals. His debut was neither foretelling considering that cinema in Spain was thought to be *cutre*, or base—a lesser form of entertainment than popular bullfighting. To say the least, then, Almodóvar faced difficult odds when he took up his Super 8 camera and began making movies (Smith 5).

Almodóvar's goal in filmmaking was not necessarily for monetary or social aggrandizement. From interviews, stories, and articles, it is clear his works were created from the pure love of movies. He recounts how much of his childhood at boarding school was spent watching movies at the local cinema; his instruction, he states, was composed just as much by the movies he watched as by the priests that taught him, if not more. After leaving Extremadura, a neighboring province to La Mancha, to live in Madrid in the late 1960s, Almodóvar began to direct his movies at night after working during the day as a telephone sales representative. He studied briefly at La Filmoteca, a liberal cinematic school, before it was shut down due to concerns by the Franco government that the school was a breeding ground for communists. His short films directed with the Super 8 camera were silent and because of little commercial advantages, shown only to small groups in his friends' apartments or, prior to the schools closing, in La Filmoteca (Smith 10).

Marvin D'Lugo endorses the claim by many critics that there is a distinct correlation between Almodóvar's works and the greater Spanish culture: "His biography (of which there is no official version) dramatizes on the individual level the metaphorical Spanish culture . . . towards integration into modern European culture, social practices, and even politics." Like his films, Almodóvar was heavily influenced by European and American cultures from an early age. He saw in these 1950s and 1960s blockbuster, film noir movies a stark contrast from what he was living and what these films portrayed, taking a particular interest in the latter. In idolizing the state of other Western movies while at the same time internalizing them to Spanish culture as well as his own life, Almodóvar "orchestrated the dissolution of the lines that (separated) the film from the filmmaker" (7).

However, it was not until the 1980s that Almodóvar began to represent, in his opinion involuntarily, Spain and Spanish culture. During these years Almodóvar had established himself as an amateur director and began showing films at various film festivals. D'Lugo explains the irony of Almodóvar representing Spain through his films on an international level given that the country and its critics both dismissed him and his works as recreational and of little potential. Soon enough, nonetheless, the same films that were criticized by Almodóvar's contemporaries were seen by others as links to Spanish social concerns that had often gone unnoticed. Of these social concerns was Almodóvar's particular attention to machismo and masculine issues in his films, most notably *¿Qué He Hecho Yo Para Merecer Esto!* and *¡Átame!*

The idea of using machismo as a lens in analyzing Almodóvar's movies is not farfetched by any means. Watching any of his movies the viewer can notice a diverse array of Spanish masculine characters that oddly exhibit traditional societal characteristics as well as new, modern ideals. His male characters take a supporting role in almost every movie to the strong, vociferous women characters. This is precisely what I wanted to study—men and their relations to women in Almodóvar's movies.

The notion of machismo was brought to my attention after spending a semester abroad in Sevilla, Spain. While preparing myself for the trip, my interest in the topic was sparked while reading literature warning of a hyper masculine attitude in the southern province, Andalusia. The literature proclaimed Andalusia as the birthplace of "macho men," the land of bullfighters and womanizers. In short, these were not dainty men in any way. However, after spending five months among Sevillanos and other Andalusians, I came to realize that these guides were simplistic in their view of what these men were and how they related to their outside environment. Sure, these men were macho and exhibited many of the traits explained in tour guides, websites, and the like, but they were not the macho I had expected.

After realizing that much of the information on macho Spanish men seemed antiquated and inadequate, I thought a good way to analyze the contemporary Spanish male was through contemporary pop culture (i.e., movies). My goal is to show that through modern movies, in particular those by Almodóvar, the role of men in Spanish society has drastically changed after the fall of the Franco regime from that of a rigid tradition to one that is currently multifaceted and malleable.

Masculinity as an academic discipline is but an infant in comparison to other social sciences; writings and lectures about masculinity have gained momentum in only the latter quarter of the twentieth century. Why, then, do many of us assume we are well versed in the makings of a man, his personality, and his role in society? Simply put, because history has always been about men talking to other men about men (Gutmann 385). As a result, gender studies as a whole has, until recently, focused its energy on the exploration and discussion of feminine-centered issues. While one might argue that the study of one gender (feminine) indirectly leads to the examination of another (masculine), the fact remains that a masculine-focused exploration is underrepresented and necessary if we plan to fully understand both sexes. Fortunately, several social anthropologists and psychologists have taken it upon themselves to examine masculinity as a social force both here and abroad. Unlike their antecedents, these men make it a point to study men as being men which leads to a more comprehensive analysis than ever before. Among these social scientists and within their results rests the discussion of a unique, particular subset of masculinity—the Iberian-Hispanic machismo.

The purpose of this essay is to introduce the makings of masculinity and, more specifically, machismo, and how these social forces affect communities, chiefly Andalusia, Spain's southern province. By analyzing and summarizing works by Brandes, Gilmore, Brogger and other, I hope to show machismo not only an offspring of the greater masculinity but also as a unique, separate social phenomenon. I begin with an introduction of general study of masculinity and then explore further machismo and its affects on Andalusian society.

To begin, let us look at the classic masculine theory. As mentioned above, masculinity in the past seemed to be a side note in many academic disciplines; we read about masculinity without knowing. What recent scholars have been able to do is unfasten the bonds that connected masculinity to these other disciplines with the hope that a free-standing discussion of masculinity will lead to better analysis and classification. What was found was that gender roles existed in a dichotomized world where masculinity was defined as anything that was not feminine, and vice versa (Gutmann 386). Realizing that the two sexes were mutually exclusive compliments of one another, Gutmann further states that a man's personal image is forged by comparing it with that of a woman. In many instances there is a ritual and practical separation of man from the world of woman (Gutmann 389; Connell 605). We will see stronger evidence of this later in discussing Andalusian society. Connell builds on Gutmann's definition by stating a male's identity is laid down from early childhood, something many can easily understand, for psychological advances have proved the lasting influence nurture has on children in later years. In synthesizing these two definitions, we can create a working classification for the remainder of this paper. Such a definition would state that masculinity is a socially enforced, learned identity which is based on the separation of the male and the female realms. While far from perfect this definition with provide us insight into more specific masculinities, above all machismo.

In further understanding broad masculinity we should briefly touch on some historic considerations. While we can go as far as the Neanderthal eras to see the workings of dominate, dichotomized males, I will focus on the European colonization era as a starting point. The fact that I do not analyze the basic humanistic qualities that can be found in these prehistoric periods does not imply there are insignificant; in fact, we will see mentions of the "natural protector" and "male rituals" that are derived from our hunting ancestors. The point here is that our general understanding of what constitutes masculine and what is feminine began, according scholars, with the conquistadores.

Conquistadores are, as any history buff might recall, servants of the Spanish throne who were sent to the New World along with ecclesiastics to conquer the natives and control the land on behalf of the Spanish throne. These soldiers, often times seen as paid thugs because of their depraved behavior, brought with them to this New World a rugged individualism and almost unparallel brutality. What ensued, of course, were the colonization of the indigenous people and the subsequent subservience of the latter to the former. Gutmann argues that this truth, that the Spanish conquistadores were able to dominate the New World, led to a demasculinization of the colonized people and a perception of hypermasculinity with everything associated with a conquistador. Among these idealizations were individuality, bravado, strength, and the militia, that is, the life of a soldier. Additionally, such traits are still widely idealized in Latin America where men prefer stoicism and bravery over emotions and rationality (Lara Cantú 387).

This distinct form of masculinity, which became known as machismo, developed into a glorification among both the conquered and Spain's peers; the indigenous watched as they were easily conquered and enslaved by these masculine conquistadores while other European nations including Portugal, England, and the Netherlands watched as their relative power fell dramatically short of that of Spain.

An important point to keep in mind, according to Torres, is that while it is true many Latin American nations faced similar suppression under Spain, and hence the same image and association of power and masculinity, we cannot assume all Iberian-Hispanic machismos are the same. Torres makes an interesting point that post-colonial independence created many nations with an equal amount of social, cultural, and political variations. This in turn contributed to rather differing points of views on the same issue. The point Torres makes here is that traditionally masculine scholars err by grouping all Latino experiences into one, creating what he calls, "inconsistent, contradictory, superficial generalizations and negative stereotypical characteristics as ambiguous and misunderstood at any other aspect of the Latino culture" (163). Torres is not, however, above stating that there are "nearly" universalities inherent in Iberian-Hispanic machismo. Among some of these universal qualities is what he calls benevolent sexism.

This benevolent sexism is described by Glick and Fiske as a "subjectively favorable, chivalrous ideology that offers protection and affection to women who embrace conventional roles" (Torres 165). This is what many other scholars have noted in their respective works both in Iberia and Latin America. Brogger, for example, deduces that because of this underlying marianismo, where women are placed on the same pedestal as the Virgin Mary, machismo is no more than "a veneer used in public places disguising gender equality, or even matriarchy" (Brogger 20). Of course, we should remember once again that the degree to which each nation or culture employs machismo and marianismo differ and that we would be mistaken if we believed the Iberian-Hispanic communities were all matriarchal. Herzfeld reiterates Brogger's idea by stating that perception in machista societies, particularly in the Mediterranean area, is of utmost importance and that being a good man is less important than "being good at being a man" (Gutmann 386).

To begin analyzing and conceptualizing machismo and its relation to Andalusia, I refer to Brandes' observation that the common factor among Andalusian men is a coherent, mutually-compatible one that dissolves differences among the male cohort (365). This is important to remember for unlike the separate, individual Latin American nations, Andalusia's common history, politics and the like, allows us to make accurate generalizations about a broad range of people without falling under Torres's ridicule. We will now apply our working understanding of machismo and see how it functions in actuality.

The works of Brandes and Gilmore provide a detailed record of social anthropological research in Andalusia. Brandes, in particular, did fieldwork in "Monteros," a pseudonym, where he begins by explaining the separate realms of men and women. As with Gilmore, Brandes noticed that men were confined to the streets and bars when not working: "Houses are for eating and sleeping; otherwise, men should be working or enjoying the company of friends [at the local bar]" (35). Gilmore, who compared two towns, "Fuenmayor" and "El Castillo," accounts that in Andalusia, "Men who linger at home are morally suspect; their manhood is questionable" (956). Again, the reoccurring idea of men and safeguarding their masculinities is introduced. Brandes goes further, however, to describe the male-only presence in bars throughout the towns, noting that women only entered to pass the occasional messages along to their fathers or husbands. In essence, these men ruled their domain and were able to maintain a homogenous environment free of anything feminine. Even male friendships were unisexual and men faced strict ostracism if they were to befriend a female; women were always the wives of *amigos*, never *amigas* themselves. A reason, according to accounts of Brandes is that "women are unrelaxed in the company of men and vice-versa" (369). Brandes formulates that the sexes are uncomfortable with each other because of underlying cultural assumptions placed on each group, such as proper women refusing sexual advances but "adequate, competent men, if given the opportunity, are supposed to make such advances" (370). The conundrum created by these social double-standards has far reaching consequences, much more than can be discussed in one paper, but I will venture to discuss the issue of power that is raised by such.

Gilmore presents a comprehensive discussion on power and sex roles in Andalusia, focusing primarily on domestic power. He uses Ernestine Friedl's works as a starting point in defining domestic power as, "the capacity to impose one's will in decisions 'concerning sex relations, marriage, residence, divorce, and the lives of children'" (Gilmore 955). He takes a methodical approach to proving, in the end, women are as powerful, if not more powerful, than men. This sweeping statement establishes, once again, that machismo is a "myth" concealing a greater matronly dominance (953). The men of Andalusia are those men who abide by social norms, whether it is to their benefit or not, simply to defend their public machismo. Examples might include Gilmore observation that Andalusian men typically hand wages over to the women to administer finances as well as relinquish child rearing and matters of the house to the *jefa*, or female boss. Even more interesting, however, are the accounts of mother-in-laws in Andalusia. The *suegra* is described by Andalusians as a necessary nuisance in the lives of men; they make men feel like "fifth wheels" and have been known to kick men out of their own houses, too (962). These women, both the wife and her mother, are forces that scheme together, in men's opinion, to get their way. In fact, social standards allow for such calculated actions because the Andalusian men are supposed to cede to living close to the *suegra* as it is important and necessary for newlywed couples; new wives typically need guidance from their mothers, men jokingly explain.

The discussion of power arises then when we consider men to be out numbered in a seemingly macho society with few means of defense. Would not men rebel and demand respect and authority? The answer in Andalusia is a surprising "no." Gilmore noticed that the notion of appeasing one's wife is necessary because men regard these matters as trivial and not worth the aggravation (960). Fighting and violence, to my surprise, are shunned; these machos prefer to express their sorrows and troubles in songs, or *coplas*, and art rather than violent outburst. They are marginalized in their own homes, but yet they do not mind so much as to retaliate. I propose that this is because men are less interested in what actually occurs in their house as much so as what their community perceives. Perception in Andalusia, hence, is vital for social survival. A man seen as macho, not necessarily being macho, gets all the respect from the neighborhood.

In conclusion, we have seen the makings of machismo from a rustic, individual social norm into a perception-oriented, quasi-tribal characterization. One might ask himself, "Where have all the men gone?" to which a response would include the assumption that quite possibly they never truly existed. Our basis for machismo, the conquistador, was a man taken away from society and allowed to loosen all social morals and guidelines. The contemporary Andalusian male, on the other hand, is more practical because he revolves his life around society. He attempts to live according to the principles created by the fifteenth century conquistadores but at the same time he has surrounded by women that the conquistadores did not have. In the end men are permitted to continue their show outside the house, but once in the domestic realm, that of a woman, they are confined to her rules.

Among the major themes in Almodóvar's films are exactly these struggles faced by Spanish women as they balance the diametric gender worlds and society's perceptions. Far too often films portray female characters, such as the housekeeper Gloria in *¿Qué He Hecho Yo Para Merecer Esto!*, as repressed. The females in his movies, while often times honored and praised, suffer under the societal machismo culture still strong in Spain. The male characters, on the other hand, like the brutal and lawless Ricki in *¡Átame!*, are shown as "real men's men." After analyzing and comparing Almodóvar's many films, I propose that while Spanish male characters possess the upper hand in male-female relationships, Almodóvar's macho men are represented in such a negative light as to leave the viewer with no other option than to be appalled by their actions. His films, therefore, serve to foster a greater understanding of Spain's transition from a generation-long repressive dictatorship to a democracy, and express the Spanish experience such a political change entails.

Almodóvar's exploration into social dilemmas began with what is widely considered to be his first realistic film, *¿Qué He Hecho Yo Para Merecer Esto!* The film revolves around the plight of an illiterate, working-class mother, Gloria, and the drama that surrounds her and her family in Madrid (Smith 51). The film begins with a scene of Gloria cleaning a martial arts studio while a class is in session. She watches the entirely masculine class from a separate room, practicing the techniques with a mop. The scene, being that it is the movie's first, establishes the separate realms of man and woman; Gloria is not only forced to imitate the men in the background but must using a mop instead of a club (52). Having associated Gloria as a cleaning lady, Almodóvar takes the character's development a step further by showing her relations with her husband and sons. Gloria's husband, Antonio, is a brutal, insensitive taxi driver who complains when his imperious requests are not executed to his liking. He scolds Gloria for the cold chicken she serves him in one scene and in the next he is brutally selfish at lovemaking (54). As he interrupts Gloria's household duties of cleaning, ironing, and arranging for sex, the song "La Bien Pagá," or "The Well-Paid One," by Miguel de Molina plays in the living room. Gloria is not only submissive and giving when ordered by her husband, she is also well paid for her services. The husband's domination of his wife is clearly shown in this scene. The interesting point to note here, according to Smith, is Almodóvar's equating of marriage to prostitution (54). Gloria is in effect no more connected with her husband than a lowly Madrileña prostitute. As we will discuss later, such references made here are clear commentaries on the old marital laws and privileges given to men under Franco Spain.

The next relation Almodóvar establishes with Gloria is that with her two sons—one a drug dealing buffoon and the other a gay, preteen prostitute. While Gloria might have failed her family by many standards (she in fact offers her son some hallucinogenic pills to take to alleviate his hunger pains), she is defined as a "good enough mother." While Antonio is busy reconnecting with his long-lost German love interest, Gloria is left to fend for the family with her lousy monthly allowances. Economic situations take such a downturn that Gloria has no other choice but to sell her son Miguel as payment to the dentist for the work the latter has done on the former. For the viewer this is an emotional scene essentially evoking images of the Third World sex trade. As a Spanish mother with many obligations and very little means, she must be resourceful and innovative, even if it means selling her son. Smith points out that Almodóvar, in shooting consistently through Gloria's point of view, refuses to make her responsible for her family's predicaments; she is never blamed for the way either of her sons turn out (60).

The character of Gloria is therefore that of a "grotesque deformation of the Catholic ideal of a married woman" (53). During Franco's reign, as any Spanish woman will recall, women were so limited in their rights that permission was needed from fathers or husbands to open up a simple *cuenta corriente*, or checking account. The repressive nature of Franco's dictatorship did not, however, stop here; marriage manuals explained the role of a perfect *casada*, or housewife. A housewife, accordingly, was to combine the traits of a woman, such as, happy, tender, and compassionate, along with selfless companion to husband, tireless homemaker, and an ideal mother (53). In reviewing the role of Gloria throughout the film one can see that she tried, successfully in many critics' opinions, to serve as a decent *casada*; she obeyed her husband and worked tirelessly but could not, regardless of how much she tried, become happy in the downtrodden Madrid given her socio-economic status. To divulge further into Spain's twentieth century feminist equality movement one notices that today's basic rights (i.e., divorce, abortion, to work outside the home) were only permitted after 1975, with the latter two examples becoming legalized in 1981 and 1985, respectively. In such a historical light, then, it is clearer that this 1984 film is criticizing the disadvantages still existent in Spanish society. Through Gloria we see that not only economic problems cause her to continue the same mundane, tiresome life but also those issues created by the machista society.

The next film by Almodóvar that clearly depicts the struggle of women under Spanish machismo is *¡Átame!*. In this movie Antonio Banderas plays Ricki, an orphaned child from a small village brought up in a mental hospital who, at age 23, is able to leave the institution and integrate himself into society. The plot revolves around Ricki's desire to have the porn- and movie star heroin addict, Marina, fall in love with him even if he has to chain her to a bed for days to accomplish his goal.

For reasons that will become obvious, many critics have denounced Ricki's actions as barbarous and unacceptable; they lamented Banderas' character as, "everything a Hollywood hero should not be, most notably, violent with women" (D'Lugo 67). His intentions after escaping are rather simple; he intends to "marry [Marina] and have [her] children" (73), but the process through which he achieves his goal, for in the end Marina does genuinely fall in love with Ricki, are despicable. He begins his journey into the unknown City with a crew cut haircut and tight jeans and shirt, a typical 1980s masculine outfit. He seems to be the epitome of machismo and the audience falls for Ricki's boyish charm and masculine physique as he plays an air guitar and imitates a rock-and-role star. The audience understands that Ricki is new to society, but at the same time believes that he serves no threat to the community. As his psychological disorientation ensues and ultimately culminates when he head butts Marina at the front door to her apartment and ties her up to her bedposts the audience realizes he is not the typical hero we might have expected. He binds Marina and asks her simply, "How long will it take you to fall in love with me?" (¡Átame!).

Unlike other characters, however, this Almodóvar character diverges from the stereotypical, one dimension role of a leading male character to be in effect a complete three dimensional character (D'Lugo 74). While earlier it was mentioned that Ricki's dress and style seemed to distinguish him as a typical macho man, his subtle actions separate him from his peers. Upon leaving the mental institution and deciding that he wanted to make Marina his, Ricki goes to a corner store to buy a heart shaped box of chocolate. The persuasive way in which he speaks with women and uncivil manner in which he treats them creates a disconnect in what the audience expects and what the audience receives; his language shows him to be a formidable mate while his actions convey his animalistic qualities. He goes as far as buying new, softer rope for Marina so that the binding does not bruise her too much! What Almodóvar accomplished, therefore, is giving Banderas' character depth that the viewer is left with no other choice than to succumb to his charm.

To this extent, then, we understand why Marina, after fleeing the apartment with her friend Lola, decides to track down Ricki at his hometown village and take him back. Lola's character serves as a mediator between the divide between the viewer's thoughts and opinions and those of Marina; Lola, like the viewer, is skeptical of Ricki's genuine ability to love Marina yet comes to understand after a brief conversation that the two do legitimately love one another. As the three characters ride back to the City the song, "Resistiré" by Manuel de la Calva plays and all join in to sing (Adelante). The song, as the name suggests, describes the singer's determination to stand his ground even when faced with the most difficult of obstacles. The application of this song, however, is not limited to the storyline of ¡Átame! but also of the larger Spanish society.

When we consider again the Spaniards' willpower and illusion following the death of Franco, it is clear that some 20 years later their dreams of a utopian society fell far short of expectations. Madrid, as shown in ¿Qué He Hecho Yo Para Merecer Esto! and ¡Átame!, became a breeding ground for drug dealers and street violence with little hope of reconciliation. The people, as one can assume, were desperate for something better with many people eventually returning back to their pueblo or hometown. The message Almodóvar wants to convey at the end of this movie, I propose, is that while Madrid and the nation might not be exactly how the people imagined, or even worse, the power is in their hands to change what they feel is lacking. Unlike the years of Franco dictatorship where a single individual could do nothing, under democracy one person or small group can. The song states, "When the world loses all its magic, when my enemy is me, when I am stabbed with nostalgia and I can hardly recognize my own voice . . . I will resist." In the end, Almodóvar compares the actual state of Spain with what he and everyone else expected from the change in democracy and criticizes the lack of progress in his movies, whether it be the social and economic state of women as in *¿Qué He Hecho Yo Para Merecer Esto!* or the brutal, continuous existence of machismo and female subordination in *¡Átame!* Almodóvar wants to remember that the Spanish should never resist in continuing to create a truly modern and progressive nation.

Works Cited

¡Átame! Internet Movie Database Inc. 27 Mar. 2007 <http://imdb.com>.

¿Qué He Hecho Yo Para Merecer Esto! Internet Movie Database Inc. 27 Mar. 2007 <http://imdb.com>.

Adelante. Dúo Dinamico. 1 Apr. 2007 <http://www.duodinamico.com/adelante.htm>.

Brandes, Stanley. "Sex Roles And Anthropological Research In Rural Andalusia." *Women's Studies* 13.4 (1987): 357–73. *Academic Search Premier.* EBSCO. Henry Birnbaum Library. 1 Mar. 2007 <http://search.ebscohost.com>.

Brogger, Jan, and David D. Gilmore. "The Matrifocal Family in Iberia: Spain and Portugal Compared." *Ethnology* 36.1 (1997): 13–31. *Academic Search Premier.* EBSCO. Henry Birnbaum Library. 26 Feb. 2007 <http://search.ebscohost.com>.

Connell, R. W. "The Big Picture: Masculinities in Recent World History." *Theory and Society* 22.5 (1993): 597–623. *Academic Search Premier.* EBSCO. Henry Birnbaum Library. 26 Feb. 2007 <http://search.ebscohost.com>.

D'Lugo, Marvin. *Pedro Almodóvar.* Ed. James Naremore. Contemporary Film Directors. Urbana: University of Illinois Press, 2006.

Esenwein, George R. "Francisco Franco." *Spain At War: The Spanish Civil War in Context, 1931–1939.* 1995. *MSN Encarta.* Microsoft Corportation. 1 Apr. 2007 <http://encarta.msn.com>.

Gilmore, David D. "Men And Women In Southern Spain: "Domestic Power" Revisited." *American Anthropologist* 92.4 (1990): 953–71. *Academic Search Premier.* EBSCO. Henry Birnbaum Library. 1 Mar. 2007 <http://search.ebscohost.com>.

Gilmore, David D. "Performative Excellence: Circum–Mediterranean." *Manhood in the Making: Cultural Concepts of Masculinity.* New Haven: Yale University Press, 1991. 30–55.

Gutmann, Matthew C. "Trafficking in Men: The Anthropology of Masculinity." *Annual Review of Anthropology* 26.1 (1997): 385–409. *Academic Search Premier.* EBSCO. Henry Birnbaum Library. 26 Feb. 2007 <http://search.ebscohost.com>.

Lara Cantú, María Asuncion. "A Sex Role Inventory with Scales for "Machismo" and "Self–Sacrificing Woman." *Journal of Cross-Cultural Psychology* 20.4 (1989): 386–98. *PsycINFO.* EBSCO. Henry Birnbaum Library. 27 Feb. 2007 <http://search.ebscohost.com>.

Mosher, Donald L., and Silvan S. Tomkins. "Scripting the Macho Man: Hypermasculine Socialization and Enculturation." *Journal of Sex Research* 25.1 (1988): 60–84. *Academic Search Premier.* EBSCO. Henry Birnbaum Library. 26 Feb. 2007 <http://search.ebscohost.com>.

Smith, Paul Julian. *Desire Unlimited: The Cinema of Pedro Almodóvar.* Critical Studies in Latin American and Iberian Cultures. London: Verso, 1994.

Sparks, Richard. "Masculinity and Heroism in the Hollywood "Blockbuster": The Culture Industry and Contemporary Images of Crime and Law Enforcement." *British Journal of Criminology* 36.3 (1996): 348–61. *Academic Search Premier.* EBSCO. Henry Birnbaum Library. 26 Feb. 2007 <http://search.ebscohost.com>.

Torres, Jose B., V. Scott H. Solberg, and Aaron H. Carlstrom. "The Myth of Sameness Among Latino Men and Their Machismo." *American Journal of Orthopsychiatry* 72.2 (2002): 163–82. *Academic Search Premier.* EBSCO. Henry Birnbaum Library. 1 Mar. 2007 <http://search.ebscohost.com>.

READING WRITING

This Text: Reading

1. How does Dushku define machismo? Is this your definition?
2. Which American director most pointedly engages or portrays ideas of machismo?
3. What do you think Ariel Levy and Pedro Almodóvar would have to say to one another?

Your Text: Writing

1. Write a short paper analyzing an action movie through the lens of masculinity.
2. Write a paper analyzing a romantic comedy through the lens of masculinity.
3. Combine the assignments of 1 and 2—which movie or even genre seems to be most concerned with reproducing stereotypical ideas of masculinity?

Photo Essay

Judith Taylor, Dolls & Mannequins

Judith Taylor's spooky but exciting photographs of dolls and mannequins offer interesting perspectives on gender and gender expectations. Magazines and billboards often teach us to see women as dolls, and Taylor's photos merely reinforce what we already know. In this short photo essay, Taylor, a poet by training, presents images not of females but of female figures and in so doing poses larger questions about bodies, women, and how we are trained to look at both.

Judith Taylor, "The Self and Others" (c 2010)

Judith Taylor, "Barbie's Eye" (c 2010)

Judith Taylor, "Incognito" (c 2010)

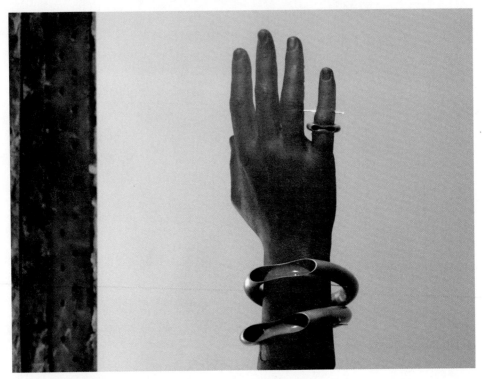

Judith Taylor, "Hand" (c 2010)

Judith Taylor, "Two Manes" (c 2010)

Judith Taylor, "Eyelashes" (c 2010)

Judith Taylor, "Wedged." (c 2010)

Judith Taylor, "Wander Woman" (c 2010)

READING **WRITING**

This Text: Reading

1. What argument do you think Taylor is trying to make by focusing on these aspects of dolls and mannequins?
2. What if Taylor had taken these very same shots of actual women and girls rather than of dolls and mannequins? How would that change your reaction to the images? What does the emphasis on *dolls* do to the project?
3. Take a look at the creepy doll photographs by Cindy Sherman from the early 1990s (*Untitled #263,Untitled #264, Untitled #302, Untitled #303*). Both photographers tend to focus on specific body parts. Why?

Your Text: Writing

1. Write an essay in which you explain what statement these photos by Taylor make about women, bodies, and how girls are trained to see both.
2. Write a comparison contrast essay on photographs by Taylor and Cindy Sherman. The Sherman photos are more overtly sexual but there is a hint of that in Taylor's images too.
3. Billboards, advertisements, and commercials teach us to objectify women's bodies. Do dolls and mannequins do this as well? Write an essay in which you explore how the practice of dressing up dolls teaches us to fetishize women's bodies.
4. Ariel Levy writes about how *Girls Gone Wild* focuses on certain parts of women's bodies. Taylor's photographs also focus on specific parts of bodies but perhaps for a different purpose. Write an essay in which you compare bodies in *GGW* and Taylor's photos.

The Third Wave Feminism Suite

Although there is no official definition or starting point of "Third Wave Feminism," most scholars place its inception in the early 1990s when a number of different writers, journalists, and critics simultaneously called into question some of the approaches of the so-called "second wave" of feminism of the 1960s and 70s. These new voices called for new notions of feminism at the end of the twentieth century. Most credit Rebecca Walker's 1992 essay about the Anita Hill/Clarence Thomas scandal in which she distances herself from previous forms of feminism by declaring, "I am the third wave" as the jumping off point for third wave feminism. Third wavers are, generally, women born in the 60s and 70s who have grown up in a world in which feminism was already part of American culture. In their 2000 book *Manifesta: Young Women, Feminism, and the Future*, Jennifer Baumgardner and Amy Richards advance a defense of contemporary "girl culture," arguing that characters like Xena, Ally McBeal, and Madonna embody the best female values—strength, determination, autonomy, liberation, and sexual freedom. Like Richards and Baumgardner, other writers and performers have argued for a more inclusive definition of feminism that allows for all kinds of femininity. For example, rap and hip-hop are often decried as sexist and demeaning, but both Bell Hooks and Eisa Davis claim those sites as locales of strong, black womanhood. Essentially, Third Wave Feminism embraces popular culture in ways previous *feminism* would have resisted; this enables new feminists to forge an individual feminism that, to them, is inclusive rather than exclusive. But there is never an uncontroversial definition of feminism, and what the term is or should be remains the topic of much and often heated discussion.

In this suite on Third Wave Feminism, we have done something unusual—we pair a professor's work with that of her students. Professor Patricia Pender has written extensively on *Buffy the Vampire Slayer*. Here, we print an essay by Dr. Pender on Buffy as a Third Wave Feminist icon. Dr. Pender also teaches a class called "Girls on Film," in which students engage films about and by women through various theoretical lenses. We include three student responses to an assignment that asks the students to look at a piece of popular culture through the lens of Third Wave Feminism.

We thought we would present some of Dr. Pender's materials for her class and paper in order for you to see the context in which these papers were prepared.

Here is a section from Dr. Pender's syllabus that explains the class's focus:

This class explores the phenomenon of "girl culture" as it has been represented in recent mainstream cinema in the United States. It examines the unlikely feminist heroines of twentieth and twenty-first century popular film; Alicia Silverstone's Cher in the classic "chick flick" Clueless, *Reese Witherspoon's rampaging Vanessa in the explosive* Freeway, *and Michelle Rodriguez's feisty Diana in Karyn Kusama's* Girl Fight. *Paying particular attention to issues of race, class, ethnicity, education, sexuality, psychology, and geography, the class will attempt to interrogate and destabilize mainstream media representations of female adolescence as predominantly white, heterosexual, and upper-middle class. We will examine recent cinematic representations of African-American (*Just Another Girl on the IRT*), Latina*

(Girlfight), *queer (All Over Me)*, *and transgender (Boys Don't Cry) adolescents,
and employ a variety of methodologies: anthropological, cinematic, psychological,
and economic.*

As part of the course, Dr. Pender requires a significant research component that culminates in a research paper that also involves an active reading of a text associated with the
class. Here were the more specific requirements:

- Focus on representations of GIRLS (not women) on FILM (including TV).
- Make sure your film is MADE and SET sometime between 1980 and now (unless
  you have talked it over with me already)
- Make explicit connections to Third Wave Feminism—either in terms of your film's
  representation of girls, its subject matter (the issues it addresses), its narrative, its
  aims, its intended audience, its reception in popular media, or a combination of
  the above.

Following are examples of completed assignments (also look at Maribeth
Theroux's paper on *NEXT* in the television chapter). In the first paper, Catherine
Kirfrides looks at *Marie Antoinette*. In the second, Lara Hayhurst writes about *Grey's
Anatomy*; and in the third, Gwendolyn Limbach looks at *Veronica Mars*. All three papers
take different approaches to the assignment, although the commonality of the subject
matter remains strong.

'Kicking Ass Is Comfort Food': Buffy as Third Wave Feminist Icon

Patricia Pender

The Third Wave Feminism Suite

*BUFFY: I love my friends. I'm very grateful for
them. But that's the price of being a Slayer . . .
I mean, I guess everyone's alone, but being a
Slayer—that's a burden we can't share.*

*FAITH: And no one else can feel it. Thank god
we're hot chicks with superpowers!*

BUFFY: Takes the edge off.

FAITH: Comforting! (Buffy the Vampire Slayer, 'End of Days')

*I definitely think a woman kicking ass is extraordinarily sexy, always . . . If I wasn't
compelled on a very base level by that archetype I wouldn't have created that character.
I mean, yes, I have a feminist agenda, but it's not like I made a chart. (Joss Whedon qtd.
in Udovitch, Rolling Stone)*

WHAT ACCOUNTS FOR THE EXTRAORDINARY FEMINIST APPEAL of the hit television series
Buffy the Vampire Slayer, and how has its ex-cheerleading, demon-hunting heroine
become the new poster girl for third wave feminist popular culture?[1] In this article

---

[1] I would like to thank the students in my Stanford class, *Girls on Film: Cultural Studies in Third Wave
Feminism,* for their creative and critical engagement with this material. Thanks also to Caitlin Delohery
and Falu Bakrania who provided invaluable comments on earlier versions of this essay.

I examine *Buffy* through the problematic lens of third wave feminism, situating the series as part of a larger cultural project that seeks to reconcile the political agenda of second wave feminism with the critique of white racial privilege articulated by women of colour and the theoretical insights afforded by poststructural analysis. I suggest that if one of the primary goals of third wave feminism is to question our inherited models of feminist agency and political efficacy, without acceding to the defeatism implicit in the notion of 'postfeminism,' then *Buffy* provides us with modes of oppositional praxis, of resistant femininity and, in its final season, of collective feminist activism that are unparalleled in mainstream television. At the same time, the series' emphasis on individual empowerment, its celebration of the exceptional woman, and its problematic politics of racial representation remain important concerns for feminist analysis. Focusing primarily on the final season of the series, I argue that season seven of *Buffy* offers a more straightforward and decisive feminist message than the show has previously attempted, and that in doing so it paints a compelling picture of the promises and predicaments that attend third wave feminism as it negotiates both its second wave antecedents and its traditional patriarchal nemeses.

'Third wave feminism' functions in the following analysis as a political ideology currently under construction. Buffy makes a similar claim about her own self-development when (invoking one of the more bizarre forms of American comfort food) she refers to herself as unformed 'cookie dough' ('Chosen' 7022). Ednie Kaeh Garrison proposes that the name 'third wave feminism' may be 'more about desire than an already existing thing' (165), and Stephanie Gilmore has suggested that, ironically, the defining feature of third wave feminism 'may well be its inability to be categorized' (218). Transforming such indeterminacy into a political principle, Rory Dicker and Alison Piepmeier state that one of the aims of their recent anthology, *Catching a Wave: Reclaiming Feminism for the 21st Century,* is to 'render problematic any easy understanding of what the third wave is' (5). While there are arguably as many variants of third wave feminism as there are feminists to claim or reject that label, the characteristics I have chosen to focus on here are those that provide the most striking parallels to *Buffy*'s season seven: its continuation of the second wave fight against misogynist violence; its negotiation of the demands for individual and collective empowerment; its belated recognition and representation of cultural diversity; and its embrace of contradiction and paradox.

Combining elements of action, drama, comedy, romance, horror, and occasionally musical, *Buffy* sits uneasily within the taxonomies of television genre. Darker than *Dawson,* and infinitely funnier than *Felicity, Buffy* was explicitly conceived as a feminist reworking of horror films in which 'bubbleheaded blondes wandered into dark alleys and got murdered by some creature' (Whedon qtd. in Fudge par. 2). From its mid-season US premiere in 1997 to its primetime series finale in 2003, the chronicles of the Chosen One have generated, in the affectionate words of its creator and director Joss Whedon, a 'rabid, almost insane fan base' (Longworth 211). Subverting the conventional gender dynamics of horror, action, and sci-fi serials, as well as the best expectations of its producers, the series has followed the fortunes of the Slayer as she has struggled through the 'hell' that is high school, a freshman year at U.C. Sunnydale, and the ongoing challenge of balancing the demands of family, friends, and relationships, and work with her inescapable duty to fight all manner of evil. As the voiceover to the show's opening credits relates: 'In every generation there is a Chosen One. She and she alone will fight the demons, the vampires and the forces of darkness. She is the Slayer.'

THE THIRD WAVE FEMINISM SUITE

Television critics and feminist scholars alike have been quick to appreciate the implicit feminist message of the series as a whole. Buffy has been celebrated as a 'radical reimagining of what a girl (and a woman) can do and be' (Byers 173); as a 'prototypical girly feminist activist' (Karras par. 15); and as a 'Hard Candy-coated feminist heroine for the girl-power era' (Fudge par. 17). Her ongoing battle with the forces of evil is seen as symbolic of several second wave feminist struggles: the challenge to balance personal and professional life (Bellafante, 'Bewitching' 83), the fight against sexual violence (Marinucci 69), and the 'justified feminist anger' young women experience in the face of patriarchal prohibitions and constraints (Helford 24). More metacritically, the series has been analysed in terms of its 'wayward' reconfiguration of the mind/body dualism (Playden 143), and its refusal of the 'inexorable logic' of binary oppositions (Pender 43). Despite the fact that the series itself has ended, the furor of attention it continues to generate both within and outside the academy assures *Buffy* an active afterlife. The last two years alone have seen an online journal, three one-day conferences, and four anthologies devoted to the burgeoning field of 'Buffy Studies' with at least another six publications, and three further conferences in the academic pipeline.[2]

But what propels such feminist fandom? What inspires this excess of affect? Rachel Fudge addresses this question directly when she writes that the impulse that propels Buffy out on patrols, 'night after night, forgoing any semblance of "normal" teenage life,' is identical to the one 'that compels us third-wavers to spend endless hours discussing the feminist potentials and pitfalls of primetime television' (par. 8). Fudge claims that Buffy 'has the sort of conscience that appeals to the daughters of feminism's second wave,' women for whom 'a certain awareness of gender and power is ingrained and inextricably linked to our sense of identity and self-esteem (par. 8). In her examination of Buffy as the third wave's 'final girl,' Irene Karras argues that Buffy's appeal lies in her intentional 'slaying [of] stereotypes about what women can and cannot do' (par. 15). Karras applauds the show's combination of sexuality and what she calls 'real efforts to make the world a better and safer place for both men and women' (par. 15). Blending an exhilarating athleticism with a compulsion to activism, Buffy's spectacular agency—her (literally) fantastic facility for kicking ass—has come to function as feminist comfort food.

When fellow Slayer Faith consoles Buffy with the thought '[t]hank god we're hot chicks with superpowers' (first epigraph), the gesture is offered as sympathy and support; it helps to 'take the edge off' the burden they 'can't share.' In this exchange, the Slayer's burden is assuaged in part by what Whedon refers to as her 'sexiness' (second epigraph); in part by the very exceptional qualities or superpowers that isolate her to begin with; and perhaps ultimately by the sharing of confidences and, by extension, of responsibilities. The 'comfort' offered here is a complex conglomerate, and one that rewards further scrutiny. The title of this chapter, 'kicking ass is comfort food,' comes from the episode 'The Prom' (3020), which occurs immediately prior to season three's apocalyptic Ascension. Buffy has just been told by her lover, Angel, that—in the event that they survive the imminent end-of-the-world—he will be abandoning their relationship and leaving town. To complicate matters, a jilted senior denied a prom date has secretly been training hellhounds to attack partygoers wearing formal attire. Buffy's mentor Giles attempts to console his devastated

---

[2] See the *Academic Buffy Bibliography,* the *Encyclopaedia of Buffy Studies* and David Lavery's '"I Wrote My Thesis on You": *Buffy* Studies as an Academic Cult.'

The particularly feminine Buffy engages in particularly masculine vampire slaying, using particularly masculine weaponry.

charge with the conventional cure for a broken heart:

GILES: Buffy, I'm sorry. I understand that this sort of thing requires ice cream of some sort.
BUFFY: Ice cream will come. First I want to take out psycho-boy.
GILES: Are you sure?
BUFFY: Great thing about being a Slayer—kicking ass is comfort food. ('The Prom')

Kicking ass becomes comfort food for Buffy when her supernatural abilities provide her with an extraordinary outlet for more conventional frustrations. Action—in this case a cathartically violent form of action—serves up a supernatural solace for a range of quotidian, human afflictions.

Kicking ass offers Buffy psychological and physical relief: it allows her to simultaneously redress straightforward social evils and to palliate more personal sorts of demons. For the feminist viewer, the spectacle of Buffy kicking ass is similarly comforting; equally, exhilarating and empowering, Buffy provides the compound pleasures of both the hot chick and her superpowers. Recent feminist critiques of the heteronormative assumptions and moral policing that underlie second wave theories of visual pleasure ensure that as feminist viewers, we too can find the spectacle of 'a woman kicking ass . . . extraordinarily sexy' (second epigraph).[3] At the same time, as Elyce Rae Helford has argued, Buffy can stand metaphorically for young women everywhere who are angered by having 'their lives directed by circumstances or individuals beyond their control' (24). In an era which can sometimes seem saturated with condemnations of feminism's increasing frivolity, Buffy's indomitable militancy—her unrelenting vigilance—can be consumed by the feminist spectator as primetime panacea. Buffy's predilection towards, and consummate abilities in, the art of kicking ass thus simultaneously soothe and sustain, and inspire and incite the compulsion to feminist activism.

While over the last seven years the series has addressed a staggering range of contemporary concerns—from the perils of low-paid, part-time employment to the erotic dynamics of addiction and recovery—it is significant that the final season of *Buffy* makes a

---

[3]For more on this see Debbie Stoller.

decisive shift back to feminist basics. Season seven eschews to a certain extent the metaphorical slipperiness and pop-cultural play that is typical of its evocation of postmodern demons and instead presents a monster that is, quite literally, an enemy of women. The principal story arc pits an amorphous antagonist, The First Evil, against the Slayer and her 'army,' a group that has swelled to include in its ranks 'Potential' Slayers from around the globe. Staging the series' final showdown with a demon that is overtly misogynist and creating an original evil with a clearly patriarchal platform, *Buffy*'s season seven raises the explicit feminist stakes of the series considerably.

Unable to take material form, The First Evil employs as its vessel and deputy a former preacher turned agent-of-evil called Caleb. Spouting hellfire and damnation with fundamentalist zeal Caleb is, of all of the show's myriad manifestations of evil, the most recognisable misogynist: 'There once was a woman. And she was foul, like all women are foul' (Dirty Girls' 7018). Dubbed 'the Reverend-I-Hate-Women' by Xander ('Touched' 7020), Caleb is a monstrous but familiar representative of patriarchal oppression, propounding a dangerous form of sexism under the cover of pastoral care. 'I wouldn't do that if I were you sweet pea,' Caleb at one point warns Buffy; 'Mind your manners. I do believe I warned you once' ('Empty Places' 7019). At other times he calls her 'girly girl' ('End of Days' 7021), a 'little lady' ('Empty Places'), and, once (but only once), 'whore' ('Touched'). Buffy's response (after kicking him across the room) is to redirect the condescension and hypocrisy couched in his discourse of paternal concern: 'You know, you really should watch your language. Someone didn't know you, they might take you for a woman-hating jerk' ('Touched'). In comparison with the supernatural demons of previous episodes, Caleb's evil might seem unusually old-fashioned or even ridiculous, but successive encounters with the Slayer underscore the fact that his power is all the more insidious and virulent for that. Mobilising outmoded archetypes of women's weakness and susceptibility—'Curiosity: woman's first sin. I offer her an apple. What can she do but take it?' ('Dirty Girls')—Caleb effectively sets a trap that threatens to wipe out the Slayer line. Within the context of the narrative, Caleb's sexist convictions—'Following is what girls do best' ('Dirty Girls')—and, more importantly, their unconscious internalisation by the Slayer and her circle pose the principal threat to their sustained, organised, collective resistance.

In its exploration of the dynamics of collective activism, *Buffy*'s final season examines the charges of solipsism and individualism that have frequently been directed at contemporary popular feminism. 'Want to know what today's chic young feminist thinkers care about?' wrote Ginia Bellafante in her notorious 1998 article for *Time* magazine: 'Their bodies! Themselves!' ('Feminism' 54). One of the greatest challenges Buffy faces in season seven is negotiating conflicting demands of individual and collective empowerment. Trapped by the mythology, propounded by the Watcher's Council, that bestows the powers of the Slayer on 'one girl in all the world,' Buffy is faced with the formidable task of training Potential Slayers-in-waiting who will only be called into their own power in the event of her death. In the episode 'Potential' (7012) Buffy attempts to rally her troops for the battle ahead:

> The odds are against us. Time is against us. And some of us will die in this battle. Decide now that it's not going to be you . . . Most people in this world have no idea why they're here or what they want to do. But you do. You have a mission. A reason for being here. You're not here by chance. You're here because you are the Chosen Ones.

This sense of vocation resonates strongly with feminist viewers who feel bound to the struggle for social justice. However, such heroism can still be a solitary rather than collective endeavour. On the eve of their final battle, after decimating her advance attack, Caleb makes fun of what he calls Buffy's 'One-Slayer-Brigade' and taunts her with the prospect of what we might think of as wasted Potential:

> None of those girlies will ever know real power unless you're dead. Now, you know the drill . . . 'Into every generation a Slayer is born. One girl in all the world. She alone has the strength and skill . . .' There's that word again. What you are, how you'll die: alone. ('Chosen' 7022)

Such references make it clear that loneliness and isolation are part of the Slayer's legacy.

Balancing the pleasures and price of her singular status, Buffy bears the burden of the exceptional woman. But the exceptional woman, as Margaret Thatcher and Condoleezza Rice have amply demonstrated, is not necessarily a sister to the cause; a certain style of ambitious woman fashions herself precisely as the exception that proves the rule of women's general incompetence. In one of the more dramatic and disturbing character developments in the series as a whole, season seven presents Buffy's leadership becoming arrogant and autocratic, and her attitude isolationist and increasingly alienated. Following in the individualist footsteps of prominent 'power feminists,' Buffy forgoes her collaborative community and instead adopts what fans in the United States and elsewhere perceived as a sort of 'You're-Either-With-Me-Or-Against-Me' moral absolutism ominously reminiscent of the Bush administration (Wilcox)—an incipient despotism exemplified by what Anya calls Buffy's 'Everyone-Sucks-But-Me' speech ('Get It Done' 7015).

The trial of Buffy's leadership is sustained up to the last possible moment, and its resolution repudiates recurring laments about the third wave's purported political apathy. 'According to the most widely publicized construction of the third wave,' describe Leslie Heywood and Jennifer Drake, '"we" hate our bodies, ourselves, our boring little lives, yet we incessantly focus on our bodies, and our boring little lives. . . . "We" believe that the glamorization of nihilism is hip and think that any hope for change is naive and embarrassing' ('We Learn America' 47). Jennifer Baumgardner and Amy Richards respond to such allegations directly when they write 'imagine how annoying it is to hear from anyone (including the media and especially Second Wave feminists) that young women aren't continuing the work of the Second Wave, that young women are apathetic, or "just don't get it"' (85). Baumgardner and Richards state that they have reacted 'by scrambling to be better feminists and frantically letting these women know how much we look up to them.' Ultimately, however, they have 'refused to accept this myth' (85).

Drawing attention to the Slayer's increasing isolation, Caleb highlights the political crisis afflicting her community, but in doing so he inadvertently alerts Buffy to the latent source of its strength, forcing her to claim a connection she admits 'never really occurred to me before' ('Chosen'). In a tactical reversal Giles claims 'flies in the face of everything . . . that every generation has ever done in the fight against evil,' Buffy plans to transfer the power of the Chosen One, the singular, exceptional woman, to the hands of the Potentials—to empower the collective not at the expense of, but by force of, the exception. In the series finale, Buffy addresses her assembled army in the following terms:

> Here's the part where you make a choice. What if you could have that power *now?* In every generation one Slayer is born, because a bunch of men who died thousands of years ago made up that rule. They were powerful men. This woman [pointing to Willow] is more powerful than all of them combined. So I say we change the rules. I say *my* power

should be *our* power. Tomorrow, Willow will use the essence of the scythe to change our destiny. From now on, every girl in the world who might be a Slayer, *will* be a slayer. Every girl who could have the power, *will* have the power. Can stand up, will stand up. Slayers—every one of us. Make your choice: are you ready to be strong? ('Chosen'; emphasis in original)

At that moment—as the archaic matriarchal power of the scythe is wrested from the patriarchal dictates of the Watcher's Council—we see a series of vignettes from around the world, as young women of different ages, races, cultures, and backgrounds sense their strength, take charge, and rise up against their oppressors. This is a 'Feel the Force, Luke' moment for girls on a global scale. It is a revolution that has been televised.

In transferring power from a privileged, white Californian teenager to a heterogeneous group of women from different national, racial, and socioeconomic backgrounds *Buffy*'s final season addresses, almost as an afterthought, the issue of cultural diversity that has been at the forefront of third wave feminist theorising. Garrison has drawn attention to the connections between Chela Sandoval's articulation of 'US Third World Feminism' and US third wave feminism, representing the latter as a movement fundamentally indebted to the feminist critique articulated by women of colour. Garrison claims that, 'unlike many white feminists in the early years of the Second Wave who sought to create the resistant subject "women," in the Third Wave, the figure "women" is rarely a unitary subject' (149). This understanding of third wave feminism is borne out by Baumgardner and Richards, who argue that 'the third wave was born into the diversity realized by the latter part of the second wave,' a diversity represented by the works of African American and Chicana feminists, Third World feminists of colour, and US Third World feminists (77). Heywood and Drake make the third wave's debts to Third World feminism explicit when they state that the arguments that women of colour scholars introduced into the dominant feminist paradigms in the 1980s 'have become the most powerful forms of feminist discourse in the 1990s' ('We Learn America' 49). They claim that while third wave feminism owes 'an enormous debt to the critique of sexism and the struggles for gender equity that were white feminism's strongest provinces, it was U.S. Third World feminism that modeled a language and a politics of hybridity that can account for our lives at the century's turn' (Introduction 13).

From some of its earliest incarnations academic third wave feminism has presented itself as a movement that places questions of diversity and difference at the centre of its theoretical and political agenda. However, as Stacy Gillis and Rebecca Munford have pointed out, the 'extent to which third wave feminism has learned how to incorporate, rather than to exclude' (5) remains an issue for ongoing concern. Examining what she sees as the serious limitations of predominantly Western third wave feminism, Winifred Woodhull warns that the third wave risks repeating the exclusionary errors of earlier feminist practices. 'Given the global arena in which third wave feminism emerges,' she writes, 'it is disappointing that new feminist debates arising in first-world contexts address issues that pertain only to women *in* those contexts' (6; emphasis in original). Woodhull claims that the significance and potential of third wave feminism 'can be grasped only by adopting a global interpretive frame, that is, by relinquishing the old frameworks of the west and developing new ones that take seriously the struggles of women the world over' (6). In its most rigorous and responsible guise, then, third wave feminism's call for cultural diversity is the political response to the critique of white racial privilege articulated by second wave feminists of colour, and the theoretical consequence of incorporating the discourse of difference elaborated by poststructural theory more broadly. In its less careful incarnations, as *Buffy* demonstrates admirably, it can perform the very strategies of occlusion and erasure that its more critical proponents are at pains to redress.

Buffy's racial politics are inarguably more conservative than its gender or sexual politics, a situation pithily summarised by one of the few recurring black characters of the show's first three seasons, Mr. Trick: 'Sunnydale' . . . admittedly not a haven for the brothers—strictly the Caucasian persuasion in the Dale' ('Faith, Hope, and Trick' 3003). While the final season of the show has seen an expansion of *Buffy*'s exclusively white, middle-class cast with the introduction of character Principal Robin Wood and the international expansion of the Slayer line, such changes can easily be dismissed as mere tokenism. Season seven makes repeated recourse to racial stereotypes—most notably in its primitivist portrayal of the 'First Slayer' and the 'Shadow Men' as ignoble savages, and its use of formulaic markers of cultural difference to distinguish the international Slayers. As Gayle Wald has warned in a slightly different context, feminist scholarship must be wary of uncritically reproducing simplistically celebratory readings of popular culture that focus on gender performance 'as a privileged site and source of political oppositionality,' in which 'critical questions of national, cultural, and racial appropriation can be made to disappear' (590). A critical analysis *of Buffy*'s racial representations need not be considered a critique of the palpable pleasures provided by the show but rather, as Wald suggests, 'a critique of the production of pleasure through gendered and racialized narratives that signify as new, transgressive, or otherwise exemplary' (595).

In extending the Slayer's powers to young girls across the globe, *Buffy*'s season seven can be seen to begin to redress—albeit belatedly and incompletely—the national, cultural and racial privilege the show has assumed through its seven-year cycle. Bringing ethnic diversity and racial difference to the Slayer story, a generous reading of *Buffy*'s finale might see it as an exemplary narrative of transnational feminist activism. A more critical reading might see it as yet another chapter in a long, repetitive story of US imperialism. I would suggest that these readings are not as inimical as they might initially seem; season seven's narrative implies that both of these readings are admissible, perhaps even mutually implicated. In her analysis of what she calls 'the globalization of Buffy's power,' for instance, Rhonda Wilcox has argued that '*Buffy* be seen as both a metaphor for and an enactment of globalization,' one that contemplates both its negative and positive aspects. Wilcox claims that the series celebrates capitalist institutions such as the mall at the same time that it recognises and critiques the 'cultural presumption' inherent in the idea of 'all-American domination of the world . . . through the spread of technological goods and through governmental aggression.' Similarly, I would suggest that the idealised vision of universal sisterhood with which *Buffy* concludes needs to be read against the immediate political context in which its final season is screened; a context that illuminates some of the same gestures of cultural imperialism that the series elsewhere successfully critiques. *Buffy*'s celebration of what is effectively an international military alliance under ostensibly altruistic American leadership demands special scrutiny in our current political climate. In the context of the indefensible arrogance of Bush's 'War on Terror' and the spurious universalism of his 'Coalition of the Willing,' *Buffy*'s final gesture of international inclusivity is imbued with unwittingly inauspicious overtones.

It would be a mistake, I think, to underestimate or to collapse too quickly the contradictions embedded in *Buffy*'s cultural politics, contradictions that are in turn indicative of the crosscurrents that distinguish the third wave of feminism. The refusal of misogynist violence, the battle against institutionalised patriarchy, and the potential of transnational feminist activism are issues that remain at the forefront of the third wave agenda, and themes that *Buffy*'s final season explores with characteristically challenging and satisfying complexity. The fact that its success in critiquing its own cultural privilege is equivocal should be read less as a straightforward sign of failure than as a reflection of the redoubtable contradictions that characterise third wave feminism itself. Fudge has suggested that *Buffy* 'constantly treads the fine line between girl-power schlock and feminist wish-fulfillment, never giving satisfaction to either one' (par. 17). Adopting one of the signature rhetorical and political strategies of feminism's third wave, *Buffy* has consistently welcomed such apparent contradiction with open arms. I suggest that in its examination of individual and collective empowerment, in its ambiguous politics of racial representation, and its willing embrace of contradiction, *Buffy* is a quintessentially third wave cultural production. Providing a fantastic resolution—in both senses of the word—to some of the many dilemmas confronting third wave feminists today, *Buffy* is comfort food for girls who like to have their cake and eat it too.

Works Cited

Academic Buffy Bibliography. Ed. Derik A. Badman. 20 Apr. 2003. 22 Sept. 2003. <http://madinkbeard.com/buffy/index.html>.

Baumgardner, Jennifer, and Amy Richards. *Manifesta: Young Women, Feminism, and the Future.* New York: Farrar, Straus and Giroux, 2000.

Bellafante, Ginia. 'Bewitching Teen Heroines.' *Time* 5 May 1997. 82–85.

———. 'Feminism: It's All About Me.' *Time* 29 June 1998. 54–62.

Buffy the Vampire Slayer. By Joss Whedon. Perf. Sarah Michelle Gellar, Alyson Hannigan, and Nicholas Brandon. Twentieth Century Fox, 1997–2003.

Byers, Michelle. 'Buffy the Vampire Slayer: The Next Generation of Television.' *Catching a Wave: Reclaiming Feminism for the 21st Century.* Ed. Rory Dicker and Alison Piepmeier. Boston: Northeastern UP, 2003. 171–187.

Dicker, Rory, and Alison Piepmeier. Introduction. *Catching a Wave: Reclaiming Feminism for the 21st Century.* Ed. Rory Dicker and Alison Piepmeier. Boston: Northeastern UP, 2003. 3–28.

Encyclopaedia of Buffy Studies. Ed. David Lavery and Rhonda V. Wilcox, I May 2003.

Slayage: The Online Journal of Buffy Studies. 22 Sept. 2003. <http://www.slayage.tv/EBS>.

Fudge, Rachel. 'The Buffy Effect: Or, A Tale of Cleavage and Marketing.' *Bitch: Feminist Responses to Popular Culture* 10 (1999). 20 June 2000. <http://www.bitchmagazine.com/archives/08_01/buffy/buffy.htm>.

Garrison, Ednie Kaeh. 'U.S. Feminism–Girl Style! Youth (Sub)Cultures and the Technologics of the Third Wave.' *Feminist Studies* 26.1 (2000): 141–170.

Gillis, Stacy, and Rebecca Munford. 'Harvesting Our Strengths: Third Wave Feminism and Women's Studies.' *Third Wave Feminism and Women's Studies.* Ed. Stacy Gillis and Rebecca Munford. Spec, issue of *Journal of International Women's Studies* 4.2 (2003). <http://www.bridgew.edu/SoAS/jiws/April03/>.

Gilmore, Stephanie. 'Looking Back, Thinking Ahead: Third Wave Feminism in the United States.' *Journal of Women's History* 12.4 (2001): 215–221.

Helford, Elyce Rae. '"My Emotions Give Me Power": The Containment of Girls' Anger in *Buffy*.' *Fighting the Forces: What's at Stake in* Buffy the Vampire Slayer. Ed. Rhonda Wilcox and David Lavery. Lanham: Rowman and Littlefield, 2002. 18–34.

Heywood, Leslie, and Jennifer Drake. Introduction. *Third Wave Agenda: Being Feminist, Doing Feminism.* Ed. Leslie Heywood and Jennifer Drake. Minneapolis: Minnesota UP, 1997. 1–20.

———. 'We Learn America Like a Script: Activism in the Third Wave; Or, Enough Phantoms of Nothing.' *Third Wave Agenda: Being Feminist, Doing Feminism.* Ed. Leslie Heywood and Jennifer Drake. Minneapolis: Minnesota UP, 1997. 40–54.

Karras, Irene. 'The Third Wave's Final Girl: *Buffy the Vampire Slayer.*' *Thirdspace* 1.2 (2002). <http://www.thirdspace.ca/articles/karras.htm>.

Lavery, David. "'I Wrote My Thesis on You": *Buffy* Studies as an Academic Cult.' Sonic Synergies/Creative Cultures Conf. University of South Australia, Adelaide. 21 July 2003.

Longworth Jr, James L. 'Joss Whedon: Feminist.' *TV Creators: Conversations with America's Top Producers of Television Drama.* Ed. James L. Longworth Jr. Syracuse: Syracuse UP, 2000.197–220.

Marinucci, Mimi. 'Feminism and the Ethics of Violence: Why Buffy Kicks Ass.' Buffy the Vampire Slayer *and Philosophy: Fear and Trembling in Sunnydale.* Ed. James B. South. Chicago: Open Court, 2003. 61–75.

Pender, Patricia. "'I'm Buffy and You're . . . History": The Postmodern Politics of *Buffy the Vampire Slayer.' Fighting the Forces: What's at Stake in* Buffy the Vampire Slayer. Ed. Rhonda Wilcox and David Lavery. Lanham: Rowman and Littlefield, 2002. 35–44.

Playden, Zoe-Jane. "'What You Are, What's to Come": Feminisms, Citizenship and the Divine.' *Reading the Vampire Slayer: An Unofficial Critical Companion to Buffy and Angel.* Ed. Roz Kaveney. London: Tauris Parke, 2002. 120–147.

Stoller, Debbie. 'Introduction: Feminists Fatale: BUST-ing the Beauty Myth.' *The BUST Guide to the New Girl Order.* Ed. Marcelle Karp and Debbie Stoller. New York: Penguin, 1999. 42–47.

Udovitch, Mim. 'What Makes Buffy Slay? *Rolling Stone*, July 2000. 40–41, 110.

Wald, Gayle. 'Just a Girl? Rock Music, Feminism, and the Cultural Construction of Female Youth.' *Signs: Journal of Women in Culture and Society* 23.3 (1998): 585–610.

Wilcox, Rhonda. "'Show Me Your World": Exiting the Text and the Globalization of *Buffy.*' Staking a Claim: Global Buffy, Local Identities Conf. University of South Australia, Adelaide. 22 July 2003.

Woodhull, Winifred. 'Global Feminisms, Transnational Political Economies, Third World Cultural Production.' *Third Wave Feminism and Women's Studies.* Ed. Stacy Gillis and Rebecca Munford. Spec. issue of *Journal of International Women's Studies* 4.2 (2003). <http://www.bridgew.edu/SoAS/jiws/April03/>.

Classically Different: Sofia Coppola's *Marie Antoinette* Takes a New Look at What It Means to Be a Girl

Catherine Kirifides

Student Essay

CROWDS GATHER, TOMATOES ARE THROWN and angry expletives are yelled in French at one young girl. Surprisingly enough this is not 1793, but 2006 and the anger is directed at Sofia Coppola whose new film *Marie Antoinette* has just been unveiled at the Cannes Film Festival. The reaction of the French people to this revisionist take on the famed teen queen binds Coppola to her main character due to the perception of Coppola as a foreign girl with status.

Like the general French public, critics pulverized Coppola's newest film for being historically inaccurate, cheesy, and mere pop fluff. "A case of never mind the history books," many have wondered, "why Coppola is bothering with reality if she's going to be so cursory about it" (Gilbey 1). These accusations came as a shock considering the young Coppola's track record of feature films, which include *The Virgin Suicides* and *Lost in Translation.* Both films dealt with heavy issues of adolescence and were heralded for their seriousness and complexity. The impression, on the other hand, of *Antoinette* as "silly fizz makes it simpler and less creepy than her [Coppola's] earlier projects" claimed *The New*

Yorker, though the opening sequence was "codified to death" (Lane 3, 1). How is it that Sofia Coppola, the golden child of Hollywood greatness, could possibly have made such a shallow film? Considering Coppola's past films and the subject matter she most likes to explore—adolescent girls—one must come to the conclusion that there is a rhyme and reason as to why *Marie Antoinette* was made the way it was. Coppola doesn't seem like a girl who makes mistakes.

Though the film does take on a more teen pop feel than her earlier works, from the cinematography to the costuming and editing, form still follows function. The pop feel of the production is used to magnify Antoinette's parallel to contemporary girlhood. These artistic decisions reflect Coppola's portrayal of Antoinette as a young vibrant girl who is discovering a new world, and growing up in it, throughout the course of the film. Focusing on Antoinette's youth, Coppola highlights the generational differences between the young Queen and her mother and other ladies at court. By being thrust into an adult life at an early age, Coppola's Antoinette tries to recapture her childhood through her more radical behavior. Coppola asks if the negative connotation of the name Marie Antoinette is justified. Based on Antonia Fraser's biography *Marie Antoinette: The Journey,* Coppola has written and directed a tale that looks at the iconic queen for what she truly was: merely a girl.

Barbara Amiel writes that Marie Antoinette's life "took place at a punctuation mark in history" (2). Coppola's film shows us a girl who did not only just happen to be at the wrong place at the wrong time, but one who challenged the norm and the institutions of the time. Though she ended up on the chopping block, Coppola's Antoinette is depicted as a rebel and a revolutionary—just not in the patriotic sense. By highlighting the generational differences between Antoinette and her mother, Empress Maria Teresa of Austria, we see how this young girl was, in a way, bucking the system. Maria Teresa said, the year Marie Antoinette was born, "They are born to obey and must learn to do so in good time" (Fraser 21). The film is narrated some of the time by the voice of Maria Teresa, as she reads pieces from the constant correspondence she kept with her youngest daughter. Like the ominous voice from above, Maria Teresa's words truly affect young Antoinette. Whether we see her try and brush off her mother's advice by diving into the French ways of doing things (for which she is being reprimanded), or slowly sink to the ground because of them, we have to take into account the fact that her mother's word and opinion has great influence over her. After one such letter from her mother Antoinette states, "Letting everyone down would be my greatest unhappiness." This need to seek approval from the women around her, and the depression the lack of this approval leads to, is very similar to the dynamic girls today have with the 2nd wave feminists many of their mothers were.

Unable to totally conform to all the rules of etiquette that Versailles required, Antoinette is depicted as someone who is constantly fighting against the older regime of royalty and prestige. The film begins with Antoinette's passage from Austria to France, showing the young girl's open compassion for her ladies in waiting, dog, and mother. She is met with an intrigued coldness by the French for this display of affection when she hugs goodbye and hello to the people around her. After arriving at Versailles she is watched by everyone and we see her engaging in easy conversation with the children around her. This fondness and ease with children foreshadows her future woes in motherhood as well as the fact that there were not many people remotely close to her age at court. Coppola also made the artistic decision to have Antoinette's close circle of friends and admirers of the young and beautiful persuasion (which is not historically correct) in order to further highlight this generational difference. Antoinette's relationship with her husband's (the dauphin, Louis Auguste) aunts is another of woman/girl strain. Unable to understand Antoinette's disinclination for intrigue and pompous etiquette, they first mock her and then try to make her the elitist queen they wish her to be. They eventually gain influence over the young girl by coaxing her to snub the king's mistress, Du Barry, who also flouts the rules of etiquette at court. Once the aunts' influence causes Antoinette trouble, she is reprimanded by her mother, she resorts to her own ways of handling people and situations. This helps in winning over the king and her husband, but hurts her in terms of friends she later makes and promotes. Antoinette is seen as a girl who is being pulled between the older generation's ways of how to gain power as a woman and how she wants to enjoy her own life. As her mother states, "Everything depends on the wife, if she is willing and sweet [. . .] never ill humor," showcasing the mentality of the older generation of women about a woman's duty, place, and influence.

Since Coppola's film generally focuses on the issue of girlhood and what it means to grow up in a specific time period, it is very telling that she chose this girl and this time. "I didn't set out on a campaign to correct the misperceptions about her; I just wanted to tell the story from her point of view," said Coppola in an interview. "I was struck by the fact that Louis and Marie were teenagers—in charge of France at the most vulnerable time in its history" (Covington 2). Highlighting Antoinette's rebellion of serious adulthood, we see her life as the flash of intoxicating glamour and fun that whirls about and that "her royal privilege is to get lost in the superficial pleasure of the moment" (Johnson 2). Coppola condenses many years of Antoinette's life, mixing up the order of events, to give us the feeling that everything was happening to the young

Kirsten Dunst as Marie; Marie as both girl and woman.

girl all at once. This consolidation of facts allows us to see the essence of her life and some of the more interesting events in it, rather than the hum drum of day to day court life. This long and tedious existence is seen by the pacing and cinematography Coppola employs in the first thirty minutes of the film. Gradually speeding up the very monotonous start to the film, the days fly by until Antoinette takes her life, or at least amusement, into her own hands. When you are sent away to be married at 14, don't consummate that marriage until age 21 and become queen of France at 18 you inevitably skip the most important time of female adolescence. This teen adolescence age is when most girls are just discovering who they are and are coping with low self-esteem, personality changes, and responsibility. Antoinette was forced to act like an adult, with no questions or wavering allowed. This stifled childhood leads to a rebellion expressed in all things girly and childish. Most girls are deemed women once they are married, have sex and children, and have a job (i.e. being queen). Antoinette refuses all of those factors and ferociously throws herself into fashion, the arts, and game playing. Always acting for her own amusement, Antoinette has no other knowledge of what life is like outside of her bubble. The extravagance associated with Antoinette is excused by the fact that "her actions would have been excessive or greedy only if she had had no sense of entitlement and believed herself to be getting away with something [. . .] She did her best at what she was supposed to do, being the leader of French style" (Amiel 5). These elements of Antoinette's influence and role in society, as well as her extravagance, are all addressed in Coppola's film.

Coppola drives home (through editing) the idea that Antoinette's fling into fashion and other stereotypical simple female pleasures are a result of her unhappiness in her pseudo-adult life. By juxtaposing scenes of domestic inadequacy and frustration with those of pleasure, we see the extremes that dominated Antoinette's life. The contrasting looks and forms of each type of scene help to highlight this difference. The dark and naturally lit scene where Antoinette is rebuffed in bed by Louis' "I'm exhausted" is directly followed by the sequence showing the fast paced life of riding, parties, and unfixed movement. Similarly, after Antoinette's sister-in-law gives birth, we see Antoinette's masked unhappiness and despair as she cries curled up in a ball of the floor of her apartment's back room. There isn't a more telling action to show a child who feels she's failed. This muted painful image directly cuts to the montage showing extravagant shoes, drink, food, and gambling to the music of "I Want Candy." With the heightened coloring and pace, Coppola's implication is, "Can't have a baby? Buy some shoes and get drunk." This escapist behavior is one way to look at Antoinette's excessive spending and flagrant personality.

How Coppola deals with Marie Antoinette's iconic image is very telling of her own experiences. All of Coppola's films have been said to have some autobiographical thread to them. Antoinette's wealth, family privilege, and youthful age while she makes a name for herself produce a compelling parallel with Coppola's life. Coppola has practically worked on films since she came out of the womb (she first appeared on film as the baby boy in the christening scene in her father's film *The Godfather*), been given chances to try many different aspects of her field (she has a clothing label, done camerawork and costume design, writes, directs, and acts), and has been heralded as a young genius. "It is, perhaps, this combination of celebrity status, privilege and talent that causes some to regard Sofia Coppola's achievements with ambivalence," writes Pam Cook (36). Born into "her own bubble of Hollywood royalty" (Johnson 2), in the extravagant 1980s, we can see her cloistered childhood as paralleling Antoinette's, which stylistically evokes the pastel frippery, obscene spending, and punk music of the 1980s. Besides this personal comparison, there is much to be said for the Paris Hilton like quality Coppola gives to Antoinette. She is portrayed as a socialite who doesn't know any better (in terms of how much she is spending and how ridiculously opulent her lifestyle is). Antoinette breaks the norm of what is expected of a proper queen of her role and stature, is dragged through the dirt by the paparazzi and tabloids, has a tight clique of other socialite friends, and even carries her dog around as if it's the latest fashion accessory. The cute blondeness and pouty look of Kirsten Dunst (who plays Antoinette, and is a Hollywood child star herself) only helps to highlight the similarities between Hilton and Antoinette, socialite sisters 200+ years apart. The stereotypical connection between Antoinette and twenty-first century socialites is an unfavorable one. Amiel addresses this connection by saying, "In modern usage, the name Marie Antoinette has become the negative sobriquet of the female consumer gone mad" (2). The negative reputation today's socialites have hits a familiar chord with audiences (mainly adolescent girls) as they watch *Antoinette*. Coppola doesn't seem to be disregarding the possible validity of some of these tabloid accusations. With the "unembarrassed devotion to the superficial" (Lane 2) elitist clique Antoinette kept around her and the flagrant disregard for politics, Coppola gives us material to decide for ourselves about Antoinette's personality. Contrarily, Coppola justifies many of the queen's extravagant actions by showing Antoinette's unhappy life and naiveté, claiming she kept her characters, "in this bubble, because none of them realized what was going on outside their world" (Johnson 2). Overall the statement that these girls are being judged extremely harshly due to their presence in the spotlight, which they were born into, is being made. The film forces the viewer to re-examine the situation and decide for themselves how much of Antoinette's bad PR was of her own doing, and how much was unfairly attributed to her. Seen as a purposefully sympathetic image of the queen by some, Amiel claims that the film's main point is to show us, "Whether it is the 18th century or the 21st, the same pitfalls await anyone who achieves any sort of social prominence" (5).

The way in which we view the socially prominent is an important factor in the film. Image, the creation and destruction of it, is commented on continually. The portrait of Antoinette and her children in the garden by Adolf Ulrik von Wertmüller is recreated in the film. This portrait was considered "unflattering and insufficiently formal," showcasing the royal family in plainer clothing and less reserved positioning (Fraser 296–297 insert). Also shown in the film is the more austere and famous portraits of the royal family and Antoinette by Louise-Elisabeth Vigée-Lebrun. The portraits are utilized as a device to illustrate the passage of time, events, and the changing sentiments towards the queen. We see the image of Antoinette as the solitary object in the film frame. Only the banners with slogans "Beware of Deficit," "Queen of Debt," and "Spending France into Ruin" change throughout the shot, marking how the image of the queen is perceived by onlookers. The personal life of the queen is also determined through images of her. The painting out of Antoinette's fourth child (third in the film version) in the Lebrun family portrait is shown to convey the passage of time and familial events as the public would have seen them. Through using the iconic portraits of the queen, we catch a glimpse of how the *image* of Marie Antoinette plays into this story.

The image, and the use of it, is very important since we are first and foremost discussing a visual representation of a historical figure, and not fact. As her mother warns in the film, "all eyes will be on you." Much of Antoinette's life was just that, watched. Antoinette described this life as a voyeur's subject in a 1770 letter when she stated, "I put my rouge on and wash my hands in front of the whole world." She was watched as she got dressed, went to church, ate, walked around her home and even gave birth. In the film, we see the famed incident where Antoinette is left standing naked for several minutes because new and more prestigious courtiers kept entering her chambers and the etiquette of who got the privilege to dress her had to be upheld. To this, Antoinette states, "This is ridiculous," and the Comtesse des Noailles retorts, "This is Versailles." The dinner ceremonies where courtiers and guests were allowed to walk by and watch the royal family eat is also depicted several times in the film. As time progresses we get the sense that Antoinette is starting to get used to this constant attention, but never as much as her husband who can furiously eat despite the confines of strict etiquette while Antoinette merely picks at her food.

Antoinette inevitably flouts this, and other standards of etiquette at Versailles, by hosting private gatherings and "handing out meats to a hunting party." Most representative of these rule-breaking behaviors is Antoinette's use of the Petit Trianon at Versailles. Although the actual time and reason she made this her second home is muddled in the film, what this place represented to Antoinette and to the public is much more important. The root of Antoinette's desire for the Petit Trianon is due to the simple fact that "She wanted a domain reserved for her intimate circle of friends" (Covington 4). In the film, we see Antoinette's love for the retreat as related to a longing for a more casual setting which she has dominion over. She plays with her daughter there, picking flowers and strawberries. The facade of this being a casual place is illustrated in the film by a scene which shows servants cleaning the chicken eggs before Antoinette takes her daughter to find them. The Petit Trianon was also the setting for many of the tabloid exploits of Antoinette. By cloistering herself off even more from the world, she had free reign to do and act as she pleased. This access to freedom is seen as a chance for wrongdoing by much of the eighteenth century press who imagined orgies, seduction, and extravagant parties at the Petit Trianon. This portion of the film is also representative of a shift in Antoinette's personality. The Petit Trianon sequence starts after she becomes a mother and we see Antoinette take pleasure in the seemingly more simple way of life. She is seen reading Rousseau to her friends asking, "What is the natural state?" as they sit in the garden in their new romantic frock dresses which, "suited Marie Antoinette's romantic idea of a simplified life" (Fraser 176). This is a contrast from her earlier character who asked, "Which sleeve do you like; with ruffles or without?" during a political briefing.

Another way Coppola uses Antoinette's disregard for etiquette is as an indictor of the public opinion of her. A scene in which Antoinette claps at the opera (which Princess de Lamballe tells her "is not usually permitted at court appearances") and everyone in the crowd happily follows her example is later juxtaposed by her acting in the same manner, though she is met with cold silence the second time. Her ability to pioneer trends, fashion, or behavior is diminishing as her rule-breaking is seen as menacing rather than refreshing.

For all of its controversy and extravagance, what exactly is Sofia Coppola trying to say with her rendition of *Marie Antoinette*? She seems not merely to be painting a more sympathetic picture of the famed queen, but to be looking closely at the girl, and what it means to be one. Exploring the allure of close female friends and safe home spaces, signified by the Petit Trianon and the de Polignac crowd, Coppola maintains an ambivalent attitude about the relationships between Antoinette and her closest friends, the Princess de Lamballe and Comtesse de Polignac. History and gossip has called them evil, lovers, and meddlesome females, but Coppola looks at them like a high school clique. The claiming and owning one's sexuality, which we see Antoinette do once she meets Count Fersen, is also a rite of passage for girls that most of society today still ignores. Coppola comments on the many ways women employ their time and resources by showing the extravagance of the shopping and beauty industries but also shows the joy it can bring as well. Power for girls is gained in this film through strong and pleasing personalities, malicious gossip and truthful exchanges, learning to play by the rules and by breaking them. Ironically, it is Coppola's refusal of the gravitas that historical dramas usually command that makes her revisionist version of Marie Antoinette as subversive and revolutionary as the girl she's portraying. This fluffier way of looking at history entices market audiences (i.e. teenage girls) and gives them something to relate to. Whether she gets the critics on her side or not, Coppola has succeeded in looking at a historical figure from a new perspective—that of the girl. Echoed by Antoinette to her newborn daughter, Coppola's *Marie Antoinette* tells us, "Poor little girl. You were not what was desired, but you are no less dear to me."

Works Cited

Amiel, Barbara. "Misunderstood Marie Antoinette." *Maclean's* 119 (2006): 48–50. Academic Search Premier. Pace U Lib., New York, NY. 24 Jan. 2007 <http://web.ebscohost.com/>.

Cook, Pam. "Portrait of a Lady: Sofia Coppola." *Sight & Sound* 16 (2006): 36–40. Academic Search Premier. Pace U Lib., New York, NY. 24 Jan. 2007 <http://ebscohost.com/>.

Covington, Richard. "Marie Antoinette." *Smithsonian* 37 (2006): 56–65. Academic Search Premier. Pace U Lib., New York, NY. 24 Jan. 2007 <http://ebscohost.com/>.

Doane, Mary Anne. *Femmes Fatales: Feminism, Film Theory, Psychoanalysis.* New York, London: Routledge, 1991.

Drake, Jennifer, and Leslie Heywood. "Introduction." *Third Wave Agenda.* Minneapolis: U of Minnesota P, 1997. 1–20.

———. "We Learn America Like a Script: Activism in the Third Wave; or, Enough Phantoms of Nothing." *Third Wave Agenda.* Minneapolis: University of Minnesota Press, 1997. 40–54.

Fraser, Antonia. *Marie Antoinette: The Journey.* New York, London: Random House, 2001.

Gilbey, Ryan. "Never Mind the Bastille, Here's a Sexy Picture." *New Statesman* 23 Oct. 2006: 43.

Grossberger, Lewis. "Film Rouge." *Media Week* 16 (2006): 13–13. Communication & Mass Media Complete. Pace U Lib. New York, NY. 24 Jan. 2007 <http://ebscohost.com/>.

Gussow, Mel. "A Resolute Biographer and a Kinder, Gentler Antoinette." *The New York Times* 4 Sept. 2001: E1.

Harris, Anita. "Introduction." *All About the Girl: Culture, Power, and Identity.* Taylor & Francis, Routledge, 2004. xvii–xxv.

Heyman, Marshall. "Kirsten." *W* Apr. 2007: 256–267.

Johnson, Brian D. "Sex and the City in Versailles." *Maclean's* 119 (2006): 72–72. Academic Search Premier. Pace U Lib., New York, NY. 24 Jan. 2007 <http://ebscohost.com/>.

Lane, Anthony. "Lost in the Revolution." *New Yorker* 82 (2006): 93–95. Academic Search Premier. Pace U Lib., New York, NY. 24 Jan. 2007 <http://ebscohost.com/>.

Mantel, Hilary. "The Perils of Antoinette." *New York Review of Books* 54 (2007): 59–63. Academic Search Premier. Pace U Lib., New York, NY. 24 Jan. 2007 <http://ebscohost.com/>.

Marie Antoinette. Dir. Sofia Coppola. Perf. Kirsten Dunst, Jason Schwartzman. DVD, 2006. Columbia Pictures, Sony Pictures, 2007.

Pastor, Jennifer et al. "Makin' Homes: An Urban Girl Thing." *Urban Girls: Resisting Stereotypes, Creating Identities.* Ed. Leadbeater, B.J.R., and N. Way. New York: New York UP, New York, 1996. 15–34.

Phillips, Lynn. *The Girls Report: What We Know & Need to Know About Growing Up Female.* New York: National Council for Research on Women, 1998.

Vigée-Lebrun, Louise-Elisabeth. *Marie Antoinette, aged twenty-eight.* 1783. Bridgeman Art Library, Versailles. *Marie Antoinette: The Journey.* By Antonia Fraser. New York: Doubleday. 296–297, second picture.

———. *The Queen with Three of Her Children.* 1787. Giraudon/Bridgeman Art Library, Versailles. *Marie Antoinette: The Journey.* By Antonia Fraser. New York: Doubleday. 360–361, second picture.

von Wertmüller, Adolf Ulrik. *The Queen with Her Children in the Park of the Trianon.* 1784. National Museum, Stockholm/Bridgeman Art Gallery, Versailles. *Marie Antoinette: The Journey.* By Antonia Fraser. New York: Doubleday. 296–297, ninth picture.

How I Wrote This Essay Catherine Kirifides

Why did you write this piece—what was the assignment or motivation for writing?

I wrote this piece as an assignment for my university class entitled "Girls on Film." The directions were to write a paper on any TV show or film created after 1980, discussing its girl characters/participants and how they related to third wave feminism.

What did you do when you got the assignment?

Since the assignment was open to many options in terms of what I could write about, I thought of my favorite TV shows and films and tried to find an interesting angle in relation to third wave feminism. Are the characters positive or do they reinforce a negative stereotype of girls? Do I want to write about something I feel needs to change, or a show I want to promote? Thinking practically, I also took into account what topics would give me enough information to write a 10 to 15 page paper on.

How did you begin?

Once I had decided to write about *Marie Antoinette*, and got permission from my professor to do a non-contemporary figure, I made a list of how this film depicted Antoinette as a type of girl feminist. Once I had a basis for my paper I searched for varying articles and references I could use to support my points about Coppola's Antoinette as a radical and feminist girl figure.

Describe the process of writing the first draft.

The way I create first drafts is to free write my thoughts and points I want to include in the paper. After this skeleton structure is formed, I go back and add in the references and cited information that support my argument. Next, I edit through the entire piece working to fuse the opinions with the references to create a cohesive voice and varying language structure. Essentially there are multiple drafts before I end up with the official "first draft" I submit.

Did you write a draft all the way through?

I free wrote a skeleton draft in one sitting that included my main points and opinions, and worked from there.

How much editing did you do as you wrote?

I didn't edit my original free write, but edited many times over as I reworked the draft into an acceptable form to turn in.

Did you do research as you wrote or before you started writing? What databases did you use?

I researched both as I wrote and before I started writing. Before writing I did minor research on databases such as Academic Search Primer, Google Scholar, and Lexis-Nexis to find what types of research I could find to support my points. During writing I looked more thoroughly into these databases to find articles from a variety of sources and mediums.

How long would you say the process took?

Completing my first draft probably took about two weeks. Since it was an assignment (and a final paper worth a large percentage of my grade) there were deadlines for paper ideas, the first draft, and the final paper. I believe I had about three to four weeks for the whole process.

How did you edit the draft?

First I edited the draft for content, then grammar and spelling, then for tone and flow. Once I was content with the paper, I edited it again for content and detail to make sure I was using every word to its fullest.

What was the response when you turned in your essay?

The response to my first draft was mainly that I needed to cut and focus my thoughts on fewer moments in the film. I have a tendency to get very interested in a topic and want to write all about it. My first draft was probably about five to ten pages too long. My professor did like my references to technical cinematic elements as well as to the narrative but pointed out places I was either getting too technical, or not reiterating the "third wave feminism" topic enough which was key to our class and assignment. The response to my final paper was positive overall and I was prompted by my professor to submit to this textbook.

Are you satisfied now with what you wrote? Would you make any changes?

I'm basically satisfied with what I wrote. Re-reading the paper now, I like the points I made but would probably rework sections. I'd concentrate on smoothing out the inconsistent tone and making some sentences more clear and descriptive.

Putting the "Me" Back in Medical Drama: *Grey's Anatomy's* Adventures in McFeminism

Lara Hayhurst

Student Essay

FEMINISM'S THIRD WAVE longs to use popular culture and the media as a weapon of empowerment for women rather than an obstacle hindering their progression. The Third Wave propagates itself as not just a compromise between strident Second Wave ideals and the gutted superficiality of the Girlie Feminism movement, but as its own, progressive breed of feminism that is integrated, inclusive, open-minded, and tangible to all females. With this in mind, analyzing specific cultural productions that should ideally be serving as Weapons of Female Empowerment is an important exercise. Television holds an important place in our contemporary media, and by analyzing a television show with a large female viewership, such as *Grey's Anatomy*, that also quietly promotes itself as a progressive and feminist piece of pop culture, we can determine if this part of contemporary media and television is beneficial or detrimental to the ideals of the Third Wave.

When perusing critical responses to *Grey's Anatomy*, one encounters conflicting critiques that alternately brush the series off as daytime drama or consider it a dynamic, culturally progressive piece of television. This leads me to believe that while *Grey's Anatomy* has certainly taken the female fantasy narrative made so popular by *Sex and the City* much further on the feminist radar by including a multiracial cast and professional, yet flawed, women, the series also misrepresents itself as a progressive piece of VIT, or Very Important Television. It seems that *Grey's Anatomy* merely satisfies the appetite of cultural norms with a suggestive gloss of progressive feminism and color-blind casting. It cannot be denied, however, that this formula, and *Grey's Anatomy*'s operation within it, certainly appeals to the sensibilities of today's average female viewer, which *Grey's Anatomy* identifies as its primary fan base: young women between the ages of 18–49 with generally upper levels of income (Lisotta 1). These women, whose ideas and writing can be read in a number of online *Grey's Anatomy* blogs and fansites, also seem to be self-identifying feminists interested in the series' portrayal of "strong, successful women" ("Feminism Friday").

Although *Grey's Anatomy* is now in its third season of prime time television on the ABC network, the program was initially a mid-season replacement that occupied a strategic time placement after the network's fantastical juggernaut, *Desperate Housewives*. However, *Grey's* soon developed enough of a fan base and high enough ratings to move into a night of its own (Gilbert 1). Set in the fantasy world of Seattle Grace Hospital, the series features a gaggle of surgical interns just beginning their residencies, and we experience their lives and loves as narrated by Meredith Grey, our protagonist. Though sometimes denigrated and brushed off as "nighttime soap opera with scalpels and condoms" (Gilbert 1), it cannot be denied that the series has momentum, significance, and a fiercely loyal and far-reaching fan base.

Ellen Pompeo, who portrays lead intern Meredith Grey on the series, claims that the girls of *Grey's* are more evolved and different from the "flawed bimbo" female stereotype that consistently appears on television (Freydkin and Keck 1), which is exactly what creator Sondra Rhimes had in mind when she began writing *Grey's Anatomy*. Rhimes, who must be credited as the first African American woman to create and produce a top-10 network series (McDowell 2), found TV drama's leading ladies existing "purely in relation to the men in their lives," and then decided that she wanted to see more women on TV like those she knew—women who were "competitive and a little snarky . . . complex, ambitious, clever, confused women" (McDowell 2). The inaccurate representation of women on TV is nothing new; "although popular TV dramas . . . appear to present characters and plotlines that defy gender stereotypes, [Susan] Douglas still finds telltale signs of cultural bias against women in such programs" (Maasik and Solomon 270). Susan Douglas, in her essay "Signs of Intelligent Life on TV," reiterates the point that modern television strives "to suck in those women

For all of its over-the-top drama, *Grey's Anatomy* remains the only television show that foregrounds strong women of many ethnicities in power positions.

[middle and upper-income folks between the ages of 18–49] whose lives have been transformed by the women's movement while keeping guys from grabbing the remote" (272). This is exactly what *Grey's Anatomy* is striving to do; it appeases and appeals to first-world feminists, but hidden contradictions abound in their devotion to both the series and Third Wave Feminism.

One extensive feminist blog on the series, *The Thinking Girl*, praises the number of female characters on *Grey's Anatomy*, and how they are portrayed as "dedicated and deserving"(2), but it later admits that the men continually have the upper hand of the girls within the show. Dr. McDreamy (a.k.a. Derek Shepard), an attending surgeon involved in a complicated relationship with Meredith, is obviously superior to her because, as the site writes:

> He holds all the cards in his *marriage* because his wife cheated on him, and he feels that gives him a moral superiority that allows him to be an asshole to her. And [Meredith] has to deal with accusations of sleeping her way to the best surgeries, and claims of favoritism, while [McDreamy's] morality is never questioned in any way. But, he's just so darn dreamy! With that floppy hair and dimples, he is oh-so-hard to resist! (2)

Although many find McDreamy hard to resist, viewers also cheered Meredith during Season Two of the series when she issues a verbal diatribe to her boss, and former lover, after he decided to return to his aforementioned wife. Meredith begins dating and pursuing one-night stands after the break-up, and McDreamy, now devoid of the "moral superiority" that *The Thinking Girl* awarded him earlier, becomes jealous that he no longer holds Meredith and Addison in the palm of his hand. Now known colloquially among fans as the "Whore Speech" (Freydkin and Keck 6), Meredith rants:

> You don't get to call me a whore. When I met you, I thought I had found the person I was going to spend the rest of my life with. I was done. So all the boys, and all the bars, and all the obvious Daddy issues—who cared? Because I was done. *You* left me. *You* chose Addison. I'm all glued back together now. I make no apologies for how I chose to repair what *you* broke (Greysanatomyinsider.com 1).

This seems like a feminist message; girl talks back to man who did her wrong and unapologetically pursues her own sexual interests in his absence. It's smatterings of occurrences like this that provides *Grey's* with a feminist vibe. But what becomes of this exchange? McDreamy storms off, later recants and dumps the wife, and we are left with a simpering Meredith pleading to His Floppy-Hairedness; "Pick me . . . choose me . . . love me" (Greysanatomyinsider.com 1).

More examples of feminist contradiction occur when one fan/blogger later complements the "smart dialogue" and "good friendships" (Greysanatomyinsider.com 1) within the series, and then a few pages later rants, "wouldn't it be incredible if some writer out there could damn well come up with some real compelling female conversation?" (Greysanatomyinsider.com 7), because she feels that the girls, although important and professional, limit their conversations amongst themselves to that suitable to a gaggle of high school girls. But my thought is: would *Grey's Anatomy* be as successful as it is if they didn't? When fans are saying things like, "The setting, the medical emergencies—that's all secondary—in the end, I'm tuning in every week to watch [the girls] find love . . . and hope they get loved in return" (Freydkin and Keck 5), and, "My favorite is Callie. She's real. She rocks a size-12 body and she's Hispanic, which is awesome . . . and she's got the best lip gloss" (8), it appears that "feminist" women may long for a more stereotypical, culturally cookie-cutter life and romance then they may let on, and they may not be interested in the altruistic somberness of *Grey's Anatomy*'s older siblings such as *ER* and even *House, MD*.

Because *Grey's* fan base is over 68% women, and it is ranked number two in female viewership (second to *Desperate Housewives*), it is clear that women are buying what *Grey's Anatomy* is selling to them, a brand of McFeminism that makes them feel like progressive peers of the ladies of Seattle Grace. In reality, however, this McFeminism is merely a dressed up version of the same old thing; girls that need the leveling weakness of a messy love life, existential angst, and unflattering blue scrubs in order to make them culturally tolerable (Stanley 1). The men of *Grey's Anatomy*, who consistently have the upper hand in their female interns' lives, also happen to be a giant McSelling Point for the female viewers. Creator Wilson herself has said of *Grey's* men; "They were my fantasy men . . . they got to say and do things I wish men would say and do" (McDowell 2). So, these "fantasy men" are doing what their creator wished all men would say and do: punishing their respective intern's sexual/romantic mistakes by assigning them inferior duties at the hospital. Countless times in the series, if Meredith or Christina are acting inappropriately to their lovers, Drs. McDreamy and Burke, they will be denied access to surgeries by their respective attending, so the doctors' control over the interns extends past the romantic and into the educational as well.

To the credit of *Grey's Anatomy*, however, it does present us with a more utopian view of humanity that varies from TV dramas of the past where, as Susan Douglas puts it:

> . . . female friendships are nonexistent or venomous . . . Asian and Latina women are rarely seen, and African American women are generally absent except as prostitutes, bad welfare moms, and unidentified nurses. In the ER emergency room, the black women who are the conscience and much-needed drill sergeants of the show don't get top billing, and are rarely addressed by name (273).

Rhimes explains the racial diversity of her cast by saying, "If you have a show in which there's only one character of color—which is what most shows do—then you have a weird obligation to make that person slightly saintly because they are representing all the people of color . . . But if you have all different races, people get to be good or bad, flawed, selfish, and competitive" (Ogunnaike 3). These advances help make *Grey's Anatomy* more progressive than some of its earlier counterparts, and the series is also sometimes credited for the defibrillation of medical dramas like *ER* and the success of medical comedies like *Scrubs*, although fans of both shows have sometimes looked down upon *Grey's* for being short on altruism and long on "Hospital High School" drama (Gilbert 2), like when Addison Shepard (McDreamy's wife) finds Meredith's panties in her husband's operating room and posts them on the hospital callboard under a sign that says "Lost and Found." Instances like these humanize the serious world of the hospital, which viewers find appealing, but some critics think that it creates mere cartoons of characters that would be better served in a more austere medical drama (Gilbert 2).

What all of this information and critique boils down to, however, is that *Grey's Anatomy*, much like its fan base, is complicated and contradictory (an interesting thought, as the show's original working title was *Complications*). These are girls and women that want professional careers, personal control, and success; all the things that the femmes of *Grey's Anatomy* seem to have, but deep down inside they, and the surgeons, may just really want dysfunctional romance and some great lip gloss. With this brand of Diet Third Wave Feminism, we have upper-middle class females that don't identify with the commercial "girls-can-do" attitude of Girlie Feminism per say, but neither do they relate to the rigidness of the Second Wave. Are these women who can become active enough to actually do something and join the ranks of what Third Wave Feminism is all about? Or do they just want to put on the glossy veneer of a Very Important Feminist, much like *Grey's Anatomy* is Very Important Television?

Grey's Anatomy may actually be fostering a generation of young females who aren't, and don't want to be, blind to the issues of race, gender, class, and socioeconomic hardship, but nor do they want to mess up their aforementioned lip gloss. This is a generation that isn't quite as self-centered or issue-blind as the Ally McBeals of yesteryear, but neither are they the great, altruistic humanitarians of today . . . and *Grey's Anatomy* seems to be catering to those McFeminists just fine.

Works Cited

Albiniak, Paige. "Why 'Grey' Seems So Bright." *Broadcasting & Cable* 30 May 2005. *Business Source Premier Database.*

Douglas, Susan. *Where the Girls Are: Growing Up Female With the Mass Media.* New York: Three Rivers Press, 2005.

THE THIRD WAVE FEMINISM SUITE

"Feminism Friday; *Grey's Anatomy.*" *The Thinking Girl.* 10 Nov. 2006. <http://www.thinkinggirl. wordpress.com/2006/11/10/feminism-friday-greys-anatomy.htm>.

Freydkin, Donna, and William Keck. "*Grey's* Ladies: Hospital Show's Appeal Lies with its Strong, but Flawed, Women." *USA Today* 21 Sept. 2006.

Gilbert, Matthew. "*Anatomy* of a Hit: It Doesn't Want to Save the World. And That's Why We Love It." *The Boston Globe* 7 May 2006.

Grey's Anatomy Insider Fansite. 26 Feb. 2007. <http://www.greysanatomyinsider.com>.

Grey's Anatomy. Internet Movie Database 26 Feb. 2007. <http://www.imdb.com/title/tt0413573>.

"*Grey's Anatomy.*" *Wikipedia.* 26 Feb. 2007. <http://www.en.wikipedia.org/wiki/Grey's_Anatomy>.

Lisotta, Christopher. "Upscale Young Viewers Go For *Anatomy.*" *Television Week.* 2 Oct. 2006 *Business Source Premier Database.*

Maasik, Sonia, and Jack Solomon. *Signs of Life in the USA: Readings on Popular Culture for Writers.* New York: Bedford/St. Martins, 2006.

McDowell, Jeanne. "A Woman and Her *Anatomy.*" *Time* 22 May 2006.

Ogunnaike, Lola. "*Grey's Anatomy* Creator Finds Success in Surgery." *The New York Times* 28 Sept. 2006.

Stanley, Alessandra. "Television Review: Male Misery Just Loves Female Company." *The New York Times* 3 Jan. 2007.

How I Wrote This Essay Lara Hayhurst

Why did you write this piece—what was the assignment or motivation for writing?

This piece was an assignment given as a final paper for a course I took my senior year at Pace University; "Girls on Film: Cultural Studies in New Wave Feminism."

What did you do when you decided to write?

The course focused around distinguishing the different waves of feminism; the second wave of the sixties, "Girlie" feminism, and how they all influenced the current third wave of feminism, which strives to use pop culture and media as a tool to advance women. When asked to write an extensive paper on a facet of media or pop culture relevant to women and the third wave of feminism, I had to choose a topic that I felt extremely familiar with, so as not to make the task too daunting. I was already a big fan of *Grey's Anatomy*, and felt that the way it treated its female characters was complex and interesting.

How did you begin?

I was already up-to-date with the current season of *Grey's* as far as knowledge and observation went, but I re-watched some favorite episodes and those that I remembered dealing specifically with the women or women's issues. I also waded through a lot of blogs, fansites, and the like to get a feel for how real women in the show's primary demographic felt about the characters, what they liked and disliked about certain episodes, and what they were drawn to discussing.

Describe the process of writing the first draft.

It was a few years ago, so I don't remember fine details, but I remember spreading all my research out in front of me and highlighting the sections that dealt with my different points of discussion in different colors. I made an outline and then filed in my bibliographic support as I went, taking it paragraph by paragraph. Going back and revisiting the paper, I find the beginning sections a little hard to read, the flow isn't as smooth and the quotations don't come naturally all the time, but around the middle of the paper I pick up speed and I quite like the way I ended it!

Did you write a draft all the way through?

Yes, I always prefer to write that way. Even if it becomes stream of consciousness rambling, it's always helpful to me to see where my mind goes and then relate back to my references for support.

How much editing did you do as you wrote?

Not a lot. I did my big edit after I submitted my first draft and got feedback from my professor.

Did you do research as you wrote or before you started writing? What databases did you use?

I did most of my research beforehand. Because my topic was so contemporary, a lot of internet searching and wading through blogs and fansites took up my time, but I also used textbook and reading materials we had been given in class, just to make sure I was relating my thesis back to the overall objective of the course. Looking back on my bibliography, it's a mix of easily accessible sites like Wikipedia, blogs, and print articles (*USA Today*, *Entertainment Weekly*, etc), and more broad resources such as *Where The Girls Are* and *Signs of Intelligent Life in the USA*. I'm hoping this made the paper topical and on-point, but also accessible.

How long would you say the process took?

We were given the assignment at the beginning of the semester, and I think I chose my topic right away. I collected research and began watching episodes for a few months, and then the actual writing probably took a week.

How did you edit the draft?

I did my edit mostly based on my professor's suggestions. I was working for a grade, after all. I also always like to read my work out loud and make sure it flows easily. I made a few changes that way, and I also read it aloud to my husband to make sure it was understandable off the page as well as on. He gave me some ideas and help that I appreciated from a layman uninvolved with my course or the project itself.

What was the response when you turned in your essay?

Favorable! I remember sending the draft to my Dad, an author, and he thought it was strong. I received a good grade on the paper, and was thrilled when my professor suggested I submit the essay to Dr. Silverman for his upcoming textbook.

Are you satisfied now with what you wrote? Would you make any changes?

This was the first time I had revisited the essay since we edited it for publication, and I think I mention above, that I found the first few pages a little jumbled and my thesis a little unclear. I think towards the middle I really settled in and it becomes clear that my thesis is really one of exploration and contradiction, not a black and white opinion. I think if I had made it more clear at the onset that my paper was about "Diet Third Wave Feminism" and the Upper Middle Class "McFeminists" that subscribe to it using shows like "*Grey's*," the paper would be more clear.

Just on a side note; I've actually fallen off the *Grey's Anatomy* wagon and haven't seen any of the past two seasons. Snippets of the episodes I've caught on TV kind of annoy me, and I think the show has lost its edge. I think it has become a little more of a nighttime soap opera in recent years, and I think other viewers agree. It has spawned its own little sub genre of television, however, which I think is interesting. Shows concerning the gaggle of new interns that arrive at the hospital/law office/university and succeed/fail/love/say snarky dialogue is prevalent, but none of the shows seem to be doing particularly well with ratings. My personal TV preference now lies with *Mad Men*, *Dexter*, and *Damages*; all shows that could have their own critiques of third wave feminism, in my opinion.

"La Femme Veronica": Intelligence as Power in Veronica Mars

Gwendolyn Limbach

Student Essay

A CRITIC FAVORITE AND CULT HIT, *Veronica Mars* is hailed simultaneously as "so not the new Nancy Drew" and younger sister of *Buffy the Vampire Slayer* (Bianco). Yet this neo-noir, teen crime drama heroine goes beyond both female predecessors in not only her investigative prowess but also her agency on screen. Whereas Buffy finds her power in super-human physical strength to vanquish demons, Veronica locates her own agency in her intelligence, which enables her to solve her life and her town's many mysteries. Veronica's world is a complex puzzle unto itself: throughout the television series' first season Veronica must solve the murder of her best friend, Lilly Kane, whose suspects include the girl's father, brother, boyfriend, and lover; find the person who drugged and raped her at a party; and discover her true paternity. As Joss Whedon, creator of *Buffy*, writes, "Welcome to the funniest and most romantic show on television." Because of its complex plot and intricate characters, *Veronica Mars* goes beyond the usual teen genre fodder of other shows to explore classic noir themes as well as class and race conflict, sexuality, and familial relationships. Through Veronica's intelligence as a detective, she is able to exploit a traditionally male genre and role and expectations of girlhood, allowing her to survive not only high school but also the precarious culture of teen girls in the media market.

From the beginning of the first episode it is obvious that Veronica Mars is not an average high school student. Only when the camera rests momentarily on her textbook and she reveals that she has a Calculus test in four hours does the viewer realize this private investigator is a teenage girl. Veronica excels in school, as is apparent when she wakes from a daydream in her Advanced Placement English class to quote Pope's "Essay on Man." Her sassy attitude also reveals itself in this scene when she sums up Pope's meaning succinctly: "Life's a bitch, and then you die" ("Pilot"). But to define Veronica's intelligence solely in terms of school-learned knowledge and good study habits would only contain her in the "smart girl" stereotype of girlhood. Instead, she shows that her intelligence encompasses the world outside of school; she does not sit in the library pouring over books for answers, but instead uses intricate ploys, advanced technology, loyal friends, and skills gleaned from her professional P.I. father to solve her cases. For example, in the episode "The Wrath of Con," Veronica exposes college-aged computer scam artists through a myriad of tricks: disguising herself at once as a Japanime-looking gamer to steal an ID and then as a nerdy freshman to break into the suspects' dorm room; bugging the suspects' room; learning the code to the students' security system by recognizing keypad tones; luring the boys out of the room to see a game demo with another (imposter) prospective student; breaking into the dorm room again and dismantling the students' hard drive and backup drive. Here, and in many other cases, Veronica employs her knowledge of technology and of other people's psyches as well as the help of trusted allies to figure out not just the whodunit but also how to catch them. Many times, as one reviewer put it, "Veronica out-savvies people" through her use of "wit, spunk, and smarts" (Armstrong).

By the end of every episode Veronica possesses the necessary knowledge to solve the mystery of the day and says so rather than retreating into silence, which many young girls are forced into. In most instances she declares "I know who did it" or "I know what happened" when she has solved the mystery. Throughout the 22-episode first season, she makes these statements 19 times; unlike non-nerd smart girls who "simply [sublimate] their intellect into achieving recognition" in the social sphere, Veronica proudly announces her knowledge regardless of how others will judge her (Shary 244). Social acceptance is clearly not Veronica's goal as she reveals that she was once a part of the popular group because of her social connections, dating rich Duncan Kane and befriending his sister Lilly, but quickly fell out of favor with the others after Lilly's murder and the ensuing investigation. As Timothy Shary notes, most films today suggest that the "more valuable assets that grant girls success (popularity and respect) are fashion sense, physical beauty, agreeable attitude, and the attainment of a boyfriend" (236). However, Veronica Mars tends to contradict, and many times manipulate, some of these preferred assets to expand her investigations. When Veronica is commissioned by the vice principal to investigate the kidnapping of the school mascot, she infiltrates the competing high school and quickly ingratiates herself with the jock in-crowd, noting, "Whoever said it's a man's world had no idea how easy it is sometimes to be a girl" ("Betty and Veronica"). By dressing like the in-crowd and acting the part of a ditzy ingenue, she quickly earns a seat at the popular table and asks questions of her suspects without suspicion. Veronica exploits cultural expectations of petite, blonde girls to get information from those that underestimate her.

In other instances Veronica utilizes her father's personal expectations of her intelligence to get away with rule-breaking in the name of investigating a mystery, at the same time living up to a rebuking patriarchal standards of gendered intelligence. Shary notes that non-nerdly smart girls are expected to be studious but not appear too smart. Veronica never shies away from appearing "too" smart, and she knows that appealing to her father's wish for her academic success allows her to accomplish more than simply telling him the truth. Four times in the season Veronica claims that she's doing a "school project" to either hide her investigations from her dad or get information from him. In one episode Veronica claims that she is trying to take a blood sample for a health class assignment on HIV. By playing on her girlish fear to prick her finger and her desire for good grades, Veronica tricks her father into giving his blood sample for what turns out to be a paternity test. Keith Mars jokes that his "bad-ass, action-figure daughter is scared to take a little tiny drop of blood" but in fact the joke is on him ("Drinking the Kool-Aid").

Like Buffy, the attractive, witty Veronica Mars, does as a teenage girl what has been tradition-ally reserved for cranky, middle-aged men.

Whereas with her father Veronica plays on the "girly" stereotype of girlhood, once she is among her peers Veronica refuses to rely on any stereotypes to survive. Part of *Buffy*'s premise, and its major appeal to teens, is that "high school is hell, literally"; a similar concept can be applied to *Veronica Mars*. As Roz Kaveney notes, high school life is not easy for Veronica because she is "stigmatized as a slut because of her behavior under the date-rape drug [actually, GHB, not Rohypnol] and because she no longer has social power as Lilly's friend, consort of Lilly's brother Duncan, and the daughter of the sheriff" (178). Until she meets Wallace, a new student who is the victim of bullying by the town biker gang, Veronica has no friends or allies at Neptune High School. She endures snide quips from the school's "obligatory psychotic jackass," Logan Echols, and even a guest-starring Paris Hilton who remarks that "no one cares what you think Veronica Mars, not anymore" ("Pilot," "Credit Where Credit's Due"). Yet rather than retreating into silence, Veronica stands up to these in-crowd kids and creates a space for herself in which she is feared by some if not respected by all. When her reputation is once again tarnished along with that of a remaining popular friend, Meg, Veronica's advice is to "get tough . . . get even"; once she asserts herself, Meg tells her "people are afraid of you" ("Like a Virgin"). Here it is apparent that Veronica refuses to be relegated to the smart-girl trope where "either the smart girl is made to minimize her intellectual qualities or those qualities negatively affect her" (Shary 244). The friendship of her popular former friends is never a goal for this heroine; she has learned all too well that the rich, white, and powerful group is the most destructive one.

According to Anita Harris's introduction to *All About the Girl*, many researchers in girls' studies have noted the "now popular idea that girls lose their resistant and authentic voices when they engage with cultural requirements to shape their identities in line with dominant femininities" (xviii). In the case of *Veronica Mars*, viewers see through flashbacks that this popular idea was true of Veronica's life before Lilly's death and her own rape. Veronica caves to Lilly's peer-pressure over skipping the homecoming dance and isolates a potential friend after a misunderstanding at a party. When Veronica interacts with popular friends during these flashbacks her customary sarcasm and "green-apple personality" are conspicuously absent (Flynn, "Life on *Mars*"). It is only after Veronica encounters a peril too common among girls, rape, that she rebukes the dominant femininities she once tried to uphold, stating, "I'm no longer that girl" ("Pilot"). The new Veronica takes an active role in her life and relationships. Later in the season Veronica investigates the night of her rape and finally receives some answers. By having the conclusion to this plot thread delayed until the penultimate episode, Thomas does not place Veronica in a victim subject position throughout the season. Unlike some rape survivors, Veronica does not lose her voice like so many other girls but rather finds a stronger voice through her experience.

Veronica's voice, its authenticity, snarkiness, and the self-assured quality it gives Veronica, is one of the protagonist's most distinctive characteristics. Her voice is also key to the show itself through her voice-over narration and flashbacks, which reveal the teen's complex world and her reactions to it, making "Veronica sound like a hurt child one minute and Philip Marlowe the next" (Kelleher). This is Veronica's show, and we see it from her point of view; her authentic voice resists societal expectations of docility from teenage girls and instead makes itself heard in a patriarchal world. In her essay on Feminist Television Criticism, Ann Kaplan contends that "radical feminists emphasize that the silencing of the female voice results from male domination (252). Though this emphasis does not seem to be a specifically "radical" type of feminism, the author's point, especially in connection to *Veronica Mars*, holds true. Neptune, and the world at large, is dominated by men who exercise their agency over women. Until her rape, Veronica seems to be unaware of the patriarchal authority she is under, unaware that she is being silenced. After this experience, she realizes the extent to which her agency has been withheld from her and therefore reclaims it through raising her voice. Rather than launching into bra-burning protests to be heard, Veronica remarks on the state of her world through pop-culture awareness and references. *Entertainment Weekly* writer Gillian Flynn describes Veronica as "blithely brushing off adversity, launching bubble-gum-flavored retorts at everyone from disappointing beaus to bullying FBI agents . . . Veronica Mars is like a cute female Fletch" ("*Mars* Attracts"). Veronica mocks the expectations of quiet, studious girls repeatedly through the series. For instance, when Keith leaves town to chase a bail-jumper he suggests that Veronica stays with a friend and she replies, "And miss the opportunity to have the apartment to myself so I can raid the liquor cabinet and watch Skinemax? No, wait, I'm a girl. I'm gonna do all my homework, secure the locks, brush, floss, and crawl into bed with an overly protective pit bull. You don't have to worry about me" ("A Trip to the Dentist"). Though it looks like she places herself in this quiet, "girly" position, statements like this one mock the silence that society tries to force upon her. Frequently we see Veronica use her pop culture sensibility and language to confront the hegemonic white upper-class group and gain agency.

The theme of this hegemonic group as corrupt appears pervasively in the series. Veronica explains in the first episode that Neptune is "a town without a middle class . . .

where your parents are either millionaires or work for millionaires" ("Pilot"). Though Veronica's character and her other lower-class friends look like and are usually coded as middle class, "her poverty status [exists] in comparison with the Kanes and Echols of her world" (Kaveney 181). One *Entertainment Weekly* writer notes that "the wealthy Southern California town of Neptune has a heightened-reality vibe" (Flynn). Veronica's class status is repeatedly the target of derision, especially by her antagonist Logan, the son of movie stars, but viewers identify with Veronica, Wallace, and computer wiz Mac rather than with the rich kids. Throughout the series, the sons and daughters of millionaires commit offenses more often than their low class counterparts that include drug trafficking, steroid use, student government election corruption, stealing money from each other, binge drinking that results in a coma, raucous parties, faking a kidnapping, extortion, and slipping GHB into drinks at parties. As Tom Gilatto notes in a review in *People*, "the show has definitely been flavored . . . by the nasty cultural down-trickle of real-life crimes of pampered West Coasters" ("Veronica Mars"). These infractions are much more visible than the crimes committed by the PCH (Pacific Coast Highway) biker gang, a group of tattooed, working class Latinos who frequently fail to graduate, yet the former group seems to evade any type of punishment. That is, of course, until Veronica Mars is on the case.

When it is up to Veronica to solve the crime, her first suspects are usually those at the top of the high school hierarchy; however, viewers see in the first two episodes that Veronica's first investigations take her to first suspect the same person, Weevil. He is the leader of the biker gang and is seen as a threat to Wallace and Veronica after he tapes the former to the school flagpole naked and taunts the latter about her reputation repeatedly. Keeping in line with the dominant cultural conceptions of the white power structure of Neptune, Veronica singles Weevil out as the "obvious" suspect after his grandmother is arrested for opening credit accounts in her employer's name. Both the grandmother's lawyer and the sheriff, and even Keith, believe that Weevil is the real culprit, so Veronica begins her investigation on this premise. Veronica has seen Weevil's criminal behavior previously, but when evidence shows that he could not have used the credit card she quickly reconsiders her position. Unlike the men around her, Veronica can shed class prejudices and expand her inquiries to other avenues. Instead of investigating someone who fits the criminal description in terms of Neptune's white upper-class standards, Veronica turns her attention to Logan Echols, noting that "80% of credit fraud is committed by a close relative" ("Credit Where Credit's Due"). Unfortunately the show fails to pursue the idea of the wayward upper-class delinquent by revealing that Weevil's cousin is guilty of fraud. However, creator Thomas does not swiftly send him to jail like so many other shows might do; instead, his crime is shown to be about betrayal of friends, family, and race (partly because the cousin used the stolen credit card to take out a rich white girl) rather than a transgression against the system. Veronica's attitudes towards race and class become more distant from those of Neptune's hegemony as the show progresses, revealing Veronica as one of the most socio-economically aware characters on teen-targeted television.

Veronica is also very aware of the existence, and dominance, of the patriarchy in Neptune and this knowledge allows her to resist containment within it. Within Veronica's world there are two main representations of patriarchal agency that she must confront: her father Keith and the school vice principal, Mr. Clemmons. Veronica's relationship with her father Keith is quite a rare one on television today and is, as magazine writer Jaime Weinman notes, "a bright spot in the world of television fatherhood." At the same time that the show is not one "in which father knows best," creator Thomas says that " '[a]s clever as we play Veronica, we always try to play Keith one step more clever' " (Weinman). This tension of who can outsmart whom sets up a struggle between not just parent and child but also dominant and dominated societal forces. Veronica as the lower-class teenage girl must work harder to gain knowledge and prove her intelligence than her already established P.I. dad, whose wealthy clients provide access to upper-class means of detecting through their ability to pay for any on-the-job expenses such as bugging equipment, etc. Even though Keith appears to know more than his daughter at times, Veronica is still a formidable force against him. She uses some of the contacts her father made as sheriff to get information and, as discussed above, can pursue investigations under Keith's nose by claiming to do mere school projects. And although Thomas wishes to play Keith as cleverer than his daughter, Veronica shows a keen detective prowess than amazes both her father and the viewer. For example, after stealing a crime scene photo of Lilly's room from her father's safe and comparing it to a video of a police press conference, Veronica proves that the evidence linking Lilly's convicted killer to the victim was planted in the killer's home. In the end, it is Veronica and not Keith who finds her friend's real murderer and turns him over to the police.

The scene in which she does this has met with criticism by some, including Kaveney. She contends that "the episode's culmination places Veronica in serious physical danger from which she does not escape by her usual intelligence—she has to be rescued by her father . . . in the season finale, it is a worrying drift away from message" (184). Though Kaveney makes a fair point that Keith must save Veronica, she fails to note that Veronica immediately then saves her father from being horribly burned. Not only this, she then takes his gun and finds Lilly's killer, Aaron Echols (Logan's father), and orders a bystander to call the authorities. In this instance Veronica possesses agency by solving Lilly's murder and controlling the resultant situation by wielding a gun. Although the series shows Keith as the main patriarchal representation in Veronica's life, it also reveals that Veronica has legitimate and successful tools to confront and defy this form of domination.

Her main device to do so, of course, is her intelligence and her use of it when others attempt to contain her, as is the case with the vice principal. Though Clemmons tries to be the authority in school, Veronica reveals in the first episode that she possesses more knowledge of Neptune High: "The [locker] searches aren't really random. I know when they're going to happen before Vice Principal Clemmons does" ("Pilot"). We realize that even though Veronica is an outcast among her peers and considered a problem student among her teachers, she still has agency in her school environment. Throughout the season we see Veronica reading students' permanent files, bugging an administrator's office, and even impersonating the school board president to get information. By the sixteenth episode Clemmons explicitly recognizes Veronica's intelligence when he hires her to investigate the disappearance of the school mascot. Though the two are positioned in traditional places of school administrator and student, with Clemmons standing behind his desk and Veronica sitting in front of him expecting to be punished for a crime she did not commit, the places of power are actually reversed. The vice principal lacks knowledge and must defer to Veronica as the most capable seeker of knowledge. Their positioning is ironic in that when a client appeals to a detective for help, the P.I. is behind the desk and the client in front. This reversal questions the physical and metaphorical positions of power within a school setting that tends to disenfranchise the working-class students.[1]

With "a girl scout's face and Philip Marlowe's jadedness" *Veronica Mars* is a singular representation of young female agency on television today (Poniewozik). With the influences of both third wave feminism and pop culture, this complex show confronts issues of class and race conflict, rape, murder, and personal identity. Through Veronica's possession and use of her intelligence, along with her continuous search for further knowledge, she is able to find an agency that would otherwise be denied to her. Her awareness of the hegemonic and patriarchal systems that attempt to control her world better equips Veronica to challenge these institutions. Although the series was canceled after its third season, fans and cultural critics alike must hope that Veronica Mars's influence can extend to female viewers as well as fellow teen girls on television.

Works Cited

Armstrong, Jennifer. "Bell of the Fall." *Entertainment Weekly* no. 796 (Dec. 2004): 36–7. OmniFile Full Text Select. H.W. Wilson. 23 Feb. 2007 <http://vnweb.hwwilsonweb.com>.

Bianco, Robert. "*Veronica Mars*: Intelligent Life." *USA Today* (Sept. 2004). Academic Search Premier. 23 Feb. 2007 <http://search.ebscohost.com>.

Flynn, Gillian. "Life on Mars." *Entertainment Weekly* no. 790 (Oct. 2004): 59–60. OmniFile Full Text Select. H.W. Wilson. 23 Feb. 2007 <http://vnweb.hwwilsonweb.com>.

———. "*Mars* Attracts." *Entertainment Weekly* no. 865 (Feb. 2006): 53. OmniFile Full Text Select. H.W. Wilson. 23 Feb. 2007 <http://vnweb.hwwilsonweb.com>.

Gilatto, Tom. "Veronica Mars." *People* 64.19 (Nov. 2005): 41. Academic Search Premier. 16 Feb. 2007 <http://search.ebscohost.com>.

Harris, Anita. "Introduction." *All About the Girl: Culture, Power, and Identity*. Ed. Anita Harris. London: Routledge, 2004. xvii–xxv.

Kaplan, Ann. "Feminist Criticism and Television." *Channels of Discourse, Reassembled*. Chapel Hill: UP of North Carolina, 1992.

Kaveney, Roz. "Watching the Teen Detective: *Veronica Mars*." *Teen Dreams: Reading Teen Films from Heathers to Veronica Mars*. London: I.B. Tauris & Co., 2006. 177–185.

Kelleher, Terry. "*Veronica Mars*." *People* 62.13 (Sept. 2004): 42. Academic Search Premier. 23 Feb. 2007 <http://search.ebscohost.com>.

Poniewozik, James. "6 Best Dramas on TV Now." *Time* 165.14 (Apr. 2005): 70. Academic Search Premier. 16 Feb. 2007 <http://search.ebscohost.com>.

Shary, Timothy. "The Nerdly Girl and Her Beautiful Sister." *Sugar, Spice, and Everything Nice: Cinemas of Girlhood*. Frances Gateward and Murray Pomerance, ed. Detroit: Wayne State UP, 2002. 235–250.

Weinman, Jaime J. "Wow! A Show with a Smart Father!" *Maclean's* 119.39 (Oct. 2006): 60. Academic Search Premier. 23 Feb. 2007 <http://search.ebscohost.com>.

Whedon, Joss. "Ace of Case." *Entertainment Weekly* no. 844 (Oct. 2005): 131. OmniFile Full Text Select. H.W. Wilson. 23 Feb. 2007 <http://vnweb.hwwilsonweb.com>.

---

[1]See episode 1.6 "Return of the Kane." School activities such as sports and student government, which require lengthy after-school commitments that many students with jobs cannot do, are awarded "Pirate Points." These accumulated points allow students special privileges, like ordering outside food for lunch among others.

Why did you write this piece—what was the assignment or motivation for writing?

The essay was a term paper assignment for an upper-level women's studies course.

What did you do when you got the assignment?

The assignment allowed us to choose a text to write about, so I first thought about what interested me. Doing research and focusing on the same text for weeks or months is much easier and more enjoyable when you really like what you're doing.

How did you begin?

Once I choose the text (*Veronica Mars*) I brainstormed about what angle I would take, or what I wanted to say about the show. There are a lot of themes within any text, so for VM I wrote down which themes would be most relevant to the course and did some research to see what was out there on the show to help me narrow down the options. Once I decided on the focus I drafted a thesis statement to give me direction while writing and researching.

Describe the process of writing the first draft.

I think I revised my thesis about 5 times to get it right and make sure it reflected my position within the paper. I outlined the draft before I started writing and organized the sources I wanted to use based on the outline. I'm a big organizer. Outlining beforehand is great because I knew exactly what I wanted to say in almost every paragraph, so doing the actual writing was more streamlined. I wrote the whole draft over the course of a couple days, giving myself breaks in between blocks of writing to relax or just think about what I had written. I'd often go back and reread a page or two out loud to myself to make sure everything sounded right. When I finished the whole draft I saved it in 2 different places, closed my computer, and didn't think about it for a night. Then I came back, edited, made corrections, and printed.

Did you write a draft all the way through?

Yes, I wrote the whole draft before turning it in, but I didn't write it all at once.

How much editing did you do as you wrote?

I tend to do a lot of unconscious editing from habit. I'll write a few sentences, and when I reach the end of the thought I go back, reread, and fix mistakes, then go on to the next part. It's easier to edit a few paragraphs as you write, then edit when you're finished, rather than saving all the edits until the very end, especially when there's a deadline.

Did you do research as you wrote or before you started writing? What databases did you use?

I did most of my research before I began writing. Sometimes as I wrote I would think of something I wanted to include and would search for articles. I used JSTOR and Ebsco Host for most of my database research.

THE THIRD WAVE FEMINISM SUITE

How long would you say the process took?

I completed research over two-three weeks.

How did you edit the draft?

I find it easier to edit on paper rather than on a screen, so I printed the draft and read through it aloud, making notations when I wanted to change or fix anything. Then I read the paper backwards, paragraph by paragraph, to make sure that each paragraph made sense and that I wasn't getting caught up in the flow of reading and missing errors.

What was the response when you turned in your essay?

My professor gave very positive feedback on the draft. She found very few mechanical errors and gave advice on developing some analysis and reorganizing the order of some paragraphs. Nothing had to be completely excised or rewritten, so my revision process was pretty simple.

Are you satisfied now with what you wrote? Would you make any changes?

I am satisfied with the essay, but I think there's always room for improvement. As cheesy as it sounds, writing *is* a process. The essay itself doesn't change over time, but I do as a person and as a writer. When I revisit essays with fresh eyes and more writing under my belt I can see sentences that could be phrased more clearly or arguments that could be made stronger, or I'm reminded of new research I've found that would be germane. As for the *Veronica Mars* essay I wrote, I certainly would change some aspects of it, but I'd have to read the essay again to decide on which ones.

READING **WRITING**

This Text: Reading

1. What is Third Wave Feminism? Which student paper most directly engages Dr. Pender's definition?
2. In what way is Third Wave Feminism related to the original ideas of feminism? In what ways is it a departure?
3. For what other television shows or movies would it be useful to use Third Wave Feminism as a lens?
4. What do you think a "Fourth Wave Feminism" might look like? What might popular culture in a fourth wave look like? Do you see any precursors now?
5. What might you find if you ventured outside the period defined by Dr. Pender and used the lens of Third Wave Feminism and examined a show like *I Love Lucy* or *The Mary Tyler Moore Show*?

Your Text: Writing

1. Do a close reading of a current television show through the lens of Third Wave Feminism.
2. Do a close reading combined with a research angle (similar to Dr. Pender's assignment).
3. Write an annotated bibliography on Third Wave Feminism or feminism in general. What trends do you note in both scholarship generally and the subject matter specifically?
4. After undertaking number 3, use this information to approach a text, and write this as a paper.

READING BETWEEN THE LINES

Classroom Activities

1. Send all of the males to another room to discuss a specific text. Now that all the guys are absent, hold a discussion for 20 minutes on one or two texts in this section. How is your classroom experience different without males around? Why is it different?
2. In class, watch a television show from the '50s or '60s like *Leave It to Beaver* or *Father Knows Best* or *Bonanza.* Compare the gender roles to those in a show like *Will & Grace, Frasier,* or *Ally McBeal.* What has changed? What hasn't? How do cultural norms and mores affect how gender gets represented?
3. Go around the room, and ask students to identify how they are themselves "marked," or ask them to provide one example of how they "do gender."
4. As a class, identify five famous women. How do they "do gender"?
5. Do the same with five famous men.
6. As a class, discuss why words like slut, whore, bitch, easy, loose, cold, frigid, and manipulative are generally reserved for females. Why are similar words used to describe males, like stud, player, gigolo, pimp, shrewd, and rational, so different from those used to describe women?
7. In previous editions, we asked if Americans would have an African American president or a female president first. Well, we now know the answer to that question. Does Barak Obama's election tell us anything about race versus gender in America? Or was the election primarily about Obama vs. Clinton?
8. Have everyone in the class bring in a magazine ad that has to do with gender or gender roles. When taken together, what emerges?
9. Break up into groups and discuss the contradictions of gender we see in television, movies, music, and magazines. Compare your answers.
10. Listen to some rap, country, pop, and folk songs in class. How are issues of gender reinforced by song lyrics, album covers, and videos?

Essay Ideas

1. Write a paper in which you examine and debunk three stereotypes about gender.
2. Most of the essays here have dealt with gender issues and women. Write an essay in which you examine how music, sports, business, movies, and even pornography determine what admirable "masculine" traits are.
3. Write a personal essay in which you examine three ways in which you "do gender." What do your means of doing gender say about you?
4. Write an argumentative essay about certain texts that you think are harmful in terms of how they perpetuate gender stereotypes.
5. Read a magazine that is aimed at another gender. If you are a woman, read *Maxim, Sports Illustrated, GQ, Details, Men's Health,* or *Field and Stream;* if you are a man, read *Cosmopolitan, Shape, Redbook, Ladies Home Journal, Martha Stewart Living, Ms.,* or *Working Woman.* Write a paper in which you give a semiotic analysis of the magazine.
6. Write a paper on daytime television. What messages do the commercials and the programming send to women (and men) about women (and men)?
7. As this book goes to press, there is a proliferation of pro-anorexia sites on the World Wide Web. Write a paper that is a reading of anorexia and/or bulimia. Why does this disease affect mostly middle-class white women? Why don't men suffer from these ailments?

8. Give a semiotic reading of male/female dating. What roles are men and women supposed to play early in the dating process? What behavior is okay? What is forbidden? How do we know these rules?

9. Go to the room or the apartment of a friend of yours of a different gender. Give a semiotic reading of that person's room. How is it different from yours? How does your friend's room reflect his or her gender?

10. Give a reading of the gender dynamics in your household. What gender roles do your parents or stepparents fall into? Your siblings?

Visualizing Writing

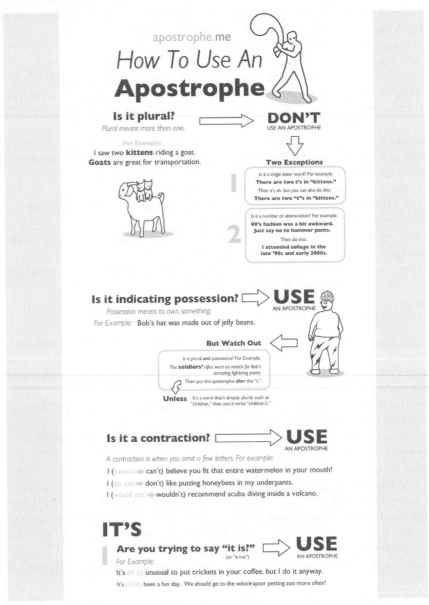

ITS

If you're unsure, simply try replacing "it's" with "it is."
If it sounds ok that way, use an apostrophe.

2 Are you indicating possession?

For Example:

The velociraptor is known for **its** cute, playful nature,
but **its** inability to sing in key is unfortunate.

DON'T
USE AN APOSTROPHE

Is it a possessive name ending in "s?"

For Example:

Charles's rocketship allowed him to have lunch on the moon.

Charles' cat is always terrified during liftoff.

⇨ **BOTH**
ARE ACCEPTABLE
JUST BE CONSISTENT

Is it a possessive __and__ plural name? ⇨ STICK IT
AFTER THE "S"

For Example: The Johnsons' moonwich recipe was very famous.

In this case, you're referring to the entire Johnson family.

TO RECAP

Remember that most apostrophes are used for possessive nouns.
So if a noun owns something, use an apostrophe:

Bob's *jellybean hat became sticky in the scorching sun.*

Or use it for contractions:

Bob's *going to the store to create a bacon hat instead.*

And if it's plural, don't use an apostrophe:

Bacon **hats** *do not melt and they smell wonderful.*

⌐ LASTLY ⌐
When in doubt

→DON'T←
USE AN APOSTROPHE

From Mathew Inman of *The Oatmeal: http://theoatmeal.com/*

7 Reading and Writing about Visual Art

L et's begin with a quick overview of what we mean by "art." Although our concept of the term has undergone transformations with technological innovations, when we use the word "art," we tend to mean paintings, sculpture, and photographs, though items like artistic installations (large works of art often taking up entire rooms) or collages are often considered art. In addition, there is public or "street art," which tends to use walls or the sides of buildings rather than traditional canvases. Examples of this type of art include murals and graffiti.

In the last decade or so, the term "visual culture" has sidled up along side "art," and now the two are often used interchangeably. "Visual culture" refers to any text that relies on visual images like comics, video games, YouTube, graphic novels, Facebook, advertising, and even iPhone apps. Traditionally, these texts make meaning through visual signs—colors, shapes, shadings, and lines—as opposed to making meaning with words or music. Like everything else we talk about in this book, works of art and visual culture are complex texts that you are encouraged and invited not simply to look at but to *read*. And, as we say elsewhere in the book, the act of writing is fundamentally linked to the act of reading. Writing comes out of the process of interpretation; so even if you are not literally taking notes when you look at visual culture, the very process of trying to figure it out is (or can be) the beginning of writing.

When you write about art, it is important to keep in mind its universality and longevity. Long before there were written languages, there were visual ones. Since human beings could hold sticks and daub them in mud, there has been art. In caves in France, on cliffs in Utah, on tablets in the Middle East, on paper in the Orient, and on tombs in Egypt, men and women have been drawing pictures. If you have visited any of these places and seen these texts, you get a sense of the artist's overwhelming urge to represent the world—that is to represent or remake the world. That is really all art of any kind is—an individual's way of presenting the world in a new way. Vincent Van Gogh's sunflowers, Claude Monet's water lilies, Pablo Picasso's musicians, Georgia O'Keefe's flowers, El Greco's Jesus, even Jackson Pollock's splatterings are attempts to make us experience some aspect of the world in a way we had not before.

For a variety of reasons, art resonates with us in ways other media do not and perhaps cannot. For one, we are visual creatures. We see millions of things every day and in so doing rely heavily on our sight. Visual artists take our enormous practice of seeing the world and use it to make us see something new. So, in some regard, there is very little to learn.

This painting by San Francisco artist Rigo is a brilliant play on traditional art, street art, public art, and standard signage. Is it art? Find out in our "Is It Art" suite beginning on page 466. (Rigo, *One Tree*, 1995).

Artists use what you already use. All you have to do is get an idea of the few tools they use to make their art do what they want it to.

Now, on to some hints for writing about art and other aspects of visual culture.

TEST YOUR FIRST REACTIONS, BOTH EMOTIONALLY AND INTELLECTUALLY.

Painting, photography, and street art often have definite advantages over poetry and fiction in that when you look at a piece of art, you don't immediately ask yourself what a certain tree symbolizes or what the blue rectangle is a metaphor for. Accordingly, you can approach reading art in different ways. Instead of trying to figure out what the painting "means," try to pay attention to what the painting or photo "evokes." What sort of reaction or response does the piece elicit? Is there a mood or tone? Does the painting or its colors create any particular emotion? You might also ask yourself how the artist works with notions of beauty. Is the picture or sculpture conventional in its use of beauty, or does he or she challenge typical ideas of beauty? If Hieronymus Bosch's *Garden of Earthly Delights* makes you uncomfortable, then the painting has succeeded as a rhetorical and semiotic text. If you thought Shepard Fairey's prints of Barack Obama were cool, then you got what he was going for. If you find Georgia O'Keefe's paintings of flowers, pistils, and stamens strangely erotic, then you are probably experiencing the kind of reaction that she intended. Works like Picasso's *Guernica* might affect you emotionally first, then begin to move you on an intellectual level—or vice versa. Either way, artists use shapes, colors, scale, and tone to make you feel a certain way. Thus, you may be reading the text of the art work on a subconscious level and not even know it.

PAY ATTENTION TO THE GRAMMAR OR SYNTAX OF VISUAL ART.

Like written language, visual art enjoys its own set of rules and structures. You don't have to know many of these terms or ideas to enjoy or understand art, but knowing some does help to decode individual artistic texts. For instance, let's look at the notion of **composition**. Chances are that you are in a composition course right now, and while artistic composition is slightly different, there are similarities. To compose means to "put together" or "assemble." It comes from two Latin words: *com*, which means "together," and *poser*, which means to "place or to put down." Accordingly, "composition" means to place together. In this way, the composition of a photograph or advertisement resembles the composition of your essays: both are texts that have been assembled from various "components" (a word with the same origin). So then the composition of a work of art is the plan or placement of the various elements of the piece. Most of the time, a painting's composition is related to the principles of design, such as balance, color, rhythm, texture, emphasis, and proportion. The same can often be said of a particularly smart advertisement or web page.

Let's say you are looking at Leonardo da Vinci's masterpiece *The Last Supper*. You might notice the symmetry or balance of the painting, how the table and the men are perfectly framed by the walls of the building, and how Jesus is framed in the very center of the piece by the open doorway. Placing Jesus in this position, lighting him from the back, gives him a certain emphasis the disciples lack. His red robe and his blue sash add to his stature, as does his posture. He looks as though he is offering a blessing, a gesture that underscores da Vinci's interpretation of

Christ as a giver and a healer. Thus, how the artist places his subject (at the center) and how he depicts him (as offering both thanks and blessing) and how his subject is contrasted against the rest of the painting (in red and almost radiating light, power, and glory) is a kind of argument or thesis to the painting, just as you will create an argument or thesis for your own composition.

Taken all together, then, the various components of a painting or a photograph contribute to the piece's effect. This is true even for visual texts that may not seem like art. Look, for example, at the web page for Four Barrel Coffee in San Francisco (http://www.fourbarrelcoffee.com) or Dot Zero Design out of Portland (http://dotzerodesign.com). In both instances, these sites play with very simple notions of composition for a dramatic effect.

HOW WE SEE, EVALUATE, INTERPRET, AND WRITE ABOUT ART IS INFLUENCED BY A NUMBER OF FORCES.

The visual arts extend beyond paintings we find in museums—they include digital images, installations, LED texts, performances, collages, comics, and a host of other media. For a long time, there has been a rift between "high" and "low" art. Some people believe that artists like Picasso, Claude Monet, Édouard Manet, Vincent van Gogh, Leonardo da Vinci, Michelangelo, Francisco Goya, Edgar Degas, and the like produce "high" art, where say, Nagel prints, photos of cars, most outdoor murals, much folk or "primitive" art, digital images, cartoons, Hummel figurines, Precious Moments statuettes, and any mass-produced design is seen by many as "low" or "populist" art. For instance, we love the Dogs Playing Poker series (Figure 1), but you are unlikely to see any of these paintings (despite how funny they are) in the Louvre, the Metropolitan Museum of Modern Art, or the Chicago Art Institute

Fig. 1 C. M. Coolidge, *A Friend In Need* (1903)

Fig. 2 William Wegman, *Jack Sprat* (1996)

because they are considered "blue collar" or "pedestrian" or "unsophisticated." That said, William Wegman's photos of dogs (Figure 2) *are* considered art. You can find calendars and postcards in the gift shops of most museums and the photos themselves on the walls.

Still, the question of why one is "art" and one is "tacky" remains. Both are color images of dogs at tables. What makes the Wegman piece art? (One reason might be that the Wegman dogs in a way are mocking the dogs playing poker. Of course, the dogs playing poker might be themselves mocking something else.) These kinds of questions are at the heart of the art world and continue to serve as cultural markers of education, sophistication, social class, and good taste. There are many, many people who would judge your sense of taste depending on which of these two images you think is the best "art." Now, if you "like" the poker dogs better than the eating dogs, that's one thing; but if you argue that the poker dogs are better *art*, that is another matter altogether.

These issues come into play in provocative ways when we consider issues of public art and street art. For some, graffiti is not "art," but for others, it is a form of social communication. A tattooed body, a tagged building, a painted van can all be seen as artistic texts—as forms of visual culture—but they may not be taken seriously as "art" by certain members of the cultural elite and can even be seen as examples of defacement. Why are murals by Diego Rivera or Rigo considered art but not Andre the Giant posters? That would be a great paper topic!

ART REFLECTS NOT ONLY THE ARTISTS THEMSELVES BUT ALSO THEIR CULTURE.

Like music, literature, and film, the visual arts are products not only of artists but also of the culture in which the artist lives and works. It should come as no surprise that during the Middle Ages and the Renaissance, when the Catholic Church dominated the religious and political landscape of Europe, that most of the paintings reflected Biblical themes. Similarly, during the Romantic period, large, dark, brooding, tumultuous paintings tended to mimic "romantic" characteristics that worked their way into both architecture and fiction. Even the earliest cave paintings and rock art focuses on themes important to the artists of the time—hunting, fishing, keeping warm, and invoking the gods. The belief that art reflects the world in which it exists is called **mimesis.** Some people may argue that artistic movements such as Surrealism and Cubism were movements away from mimetic art because people like Marcel Duchamp, Georges Braque, Picasso, and Man Ray distorted reality in their work. However, if we consider that, at this time, most artists, writers, and thinkers found the early twentieth century to be a time of chaos, disorder, violence, alienation, and fragmentation, then one can make a compelling argument that Picasso's and Braque's fissured pictoral landscapes reflected a fissured cultural and political landscape.

Currently, as our culture becomes more politically conscious, so too does our art. Andres Serrano has become famous for his photographs of guns, murdered corpses, and Ku Klux Klan members; Native American artist Jaune Quick-to-See Smith assembles journalism articles about violence toward American Indians, sports mascots from teams whose mascots are Indians, and stereotypes of "natives" such as toy tomahawks and moccasins to make comments on contemporary American Indian life; photographer Cindy Sherman did a series of disturbing photographs of mutilated female mannequins as a commentary on the violence toward and objectification of women; and Michael Ray Charles, an African American painter, has made a career out of augmenting representations of "Sambo," a disturbing stereotype used to mock African Americans. In each of these situations, art crosses over from the aesthetic world and into the world of ethics, becoming not just artistic statements but political statements.

We mentioned Shepard Fairey above because his posters of Barack Obama became national icons during the presidential campaign. It was a rare moment when someone with a street art background successfully entered into the world of high art and political culture, and it is worth asking how and why *these* images of *this* man struck a chord. When you write your paper, do not be afraid to consider all of the non-art forces that have shaped attitudes about your topic.

OFTEN THERE IS A GAP BETWEEN THE ARTIST AND THE PUBLIC.

It is somewhat of a cliché by now, but what an artist finds appealing is not always what the public finds appealing. The furor over the *Sensation* exhibition in 1999 is one of the most recent in a long line of controversial artistic moments. In 1989, three men—Jesse Helms (a Republican senator from North Carolina), the conservative politician and commentator

Patrick Buchanan, and art critic Hilton Kramer—launched an all-out attack on *The Perfect Moment*, a traveling exhibit of photographs by Robert Mapplethorpe that was funded by the National Endowment for the Arts (which gets some of its money from tax dollars). Some of Mapplethorpe's photographs crossed the line of decency, according to those critics and others, because of their explicit homoerotic themes and because two photographs were of naked children. What resulted was a long legal and cultural battle over pornography, public funding for the arts, morality, and artistic freedom. Similarly, Andres Serrano's wildly controversial photograph *Piss Christ* nearly got the NEA shut down for good. The 1987 photograph of a crucifix dropped in urine angered so many people that it brought about the most thorough scrutiny of public financial support for the arts in American history. But America is not the only battleground for art and culture. To this day, if you visit Picasso's famous painting *Guernica* in Madrid, you will likely be accosted by locals who will want to give you a revisionist reading of the painting, which still remains behind glass to protect it from vandalism.

Photography tends to draw more fire than other art forms because people do not always see photographs as texts but as a reflection of the actual world (see our photography suite in this chapter for more about this subject). Along these same lines, think about how public art can be. Paintings and photos hang on walls of hotels and libraries, and grace the walls of museums. We encourage our children to go to museums to get "enlightened." If what parents find at the museum disturbs them, then the public role of art often gets called into question. As readers of the world, be aware of the various forces that determine how we see art and how we see art's role in forging a vision of contemporary culture.

In the case of public art (art that is in an outdoor public space as opposed to a private residence or museum), community standards can affect how a visual text is received. Public art like murals, memorials, and sculptures on public land are often funded by local taxpayer dollars. If residents do not agree either with the political message or the aesthetic design of art funded with their tax dollars, there can be big problems. However, this also happens on smaller scales. Most of you can think of an over-the-top Christmas decoration, a controversial poster, a questionable advertisement, an offensive sign, or a religiously divisive installation from your hometown that got people all worked up. Good paper topics are those than enable you to write not just about the formal aspects of visual culture but social and political aspects as well.

WORKS OF MODERN AND CONTEMPORARY ART DESERVE YOUR ATTENTION BECAUSE THEY ARE OFTEN IMPORTANT TEXTS ABOUT THE CONTEMPORARY WORLD.

Chances are, if you are like most people, you are totally confused by modern art, which often seems like an endless series of nonsensical images: people with square heads, splatters of paint, chaos. What is important to recognize about modern art is the audience's role in constructing the text. While modern artists do create work that may reflect their perspective and their culture, they also rely on the viewer to bring to their work an idea about what art is and how art functions. Frequently, viewers of modern art complain that they could have done the work themselves; they focus on the craftsmanship of modern art. But the artist might argue that the conception of art and the discussion of what art is and what it means is what makes modern art so compelling, and being a good reader of modern and contemporary art can give you valuable insights into recent social, political, and artistic moments.

Modern art saw the rise of the most recognizable schools: cubism, expressionism, fauvism, futurism, abstract expressionism, pop art, and collage. Figures like Pablo Picasso, Paul Klee, Wassily Kandinsky, Joan Miro, Gustav Klimt, Georges Braque, Edvard Munch, Henri Rousseau, Henri Matisse, Jackson Pollock, Robert Motherwell, Andy Warhol, and a host of others ushered in an entirely new way of looking at art. Much of modern art is abstract or **nonrepresentational,** which means that the subjects of the paintings may not be nature or people but ideas, politics, or art itself (but they might just look like shapes). It is no coincidence that art took such a radical turn in the twentieth century: The innovations in technology, literature, film, psychology, and communication found commensurate innovations in the art world; those innovations, like art itself, tend to focus on destabilizing traditional forms and narratives. Modern artists believe that if you change the way you see the world, you change the world. So you have artists playing with reality: Paul Klee said he wanted to make the nonvisible visible; Kandinsky claimed that form was the outer expression of inner content; Picasso once wrote that if he wanted to express the roundness of a glass, he might have to make it square. Thus the changes in the world, the growths in perspective and innovation, get reflected and chronicled in our art.

More recent pieces like Claes Oldenburg's big funny sculptures of clothespins and erasers, Andy Goldsworthy's works made out of leaves, sticks, and his own saliva, and the street art of people like Jean-Michel Basquiat, Keith Haring, and Lee Quinones have radically altered even modern ideas about what "art" is. Street art in particular has exploded in the past ten years. For example, in 2001 IBM hired people in San Francisco and Chicago to paint the Linux symbol (a penguin) and a peace sign on sidewalks around town to promote Linux computer systems. Sony launched similar campaigns to draw attention to its PSP gaming system, and clothing designer Marc Ecko has praised street art as a valid form of creative expression. For your own assignments, think about what you think art should do and be. What *is* art? Such a definition paper may work well in addressing modern art.

REPRODUCTION AND TECHNOLOGY HAVE CHANGED HOW WE SEE AND VALUE ART.

One of our favorite books is *Ways of Seeing* by British writer John Berger. Based on a BBC television series, *Ways of Seeing* walks the reader through various "ways" we see the world. Berger's analysis ranges from looking at landscape to art to advertisements to fashion. For example, Berger makes a compelling argument about how women are posed and presented in modern ads. According to Berger, these seductive images are a reproduction of the way male artists would position the "ideal" woman in Renaissance and Enlightenment paintings. Notice, for example, how many early nude paintings feature women in unnatural and uncomfortable poses and how, quite often, they look directly at the viewer (assumed, at the

Fig. 3 Grant Wood, *American Gothic* (1930). Oil on Beaver Board.
29 7/8" × 24 7/8". Friends of American Art. The Art Institute of Chicago.

time, to be male). Contemporary artist Cindy Sherman plays with this tradition in many of her photographs.

Another of Berger's more enduring observations involves what happens to a work of art when it is reproduced over and over and over again. For Berger, the ability to reproduce art—to put the *Mona Lisa* on T-shirts, to place Van Gogh paintings on coffee mugs, to make huge blow-up dolls of Edvard Munch's *The Scream*, to be able to hang a poster of Gustav Klimt's *The Kiss* in every residence hall in the United States—translates into the ability to change the meaning of that art based on how it is used. For example, one of the most famous American paintings—perhaps *the* most famous American painting—is Grant Wood's *American Gothic* (Figure 3).

You have likely seen an image of the painting hundreds of times, though you probably have never stood before the *actual* work of art. Indeed, even though the original hangs in the Chicago Art Institute, you don't have to travel to the Windy City to see *American Gothic*—you can just search the web.

But is double-clicking on a photo of *American Gothic* on Google really "seeing" *American Gothic?* For instance, what is the painting made of? What are its dimensions? Thousands of people visit Chicago to see it every year; however, by the time they get there, they have probably been exposed to reproductions and alterations of the painting hundreds of times over the course of their lives. These issues make some wonder about the specialness or uniqueness of a work of art in the age of reproduction.

The famous German thinker Walter Benjamin first posed these questions in a remarkably influential essay called "The Work of Art in the Age of Mechanical Reproduction" (1936). According to Benjamin, even the best, most perfect reproduction lacks the original work's "presence in time and space, its unique existence at the place where it happens to be." For Benjamin, this raises important questions about authenticity (which we talk about later in the Authenticity Suite in Chapter 9), particularly in regard to photography's ability to print images over and over again. Can a photograph be a unique, original work of "art" if you can print hundreds of them?

One of Benjamin's most enduring arguments is that the mass reproduction of art changes how the masses respond to art. Or, put another way, the ability to reproduce famous paintings can turn high culture into popular culture. For instance, people who wear *American Gothic* ties might be honoring the painting, or they might see it as an ironic gesture. Twenty years ago, Gustav Klimt was a sort of fringe artist, but the proliferation of *The Kiss* has transformed him into another Monet or Degas or Picasso—not because thousands were wowed by the painting while visiting the Österreichische Galerie Belvedere in Vienna—but because folks have been wowed by the reproduction of the painting they have seen on cards and posters around the world. In fact, the great irony is that most who love the *image* have never seen the original *painting*.

On one hand, this is great for art, artists, and museums. On the other hand, however, Berger and Benjamin argue that these instances of reproduction strip the original of its power (what Benjamin calls **aura**). For example, how does it change your regard for the "authentic" *American Gothic* when you see the image on the next page.

A quick Google image search for "American Gothic" returns dozens of hits for crazy versions of this classic image. Neither Berger nor Benjamin could have predicted the proliferation and alteration of artistic images in the digital age. What's more, computer programs like Photoshop make it easy to take Wood's painting in all sorts of directions.

What makes these images funny is that they not only play on the original painting, they also play on the overuse of the original painting—proving Berger's and Benjamin's points. The repetitive use and overexposure of *American Gothic* has altered the meaning of the original painting, transforming it into a kind of icon to be parodied.

Even the images you see in this chapter are reproductions; in fact, they are reproductions of reproductions. And yet, the ability for Pearson to print these images relatively cheaply means you get to see the works of Marnie Spencer, Chris Ofili, Warhol, and, of course, dogs playing poker from the comfort of your dorm room, library, or favorite coffee shop. The question is, now that you have seen reproductions of an Andy Warhol piece, will you be more likely or less likely to seek out the original? Does it even matter? Is art more or less than the original work? What is important to remember is that the ubiquity of an image affects how we see and think about that image—for better or worse.

AMERICAN GOTH

Again, look at the perspective of the piece in question. Has the artist made you see the world or nature or a person or an object differently? If so, how? Ask yourself how the artist has represented the world, that is, how has he or she re-presented the world? Why might an artist be interested in altering your perception of something? Perhaps because if you learn to see the world in a new way fairly often, then looking at the world will be a way of creating your own art.

A CHAPTER OF SUITES.

Rather than present a menu of various essays, we decided to cluster the readings in this chapter and offer, in essence, a chapter of two different suites plus a photo essay. We found we kept coming back to the biggest question of all, what makes art?

THIS TEXT

1. While it will be impossible for you to know this fully, try to figure out the writing situation of each author. Who is the audience? What does the author have at stake? What is his or her agenda? Why is she or he writing this piece?

2. What are the main points of the essay? Can you find a thesis statement? Remember, it doesn't have to be one sentence—it can be several sentences or a whole paragraph.

3. What textual cues does the author use to help get his or her point across?

Worksheet

4. How does the author support his or her argument? What evidence does the author use to back up any claims he or she might make?
5. Is the author's argument valid? Is it reasonable?
6. Do you find yourself in agreement with the author? Why or why not?
7. Does the author help you read the visual arts better than you did before reading the essay? If so, why?
8. What issues about race, ethnicity, class, and gender does the writer raise? Do you think the writer has an agenda of sorts?
9. Did you like the piece? Why or why not?

BEYOND THIS TEXT

1. What are the major themes of the work? What is the artist trying to suggest?
2. What techniques does the artist use to get his or her message across? Why *these* techniques?
3. What are we to make of the characters in the painting or photograph? What is their function? What is their race? Their social class? Are they like you? How?
4. Where does the text take place? When is it set?
5. What are the main conflicts of the text? What issues are at stake?
6. What kinds of issues of identity is the artist working on in the text?
7. Is there tension between the self and society in the text? How? Why?
8. What is the agenda of the artist? Why does she or he want me to think a certain way?
9. How is the text put together? What is its composition? How does it make meaning?
10. What techniques is the author using? How does it adhere to issues of artistic design?
11. Did you like this artwork? Why or why not?

QUICK GUIDE TO WRITING ABOUT ART

1. Make sure if you going to a museum that you take a notebook or pad. Carefully note the name of the work and the artist.
2. If you take interpretive information from the artwork, write down the source. If you do not know the source, write down the name of the museum.
3. If you can take a photograph of the artwork, do so (many museums do not allow photographs, but some do—ask). If not, outline the work on your pad.
4. Note your initial and final emotional responses to the artwork.
5. Write down, at least in key words, what work you think the artist is doing.
6. If you are writing about public art, note the surroundings. Does the art fit with the surroundings? And vice-versa?
7. Finally, think about what you would tell a friend about the piece of work you just viewed. Sometimes the most important thing jumps out when storytelling.

The "Is It Art"? Suite

As we discussed earlier, art often frustrates us. Given a piece of modern art or even folk art, we might exclaim, "That isn't art!" This is true especially if the work seems to rely on idea rather than craftsmanship. But what we're really saying is, "That isn't *good* art." It's not hard to argue that someone who intends to create art is indeed creating art of one kind or another. This suite—our largest—looks at the provocative question, "Is it art?" and encourages you to come up with an answer.

What makes something *art*? Is it technique, theme, the support of famous people, or the adherence to specific criteria? Can "popular" art be "good" art? Can texts not intended as art objects be art? What is at stake if something is or is not art? The following essays discuss these questions and others as they explore the nature of art and criteria for judging it.

There is a lot at stake with this question, both for the artist and for the culture at large. Artists hold special places in our culture, so being an "artist" can mean more money, more commissions, a higher profile, museum collections, and eventually, maybe even postcards, neckties, magnets, and totebags with reproductions of one's work. If a text gets elevated to the level of "art," it is often assumed to have some sort of relevance to or comment on our culture. If a text becomes art, then the values embodied by that text are often seen as sanctioned, even valuable. For example, in previous editions of this book, we published a fantastic essay by E. G. Chrichton in which he argues that the NAMES AIDS quilt meets the definition of "art," as opposed to "craft" or "textile." It's a controversial argument because it signals for some that high culture approves of gay culture—even aestheticizes it. In other words, if we decide that something is art, we place it in an important place in our culture.

Murals, for example, have always had an odd place in art culture—are they "high art" or "street art?" We begin this suite with a short, accessible reading that gets at this important question. In the fall of 2010 all incoming students to the University of San Francisco were required to "read" *A Man at the Crossroads*, a famous and controversial mural by the Mexican artist Diego Rivera as part of their orientation to USF, its mission, and its academic trajectory. Erig Hongisto, himself a painter and a professor at USF, was instrumental in framing and coordinating the project. Hongisto received his MFA in Painting/Printmaking from the Yale University School of Art, 1999, and his BFA in Painting from the Maine College of Art, 1997. He is the recipient of a Pollock-Krasner Foundation Grant, a 2005 Guggenheim Fellowship in Installation and a 2002 New York Foundation of the Arts Painting Fellowship. He makes a case for Rivera's painting as art, and he argues that the techniques we use to determine its artfulness can help students in other aspects of college.

Similarly, Diana Mack (1999) argues that questions surrounding "good" art have resonances beyond the art world. In writing about the *Sensation* exhibition, she wonders who can and should define the standards for good or even acceptable public art. In classic definitional manner, Mack lays out three principles for evaluating art. Anna Rose Tull, a student at the University of San Francisco (and a student of Hongisto's), follows Mack with her own take on the controversial artist Damien Hirst. She wrote this paper in 2008 as part of the freshman writing sequence at USF. The next two essays also deal with street art. Steve Grody is a martial arts specialist and a choreographer who has also become a specialist on Los Angeles graffiti. In this 2006 piece, an excerpt from his fine book *Graffiti L.A.*, he offers a close semiotic reading of two works of graffiti art, and he introduces this art with an original piece written especially for *The World Is a Text*. Similarly, Theresa George argues for reading graffiti through an inclusive lens in her essay for Professor Devon Holmes's Rhetoric and Composition 210 class at the University of San Francisco in 2007.

Lastly, we finish off this suite with a short photo essay we're calling "Pubic Art." Some of the pieces might be considered "high art," others "street art," and still others almost no one would define as art. We're not necessarily making artistic claims for or against any of the images, but we hope to inspire you to think and talk and write about these objects in terms of how they enter into conversation with the world around them.

A quick note of explanation: since this chapter is a suite of suites, questions about the readings come at the end of the entire suite rather than at the end of each reading.

Reading A Mural: Diego Rivera's *Man at the Crossroads*

Eric Hongisto

THERE IS NO EXPERIENCE QUITE LIKE READING A MURAL. Most murals are outside, often painted on the side of a building, so as art objects, they interact with the daily activities of people, the neighborhood, and the visual landscape. Visually a mural relies on the techniques of painting, but because murals contain a narrative, they also rely on storytelling techniques of short stories and novels. Most murals tend to have a political or social function, so part of decoding them involves focusing your time around observing an image and contemplating visual relationships between society and culture. We'll be converging around a large-scale mural painting by the Mexican artist, Diego Rivera. This picture, titled *Man at the Crossroads*, was censored and destroyed; it was also later repainted and retitled *Man at the Center of the Universe*.

The original mural was created in 1933. You should imagine that we're in the heart of the Great Depression, a time period of 25% unemployment, widespread poverty and

social collapse following the plummet of the stock market in 1929. This time period also follows the slaughter of millions in World War I and is the framework for the run-up to World War II, with multiple fascist leaders beginning to garner control of their respective countries.

This particular mural has a complex history. The Rockefellers, who were the wealthiest family in America, commissioned Rivera to come to New York City and create *Man at the Crossroads* directly on the walls inside Rockefeller plaza. This fresco painting was a huge, complex undertaking. Many assistants and materials were required to create this work of art. And this permanent painting required the artist to have an entire team of assistants to be on site while creating the public artwork.

The Rockefeller family was surely aware of the rich history of Diego Rivera's complex visual imagery. He was well known as a champion Social Realist painter who frequently intertwined relationships between modernism, nationality, identity, and righting repression. He gave power and representation to workers' rights, and he was an unabashed Communist, but the Rockefellers were less than impressed when an unplanned portrait of Vladimir Lenin (the famous/infamous Russian-Communist leader) ended up in the painting.

This is one of the only photographs of the original mural while it was being created—because before this painting was finished, John D. Rockefeller Jr., asked Rivera to paint out the image of Lenin. Rivera defiantly would not alter the fresco so Rockefeller froze the project, paid him in full and then had the painting secretly hammered and destroyed overnight. The history surrounding this event is an amazing act of creativity and destruction. In his autobiography written in 1960, Rivera recalled this as censorship, saying "In human creation there is something which belongs to humanity at large, and . . . no individual owner has the right to destroy it or keep it solely for his own enjoyment."

However, to the world's benefit, Rivera later repainted a very similar mural at the Palace of Fine Arts in Mexico City. After the Rockefeller misfortune, Rivera's commission to paint another large-scale mural at General Motors in Detroit was cancelled, and indeed he had a decade of lost American commissions. We are very fortunate that he did return to America and created two world-class murals in San Francisco.

I suppose you're familiar with texting, emailing pictures and using other communication devices. And I would bet that you use these on a daily if not hourly basis. When we do this, we're utilizing our visual intelligence. Let's guess that many of you have texted in a classroom or maybe while your teacher was speaking. Or maybe you've driven a car while talking on a cell phone. When this happens, our attention span slows down, and our ability to focus is diminished.

Sometimes we choose to rush, like when we're reading a blog, which is usually done quickly. We scan for information or go right for the juicy comments section. Alternatively, when we're reading a challenging novel, we slow down, savoring the plot development through sympathetic chararacters unfolding over time. Let's try and understand what 'reading' a painting might entail and to develop a comparison to the blog and to the novel as modes of careful analysis.

Let's stress something about pictures . . . because it's very important that you are developing your own opinion about images. It's also critical to look from multiple vantage points. When you place yourself into a different perspective it can be easier to grasp new ideas and to further develop your sensibilities. In *Man at the Center of the Universe,* Rivera has painted an array of complexities with layers of meaning. We do need to step back because of this dizzying array of information. If we jumped in too quickly we'd see: an isolated individual, displays of wealth and economics, leaders of politics, labor groups, education, medicine, war, and agriculture.

✳ We want to understand the power of pictures—and as viewers, it's important to read paintings with the leading question: how and why have certain decisions been made? First, observe the colors, shapes and lines painted by the artist. We'll call these factors—the formal aspects of a composition. Alternatively, we'll also look at the central idea of pictures— which we'll call subject matter or the content of a painting. These choices, purposeful by the artists, accentuate meaning and subject matter depicted in their illusions. And as you can sense, we have a difficult time separating the forms from the content that each picture conveys. Let's go back to the metaphor of driving with a cell phone. When we slow down we can utilize our visual intelligence to see both the form and the meaning simultaneously, pulling together a stronger reading of a picture.

Let's stress that to read into this mural further, you do not need a reference book, a Wikipedia entry or be an art history major. Like a film director, novelist or an architect, think of Rivera as he organized the elements of the picture. Walk your eyes around the mural, look up, look down, compare both sides, see the quadrants, notice the special symbols inside these compartments. Make a closer inspection of the center of this composition, and try to find the central motif or theme in which the other characters play out from this entrance point. Remember how big a mural is—sometimes 30 feet by 40 feet in the case of Rivera's murals. How does this change your relationship as you stand there looking at the equivalent of a movie screen?

Even without knowing what is happening historically, and knowing the title of a painting or who made it or what genre or art period something is from, your visual intelligence can 'read' formal choices of size, color, shape and placement. You can use your intuition and see into the emotion of the characters. You can also compare symbols that allow you to assemble parts to the whole. And to help yourself, use your computer, try zooming into an area of the picture, looking for the sub-themes and messages Rivera has encoded into various quadrants.

In ending, we'd also like you to consider this mural in the light of current contemporary issues. Today is not that different from the 1930's. We are suffering from high unemployment and stagnant wages. We are fighting various wars in foreign countries, witnessing environmental disasters and revisiting complex immigration issues. Read this painting with special consideration to these issues of social justice. Treat the painting like a blog and a novel: read it intuitively, step back, and analyze.

It Isn't Pretty . . . But Is It Art?

Diana Mack

FEW AMERICANS WAKE UP MORNINGS contemplating the question of what makes a good work of art. But surprisingly enough, three belligerent public disputes have recently centered on this very question.

New York Mayor Rudolph Giuliani made headlines last month when he vowed to withhold municipal funding if the Brooklyn Museum of Art went through with its controversial British art exhibition, *Sensation*. The major object of contention: an image of the Virgin Mary, her breast rendered in elephant dung (see p. 471).

Then, a few weeks later, parents in South Carolina, Georgia, and Minnesota protested the presence in public school classrooms of J. K. Rowling's bestselling Harry Potter series, one mother claiming this fantasy literature carried "a serious tone of death, hate . . . and . . . evil."

Finally, there was the public uproar in Seattle over the heavily bosomed and pregnant *Picardo Venus*, a community garden statue many find too suggestive.

In each case, those objecting to the disbursement of public funds for the display of art they find offensive insist they are not for censorship. They claim they merely want publicly funded and publicly presented artwork to reflect community standards of taste, decency, and respect for religious faith. All well and good; but who is to define those standards? Chris Ofili, painter of the *Sensation* exhibition's much maligned *Holy Virgin Mary*, claims that Mr. Giuliani falsely assigned deprecatory motives to his work. He is not out to desecrate the image of the Virgin Mary, he says.

Rather, he's a Roman Catholic earnestly coming to terms with his faith, his African heritage, and a long Western tradition of representing the Madonna.

Similarly, J. K. Rowling might claim that the Harry Potter books also stand in a long "pre-apologetic" literary tradition: Yes, they deal with magic and witchcraft. Their tone is dark. But no less a devout Christian than C. S. Lewis understood the power of pagan imagery in preparing the young imagination for the moral rigors and spiritual comforts of biblical religion. Indeed, if there is something wrong with a "tone of death" in children's literature, then we might as well jettison all our volumes of fairy tales. For these distilled popular narratives exert their charm and power precisely, as Bruno Bettelheim pointed out, because they allow children a reality-removed way to confront the "existential predicament."

And what of the *Picardo Venus?* Must she be rejected, as one citizen–critic contended, because she "glorifies fertility a little too much for kids," or because, as another said, "no normal woman looks like that"?

Do "normal" women look like Picasso painted them? Or Rubens? Did not Botticelli's immortal *The Birth of Venus* also glorify fertility? The point is that almost all the arguments we bring against public support of controversial new works are at best specious, at worst manifestly wrongheaded. Informed aesthetic judgments seem to elude us.

Faced with creative works that seem to us alien and unappealing, we are forced to fall back on that proverbial disclaimer, "I don't know much about it . . . I only know what I like."

Just because an artwork doesn't make us feel warm and fuzzy doesn't mean it's worthless. The Seattle man who protests against the *Picardo Venus* on the basis that "art is supposed to evoke all these good feelings" is wrong. Good art is not necessarily pleasing. It is, however, disciplined. It is about mastery of medium, form, and style. And good art must communicate something comprehensibly worthwhile, something worthy of contemplation. And here we get closer to the aesthetic problem facing the American public today. More and more so-called artists today call attention to themselves by shocking and

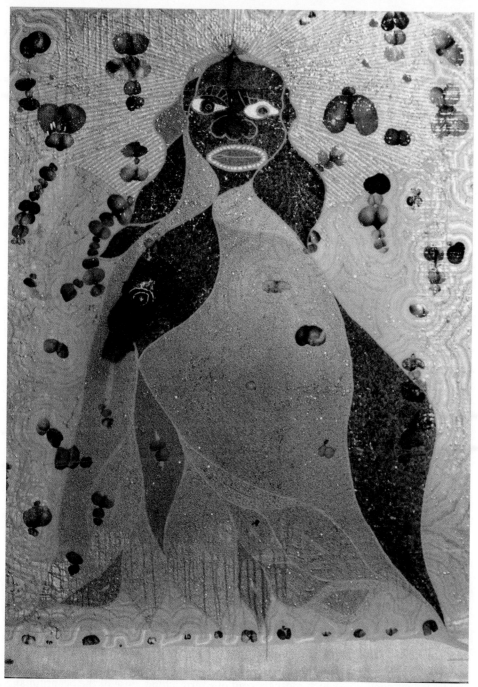

Chris Ofili, *Holy Virgin Mary* (1996).

agitating rather than by promoting reflection. In reaction to these salvos, the public has come to anticipate offense.

How do we move past the disturbing impasse of public contention over art and toward a healthier, more vital cultural life? One answer is to be guided in our aesthetic judgments by three important principles:

1. Art doesn't do. It says. Art is not action; it is speculation. It is looking, listening, digesting, speaking. Art can make a controversial statement; but it cannot do controversial things. If the primary effect of a so-called artwork is physical repulsion or titillation, if it acts on us rather than speaks to us, it is simply not up to the standards of art. If it makes us think, however, we should take up the challenge.
2. Art is about content, not context. Art is the schematic arrangement of forms and symbols through specific, culturally recognized mediums. If we exhibit, say, a cow's embryo in an art museum, it does not suddenly become a work of visual art simply by virtue of its surroundings.
3. Similarly, if we hung a print of Titian's *Woman on a Couch* in a biology lab, it would scarcely transform that painting into a science display. We need to be open to the possibilities of the creative process; yet, we must recognize that not everything offered up in the artistic arena is art.

The greater the knowledge, the sounder the judgment. When we venture onto the battlefield of the culture wars, we owe it to our artists and ourselves to come armed with knowledge. In a multicultural society such as America's, that means making the attempt to familiarize ourselves with the major artistic traditions of Europe, Asia, and Africa. Before we criticize, we need first to understand. Indeed, there is nothing more inspiring to good artists than a public that can be communicated with on the highest and most subtle levels of creativity and skill.

Graffiti: The Anatomy of a Piece

Steve Grody

BEFORE LOOKING AT THE DIAGRAM ON PAGE 473, it is useful to acknowledge the human tendency towards snobbery and how that can put on blinders. The development of aesthetic sensitivity tends to be specific to an individual's focus. While a modern jazz fan would immediately recognize an Eric Dolphy solo as distinct from John Coltrane, those with no appreciation of jazz might not hear any difference, even if they had a sensitivity to orchestral or pop music. Bringing the issue closer to home, even artists familiar with modernist abstract artists such as Robert Motherwell or Franz Kline tend to regard modern graffiti pieces (such as those in the diagram on p. 473) with condescension, even while grudgingly acknowledging their craft as contemporary urban folk practice.

Because graffiti is vernacular, it is rarely seen by outsiders as something expressing "transcendent poetics"—which means a kind of overreaching sense of the beautiful and often, a dividing line between "high" and "low" art. The difference between snobbery and simply having individual preference for one aesthetic mode or another is the moral presumption carried. That is, those doing gallery-career oriented art often (albeit unconsciously)

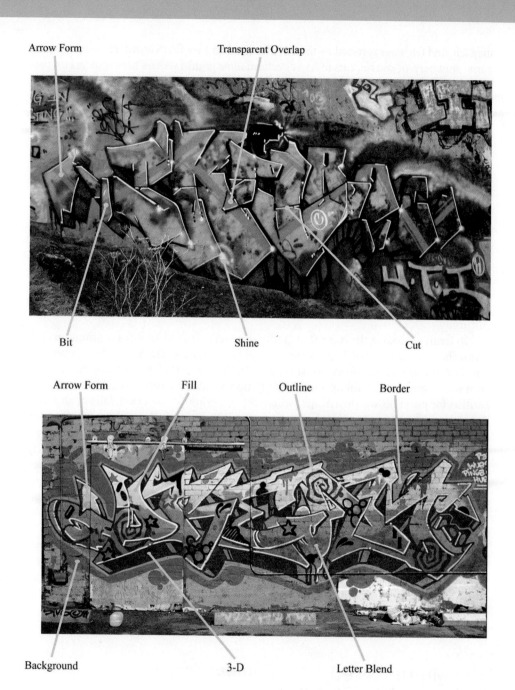

Arrow Form   Transparent Overlap

Bit   Shine   Cut

Arrow Form   Fill   Outline   Border

Background   3-D   Letter Blend

presume that a high-art or gallery-based endeavor is intrinsically more worthy, of greater moral value, than graffiti (and here we are referring to the technically sophisticated high-end spray can work). It is that moral stance that keeps one from engaging less familiar modes of expression. Interestingly, most veteran graffiti writers speak of the emotional impact that they felt, and felt was expressed by the work seen, when they first viewed a powerful graffiti piece. Snobbery, of course, cuts in any direction: most graffiti writers have blinders on preventing them from appreciating or deeply understanding much of the art done throughout history. While some might recognize a Matisse, for example, it would be rare for any to understand how radical his art is in its treading the line between representation and abstraction, as well as his exquisite color formalism. (Of course most art history Ph.Ds know Matisse's formalism as well.)

Critic Christopher Knight makes a strong argument that the prominent art critic from the 50s and 60s, Clement Greenberg, did a great disservice to following generations of artists and critics by proposing a cultural dividing line between High Art and popular art: since we can easily see examples of supposedly High Art that are empty and sterile in effect and can also see examples of Pop forms of art that are emotionally moving, should we not, Knight argues, throw out those categories with and simply look at a given piece of art and judge it for how it works on its own terms? This is not the same as a nihilistic view that argues against High/Low categories, stemming from a belief that work made from a moral basis (read: life affirming) is empty cultural pretense—that is, morality is merely a concept relative to a particular dominant culture.

In terms of reading the context of graffiti, it's useful to think of three continuums. The first is the continuum from legal to illegal; legal being those spaces where there is permission to paint, and illegal where arrest is possible. Within the "illegal" part of that continuum is a second continuum of vandalistic to non-vandalistic intention. That is, there is graffiti (for example, on storefronts) where the intention is clearly vandalism, and then there is a great deal of illegal work that is on a back alley wall, industrial rooftop or abandoned sites where it would be hard to classify the work as defacing anything. In this regard, the terms "damage" or "destruction" which are often used in relation to graffiti are entirely inappropriate: a construction barrier or formerly bare freeway wall has never been "destroyed" by graffiti. The wall fully maintains its function. This is not to say that people should like graffiti, just a clarification of a fact. The third continuum is simply that of legibility, from easy to read block fonts, to letters only the writer of the piece would be able to decipher.

There is no doubt that the two pieces on p. 473 contain some of the same compositional techniques of high art. One could draw comparisons between these works and large-scale paintings by Juan Gris and Willem de Kooning. Ultimately, if these works and those of so-called high art are both thoughtful, technically astute, aesthetically constructed texts, why ask if one is intrinsically superior than another?

The Multifaceted Nature of Street Art

Theresa George

Student Essay

"THESE MYSTERIOUS HEROES of wild communication, these spontaneous artists whose signs were volatile and abrupt, tough and angry, vehement and vital, created a great fresco . . . irreverent and complicit, committed and contrary, implicated and distant, sentimental and caustic." Here, Lea Vergine, author of *Art on the Cutting Edge: A Guide to*

Contemporary Movements, speaks of graffiti, a passionate form of art and expression that is rarely regarded as such. This unique art form provides a feeling of social belonging, literacy practice, and political and educational outreach for many of its creators. Unfortunately, a great number of city planners and criminologists have worked together in efforts to try to eliminate street art and in effect the stigmas that allegedly go along with it. The problem we must face is not how to control these spontaneous, and many times planned, events of artistic ability but how to approach each of these works as authentic and meaningful as they relate to their creators and their environments.

Just like many other socially accepted phenomena, street art can and does take many different forms, from innocent public displays of individuality to upscale alternative art. It takes on names of "tagging," "graffiti," and even "writing," all of which will be used synonymously in this paper to refer to street art for the sake of discussion. As Lea Virgine describes, graffiti includes "graphic-isms, graphemes, scratches, clashes, grazes, twistings and lacerations of the world or the surface on which they are applied" (215). She passionately declares that they are the "grapho-spasms of love" (215). Regrettably, the majority of graffiti's onlookers do not regard it with the same respect and admiration. What Virgine believes is "the painting of desire or wild communication" (215) is seen as "symbolic of the collapse of the [societal] system" (qtd. in Gladwell 183) by New York City subway director David Gunn. His remark surfaced amidst a citywide effort to eliminate graffiti from the subway stations and cars. Graffiti was believed to be a significant contributor to the high crime rate in New York City at the time. On behalf of criminologists James Q. Wilson and George Kelling, the "Broken Windows theory" explains,

> If a window is broken and left unrepaired, people walking by will conclude that no one cares and no one is in charge. Soon, more windows will be broken, and the sense of anarchy will spread . . . relatively minor problems like graffiti . . . are . . . the equivalent of broken windows (Gladwell 182).

And with the birth of this sociological theory came swift yet diligent action to rid New York City of street art. Subway cars with graffiti were labeled "dirty cars" while those lacking any signs of life were clean cars (Gladwell 183). In effect, indication of any creativity or interpersonal memos from city dwellers was associated with filth and the undesirable. This is not, however, the correct representation street artists would like their art to be identified with. In photographing and assessing the street art in New York City, David Robinson states in the introduction of his book, *SoHo Walls: Beyond Graffiti*:

> Whereas the city establishment sponsored or at least tolerated community murals, it viewed graffiti as defacement and vandalism. For the writers themselves . . . the graffiti created points of beauty and something positive amid the pervasive decay, desolation and brutal ugliness of their neighborhoods (6).

It is crucial for onlookers to understand that street art does not serve just one purpose or create only one reaction. It does more than merely exist on a wall for visual pleasure or disgust. Not only does graffiti create beauty for those living in hostile environments, it can be a source of educational outreach for those same inhabitants. Laurie MacGillivray, author of "Tagging as a Social Literacy Practice," explains,

THE "IS IT ART"? SUITE

In vilifying the practice of tagging, society too easily overlooks its evolving symbol system and the complexities of the phenomenon. The public's misunderstanding is particularly relevant for . . . teens from working-class backgrounds because of their historical academic underachievement . . . (354).

The inaccessibility to canvases for artistic expression and other activities that middle and upper class adolescents usually have leads lower class adolescents to the streets to utilize "public canvases" of walls and sidewalks. In this sense, graffiti holds special significance for the creators and their creators' communities. Many associate graffiti with gang communities since many violent gangs mark their territory with types of graffiti. But MacGillivray clarifies that there is a well-defined difference between gangs who tag to inform other gangs of their territory and those who tag because of the innocent desire to tag: "Taggers are not gang members . . . tagging is a social practice. Tagging has its own rules and codes, it is a literacy practice imbued with intent and meaning" (354). This statement may be a shock to those who generally see street art as random, undisciplined, and meaningless. However random acts of graffiti may be, they are surely not undisciplined, as MacGillivray discovers when researching and interviewing taggers.

Just as subway directors and criminologists see graffiti as undesirable, street artists see poor and meaningless art or tags as extremely unwanted as well. It is of great significance to the street art community that every piece of writing on walls, sidewalks, or subways possesses meaning and signs of talent. In interviewing taggers educated on the subject, MacGillivray finds, "While anyone can participate in tagging, it is only those who display talent that are valued in the tagging culture" (363). She cites that one tagger even stated, "if individuals are not talented, they should not engage in tagging" (363). MacGillivray continues on with this idea: "Most of our participants talked with disdain of those who tag poorly and explained that it hurts the reputation of taggers as artists" (363). This attitude towards their way of life illustrates the "social responsibility and non-elitism advocated by most graffiti artists" that Robinson experienced while photographing their work (Robinson 8). In assessing the artists' system of tagging MacGillivray expands on this idea of responsibility within their community: "In choosing the nature of their message and deciding on placement, taggers displayed sophisticated decision making which parallels the values of conventional writers" (367). This recognition of street artists as comparable to "conventional writers" qualifies them for a place in society far beyond what the average onlooker would imagine. Perhaps if more people were aware and understanding of the codes of conduct that exist within the graffiti community, as does exist with mural communities, then street art might be more welcomed and perhaps respected.

There are many similarities between murals—communal art completed on public spaces by a group of people with permission—and graffiti. Malcolm Miles, author of *Art, Space and the City: Public Art and Urban Futures,* even categorized graffiti as "unofficial street murals" (206). Of his observations, Robinson adds, "The motives of graffiti writers seem to have been similar to those of the community muralists: self-assertion, pride and self-expression" (6). These comments are quite foreign to the paradigm of public art that Jane Golden, author of *Philadelphia Murals and the Stories They Tell* and an active member of the Philadelphia Anti-Graffiti Network, accepts.

Her value of murals stands high above her regard for graffiti and tagging. She has the following admirable remarks to say about murals in the preface of her book: "Murals work on a symbolic level, providing opportunities for communities to express important concerns, values, and aspirations . . ." (2). In the foreword of Golden's book, Timothy W. Drescher states, "murals express community, but they also help create it . . . sometimes designing and producing a local mural begins a process of social connections and political activism that previously did not exist" (8–9). However distinct Golden and Drescher may find their observations of murals to be from that of graffiti, let's recall and compare comments made by Laurie MacGillivray in assessing the purposes and consequences of tagging:

> Tagging . . . can be conceived of as a local literacy practice and as an avenue into the construction of youth identity and group affiliation . . . [it is able] to sustain social relationships; it is a form of dialogue and conversation . . . Another purpose of tagging can be to provide commentary on larger social issues (355, 360, 362).

The word use of Golden and Drescher ("community," "values," "concerns," and "social connections") to describe murals closely identifies with that of MacGillivray's in regards to graffiti ("identity," "group affiliation," "social issues," and "social relationships"). Most appropriately in this sense and for the respect of varying ways of expression in our culture, the two should be regarded with similar, if not the same, value. It appears here that street art provides just as much community building and strengthening as does mural creation. Onlookers, sociologists, and criminologists must not forget the crucial value that street art holds for those who have little if nothing else in their lives.

As stated above, graffiti can be a means of expressing views on larger social issues when no other means is available, especially to young adults with low-income and undereducated backgrounds. Graffiti is the result of "an individual event [that] takes place in response to the social relationships with the expectations and norms of others" (MacGillivray 367). This unique style of communication between people of limiting backgrounds developed from "a need to express shared urban experiences" (MacGillivray 357) as well as to educate each other on social and world events. Images that MacGillivray came across in her observations included genuine reactions to political occurrences such as the recent bombings in Iraq and the "negative effects of corporate-sponsored deforestation on the environment" (362). It is an amazing ability of young urban dwellers to communicate such information to each other and to the public when the common means of obtaining it are generally inaccessible to them. Joe Austin, author of *Taking the Train: How Graffiti Art Became an Urban Crisis in New York City,* believes graffiti's

> development follows one of several pathways by which young people's political education became transformed . . . demonstrating some of the ways that youth cultures have continued to create and appropriate cultural and physical spaces of relative autonomy (270).

Rather than seeing graffiti as "dirty" and representative of a lack of education and discipline, it should be viewed as the collective experiences, desires, and desperation for communication between city dwellers and their peers. Whether or not these progressive feelings towards graffiti infiltrate the mainstream way of thought, graffiti will remain active: "In all likelihood the . . . effort will continue, undertaken by individual artists outside the mainstream who want to express themselves, make a point and provoke others while claiming their own freedom" (Robinson 15). The freedom to express oneself or one's experiences in an artistic way is a highly respected manner in the United States; it is only just that this freedom be granted to persons of all ages, education level, and socioeconomic backgrounds.

Among the profound purposes of street art such as political and education outreach lies an aesthetic purpose—the expression of the organic nature of art. While David Robinson photographed the art-covered walls of SoHo, New York City, he discovered an intense nature possessed by graffiti that he had not expected:

> Art was in the SoHo air, its energy palpable, spilling out of the lofts onto the streets—and onto the walls . . . I found the "public galleries," out on the streets, just as compelling as the art displayed indoors . . . the art . . . was organic, not restricted to white walls and neutral space (8, 5).

His experiences with the art in New York City were so powerful that he compared the essence of the art on the walls to that of Abstract Expressionism. There are even many art critics who see graffiti as a form of modem art, hence its presence in numerous galleries around the world, including the famous Museum of Modern Art in New York City.

If the great importance of graffiti art to the art community can be recognized by the prestigious taste of famous galleries, then the public too can recognize its societal, educational, and political importance to the communities that create it. From literacy practice to social belonging, street art serves multiple essential purposes to its creators and their surrounding environments. Whether the public chooses to accept the messages that artists display on walls and subway cars or continue to refute their art as legitimate, street art will not relinquish its existence. And as David Robinson so vehemently declares, "Their voices cannot be silenced, their creativity cannot be erased" (15).

Works Cited

Austin, Joe. *Taking the Train: How Graffiti Art Became an Urban Crisis in New York City*. New York: Columbia University Press, 2001.

Gladwell, Malcolm. "The Power of Context." *The Tipping Point: How Little Things Can Make a Big Difference*. 2000. Rpt. in *The New Humanities Reader*. Ed. Richard E. Miller and Kurt Spellmeyer. 2nd ed. Boston: Houghton Mifflin Company, 2006. 178–195.

Golden, Jane, Robin Rice, and Monica Yant Kinney. *Philadelphia Murals and the Stories They Tell*. Philadelphia: Temple University Press, 2002.

MacGillivray, Laurie, and Margaret Sauceda Curwen. "Tagging as a Social Literacy Practice." *Journal of Adolescent and Adult Literacy* 50.5 (Feb. 2007): 354–369.

Miles, Malcolm. *Art, Space and the City: Public Art and Urban Futures*. New York: Routledge, 1997.

Robinson, David. *Soho Walls: Beyond Graffiti*. New York: Thames and Hudson Inc., 1990. 5–15.

Vergine, Lea. *Art on the Cutting Edge: A Guide to Contemporary Movements*. Milan: Skira, 1996.

No Sense of Absolute Corruption: Damien Hirst and the Art Question

Anna Rose Tull

Student Essay

MILLIONS OF PEOPLE FROM ALL CULTURES AND BACKGROUNDS, all speaking different tongues, can look at da Vinci's *Mona Lisa* and appreciate both her mystery and her majesty. The language of fine art is such that a single masterpiece can touch viewers across the ages in the most profound and incredible ways. For millennia, people of all cultures, all nations, and all continents have utilized artistic vision to create countless works of human expression. Art, much like the human race, has gone through many cycles of change throughout history and continues to evolve today; yet, the common thread of art's ability to touch the core of the human spirit continues unchanged. Since the beginning of mankind, marked by stick-figure representations on cave walls, there has been something about artistic expression that resonates with all human beings—something that reaches the very core of human existence and provides all humanity with the common ability to relate art to life.

In the early nineties, though, a young artist emerged from the British popular art movement and began to change the way his contemporaries viewed art. Before Damien Hirst, art was gracefully provocative and, in some way or another, aesthetically pleasing to all. Whether by an act of intellectual and revolutionary genius, or by a pure urge for rebellion, Hirst made history in art by throwing out all the old conventions of what people believed art should look like and did his own thing, creating works equally as provocative as those of his precursors, but in a wholly different manner. Instead of making things that viewers want to look at, Hirst puts together repulsive "sculptures" that force the viewers to look at them, and even when they think they can't stand to look at the maggot-infested dead cow's head any longer, they feel compelled to steal a last glance at this incredible parody before moving on to the Warhol prints in the next gallery, which, although completely outrageous for the '60s, by comparison seem wholesome, tasteful and tame. There seems to be a dramatic rift in today's contemporary art between the hard-working, well-trained yet depressingly poor artists and fellows like Damien Hirst who throw dead animals into tanks of formaldehyde, give them names like *The Physical Impossibility of Death in the Mind of Someone Living*, call it "art," and garner millions of dollars as well as exhibitions in the Metropolitan Museum of Art.

It might very possibly be unanimously agreed that what Hirst does is not aesthetically pleasing in the least, but might he be making some sort of philosophical or existential statement by creating such "art" that breaks the socially-accepted ideas of what art looks like or should be? If he is trying to be provocative in some way other than to be aesthetically pleasing, is what he is doing, then, actually art? After all, isn't art supposed to be provocative? So then where does one draw the line between what is and what is not "art"? Does any artist, art critic, or art-lover have the authority to do this? If this were possible, how would one define art anyway? Isn't art indefinable, and isn't "beauty in the eye of the beholder"?

In order to even partially understand Hirst's motives, his purpose, or his statement (if he is indeed making one), one must first discern what art really is—how, if definition is actually possible, it might be defined in order to establish a future standard for discrimination—and who, if anyone, has the authority to decide what can or cannot be considered art. Next, one must explore whether Damien Hirst is conforming to that definition of art, or if he is rebelling against the determined norms, is this, then, art in itself? Or does Mr. Hirst's use of gruesome media defy artistic merit completely? Finally, one should discuss the theory of existentialism in relation to art and Damien Hirst's artistic experience as it relates to both the artist and his viewers in order to discover what existential message Mr. Hirst is trying to share with the world in which he lives and works.

So how does one determine the difference between what is "art" and what is just a "sick joke"? Although many theorists have put in more than their two cents about what they believe art to be, there has never been any clearly articulated definition of art. Art is a deeply personal experience, and, like beauty, it is in the eye of the beholder. Therefore, anyone can call anything art, but, ultimately, the work's ability to evoke an intellectual response from its viewers (as Mr. Hirst's work does), and the attraction of more and more viewers to that work, transforms a particular piece into valuable, justified art. If, then, art is supposed to be provocative, perhaps Mr. Hirst is, in fact, the best contemporary artist there is, as he provokes emotions that one does not normally get to release at all, let alone on art. Still, almost every self-proclaimed art lover can agree that what Hirst does is not pretty, and these connoisseurs struggle every day to discern whether there is a greater purpose behind Hirst's grotesque art, and if there is, what that purpose could possibly be. As much difficulty as one might have trying to make any sort of sense out of Hirst's works, though, he can be sure that the artist is not simply throwing animals into formaldehyde because he likes the way it looks; there is certainly some sort of philosophical or existential movement being created here.

Works Cited

Alberro, Alexander. *Conceptual Art and the Politics of Publicity.* Cambridge: MIT, 2003.

Danto, Arthur C. "*Damien Hirst.*" *Unnatural Wonders: Essays from the Gap Between Art and Life.* New York: Farrar, Straus, and Giroux, 2005.

Dery, Mark. *The Pyrotechnic Insanitarium: American Culture on the Brink.* New York: Grove, 1999.

Seattle Art Museum. Museum label for Andy Warhol, *Rorschach Painting.* Seattle, 28 Nov. 2008.

Warburton, Nigel. *The Art Question.* New York: Routledge, 2003.

Young, Quentin. "Beautiful Inside his Head." *The Longmont Time-Call* (7 Nov. 2008). 18 Nov. 2008 <http://timescall.com>.

PHOTO ESSAY: PUBLIC "ART"?

"It is not possible to separate art from non-art," writes Esther Pasztory in her book *Thinking with Things: Toward a New Vision of Art*, "there are only things of various sorts, functions, forms, and meanings" (10). This is especially the case with public and street art since their placement out in the public sphere makes interaction with our lives more immediate and more regular. In this short visual essay, the authors and some other contributors provide a few examples of public art—murals, paintings, sculptures, and statues. We have decided to print these images without comment and without making connections among them. Rather, we leave it up to you to think about the kinds of conversations these images might have with each other (and with you).

Some readers may not think everything in this essay is "art," while others will claim we have left out many other examples of public art. Both may be correct. But, as you look at these images, revisit some of the previous essays and ask yourself if these visual texts meet the criteria of "art"—either for others or for yourself.

In order of presentation:

Fig. 1 *The Guardian*, sculpture by Enoch Kelly Haney atop the Oklahoma State Capitol Building, Oklahoma City (photo Dean Rader c2008)

Fig. 2   Howe Chevrolet Indian, Clinton, OK (photo by Dean Rader c2007)

Fig. 3   *The Women of World War II* monument, London, England (photo by Dean Rader c2010)

Fig. 4 Public monument and topiary sculptures, Puno, Peru (photo by Dean Rader c2005)

Fig. 5 Mural, El Gabacho, Barrio Logan, San Diego, CA (photo by Martin Padgett)

Photo Essay: Public "Art"?

Fig. 6 Mural, San Luis, CO (photo by Martin Padgett)

Fig. 7 Artist Moving Systems Truck painted by Noah Ptolemy, San Francisco, CA (photo by Dean Rader c2009)

Fig. 8 Street art, taken from the train, London, England (photo by Dean Rader c2010)

Fig. 9 Mural, Los Angeles, CA (photo by Dean Rader c2010)

Photo Essay: Public "Art"?

Fig. 10 Obama sidewalk art, San Francisco, CA (photo by Dean Rader c2008)

Fig. 11 Birds/Cars with Graffiti in front, Rigo, San Francisco, CA (photo Dean Rader c2002)

CHAPTER 7 • Reading and Writing about Visual Art

Fig. 12   Sculpture by T. Paul Hernandez in front yard, Austin, TX (photo by Dean Rader c1999)

Fig. 13   Sculpture, Beddgelert, Wales (photo by Dean Rader c2010)

Fig. 14 Sculpture, Ubud, Bali (photo by Dean Rader c2007)

Fig. 15 Rock art, Hawaii, Hawaii (photo by Dean Rader c2008)

Fig. 16   Sculpture, Vancouver, British Columbia (photo by Dean Rader c2006)

Fig. 17   Abandoned house as sculpture, Post Katrina, New Orleans, LA (photo Dean Rader c2008)

READING **WRITING**

This Text: Reading

1. According to Hongisto, how should one "read" a mural?
2. Why does Hongisto claim it is important to place yourself in multiple vantage points when decoding pictures?
3. Do you agree with Mack's three principles for evaluating art?
4. What is Mack's thesis statement? Does she rely on ethos, pathos, or logos for her argument?
5. How are Grody's and George's arguments similar? Different?
6. In what way can we consider murals street art? In what way are they not?
7. Anna Rose Tull makes provocative claims about Damien Hirst. Look up images of Hirst's work on Google Images. Do you agree with Tull that his work is good art? Is she convincing?
8. Which of the "art objects" in the Public Art photo essay are the most and least artistic? Does public art have a different criteria for artfulness than paintings or sculptures found in galleries and museums?

Your Text: Writing

1. Write an essay in which you define art. Then look at two or three different texts and explain why they either are or are not art, according to your definition.
2. Look at the work of some the artists mentioned in this chapter—Ofili, Hirst, Rivera. What makes their work stand out? Write an essay in which you compare and contrast the work of two of these artists.
3. Write your own essay on art. Give 2–3 criteria for what makes good art. Be sure to explain and support your assertions.
4. Write an essay on a piece of public art in your city. Find a sculpture or a mural and talk about its relationship to its environs. What makes good *public* art?
5. Using the criteria of Mack, write an essay on street art/graffiti.
6. Write your own definition of art based on your experiences as a reader.
7. Write about your own experience as a reader in participating in making meaning.
8. If your campus has an art museum or a prominent work of art, write about it. How are the characteristics of the art in concert with the values of your institution?
9. Find a coffee mug or a tie or a T-shirt or a mouse pad with an image of a famous painting. Write an essay in which you talk about how the impact of that painting is changed as it gets endlessly reproduced.

The Reading a Photograph Suite

When photography entered the world of the visual arts, it was denigrated for being imitative, derivative, and not original—after all, it was merely reflecting what was already there. Later, however, critics praised it for some of the same reasons they had dismissed it before—photographs could truly capture reality in a way "artist-driven" work could not. Like writing, photography can be both commonplace and artistic. It can grace our scrapbooks, splash the front pages of a newspaper, and be displayed in a gallery or museum. But the question of whether photography captures reality is one that many critics struggle with.

As several recent examples have shown, photography—especially in the age of Photoshop—may be more open to manipulation than painting. With the ability to crop, erase, and superimpose, we wonder how reliable photographs are any more. In one prominent case, *Time* magazine was criticized for altering O. J. Simpson's face on its cover, making him look more menacing than in the original photograph. Indeed, in some court cases, photographs are inadmissible evidence because they can be so easily tampered with.

Reading a photograph also presents its own challenges. When one encounters a painting or a sculpture, one assumes the piece was intentionally designed a certain way, with artistic traces that indicate a signature style and help the viewer with a possible interpretation. Additionally, we are prepared to read sculpture and painting as fiction— imaginative renderings of the world. Photographs carry more overt connotations of reality, even if they have been altered in a studio. On the other hand, photographs can be candid in a way painting and sculpture cannot. Renoir, for all of his talents, would have problems busting out a quick and secret sculpture of someone exiting a limo, but photographers can snap several speedy photos without anyone noticing.

This issue of candor and intention is at the heart of this suite on photographs. We begin with a special essay new to this edition, "Reading a Photograph." Cheryl Aaron is a London-based visual artist who has had numerous shows both in the United States and England and whose work is in the collection of museums in New York and London. She is the author of two books of photography, *Laundry*, which has as its subject London laundries, and *Cafe*, which looks at the city's small cafes. In previous editions, we have featured her work in our interchapter; for this edition, we asked her to look at one of her photographs from two perspectives—the photographer and the viewer of the photograph. Following Aaron's essay are two photographs (and essays) of seemingly shocking photos of young people appearing to be unmoved by disaster. On September 10, 2006, *The New York Times* columnist Frank Rich used Thomas Hoepker's now famous (infamous?) photograph of five New Yorkers lounging on the Brooklyn waterfront during 9/11 as a kind of window into the state of America (see our section windows and lenses in the introduction). Three days later, David Plotz, the deputy editor of *Slate*, offered an entirely different reading of the same photograph. Here, we print Hoepker's photo and the columns by both Rich and Plotz. Notice how both writers rely on semiotic cues in the photo to arrive at their (differing) interpretations of the photo and America.

When American photographer Spencer Platt won the coveted World Press Photo of the Year Award in 2006 for his photograph, controversy erupted—not only because of the behavior of the well-groomed people in the car ("disaster tourism") but also because of the aesthetic quality of the photograph. Reading Platt's photo through the lens of semiotics raises a series of questions, but so, too, does reading the photo through the lenses of class, gender, war, and race. Testing your reaction toward the subjects between photograph one and photograph two speaks to how visual (and cultural) rhetoric affects our emotions and our ideas.

Errol Morris is, perhaps, the most important documentary filmmaker in the United States. Much of his work, such as the film *The Thin Blue Line,* focuses on the difficulty of certainty when interpreting what appears to be objective evidence. In his piece that appeared in *The New York Times* in the summer of 2007, Morris asks how "true" photographs and images can really be.

We close with a student essay on perhaps the most important American photographer—Cindy Sherman. Among the most well known of Cindy Sherman's works is her *Untitled Film Stills* in which, using herself as a model, she creates staged scenes that could have been derived from black and white movies from the 1950s. None of these photographs were based on any specific film; they were meant to portray stereotypical female roles as created by or perpetuated by these movies in particular. Virginia Commonwealth University student Anne Darby reads a particular Sherman photograph not through the lens of art but through the lens of gender. To view her work, we encourage you to do a Google image search for Sherman's "Untitled Film Stills."

Reading a Photograph

Cheryl Aaron

COMPARABLE TO COMPLETING A THOUGHT, photographing in the form of a series enables me to fully explore the subject matter. For my cafe series, I researched potential venues, met the proprietors, discussed my proposed project, and received permission to take photographs in their cafe.

The warmth of the Pellicci's Cafe drew me to take this photograph. It represented home away from home for me and was not dissimilar to the diners I frequented during my childhood. I planted myself at a table with a good vantage point, ordered a cup of coffee and began to take in the environment. I visited on several occasions at different times of day to gage the rhythm of the cafe, to get to know a few regulars and hopefully become slightly invisible in the hope of diminishing the self consciousness of the people I would be shooting. I used my Nikon FA with a high ASA (800) film so I didn't need to use a flash. I don't take vast amounts of shots because I feel that it inundates the subject and interferes with our relationship.

Pellicci's Cafe is a family business and the staff are used to working as a team in close quarters. I hope the audience picks up the ambiance of this splendid place. Unfortunately, they can not taste the home cooking by Mrs. Pellicci, but may notice the inlaid wooden decor constructed by a local carpenter in 1900, and little nuances including photos of the Pope circa 1985.

When I look at photographs, I am drawn in by the composition, the movement of the lights and darks, and sometimes intrigued by the cast of characters. After a long absence, it

was great to revisit this photograph. Of course I still go to Pellicci's Cafe so I know that Nevio passed away last year at the age of 80. The Cafe has now received English Heritage status so unlike its fading rivals, it will be with us for many years to come.

■ One Photo, Two Lenses: Frank Rich and David Plotz on One of the Most Controversial Photos of 9/11.

Whatever Happened to the America of 9/12?

Frank Rich

"THE MOST FAMOUS PICTURE NOBODY'S EVER SEEN" is how the Associated Press photographer Richard Drew has referred to his photo of an unidentified World Trade Center victim hurtling to his death on 9/11. It appeared in some newspapers, including this one [*The New York Times*], on 9/12 but was soon shelved. "In the most photographed and videotaped day in the history of the world," Tom Junod later wrote in *Esquire*, "the images of people jumping were the only images that became, by consensus, taboo."

Five years later, Mr. Drew's "falling man" remains a horrific artifact of the day that was supposed to change everything and did not. But there's another taboo 9/11 photo, about life rather than death, that is equally shocking in its way, so much so that Thomas Hoepker of Magnum Photos kept it under wraps for four years. Mr. Hoepker's picture can now be found in David Friend's compelling new 9/11 book, "Watching the World Change," or on the book's Web site, watchingtheworldchange.com. It shows five young friends on the waterfront in Brooklyn, taking what seems to be a lunch or bike-riding break, enjoying the radiant late-summer sun and chatting away as cascades of smoke engulf Lower Manhattan in the background.

Lounging or mourning? Thomas Hoepker's photo can be read many ways. (Thomas Hoepker 2001).

Mr. Hoepker found his subjects troubling. "They were totally relaxed like any normal afternoon," he told Mr. Friend. "It's possible they lost people and cared, but they were not stirred by it." The photographer withheld the picture from publication because "we didn't need to see that, then." He feared "it would stir the wrong emotions." But "over time, with perspective," he discovered, "it grew in importance."

Seen from the perspective of 9/11's fifth anniversary, Mr. Hoepker's photo is prescient as well as important—a snapshot of history soon to come. What he caught was this: Traumatic as the attack on America was, 9/11 would recede quickly for many. This is a country that likes to move on, and fast. The young people in Mr. Hoepker's photo aren't necessarily callous. They're just American. In the five years since the attacks, the ability of Americans to dust themselves off and keep going explains both what's gone right and what's gone wrong on our path to the divided and dispirited state the nation finds itself in today.

What's gone right: the terrorists failed to break America's back. The "new" normal lasted about 10 minutes, except at airport check-ins. The economy, for all its dips and inequities and runaway debt, was not destroyed. The culture, for better and worse, survived intact. It took only four days for television networks to restore commercials to grim news programming. Some two weeks after that Rudy Giuliani ritualistically welcomed laughter back to American living rooms by giving his on-camera imprimatur to *Saturday Night Live*. Before 9/11, Americans feasted on reality programs, nonstop coverage of child abductions and sex scandals. Five years later, they still do. The day that changed everything didn't make Americans change the channel, unless it was from "Fear Factor" to "American Idol" or from Pamela Anderson to Paris Hilton.

For those directly affected by the terrorists' attacks, this resilience can be hard to accept. In New York, far more than elsewhere, a political correctness about 9/11 is still strictly enforced. We bridle when the mayor of New Orleans calls ground zero "a hole in the ground" (even though, sadly, he spoke the truth). We complain that Hollywood movies about 9/11 are "too soon," even as *United 93* and *World Trade Center* came and went with no controversy at multiplexes in middle America. The Freedom Tower and (now kaput) International Freedom Center generated so much political rancor that in New York freedom has become just another word for a lofty architectural project soon to be scrapped.

The price of all New York's 9/11 P.C. is obvious: the 16 acres of ground zero are about the only ones that have missed out on the city's roaring post-attack comeback. But the rest of the country is less invested. For tourists—and maybe for natives, too—the hole in the ground is a more pungent memorial than any grandiose official edifice. You can still see the naked wound where it has not healed and remember (sort of) what the savage attack was about.

But even as we celebrate this resilience, it too comes at a price. The companion American trait to resilience is forgetfulness. What we've forgotten too quickly is the outpouring of affection and unity that swelled against all odds in the wake of Al Qaeda's act of mass murder. If you were in New York then, you saw it in the streets, and not just at ground zero, where countless thousands of good Samaritans joined the official responders and caregivers to help, at the cost of their own health. You saw it as New Yorkers of every kind gathered around the spontaneous shrines to the fallen and the missing at police and fire stations, at churches and in parks, to lend solace or a hand. This good feeling quickly spread to Capitol Hill, to red states where New York had once been Sodom incarnate and to the world, the third world included, where America was a nearly uniform object of sympathy and grief.

At the National Cathedral prayer service on Sept. 14, 2001, President Bush found just the apt phrase to describe this phenomenon: "Today we feel what Franklin Roosevelt called 'the warm courage of national unity.' This is the unity of every faith and every background. It has joined together political parties in both houses of Congress." What's more, he added, "this unity against terror is now extending across the world."

The destruction of that unity, both in this nation and in the world, is as much a cause for mourning on the fifth anniversary as the attack itself. As we can't forget the dead of 9/11, we can't forget how the only good thing that came out of that horror, that unity, was smothered in its cradle.

When F.D.R. used the phrase "the warm courage of national unity," it was at his first inaugural, in 1933, as the country reeled from the Great Depression. It is deeply moving to read that speech today. In its most famous line, Roosevelt asserted his "firm belief that the only thing we have to fear is fear itself—nameless, unreasoning, unjustified terror which paralyzes needed efforts to convert retreat into advance." Another passage is worth recalling, too: "We now realize as we have never realized before our interdependence on each other; that we cannot merely take but we must give as well; that if we are to go forward, we must move as a trained and loyal army willing to sacrifice for the good of a common discipline, because without such discipline no progress is made, no leadership becomes effective."

What followed under Roosevelt's leadership is one of history's most salutary stories. Americans responded to his twin entreaties—to renounce fear and to sacrifice for the common good—with a force that turned back economic calamity and ultimately an axis of brutal enemies abroad. What followed Mr. Bush's speech at the National Cathedral, we know all too well, is another story.

On the very next day after that convocation, Mr. Bush was asked at a press conference "how much of a sacrifice" ordinary Americans would "be expected to make in their daily lives, in their daily routines." His answer: "Our hope, of course, is that they make no sacrifice whatsoever." He, too, wanted to move on—to "see life return to normal in America," as he put it—but toward partisan goals stealthily tailored to his political allies rather than the nearly 90 percent of the country that, according to polls, was rallying around him.

This selfish agenda was there from the very start. As we now know from many first-hand accounts, a cadre from Mr. Bush's war cabinet was already busily hyping nonexistent links between Iraq and the Al Qaeda attacks. The presidential press secretary, Ari Fleischer, condemned Bill Maher's irreverent comic response to 9/11 by reminding "all Americans that they need to watch what they say, watch what they do." Fear itself—the fear that "paralyzes needed efforts to convert retreat into advance," as F.D.R. had it—was already being wielded as a weapon against Americans by their own government.

Less than a month after 9/11, the president was making good on his promise of "no sacrifice whatsoever." Speaking in Washington about how it was "the time to be wise" and "the time to act," he declared, "We need for there to be more tax cuts." Before long the G.O.P. would be selling 9/11 photos of the president on Air Force One to campaign donors and the White House would be featuring flag-draped remains of the 9/11 dead in political ads.

And so here we are five years later. Fearmongering remains unceasing. So do tax cuts. So does the war against a country that did not attack us on 9/11. We have moved on, but no one can argue that we have moved ahead.

Frank Rich Is Wrong About That 9/11 Photograph: Those New Yorkers Weren't Relaxing!

David Plotz

SOON AFTER THIS ARTICLE WAS POSTED, one of the people in the photograph e-mailed Slate to respond. A day later, photographer Thomas Hoepker joined the debate.

In his Sept. 10 column, Frank Rich of the *New York Times* describes a "taboo 9/11 photo," one so "shocking" that photographer Thomas Hoepker didn't publish it for four years. The photo, which the *Times* did not run but which is reproduced here (and which *Slate* also wrote about here), shows five people on the Brooklyn waterfront, engaged in conversation while the smoke from the fallen towers billows over Manhattan behind them.

In an interview with David Friend—who published the photo in a new book, *Watching the World Change: The Stories Behind the Images of 9/11*—Hoepker said his subjects "were totally relaxed like any normal afternoon" and that he didn't publish the picture in 2001 because "we didn't need to see that, then." Rich, who quotes the Hoepker interview, evidently agrees with the photographer's characterization of the image, writing, "What he caught was this: Traumatic as the attack on America was, 9/11 would recede quickly for many. This is a country that likes to move on, and fast. The young people in Mr. Hoepker's photo aren't necessarily callous. They're just American. In the five years since the attacks, the ability of Americans to dust themselves off and keep going explains both what's gone right and what's gone wrong on our path to the divided and dispirited state the nation finds itself in today."

But wait! Look at the photograph. Do you agree with Rich's account of it? Do these look like five New Yorkers who are "enjoying the radiant late-summer sun and chatting away"? Who have "move[d] on"? Who—in Rich's malicious, backhanded swipe—"aren't necessarily callous"? They don't to me. I wasn't there, and Hoepker was, so it may well be that they were just swapping stories about the Yankees. But I doubt it. The subjects are obviously engaged with each other, and they're almost certainly discussing the horrific event unfolding behind them. They have looked away from the towers for a moment not because they're bored with 9/11, but because they're citizens participating in the most important act in a democracy—civic debate.

Ask yourself: What are these five people doing out on the waterfront, anyway? Do you really think, as Rich suggests, that they are out for "a lunch or bike-riding break"? Of course not. They came to this spot to watch their country's history unfold and to be with each other at a time of national emergency. Short of rushing to Ground Zero and digging for bodies, how much more patriotic and concerned could they have been?

So they turned their backs on Manhattan for a second. A nice metaphor for Rich to exploit, but a cheap shot. I was in Washington on 9/11. I spent much of the day glued to my TV set, but I also spent it racing home to be with my infant daughter, calling my parents and New York relatives, and talking, talking, talking with colleagues and friends. Those discussions were exactly the kind of communal engagement I see in this photo. There is nothing "shocking" in this picture. These New Yorkers have not turned away from Manhattan because they have turned away from 9/11. They have turned away from Manhattan because they have turned toward each other for solace and for debate.

Rich and Hoepker and I have all characterized what these five people were doing and how they were feeling, but none of us really know. Wouldn't you like to hear from the five themselves? I would. If they're out there and they'd like to respond to Rich or me, they can e-mail me at plotzd@slate.com.

Editors' note: After Plotz's column ran in *Slate,* one of the men from the photo e-mailed the magazine. You can read his letter here: http://www.slate.com/id/2149578/.

Award-Winning Photo Puts Subjects on Defensive

Gert Van Langendonck

Editor's Note: Spencer Platt's image of Lebanese residents driving through South Beirut on Aug. 15, 2006, won the World Press Photo of the Year award. A reporter later identified the subjects in the photo.

Some saw the image as a symbol of how war affects rich and poor, while others saw the subjects as callously indifferent to the mayhem around them; PDNOnline referred to them as "cavalier." Platt himself never spoke to the subjects.

But in an interview with freelance journalist Gert Van Langendonck, the people in the car tell their side of the story. Van Langendonck, on assignment for the Belgian newspaper *De Morgen,* says he showed Platt's photo to everyone he met, and eventually someone recognized one of the women in the car, Bissan Maroun, who works as a bank teller.

A former foreign editor and U.S. correspondent for *De Morgen,* van Langendonck also has written for *NRC Handelsblad* in the Netherlands, *Die Zeit and Die Welt* in Germany, and other papers in Europe, as well as GNN.TV, a left-wing blog based in the U.S. A translation of Van Langendonck's story follows.

It was around 1 p.m. on August 15th, the second day of the ceasefire that ended the 33-day war between Israel and the armed Shia resistance group Hezbollah, and all of Lebanon was in upheaval. While tens of thousands of refugees from the South were clogging the roads on the way back to their homes, many others headed for the Dahiye, the Hezbollah-controlled southern suburbs of Beirut. Some wanted to check if their houses had survived the massive bombing campaign by the Israeli air force; others were simply curious.

It was at that moment that a red car caught photographer Spencer Platt's eye. He shot four or five frames, he says, but this was the only one he sent to his agency.

"I liked it because it showed another, fabulous side to Beirut," Platt says from his home in New York City. "It is important to show the cliches, the refugees, because that was the reality of what was happening. But this is Beirut too. It is this dichotomy that makes Lebanon such a fascinating place. But I never thought it was the picture."

Affluent Lebanese drive down the street to look at destroyed neighborhood August 15, 2006 in southern Beirut, Lebanon. As the United Nations brokered cease fire between Israel and Hezoballah enters its first day, thousands of Lebanese returned to their homes and villages. (photo Spencer Platt, 2006)

Jad Maroun, 22, and his sisters Bissan, 29, and Tamara, 26, were not feeling all that fabulous on that sunny day in August. Despite the fact that they are Christian, they all lived in the Dahiye, which was once a Christian neighborhood. At the start of the war they had fled the bombing and settled in the Plaza Hotel in Hamra, a Sunni part of Beirut. It was there that they had met Noor Nasser, 21, a Muslim, and Liliane Nacouzi, 22, a Christian, who were working as waitresses in a sandwich shop in the hotel. They too were refugees from Beirut's Southern suburbs.

It was also where they ran into Lana El Khalil, 25, the owner of the Mini Cooper in Platt's picture. El Khalil, who calls herself an atheist, had given up her apartment in Hamra to make room for Shia refugees from the South and moved back to her parents' house. But she was hardly ever at home. When the war began, she was part of a sit-in in downtown Beirut to call attention to the Palestinian cause. As soon as the bombing started, she threw herself into relief work. She joined an NGO called Samidoun that was set up specifically to help the displaced people from the South. During the first days of the war, El Khalil helped evacuate people who were trapped in the Dahiye. Later on she would ferry food and medical supplies to the neighborhood. The little convertible came in handy.

But on August 15, two days into the ceasefire, it had served its purpose. When Jad and the others asked if they could borrow the Mini Cooper to go check on their houses in the Dahiye, El Khalil was happy to oblige them.

Six months later, they are all gathered in the apartment of Bissan's fiance in the Christian neighborhood of Achrafieh. Only Tamara, the blonde girl in the picture, is missing; she is getting ready for her engagement the next day. Jad, who was driving the car that day, admits that he had second thoughts about opening up the convertible. "I was worried that it would give people the wrong idea. But it was a hot day. There were five of us in a tiny car and we all wanted to get a good look at what had happened to the neighborhood."

They never saw Spencer Platt. The first they heard about his picture was when it was published in *Paris Match* in September. It is not so much the picture that bothered them; it was the caption that often went with it in publications around the world: rich Lebanese Christians doing war tourism in the ravaged suburbs of Beirut.

"Take a good look at the picture," says Bissan Maroun, a bank employee, "I can assure you that we were not having fun. The looks on our faces show consternation at what was done to our neighborhood. And I can tell you that not one person in this photo belongs to the Christian bourgeoisie."

There is the obvious question. What were they thinking dressing up in tight t-shirts and designer sunglasses on a day like this, and in a conservative part of town? "Hey, we're Lebanese," says Noor. "It's not like we dressed up like this to go visit the Dahiye. We dress like this every day. On any other day, nobody would have given us a second glance. It was the contrast with the destruction in the background that made the difference." There is something the world needs to understand about Lebanon, adds El Khalil. "Glamour is a very important part of life here. It transcends class. Even if you're poor, you want to look glamorous."

A lot has been read into Platt's picture based on what viewers thought it conveyed. But such are the intricacies of life in Lebanon that they don't entirely disagree with its message, either. "It is a very interesting picture," says El Khalil. "And, yes, there was war tourism going on in Lebanon at the time; just not in this case."

It can be difficult for people in the West to grasp what life in a war zone is like. During the last war with Israel, many Lebanese who could afford it went up to places like Faraya, a ski resort in winter time. They settled in five-star hotels there and spent the day shopping or lounging around the swimming pool while the Southern suburbs were being bombed. Many of Beirut's designer boutiques and even some of its trendy night clubs followed their clientele to the mountain resorts. "I went to Faraya myself one week-end during the war," says El Khalil, "and I too was shocked by some of the things I saw there." But she doesn't judge. "Everybody reacts to war in their own way. Me, I chose to help people. Others went to la-la-land and partied. There is a survival instinct that kicks in. It's another form of resistance, to try and keep living your life the way you want to despite the war."

The choice of Platt's picture for the World Press Photo has stirred up quite a debate in the photojournalism community. Some critics applauded the break from more traditional war photography. In interviews with *Le Monde* in France and *Hebdo* magazine in Lebanon, Lebanese photographer Samer Mohdad described the jury's choice as "an insult to all news photographers who have risked their lives to cover this horrible war."

The young Lebanese in the picture are not quite that angry. But they ask themselves why Platt's picture was chosen, "and not, for instance, the picture of a dead young boy being taken from the rubble after an Israeli bombing in Qana." Could it be, asks El Khalil, "that the photo of the dead boy shows the reality of a war, and that this makes people in the West uncomfortable?" This is why she feels Platt's photo is dangerous. "It distracts

Reporter Gert Van Langendonk located the subjects of Spencer Platt's prize-winning photo from the Lebanon War. From left to right: Bissan Marou, 29, Noor Nasser, 21, Jad Maroun, 22, Lana El Khalil, 25 (the owner of the car, not seen in Platt's photograph), and Liliane Nacouzi, 22. Not shown here is Tamara Maroun, 26, who was in the front seat of the car. (photo Karium Ben Khelifa, 2007)

attention from the harsh reality of war. It confirms what many people in the West think already, that war only happens to people who don't look like them."

Bissan Maroun's boyfriend Wissam Awad, 32, takes the argument one step further. "Giving the award to the picture of the dead boy would have harmed the reputation of Israel in the world. Platt's picture doesn't do that. On the contrary, it suggests that the Christians had nothing to do with the war, that they were all against Hezbollah and on the side of Israel. And that's just not true."

Spencer Platt never knew who the people in his picture were. He wants it known that he never meant to judge them. "I never talked to them. For all I knew, they might have lost members of their family. No one was immune to hardship in that conflict. And I certainly didn't mean to make a political statement, as some have said. My fixer, Wafa, was of a very similar type to the people in the car, and her life had been turned upside down by the war." In the end, he says, "What I think this image partly asks us, the viewer, is to challenge our stereotypes of victims of war."

Liar, Liar Pants on Fire

Errol Morris

PICTURES ARE SUPPOSED TO BE WORTH a thousand words. But a picture unaccompanied by words may not mean anything at all. Do pictures provide evidence? And if so, evidence of what? And, of course, the underlying question: do they tell the truth?

I have beliefs about the photographs I see. Often—when they appear in books or newspapers—there are captions below them, or they are embedded in explanatory text. And even where there are no explicit captions on the page, there are captions in my mind. What I think I'm looking at. What I think the photograph is about.

I have often wondered: would it be possible to look at a photograph shorn of all its context, caption-less, unconnected to current thought and ideas? It would be like stumbling on a collection of photographs in a curiosity shop—pictures of people and places that we do not recognize and know nothing about. I might imagine things about the people and places in the photographs but know nothing about them. Nothing.

This collection could even involve my own past. I recently was handed a collection of photographs taken by my father—dead now for over fifty years.

I looked at it, somewhat confused. I suppose saddened by the passage of time. Even though I am in the photographs, the people in them are mysterious, inherently foreign. Maybe because photographs tamper with the glue that holds life and memory together.

Who are these people? Do they have anything to do with me? Do I really know them?

As disconnected from the present as these photographs might be, they do not seem devoid of context. I know too much about them—even if I know very little. They are pictures of my own family. It's too easy for me to concoct some story about them. To find a picture shorn of context, it would be important to pick a photograph that's sufficiently removed for me in time and context—a photograph preternaturally unfamiliar. Perhaps a war photograph, but a war photograph from an unfamiliar war. It should be a war six or seven wars ago. Passions, presumably, have been diminished. No one in the photographs will still be alive.

I want to ask a relatively simple question. Are these photographs true or false? Do they tell the truth?

Look at the next photograph. Is it true or false?

I find the question ridiculous: "True or false in regard to what?"

Without a caption, without a context, without some idea about what the picture is a picture of, I can't answer. I simply cannot talk about the photograph as being true or false independently of beliefs about the picture. A captionless photograph, stripped of all context, is virtually meaningless. I need to know more.

The Lusitania

And yet, this idea that photographs can be true or false independent of context is so ingrained in our thinking that we are reluctant to part with it.

Let's add a caption to the photograph.

Only now can we ask questions that have true or false answers. The caption asserts that this is a photograph of the *Lusitania,* a British ship launched in 1907. I found the photograph on a website entitled "Maritime Quest." I made no effort to check it; I simply took their word for it. That could be a mistake on my part. With no malice intended, the wrong caption could have inadvertently been placed under the photograph. The photograph could actually be a photograph of the *Titanic.* Or malice could have been involved. Someone could have maliciously switched the captions of pictures of the *Lusitania* and the *Titanic.*

But one thing is clear. When I look at these pictures—whether it is a picture of the *Lusitania* or the *Titanic*—I imagine that someone stood on a dry dock, or some vantage point, looked through the viewfinder of the camera, and took a photograph of something that was floating out there in the water. If it was the *Lusitania,* then he took a photograph of the *Lusitania.* If it was the *Titanic,* then he took a picture of the *Titanic.* This may seem hopelessly obvious, but I have this saying—and I believe there's something to it—that there is nothing so obvious that it's obvious.

But we need language, and we need context, in order to know which ship it is, and a host of other sundry facts.

In discussing truth and photography, we are asking whether a caption or a belief—whether a statement about a photograph—is true or false about (the things depicted in) the photograph. A caption is like a statement. It trumpets the claim, "This is the *Lusitania.*" And when we wonder "Is this a photograph of the *Lusitania*?" we are wondering whether the claim is true or false. The issue of the truth or falsity of a photograph is only meaningful with respect to statements about the photograph. Truth or falsity "adheres" not to the photograph itself but to the statements we make about a photograph. Depending on the statements, our answers change. All alone—shorn of context, without captions—a photograph is neither true nor false.

But why this photograph? It's so terribly bland. I wanted to begin this series of essays on photography with an image chosen particularly for its blandness. Removed in time, far from our core knowledge, it is unfamiliar. We know little about it. We most likely do not recognize it as the *Lusitania.* We might think it's an early-20th-century ocean liner, and perhaps even imagine it may be the *Titanic*—at which point we have placed a kind of mental caption under the photograph, and we begin to see the photograph in terms of our associations and beliefs, about what it seems to say about reality.

It is also interesting how a photograph quickly changes when we learn more about what it depicts, when we provide a context, when we become familiar with an underlying story. And when we make claims about the photograph using language. For truth, properly considered, is about the relationship between language and the world, not about photographs and the world.

So here's a story.

On the evening of May 7th, 1915, the RMS *Lusitania* was off the coast of Ireland en route to Liverpool from New York when it was torpedoed by a German U-Boat and sank. Nearly 2,000 passengers and crew drowned, including 128 Americans. The loss of life provoked America out of a hereunto neutrality on the ongoing war in Europe. With cries of "Remember the *Lusitania*" the U.S. entered into WWI within two years.

ENLIST

Fred Spear

Watch's Fixed Hands Record Lusitania's Last 30 Minutes

At 2.30 p.m. today it will be exactly 27 years since a small pocket watch owned by Percy Rogers, Toronto, was stopped by the action of a German submarine.

It was 2 o'clock on the afternoon of May 7, 1915. The giant Cunard liner, Lusitania, with 1,906 aboard, was eight miles off the south coast of Ireland, and New York bound. In the domed dining saloon, Percy Rogers, then secretary of the C.N.E., had just finished lunch.

Mr. Rogers got up from the table, glanced at his watch and walked to his stateroom. At the very moment he was reaching to pick up a letter, he heard a "tremendous thud." He rushed on deck.

"People were running around like a flock of sheep with no one to direct them," he recalls. "Some of them clambered into lifeboats. The ship took a heavy list." His watch ticked off the fateful minutes. It was 2 15.

"I helped women and children near me into a boat. Then, as there were no more there, I got in. We had barely pulled a little way off before the ship turned on its side and sank." Five minutes had ticked by. It was 2.20.

"There was very little suction from the ship's sinking. But our boat upset. I struck out. Women and children were floating, mothers seeking to hold babies up. . . ." The watch ticked on, minute after minute. More than 1,000 lives were being snuffed out, and as the cold salt water seeped through Percy Rogers' clothes and finally into the delicate mechanism, his watch stopped. The minute hand, which had ticked off 30 of the most terrible minutes in history, was turned downward in defeat. It was exactly 2.30.

Mr. Rogers floated with the help of a cupboard for an hour and a half. He was then picked up by a trawler and taken to Queenstown. When he looks at his watch today, one thing sticks in his mind. It is the official German statement at the time of the torpedoing: "Every German heart is filled with joy, pride and gratification." Mr. Rogers has never had the watch repaired. The hands have remained where they stopped as a reminder of the Lusitania.

To modern viewers, this image of the Lusitania is emotionally uncharged, if not devoid of interest. But to a viewer in the summer of 1915, it was charged with meaning. It was surrounded by many, many other photographs, images and accounts of the sinking of the *Lusitania,* a cause cèlébre.

Let's look at some of these other images.

"ENLIST" was a WWI Recruitment poster designed by Fred Spears. Spears' design was inspired by a news report from Cork, Ireland, that described, among the recovered bodies from the *Lusitania,* "a mother with a three-month-old child clasped tightly in her arms. Her face wears a half smile. Her baby's head rests against her breast. No one has tried to separate them."

And here is a photograph from the same period with the following caption.

"SOME OF THE SIXTY-SIX COFFINS BURIED IN ONE OF THE HUGE GRAVES IN THE QUEENSTOWN CHURCHYARD."

The caption is from a two-page pictorial spread in the May 30, 1915, *New York Times*: "BURYING THE LUSITANIA'S DEAD AND SUCCORING HER SURVIVORS."

One more photograph and an accompanying article from the *Toronto Star.*

The photograph is of a pocket watch. We learn from the accompanying article that the watch belonged to Percy Rogers and that the watch stopped at exactly 2:30 after "ticking off 30 of the most terrible minutes in history." Mr. Rogers was in a stateroom when the torpedo struck the *Lusitania.* He spent his last minutes on board helping women and children climb into lifeboats. Then he climbed into a lifeboat as well. And then the ship sank. The last paragraph of the article is memorable. It quotes "the official German statement" following the sinking of the *Lusitania*: "Every German heart is filled with joy, pride and gratification."

Now look at the photograph of the ship one more time.

The image remains the same, but clearly we look at it in a different way.

Is that really a photograph of the *Lusitania*? When was it taken? Could it have been taken on May 7, 1915? If it was, what was the exact time that it was taken? Two o'clock? Two fifteen? Just seconds before the German torpedo hit? Ah, can we see the torpedo in the water? Is that the mother and her child (depicted in the poster) standing on the deck looking out over the water? Is that Percy Rogers with his pocket watch, helping that same woman and child climb into a lifeboat?

The idea that photographs hand us an objective piece of reality, that they by themselves provide us with the truth, is an idea that has been with us since the beginnings of photography. But photographs are neither true nor false in and of themselves. They are only true or false with respect to statements that we make about them or the questions that we might ask of them.

The photograph doesn't give me answers. A lot of additional investigation could provide those answers, but who has time for that?

Pictures may be worth a thousand words, but there are two words that you can never apply to them: "true" and "false."

#27: Reading Cindy Sherman and Gender

Anne Darby

Student Essay

THE WOMAN IS SEATED, and the photograph is cropped from the middle of her forehead to the table on which her hands are resting. In her right hand she holds a half-smoked cigarette, and her left hand is curled distractedly around some indistinguishable object. In front of her right hand are a glass of champagne and a decorative ashtray. Before her left hand lies a pack of wooden matches, and on the ring finger of that hand there is a ring with a dark stone. It is impossible to discern whether it is merely a piece of jewelry or an indication of engagement, but either way it is enough to make the viewer speculate about her future marital status and, by association, her future in general.

The table is strewn with cigarette ash, which alludes to her preoccupation. She is wearing a low cut dress with a faux leopard fur collar that spans almost the width of her shoulders. The most noticeable aspect of the photograph is the emotion displayed on her face. Her heavy eye makeup is smeared by the tears which have run down her face in dark lines. Tears have caught on her eyelashes, held there by the heavy mascara. Light glints off of the excessive liquid, distorting and accentuating her eyes. Her mouth is partially open and her collarbones protrude, which indicate that she is in mid-gasp.

We are all familiar with that moment, near the end of a heavy cry, when we begin to try to compose ourselves and regain the oxygen we have lost. It is my assumption that the moment portrayed will be more poignant and powerful to female viewers, though it is possible male viewers would be able to relate on some level. The photograph stands for me as a symbol of the struggle between a person's façade and their soul. The symbols shown can be divided into those that stand as signifiers of façade and those that portray the true self coming through.

The dress, specifically the low neckline, suggests that this woman has dressed for someone other than herself. The idea that a woman, seen as a sexual object, lets (whether passively or actively, consciously or not) other parts of her character and psyche suffer is a predominant theme in Sherman's early work. For example, her *Centerfolds* series acts as commentary on pornographic images of women, and many of those images depict women in what could be sensual poses, were it not for the emotion or in some cases fear or sickness, that pervades the scene.

It has been my experience that the great majority of women to some extent project an image of who they think they are expected to be. (I know that this is also an issue with men, but that is a whole different topic, about which I am not qualified to write.) We *want* to be all of these things: beautiful, collected, intelligent, happy, witty (yet demure!) and successful. Furthermore the presence of the alcohol and the cigarette, as well as the subject's outfit, lead me to believe that she is involved in a certain lifestyle in which a woman plays a slightly different role than she does in the home or the workplace.

In a bar, at a party, or at any sort of gathering which is meant on the surface to be celebratory, most of us switch gears, and attempt to maintain a pleasant front. At a party one drinks, smokes, and talks about nothing. One is attractive and easy to get along with, never tired or moody, never undergoing stressful situations or tragedy. For a little while, that is amusing, even positive, but any length of time spent in that world causes detriment to the body and the soul. Again, this is more applicable to women than to men, and especially in the movies on which this photograph was based, but certainly not specific to those.

Alcohol and cigarettes are crutches on which one may rely to numb pain, pass time, or ignore real issues. Drinking makes one dull, and in the long term, stunts emotional growth. It causes one to lose touch with one's self. The juxtaposition of the tears with the traditional meanings associated with champagne is what makes the photograph so real. In fact, the champagne works more effectively to make this comparison than any other form of alcohol would.

The theme of a woman's misery threatening her façade has found its way many times into art and literature. I am automatically reminded of Justine, a character in Lawrence Durell's *Alexandria Quartet*. Succinctly, Justine is a beautiful woman, married to a wealthy banker, who is haunted by events of her past, most of which she is not at liberty to talk about. She had a child that was stolen from her, and she was constantly reminded of the presence of a man who had taken advantage of her in her youth, to name just a few of her woes. On the surface, she was highly visible socially, and in a position to be envied; she was untouchably beautiful, was the wealthiest woman in the city, had a husband who loved her, but inside she was ravaged by her regrets and neuroses. In a similar vein, Neil Jordan wrote a short story about a woman making idle conversation at a party while in the back of her mind wondering where it was that her soul had gone. Granted, all of the stories here have very different elements, but that particular theme ties them all together.

For me, and possibly for many other women, the smeared makeup is the most powerful single signifier of this woman's self breaking through her projected persona. When a woman prepares herself to face the world, she puts on a mask. It is a defense mechanism, as well as a beauty aid. Some women rely on this more than others, some are more conscious of it than others, but the effect is essentially the same. The activities that smear eye makeup are the activities that threaten our façade of coolness. Sleeping, crying, or a mistake in application all reveal our real human qualities. If the photograph were to be narrowed down to just the eyes and the streaks of stained tears, it would still be a loaded visual text; the rest of the photograph only elaborates on what the eyes have already said.

This photo is of Sherman herself, but because she uses herself in every image she creates, through repetition she herself is phased out of significance, giving the spotlight to each specific persona. Sherman becomes a non-element in each photograph. The significance is placed on the aspects that are different from picture to picture, which create the person, or the stereotype. Of course, if the viewer sees only one of Sherman's photographs, this is not an issue. The image is so strikingly genuine that it is difficult, even with knowledge of the subject, to imagine its staging. Also, the woman's failure to acknowledge the camera makes us believe that we really are glimpsing straight into the scene, uninvited and unnoticed.

Through staged photographs Sherman is able to solidify this nebulous concept. The success of the photograph is in the fact that it has pinpointed the perfect image to display such a moment, and such an emotion. Its delivery relies on the viewer to make it anything other than thoughtless voyeurism, but it is unlikely that an image this powerful will miss its mark.

Works Cited

Durrell, Lawrence. *The Alexandria Quartet*. 4 vols. New York: Dutton, 1957.
Jordan, Neil. *The Collected Fiction of Neil Jordan*. London: Vintage, 1997.
Krauss, Rosalind. *Cindy Sherman, 1975–1993*. New York: Rizzoli International, 1993.
Photography Exhibitions: Videocassette #No. 11. Writ. Mark Miller. Art/New York, 1982.
Sherman, Cindy. *Centerfolds*. New York: Skarstedt Fine Art, 2003.
———. *Untitled Film Stills*. New York: Rizzoli, 1990.

READING WRITING

This Text: Reading

1. What argument is Aaron subtly making about art?
2. Why did she choose a cafe as a subject? What type of ordinary place do you think is worth photographing?
3. How is it possible that two smart people like Rich and Plotz can have such different reactions to the same photograph? To what degree is the Hoepker photo misleading?
4. Whose opinion to you agree with—Rich or Plotz? Who makes the most compelling argument?
5. Plotz relies on classic semiotic techniques—paying close attention to the details of the photo—in order to arrive at his interpretation. Does he give an accurate reading of Hoepker's photo?
6. Why do you think Platt's photo—of all of the photographs taken in 2006—won this award?
7. Does this photograph say something about war that traditional "war photography" does not? If so, what does it say?
8. To what degree does Platt's photograph make an argument? Does it invite you to "read into" the photo? Is the photo value free?
9. Find two or three family photos or some of you and your friends and give a reading of these texts. What do the photos say about the people in them if you read the texts through the lens of race? Culture? If you give a semiotic reading of them, what does that suggest? Do the photos make an argument?
10. Darby does not really make an argument about Cindy Sherman's photograph as "art," rather as a document of gender. Does this affect its artistry? What about the fact that it is a staged photograph?

11. Look at some of the photographs in this book. Now imagine them without captions. How does this change how you *see* the photos?
12. Go onto Flickr or Facebook or some other site and look at photos with and without captions. How do captions alter our emotional reaction to an image? For that matter, look at some of the photo essays in this book—both with and without captions. Do words change how we read visual texts?

Your Text: Writing

1. Write an essay in which you evaluate Rich's and Plotz's reading of the photograph. Identify each writer's main thesis. What sort of argument is each making?
2. Give your own reading of Hoepker's photograph. Based on the semiotic cues in the photo, what do *you* think the photo suggests? How would you interpret either the behavior of the people or the motives of Hoepker?
3. Write an essay in which you compare Hoepker's photo with Seymour Platt's controversial photo of several young people cruising through war-torn Lebanon in a convertible. Why did these photos create such controversy? What do they tell us about the expectations of people after and during disaster?
4. Write a comparison/contrast essay in which you read the two photographs alongside each other. Each is a kind of portrait, but each uses context to send a different message. Describe your emotional reactions to each.
5. Write an essay in which you read Platt's photo and Hoepker's photo of the young people lounging during the 9/11 attacks.
6. Write an essay using old family photos as a point of departure. How hard is it to read texts from the past through the lens of the present?
7. Go to a local diner and take some photographs—candid photographs if possible. What stands out in the subjects?
8. Go to a library and look at some books of art and photography. How many of the photographs and paintings focus on everyday life? When does this become more prevalent? Why do you think that is so?
9. Write a paper (using photos if possible) about the everyday beauty of a place familiar to you.
10. Track down some Cindy Sherman photographs and write about her work as "art" using some of the criteria in this chapter. For an interesting comparison, see Judith Taylor's photo essay in the chapter on Gender—how is Sherman's and Taylor's work similar?

READING BETWEEN THE LINES

Classroom Activities

1. Bring in a slide or a photograph of a famous work of art. As a class, read the artistic text. How does reading it as a group change how you see it? Now discuss a piece of street art. What informs opinions about these issues?
2. As a class, select an image from the book. Then, spend 15 minutes trying to redraw or reproduce the image. How does that change the image? How does it change how you see the image?
3. Bring a reproduction of a painting by Elsworth Kelley or Barnett Newman or Morris Louis to class. Or, look at a sculpture by Claes Oldenburg or Jeff Koonz. Have a discussion on whether these pieces are art. Why? Why not?
4. Track down a particularly incendiary artistic text in class, like Andres Serrano's *Piss Christ* or a Robert Mapplethorpe photograph or the Chris Ofili painting from the *Sensation* exhibit. What is the role of art, decency, and public opinion? Where and how do aesthetics and ethics meet? What cultural forces might prompt this kind of art?
5. Look at some Andy Warhol prints in class. Are his pieces art? Why or why not?
6. Talk about the differences between painting and photography. What can one do that the other cannot?
7. Take a field trip to look at some pieces of sculpture near or on your campus. How does sculpture adhere to the principles of artistic design?
8. Talk about the role of art in American culture. Compare how you think about art to how you think about television, film, and literature.
9. Take a class field trip and "read" some examples of street art—murals, graffiti, home-made sculptures. Write about how these text are or are not art.
10. Bring some examples of visual culture to class—advertisements, comics, Animae, graphic t-shirts, screen grabs of video games and websites—and read them.

Essay Ideas

1. Write a paper in which you define art, then show why three paintings, photographs, or sculptures meet your definition of art. Feel free to use street art as one of your examples.
2. Write a poem about one of the images in this chapter, and then write an essay about the process of writing a poem about the image.
3. What is the relationship between gender and art? Many of the most famous paintings, photographs, and sculptures are of nude women. How has art altered how men and women see the female body?
4. In what way is how we see the world affected by what we believe or what we know? How does our background, our beliefs, our interests, and our personality affect how we see art? How does the political climate of our society affect how we see art?
5. Google Diane Arbus and look at her photographs. Compare a Diane Arbus photograph with a classic portrait. Are both art? Compare what della Francesca or da Vinci or Vermeer tries to do in his art with what Arbus tries to accomplish in hers. How might their respective cultures influence their ideas of what art should do?
6. Write an essay comparing Chrichton's questions about art and the NAMES quilt with Mack's questions about art and the *Sensation* exhibit. How do both pieces rise out of social or political unrest?

7. Look at some of the images in this book. Look at the cover. What arguments do these images make?
8. Write an essay in which you demonstrate and explain how a work of art makes a political statement.
9. Do you believe that public funding for the arts should be cut if the public finds the art objectionable? Can the public, if it supports an exhibit with its tax dollars, censor a work of art?
10. Write an essay on the artistic situation for one of the texts. What cultural or societal forces may influence what or how an artist creates?

Visualizing Writing

Thanks to Chris Duval at Apostrophe Abuse: http://www.apostropheabuse.com/.

8 Reading and Writing about Music

We can not escape music. Almost any place we go music is playing—in the supermarket, at Starbucks, in the car, and on television. In fact, as we write this, we're listening to the Magnetic Fields and the Avett Brothers. Accordingly, music often serves as the soundtrack for our lives; we attach memories to particular songs, and those song-memory attachments tend to be long lasting.

Music too is one medium we are at once reading actively and passively as we emotionally connect to the sounds and tones—we do not think so much about the mood a song evokes as much as how it makes us feel. Accordingly, we actively read music, if we read it at all, by focusing on its lyrics—after all, the content of what's sung in a song is the easiest element to interpret. In addition, we have the tools for interpreting words already: We know how to read and make sense of language or literature. And such tools can be useful in understanding music.

Still, writing about music has its difficulties. Of all the texts in this book, music may be the most emotionally powerful. We can argue about books and movies and television shows, but discussions about music—favorite artists, what albums you would take to a desert island, who is better, the Beatles or the Stones—elicit the most passionate responses. And we often put that passion to good use. We turn to music to put us in a romantic mood, to celebrate events, to announce the arrival of the bride, to begin graduation ceremonies, to initiate all sporting events. Our lives are framed by music—it may be the text we are the most unable to live without, which is why it is particularly important to be a good reader of it. And in the case of your courses, be a good writer about it.

But we have any number of other considerations to decipher a song's intentional meanings, as well as some of its unintentional ones. Here are some to keep in mind when listening to and writing about music.

MUSIC IS MADE UP OF GENRES.

Both professional and amateur listeners often classify a music's type in trying to understand or enjoy it. There are many genres of music—classical, rhythm and blues, rock and roll, rap, country, jazz, and "pop," as well as numerous subgenres within these groups (alternative, emo, trip-hop, fusion, etc.). Bands often combine genres, transcend genres, or even comment on them as they play within them. Sometimes, for example in the case of rap music, the commentary is part of the music itself. Some people place an enormous amount of importance on genres when deciding to listen to particular music—they want ways to understand

◀ Is Johnny Cash authentic? Find out why that might not be the question to ask in our authenticity suite beginning on page 539.

what experience is ahead of them, and whether, based on past experience, they will like a particular song or band.

Of the genres we have listed, the one hardest to qualify is "pop music" (which is why we place it in quotes). For many, the term has negative connotations—it stands for "popular," which in some circles means "unsophisticated" or that it panders to a popular sensibility instead of artistic integrity. For the authors, pop music is an umbrella that often covers parts or wholes of entire genres at one time or another—classical music was the pop music of its day, as was early jazz or swing. Even much of "classic rock" was once popular. Having said that, what is popular oftentimes is worth studying for the light it may shed on our contemporary world.

Yet, musical genres are not value free. We tend to associate certain traits with particular genres. If we see a number of country and western CDs in someone's car, we may (often incorrectly) assume something about them or their socioeconomic class. Genres are themselves complex texts whose significations change over time as culture, tastes, and people change.

One of the most straightforward papers you can write is one about whether a song, album, or artist fits into a particular genre. This lends itself to an arguable thesis. One thing you likely should think about when doing this type of paper is defining the characteristics of the genre. In other words, you might ask yourself what muscial characteristics such as guitar, rhythm, and other instruments define a particular genre. Or do its lyrics define the genre? When it comes to country music and rap music, for example, they are often easily defined by recognized characteristics such as steel guitar and straightforward lyrics in country music, and sampled music and more explicit lyrics in rap. But often artists write and perform music that has some characteristics of a genre and not others; this instability can often lead to a productive writing situation.

MUSIC IS (OR IS NOT) A REFLECTION OF THE CULTURE THAT SURROUNDS IT.

Music is often of a time and place and can offer clues to the society in which it is written. For example, much of Bob Dylan's work in the turbulent 1960s directly reflects the world around it; his songs frequently engage the protest movements of the time. Gangsta rap also seemingly helps tell stories from disadvantaged areas with its focus on the dilemmas of living in such areas. These forms of music can bring a broader understanding of various social ailments to the "average" listener. By a bizarre and unfortunate coincidence, Ryan Adams's catchy tribute to New York City, "New York, New York," was just gaining popularity when the events of September 11, 2001, occurred. The song became an unintended anthem and tribute that has, for many, come to symbolize the hope and sacrifice that New Yorkers felt after the attacks.

But making automatic leaps from music to culture and vice versa can be problematic. Songwriters sometimes have social aims that go along with their music, and sometimes they do not. Even if they do, there can be unintended messages that flow from their music; music may unintentionally reflect society as well. For example, some people believe that disco music with its programmed beats and the sexual innuendo in many of its lyrics reflected the so-called shallow values of the 1970s, though those writing the music probably did not intend their music to have this effect. Similarly, since Kurt Cobain's suicide, some critics have associated the entire grunge sound with nihilism—something Cobain never would have wanted.

On a purely musical level, we can also listen to a song and place it in a particular era because of certain musical conventions of the period—identifiable instruments or sounds in general often give this away. Can you think of some conventions used today? Some we associate with a previous era? Think not only of songs but also of commercials. Do you remember when rap beats became a big part of commercials? It was not always so. . . .

Finally, sometimes musicians write songs that seem not to be of a time and place. Gillian Welch's popular album *Revival* sounds as though it is a relic from early twentieth-century Appalachia, yet Welch, a Californian with classical music training, recorded the record in 1995. Smash Mouth could fool some into believing they were around in the early '60s. What qualities do these artists convey in their songs? What do they avoid?

THE PACKAGING OF MUSIC REFLECTS THE AIMS OF THE BANDS, OR THE RECORD COMPANIES, OR BOTH, AND IT HAS AN EFFECT ON THE WAY WE VIEW THE MUSIC.

The packaging of music involves a variety of things. Consumers are presented bands not only with their music, but their record cover, their band name, the album or song name—components that sit outside of the actual music itself. As you know, how musicians present themselves can be crucial to how we perceive them and probably how we perceive their music. For example, how would we view the music of Britney Spears coming from Tupac Shakur, and vice versa? Would Justin Timberlake be as popular if he looked like Dick Cheney? The persona of each of these artists contributes to the way we perceive them and their work.

Often we read performers not only from the packaging of an album but also visually through photographs in rock magazines, reports on entertainment shows, live concerts, and videos. In particular, the handlers of the musician or the musician himself or herself use the music video to provide another way of determining how potential consumers see the artist. Web sites do similar work but may offer different portrayals of the performer if the artist, a fanatical listener, or the record company sponsors the site.

Sometimes the packaging of an artist helps us understand what musicians think they are doing; other times the package is a wall that interferes with our experiencing music honestly or directly. Accordingly, we have to recognize that packaging comes as a part of listening to the music, and we can do with that information as we will. For example, many fans of musicians assume that these musicians "sell out" when they sign a record deal with a large corporation, often looking for evidence of such behavior in the music, as did the fans of the band R.E.M. in the 1990s when they moved from the independent label I.R.S. to the mega-label Warner Brothers. Others just listen to the music with little regard to packaging, marketing, or in some instances, lyrics.

Packaging also can reflect the times—if we see an image of a band from a different decade we may understand a more complex relationship between the band and its era. But in reading packaging of bands from past eras we have to take into account the same factors we do in evaluating packaging from our own era.

When writing about the materials surrounding music, describing the materials is an important step, similar to the steps needed when writing about the songs or albums themselves. A detailed visual description of what the cover looks like as well as a shot-by-shot description of the video is useful. While not all of this might make it into the paper, writing about the materials will likely help you understand it.

WHILE THE MUSIC WE LIKE MAY REFLECT PERSONAL TASTE, IT MAY ALSO REFLECT CULTURAL TASTES.

How many of you have heard of Toni Price? The Derailers? The Gourds? The Damnations? Dale Watson? Texan students may recognize these names, as all of these performers are hugely popular in the Austin, Texas area, selling out concerts and receiving considerable air time on local radio stations. Yet, few people outside of Austin and even fewer outside of Texas know this music, despite the fact that Austin enjoys a reputation as a progressive musical city. Similarly, if you have grown up in a small town outside of Austin, rap, grunge, and trip-hop may never make it to local radio stations or to the record collections of your friends, and, therefore, by extension, it may never make its way into your life (although MTV's presence now makes that less likely). Even worse, if you are from the United States, you may never get exposure to British punk bands, fado music from Portugal, or Bulgarian *a cappella* choruses. Record stores and video music channels have gotten much better at featuring international music in the past few years, and the Internet provides much more opportunity for fans to find this music, but there remain vast quantities of music we will never hear, simply because those forms of music belong to other cultures and places.

In addition, for many people, what they encounter on television, the Internet, and in print determines their musical tastes. If bands do not make videos or are not featured in popular magazines, we may never know they exist. Many forms of alternative music never make it onto the airwaves; accordingly, potential listeners never find music outside of the mainstream. American trends toward playing and replaying market-tested music like pop, rock, country, and rap tends to reinforce listening tastes and habits. In short, you may like the music you do simply because that's all you have been exposed to. Thus, our tastes may depend less on comparison shopping or eclectic listening than the demands of the marketplace.

Some of your professors might be amenable to you writing about the evolution of your musical taste as a type of personal essay. If you write this type of essay, you should still think about the traditional aspects of essay writing—an argument, evidence, and focus.

THE MUSIC ITSELF CONTAINS READABLE ELEMENTS THAT CONTRIBUTE TO THE LISTENER'S EXPERIENCE.

Music creates moods as well as meaning. It is often hard to isolate the aspects of songs that make us feel a particular way. Often, performers intend the pace of a song, its intensity, or the sounds of the notes to affect listeners in specific ways. Hard-driving punk, smooth jazz, rap with samples and scratches, and string concertos with a lot of violins spark conscious and subconscious reactions. Sometimes, these reactions are strong and mysterious; other times, we know all too well why we feel what we do. Music functions much like poetry in that it evokes as much as it overtly states.

We can often tell by the pace of a song what the mood is—a fast song means something different than a slow song. The instruments in a song indicate/signify something (for example, the presence of trumpets or violins tells the listener something about the intentions of the artist). They are there to make the song sound better, but the way they sound better is often indicative of something else as well. Similarly, how the lyrics are sung may indicate how we are to read the song. For instance, Kurt Cobain's voice demands a kind of response that Celine Dion's does not; how we read Johnny Cash's voice will differ from how we read Aretha Franklin's.

The recent popularity of MP3 players such as the iPod have completely altered our relationship to music and public space. On the bus, the subway, while walking down the street or across campus, we see people bobbing their heads in giddy oblivion, and until we see the headphones protruding from their ears, we may think they are suffering some kind of seizure from an unknown malady. But these compact players have increased our ability to add soundtracks to our days. In fact, in the past few months, psychologists have argued that listening to music this way actually makes people happier—and if you listen in the morning, it can dramatically affect your mood for the entire day.

In writing about music, separating the emotional response from the intellectual one can be difficult. And we are not sure you have to—by describing the way music makes you feel, you get at the heart of one of the crucial aspects of interpreting music. Even professional writers about music sometimes describe the emotional aspects of music when writing about it.

Making an argument about music can be as simple as defending a song, album, or artist or as complicated as analysis through musicology. The key is remembering to be concrete in describing the music and above all, make an argument.

THE LISTENERS CREATE THE MUSIC.

What we as listeners make of this sound, the packaging, and lyrics is largely up to us. We can choose to ignore the packaging, the lyrics, or the music, or a combination of the above, and arrive at one kind of interpretation. We can read biographies of musicians, watch their videos, or read the lyric sheets in a CD to get at a more complete reading of a musician or band. We can choose to listen to music on an expensive system that enhances the effects of a CD, listen to them on a car stereo, or a Walkman, and have that transform our understanding of the song. Or we can put our car radios on scan and find the first song that we like. . . .

THIS TEXT

1. Notice how each writer approaches the music generally, or a song or artist differently. Why do you think that's the case?

2. Do you think all the writers are music critics? What distinguishes a critic from a writer?

3. Do you think the writers are fans of the music they are writing about? What about their writing makes you draw that conclusion? Do you think writers should be fans of the music about which they write?

4. Notice whether you can get the criteria for each writer's idea of what a good song or album would be.

5. How much do these writers think about the social impact of the music they write about? Do you think they think about it enough, or too much?

6. How are elements such as race and gender a part of the analysis here?

7. How does the background of the authors influence their ideas about music?

8. While it will be impossible for you to know this fully, try to figure out the writing situation of each author. Who is the audience? What does the author have at stake?

9. What social, political, economic, and cultural forces affect the author's text? What is going on in the world as she is writing?

10. What are the main points of the essay? Can you find a thesis statement anywhere?

11. How does the author support his argument? What evidence does he use to back up any claims he might make?

12. Is the author's argument valid and/or reasonable?

13. Do you find yourself in agreement with the author? Why or why not?

14. Does the author help you read music better than you did before reading the essay? If so, why?

15. How is the reading process different if you are reading a song, as opposed to a short story or poem?

16. What is the agenda of the author? Why does she or he want me to think a certain way?

17. Did you like this? Why or why not?

BEYOND THIS TEXT

Lyrics

Theme: What are some of the themes of the song (themes are generally what the author thinks of the subject)? Are there both intentional and unintentional themes?

Plot: Is there a plot to the song? Does the song tell a story or convey a narrative?

Literary devices: Do you notice any devices such as the use of figurative language (metaphor, simile) or repetition or rhyme? Are there notable symbols? Are these devices effective? Do they add to your enjoyment?

"Literariness": Do you think the lyrics have literary quality? Would the lyrics stand alone as a poem? Why or why not?

Music

The instruments: What instruments does the band use? Does it use them effectively? Does their use symbolize anything outside of normal use?

Mood: What is the mood of the song? How does the music reflect this—through the makeup of its instruments, its speed, its tone (minor or major), or a combination of factors?

Technology: Are there technological aspects in the song? What are they? What effects do they have on the song?

The Whole Package

Genre: How would you classify this song by genre? Would you do so by the lyrics or music? Why? Are there ways that songs resist classification? If so, in what ways?

Effectiveness: Does this song "work"? Why or why not? Is there an element of the song that's stronger than the others?

How and where it's played: Unlike a poem, you can hear songs in the car, in a dance club, in the elevator, on a date, in the doctor's office, and at church. How does setting influence how you hear a song?

A QUICK GUIDE TO WRITING ABOUT MUSIC

1. **Make sure you have a place to write down notes.** Sketch out some preliminary questions you want to answer when listening (we have a worksheet in this chapter that you could use.)
2. **Listen to the album or song all the way through.** Listen to it taking notes. If you think there is a particularly important part of the song or album, note the time of that part.
3. **Read over your notes. Highlight or bold parts you think are useful.** See if you have an argument.
4. **Think about the way the paper might be split into paragraphs.** Try to connect the notes to the paragraphs.
5. **Alternatively—as some of the writers have indicated they have done—write an entire draft after listening to the song.** And THEN go through and take some of these steps.
6. **Researching information (see the introduction for more general tips) on music will often require using a mix of academic or scholarly sources, magazines and newspapers, Internet postings, and encyclopedias.** You will have to be extra careful about researching music because you may have to use sources or at least evaluate some that may not be reliable.
7. **We prefer engaging the primary text before doing research; we like writing our thoughts down before we search out information.** It often allows us to focus the research process and avoid the inclusion of random bits of information. Research should help an argument you are making; seldomly do your professors just want research; this is a difference between some college writing and writing in high school.

"Coal Miner's Daughter"

Alessandro Portelli

Alessandro Portelli teaches American Literature at the University of Rome–La Sapienza. Noted for his work on oral history, Portelli has written a number of books, including his landmark work, The Text and the Voice *(1994), and his most recent book,* The Order Has Been Carried Out: History, Memory, and Meaning of a Nazi Massacre in Rome *(2007).*

> When I state myself, as the Representative of the Verse—it does not mean me—but a supposed person.
>
> —*Emily Dickinson*

1.

There is a scene in Robert Altman's *Nashville,* in which a singer with long wavy black hair steps on the stage at Opryland, sings a song and then, as the band starts vamping for the next number, breaks into a rambling speech, which soon turns into a loose reminiscence of childhood:

> I think there's a storm a-brewing. That's what my granddaddy used to say before he lost his hearin' and sometimes he'd say, "Oh gosh," or "Durn it," or "My word" . . . My granny, she'd go round the house clickin' her false teeth to the radio all day. She was a lot of fun, and always cooked my favorite roast beef and she was a sweetheart. She raised chickens, too. She, uh—in fact, did ya ever hear a chicken sound?[1]

This scene is a fictionalized account of the most famous crackup in country-music history: that of Loretta Lynn in the early '70s. An authorized version of the same episode appears in a later film, Michael Apted's *Coal Miner's Daughter,* based on Loretta Lynn's autobiographical book by the same title (the episode, however, is not discussed in the book). Both films concur in showing the breakdown as an eruption of private memories: a compulsive autobiographical act.

2.

The book takes its title, in turn, from Loretta Lynn's best and most successful song, "Coal Miner's Daughter." The song appears at first hearing as another autobiographical act, containing many features of Lynn's later descriptions of her own life: the sentimental cliché ("We were poor but we had love"), the precise description of background details, the relish in the sound of vernacular speech. In her book, Lynn says:

> I'd always wanted to write a song about growing up, but I never believed anybody would care about it. One day I was sitting around the television studio at WSIX, waiting to rehearse a show . . . I went off to the dressing room and just wrote the first words that came into my head. It started: "Well, I was borned a coal miner's daughter . . .", which was nothing but the truth.[2]

Before we go on to examine her autobiographies, let us take a quick look at Loretta Lynn's life. She was in fact born a coal miner's daughter in the mid-Thirties in Western Kentucky; she barely learned to read and write, married at thirteen, followed her husband to Washington state, worked hard, lived poor, had four children by the time she was eighteen (was a grandmother at twenty-nine), and never thought of a career in music until she was twenty-four. Since then, she has moved to Nashville, had two twin daughters, and worked her way up to be the most successful female country singer and one of the most successful entertainers in the history of show business.

It was more than a year before Lynn and her entourage could bring themselves to issue "Coal Miner's Daughter" as a record. The time in which the song was "kept . . . in the

---

[1] *Nashville,* screenplay by Joan Tewkesbury (New York: Bantam Books, 1976), no page numbers.
[2] Loretta Lynn with George Vecsey, *Coal Miner's Daughter* (New York: Warner Books, 1980), p. 201. All further quotations will be indicated in the text with page numbers.

can" seems like a metaphor for a repressed autobiographical urge. Lynn says that she did not think that people would be interested in a song about her life; in fact, the first important decision in autobiography is always accepting that one's life is worth telling in public. Once the song hit the charts, however, all doubts were removed, and the floodgates of autobiography were thrown open. In further songs, interviews, ceremonies, and finally in a book and a film, the story of the coal miner's daughter, the Washington housewife, the Nashville Opry star was told over and over, in a variety of media but with remarkable consistency.

> I was given up when I was a baby. I came close to drowning near my ranch a few years ago. I never told anybody about that until now. And the doctors told me that my heart stopped on the operating table when I had chest surgery in 1972. Ever since then, I've wanted to tell my life story (p. 18).

Autobiography as a response to a death threat is a standard concept not necessarily to be taken at face value. In fact, the song "Coal Miner's Daughter" was composed before Lynn's surgery. It is a fact, however, that telling her life story means more to Loretta Lynn than the public relations gesture it is for many other public figures.

In 1974, an interviewer asked her how country music had changed since she came to Nashville. Most musicians would be content to give a professional answer to this professional question. But terms like "change" and memories of coming to a new place start a whole other chain of associations in Loretta Lynn's mind:

> I didn't live in Nashville. Of course I had never been any place except I went to the state of Washington—my husband sent for me and I went on the train. I was pregnant. . . .[3]

The interviewer comes back to the original question shortly afterwards, asking "How has country music changed?"—and again Lynn digresses freely, associating autobiographical thoughts:

> It seems like everything has changed. When I was growing up . . . like for me to see a loaf of bread [. . .] There ain't many people live the way we did in Butcher Holler, and Butcher Holler has changed.

When asked about career and business, Lynn almost compulsively responds in terms of her early life, of before she became a professional musician. There is an undeniable degree of authenticity in this urge, as the episode of the breakdown confirms, an inner need. On the other hand, the autobiographical urge also sells. Within a year after "Coal Miner's Daughter," she had three more singles out with songs of an autobiographical nature, signaling both the open floodgates of autobiography and the sequels to a commercial hit—from coal mine to gold mine, as it were. "Coal Miner's Daughter" becomes a trademark, designating a song, a bestselling book, a major movie, a publishing company (Coal Miner Music), a band (Lynn's backup group changed names, from Western—Trailblazers—to Appalachian—Coal Miners).

On the other hand, some members of the band did come from coal mining families, and all were supposed to have been factory workers at one time (at least, this is the point she

---

[3]Rick Broan and Sue Thrasher, "Interview with Loretta Lynn," February 25, 1974, typescript (courtesy of Sue Thrasher). The interview appeared in *The Great Speckled Bird;* Lynn refers approvingly to it in *Coal Miner's Daughter,* p. 91.

was making at the time her autobiography was written). The same sign, then, designates a commercial gimmick, and a factual truth: the constant tension in all of Loretta Lynn's autobiographical image-making and soul-searching. The most obvious example of this process is, of course, her name. Contrary to the practice of many stars, she did not change her name (which happens to possess the feature of alliteration, highly prized in advertising); on the other hand, her name increasingly designates objects other than her person—her voice, her image, her records, all the way to Crisco shortening and franchised western wear stores.

3.

If we look at the front and back cover of a paperback edition of *Coal Miner's Daughter* (in this case, the 1977 Warner paperback), we find there one of the most concise statements of the nature of autobiography anywhere. The two pictures—the glamorous star on the front, the bucktoothed little girl on the back—are the same person, and yet two different people. The contrast shows the distinction between past and present selves, public and private lives, which creates the inner tension in the autobiographical genre; and it also underlies that this contrast takes place within what remains, after all, one and the same person.

Structurally, this means that autobiography has much in common with metaphor. A metaphor is the discovery of similarity in a context of difference: "Achilles is a lion" makes sense as a metaphor precisely because Achilles is not a lion. Jean Starobinski has pointed out that in order for autobiography to exist, there must have been a change, a dramatic development in the subject; I would stress the fact that the change is only significant because the subject remains the same. The difference between the narrating and the narrated self is worthy of our attention because these two selves happen to belong to the same person.

This is true also at another level. Autobiography is a public performance; but the story teller is expected to reveal the private self in it. On one level, the autobiographer is supposed to abolish the difference between public and private self; on another, this act is only relevant inasmuch as the reader is constantly reminded that the two selves are logically distinct. "One does not dress for private company as for a public ball," says Benjamin Franklin, the founding father of modern autobiography; and Nathaniel Hawthorne muses that "it is scarcely decorous to speak all."

This double metaphorical structure is best expressed in the autobiographies of stars. Their success story enhances difference and change, but they always strive to prove continuity and identity insisting that success has not changed them; they build an elaborate public image, but must persuade their fans that it also coincides with their private selves. Country music as a genre claims sincerity to a very high degree, linking it closely with autobiography: "A hillbilly is more sincere than most entertainers," Hank Williams used to say, "because a hillbilly was raised rougher."

In fact, the ideal country star must be born in a cabin and live in a mansion, like Loretta Lynn; and, as she does, must travel back and forth between them, at least in imagination. Most importantly, they are expected to live in a mansion as they would in a cabin. Stars must look dazzlingly glamorous on the stage, declaring distance; but must open their homes to visiting fans and tourists, stressing familiarity. No wonder autobiography is also a thematic staple in so many country songs.

> My fans and writers—says Lynn—are always making a big deal about me acting natural, right from the country. That's because I come from Butcher Holler, Kentucky, and I ain't never forgot it. [. . .] We're country musicians; I don't think we could play our kind of music if we didn't come from little places like Butcher Holler (p. 59).

In her book, Lynn presents herself as a regular housewife (an image doubled by her Crisco commercials), who has some problems with her husband but still understands and loves him, who hangs drapes and even worries about where the money for the children's braces is coming from. "When you're lookin' at me, you're lookin' at country," she sings; "I was Loretta Lynn, a mother and a wife and a daughter, who had feelings just like other women," she says (p. 151). And yet—if she were just another housewife, mother, and daughter, who would buy her book and see her movie? But then—*who* is she? As in most autobiographies, the answer is blowing somewhere along the continuum of past and present, public and private.

4.

Let us begin with public and private. *Coal Miner's Daughter* opens in the bedroom; there's another bedroom scene two pages later, and early in the book Lynn describes her wedding night in detail. These, however, are not love scenes. In the opening episode, she has a nightmare and winds up bloodying her husband's nose with her wedding ring; the next thing she mentions is the gun her husband keeps on the night table. The wedding night scene, though ostensibly humorous, describes a rape: "He finally more or less had to rip off my panties. The rest of it was kind of a blur" (p. 78).

On one level, Lynn is grappling with inner dreams and deepseated fears; on another, she is casting herself in the folksy role of the country girl whose mother never told her about the facts of life and who—"just like other women"—had to find out the hard way. The autobiographical urge merges with the commercial image-making: Lynn takes her fans into her bedroom, but then resents the invasion and hides.

This is true also literally. When she was in the hospital, "the fans heard I was in bed [and] they trooped right into my room and started taking pictures" (p. 163). Every year, Loretta Lynn opens her house to thousands of fans, in a ritual of reunion between the star and her social constituency that blurs the line where the public ends and the private begins. Fans "just pop into my kitchen when we're sitting around. It sounds terrible, but I can't relax in my own home," she complains. So she winds up checking in at a motel— leaving her private residence to seek shelter in public places. The same process functions in the autobiographies: the need to show and the need to hide establish a constant tension. She displays her inner self to the public, but when the public gets there she has retired somewhere else—and regrets it, and thinks "it's terrible."

A similar contradiction occurs in the relationship between past and present. Being a coal miner's daughter is both an inner identity actively sought and a mask imposed by business associates and fans. Fidelity to roots is an authentic part of herself as well as a role imposed from outside. Thus, in order to play up continuity she is forced to repress the changes that make her what she is. She speaks dialect freely and spontaneously, but a critic has noticed that "from time to time, she will repeat a word which she has pronounced correctly, only to repeat it *incorrectly* (as *born* to *borned*), almost as though she were reminding herself."[4]

Thus, the same sets of signs designate truth and fiction, spontaneity and manipulation. Loretta Lynn does artificially what comes naturally—like speaking dialect—and does naturally what comes artificially—like wearing a mask.

---

[4]Dorothy A. Horstman, "Loretta Lynn," in Bill C. Malone and Judith McCulloch, eds., *Stars of Country Music* (Urbana: University of Illinois Press, 1975), p. 32.

5.

All the theory and practice of autobiography revolve around the first person pronoun, "I." The question is, what does Loretta Lynn mean, to what exactly does she refer, when she uses that word?

Let us consider the songs first. When she sings "I was borned a coal miner's daughter," she is using the autobiographical first person; but when she sings "I'm a honky tonk girl," her first hit, she is using the fictional-lyrical first person of popular song. These two meanings of "I" interact intensively in her work. Because she uses autobiography so much, many songs that are not about herself have been taken for autobiography: an exchange favored by the fact that in all her repertoire Lynn consistently projects a character based very much upon herself, the spunky woman who does not question the system but won't take no nonsense from nobody—"Don't Come Home a-Drinkin' with Lovin' on Your Mind" because "Your Squaw's on the Warpath Tonight."

The interaction of autobiographical and fictional–lyrical "I" generates intermediate forms: first-person songs, written by herself, but not autobiographical; first-person songs, written by others, but based on aspects of her life. She wrote "The Pill," a song about contraceptives which was one of her most controversial hits, though she says she hardly ever used it herself (it would have been harder to write, and sell, a song about her husband's vasectomy, which she talks about in the book). On the other hand, "One's On the Way"—a vivid description of a housewife with four kids, a careless husband, maybe twins on the way, the pot boiling over, and the doorbell ringing—is based on recollections of her early married life, but was written by Shel Silverstein. There is even another Shel Silverstein song, called "Hey, Loretta," in which Lynn sings to herself as if she were somebody else.

To further confuse matters, there is the problem of performance. Singers—like all oral performers—present even the most impersonal material through their body and their voice, thus making it intrinsically personal. Even when she performs someone else's songs, Lynn steps closer to an autobiographical act, although it might not be technically described as such. On the other hand, when Emmylou Harris records Lynn's "Blue Kentucky Girl," the autobiographical overtones are lost.

In conclusion, there are at least four meanings of the word "I" as used in Lynn's repertoire and performances, going from the purely autobiographical to the purely fictional lyrical, through at least two intermediate forms. Each of these forms shades or may turn into another through the processes of performance and reception.

Much the same can be said about the book. A capsule definition of autobiography is based on the coincidence between the hero and the narrator inside the book's covers and the author outside: they all have the same name. But if we look at the cover of *Coal Miner's Daughter*, we see that the names on the cover are split: "by Loretta Lynn with George Vecsey." *Coal Miner's Daughter* is one of those "as told to" autobiographies in which famous people delegate the writing to a professional when they are too busy or unable to take care of it themselves. Although these books are billed as autobiographies, the person who says "I" in them is not the same person that does the actual writing. Loretta Lynn makes no pretense about it: George Vecsey is frequently mentioned in the text as "my writer," in the third person. In quite a postmodern fashion, Vecsey writes about himself in the third person, about somebody else in the first, and enters his own text as a character in someone else's story: while he writes his own name, he pretends that this is Loretta Lynn talking about him. One assumes that, when the "I" character is different from the author, we are dealing with fiction; *Coal Miner's Daughter,* however, is supposed to be factually straight. The only fiction about it has to do with the uses of the first person.

With the film, we take another step. By definition, there can be no autobiographical film in the strict formal sense. When a book is turned into a film, the first consequence is the disappearance of the first-person narrator: films are always in the third person. In the movie *Coal Miner's Daughter* (whose credits are reproduced on the back cover of the paperback) the "author's" name on the cover is Michael Apted, filming a screenplay by Tom Rickman based on the book written by George Vecsey as told by Loretta Lynn. The face and voice on the screen belong to Sissy Spacek. Yet, the name is still Loretta Lynn: the film is clearly intended as a "true" statement, largely meant to "set the record straight" after *Nashville.* Many side characters in *Coal Miner's Daughter* actually play themselves, reinforcing the "documentary" overtones.

We come full circle when we turn to the paperback and discover that the film has been incorporated into the book. First of all, as we have already pointed out, the book displays the film credits, making it look as if the book was a novelization of the film: the written autobiography is somehow validated by having been the subject of a fictional movie. In the second place, the images from the film are also included in the book.

In the book, indeed, Loretta Lynn tells her story not one, but three times: with words, with photographs from her family album, with stills from the movie. The two sets of photographs are almost interchangeable: the family album's captions, however, are in the first person, while those of the movie stills are in the third. But the pictures themselves are sometimes hard to tell apart. The picture of Loretta Lynn in her first stage outfit is so similar to the one of Sissy Spacek wearing the replica of it that they perform a sort of reversal of the autobiographical process: while the pictures on the cover portray two different people who are yet the same person, those two photographs inside portray one character who is in fact two different persons. It may not be irrelevant, in the book's rhetorical structure, that the film stills come before the family album: it looks as though Loretta Lynn's photos were patterned after Sissy Spacek's. Which, of course, has been the problem all along: which of the two, the image or the person, is the real one, which one comes first.

6.

In a passage in *The Day of the Locust,* Nathanael West describes the main female character, Faye Greener, as she tries out one identity after another:

> She would get some music on the radio, then lie down on her bed and shut her eyes. She had a large assortment of stories to choose from. After getting herself in the right mood, she would go over them in her mind, as though they were a pack of cards, discarding one after another until she found one that suited. On some days, she would run through the whole pack without making a choice [. . .] While she admitted that her method was too mechanical for best results [. . .] she said that any dream was better than no dream.[5]

Let us compare this passage to one from *Coal Miner's Daughter,* in which Lynn describes her belief in reincarnation—a subject clearly related to the question of the mutable and multiple self.

---

[5]Nathanael West, *The Day of the Locust,* in *The Collected Works of Nathanael West* (Harmondsworth, Midds.: Penguin, 1975), pp. 60–61.

I once read that you could feel your past lives if you concentrated real hard. So I tried it in my hotel room. I wasn't asleep but kind of in a trance. I lay down quiet and let my mind drift.

All of a sudden I was an Indian woman wearing moccasins and a long buckskin dress and I had my hair in pigtails. Even the sound and smell were vivid to me. All around me there was a huge field with Indians riding horseback. I was standing next to a mounted Indian. I sensed that he was about to go off into battle, and I was saying good-bye to him. Then a shot rang out, and my husband fell off his horse [. . .] In the second such experience, I saw myself dressed up in an Irish costume, doing an Irish dance down a country lane in front of a big white house (p. 98).

Loretta Lynn is part Cherokee, and almost as proud of her Indian blood as she is to be a coal miner's daughter. The rest of her ancestry is the Scots–Irish stock prevalent in Appalachia. As she thumbs through her past lives, she meets her ancestors: the idea that one's past lives are those our ancestors lived is not as flat a banality as one would expect in the autobiography of a star. Like Faye Greener's second-hand dreams, however, Loretta Lynn's earlier selves are fashioned after artificial patterns. The Indian warrior chief on horseback is more reminiscent of plains Indians, of Western movie Sioux, that of a mountain Cherokee. The "big white house" is a plantation house, and in anybody's book an Irish girl in front of a Southern plantation house is named Scarlett O'Hara. "I never picture myself after Scarlett O'Hara," says Lynn later in the book—but she makes this claim in the context of buying her new house because its "huge white columns" remind her of Tara (p. 136). The more she seeks inside to find her true self, the more she encounters someone else's fictions.

The paradox in *The Day of the Locust* is that, by having only masks and no face, Faye Greener achieves a sort of purity: she hides nothing, because there is nothing to hide. She is incapable of deceit because she lives in a world (Hollywood, which is to her what Nashville is to Loretta Lynn) in which deceit is real life and fiction is the only truth.

The Day of the Locust anticipates many developments which would later be labelled as "postmodern"; it concerns the relationship between mass culture, the fragmentation of the self, the erasure of distinctions between image and substance, sign and referent, truth and fiction in a universe in which image is the only substance and signs are the only referents of signs.

"In country music," Lynn complains, "we're always singing about home and family. But because I was in country music, I had to neglect my home and my family" (p. 140). Let us not be deceived by the sentimental wording: these are the only words she has, but her problem is serious. She is dealing with the disappearance of reality in a sign-dominated universe. Success in country music is based on foregrounding the autobiographical ingredient (one need only think of the early Dolly Parton and Merle Haggard); but the more an artist achieves success, the less "life" there is to talk about. In many cases, this erosion of reality turns the autobiographical urge of country music toward the writing of songs about being a country-music singer—metasongs like self-reflexive postmodern metanovels about novels, composed much for the same causes.

In Loretta Lynn, we can see the autobiographical impulse grow stronger while her career develops, as if she were groping back toward a time when she was a nobody but knew who she was (or now thinks she did). She lives through some of the basic problems with which many contemporary intellectuals are concerned, and deals with them with her limited means and ambitions, in the most direct way there is: by trying her level best, over and over again, to tell the story of her life.

How I Wrote This Essay Alessandro Portelli

Why did you write this piece—what was the assignment or motivation for writing?

I was intrigued after some radical friends in Atlanta told me that they loved country music, which I had always thought was intrinsically reactionary, and after I saw the movie and read the book. I had arranged to also do an interview with Loretta Lynn but at the last moment I was unable to go. When my department at the U. of Rome organized a conference on autobiography I presented this as a paper.

What did you do when you decided to write?

I guess I just followed Woody Guthrie's advice: I sat down at the typewriter and JUST WROTE.

How did you begin?

The order of the text is by and large the same as that of the composition process. I thought starting with a scene and a visual image would be a good way to get the reader's attention.

Describe the process of writing the first draft.

Basically, the first draft is also the final draft.

Did you do research as you wrote or before you started writing? What databases did you use?

This was written before there were any databases. Because it is conceived as an essay in literature rather than history, my sources were the texts themselves—the book, the film, the songs, and the interview with Ms. Lynn my Atlanta friends made available to me.

How long would you say the process took?

A few days.

How did you edit the draft?

I reread, tightened some sentences, and tried to correct typos.

What was the response when you turned in your essay?

The presentation at the conference was well received. It then appeared in the conference proceedings, which I don't think many people read.

Are you satisfied now with what you wrote? Would you make any changes?

As satisfied as one usually is with things written almost thirty years ago. I just went over it to translate it for an Italian publication and I saw no reason to change anything.

READING WRITING

This Text: Reading

1. How important is biography in understanding an artist? Does Portelli make a case one way or another?
2. How can one describe a song as an "autobiography"? Does Portelli make a good case?
3. Listen to "Coal Miner's Daughter." How do you think reading Portelli's piece affected your listening?

Your Text: Writing

1. Listen to a rap or country song in which the artist speaks in the first person about their experiences. Now go to an electronic database or a newspaper or magazine archive and find out something about the artist. Write a paper about what differences emerge and why or whether that matters.
2. Do an examination of an autobiographical song (or one that sounds like one). Do a literary analysis of the way the artist constructs the self.
3. In one of the two papers above, see how structuring the paper in multiple pieces in the way Portelli does affects your writing and might affect the reader's response to it.

The Rock Lexicon

Chuck Klosterman

Chuck Klosterman is one of America's most prominent commentators on popular culture. The author of four books, Fargo Rock City; Sex, Drugs, and Cocoa Puffs; Killing Yourself to Live; *and the recently released* Chuck Klosterman IV, *Klosterman has written for* Spin, Esquire, *and* ESPN.com, *among many outlets. Here (2005) he writes about the arcane definitions of genres he encountered as a writer for* Spin.

"I DON'T READ YOUR MAGAZINE ANYMORE," says my 36-year-old sister as we ride in a rental car. "I don't read your magazine anymore because all you guys ever write about is emo, and I don't get it."

Now, for a moment, I find myself very interested in what my sister is saying. I absolutely cannot fathom what she could possibly hate about emo, and (I suspect) this subject might create an interesting ten minutes of rental-car discussion. Does she find emo too phallocentric? Do the simplistic chord progressions strike her as derivative? Why can't she relate to emo? I ask her these questions, and I await her answer. But her answer is not what I expect.

"No, no," she says. "When I say I don't get emo, I mean I literally don't know what it is. The word may as well be Latin. But I keep seeing jokes about emo in your magazine, and they're never funny, because I have no idea what's supposed to be funny about something I've never heard of."

This, of course, leads to a spirited dialogue in which I say things like "'Emo' is short for emotional," and she says things like "But all pop music is about emotions," and I respond by saying, "It's technically a style of punk rock, but it's actually more of a personal, introspective attitude," and she counters with "That sounds boring," and then I mention

Andy Greenwald (author of *Nothing Feels Good: Punk Rock, Teenagers, and Emo*), and she asks, "Wasn't Andy Greenwald a defensive end for the Pittsburgh Steelers in the late '70s?" and I say, "No, that was L.C. Greenwood, and I'm pretty sure he doesn't know any of the members of Senses Fail."

But anyway, I learned something important from this discussion: that reading rock magazines must be very confusing to people who only listen to rock music casually. Whenever journalists write about music, we always operate under the assumption that certain genres are self-evident and that placing a given band into one of those categories serves an expository purpose. Just as often, an artist will be described as a synthesis of two equally obscure subgenres, and we're all supposed to do the sonic math ourselves. However, this only helps the informed; that kind of description is useful to those who have already conquered the rock lexicon. What we need is a glossary of terms so we can all share an equal playing field.

I will do my best.

DISCO METAL: This is up-tempo, semiheavy guitar rock that someone (usually a stripper) could feasibly dance to. White Zombie made a lot of songs in this style. Weirdly, it does not seem to apply to straightforward metal bands (Kiss, Van Halen) who overtly write disco songs ("I Was Made for Lovin' You," "Dance the Night Away"). No one knows why.

SHOEGAZE: Music by artists who stare at their feet while performing—presumably because they are ashamed to be playing such shambolic music to an audience of weirdos.

POST-ROCK: This is when a group of rock musicians employ traditional rock instrumentation to perform music for people who traditionally listen to rock—except these musicians don't play rock and the songs don't have any vocals. I don't get it either. The premier band of this genre is Tortoise, and the kind of people who like post-rock are the same kind of people who think it's a good idea to name a band Tortoise.

PSYCH: (as in "psychedelic") The modifier psych has only recently come back in vogue, which is interesting. You have possibly heard the terms "psych folk" (sometimes applied to artists in the vein of Devendra Banhart) or "psych country" (which is vaguely similar to what used to be called "outlaw country") or "psych rock" (which is what Courtney Taylor of the Dandy Warhols calls his band's sound in the documentary DIG!). I've made a great effort to try to find the unifying principle among these permutations of psych music, and the answer is probably what you'd expect: This is music for drug addicts, made by drug addicts. If you are in a Tejano quartet and all four of you start taking mescaline (and if all the kids who come to your shows drop acid in the parking lot before entering the venue), you now play "psych Tejano." That's the whole equation.

GRIME: Almost two years ago, I asked two learned people at *Spin* to explain to me what grime is. They both said, "Don't worry about it. You will never need to know. It's completely unnecessary knowledge." Then, over the next few weeks, grime came up in conversation on three separate occasions. And it would always come up in the same manner: Someone would mention either Dizzee Rascal or the Streets, refer to them as grime artists, and immediately be told, "Those aren't real grime artists. That's not real grime." As such, this is all I know about grime—it's British rap (but not really) that is kind of "like garage and 2-step" (but the word garage is pronounced like marriage), and it's supposedly a reflection of life in lower-class London neighborhoods like Brixton. If anyone out there knows what grime is, e-mail me at cklosterman@spin.com. But make sure you write "This is about grime" in the subject line so I will know to ignore it completely.

FASHION ROCK: The concept of fashion rock revolves around (a) appearing to be impoverished while (b) spending whatever little money you possess on stylish clothing (and possibly cocaine). In short, fashion rockers aspire to look like superfancy hobos, which is obviously nothing new (this look was called "gutter glam" by L.A. hair bands in the 1980s and "mod" by British goofballs in the late 1960s). What's curious, however, is that fashion rock—though defined by clothing—does seem to have an identifiable sound, which is a kind of self-conscious sloppiness that translates as a British version of the Strokes (this is best illustrated by the Libertines, but even more successfully by the Killers, possibly because they are not even British).

RAWK: This is how people who start bands in order to meet porn stars spell rock. It is also applied to long-haired guitar players who can't play solos.

PROG: There was a time when "progressive rock" was easy to define, and everybody knew who played it—Jethro Tull, ELP, Yes, and other peculiar, bombastic men who owned an inordinate number of Moog synthesizers during the mid-1970s. This was an extremely amusing era for rock; the single best example from the period was King Crimson's 1969 song "21st Century Schizoid Man," a track built on a spooky two-pronged premise: What would it be like to encounter a fellow who was not only from the distant future, but also suffering from an untreated mental illness? At the time, "21st Century Schizoid Man" was the definition of progginess. However, just about anything qualifies as prog in 2005. An artist can be referred to as "kind of proggy" if he or she does at least two of the following things: writes long songs, writes songs with solos, writes songs about mythical creatures, writes songs that girls hate, grows a beard, consistently declines interview requests, mentions Dream Theater as an influence, claims to be working on a double album, claims to be working on a rock opera, claims to have already released a rock opera, appears to be making heavy metal for people who don't like heavy metal, refuses to appear in his or her own videos, makes trippy music without the use of drugs, uses laser technology in any capacity, knows who Dream Theater is.

MUSK OX ROCK: Combining woolly '90s grunge with the ephemeral elasticity of Icelandic artists like Björk and Sigur Rós, so-called oxenheads deliver thick, nurturing power riffs that replicate the experience of melting glaciers, troll attacks, and political alienation. The genre includes bands such as Switchfoot, Radiohead, and Bettie Serveert.

IDM: This is an acronym for "Intelligent Dance Music." Really. No, really. I'm serious. This is what they call it. Really.

READING **WRITING**

This Text: Reading

1. How familiar are you with the genres that Klosterman writes about? Are there others that you know that are similarly obscure? Why do you think we categorize music this way?

2. In what ways does Klosterman use humor to make his point?
3. What purpose does the conversation with his sister serve?

Your Text: Writing

1. Write a short definitional paper about a particular genre, using examples to define it. Or make up your own genre and define it.
2. Write a persuasive paper arguing for abolishment of genre considerations. What would the musical world look like in such a scenario?
3. Invent your own genre and write a speculative piece defining it. What would it sound like? Who would listen to it?

We Are the Champions, Another One Bites the Dust

Daniel Nester

Daniel Nester wrote a poem in response to every Queen song, filling two volumes, God Save the Queen *and* God Save the Queen II. *These are taken from his first collection. He is an assistant professor of English at the College of Saint Rose and he edits* Unpleasant Event Schedule, *an online literary journal.*

We Are the Champions

In 1977, legend has it that the Sex Pistols were recording in a studio adjacent to Queen's. Pistols bassist Sid Vicious wanders into the wrong room, and bumps into Freddie Mercury, who sits at his piano with four fingers of vodka.

"Ah, Freddie Mercury," Sid says smugly, staggering.[1] "Bringing ballet to the masses then?" Freddie takes a sip, looks up from his instrument.

"Oh yes, Mister Ferocious," Freddie says. "Well, we're doing our best, my dear."[2]

Another One Bites the Dust

Every man runs the same line, tries real hard to see how it would have all crashed down, which it most certainly does. Another defeated genre, another wide-eyed and wide-tied analyst.[3]

But this man completely hates metronomic duties as he fills another's coffers—*at least that's what I'm thinking right now,* the speaker thinks. So they go skiing together, and everything will be OK.

Another firearm-themed ditty, Michael Jackson's disco business advice.[4]

---

[1]Liza Minelli's version of WATC, Freddie Mercury memorial concert, Wembley Arena (London, April 19, 1992). Billie Jean King and Freddie Mercury at Studio 54, *New York Post* reports rumor of "romance," 1978.

[2]"They were *both afraid* of each other, actually."—Jim Jenkins, Breakthru 2002 Fan Club Convention (Q&A session, August 17, 2002).

[3]Single released August 1980. "Disco? Queen ate it up and spit it out for breakfast"—Kal Rudman, editor of the Cherry Hill, NJ–based radio tip sheet *Friday Morning Quarterback* (1980). Chic, "Good Times" (single released June 1979, also on *Risqué,* 1979). Sugar Hill Gang, "Rapper's Delight" (single only, September 1979).

[4]Michael Jackson urges Roger Taylor to make AOBTD the next single (New York City, Studio 54, late 1979). Michael Jackson, *Off The Wall* (1979).

How I Wrote My Poems Daniel Nester

Why did you write this piece—what was the assignment or motivation for writing?

I gave myself an assignment, which was to write notes on every song ever recorded by my favorite rock band, Queen. I had been obsessed with them for so long—collecting records, memorabilia, fan conventions—that when it came down to writing about them, I didn't know where to start.

What did you do when you got the assignment or decided to write?

It was like a challenge I made to myself: OK, you have always wanted to write about one of the main obsessions in your life, how are you going to write about it? I wanted the writing, at least at first, to be as automatic as possible. So that's why I decided to employ the song-by-song method.

How did you begin?

This is going to sound freaky. I got all my old vinyl records out—albums, 45s, CDs, bootlegs. I hung up a couple of my old Queen posters in my room.

Describe the process of writing the first draft.

I was listening to each song as I wrote the first draft. Sometimes I would doodle. Other times I would write really fast. Sometimes, if I had to keep going and couldn't be at home, I had my iPod and wrote in a café. Other times I had the full run of the house and could blast my stereo. Those were the most fun.

Did you write a draft all the way through?

I didn't stop until I did the entire book. Then I went back to revise.

How much editing did you do as you wrote?

For this writing project, absolutely none. At first, it was writing I was doing only for myself—I wanted to get down all those seemingly random but to me related thoughts on each Queen song.

Did you do research as you wrote or before you started writing? What databases did you use?

I conducted research in the editing process—I used all the books written on Queen, magazine articles. I used a lot of interlibrary loan during this stage.

How long would you say the process took?

Two years, from first draft to signing off on the galleys.

How did you edit the draft?

I took special care to edit, proofread, and fact-check, more than any other writing project I have done, because the first draft was written in such an automatic way. I wanted it that way.

What was the response when you turned in your essay?

The first time I presented this project in public was a reading at a bar. I explained what I had done and was doing, read about 12-15 songs' worth of the book, and it seemed people "got it." That was really gratifying and cool.

Are you satisfied now with what you wrote? Would you make any changes?

Sometimes I think I should explain what I wrote more—what makes total sense to me might seem random to others. But using titles that correspond to Queen songs, often really popular ones, at least gives readers and I some kind of common ground.

READING WRITING

This Text: Reading

1. What do you think of Nester's poems? How related to the Queen songs are they?
2. What qualities about music do Nester's poems demonstrate?
3. Why does Nester use footnotes here?

Your Text: Writing

1. Listen to a favorite album of yours and write responses to a few songs. Are you surprised by the associations that come up during listening?
2. Write a paper that compares Nester's poem to the actual lyrics of a Queen song. In what ways does Nester engage the lyrics?

Right on Target: Revisiting Elvis Costello's *My Aim Is True*

Sarah Hawkins

Student Essay

Sarah Hawkins wrote this review/re-evaluation for an advanced composition class at the University of San Francisco in 2001. A persuasive piece of sorts, she tries to reintroduce an artist (with whom many of her professors are familiar) to a younger audience.

ELVIS COSTELLO IN A NUTSHELL: a frustrated, neurotic, nonconformist who just so happens to be endlessly talented. With a song-writing capability second only to John Lennon and an Ani Difranco–esque tenacity, Elvis Costello is a pop music figure that cannot be ignored. *My Aim Is True* blends the personal with the political, shapes music to emotion, and captures moods ranging from stark depression to danceable irony. Costello writes songs on edge, displaying the sensitivity and conceit of any true elitist. Ever feel a little at odds with society? Feel left out by the mainstream? Feel simultaneously rejected and superior? Well, Elvis Costello has and he is not going to take it lying down. Successfully, he throws all of these feelings in a bag with a dry sense of humor, adds more than a pinch of cynicism, and blends them with musical accuracy. The result? A musical masterpiece that deserves attention even twenty-four years after its release.

The underdog offbeat brilliance of *My Aim Is True* has aged like fine wine, creating a modern cult following much like that of actor John Cusack. Both speak a familiar language—that of the common man experiencing failure. Costello through his lyrics, Cusack through roles such as the down-trodden record store owner Rob in the movie *High Fidelity,* or the awkward teens he plays in both *Say Anything,* and *Better Off Dead.* Part of the attraction to figures such as Costello and Cusack is that people of an ordinary nature can relate to them. Everyone wants to see pop stars that are not perfect looking, perfectly graceful, or perfectly happy. And everyone likes to see the underdog represented in a way that is unique rather than stereotypical. Both Elvis Costello and John Cusack do this and do it well.

Take for example the opening song from Costello's *My Aim Is True.* He launches into the album singing, "Welcome to the Working Week," and reaching out to any unsatisfied employee. One of the album's simplest moments, this song places the chorus "Welcome to the working week, I know it don't thrill ya I hope it don't kill ya," against a fierce yet sing-along tune, automatically winning the hearts of all those disgruntled, tired and unsure. A manifesto of the working class, this song portrays the life of pre-fame Elvis. Just an average Joe working a passionless day job as a computer operator, straining his eyes day in and day out to the point where he needs those now infamous thick-rimmed glasses reminiscent of Buddy Holly and favored among members of his current cult following.

The glasses might have helped a man born Declan McManus to see, but they framed the style and stage presence of Elvis Costello, making Declan the computer operator look every bit Elvis's intellectual/outcast/critic of society. Yes, even the stage name, taken from "the King" of popular rock 'n roll, is an attack on the music industry. In the face of an emerging, dance-happy new wave, *My Aim Is True* threw a monkey wrench in the commercialized system. While pseudo-angry, underground, punk rock bands only managed to reinforce the traditional conventions of the music industry, Elvis Costello and his band the Attractions presented a vastly talented, deliriously fresh voice for stale angst. Only an album with such sophisticated musical influences—think British Rock classics: the Beatles, the Kinks, and the Who meet Motown—could possibly be taken seriously when fronted by such a funny looking guy. No glam rock. No gimmick. No apologies. No love songs.

Well—no love songs in the traditional sense, anyway. There is "Allison," the fifth track, and the reflective breath amidst a furious storm, the bluesy phantom that promises in its opening lines not "to get too sentimental like those other sticky Valentines." The music strikes a sorrowful chord, one any regretful lover could appreciate. Proving more elusive, the lyrics refuse the position of the heartbroken crooning for lost love. Instead, Costello once again widens the scope by reaching out for his more comfortable position as a keen observer, obscuring this obviously personal experience—so personal, in fact, that he no longer performs the song live. While affectionate and regretful, the song is also edgy and controlled. Using the encounter with a past flame to cynically portray marriage, Costello huskily vocalizes his disapproval, "Well I see you've got a husband now/did he leave your pretty fingers lying in the wedding cake/you used to hold him right in your hand/I bet it took all that he could take."

As quickly and comfortably as Elvis slipped into the introspective shoes of Allison, he ditches them for the furious funk of "Sneaky Feelings." One would get the impression that Mr. Costello must indeed have a closet full of shoes he fills quite perfectly. In "I'm Not

Angry"—yeah, right—he sports a good pair of trainers. The first five seconds of fast guitar, intense keyboard and oddly timed cymbals are enough to get anyone running. No, Elvis Costello is not angry, he's irate. While some might mistake this as a chip on his embittered shoulder, the truth is that Elvis Costello's songs extend far beyond self-deprecation and personal failures. Take "Less Than Zero" for example—a song written in response to a disturbing broadcast he saw on T.V., the BBC segment on the supposed reform of Oswald Moseley, one of the British leaders of the fascist regime. Capturing what he sees as the ultimate decline of an already unraveling society, Costello creates a narrative in which Moseley is the main character, representing not only himself but consumer society at large. "Mr. Oswald has an understanding with the law/he said he heard about a couple living in the USA/they traded in their baby for a Chevrolet/let's talk about the future/we'll put the past away." This song shows that if London is welcoming the likes of Moseley back with open arms, it is no place for Elvis Costello.

Similar bitter irony is reflected in the songs "Waiting for the End of the World," "Cheap Reward," "No Dancing," and "Pay it Back." Okay, so Mr. Costello may never get the award for most happy camper. He *admits* in an interview that most of his songs are inspired by "regret and guilt." He *does* sing about failure and misunderstanding and bitterness and all the things people never want to talk about but feel all the time. He *really* used to keep a list—a blacklist—of all the record executives and industry bigwigs he saw as the root of musical evil. BUT. He managed to break the system. He got the last laugh. He made it. Unleashing his fury in the form of *My Aim Is True*, he broke musical ground. He blended jazz, funk, rock and new age with impeccable perfection. He said something that mattered at a time when no one was saying anything. He mastered language and music, introduced them, made them shake hands, then fight, then dance together and laugh about it all.

Most importantly, he didn't stop there. He went on to build a musical legacy. Not only did he record an expansive body of work showcasing his varying talents, he became a producer, guiding other brilliant bands. As a producer, Costello worked with bands as diverse as his own influences. One of these bands, the Specials, embodies the soul of two-tone ska, a musical genre emphasizing the importance of racial diversity and social consciousness. Another band that he worked with—The Clash—has been an instrumental part of the punk rock scene. Echoes of Costello can be heard in much of today's experimental indie rock. Elliot Smith, indie rock darling, cites Costello as a major influence. One of the most impressive contemporary songwriters, Smith wrote songs that while of a mellower and more melodic musical variety, echo the underdog sentiments popularized by Costello.

Perhaps his contribution to indie sensibilities of attitude and style are equal if less tangible than those he made in music. To be indie is to have a love of irony and embrace—on multiple levels—social awkwardness. In fact, indie owes much of this attitude to Costello. This "antiking" of pop was the first one to successfully bring these two elements into the spotlight. Traces of his fashion statement, namely the trademark glasses, can be seen among geek rock favorites like Weezer and on the faces of infinite "indie kids." And it all started twenty-four years ago. One little record untouchable in the eyes of major record labels. A record heralded by *Rolling Stone* as 1977's album of the year and remembered by VH1 as one of the best rock albums of all time. If the industry originally believed he had missed the mark, at least Elvis Costello knew he was right on target.

READING **WRITING**

Your Text: Reading

1. How would you describe the tone of this piece? Does it work for you? Why or why not? Is it appropriate for the type of writing she's doing?
2. How would you classify this piece? Is it a review? An essay? A paper? An appreciation? What makes you think so?
3. Why does the writer like Elvis Costello? How does she try to make others like him? Who does she think will like him? Look at specific places in the text where she does this work.
4. What other albums of a certain age deserve this type of revisiting? Name a few and talk about them in class.

Your Text: Writing

1. Do an assignment similar to Hawkins: Find an older album and re-introduce it to a younger crowd. What things might you have to consider about "youth" and "age" when doing this assignment?
2. Think about your criteria when choosing to listen to an album. How does that change when looking at an older album? Write a short paper about why you choose what you listen to.
3. If it's possible, go to the record collection of an older friend or relative and interview them about the experience with one of their favorite albums. Now go back and listen to it on your own and write a paper about your experience.

The Authenticity Suite

One of the dominant issues in American musical culture is the concept of **authenticity**, especially how it relates to musical taste. Critics often judge artists' quality and stature by how well they seem to reflect criteria seemingly unchanged since the 1960s, when rock and roll emerged as a dominant music genre. Music that is generated by artists rather than professional songwriters, music whose production seems organic, bands at the early stages of their career before they "sell out," and music that seems thematically sophisticated rather than simple is generally taken more seriously by music critics—and probably your friends and classmates as well. Indeed, there is a certain cachet in college to knowing, liking, and listening to alternative bands and singers on the fringe. Ironically, the most popular musical act in the culture at large is rarely the most popular on college campuses. Often, budding critics, DJs at college radio stations, and club owners tend to prioritize musical acts that go out of their way to sound different than mainstream music heard on Clear Channel radio stations or promoted in Wal-Mart.

Of course, this is not the only way to judge music, as Britney Spears, Justin Timberlake, and Kelly Clarkson fans have demonstrated. Most of the music by these artists goes through extensive production and is not written by the artists themselves. Not surprisingly, their music is also immensely popular, and such popularity is often taken as a sign of being fake—after all, those concerned with authenticity ask, how can something that is any good be liked by so many people? Or, phrased in the lingo of authenticity, how can anything popular be *real*? Arguably these fans are judging the music by how it sounds, even if the associated phenomena—videos, interviews, media incidents—affects their opinions. Moreover, how a song sounds is an inherently emotional reaction whereas judging via authenticity is an intellectual one. We could argue that in fact hearing songs is much more organic than thinking them. While these distinctions are still in place, things are changing—witness the four stars given to Timberlake's *Justified* album by *Rolling Stone*.

At the heart of any discussion of musical authenticity lies a complicated mix of race, class, autonomy, and sincerity. For example, Amy Winehouse gets points on the authenticity scale because songs about being a tortured, troubled woman mirror her life as a troubled, tortured woman. Critics consider classic performers such as Johnny Cash and Hank Williams models of authenticity because they stuck to a sound and to themes that seemed to reflect their personalities. On the other hand, bands like R.E.M. lost many fans when they moved from their independent label IRS to the more mainstream Warner Brothers, despite the fact that some of their most interesting and edgy music has come in the Warner Brothers years. Similarly, critics tend to lionize blues singers and jazz players for their adherence to traditional and innovative forms.

In this suite, we print several essays about authenticity. David Sanjek, professor of the University Salford in England, writes about the use of authenticity as a trope in *Ghost World*, as well as the implications for listeners generally. Carrie Brownstein, of the late great band Sleater-Kinney, writes about the authenticity of live music versus recorded music. Finally, Stephen Metcalf writes about Bruce Springsteen's use of authenticity as a marketing tool.

All the Memories Money Can Buy: Marketing Authenticity and Manufacturing Authorship

David Sanjek

A Bargain at $1.75

THE CRITICAL PLAUDITS EARNED by Terry Zwigoff's 2001 motion picture *Ghost World* have focused for the most part upon its astute depiction of adolescent life and the difficult transition into the precarious independence of adulthood. Few notices, however, commented upon the important role music plays in the film unlike the source material, Daniel Clowes's 1998 graphic novel. There, one of the central female protagonists, Enid, is drawn back to the comforting support of her childhood by the 45RPM recording of a ditty entitled "A Smile and a Ribbon." ("A smile is something special, A ribbon is something rare/So I'll be special and I'll be rare, with a smile and a ribbon in my hair.")[1] The appeal of the material is altogether retrospective, for its presence in the plotline of the graphic novel underscores the disparity between the cloying sentiments of the song and the incomprehensible entanglements of Enid's day-to-day life.

Zwigoff jettisons this episode altogether, for his interest in the influence of music exceeds simply the invocation of lost innocence. He is drawn instead to the manner in which music can function as a foundation for the establishment of personal identity, particularly when the material under consideration lies outside the commercial mainstream. Think in this context of the opening shot of *Ghost World*. As the camera pans by a variety of windows of an urban apartment complex, we see one resident after another engaged in some manner of mind-numbing behavior. [Kind of an homage to Hitchcock's *Rear Window* (1954), in that Zwigoff emulates that film's voyeuristic engagement with human behavior, particularly in the subsequent moments when Enid (Thora Birch) and her girlfriend Rebecca (Scarlet Johansson) gaze with sarcastic wonder at a variety of subsidiary characters, like the Satanist couple at the diner.] Then, we discover Enid, bopping away happily to Ted Lyons and his Cubs' rendition of "Jaan Pehechaan Ho" in the Bollywood vehicle *Gumnaam* (1965). Not only is she alone and enraptured, but she also appears to be the sole viewer of some television channel one imagines does not appear in the common cable guide. Unlike the other figures shown in the sequence, she fails to come across as weighed down by anomie, but, instead, buoyed up by her uncommon cultural sensibility.

This scene is elaborated upon by the introduction of the character of Seymour (Steve Buscemi), the sad sack record collector whom Enid befriends. Seymour does not appear in the graphic novel, and while he first enters the narrative as simply an object of the girls' contempt, he soon thereafter comes to embody Enid's access to the musical culture upon which she begins to determine her path in life. They first encounter one another face-to-face when Seymour sells Enid a vinyl reissue collection that contains Skip James's 1932 recording "Devil Got My Woman" for the bargain basement price of $1.75. If Enid initially buys the LP as a lark, once it begins to play on her stereo, the music affects a transformation upon her. As Zwigoff comments, "She's trying to find her identity in the world, and then she plays this weird eerie thing, and thinks maybe there *is* something this guy has to offer."[2] The singer's otherworldly falsetto and evocative depiction of the torments of

---

[1] Daniel Clowes, *Ghost World* (Seattle: Fantagraphic Books, 1998), p. 62.

[2] Simon Reynolds, "In Between Days," *Village Voice*, July 18-24, 2001 http:www.villvoice.com (access April 3, 2002).

affection amount to the farthest possible thing from the au courant material Enid's peers live by. Moreover, the manner in which James strips his material of any form of false sentiment parallels Enid's seemingly affectless approach to her own feelings. You can imagine she would be drawn by Stephen Calt's description of James's material: "His songs were expressions of his own bleak temperament. He was an aloof person who begrudged banter and mistrusted merriment."[3] Even if the song is played only once in the film, its influence upon Enid and the fact that Seymour has been her access to it resonates throughout the rest of the narrative. For through "Devil Got My Woman" and him, Enid has sampled the most tantalizing of cultural categories: authenticity. All for just $1.75.

Enid may not use this term specifically nor does Zwigoff draw it into the film, yet the notion of authenticity resonates from beginning to end. Enid defines it, or at least one version of the phenomenon, when she explains to Rebecca why she is attracted to Seymour: the fact that he's so square that he transcends the sphere of hip. However, what Seymour has to offer the young woman is as much a form of negation as any kind of affirmation or indication of what Enid should do with her life. Even though the consequences of his behavior make Seymour alienated and unhappy, he has deliberately and energetically erased any interest in or connection to the vast majority of contemporary life. (We'll leave unanswered the question of exactly when *Ghost World* takes place. The film seems at one and the same time set in the present day and a near-distant past. Why a stereo and not a CD player?) He epitomizes a state of disaffiliation whose only sense of meaning emerges when in contact with music or other forms of culture related to the 1930s or earlier. Seymour does not indicate that access to this body of material satisfies his life—he dismisses his hobbies with the most melancholy declaration, "Go ahead and kill me. You think it's healthy to obsessively collect things?"—yet he fails to give one the sense that he could live without either his vintage disks or memorabilia. Enid in turn does not take up his obsessive dedication to collecting nor listen intently to another historic piece of material other than Skip James. No matter, the one song and the interaction with Seymour have made an indelible impact. Both offer her access to something substantial and satisfying that neither her peers nor the society about her embody. They each have triggered in Enid a need to retain her independence, whatever the cost.

Zwigoff's fascination with the authentic as embodied by a certain sphere of musical culture resonates through his other two pictures, the 1985 documentary on the string musician Howard Armstrong, *Louie Bluie*, and the 1994 portrait of the artist Robert Crumb. In the first case, Zwigoff not only pays tribute to a rare and unforgettable character but also a form of performance—the African American string band—that has by and large been written out of most history books for being, it appears, unfashionable and somehow unaffiliated with customary notions of racially-determined forms of performance.[4] Armstrong

---

[3]Stephen Calt, *I'd Rather Be The Devil. Skip James and the Blues* (New York: Da Capo Press, 1994), p. 18.

[4]It is a mistake to correlate what we can hear on recordings and what was played concurrently in the sphere of daily life. The kind of string-based dance music that Armstrong and others created was judged by A&R men of the period as being somehow not sufficiently parallel with what they determined "race" music to be. As the blues scholar Paul Oliver has stated, "the phases of recording black music do not correspond in all details with the changing nature of the music itself. . . . Few attempts have been made to make a comprehensive analysis of all the forms of black song (let alone of instrumental music) which appeared on disc through all these phases. Nor has there been adequate consideration of how representative these were of the music in both the urban and the rural contexts of the times, nor whether their appearance or absence from record was a reflection of their popularity within the black community." Paul Oliver, *Songsters and Saints. Vocal Traditions on Race Records* (Cambridge: Cambridge University Press, 1984), pp. 11–12.

therefore is made heroic by Zwigoff because he stuck to his guns in the face of arbitrary definitions of how and what he should play. In effect, Armstrong and his fiddle come across as being more authentic than what we are accustomed to hearing of music at that time, for the material simultaneously breaks with our very notion of what it meant to be black and musically inclined in the period before and during the Depression. In the case of *Crumb*, Zwigoff illustrates how for the cartoonist, as for the filmmaker, the sphere of the 78 constitutes one of the precious few precincts untouched and undefiled by the crass influence of present-day culture. Zwigoff at one point interpolates a telling, if misguided strip by Crumb that condemns technology for replacing live performance with sterile copies.[5] This position fails to take into account Crumb's own fetishizing of certain select recordings as well as uncritically valorizes a simplified notion of vernacular culture. Nonetheless, both the set of drawings and the memorable sequence in which the artist's collection is packed for shipping to his new home in France vividly conjure up the defense of authenticity that Zwigoff dramatizes in *Ghost World*.

The conviction shared with equal vigor by Enid, Seymour, Crumb and Zwigoff that certain kinds of music are authentic and others ersatz encapsulates the fundamental parameters of a familiar debate. This tussle of perspectives all too often reduces the discussion of music to nothing more or less than a collision of incompatible and absolute categories. Each time one encounters a performance, it becomes appraised as if one were examining raw ore in search of rare metals. The frequency with which the object is determined to be bogus therefore leads to interminable cycles of despair, as if the vast majority of recording artists engage in a deliberate exercise in deceit, pawning off fool's gold for the real thing. Moreover, the propensity on the part of many people to assume that most music fails the test of authenticity by virtue of its institutionalization at the hands of commercial interests unnecessarily complicates the matter. Where can one go with such an *ad hominem*, and therefore debateable, proposition such as that made by Charles Keil: "Everything mediated is spurious until proven genuine."[6] This kind of absolutism equates all manner of packaging with desecration. From my perspective, I do not know of any commercial music that lacks dirty hands, so to speak. Rather than a cut-and-dried category, authenticity amounts in my mind to a constructed determination that must encompass the commodified with the non-commercial, the immediate with the mediated, the raw with the cooked. Seldom are we in a position to isolate these domains from one another. The circumstances under which we assess recorded music for its quantity of authenticity parallels the proposition that the character actor Walter Brennan would put before directors: did they want him to play a particular part with or without his dentures. Same man, with or without the incisors. Same music, with or without the apparatus that we associate with the mass media.

---

[5]Crumb's piece "Where Has It Gone, All the Beautiful Music of Our Grandparents" appears in *R. Crumb Draws the Blues* (London: Crack Editions, 1992). It is also reproduced in the tandem collection by Charles Keil and Steve Feld, *Music Grooves* (Chicago: University of Chicago Press 1994), pp. 233–37. As he states in one panel, "Wherever technology invades a culture, you find the youth embracing it, going for it, disdaining the old ways. They want the goodies, the shiny toys, the promise of all that glitter, the comfort and, the convenience, the sophistication . . . it's only natural . . ."
[6]Charles Keil and Steven Field, *Music Grooves: Essays and Dialogues* (Chicago: University of Chicago Press, 1995), 313.

I wish therefore to proceed in this discussion by assenting to the proposition put forth by Simon Frith some time ago that

> Because it cannot be denied that rock and pop [or any other musical genre, in my mind] are indeed "commodities," [the] problem is to show that there is, nevertheless, something "authentic" to that commodity . . . My starting point is that what is possible for us as consumers—what is available to us, what we can do with it—is a result of decision made in production, made by musicians, entrepreneurs, and corporate bureaucrats, made according to governments' and lawyers' rulings, in response to technological opportunities. The key to "creative consumption" remains an understanding of those decisions, the constraints under which they are made, and the ideologies that account for them. Such understanding depends on both industrial research and the intelligence revealed in single songs.[7]

It does us no good to proceed as if we were Dorothy on the emerald road and find out, time and again, that the Mighty Oz has rigged the machinery behind the scenes, thereby clamping down upon any undiluted access to self-expression. Should we proceed down this path, we can only end up as dyspeptic as Seymour, Crumb and Zwigoff, convinced that we are surrounded by charlatans who operate at the behest of confidence men. We can come to some understanding of the forces against which musicians must contend and regardless of which they occasionally remain true to some value system only by examining individual instances of cultural production.

As even *Ghost World* indicates, the definition of authenticity has to be as flexible as the material to which it applies. No master template of characteristics exists that can be checked off and tallied up so as to determine where on the scale a particular piece of music lies. Much as many of us scorn the rating practices typified by the weekly analysis conducted on Dick Clark's *American Bandstand*, the fixation upon authenticity is, to me, only a slightly more sophisticated version of that enterprise. Our reasons for preferring one piece of music or another or one genre above all else may be an interesting arena of investigation, but, in the end, the exercise amounts to a pissing contest over taste. Not an activity I prefer to engage in, for, as compelling as it might be, someone simply acquires a wet shoe in the end.

Even more to the point, debates over authenticity really come down to distinctions about repertoire, which person's list is superior to another's. It's nothing short of a collector's reflex, a conviction that catalog outweighs content. Whenever the mainstream taste of the wider public descends into a pattern that the cognoscenti consider debased, the obsession with repertoire emerges in full force. Preserving material that blows the current Top Ten out of the water bears a less than appetizing analogy to the educated classes in the Middle Ages barricading themselves against the barbarians at the gates. Gina Arnold's metaphor comes to mind in this context: "That, after all, is my generation's symbol of a roving mind: great record collections in cardboard boxes, kept the way monks hoarded literature from marauding pagan masses."[8] I cannot share her, and others', conviction that the world could be transformed by a better playlist. When she argues that the presence of Nirvana on the radio meant that "my own values are winning: I'm no longer in the opposition," my rejoinder is that I never really wanted to start a fight over what's on the jukebox

---

[7]Simon Frith, *Music for Pleasure. Essays in the Sociology of Pop* (New York: Routledge, 1988), 6–7.

[8]Gina Arnold, *Route 666. On the Road to Nirvana* (New York: St. Martin's Press, 1991), p. 6.

THE AUTHENTICITY SUITE

in the first place.[9] Taste is transitory, and the belief that when someone shares my preferences, the chance of better things emerging on the horizon increases does not parallel my sense of social transformation. In the end, I'm more interested in what music people like and the role it plays in their lives than whether or not I get off on the same material. Their authenticity could easily be my ersatz.

Therefore, I have to concede that, in the end, I share Nick Tosches's admonition that "meaning is the biggest sucker's-racket of all; and any regard for it, no matter how fleeting, befits a middle-aged fool like me."[10] Seeking out this elusive category may be a quixotic crusade, yet, to return to Enid in *Ghost World*, otherwise how can I make sense out of why Bollywood soundtracks make a young girl dance and the scratchy vocalizing of a long-dead delta cynic nearly drive her to tears?

More Rock, Less Talk: Live Music Turns Off the Voices in Our Heads

Carrie Brownstein

AS AN ARTIST, IT IS MOST FRIGHTENING to feel that the meaning in your work is slipping away from you. I think that this is a natural by-product of placing art into the world. But it's especially true in a medium like music, one that is populist— where the audience naturally adopts it as their own. In some ways it should belong to them. Listeners are each allowed their own interpretation, without the need for any kind of theoretical or technical understanding.

Their belief that they can have a unique response or a visceral relationship to the art is what removes it from an elitist, academic realm. However, for every individual vision of the art there is also an individual definition of who the artists are and what they represent. If the audience for the work is large, you wind up with a multitude of definitions, and these are likely to vary enormously. Eventually there comes to exist, separate from the artist, an entity that is externally defined, one that embodies the expectations inhabited by the outside world. This external entity, a veritable artistic doppelgänger, is difficult to ignore. It can feel like a demanding evil twin, and artists can begin to ignore or lose sight of their own motivations.

Since my own goals in music lie in forging a connection with people, with an audience, it's disheartening to feel as though my message is misinterpreted or no longer of my own design. I struggle to tune out the external expectations and definitions. At the same time, I cannot wholly ignore those to whom I am trying to relate, who are sharing the experience along with me. It is a precarious position.

Recorded music, by fixing the sound in a specific time and place, can't help but form a definitive sonic blueprint for a band. The recorded medium is much more likely to be categorized and posited within the ever-growing and ever-limiting list of genres. We can hear the same instance replayed over and over, and though the listeners bring their own experience to the songs, and may hear new textures with each pass, the sonic nature of the song is fixed.

---

[9]Arnold, p. 4.

[10]Nick Tosches, *Where Dead Voices Gather* (New York: Little Brown, 2002), p. 6.

In contrast, the context of playing live allows for fluidity and continuity between the otherwise disparate past and present, the fixed (recorded) and the ephemeral, and the artist's private and public identities. The live experience elevates the art of music by making it permeable and improvisational. To me, the dialogue in a live context exists in the sonic and visceral relationship between the artist and the song and between the artist and the audience.

Essentially, the live show is nothing more than an impromptu conversation. It's a moment that lets us connect on a level free from the restraints of everyday discourse. It welcomes as opposed to shuns lexical ambiguities. Our translation of the experience is not reliant on our intellectual grasp of the moment; it operates more spontaneously, as an intuitive and physical response. In addition, the language of any given live show is unique, a spontaneous and instantaneous negotiation of sound, utterance, and gesture. It is useful only in this moment. Few other forms of communication or art achieve this evanescent beauty.

For myself, the moment when the live aspect became the most crucial was when the identity of my band, Sleater-Kinney, became uncertain, when there became a joint owner-ship between us and the audience. We had been split into two: there were two distinct defi-nitions of the band, our own and that of the audience. Often, the dichotomy felt irreconcilable.

To us, Sleater-Kinney was a dialogue among three people. It was our source of salva-tion, escape, strength, and joy. Sleater-Kinney was nothing more than the sounds that trav-eled from our mouths, fingers, hands, and our hearts. It traveled no further than the walls of our practice space. All of the meaning was both surrounding us and inside of us; there existed little disparity between the internal and external worlds of the band. Whatever sounds came out of us at that moment, that was who we were, we owned it. Yet the mo-ment we left the practice space, recorded the songs, and placed them into the world, our formerly insular identity, or lack of conscious identity, became public and therefore open to debate.

Though we had no intention of remaining obscure, we also had no way of preparing for the outside definitions and expectations. Suddenly, we were defined by specific songs, albums, photographs, quotes, politics, and genders. We were a "girl group," a "feminist band," we had "risen from the riot grrrl ghetto," we were Call the Doctor, we were Dig Me Out. We went from mutable to fixed identities.

But live we remained and remain nothing except the moment itself. The audience, hearing it brought together in front of them, senses the congruencies in the music. Two seemingly disparate songs suddenly come off as unified. People tend to fear growth and change in artists, but live performance has a way of proving that this evolution contains a common thread, a core that is true to the original artistic vision.

My early relationship to performing live music is best described in the song "I Wanna Be Your Joey Ramone," which we wrote in 1995. Joey Ramone was a performer who em-bodied both diffidence and grandiosity. To me, he was a man who was simultaneously awkward, with his spindly legs and his hair falling into his face, and also larger than life. This contradiction seemed to be an ideal metaphor for my own relationship to performing and music. Part of me wanted to own the stage while the other part of me remained un-comfortable with such power. The song was also about stepping into someone else's shoes (in this case Joey's) as a means of exploring my own fears and dreams.

THE AUTHENTICITY SUITE

When Sleater-Kinney first began, it seemed to me that the only way to get a sense of rock 'n' roll was to experience it vicariously. At least that was the message coming to us from the outside world: the archetypes, the stage moves, the representations of rebellion and debauchery were all male. The song has us exploring a role typically associated with male performers. By doing so, we get a glimpse of the absurdity, the privilege, and the decadence that wasn't inherently afforded to us.

Some people are born with the certainty that they own sound or volume; that the lexicon of rock music is theirs to borrow from, to employ, to interpret. For them, it might be nothing to move around on stage, to swagger, to sing in front of people, to pick up a guitar, to make records. I set out from a place where I never assumed that those were acceptable choices or that I could be anything but an accessory to rock 'n' roll. Coming out of a tradition that historically didn't allow women much of a voice, then finding myself helping to create a sound that filled an entire room, that reached into every person in that room, that is a power that I had to learn. I needed to try it on before I could call it mine. I had to find a means to make it my own.

The transition from a vicarious exploration of power to empowerment could happen only in live environments. There one faces not only the audience's expectations of what it means to be a performer on stage but also one's own mental catalog of the archetypal images of rock, which are often affirmations of adolescent male sexual identity. Playing live felt like battling history, icons, images. It is hard not to be reduced to the category of "women in rock." I didn't feel like I could be rock 'n' roll.

Instead, we were women imitating and participating in rock 'n' roll, something we didn't create. To feel comfortable with the power, I couldn't feel like it was being lent to me, and certainly no one was passing it to me. I had to claim it. I had to carve a space for myself in my own imagination and in the imagination of the audience.

Because the live moment is fluid, so too is the identity: it passes back and forth from audience to performer; it presents a form and then turns that form on its head. On stage, questions of identity, gender, or categorical indexing begin to feel obsolete. They are obliterated by the visceral. The live performance allows gender to take on an ambiguous or even androgyne role; it smashes the historical assumptions about who owns rock 'n' roll. Whoever is on stage at that moment owns the music; whoever is watching and hearing it at that moment owns it as well.

Live music also frees me from the restraints of the rhetorical. Art historian Anne Middleton Wagner writes: "It is a necessary consequence for working 'as a woman.' Making art from such a position is inevitably rhetorical; it must often be strategic, must often employ assertion, denial, tactical evasion, subterfuge, deception, refusal." I certainly feel that this is the case with Sleater-Kinney: talking about the experience has become part of the experience itself. In interviews, we are constantly asked the question, "What is it like to be a woman playing rock?" More than anything, I feel that this metadiscourse, talking about the talk, is part of how it feels to be a "woman playing rock."

There is the music itself, and then there is the ongoing dialogue about how it feels. The two seem to be intertwined and also inescapable. This dialogue also began to appear in our own songwriting. The songs responded to and addressed the fans, the critics, and even our own work: the new songs (such as "Male Model" or "#1 Must Have") explaining the old ("I Wanna Be Your Joey Ramone," "Little Babies"), discussing what we had already done and why we had done it.

THE AUTHENTICITY SUITE

The metadiscourse and the rhetorical form a disconnect; a psychological, linguistic, and identity fissure. However, these elements are made congruent and whole in the live context. Here the rhetoric ceased; there is no explanation but the sound itself. I am not talking about the music, I am the music.

For all the freeing possibilities that live performance opens up, it also introduces another dynamic that is more problematic: the inherent hierarchy assumed between performer and audience. There are few moments when this imbalance is effectively dismantled. Recently, however, I experienced a disruption of this dynamic. It was at an outdoor show, at the moment when night fell upon the stage, when the sky was fixed for an instant, holding elements of both night and day in its hues. This was a moment that could never happen indoors, a straddling of two contrasting environments and moods. It came to me that you could see it as nature's way of illustrating how a concert is simultaneously a public and a private experience.

Whatever form it takes, live music draws on both individual and collective elements, for performer and audience alike. Outdoors, however, the dichotomy is exaggerated. During the day, everyone is made much more aware of just how public and shared the experience really is. Not only can you sense how close you are to the strangers in front of or next to you, but after a few hours you know every detail of their faces, every whisker, every blemish, every twitch. In the midst of a song, you can watch their faces change in response to the lyrics and the music; you know how they look with their eyes closed, mouthing the words. In the light of day, the private experience is exposed and the collective experience is no longer merely visceral—it is also visible.

When I play outside I am constantly aware of this visibility. I like the way the environment lends itself to demystifying the performer and removes some of the artifice. Aside from the stage itself, there exists less of the performer-fan hierarchy perpetuated by elements such as elaborate lighting. Everyone is under the same indiscriminate glare of the sun. I can look out into the crowd and see individual faces and expressions, I can see the dimensions of the space, where the crowd begins, where it ends; there is nowhere to hide for me or for them.

Naturally, there is a drawback to a heightened awareness of one another and the fact that the private has been made public. Many people come to rock 'n' roll and punk out of desperation. They like the anonymity provided by a dark room, where emotions are less transparent, where appearances can be obfuscated. Thus, there is often a feeling of reservation at a summer concert, a reluctance to allow oneself to be exposed. And this brings me back to my favorite moment, which is when the spotlight of the sun begins to fade.

Often, by the time night falls, we have been participants long enough to be acutely aware of the collective nature of the event. By this time we are yearning for a moment that is our own, a moment that goes unseen. The onset of darkness is that moment, the one where the private and public experience converge. We at last have the privacy to feel and express ourselves without anyone watching. At the same time, there is a relief in knowing that we're not alone.

In general, I feel that live performance is the truest and most organic way to experience the tradition of music, for the listener and for the artist. It frees us from our own intellectual restraints—the kind of analytical discourse that we use on a daily basis that distances us from an interior emotional landscape. Appearing live is also a way for artists to ward off static or reductive definitions. The moment relies on movement, connection, continuity, spontaneity. We are reminded that music is an experience, not merely an object, and thus it becomes difficult to separate it from our own bodies. It feels crucial to form connections with one another, to be aware of how our private and public selves intertwine. Lastly, live music is about breaking free of restraints, of tradition, of roles. This is possible because the live moment is ephemeral, it leaves no singular residue. All that exists once it is over is the potential in ourselves to be transformed.

Faux Americana: Why I Still Love Bruce Springsteen

Stephen Metcalf

IN HIS EARLY LIVE SHOWS, Bruce Springsteen had a habit of rattling off, while the band vamped softly in the background, some thoroughly implausible story from his youth. This he punctuated with a shy, wheezing laugh that let you know he didn't for a second buy into his own bullshit. Back then, in the early 1970s, Bruce was still a regional act, touring the dive bars and dive colleges of the Atlantic coast, playing any venue that would have him. As a matter of routine, a Springsteen show would kick off with audience members throwing gifts onto the stage. Not bras and panties, mind you, but gifts—something thoughtful, not too expensive. Bruce was one of their own, after all, a scrawny little dirtbag from the shore, a minor celebrity of what the great George Trow once called "the disappearing middle distance." By 1978, and the release of *Darkness on the Edge of Town,* the endearing Jersey wharf rat in Springsteen had been refined away. In its place was a majestic American simpleton with a generic heartland twang, obsessed with cars, Mary, the Man, and the bitterness between fathers and sons. Springsteen has been augmenting and refining that persona for so long now that it's hard to recall its status, not only as an invention, but an invention whose origin wasn't even Bruce Springsteen. For all the po-faced mythic resonance that now accompanies Bruce's every move, we can thank Jon Landau, the ex-*Rolling Stone* critic who, after catching a typically seismic Springsteen set in 1974, famously wrote, "I saw rock and roll future, and its name is Bruce Springsteen."

Well, Bruce Springsteen was Jon Landau's future. Over the next couple of years, Landau insinuated himself into Bruce's artistic life and consciousness (while remaining on the *Rolling Stone* masthead) until he became Springsteen's producer, manager, and full-service Svengali. Unlike the down-on-their-luck Springsteens of Freehold, N.J., Landau hailed from the well-appointed suburbs of Boston and had earned an honors degree in history from Brandeis. He filled his new protégé's head with an American Studies syllabus heavy on John Ford, Steinbeck, and Flannery O'Connor. At the same time that he intellectualized Bruce, he anti-intellectualized him. Rock music was transcendent, Landau believed, because it was primitive, not because it could be avant-garde. *The White Album* and Hendrix and the Velvet Underground had robbed rock of its power, which lay buried in the pre-Beatles era with Del Shannon and the Ronettes. Bruce's musical vocabulary accordingly shrank. By *Darkness on the Edge of Town,* gone were the *West Side Story*–esque jazz suites of *The Wild, the Innocent, and the E Street Shuffle.* In their place were tight, guitar-driven intro-verse-chorus-verse-bridge-chorus songs. Springsteen's image similarly transformed. On the cover of *Darkness,* he looks strangely like the sallower cousin of Pacino's

Sonny Wortzik, the already quite sallow anti-hero of *Dog Day Afternoon*. The message was clear: Springsteen himself was one of the unbeautiful losers, flitting along the ghostly fringes of suburban respectability.

Thirty years later, and largely thanks to Landau, Springsteen is no longer a musician. He's a belief system. And, like any belief system worth its salt, he brooks no in-between. You're either in or you're out. This has solidified Bruce's standing with his base, for whom he remains a god of total rock authenticity. But it's killed him with everyone else. To a legion of devout nonbelievers—they're not saying Bruuuce, they're booing—Bruce is more a phenomenon akin to Dianetics or Tinkerbell than "the new Dylan," as the Columbia Records promotions machine once hyped him. And so we've reached a strange juncture. About America's last rock star, it's either Pentecostal enthusiasm or total disdain.

To walk back from this impasse, we need to see Springsteen's persona for what it really is: Jon Landau's middle-class fantasy of white, working-class authenticity. Does it derogate Springsteen to claim that he is, in essence, a white minstrel act? Not at all. Only by peeling back all the layers of awful heartland authenticity and rediscovering the old Jersey bullshitter underneath can we begin to grasp the actual charms of the man and his music. A glimpse of this old bullshitter was recently on display when Springsteen inducted U2 into the Rock 'n' Roll Hall of Fame on March 14. Springsteen had recently caught the new iPod commercial featuring the Irish rockers. "Now personally, I live an insanely expensive lifestyle that my wife barely tolerates," the old BSer confided to the audience of industry heavyweights, adding,

> Now, I burn money, and that calls for huge amounts of cash flow. But, I also have a ludicrous image of myself that keeps me from truly cashing in. You can see my problem. Woe is me. So the next morning, I call up Jon Landau . . . and I say, "Did you see that iPod thing?" and he says, "Yes." And he says, "And I hear they didn't take any money." And I said, "They didn't take any money?" and he says, "No." I said, "Smart, wily Irish guys. Anybody—anybody—can do an ad and take the money. But to do the ad and not take the money . . . that's smart. That's wily." I say, "Jon, I want you to call up Bill Gates or whoever is behind this thing and float this: a red, white and blue iPod signed by Bruce 'The Boss' Springsteen. Now remember, no matter how much money he offers, don't take it!"

Every now and again, the majestic simpleton breaks character, and winks; and about as often, he works his way back to subtlety and a human scale and cuts a pretty great song or album. From the post-Landau period, the harrowing masterpiece *Nebraska* is the only record you can push on the nonbelievers, followed by the grossly underrated *Tunnel of Love*. The Oscar-winning "Streets of Philadelphia," an account of a man with AIDS slowly fading into his own living ghost, is the equal of any song he's written. In 1995 Springsteen produced *The Ghost of Tom Joad*, the culmination of a 15-year obsession with Woody Guthrie, whose biography he had been handed the night after Reagan defeated Carter, in 1980. The album is stronger than its popular reception might lead one to believe. "Across the Border" and "Galveston Bay" are lovely and understated and bring home the fact that Springsteen—a man who wrote monster hits for acts as diverse as Manfred Mann, the Pointer Sisters, and Patti Smith—remains a skilled melodist. Nonetheless, the record is a little distant in its sympathies, as if Springsteen had thumbed through back issues of *The Utne Reader* before sitting down to compose.

His new album, *Devils & Dust*, is a sequel to *The Ghost of Tom Joad*. It's mostly acoustic and intimate in scale; but Springsteen appears to have taken criticism of Tom Joad to heart, and *Devils & Dust* is warmer, and in patches, fully up-tempo. It's hard to describe how good the good songs are. The title song is classic Springsteen—"a dirty wind's blowing," and a young soldier may "kill the things he loves" to survive. And on "Black Cowboys," Springsteen unites a visionary concision of detail with long lines in a way that channels William Blake:

> Come the fall the rain flooded these homes, here in Ezekiel's valley of dry bones, it fell hard and dark to the ground. It fell without a sound. Lynette took up with a man whose business was the boulevard, whose smile was fixed in a face that was never off guard.

Though initially signed as a folkie, Springsteen has never been much of a technician on the acoustic guitar, compared to, say, the infinitely nimble Richard Thompson. But on *Devils & Dust* there's a new comfort with the instrument; and he decorates many of the songs with a lovely, understated filigree. Ah, but how hard the lapses in taste! The strings and vocal choruses used to punch up the sound are—what other word is there?—corny. Next to, say, *Iron and Wine*, *Devils & Dust* too often sounds like a chain store selling faux Americana bric-a-brac. One always suspects with Springsteen that, in addition to a blonde Telecaster and "the Big Man," a focus group lies close at hand. The album is suspiciously tuned in to two recent trends, the exploding population of the Arizona and New Mexico exurbs; and the growing religiosity of the country as a whole. *Devils & Dust* is very South by Southwest—Mary is now Maria, there's a lot of mesquite and scrub pine, and one song even comes with a handy key to its regional terminology (Mustaneros: Mustangers; Pradera: Prairie; Riata: Rope). It's also crammed with Biblical imagery, from a modern re-telling of the story of Leah to Christ's final solacing of his mother. The first is a silly throwaway; the second is a fetching, Dylan-inspired hymn that ends with the teasing rumination, "Well Jesus kissed his mother's hands/ Whispered, 'Mother, still your tears,/ For remember the soul of the universe/ Willed a world and it appeared.'"

The high watermark for Springsteen commercially, of course, was 1984, when "Born in the USA" somehow caught both the feelings of social dislocation and the euphoric jingoism of the Reagan era. Landau's mythic creation, the blue-collar, rock 'n' roll naif, has never held such broad appeal since. In recent years, Springsteen has settled into a pattern of selling a couple million albums (*Born in the USA* sold 15 million) to the Bruce die-hards. A clue to who these people are can be found in Springsteen's evolving persona, which is no longer as structured around his own working-class roots. On a short DV film on the CD's flip side, Springsteen says he tries to "disappear" into the voices of the migrant workers and ghetto prisoners whose stories make up *Devils & Dust*: "What would they do, what wouldn't they do, how would they behave in this circumstance, the rhythm of their speech, that's sort of where the music comes in." With Landau nowhere in evidence (he's thanked, but excluded from the album's formal credits), it is up to Springsteen alone to impersonate the voices of the dispossessed. The pupil has finally surpassed the master.

Nonetheless, here I am, starting to hum its tunes, growing a little devil's patch, hitting the gym, and adding a distant heartland twang to my speech. (My wife, meanwhile, curls up on the sofa in shame.) You old bullshitter, you got me again.

READING WRITING

This Text: Reading

1. How do all the authors define authenticity? Where do they differ?
2. Do you agree with any of the definitions of authenticity? More importantly, do you agree with the concept of authenticity—or do you know people who do?
3. What do you think the criteria for judging music should be?
4. Write down ten people or things you think are authentic. Now look at the list and think about what are the common links between them. Then compare your definition with those of the writers.
5. Which demographic do you think is most vulnerable to the authenticity argument?
6. What is the relationship between authenticity and cool?

Your Text: Reading

1. Write a persuasive paper about why authenticity should be the guiding principle in choosing which art to view or buy.
2. Or take the opposite tack—write about why authenticity is overrated.
3. Write a definitional paper about the criteria people use to judge art. (You might refer to the "Is It Art?" suite in the visual art chapter.)
4. Write a paper about the future of the use of authenticity.

READING BETWEEN THE LINES

Classroom Activities

1. Compare your experiences listening to songs and reading the lyrics. First listen to a song, then read its lyrics. For a different song, reverse the procedure. What differences in understanding the song does this make?

2. If possible, listen to a song, then watch a video. What differences in understanding the song does this make?

3. Before listening to its content, read its album/CD cover. What symbols and themes does the band use in designing the cover? What do they suggest about the album's content? About the nature of the band? Now listen to some of the music. How do your preconceived ideas about the music compare to those presented by the music itself?

4. Watch a section of a movie with a soundtrack. What emotions does the soundtrack try to convey? Now watch the same movie with the sound lowered. Do you get the same ideas without the music? Does the music enhance your understanding of the movie? Detract from it?

5. Come up with some sample band names. Name genres for which the band's name would be appropriate. What does this exercise say about the way we view a band's name?

Essay Ideas

1. Pick a song. What is the mood of the music compared to its lyrics? Do they work well together? Why or why not? Are the lyrics more sophisticated than the music or vice versa? Write a paper that makes an argument about the compatibility of music and lyrics.

2. Find a CD you do not know well. Study its cover, making notes on what the cover is "saying" to a potential listener. Now listen to the songs (reading the lyrics if you wish). Does the message behind the cover reflect the music? Why or why not? You can also do similar work with the band's name.

3. Find a well-known song you like. How would you find out information about the song? What sources might be appropriate? How might you approach writing a paper if you had this information? As you think about this question, look for information on the song. When you have gathered enough information, think of arguments or ideas about the song about which you could write.

4. Take a band you like that has produced more than one album. Trace its critical history. What elements of the band's work do the critics pick up on on a consistent basis? What is their general opinion of the band? How do they classify its genre? Now sit and think about whether you agree or disagree with these critics—and why.

5. Find two songs that have similar subjects. Compare and contrast their approaches to the subject, through both their music and lyrics. What approach do you favor, and why?

6. Find a band or bands with an explicitly political approach. Do you know their politics through their music or outside of it? Does their outside behavior agree with their music? How do critics and other members of the media approach their relationship between politics and music? What do their fans think?

7. Find a movie or television show with a prominent soundtrack—does the music work well with the movie or TV series? What are your criteria? Is there a specific moment in the movie or television show that embodies the success or failure of the director's use of music?

Visualizing Writing

We enjoyed showing you one quotation error so much, here's another!

Thanks again to Emily Desmet who took the photo and curator Bethany Keeley at *The Blog of Unnecessary Quotations*: http://www.unnecessaryquotes.com.

9 Writing about the Media

I n the past twenty years, the word *media* has become almost an obscenity, particularly to those who are caught in its gaze. Such a sticky word demands a definition.

Anything from books to magazines to news programs to radio shows to films is technically a medium (media is the plural of medium). For the purposes of this chapter, we will define the media as organizations or companies that seek to cover any kind of news in whatever form. Probably the most technically correct way to refer to news organizations would be just that—news organizations—but because "media" is itself a word that is often discussed, we want to engage it here. We include advertising in this chapter as well, because it often helps pay for the coverage we see. "The media" has become a symbol of a world whose happenings are broadcast 24 hours a day, where no subject seems too trivial to be covered. Everyone seems to think the media are too intrusive. And yet . . . we watch and we read. If we did not watch or read, the media would change because the media are not one entity but many, which are always changing. For instance, there was no cable television when the authors of this book were born, and thus no CNN. Moreover, when many of you were born, the Internet was only a military communications system, hardly the consuming force it is today. So, whatever we write and think about the media now is destined to change for better or worse as our world changes.

You might also be wondering why we have decided to combine advertising, journalism, and the media in one chapter, when each could be its own chapter or its own book. For better or worse, the distinctions between media, advertising, and journalism are fuzzy at best. Is an infomercial news, an advertisement, or a form of television media? On the CNN.com Web site, one finds a news story about America's favorite cities to visit within eyeshot of an ad for Orbitz—is this coincidence? In 2004, CBS ran a segment on *60 Minutes* in which Dan Rather interviewed Bill Clinton about his forthcoming memoir; however, the network came under fire when some blogs explained that CBS would receive a cut from the sales of the book if it was purchased through an Amazon.com link on the CBS.com Web site.[1] Even beyond these instances, the texts of media and advertising and the media are so interdependent, that it seems responsible to link them semiotically.

Even though the media are diverse in nature, they share a number of concerns that connect them. Almost all forms of media struggle to balance various concerns: public interest versus profit, fairness and objectivity versus bias, national coverage versus local, depth of coverage versus breadth of coverage, the need to report quickly versus the imperative to

Google lets us easily search the Internet, but does it make us stupid? See our suite starting on page 601 to find out.

---

[1]David Shaw, "*My Life*' in the Eye of the Perfect Marketing Storm," *The Los Angeles Times* 4 July 2004 <http://articles.latimes.com/2004/jul/04/entertainment/ca-shaw>.

report accurately. Some newer forms of media, particularly partisan blogs, in their role in both advocating positions and criticizing more traditional media, are deliberately biased, and certainly part of the media landscape today. All the conflicts sometimes lead to our sense that there is something wrong with the media, that something is not working right. Still, while the media are far from perfect (what is, after all?), they perform a crucial role in American life and American culture. This introduction will begin to explain some of the difficulties and misconceptions attached to the media before going into articles that explore the media in more depth.

Separate but related elements of the media are advertisers and marketers who have a crucial financial relationship with newspapers, magazines, web pages, television news, and television shows. In essence, advertising pays for our free television and subsidizes our purchase of magazines and newspapers—without ads, we would pay for broadcast television (it is why cable television generally and premium channels like HBO cost money) and pay a lot more for newspapers and magazines. What do advertisers get in return for their ads? The simple answer is public exposure for their products or services. The more complicated (and perhaps unintended) one is an influence in public life. Although some critics object to the very existence of advertising in public life, most everyone acknowledges that advertising is the price we pay for living in a capitalist society. What is most criticized about advertising is the way advertising seeks to sell us products through manipulation and base appeals—its use of implicit and often inflated promises of various forms of happiness (sexual gratification, satiation of hunger, thinness, coolness) with the purchase of advertised items. When we consider these issues plus the sheer proximity of where and how ads and other media appear, it makes sense to think of these two entities as two sides of the same coin. While advertisers are not what people automatically think of as the media, their influence and importance in American society and their impact on various media outlets cannot be denied.

This introduction may seem one of our more political ones, but there is a reason for that: everyone, from liberals to conservatives, from the rich to the poor, from young to old, seems to criticize what the media do. Our purpose in asking you to read media and advertising in a complex way is to help you broaden and complicate your view of them.

In terms of writing about the media, one of the things that the Internet has fostered is a vibrant media criticism, a type of writing you could undertake as well. If you choose to write about the media, you could critique how various media cover news or even the semiotics of a particular form of media. But you are probably more likely to write about advertising. Advertisements use a lot of symbols, and they often telegraph who their intended audience is through these symbols. And they are good candidates to be analyzed with some of the lenses we wrote about in the introduction, such as race, gender, and class. Following are some things to consider about the media.

THE MEDIA ARE BUSINESSES, NOT A PUBLIC SERVICE.

Although the media *are* in the business of selling newspapers or garnering ratings points, they also have obligations to the public. Some argue that because of the advantages given to television and radio networks by the government—exclusive use of broadcast frequencies for radio stations and various broadcast advantages to the big three television networks (NBC, CBS, and ABC)—that media outlets have further obligations to the public interest.

And yet, at the heart, the media are business organizations. As a way of trying to maintain some distance between the business side and the editorial (news) side, media organizations often try to separate the two divisions: the editorial side covers the news; the business side gets advertising and does accounting work. Those businesses that try to intimidate the editorial side by threatening to withdraw advertising are likely to get frosty receptions from both the editorial side AND the business side. Part of that has to do with the newspaper having the reputation that their coverage cannot be bought or sold as part of their credibility.

However, the business and editorial sides often do have connections. Special sections in magazines and in newspapers in which coverage is devoted to a particular event or phenomenon are the most obvious examples, but when we watch television some decisions seem motivated by the business component; local coverage of a business opening or prominently mentioning sponsorship of local events are examples of this interchange. Even the editorial side of large newspapers like *The New York Times* and *The Washington Post* may have unconscious motivations toward the business end; a newspaper is generally designed toward highlighting the most important stories, a tactic that "sells" the newspaper to the patron. Small-town papers may make even less of a distinction between the editorial and business side. In smaller communities, the publisher, who either represents the owner or is the owner, *does* often influence editorial decisions, especially in the editorials of a paper.

Given the fact that the basic structures of media organizations are unlikely to change, the most important thing to do is to watch or read news with an active, sometimes skeptical eye, looking for links between business interests and media outlets. Even more importantly, read news widely. Look at alternative papers or read media criticism. Taking such steps will help you become a better reader of the media.

THE MEDIA ARE MADE UP OF A VARIETY OF PEOPLE.

Do you think Katie Couric and the local weekly's columnist have similar roles in the media? Of course not—but the latter is as much a media member as the former. When columnists, politicians, or sports figures refer to the media, whom, specifically, do they mean? Miss Manners? National Public Radio? The folks at the History Channel? The obituary writer of your hometown newspaper? Probably they are thinking of the very public media outlets like the major television networks, the overly aggressive talk radio personalities, and perhaps some writers for national newspapers and magazines. However, most members of "the media" are regular, virtually anonymous people who try to bring you interesting, important stories.

Although many members of the media have similar aims, their format and their audience shape their content. Radio news can only read a few paragraphs of a traditional newspaper story in its allotted time and has to rely on taped interviews to enhance it. A television news report has to focus on visual material, and national newspapers have different expectations attached to them than does the local weekly. Newspapers analyze long-term events better than television does, and magazines do it even better. But in covering house fires and the weather, and showing sports highlights, television is more effective. Overall, the media have different elements that make various organizations better suited to do one job rather than another.

In addition, there are very few absolutes when it comes to the media. Some newspapers and television stations are civic-minded organizations dedicated to upholding the public trust. Sometimes newspapers seem motivated more by financial concerns. Some ads are very entertaining. Some are offensive. Some media outlets try to present the news in the most balanced, most objective way they can. Other sources make no bones about being biased. The crucial thing is to be able to view the media generally, and advertising and the news specifically, with a critical eye.

DESPITE WHAT YOUR FAVORITE CONSERVATIVE RADIO OR TELEVISION TALK SHOW HOST SAYS, THE MEDIA ARE NOT PARTICULARLY LIBERAL.

You may not be familiar with the ongoing controversy of the supposed "liberal bias" of the media, but if you spend any time watching or reading columnists—both from the left (liberal) and right (conservative)—you will encounter claims of a liberal media. Actually, the fact that someone points out that there is a liberal bias itself undermines the idea of one. If there is such a liberal bias, then how have we heard about it? Through the conservative media.

You may think we exhibit a so-called liberal bias in taking this stance, but the business element that often shapes editorial content, especially in small communities and perhaps the networks as well, tends to be more sympathetic to conservative political ideals. In addition, the fact that most media outlets recognize many conservative commentators probably shows how baseless this idea of a liberal media really is. Most publications also do not foreground information that is of concern to liberals or liberal organizations. For instance, do you know of any major news publication with a "Labor" section? How about a section entitled "Feminism"? Or, for that matter, "Racial Equality"? Does your local radio station give an environmental awareness update? Probably not (though with the rise of awareness about global warming, perhaps that may change). However, every major paper devotes a great deal of time to its business section, and just about every radio station gives some kind of market news or stock report. Many sportswriters, owners of sports franchises, and many athletes themselves tend to be both politically and socially conservative. Finally, simple coverage of events can reflect bias. In the September 2002 issue of *Harper's Magazine*, for example, the *Harper's* index lists the number of appearances made by corporate representatives on U.S. nightly newscasts in 2001 at 995, while the number of appearances of labor representatives was 31.

On the other hand, it may be unfair to accuse the media of leaning too far to the right. Most actors, filmmakers, and singers find affinity with left-leaning causes and, as you know, entertainment always makes the news. Both liberal and conservative groups assail the media for bias, which probably indicates that the media's bias falls somewhere in the middle. The media's political bias may or may not be of concern to you now, but it is one aspect of the media you will continually hear about as they play a larger and larger role in public discourse.

THE MEDIA ARE NOT OBJECTIVE, BUT ITS MEMBERS TRY TO BE FAIR.

Reporters and editors are human beings with political, social, and cultural preferences that they hope to acknowledge and put away when reporting. Reporters quickly learn they have to ask both (or many) sides of questions when it comes to an issue. News stories often have this "she said, he said" quality. Does that mean the media always do a good job of being objective or fair? Definitely not, but they generally aim to do so. Those outlets with a specific political agenda are usually responsible enough to make that orientation clear in their editorial page or early in the publication or program. It is also worth noting that editorial writers and columnists are under no obligation to be fair or objective; their object is to deliver their opinion for better or worse. Calls for their objectivity miss the point of what an editorial is supposed to do—deliver opinions.

Questions of objectivity and fairness are not only important when talking about the media but also in your own work. As writers and researchers, we hope we are being objective when we undertake a subject, but we naturally come to any subject with a viewpoint that is shaped by our experiences and the ideas that come from them. That is why we may disagree with each other over whether we liked a movie or a book, or over which candidate we support in an election (or even who we find attractive or not). In fact, one of the reasons we discuss the idea of lenses so insistently throughout the book is that a lens, whether it be liberal, conservative, about race, class, or gender, or through a particular geography, allows us to acknowledge a particular point of view.

Though reporters come to the news with biases, they generally understand their obligations to report fairly and generally serve the public interest, just as editorial writers and columnists understand their *mission* to seek to influence public opinion. The bigger point here is that critics who claim a lack of objectivity from the media are uninformed about the reality of the media (sometimes deliberately so). The media often deserve the criticism they get from both liberals and conservatives, but an imperfect media is destined in any system—in particular, one whose primary focus is business. Understanding these concerns will help you understand the media in a more inclusive and a more informed way.

ADVERTISERS REFLECT CONSUMERS' DESIRES AS WELL AS BUSINESS'S DESIRE TO SELL TO THEM.

There is a long-standing belief that advertising is manipulative and somehow unsavory. While we will not argue fully with those ideas, we believe it is important to think about what exactly advertising does. For one, we do think that advertising generally tries to sell us things we want (even if we "should not" want them). Advertising items that consumers do not want is not a particularly effective use of advertiser's dollars. If you look at the majority of what advertisers sell, they consist of consumer items such as food, cars, clothing, electronics, and services—things that people want, though again the issue of how many of these things we should have or want is another question. Advertising can only influence a consumer so much—if a new snack food tastes like soap or broccoli, endorsements by every celebrity will still fail to sell it. Accordingly, some advertising experts believe that the greatest influence happens in choosing a brand at the point of sale, not in actually choosing to buy the product itself. Most of the marketing research that businesses do is not geared toward learning how to manipulate but learning what consumers will buy.[2]

---

[2]See Michael Schudson, *Advertising, the Uneasy Persuasion: Its Dubious Impact on American Society* (New York: Basic Books, 1986).

Yet the question of how far advertisers go in changing our attitudes about our world and what we should want is an open question that researchers continue to try to answer. We think that blaming advertisers for the perceived shallowness of human desire oversimplifies the role advertisers and consumers play in deciding what they want.

In addition, both authors have been confronted in the classroom with the idea that the public is not very smart compared to the students themselves. This kind of thinking on the part of students probably underestimates the intelligence of the public. If you assume the public is as savvy as you are, you will avoid many pitfalls.

ADVERTISING AND GRAPHIC DESIGN CAN BE CONSIDERED ARTISTIC.

Artistic components abound in advertising. Advertisers and directors of commercials compose their ads so that they are both aesthetically pleasing and effective at getting us to buy. Advertisers often use the same principles as artists by seeking tension, drama, comedy, and beauty in their work. And sometimes directors and artists do both commercial and more "artistic" work. For instance, film directors such as David Lynch and the Coen brothers have all done television commercials, and many artists do graphic design (including those involved in the Absolut Vodka campaign). What complicates graphic design and television commercials as art is their associations with commercial interests. Americans like to separate art from commerce; we would rather have our artists make their money from selling their art to the community, not to companies. However, increasingly, the two worlds are merging.

What do we do when we see a funny or clever commercial or a piece of advertising that is particularly striking? Perhaps we feel at war with ourselves in trying to place within a context what is clearly artistic expression and yet is trying to sell us something. Can we enjoy the art of advertising while decrying its influence? It is a difficult question. There are a lot of creative advertisements and interesting graphic designs out there; to make a false distinction between high art and commercialism is to ignore how the texts of advertising and the texts of art work.

ADVERTISERS APPEAL TO US THROUGH COMMON IMAGES WHOSE MEANING WE HAVE ALREADY LEARNED.

Advertisers appeal to us through images that are iconic—standing directly in for something—or symbolic. Diamond manufacturers do not have to tell us that diamonds serve as an icon for sophistication and wealth—we already know that. Thus, the diamond ring has become an icon for luxury, as has a spacious car with a leather interior and adjustable seats. We have learned what manicured lawns, Bermuda shorts, and gold jewelry mean by association. We know what it means to see a beach, golf clubs, a city, or any number of settings in a commercial. Because advertisers communicate through images as much as they do words, and these images seem to convey what they want without too much effort, looking at the visual language they use can tell us more about the role these images play in American culture.

RESEARCHERS DISAGREE ABOUT ADVERTISING'S EFFECTS ON CONSUMERS.

Many researchers, including some of the writers included here, believe there is a connection between advertisements and harmful behavior. Jean Kilbourne (not included here), for example, suggests that ads influence our children in harmful ways, particularly young women. William Lutz argues that the way in which advertisers alter the meaning of words can have a harmful effect on language and how we use it. Others are not so sure.

The authors are not convinced in one particular way, with this caveat. We believe the relationship between humans and any form of culture is complicated. We are not denying that there is a relationship between advertising and behavior—we are just not convinced about how direct it is. Similarly, we are not making any specific claims about the relationship between the media and advertising except to say that the two are increasingly intimately related and that we urge you to continue to be literate readers of both.

NEWS MEDIA

Medium: What form of media are you watching or reading? How does form contribute to coverage?

Bias: What point of view does the story seem to have? Are there some key words that indicate this? Do all the same stories seem to have the same viewpoint? If there is a bias, is the story still "fair"–does the reporter seek multiple perspectives?

Signs: When watching a newscast, how does the program communicate in image (video, photograph, graphic)? What symbols does it use? Are there any unintended meanings? How does the clothing of the reporters and anchors contribute to what we take from the newscast?

Audience: To what audience does the news article or news report appeal? How can you tell? Will others outside the target audience feel alienated by the report or article? What are news organizations assuming about their audience in a particular piece or the newscast, magazine, Web site, or newspaper as a whole?

Reality: Do the images and ideas match your idea of reality? Are they supposed to? Do they (the people reporting and presenting the news) see the world the way you do?

Race, ethnicity, gender, class: How are images of any or all of these groups presented? Can you tell the bias of the reporter or news organization from their presentation?

ADVERTISING

Signs: How does the advertisement speak to you through images? What do the images symbolize? Are there unintended meanings attached to the symbols? Can you classify the symbols into types? What do advertisers assume about the connections you will make between the signs presented and what researchers call "the point of purchase"?

Audience: What is the target audience of this advertisement? How do you know? What assumptions are advertisers making about their audience?

RACE, ETHNICITY, GENDER, CLASS

How are images of any or all of these groups presented? Can you tell what advertisers think of these groups through their portrayal? Or their absence?

THE RHETORICAL ANALYSIS

One of the easiest ways of analyzing an advertisement is by using Aristotle's three appeals; the appeals provide a natural organization of the paper.

ARISTOTLE'S THREE APPEALS: ETHOS, PATHOS, LOGOS
ETHOS—THE ETHICAL APPEAL

An advertisement or other visual text uses the trustworthiness and credibility of the author to make its appeal. The ethos many times is the brand name itself—a brand we are familiar with may bring credibility. Or the advertiser may use someone famous or with expertise to present the advertisement. Politicians often use endorsements to provide credibility. Many times the ethical appeal is the weakest in an advertisement, however.

PATHOS—APPEAL TO EMOTIONS

This appeal tries to get the reader to feel a particular emotion through the use of images or words, or both. An advertisement typically wants us to be motivated to purchase the particular item. The copywriters may do this by presenting images, colors, people, letters, or a combination of the above to evoke feelings of intrigue, happiness, or pleasure in some form. The images are often aimed at reminding us of other ideas or images. The appeal to emotions is often the strongest in an advertisement.

LOGOS—APPEAL TO REASON OR LOGIC

Advertisements often try to present a logical appeal, using facts of one sort or another. For example, an advertisement might use claims that it is the most popular brand or has won the most awards. It might claim the time to purchase the item is sooner rather than later because of the discounts its manufacturer is providing.

THE TARGET AUDIENCE

When talking about visual texts, you might also talk about who its target audience is—how old or young, how rich or poor, where they are from, and so on.

A TYPICAL PAPER

1. An introduction talking about advertising.
2. A thesis statement describing the argument you are making about the ad.
3. A paragraph providing an organized general description of the ad.
4. Three or more paragraphs about the strengths and weaknesses of the three appeals.
5. A paragraph that talks about the target audience.
6. A concluding paragraph that explains why one appeal is stronger than the other.

Before Jon Stewart: The Growth of Fake News. Believe It.

Robert Love

The Daily Show with Jon Stewart has altered how an entire demographic approach television news. The satirical news program has won dozens of awards, including an Emmy and a Peabody, and has spurred interest in "fake news." Robert Love's article on the history and rise of fake news originally appeared in the Columbia Journalism Review *(2007). He is the executive editor of* Best Life *and an adjunct professor at Columbia University's Graduate School of Journalism.*

JUST BEFORE HIS FAMOUS CONFRONTATION with Tucker Carlson on CNN 's *Crossfire* two years ago, Jon Stewart was introduced as "the most trusted name in fake news." No argument there. Stewart, as everyone knows, is the host of *The Daily Show*, a satirical news program that has been running since 1996 and has spun off the equally funny and successful *Colbert Report*. Together these shows are broadcast (back to back) more than twenty-three times a week, "from Comedy Central's World News Headquarters in New York," thus transforming a modest side-street studio on Manhattan's West Side into the undisputed locus of fake news.

The trope itself sounds so modern, so hip, so *Gawkerish* when attached to the likes of Stewart or Stephen Colbert, or dropped from the lips of the ex-*Saturday Night Live* "Weekend Update" anchor Tina Fey, who declared as she departed SNL, "I'm out of the fake news business." For the rest of us, we're knee deep in the fake stuff and sinking fast. It comes at us from every quarter of the media—old and new—not just as satire but disguised as the real thing, secretly paid for by folks who want to remain in the shadows. And though much of it is clever, it's not all funny.

Fake news arrives on doorsteps around the world every day, paid for by You, *Time* magazine Person of the Year, a.k.a. Joe and Jane Citizen, in one way or another. Take for instance, the U.S. government's 2005 initiative to plant "positive news" in Iraqi newspapers, part of a $300 million U.S. effort to sway public opinion about the war. And remember Armstrong Williams, the conservative columnist who was hired on the down low to act as a $240,000 sock puppet for the president's No Child Left Behind program? Williams's readers had no idea he was a paid propagandist until the Justice Department started looking into allegations of fraud in his billing practices.

Fake news has had its lush innings. The Bush administration has worked hand-in-glove with big business to make sure of it. Together, they've credentialed fringe scientists and fake experts and sent them in to muddy scientific debates on global warming, stem cell research, evolution, and other matters. And as if that weren't enough, the Department of Health and Human Services got caught producing a series of deceptive video news releases—VNRs in p.r.-industry parlance—touting the administration's Medicare plan. The segments, paid political announcements really, ended with a fake journalist signing off like a real one—"In Washington, I'm Karen Ryan reporting," and they ran on local news shows all over the country without disclosure. All of this fakery taken together, it may be fair to say that the nation's capital has been giving Comedy Central a run for its money as the real home of fake news.

But let's dispense with the satire, whose intentions are as plain as Colbert's arched eyebrow. And let's step around the notion of fake news as *wrong* news: The 1948 presidential election blunder DEWEY DEFEATS TRUMAN, for instance, or even the *New York Post*'s howler from the 2004 campaign, DEM PICKS GEPHARDT AS VP CANDIDATE. Those are honest mistakes, set loose by overweening editors perhaps, but never with the intention to deceive. That wasn't always the case, as we shall see. In the early days of American journalism, newspapers trafficked in intentional, entertaining hoaxes, a somewhat puzzling period in our history. In modern times, hoaxes have migrated from the mainstream papers to the tabloid outriders like the old *National Enquirer*, the new *Globe*, and the hoaxiest of them all, *The Weekly World News*, purveyor of the "Bat Boy" cover stories.

The mainstream press covers itself with the mantle of authority now. Six of ten Americans polled in 2005 trusted "the media" to report the news "fully, fairly and accurately," a slight decline from the high-water mark of seven-in-ten during the Woodward-and-Bernstein seventies. What's more, in a veracity dogfight between the press and the government, Americans say they trust the media by a margin of nearly two to one.

But here's a question: Can we continue to trust ourselves? Are we prepared for the global, 24-7 fake news cage match that will dominate journalism in the twenty-first century? Let's call it *Factual Fantasy: Attack of the Ax-Grinding Insiders*. The boundaries have vanished, the gloves are off, our opponents are legion and fueled with espresso. Both CNN and *The New York Times* were used by the U.S. military as unwitting co-conspirators in spreading false information, a tactic known as *psychological operations*, part of an effort to convince Americans the invasion of Iraq was a necessary piece of the war on terror.

But let's not leave out the technology. Leaks may be the time-tested tactic for manipulating the press, but the new digital toolbox has given third-party players—government, industry, politicians, you name 'em—sleeker weapons and greater power to turn the authority of the press to their own ends: to disseminate propaganda, disinformation, advertising, politically strategic misinformation—to in effect use the media to distort reality. Besides a vast and sophisticated degree of diligence, the rising generation of journalists would be wise to observe two rules for working in this new environment: Beware of profiteers and hyper-patriots, and check out a little history—lest it repeat itself.

Fake news has been with us for a long time. Documented cases predate the modern media, reaching as far into the past as a bogus eighth century edict said to be the pope-friendly words of the Roman emperor Constantine. There are plenty of reports of forgeries and trickeries in British newspapers in the eighteenth century. But the actual term "fake news"—two delicious little darts of malice (and a headline-ready sneer if ever there was one)—seems to have arisen in late nineteenth century America, when a rush of emerging technologies intersected with newsgathering practices during a boom time for newspapers.

The impact of new technology is hard to overestimate. The telegraph was followed by trans-Atlantic and transcontinental cables, linotype, high-speed electric presses and halftone photo printing—wireless gave way to the telephone. The nation, doubled in population and literacy from Civil War days, demanded a constant supply of fresh news, so the media grew additional limbs as fast as it could. Newly minted news bureaus and press associations recruited boy and girl reporters from classified ads—"Reporting And Journalism Taught Free Of Charge"—and sent their cubs off to dig up hot stories, truth be damned, to sell to the dailies.

By the turn of the century, the preponderance of fakery was reaching disturbing proportions, according to the critic and journalist J.B. Montgomery-M'Govern. "Fake journalism," he wrote in *Arena*, an influential monthly of the period, "is resorted to chiefly by news bureaus, press associations and organizations of that sort, which supply nearly all the metropolitan Sunday papers and many of the dailies with their most sensational 'stories.'"

Montgomery-M'Govern delivers a taxonomy of fakers' techniques, including the use of the "stand-for," in which a reputable person agrees to an outrageous lie for the attendant free publicity; the "combine," in which a group of reporters concoct and then verify a false story; the "fake libel" plant, in which editors are duped by conspirators into running false and litigious articles; the "alleged cable news" story, in which so-called "foreign reports," dashed off in the newsroom or a downtown press association, are topped with a foreign dateline and published as truth. The editors of huge Sunday editions, with their big appetites for the juiciest stuff (what M-M calls "Sunday stories") naturally set the bar lower for veracity than they did for hot-blooded emotional impact.

Have I mentioned that news was suddenly big money? By the century's turn, the tallest buildings in New York and San Francisco were both owned by newspapers. And the business became so hypercompetitive that some reporters not only made things up but stole those fake scoops and "specials" from one another with impunity. The Chicago Associated-Press fell into a trap set by a suspicious client, who set loose a rumor at two in the morning that President Grover Cleveland had been assassinated! True to its reputation, Chicago AP ran with it—no fact-checking here—and put it up on the wires. The assassination story ran in newspapers all over the country the next day, amid much chuckling and finger pointing.

The further away the newsworthy event, the more likely it was to involve fakery. BOGUS FOREIGN NEWS ran the headline in *The Washington Post* of February 22, 1903, but the subheads that followed it are so illustrative as to deserve full reproduction below.

POPE HAS DIED TWENTY-TWO TIMES IN FIVE YEARS

YELLOWNESS ACROSS THE SEA

AMERICANS OUTSTRIPPED IN THIS SORT OF THING BY ENGLISH AND GERMAN MANUFACTURERS-EDITORS VICTIMS

BECAUSE REPORTS ARE SOMETIMES TRUE-RIVALRY FOR NEWS AMONG ORIENTAL ENGLISH DAILIES

It was a global problem. Even twenty true words cabled from London about an Indian Ocean hurricane could grow to a story ten times that length, padded out with imaginary details and encyclopedia facts. Mo' words, mo' money.

The loudest whoops at the fake news fiesta were shouted at William Randolph Hearst's *New York Journal*. Hearst, the legendary publisher and proud leading light of the "yellow press," propounded two combustible ideas at the height of his influence in the late 1890s. First, he believed in the "journalism of action," an activist press solving crimes, supporting charities, investigating corruption—taking charge in the arenas of national and international affairs. Second, he held unvarnished truth to be a somewhat negotiable commodity, especially when its subversion could lead to profit or power.

By 1897, the stage was set for a little international combustion. Cuba, ruled as a Spanish colony since 1511, had grown an insurgency, which was put down with terrific cruelty by its European overlords. In the U.S. there was a growing sentiment for a free and independent Cuba, along with the feeling that we should be mobilized for war to help out. Teddy Roosevelt, Joseph Pulitzer, and Hearst, among many others, felt that aggression was the proper response, but President McKinley was slow to act. And so began the first privately funded propaganda push to war in modern media history.

It kicked off in earnest on February 15, 1898, when the warship *USS Maine*, docked in Havana Harbor, exploded, killing 266 crewmen. Hearst first placed an ad offering $50,000 REWARD! FOR THE DETECTION OF THE PERPETRATOR OF THE MAINE OUTRAGE! He then threw all of his paper's resources at covering the explosion and its investigation, sending boatloads of reporters and illustrators to Cuba and Key West. Hearst's *Journal*—along with Pulitzer's *World*—not only produced the bulk of the news coming out of Cuba, but within days began spinning it to blame Spain for the explosion.

Competing papers cried foul! "Nothing so disgraceful as the behavior of these two newspapers has ever been known in the history of journalism," wrote E. L. Godkin in the *New York Evening Post*. He alleged "gross misrepresentation of the facts, deliberate intervention of tales calculated to excite the public and wanton recklessness in construction of headlines."

Nevertheless it was headlines that propelled the United States to war with Spain, headlines that swayed the populace with somewhat dubious evidence. War was declared and in two weeks it was over; we had freed Cuba, gained three new territories, and ended Spain's influence in the Western Hemisphere.

Okay, headlines can lie, but can you better determine the truth in a photo or the voice of a trusted colleague? With the advent of faster and easier halftone reproduction in the 1920s came the photo-driven tabloid newspapers like the *New York Illustrated Daily News*. In 1924 the most tabloidy of all tabloids arrived, the *New York Evening Graphic* (nicknamed the Porno-graphic), which launched the gossip careers of Ed Sullivan and Walter Winchell and the vaunted Composograph photo. The Composograph was actually a technique that combined real and staged pictures to depict events where no cameras had ventured. *The Graphic*'s editors had a blast with the pop star Rudolph Valentino, documenting the singer's unsuccessful surgery, funeral, and his meeting in heaven with the departed Enrico Caruso—the headline: RUDY MEETS CARUSO! TENOR'S SPIRIT SPEAKS!

Telephones meant faster, more accurate newsgathering at a time when speed was prized and "extra" editions meant extra profits. The telephone necessitated the creation of two-man urban reporting teams—leg men and rewrite men—which irritated H. L. Mencken to no end. "Journalism," he wrote in 1927, "is in a low state, mainly due to the decay of the old-time reporter, the heart and soul of the American newspapers of the last generation. The current rush to get upon the streets with hot news, even at the cost of printing only half of it, has pretty well destroyed all his old qualities. He no longer writes what he has seen and heard; he telephones it to a remote and impersonal rewrite man. . . . But it must be manifest that, hanging on his telephone, maybe miles away from the event he is describing, he is completely unable to get into his description any of the vividness of a thing actually seen. He does the best he can, but that best is to the reporting of a fairer era as a mummy is to a man."

Of course Mencken's selective memory harks back to the glory days of yellow journalism, when the worst (or best) fakery in history took place, but never mind that. He seems to have completely forgotten his own role ten years earlier in a great classic newspaper hoax, "A Neglected Anniversary," a fake history of the bathtub, which ran in the *New York Evening Mail* on December 28, 1917.

"Not a plumber fired a salute or hung out a flag," Mencken lamented. "Not a governor proclaimed a day of prayer. Not a newspaper called attention to the day," the purported seventy-fifth birthday of the bathtub. Mencken's piece provided a vivid and full history of the introduction of the tub to American life. It singled out for praise Millard Fillmore for his role in bringing one of the first tubs to the White House, giving it "recognition and respectability in the United States."

"A Neglected Anniversary" was so finely rendered that it literally sprang back to life—like a reanimated mummy—and found its way into print dozens of times, criticized, analyzed, and repeated as a real chapter in American history.

Hoaxes like this seem so *Colbert* now, like mutant cousins to his notion of "truthiness." But hoaxers are historically not comedians; they are, like Mencken, journalists who write entertaining stuff that sounds vaguely true, even though it's not, for editors who are usually in on the joke. The hoaxing instinct infected newsrooms throughout the early days of modern newspapers to a degree that most of us find puzzling today. Newspapers contained hundreds, if not thousands of hoaxes in the late nineteenth and early twentieth centuries, most of them undocumented fakes in obscure Western weeklies. The subjects were oddball pets and wild weather, giants, mermaids, men on the moon, petrified people (quite a few of those), and (my favorite) the Swiss Navy. As a novice editor at the Virginia City, Nevada, *Territorial Enterprise*, a young Mark Twain put his talent to the test with a hoax of hoaxes. "I chose to kill the petrification mania with a delicate, a very delicate satire," he wrote. He called it "A Petrified Man."

Who knew? The twinning of news and entertainment that plagues us today grew not from some corporate greedhead instinct of the go-go eighties, but from our own weird history. The reasons for hoaxing were mostly mercenary: for the publisher, it was to fill column inches and bring in eyeballs. For the journalist, it was sport, a freelance fee or a ploy to keep his job. Strange to say, readers didn't seem to mind too much.

The first major fake news event of the modern media age was the Great Moon Hoax of 1835. A series of articles began appearing in the *New York Sun* on August 25, the late-summer brainchild of its ambitious publisher, Benjamin Day. Day wanted to move papers, like every publisher, and came up with a novel method. He began publishing a series of articles, allegedly reprinted from a nonexistent scientific journal, about Sir John Herschel, an eminent British astronomer on his way to the Cape of Good Hope to test a powerful new telescope.

What Herschel saw on the moon was . . . Life! Not just flora and fauna but living men— hairy, yellow-faced guys, four feet tall with enormous wings that "possessed great expansion and were similar in structure of those of the bat." It was all too much, but New Yorkers had to see for themselves and the *Sun*'s circ hit a new high of 15,000. Even after its men-in-the-moon story was revealed to be a hoax, the paper retained its popularity with readers.

Edgar Allan Poe, famous but destitute in 1844, wrote another well-known hoax for the *Sun*. THE ATLANTIC CROSSED IN THREE DAYS! Poe's story began, and it went on to describe a lighter-than-air balloon trip that wouldn't actually take place for another sixty years. Thirty years later, at the behest of its publisher, James Gordon Bennett Jr., the *New York Herald* ran what's often been called the Central Park Zoo Hoax. ESCAPED ANIMALS ROAM STREETS OF MANHATTAN the headline warned. The article maintained that twenty-seven people were dead and 200 injured in terrible scenes of mutilation. State militiamen were called in to control the situation, and sensible New Yorkers barricaded themselves in their homes.

In 1910, *The Washington Post* waxed nostalgic over the old men-on-the-moon hoax, with a short item under a no-nonsense headline: THIS WAS A FAMOUS HOAX. In fact, that kind of warm retrospective began to appear as an occasional column or feature, illustrating a growing trend among newspapers to look back with a smile on the bad old days of great hoaxes. In the intervening years, the newspaper business had grown up into the Fourth Estate; hoaxes, for better or worse, were a part of its wild-child adolescence. By 1937, it was pretty much over, at least according to Marvin H. Creager, the president of the American Society of Newspaper Editors who addressed the group's fifteenth annual convention. "The day of the fake and the hoax . . . seems to have passed," he said, "and with it the reporters and editors who delighted in perpetrating them."

Creager, speaking to his confident colleagues at a time of rising circulation, added, "The reporter with a box of tricks is out of place in the newspaper world today."

Times change and so do the tricksters. The newspaper, the first mass-marketed medium to enter American living rooms, was a jack of all trades, a witty parlor guest with a deck of cards. Over time, mass distribution of movies, radio, TV, and the Internet arrived to entertain Americans and eventually to eat the lunch of the great newspaper dynasties. From the days of the Yellow Press onward, publishers began to see themselves as public servants and guardians of truth; editors learned the wisdom of marking off news columns from opinion pages and imparting a higher level of veracity even to soft features. Hoaxes? The Fourth Estate has no use for hoaxers, even of the pathetic dysfunctional variety; our tribal councils cast out fabulists like Jayson Blair or Stephen Glass with great harrumphing fanfare.

Today, people expect the news media to give them relevant, accurate information. Serious journalists have for decades thought of themselves as the descendants of muckrakers, reformers, and watchdogs.

But hold the applause for a moment. This presumption of good faith makes us the perfect marks for the new agenda-based fakers. Just last year, the Center for Media and Democracy identified sixty-nine news stations that ran clearly marked government- or industry-produced VNRs as unbiased news during a ten-month period. Many station managers, it was reported, even disguised those advertisements to look like their reporters' own work and offered no public disclosure.

Doctored pictures from war zones? The *Los Angeles Times* ran one in 2003, and Reuters ran one last year. Grassroots organizations with Orwellian names like Project Protect, funded not by conservation-minded voters, but the timber industry? The investigative reporter Paul Thacker brought that one to light, along the way revealing that a Fox News science reporter named Steven Milloy had undisclosed ties to the oil and tobacco industries. Milloy discredited reports of the danger of secondhand smoke as "junk science" on foxnews.com, never letting on he was on the payroll of Phillip Morris.

Welcome to journalism's latest transitional phase, where another rush of technology is changing the business in ways not imaginable ten years ago. Picture, cell, and satellite phones, wireless Internet, cheap digital cameras, Photoshop, and blogger software make it easier to deliver the news and also easier to fake it. If you're the kind of person who thinks there ought to be a law, there is one, at least for the conduct of our elected officials. Federal statutes prohibit the use of funding for "publicity or propaganda purposes" not authorized by Congress. The ban seems to have been observed as closely as speeding laws in recent years. For the rest of us, however, it's what they call a self-policing situation.

Late last year, Armstrong Williams, the conservative commentator who took undisclosed payments to promote President Bush's education agenda, settled his case with the Justice Department. The feds had pursued him not for propaganda violations, though they might have, but under the False Claims Act, for false or fraudulent billing. A weary Armstrong agreed to repay $34,000 to the government and said he was happy to be done with it. He admits no wrongdoing and has committed no crime.

In the exposure, however, he lost his syndicated column and suffered an eighteen-month investigation. The notoriety of his case jump-started a government-wide inquiry into the use of fake news as propaganda, which may actually have done some good.

According to *USA Today*, "the Government Accountability Office, Congress's nonpartisan watchdog, in 2005 found that the deal violated a ban on 'covert propaganda.'"

But make no mistake; it's a small, isolated victory. In a time of falling circulation, diminishing news budgets, and dismantled staffs, the fakers are out there, waiting for their opportunities to exploit the authority that modern journalism conveys. Some of us, I fear, aren't doing all we can to help readers and viewers know the difference between the fake and the honest take. In early January, *The Huffington Post* reported that *The Washington Post*'s Web site was talking to Comedy Central about enlisting *The Daily Show* staff to cover the 2008 presidential campaign. Jon Stewart, the elder statesman of fake news, working for *The Washington Post*? There was no confirmation of a deal at press time.

So, here's my totally mock serious signoff: If General Pervez Musharraf, the president of Pakistan, who has already appeared once on *The Daily Show*, returned to announce that he had captured Osama bin Laden, would that be fake news? And what would we call it when it ran in *The Washington Post*?

Just asking.

READING **WRITING**

This Text: Reading

1. What does Love think of "fake news"? Do you agree with him?
2. Do you think he fairly characterizes Jon Stewart and Comedy Central? In what ways do those entities differ from mainstream media organizations?

Your Text: Writing

1. Watch *The Daily Show* one night and critique the presentation of news.
2. Compare *The Onion* to *The Daily Show*. What functions do each perform?
3. Watch *The Daily Show* and a network news evening broadcast. In what ways do they differ in their presentation? Where does *The Daily Show* borrow from network news? Which show informs you better?

The Long Tail

By Chris Anderson

Chris Anderson is Wired's *editor in chief and writes the blog* The Long Tail.

Forget squeezing millions from a few megahits at the top of the charts. The future of entertainment is in the millions of niche markets at the shallow end of the bitstream. In 1988, a British mountain climber named Joe Simpson wrote a book called *Touching the Void,* a harrowing account of near death in the Peruvian Andes. It got good reviews but, only a modest success, it was soon forgotten. Then, a decade later, a strange thing happened. Jon Krakauer wrote *Into Thin Air,* another book about a mountain-climbing tragedy, which became a publishing sensation. Suddenly *Touching the Void* started to sell again.

Random House rushed out a new edition to keep up with demand. Booksellers began to promote it next to their *Into Thin Air* displays, and sales rose further. A revised paperback edition, which came out in January, spent 14 weeks on the *New York Times* best-seller list. That same month, IFC Films released a docudrama of the story to critical acclaim. Now *Touching the Void* outsells *Into Thin Air* more than two to one.

What happened? In short, Amazon.com recommendations. The online bookseller's software noted patterns in buying behavior and suggested that readers who liked *Into Thin Air* would also like *Touching the Void*. People took the suggestion, agreed wholeheartedly, wrote rhapsodic reviews. More sales, more algorithm-fueled recommendations, and the positive feedback loop kicked in.

Particularly notable is that when Krakauer's book hit shelves, Simpson's was nearly out of print. A few years ago, readers of Krakauer would never even have learned about Simpson's book—and if they had, they wouldn't have been able to find it. Amazon changed that. It created the *Touching the Void* phenomenon by combining infinite shelf space with real-time information about buying trends and public opinion. The result: rising demand for an obscure book.

This is not just a virtue of online booksellers; it is an example of an entirely new economic model for the media and entertainment industries, one that is just beginning to show its power. Unlimited selection is revealing truths about what consumers want and how they want to get it in service after service, from DVDs at Netflix to music videos on Yahoo! Launch to songs in the iTunes Music Store and Rhapsody. People are going deep into the catalog, down the long, long list of available titles, far past what's available at Blockbuster Video, Tower Records, and Barnes & Noble. And the more they find, the more they like. As they wander further from the beaten path, they discover their taste is not as mainstream as they thought (or as they had been led to believe by marketing, a lack of alternatives, and a hit-driven culture).

An analysis of the sales data and trends from these services and others like them shows that the emerging digital entertainment economy is going to be radically different from today's mass market. If the 20th-century entertainment industry was about hits, the 21st will be equally about misses.

For too long we've been suffering the tyranny of lowest-common-denominator fare, subjected to brain-dead summer blockbusters and manufactured pop. Why? Economics. Many of our assumptions about popular taste are actually artifacts of poor supply-and-demand matching—a market response to inefficient distribution.

The main problem, if that's the word, is that we live in the physical world and, until recently, most of our entertainment media did, too. But that world puts two dramatic limitations on our entertainment.

The first is the need to find local audiences. An average movie theater will not show a film unless it can attract at least 1,500 people over a two-week run; that's essentially the rent for a screen. An average record store needs to sell at least two copies of a CD per year to make it worth carrying; that's the rent for a half inch of shelf space. And so on for DVD rental shops, videogame stores, booksellers, and newsstands.

In each case, retailers will carry only content that can generate sufficient demand to earn its keep. But each can pull only from a limited local population—perhaps a 10-mile radius for a typical movie theater, less than that for music and bookstores, and even less (just a mile or two) for video rental shops. It's not enough for a great documentary to have a potential national audience of half a million; what matters is how many it has in the northern part of Rockville, Maryland, and among the mall shoppers of Walnut Creek, California.

There is plenty of great entertainment with potentially large, even rapturous, national audiences that cannot clear that bar. For instance, *The Triplets of Belleville,* a critically acclaimed film that was nominated for the best animated feature Oscar this year, opened on just six screens nationwide. An even more striking example is the plight of Bollywood in America. Each year, India's film industry puts out more than 800 feature films. There are an estimated 1.7 million Indians in the US. Yet the top-rated (according to Amazon's Internet Movie Database) Hindi-language film, *Lagaan: Once Upon a Time in India,* opened on just two screens, and it was one of only a handful of Indian films to get any US distribution at all. In the tyranny of physical space, an audience too thinly spread is the same as no audience at all.

The other constraint of the physical world is physics itself. The radio spectrum can carry only so many stations, and a coaxial cable so many TV channels. And, of course, there are only 24 hours a day of programming. The curse of broadcast technologies is that they are profligate users of limited resources. The result is yet another instance of having to aggregate large audiences in one geographic area—another high bar, above which only a fraction of potential content rises.

The past century of entertainment has offered an easy solution to these constraints. Hits fill theaters, fly off shelves, and keep listeners and viewers from touching their dials and remotes. Nothing wrong with that; indeed, sociologists will tell you that hits are hard-wired into human psychology, the combinatorial effect of conformity and word of mouth. And to be sure, a healthy share of hits earn their place: Great songs, movies, and books attract big, broad audiences.

But most of us want more than just hits. Everyone's taste departs from the main-stream somewhere, and the more we explore alternatives, the more we're drawn to them. Unfortunately, in recent decades such alternatives have been pushed to the fringes by pumped-up marketing vehicles built to order by industries that desperately need them.

Hit-driven economics is a creation of an age without enough room to carry everything for everybody. Not enough shelf space for all the CDs, DVDs, and games produced. Not enough screens to show all the available movies. Not enough channels to broadcast all the TV programs, not enough radio waves to play all the music created, and not enough hours in the day to squeeze everything out through either of those sets of slots.

This is the world of scarcity. Now, with online distribution and retail, we are entering a world of abundance. And the differences are profound.

To see how, meet Robbie Vann-Adib, the CEO of Ecast, a digital jukebox company whose barroom players offer more than 150,000 tracks—and some surprising usage statistics. He hints at them with a question that visitors invariably get wrong: "What percentage of the top 10,000 titles in any online media store (Netflix, iTunes, Amazon, or any other) will rent or sell at least once a month?"

Most people guess 20 percent, and for good reason: We've been trained to think that way. The 80-20 rule, also known as Pareto's principle (after Vilfredo Pareto, an Italian economist who devised the concept in 1906), is all around us. Only 20 percent of major studio films will be hits. Same for TV shows, games, and mass-market books—20 percent all. The odds are even worse for major-label CDs, where fewer than 10 percent are profitable, according to the Recording Industry Association of America.

But the right answer, says Vann-Adib, is 99 percent. There is demand for nearly every one of those top 10,000 tracks. He sees it in his own jukebox statistics; each month, thousands of people put in their dollars for songs that no traditional jukebox anywhere has ever carried.

People get Vann-Adib's question wrong because the answer is counterintuitive in two ways. The first is we forget that the 20 percent rule in the entertainment industry is about *hits,* not sales of any sort. We're stuck in a hit-driven mindset—we think that if something isn't a hit, it won't make money and so won't return the cost of its production. We assume, in other words, that only hits deserve to exist. But Vann-Adib, like executives at iTunes, Amazon, and Netflix, has discovered that the "misses" usually make money, too. And because there are so many more of them, that money can add up quickly to a huge new market.

With no shelf space to pay for and, in the case of purely digital services like iTunes, no manufacturing costs and hardly any distribution fees, a miss sold is just another sale, with the same margins as a hit. A hit and a miss are on equal economic footing, both just entries in a database called up on demand, both equally worthy of being carried. Suddenly, popularity no longer has a monopoly on profitability.

The second reason for the wrong answer is that the industry has a poor sense of what people want. Indeed, we have a poor sense of what we want. We assume, for instance, that there is little demand for the stuff that isn't carried by Wal-Mart and other major retailers; if people wanted it, surely it would be sold. The rest, the bottom 80 percent, must be subcommercial at best.

But as egalitarian as Wal-Mart may seem, it is actually extraordinarily elitist. Wal-Mart must sell at least 100,000 copies of a CD to cover its retail overhead and make a sufficient profit; less than 1 percent of CDs do that kind of volume. What about the 60,000 people who would like to buy the latest Fountains of Wayne or Crystal Method album, or any other nonmainstream fare? They have to go somewhere else. Bookstores, the megaplex, radio, and network TV can be equally demanding. We equate mass market with quality and demand, when in fact it often just represents familiarity, savvy advertising, and broad if somewhat shallow appeal. What do we really want? We're only just discovering, but it clearly starts with *more.*

To get a sense of our true taste, unfiltered by the economics of scarcity, look at Rhapsody, a subscription-based streaming music service (owned by RealNetworks) that currently offers more than 735,000 tracks.

Chart Rhapsody's monthly statistics and you get a "power law" demand curve that looks much like any record store's, with huge appeal for the top tracks, tailing off quickly for less popular ones. But a really interesting thing happens once you dig below the top 40,000 tracks, which is about the amount of the fluid inventory (the albums carried that will eventually be sold) of the average real-world record store. Here, the Wal-Marts of the world go to zero—either they don't carry any more CDs, or the few potential local takers for such fringy fare never find it or never even enter the store.

The Rhapsody demand, however, keeps going. Not only is every one of Rhapsody's top 100,000 tracks streamed at least once each month, the same is true for its top 200,000, top 300,000, and top 400,000. As fast as Rhapsody adds tracks to its library, those songs find an audience, even if it's just a few people a month, somewhere in the country.

This is the Long Tail.

You can find everything out there on the Long Tail. There's the back catalog, older albums still fondly remembered by longtime fans or rediscovered by new ones. There are live tracks, B-sides, remixes, even (gasp) covers. There are niches by the thousands, genre within genre within genre: Imagine an entire Tower Records devoted to '80s hair bands or ambient dub. There are foreign bands, once priced out of reach in the Import aisle, and obscure bands on even more obscure labels, many of which don't have the distribution clout to get into Tower at all.

Oh sure, there's also a lot of crap. But there's a lot of crap hiding between the radio tracks on hit albums, too. People have to skip over it on CDs, but they can more easily avoid it online, since the collaborative filters typically won't steer you to it. Unlike the CD, where each crap track costs perhaps one-twelfth of a $15 album price, online it just sits harmlessly on some server, ignored in a market that sells by the song and evaluates tracks on their own merit.

What's really amazing about the Long Tail is the sheer size of it. Combine enough non-hits on the Long Tail and you've got a market bigger than the hits. Take books: The average Barnes & Noble carries 130,000 titles. Yet more than half of Amazon's book sales come from *outside* its top 130,000 titles. Consider the implication: If the Amazon statistics are any guide, the market for books that are not even sold in the average bookstore is larger than the market for those that are (see "Anatomy of the Long Tail"). In other words, the potential book market may be twice as big as it appears to be, if only we can get over the economics of scarcity. Venture capitalist and former music industry consultant Kevin Laws puts it this way: "The biggest money is in the smallest sales."

The same is true for all other aspects of the entertainment business, to one degree or another. Just compare online and offline businesses: The average Blockbuster carries fewer than 3,000 DVDs. Yet a fifth of Netflix rentals are outside its top 3,000 titles. Rhapsody streams more songs each month *beyond* its top 10,000 than it does its top 10,000. In each case, the market that lies outside the reach of the physical retailer is big and getting bigger.

When you think about it, most successful businesses on the Internet are about aggregating the Long Tail in one way or another. Google, for instance, makes most of its money off small advertisers (the long tail of advertising), and eBay is mostly tail as well—niche and one-off products. By overcoming the limitations of geography and scale, just as Rhapsody and Amazon have, Google and eBay have discovered new markets and expanded existing ones.

This is the power of the Long Tail. The companies at the vanguard of it are showing the way with three big lessons. Call them the new rules for the new entertainment economy.

Rule 1: Make everything available

If you love documentaries, Blockbuster is not for you. Nor is any other video store—there are too many documentaries, and they sell too poorly to justify stocking more than a few dozen of them on physical shelves. Instead, you'll want to join Netflix, which offers more than a thousand documentaries—because it can. Such profligacy is giving a boost to the documentary business; last year, Netflix accounted for half of all US rental revenue for *Capturing the Friedmans,* a documentary about a family destroyed by allegations of pedophilia.

Netflix CEO Reed Hastings, who's something of a documentary buff, took this new-found clout to PBS, which had produced *Daughter From Danang,* a documentary about the children of US soldiers and Vietnamese women. In 2002, the film was nominated for an Oscar and was named best documentary at Sundance, but PBS had no plans to release it on DVD.

Hastings offered to handle the manufacturing and distribution if PBS would make it available as a Netflix exclusive. Now *Daughter From Danang* consistently ranks in the top 15 on Netflix documentary charts. That amounts to a market of tens of thousands of documentary renters that did not otherwise exist.

There are any number of equally attractive genres and subgenres neglected by the traditional DVD channels: foreign films, anime, independent movies, British television dramas, old American TV sitcoms. These underserved markets make up a big chunk of Netflix rentals. Bollywood alone accounts for nearly 100,000 rentals each month. The availability of offbeat content drives new customers to Netflix—and anything that cuts the cost of customer acquisition is gold for a subscription business. Thus the company's first lesson: Embrace niches.

Netflix has made a good business out of what's unprofitable fare in movie theaters and video rental shops because it can aggregate dispersed audiences. It doesn't matter if the several thousand people who rent *Doctor Who* episodes each month are in one city or spread, one per town, across the country—the economics are the same to Netflix. It has, in short, broken the tyranny of physical space. What matters is not where customers are, or even how many of them are seeking a particular title, but only that some number of them exist, anywhere.

As a result, almost anything is worth offering on the off chance it will find a buyer. This is the opposite of the way the entertainment industry now thinks. Today, the decision about whether or when to release an old film on DVD is based on estimates of demand, availability of extras such as commentary and additional material, and marketing opportunities such as anniversaries, awards, and generational windows (Disney briefly rereleases its classics every 10 years or so as a new wave of kids come of age). It's a high bar, which is why only a fraction of movies ever made are available on DVD.

That model may make sense for the true classics, but it's way too much fuss for everything else. The Long Tail approach, by contrast, is to simply dump huge chunks of the archive onto bare-bones DVDs, without any extras or marketing. Call it the Silver Series and charge half the price. Same for independent films. This year, nearly 6,000 movies were submitted to the Sundance Film Festival. Of those, 255 were accepted, and just two dozen have been picked up for distribution; to see the others, you had to be there. Why not release all 255 on DVD each year as part of a discount Sundance Series? In a Long Tail economy, it's more expensive to evaluate than to release. Just do it!

The same is true for the music industry. It should be securing the rights to release all the titles in all the back catalogs as quickly as it can—thoughtlessly, automatically, and at industrial scale. (This is one of those rare moments where the world needs more lawyers, not fewer.) So too for videogames. Retro gaming, including simulators of classic game consoles that run on modern PCs, is a growing phenomenon driven by the nostalgia of the first joystick generation. Game publishers could release every title as a 99-cent download three years after its release—no support, no guarantees, no packaging. All this, of course, applies equally to books. Already, we're seeing a blurring of the line between in and out of print. Amazon and other networks of used booksellers have made it almost as easy to find and buy a second-hand book as it is a new one. By divorcing bookselling from geography, these networks create a liquid market at low volume, dramatically increasing both their own business and the overall demand for used books. Combine that with the rapidly dropping costs of print-on-demand technologies and it's clear why any book should always be available. Indeed, it is a fair bet that children today will grow up never knowing the meaning of out of print.

Rule 2: Cut the price in half. Now lower it.

Thanks to the success of Apple's iTunes, we now have a standard price for a downloaded track: 99 cents. But is it the right one?

Ask the labels and they'll tell you it's too low: Even though 99 cents per track works out to about the same price as a CD, most consumers just buy a track or two from an album online, rather than the full CD. In effect, online music has seen a return to the singles-driven business of the 1950s. So from a label perspective, consumers should pay more for the privilege of purchasing a la carte to compensate for the lost album revenue.

Ask consumers, on the other hand, and they'll tell you that 99 cents is too high. It is, for starters, 99 cents more than Kazaa. But piracy aside, 99 cents violates our innate sense of economic justice: If it clearly costs less for a record label to deliver a song online, with no packaging, manufacturing, distribution, or shelf space overheads, why shouldn't the price be less, too? Surprisingly enough, there's been little good economic analysis on what the right price for online music should be. The main reason for this is that pricing isn't set by the market today but by the record label demicartel. Record companies charge a wholesale price of around 65 cents per track, leaving little room for price experimentation by the retailers.

That wholesale price is set to roughly match the price of CDs, to avoid dreaded "channel conflict." The labels fear that if they price online music lower, their CD retailers (still the vast majority of the business) will revolt or, more likely, go out of business even more quickly than they already are. In either case, it would be a serious disruption of the status quo, which terrifies the already spooked record companies. No wonder they're doing price calculations with an eye on the downsides in their traditional CD business rather than the upside in their new online business.

But what if the record labels stopped playing defense? A brave new look at the economics of music would calculate what it really costs to simply put a song on an iTunes server and adjust pricing accordingly. The results are surprising.

Take away the unnecessary costs of the retail channel—CD manufacturing, distribution, and retail overheads. That leaves the costs of finding, making, and marketing music. Keep them as they are, to ensure that the people on the creative and label side of the business make as much as they currently do. For a popular album that sells 300,000 copies, the creative costs work out to about $7.50 per disc, or around 60 cents a track. Add to that the actual cost of delivering music online, which is mostly the cost of building and maintaining the online service rather than the negligible storage and bandwidth costs. Current price tag: around 17 cents a track. By this calculation, hit music is overpriced by 25 percent online—it should cost just 79 cents a track, reflecting the savings of digital delivery.

Putting channel conflict aside for the moment, if the incremental cost of making content that was originally produced for physical distribution available online is low, the price should be, too. Price according to digital costs, not physical ones. All this good news for consumers doesn't have to hurt the industry. When you lower prices, people tend to buy more. Last year, Rhapsody did an experiment in elastic demand that suggested it could be a lot more. For a brief period, the service offered tracks at 99 cents, 79 cents, and 49 cents. Although the 49-cent tracks were only half the price of the 99-cent tracks, Rhapsody sold three times as many of them.

Since the record companies still charged 65 cents a track—and Rhapsody paid another 8 cents per track to the copyright-holding publishers—Rhapsody lost money on that experiment (but, as the old joke goes, made it up in volume). Yet much of the content on the Long Tail is older material that has already made back its money (or been written off for failing to do so): music from bands that had little record company investment and was thus cheap to make, or live recordings, remixes, and other material that came at low cost.

Such "misses" cost less to make available than hits, so why not charge even less for them? Imagine if prices declined the further you went down the Tail, with popularity (the market) effectively dictating pricing. All it would take is for the labels to lower the whole-sale price for the vast majority of their content not in heavy rotation; even a two- or three-tiered pricing structure could work wonders. And because so much of that content is not available in record stores, the risk of channel conflict is greatly diminished. The lesson: Pull consumers down the tail with lower prices.

How low should the labels go? The answer comes by examining the psychology of the music consumer. The choice facing fans is not how many songs to buy from iTunes and Rhapsody, but how many songs to buy rather than download for free from Kazaa and other peer-to-peer networks. Intuitively, consumers know that free music is not really free: Aside from any legal risks, it's a time-consuming hassle to build a collection that way. Labeling is inconsistent, quality varies, and an estimated 30 percent of tracks are defective in one way or another. As Steve Jobs put it at the iTunes Music Store launch, you may save a little money downloading from Kazaa, but "you're working for under minimum wage." And what's true for music is doubly true for movies and games, where the quality of pirated products can be even more dismal, viruses are a risk, and downloads take so much longer.

So free has a cost: the psychological value of convenience. This is the "not worth it" moment where the wallet opens. The exact amount is an impossible calculus involving the bank balance of the average college student multiplied by their available free time. But imagine that for music, at least, it's around 20 cents a track. That, in effect, is the dividing line between the commercial world of the Long Tail and the underground. Both worlds will continue to exist in parallel, but it's crucial for Long Tail thinkers to exploit the opportunities between 20 and 99 cents to maximize their share. By offering fair pricing, ease of use, and consistent quality, you can compete with free.

Perhaps the best way to do that is to stop charging for individual tracks at all. Danny Stein, whose private equity firm owns eMusic, thinks the future of the business is to move away from the ownership model entirely. With ubiquitous broadband, both wired and wireless, more consumers will turn to the celestial jukebox of music services that offer every track ever made, playable on demand. Some of those tracks will be free to listeners and advertising-supported, like radio. Others, like eMusic and Rhapsody, will be subscription services. Today, digital music economics are dominated by the iPod, with its notion of a paid-up library of personal tracks. But as the networks improve, the comparative economic advantages of unlimited streamed music, either financed by advertising or a flat fee (infinite choice for $9.99 a month), may shift the market that way. And drive another nail in the coffin of the retail music model.

Rule 3: Help me find it

In 1997, an entrepreneur named Michael Robertson started what looked like a classic Long Tail business. Called MP3.com, it let anyone upload music files that would be available to all. The idea was the service would bypass the record labels, allowing artists to connect directly to listeners. MP3.com would make its money in fees paid by bands to have their music promoted on the site. The tyranny of the labels would be broken, and a thousand flowers would bloom.

Putting aside the fact that many people actually used the service to illegally upload and share commercial tracks, leading the labels to sue MP3.com, the model failed at its intended purpose, too. Struggling bands did not, as a rule, find new audiences, and independent music was not transformed. Indeed, MP3.com got a reputation for being exactly what it was: an undifferentiated mass of mostly bad music that deserved its obscurity.

The problem with MP3.com was that it was *only* Long Tail. It didn't have license agreements with the labels to offer mainstream fare or much popular commercial music at all. Therefore, there was no familiar point of entry for consumers, no known quantity from which further exploring could begin.

Offering only hits is no better. Think of the struggling video-on-demand services of the cable companies. Or think of Movielink, the feeble video download service run by the studios. Due to overcontrolling providers and high costs, they suffer from limited content: in most cases just a few hundred recent releases. There's not enough choice to change consumer behavior, to become a real force in the entertainment economy.

By contrast, the success of Netflix, Amazon, and the commercial music services shows that you need *both* ends of the curve. Their huge libraries of less-mainstream fare set them apart, but hits still matter in attracting consumers in the first place. Great Long Tail businesses can then guide consumers further afield by following the contours of their likes and dislikes, easing their exploration of the unknown.

For instance, the front screen of Rhapsody features Britney Spears, unsurprisingly. Next to the listings of her work is a box of "similar artists." Among them is Pink. If you click on that and are pleased with what you hear, you may do the same for Pink's similar artists, which include No Doubt. And on No Doubt's page, the list includes a few "followers" and "influencers," the last of which includes the Selecter, a 1980s ska band from Coventry, England. In three clicks, Rhapsody may have enticed a Britney Spears fan to try an album that can hardly be found in a record store.

Rhapsody does this with a combination of human editors and genre guides. But Netflix, where 60 percent of rentals come from recommendations, and Amazon do this with collaborative filtering, which uses the browsing and purchasing patterns of users to guide those who follow them ("Customers who bought this also bought . . ."). In each, the aim is the same: Use recommendations to drive demand down the Long Tail.

This is the difference between push and pull, between broadcast and personalized taste. Long Tail business can treat consumers as individuals, offering mass customization as an alternative to mass-market fare.

The advantages are spread widely. For the entertainment industry itself, recommendations are a remarkably efficient form of marketing, allowing smaller films and less-mainstream music to find an audience. For consumers, the improved signal-to-noise ratio that comes from following a good recommendation encourages exploration and can reawaken a passion for music and film, potentially creating a far larger entertainment market overall. (The average Netflix customer rents seven DVDs a month, three times the rate at brick-and-mortar stores.) And the cultural benefit of all of this is much more diversity, reversing the blanding effects of a century of distribution scarcity and ending the tyranny of the hit. Such is the power of the Long Tail. Its time has come.

READING WRITING

This Text: Reading

1. What is Anderson's argument?
2. How much of what he observes do you see in your own consumption of culture? Which part of the long tail do you do most of your consuming?
3. Is there any form of culture do you think is not covered by his argument?

Your Text: Writing

1. Write a short paper about your collection of music. Where do most of your songs and CDs fit on the tail? (You can check by seeing their popularity on Amazon.)
2. Try to find the end of the longest tail on Amazon. What is the least popular book? Why do you think it does not get buyers?

Advertising and People of Color

Clint C. Wilson and Felix Gutierrez

By giving semiotic readings of some disturbing advertisements, Wilson and Gutierrez demonstrate how people of color and stereotypes about ethnicities have been exploited to sell various items (1995). As you read, pay attention to how the authors blend research and their own interpretation of visual texts.

Editor's Note: Also, as we mention in "Reading an Advertisement" in Chapter One, it is often difficult to obtain permission to reprint advertisements. As it turns out, we were denied permission to print all three ads that appear in the original version of this essay—most likely because companies have become more sensitive to the personal and legal ramifications of racial stereotyping. In one ad for Cream of Wheat, Rastus, a black servant in a chef's cap, holds a blackboard containing information about Cream of Wheat written in African American dialect. The other, an ad for Crown Royal aimed at Hispanic audiences, shows five clearly wealthy, well-dressed Latinos and Latinas drinking Crown Royal at what appears to be a fancy birthday party. The text for the ad, "Comparta sus riquezas" ("Share the Wealth") is in Spanish. Finally, though AT&T did deny us permission to print the original ad, they did agree to let us run an updated one. The original shows a young Chinese girl holding a phone. Appearing in Chinese newspapers in the United States, the ad ran only in Chinese.

GIVEN THE SOCIAL AND LEGAL RESTRICTIONS on the participation of racial minorities in the society of the United States during much of this country's history, it is not hard to see how the desire to cater to the perceived views of the mass audience desired by advertisers resulted in entertainment and news content that largely ignored people of color, treated them stereotypically when they were recognized, and largely avoided grappling with such issues as segregation, discriminatory immigration laws, land rights, and other controversial issues that affected certain minority groups more than they did the White majority. Although the entertainment and editorial portrayal of non-Whites is amply analyzed in other chapters of this book, it is important to recognize that those portrayals were, to a large extent, supported by a system of advertising that required the media to cater to the perceived attitudes and prejudices of the White majority and that also reinforced such images in its own commercial messages. For years advertisers in the United States reflected the place of non-Whites in the social fabric of the nation either by ignoring them or, when they were included in advertisements for the mass audience, processing and presenting them in a way that would make them palatable salespersons for the products being advertised. These processed portrayals largely mirrored the stereotypic images of minorities in the entertainment media that, in turn, were designed to reflect the perceived values and norms of the White majority. In this way, non-White portrayals in advertising paralleled and reinforced their entertainment and journalistic images in the media.

The history of advertising in the United States is replete with characterizations that, like the Frito Bandito, responded to and reinforced the preconceived image that many White Americans apparently had of Blacks, Latinos, Asians, and Native Americans. Over the years advertisers have employed Latin spitfires like Chiquita Banana, Black mammies like Aunt Jemima, and noble savages like the Santa Fe Railroad's Super Chief to pitch their products to a predominately White mass audience of consumers. In 1984 the Balch Institute for Ethnic Studies in Philadelphia sponsored an exhibit of more than 300 examples of racial and ethnic images used by corporations in magazines, posters, trade cards, and storyboards. In an interview with the advertising trade magazine *Advertising Age,* institute director Mark Stolarik quoted the catalog for the exhibit, which capsulized the evolution of images of people of color and how they have changed.

"Some of these advertisements were based on stereotypes of various ethnic groups. In the early years, they were usually crude and condescending images that appealed to largely Anglo-American audiences who found it difficult to reconcile their own visions of beauty, order and behavior with that of non-Anglo-Americans," said Stolarik. "Later, these images were softened because of complaints from the ethnic groups involved and the growing sophistication of the advertising industry."[1]

The advertising examples in the exhibit include positive White ethnic stereotypes, such as the wholesome and pure image of Quakers in an early Quaker Oats advertisement and the cleanliness of the Dutch in a turn-of-the century advertisement for Colgate soaps. But they also featured a late 19th century advertisement showing an Irish matron threatening to hit her husband over the head with a rolling pin because he didn't smoke the right brand of tobacco. Like Quaker Oats, some products even incorporated a stereotypical image on the package or product line being advertised.

"Lawsee! Folks sho' whoops with joy over AUNT JEMIMA PANCAKES," shouted a bandanna-wearing Black mammy in a magazine advertisement for Aunt Jemima pancake mix, which featured a plump Aunt Jemima on the box. Over the years, Aunt Jemima has lost some weight, but the stereotyped face of the Black servant continues to be featured on the box. Earlier advertisements for Cream of Wheat featured Rastus, the Black servant on the box, in a series of magazine cartoons with a group of cute but ill-dressed Black children. Some of the advertisements played on stereotypes ridiculing Blacks, such as an advertisement in which a Black school teacher standing behind a makeshift lectern made out of a boldly lettered Cream of Wheat box, asks the class "How do you spell Cream of Wheat?" Others appeared to promote racial integration, such as a magazine advertisement captioned "Putting it down in Black and White," which showed Rastus serving bowls of the breakfast cereal to Black and White youngsters sitting at the same table.

---

[1]"Using Ethnic Images," p. 9.

Racial imagery was also integrated into the naming of trains by the Santa Fe railroad, which named one of its passenger lines the Super Chief and featured highly detailed portraits of the noble Indian in promoting its service through the Southwestern United States. In another series of advertisements, the railroad used cartoons of Native American children to show the service and sights passengers could expect when they traveled the Santa Fe line.

These and other portrayals catered to the mass audience mentality by either neutralizing or making humor of the negative perceptions that many Whites may have had of racial minorities. The advertising images, rather than showing people of color as they really were, portrayed them as filtered through Anglo eyes. This presented an out-of-focus image of racial minorities, but one that was palatable, and even persuasive, to the White majority to which it was directed. In the mid-1960s Black civil rights groups targeted the advertising industry for special attention, protesting both the lack of integrated advertisements including Blacks and the stereotyped images that the advertisers continued to use. The effort, accompanied by support from federal officials, resulted in the overnight inclusion of Blacks as models in television advertising in 1967 and a downplaying of the images that many Blacks found objectionable.

"Black America is becoming visible in America's biggest national advertising medium," reported the *New York Times* in 1968. "Not in a big way yet, but it is a beginning and men in high places give assurances that there will be a lot more visibility."[2]

But the advertising industry did not generalize the concerns of Blacks, or the concessions made in response to them, to other groups. At the same time that some Black concerns were being addressed with integrated advertising, other groups were being ignored or singled out for continued stereotyped treatment in such commercials as those featuring the Frito Bandito.

Among the Latino advertising stereotypes cited in a 1969 article[3] by sociologist Tomás Martínez were commercials for Granny Goose chips featuring fat gun-toting Mexicans, an advertisement for Arrid underarm deodorant showing a dusty Mexican bandito spraying his underarms after a hard ride as the announcer intones, "If it works for him it will work for you," and a magazine advertisement featuring a stereotypical Mexican sleeping under his sombrero as he leans against a Philco television set. Especially offensive to Martínez was a Liggett & Meyers commercial for L&M cigarettes that featured Paco, a lazy Latino who never "feenishes" anything, not even the revolution he is supposed to be fighting. In response to a letter complaining about the commercial, the director of public relations for the tobacco firm defended the commercial's use of Latino stereotypes.

"'Paco' is a warm, sympathetic and lovable character with whom most of us can identify because he has a little of all of us in him, that is, our tendency to procrastinate at times," wrote the Liggett & Meyers executive. "He seeks to escape the violence of war and to enjoy the pleasure of the moment, in this case, the good flavor of an L&M cigarette."[4] Although the company spokesman claimed that the character had been tested without negative reactions from Latinos (a similar claim was made by Frito-Lay regarding the Frito Bandito), Martínez roundly criticized the advertising images and contrasted them to what he saw as the gains Blacks were then making in the advertising field.

---

[2]Cited in Philip H. Dougherty, "Frequency of Blacks in TV Ads," *New York Times*, May 27, 1982, p. D19.
[3]Martìnez, "How Advertisers Promote," p. 10.
[4]Martìnez, "How Advertisers Promote," p. 11.

"Today, no major advertiser would attempt to display a black man or woman over the media in a prejudiced, stereotyped fashion," Martínez wrote.

Complaints would be forthcoming from black associations and perhaps the FCC. Yet, these same advertisers, who dare not show "step'n fetch it" characters, uninhibitedly depict a Mexican counterpart, with additional traits of stinking and stealing. Perhaps the white hatred for blacks, which cannot find adequate expression in today's ads, is being transferred upon their brown brothers.[5]

In 1970 a Brown Position Paper prepared by Latino media activists Armando Rendón and Domingo Nick Reyes charged that the media had transferred the negative stereotypes it once reserved for Blacks to Latinos, who had become "the media's new nigger."[6] The protests of Latinos soon made the nation's advertisers more conscious of the portrayals that Latinos found offensive. But, as in the case of the Blacks, the advertising industry failed to apply the lessons learned from one group to other racial minorities.

Although national advertisers withdrew much of the advertising that negatively stereotyped Blacks and Latinos, sometimes replacing them with affluent, successful images that were as far removed from reality as the negative portrayals of the past, the advances made by those groups were not shared with Native Americans and Asians. Native Americans' names and images, no longer depicted either as the noble savage or as cute cartoon characters, have all but disappeared from broadcast commercials and print advertising. The major exceptions are advertising for automobiles and trucks that bear names such as Pontiac, Dakota, and Navajo and sports teams with racial nicknames such as the Kansas City Chiefs, Washington Redskins, Florida State University Seminoles, Atlanta Braves, and Cleveland Indians. Native Americans and others have protested these racial team names and images, as well as the pseudo-Native American pageantry and souvenirs that accompany many of them but with no success in getting them changed.

Asians, particularly Japanese, continue to be dealt more than their share of commercials depicting them in stereotypes that cater to the fears and stereotypes of White America. As was the case with Blacks and Latinos, it took organized protests from Asian American groups to get the message across to the corporations and their advertising agencies. In the mid-1970s, a Southern California supermarket chain agreed to remove a television campaign in which a young Asian karate-chopped his way down the store's aisles cutting prices. Nationally, several firms whose industries have been hard-hit by Japanese imports fought back through commercials, if not in the quality or prices of their products. One automobile company featured an Asian family carefully looking over a new car and commenting on its attributes in heavily accented English. Only after they bought it did they learn it was made in the United States, not Japan. Another automobile company that markets cars manufactured in Japan under an English-language name showed a parking lot attendant opening the doors of the car, only to find the car speaking to him in Japanese. For several years Sylvania television ran a commercial boasting that its television picture had repeatedly been selected over competing brands as an off-screen voice with a Japanese accent repeatedly asked, "What about Sony?" When the announcer responded that the Sylvania picture had also been selected over Sony's, the off-screen voice ran off shouting what sounded like a string of Japanese expletives. A 1982 *Newsweek* article observed that "attacking

---

[5]Martìnez, "How Advertisers Promote," pp. 9–10.
[6]Domingo Nick Reyes and Armando Rendòn, *Chicanos and the Mass Media* (Washington, DC: The National Mexican American Anti-Defamation Committee, 1971).

Japan has become something of a fashion in corporate ads" because of resentment over Japanese trade policies and sales of Japanese products in the United States, but quoted Motorola's advertising manager as saying, "We've been as careful as we can be" not to be racially offensive.[7]

But many of the television and print advertisements featuring Asians featured images that were racially insensitive, if not offensive. A commercial for a laundry product featured a Chinese family that used an "ancient Chinese laundry secret" to get their customer's clothes clean. Naturally, the Chinese secret turned out to be the packaged product paying for the advertisement. Companies pitching everything from pantyhose to airlines featured Asian women coiffed and costumed as seductive China dolls or exotic Polynesian natives to pitch and promote their products, some of them cast in Asian settings and others attentively caring for the needs of the Anglo men in the advertisement. One airline boasted that those who flew with it would be under the care of the Singapore Girl.

Asian women appearing in commercials were often featured as China dolls with the small, darkened eyes, straight hair with bangs, and a narrow, slit skirt. Another common portrayal featured the exotic, tropical Pacific Islands look, complete with flowers in the hair, a sarong or grass skirt, and shell ornament. Asian women hoping to become models sometimes found that they must conform to these stereotypes or lose assignments. Leslie Kawai, the 1981 Tournament of Roses Queen, was told to cut her hair with bangs by hairstylists when she auditioned for a beer advertisement. When she refused, the beer company decided to hire another model with shorter hair cut in bangs.[8]

The lack of a sizable Asian community, or market, in the United States was earlier cited as the reason that Asians are still stereotyped in advertising and, except for children's advertising, are rarely presented in integrated settings. The growth rate and income of Asians living in the United States in the 1980s and 1990s, however, reinforced the economic potential of Asian Americans to overcome the stereotyping and lack of visibility that Blacks and Latinos challenged with some success. By the mid-1980s there were a few signs that advertising was beginning to integrate Asian Americans into crossover advertisements that, like the Tostitos campaign, were designed to have a broad appeal. In one commercial, television actor Robert Ito was featured telling how he loves to call his relatives in Japan because the calls make them think that he is rich, as well as successful, in the United States. Of course, he adds, it is only because the rates of his long distance carrier were so low that he was able to call Japan so often.

In the 1970s mass audience advertising in the United States became more racially integrated than at any time in the nation's history. Blacks, and to a much lesser extent Latinos and Asians, could be seen in television commercials spread across the broadcast week and in major magazines. In fact, the advertisements on network television often appeared to be more fully integrated than the television programs they supported. Like television, general circulation magazines also experienced an increase in the use of Blacks, although studies of both media showed that most of the percentage increase had come by the early 1970s. By the early 1970s the percentage of prime-time television commercials featuring Blacks had apparently leveled off at about 10%. Blacks were featured in between only 2% and 3% of

---

[7]Joseph Treen, "Madison Ave. vs. Japan, Inc.," *Newsweek* (April 12, 1982), p. 69.
[8]Ada Kan, *Asian Models in the Media*, Unpublished term paper, Journalism 466: Minority and the Media, University of Southern California, December 14, 1983, p. 5.

magazine advertisements as late as 1978. That percentage, however small, was a sharp increase from the 0.06% of news magazine advertisements reported in 1960.[9]

The gains were also socially significant, because they demonstrated that Blacks could be integrated into advertisements without triggering a White backlash among potential customers in the White majority. Both sales figures and research conducted since the late 1960s have shown that the integration of Black models into television and print advertising does not adversely affect sales or the image of the product. Instead, a study by the American Newspaper Publishers Association showed, the most important influences on sales were the merchandise and the advertisement itself. In fact, while triggering no adverse effect among the majority of Whites, integrated advertisements were found to be useful in swaying Black consumers, who responded favorably to positive Black role models in print advertisements.[10] Studies conducted in the early 1970s also showed that White consumers did not respond negatively to advertising featuring Black models, although their response was more often neutral than positive.[11] One 1972 study examining White backlash, however, did show that an advertisement prominently featuring darker-skinned Blacks was less acceptable to Whites than those featuring lighter-skinned Blacks as background models.[12] Perhaps such findings help explain why research conducted later in the 1970s revealed that, for the most part, Blacks appearing in magazine and television advertisements were often featured as part of an integrated group.[13]

Although research findings have shown that integrated advertisements do not adversely affect sales, the percentage of Blacks and other minorities in general audience advertising did not increase significantly after the numerical gains made through the mid-1970s. Those minorities who did appear in advertisements were often depicted in upscale or integrated settings, an image that the Balch Institute's Stolarik criticized as taking advertising "too far in the other direction and created stereotypes of 'successful' ethnic group members that are as unrealistic as those of the past."[14] Equally unwise, from a business sense, was the low numbers of Blacks appearing in advertisements.

"Advertisers and their ad agencies must evaluate the direct economic consequences of alternative strategies on the firm. If it is believed that the presence of Black models in advertisements decreases the effectiveness of advertising messages, only token numbers of Black models will be used," wrote marketing professor Lawrence Soley at the conclusion of a 1983 study.

"Previous studies have found that advertisements portraying Black models do not elicit negative affective or conative responses from consumers. . . . Given the consistency of the research findings, more Blacks should be portrayed in advertisements. If Blacks continue to be under-represented in advertising portrayals, it can be said that this is an indication of prejudice on the part of the advertising industry, not consumers."[15]

---

[9]Studies on increase of Blacks in magazine and television commercials cited in James D. Culley and Rex Bennett, "Selling Blacks, Selling Women," *Journal of Communication* (Autumn 1976, Vol. 26, No. 4), pp. 160–174; Lawrence Soley, "The Effect of Black Models on Magazine Ad Readership," *Journalism Quarterly* (Winter 1983, Vol. 60, No. 4), p. 686; and Leonard N. Reid and Bruce G. Vanden Bergh, "Blacks in Introductory Ads," *Journalism Quarterly* (Autumn 1980, Vol. 57, No. 3), pp. 485–486.

[10]Cited in D. Parke Gibson, *$70 Billion in the Black* (New York: Macmillan, 1979), pp. 83–84.

[11]Laboratory studies on White reactions to Blacks in advertising cited in Soley, "The Effect of Black Models," pp. 585–587.

[12]Carl E. Block, "White Backlash to Negro Ads: Fact or Fantasy?" *Journalism Quarterly* (Autumn 1980, Vol. 49, No. 2), pp. 258–262.

[13]James D. Culley and Rex Bennett, "Selling Blacks, Selling Women."

[14]"Using Ethnic Images," p. 9.

[15]Soley, *The Effect of Black Models*, p. 690.

READING WRITING

This Text: Reading

1. It's likely that you found the descriptions of some of these ads shocking. What do these advertisements tell you about how America and Americans used to see people of color?
2. This is one of the few essays that examine how all people of color have been represented. Were you surprised to read about images of Hispanics and American Indians? If so, why?
3. What is the argument of the essay?

Your Text: Writing

1. With some research, you should be able to track down some images of a similarly disturbing nature. What is the semiotic setting of these ads? Write a paper in which you analyze the ads from today's perspective but are mindful of the ad as being a cultural document.
2. Write an essay on advertising and white people. Based on ads, what assumptions can we make about Anglos?
3. Write a comparative paper examining what Wilson and Gutierrez say about race with a similar essay from the Race chapter.

Hanes Her Way

Student Essay

Brittany Gray

Brittany Gray was a freshman at Virginia Commonwealth University in Richmond when she wrote this analysis of a "Hanes Her Way" ad in 2001. In her analysis of an ad piece, Gray reads her ad through the lens of the familiar vs. fantasy.

IT KNOWS WHO YOU ARE. It knows what you want. It gets into your psyche, and then—onto your television, your computer screen, your newspapers and your magazines. It is an advertisement, folks, and it's studying every little move you make, be it in the grocery store or the outlet mall. These advertisement executives know just what the consumer needs to hear to convince him or her to buy the product. Grocery stores even consult such advertisement firms on matters such as just how to set up the store in order to maximize consumer purchase. It has been watching, and it knows just what mood to set to get into the head of the consumer, and just how to set the scene.

This particular scene is a mild, relaxed morning. The sun streams in through the windows. The lighting is a tranquil yellow, and the background music is "Fade Into You" by Mazzy Star, a soft and haunting ballad which perfectly complements the temperate setting. Through a doorway a man watches a woman who is wearing a white t-shirt and white cotton underwear as she makes a bed, snapping a sheet into the air and watching it drift back down onto the bed in slow motion. Then a voiceover begins. The man talks over the music about how when they were dating, his girlfriend used to wear such tiny, sexy underwear. Then he says that now that they are married she just wears old worn cotton underwear by Hanes. He goes on to say that there is something comforting about the cotton underwear.

He says he loves when he opens the laundry hamper and sees the worn out underwear in there waiting to go into the wash, because it reminds him of his mother and his childhood. The commercial then fades out on the Hanes trademark.

The ethical appeal in this commercial is particularly strong. For starters, the brand name of Hanes goes back a long way and has been trusted for years. There is nothing more comforting about buying a product than knowing that millions of people aside from oneself also trust the product. Also, the people in the ad seem to trust the product. It seems that trust and stability are the qualities that Hanes wants the customer to attribute to their underwear.

The pathos in this commercial was the strongest of all the appeals. The fact that, first of all, the couple is married, and also that the man seems to love and accept his wife so openly plays a part in the emotional appeal. It is not often that couples on television are married anymore, and when they are, their lives and marital stress are often the topic of comedy. This couple is not only happily married, but obviously has been married for a while as well, given the fact that the wife has had time to change her style of underwear *and* the fact that her Hanes Her Way cotton briefs are well worn.

Another aspect of the pathos is the setting of the scene. The tranquility of the lighting, the airy atmosphere consisting of so much white cotton and linen, and the relaxing background music all play a role in the manipulation of emotion. The way the man stands there with such a nostalgic look on his face, watching his wife and speaking about her so wistfully is meant to really touch something inside—and it does. Not only that, but the man still finds his wife beautiful, even after so many years, and even after the underwear that he initially found so attractive is gone. The entire ad evokes a sense of tranquility and comfort, seeming to say, "our product will fulfill you just the way these people are fulfilled."

The appeal to logic in this ad was for the most part absent, aside from one thing. After all, there is no real logic to a man liking his wife's underwear, nor is there any rhyme or reason behind the comfort that seeing the underwear lying in the hamper brings him, reminding him of his childhood and his mother. Hanes underwear does not make the sun come out in the morning, and it certainly won't find someone a spouse. The logic of the commercial, as well as the fact of the matter, is that Hanes underwear is comfortable—especially Hanes Her Way white cotton briefs.

The audience targeted in this commercial was without question middle-class women, probably aged 12 and up. Most men do not get misty-eyed hearing pretty music, and they are not particularly struck watching a man speak so fondly of his wife. However, women thrive on such things. Every woman loves to see a man talk about his wife as though she were the only woman on the earth, because it is such a rare occurrence.

That is not the only aspect of the ad directed at women, however. The lighting in the commercial, paired with the beautiful sunny morning, as well as the crisp white linens shown throughout the commercial, are all aimed at women in middle-class families. Women love to see that level of comfort and cleanliness within a home, as it all touches on a woman's romantic, idealistic side. Also, the fact that the couple and their home is so completely average shows that Hanes is for average, normal people. Everyone wants to feel that what they do is normal and accepted, especially women trying to run a home. It is one less thing to worry about, one less thing that can be criticized when it comes to a woman's running of her home. It also shows that the happiness of the couple is not out of reach—they are just like every other working class American couple.

These audience clinchers are not entirely in opposition to the ones used in men's underwear commercials. Many men's underwear commercials portray scenes containing rumpled beds in the morning, and fresh white linen. Underwear commercials in general seem to abound in their portrayal of morning sunrises and beautiful people making beds. In men's commercials, though, it seems that there is always that bittersweet touch of masculinity. There is constantly some muscular role model, doing the types of things that strong, ideal men should do. The man in the commercial always seems to do the same stereotyped things. He gives the dog a bath, he plays with the kids. He does the dishes with a smile, pausing to toss a handful of bubbles at his adoring wife. He goes jogging in the morning before his coffee. He shows his son how to throw a baseball just right, and of course he doesn't neglect his daughter—he tosses her into the air, and playfully dodges her blows during a pillow fight. And of course, he feels perfectly comfortable sitting around in nothing but his white cotton briefs.

Women on the other hand don't need examples of femininity. They know how to be women, and showing what the typical woman does in a day would be cheesy and clichéd. Just show a woman a good old fashioned love scene and most likely she's sold.

This commercial probably shouldn't appeal to me so strongly. It is exactly like most other commercials for women's underwear I have seen. They all have the same basic elements: white linen, sunny mornings, happy families, and beautiful, smiling people. I'm not sure if I can place my finger on exactly what made this commercial stand out for me. I think it was the combination of the music and the couple. I've never heard music like that in an underwear commercial. The music used is normally that sunny, get-up-and-go type of music, but this commercial utilized the softer sound of Mazzy Star. The voiceover and the utilization of romance really struck me too. Though the ad was not particularly original, I still felt that it was a beautifully done commercial.

The ethos of this commercial was definitely strong. The name of Hanes is one of the most trusted in underwear, and the advertisers used the stability of the marital relationship to illustrate this. However, the pathos was the most outstanding of the appeals in this ad. The fact that the underwear was made by Hanes was made known, as well as the reasons why Hanes should be trusted. However, the vivid sensory imagery in this commercial which made it so pleasing to the eye and such a joy to watch rules over the ethical appeal. A sunny morning means much more to me personally than the comfort of knowing that I'm wearing sturdy underwear, which is a comfort that is forgotten soon after putting the underwear on. A morning as beautiful as the one on TV is not commonly seen, nor is a couple more obviously in love. It is simple joys such as these that the commercial strikes at, and the joys seem to overpower the main ethical and logical appeal—that Hanes makes good underwear.

READING **WRITING**

This Text: Reading

1. What qualities of the advertising does Gray identify as worthy of discussion? If you have seen the ad, do you agree with her emphasis?
2. Have you purchased underwear based on commercials? Where do you think your influences to purchase come from?
3. In what ways do the home generally and bedroom specifically serve as a sign? What products are most appropriate for this approach? Can you think of other places that serve similar purposes?

Your Text: Writing

1. Perform a similar sign analysis using an advertisement that uses another familiar place (a front lawn, an office, sports field, etc.). What about the place's familiarity is part of the appeal?

2. Write a paper discussing the presence of fantasy and familiarity in a typical advertisement. What types of ads rely more on fantasy? Which on familiarity?

3. Examine the types of intimate relationships portrayed in advertisements. Write a paper examining how advertisers use those relationships to appeal to their target audience.

Weasel Words

William Lutz

In his classic essay on words in advertising, taken from his book Doublespeak *(1989), William Lutz, a professor of English at Rutgers University, points out code words that advertisers use to make false claims about their products.*

ONE PROBLEM ADVERTISERS HAVE when they try to convince you that the product they are pushing is really different from other, similar products is that their claims are subject to some laws. Not a lot of laws, but there are some designed to prevent fraudulent or untruthful claims in advertising. Even during the happy years of nonregulation under President Ronald Reagan, the FTC did crack down on the more blatant abuses in advertising claims. Generally speaking, advertisers have to be careful in what they say in their ads, in the claims they make for the products they advertise. Parity claims are safe because they are legal and supported by a number of court decisions. But beyond parity claims there are weasel words.

Advertisers use weasel words to appear to be making a claim for a product when in fact they are making no claim at all. Weasel words get their name from the way weasels eat the eggs they find in the nests of other animals. A weasel will make a small hole in the egg, suck out the insides, then place the egg back in the nest. Only when the egg is examined closely is it found to be hollow. That's the way it is with weasel words in advertising: Examine weasel words closely and you'll find that they're as hollow as any egg sucked by a weasel. Weasel words appear to say one thing when in fact they say the opposite, or nothing at all.

"Help"—The Number One Weasel Word

The biggest weasel word used in advertising doublespeak is "help." Now "help" only means to aid or assist, nothing more. It does not mean to conquer, stop, eliminate, solve, heal, cure, or anything else. But once the ad says "help," it can say just about anything after that because "help" qualifies everything coming after it. The trick is that the claim that comes after the weasel word is usually so strong and so dramatic that you forget the word "help" and concentrate only on the dramatic claim. You read into the ad a message that the ad does not contain. More importantly, the advertiser is not responsible for the claim that you read into the ad, even though the advertiser wrote the ad so you would read that claim into it.

The next time you see an ad for a cold medicine that promises that it "helps relieve cold symptoms fast," don't rush out to buy it. Ask yourself what this claim is really saying. Remember, "helps" means only that the medicine will aid or assist. What will it aid or assist in doing? Why, "relieve" your cold "symptoms." "Relieve" only means to ease, alleviate, or mitigate, not to stop, end, or cure. Nor does the claim say how much relieving this medicine will do. Nowhere does this ad claim it will cure anything. In fact, the ad doesn't even claim it will *do* anything at all. The ad only claims that it will aid in relieving (not curing) your cold symptoms, which are probably a runny nose, watery eyes, and a headache. In other words, this medicine probably contains a standard decongestant and some aspirin. By the way, what does "fast" mean? Ten minutes, one hour, one day? What is fast to one person can be very slow to another. Fast is another weasel word.

Ad claims using "help" are among the most popular ads. One says, "Helps keep you young looking," but then a lot of things will help keep you young looking, including exercise, rest, good nutrition, and a facelift. More importantly, this ad doesn't say the product will keep you young, only "young *looking.*" Someone may look young to one person and old to another.

A toothpaste ad says, "Helps prevent cavities," but it doesn't say it will actually prevent cavities. Brushing your teeth regularly, avoiding sugars in foods, and flossing daily will also help prevent cavities. A liquid cleaner ad says, "Helps keep your home germ free," but it doesn't say it actually kills germs, nor does it even specify which germs it might kill.

"Help" is such a useful weasel word that it is often combined with other action-verb weasel words such as "fight" and "control." Consider the claim, "Helps control dandruff symptoms with regular use." What does it really say? It will assist in controlling (not eliminating, stopping, ending, or curing) the *symptoms* of dandruff, not the cause of dandruff nor the dandruff itself. What are the symptoms of dandruff? The ad deliberately leaves that undefined, but assume that the symptoms referred to in the ad are the flaking and itching commonly associated with dandruff. But just shampooing with *any* shampoo will temporarily eliminate these symptoms, so this shampoo isn't any different from any other. Finally, in order to benefit from this product, you must use it regularly. What is "regular use"—daily, weekly, hourly? Using another shampoo "regularly" will have the same effect. Nowhere does this advertising claim say this particular shampoo stops, eliminates, or cures dandruff. In fact, this claim says nothing at all, thanks to all the weasel words.

Look at ads in magazines and newspapers, listen to ads on radio and television, and you'll find the word "help" in ads for all kinds of products. How often do you read or hear such phrases as "helps stop . . . ," "helps overcome . . . ," "helps eliminate . . . ," "helps you feel . . . ," or "helps you look . . ."? If you start looking for this weasel word in advertising, you'll be amazed at how often it occurs. Analyze the claims in the ads using "help," and you will discover that these ads are really saying nothing.

There are plenty of other weasel words used in advertising. In fact, there are so many that to list them all would fill the rest of this book. But, in order to identify the doublespeak of advertising and understand the real meaning of an ad, you have to be aware of the most popular weasel words in advertising today.

Virtually Spotless

One of the most powerful weasel words is "virtually," a word so innocent that most people don't pay any attention to it when it is used in an advertising claim. But watch out. "Virtually" is used in advertising claims that appear to make specific, definite promises when there is no promise. After all, what does "virtually" mean? It means "in essence of effect, although not in fact." Look at that definition again. "Virtually" means *not in fact*. It does *not* mean "almost" or "just about the same as," or anything else. And before you dismiss all this concern over such a small word, remember that small words can have big consequences.

In 1971 a federal court rendered its decision on a case brought by a woman who became pregnant while taking birth control pills. She sued the manufacturer, Eli Lilly and Company, for breach of warranty. The woman lost her case. Basing its ruling on a statement in the pamphlet accompanying the pills, which stated that, "When taken as directed, the tablets offer virtually 100 percent protection," the court ruled that there was no warranty, expressed or implied, that the pills were absolutely effective. In its ruling, the court pointed out that, according to the *Webster's Third New International Dictionary*, "virtually" means "almost entirely" and clearly does not mean "absolute" (*Whittington v. Eli Lilly and Company*, 333 F. Supp. 98). In other words, the Eli Lilly company was really saying that its birth control pill, even when taken as directed, *did not in fact* provide 100 percent protection against pregnancy. But Eli Lilly didn't want to put it that way because then many women might not have bought Lilly's birth control pills.

The next time you see the ad that says that this dishwasher detergent "leaves dishes virtually spotless," just remember how advertisers twist the meaning of the weasel word "virtually." You can have lots of spots on your dishes after using this detergent and the ad claim will still be true, because what this claim really means is that this detergent does not *in fact* leave your dishes spotless. Whenever you see or hear an ad claim that uses the word "virtually," just translate that claim into its real meaning. So the television set that is "virtually trouble free" becomes the television set that is not in fact trouble free, the "virtually foolproof operation" of any appliance becomes an operation that is in fact not foolproof, and the product that "virtually never needs service" becomes the product that is not in fact service free.

New and Improved

If "new" is the most frequently used word on a product package, "improved" is the second most frequent. In fact, the two words are almost always used together. It seems just about everything sold these days is "new and improved." The next time you're in the supermarket, try counting the number of times you see these words on products. But you'd better do it while you're walking down just one aisle, otherwise you'll need a calculator to keep track of your counting.

Just what do these words mean? The use of the word "new" is restricted by regulations, so an advertiser can't just use the word on a product or in an ad without meeting certain requirements. For example, a product is considered new for about six months during a national advertising campaign. If the product is being advertised only in a limited test market area, the word can be used longer, and in some instances has been used for as long as two years.

What makes a product "new"? Some products have been around for a long time, yet every once in a while you discover that they are being advertised as "new." Well, an advertiser can call a product new if there has been "a material functional change" in the product. What is "a material functional change," you ask? Good question. In fact it's such a good question it's being asked all the time. It's up to the manufacturer to prove that the product has undergone such a change. And if the manufacturer isn't challenged on the claim, then there's no one to stop it. Moreover, the change does not have to be an improvement in the product. One manufacturer added an artificial lemon scent to a cleaning product and called it "new and improved," even though the product did not clean any better than without the lemon scent. The manufacturer defended the use of the word "new" on the grounds that the artificial scent changed the chemical formula of the product and therefore constituted "a material functional change."

Which brings up the word "improved." When used in advertising, "improved" does not mean "made better." It only means "changed" or "different from before." So, if the detergent maker puts a plastic pour spout on the box of detergent, the product has been "improved," and away we go with a whole new advertising campaign. Or, if the cereal maker adds more fruit or a different kind of fruit to the cereal, there's an improved product. Now you know why manufacturers are constantly making little changes in their products. Whole new advertising campaigns, designed to convince you that the product has been changed for the better, are based on small changes in superficial aspects of a product. The next time you see an ad for an "improved" product, ask yourself what was wrong with the old one. Ask yourself just how "improved" the product is. Finally, you might check to see whether the "improved" version costs more than the unimproved one. After all, someone has to pay for the millions of dollars spent advertising the improved product.

Of course, advertisers really like to run ads that claim a product is "new and improved." While what constitutes a "new" product may be subject to some regulation, "improved" is a subjective judgment. A manufacturer changes the shape of its stick deodorant, but the shape doesn't improve the function of the deodorant. That is, changing the shape doesn't affect the deodorizing ability of the deodorant, so the manufacturer calls it "improved." Another manufacturer adds ammonia to its liquid cleaner and calls it "new and improved." Since adding ammonia does affect the cleaning ability of the product, there has been a "material functional change" in the product, and the manufacturer can now call its cleaner "new," and "improved" as well. Now the weasel words "new and improved" are plastered all over the package and are the basis for a multimillion-dollar ad campaign. But after six months the word "new" will have to go, until someone can dream up another change in the product. Perhaps it will be adding color to the liquid, or changing the shape of the package, or maybe adding a new dripless pour spout, or perhaps a _____. The "improvements" are endless, and so are the new advertising claims and campaigns.

"New" is just too useful and powerful a word in advertising for advertisers to pass it up easily. So they use weasel words that say "new" without really saying it. One of their favorites is "introducing," as in, "Introducing improved Tide," or "Introducing the stain remover." The first is simply saying, here's our improved soap; the second, here's our new advertising campaign for our detergent. Another favorite is "now," as in, "Now there's Sinex," which simply means that Sinex is available. Then there are phrases like "Today's Chevrolet," "Presenting Dristan," and "A fresh way to start the day." The list is really endless because advertisers are always finding new ways to say "new" without really saying it. If there is a second edition of this book, I'll just call it the "new and improved" edition. Wouldn't you really rather have a "new and improved" edition of this book rather than a "second" edition?

Acts Fast

"Acts" and "works" are two popular weasel words in advertising because they bring action to the product and to the advertising claim. When you see the ad for the cough syrup that "Acts on the cough control center," ask yourself what this cough syrup is claiming to do. Well, it's just claiming to "act," to do something, to perform an action. What is it that the cough syrup does? The ad doesn't say. It only claims to perform an action or do something on your "cough control center." By the way, what and where is your "cough control center"? I don't remember learning about that part of the body in human biology class.

Ads that use such phrases as "acts fast," "acts against," "acts to prevent," and the like are saying essentially nothing, because "act" is a word empty of any specific meaning. The ads are always careful not to specify exactly what "act" the product performs. Just because a brand of aspirin claims to "act fast" for headache relief doesn't mean this aspirin is any better than any other aspirin. What is the "act" that this aspirin performs? You're never told. Maybe it just dissolves quickly. Since aspirin is a parity product, all aspirin is the same and therefore functions the same.

Works Like Anything Else

If you don't find the word "acts" in an ad, you will probably find the weasel word "works." In fact, the two words are almost interchangeable in advertising. Watch out for ads that say a product "works against," "works like," "works for," or "works longer." As with "acts," "works" is the same meaningless verb used to make you think that this product really does something, and maybe even something special or unique. But "works," like "acts," is basically a word empty of any specific meaning.

Like Magic

Whenever advertisers want you to stop thinking about the product and to start thinking about something bigger, better, or more attractive than the product, they use that very popular weasel word, "like." The word "like" is the advertiser's equivalent of a magician's use of misdirection. "Like" gets you to ignore the product and concentrate on the claim the advertiser is making about it. "For skin like peaches and cream" claims the ad for a skin cream. What is this ad really claiming? It doesn't say this cream will give you peaches-and-cream skin. There is no verb in this claim, so it doesn't even mention using the product. How is skin ever like "peaches and cream"? Remember, ads must be read literally and exactly, according to the dictionary definition of words. (Remember "virtually" in the Eli Lilly case.) The ad is making absolutely no promise or claim whatsoever for this skin cream. If you think this cream will give you soft, smooth, youthful-looking skin, you are the one who has read that meaning into the ad.

The wine that claims "It's like taking a trip to France" wants you to think about a romantic evening in Paris as you walk along the boulevard after a wonderful meal in an intimate little bistro. Of course, you don't really believe that a wine can take you to France, but the goal of the ad is to get you to think pleasant, romantic thoughts about France and not about how the wine tastes or how expensive it may be. That little word "like" has taken you away from crushed grapes into a world of your own imaginative making. Who knows, maybe the next time you buy wine, you'll think those pleasant thoughts when you see this brand of wine, and you'll buy it. Or, maybe you weren't even thinking about buying wine at all, but now you just might pick up a bottle the next time you're shopping. Ah, the power of "like" in advertising.

How about the most famous "like" claim of all, "Winston tastes good like a cigarette should"? Ignoring the grammatical error here, you might want to know what this claim is saying. Whether a cigarette tastes good or bad is a subjective judgment because what tastes good to one person may well taste horrible to another. Not everyone likes fried snails, even if they are called escargot. (*De gustibus non est disputandum*, which was probably the Roman rule for advertising as well as for defending the games in the Colosseum.) There are many people who say all cigarettes taste terrible, other people who say only some cigarettes taste all right, and still others who say all cigarettes taste good. Who's right? Everyone, because taste is a matter of personal judgment.

Moreover, note the use of the conditional, "should." The complete claim is, "Winston tastes good like a cigarette should taste." But should cigarettes taste good? Again, this is a matter of personal judgment and probably depends most on one's experiences with smoking. So, the Winston ad is simply saying that Winston cigarettes are just like any other cigarette: Some people like them and some people don't. On that statement, R. J. Reynolds conducted a very successful multimillion-dollar advertising campaign that helped keep Winston the number-two-selling cigarette in the United States, close behind number one, Marlboro.

Can't It Be Up to the Claim?

Analyzing ads for doublespeak requires that you pay attention to every word in the ad and determine what each word really means. Advertisers try to wrap their claims in language that sounds concrete, specific, and objective, when in fact the language of advertising is anything but. Your job is to read carefully and listen critically so that when the announcer says that "Crest can be of significant value . . . ," you know immediately that this claim says absolutely nothing. Where is the doublespeak in this ad? Start with the second word.

Once again, you have to look at what words really mean, not what you think they mean or what the advertiser wants you to think they mean. The ad for Crest only says that using Crest "can be" of "significant value." What really throws you off in this ad is the brilliant use of "significant." It draws your attention to the word "value" and makes you forget that the ad only claims that Crest "can be." The ad doesn't say that Crest *is* of value, only that it is "able" or "possible" to be of value, because that's all that "can" means.

It's so easy to miss the importance of those little words, "can be." Almost as easy as missing the importance of the words "up to" in an ad. These words are very popular in sales ads. You know, the ones that say, "Up to 50 percent off!" Now, what does that claim mean? Not much, because the store or manufacturer has to reduce the price of only a few items by 50 percent. Everything else can be reduced a lot less, or not even reduced. Moreover, don't you want to know 50 percent off of what? Is it 50 percent off the "manufacturer's suggested list price," which is the highest possible price? Was the price artificially inflated and then reduced? In other ads, "up to" expresses an ideal situation. The medicine that works "up to ten times faster," the battery that lasts "up to twice as long," and the soap that gets you "up to twice as clean" all are based on ideal situations for using those products, situations in which you can be sure you will never find yourself.

Unfinished Words

Unfinished words are a kind of "up to" claim in advertising. The claim that a battery lasts "up to twice as long" usually doesn't finish the comparison—twice as long as what? A birthday candle? A tank of gas? A cheap battery made in a country not noted for its technological achievements? The implication is that the battery lasts twice as long as batteries made by other battery makers, or twice as long as earlier model batteries made by the advertiser, but the ad doesn't really make these claims. You read these claims into the ad, aided by the visual images the advertiser so carefully provides.

Unfinished words depend on you to finish them, to provide the words the advertisers so thoughtfully left out of the ad. Pall Mall cigarettes were once advertised as "A longer finer and milder smoke." The question is, longer, finer, and milder than what? The aspirin that claims it contains "Twice as much of the pain reliever doctors recommend most" doesn't tell you what pain reliever it contains twice as much of. (By the way, it's aspirin. That's right; it just contains twice the amount of aspirin. And how much is twice the amount? Twice of what amount?) Panadol boasts that "nobody reduces fever faster," but, since Panadol is a parity product, this claim simply means that Panadol isn't any better than any other product in its parity class. "You can be sure if it's Westinghouse," you're told, but just exactly what it is you can be sure of is never mentioned. "Magnavox gives you more" doesn't tell you what you get more of. More value? More television? More than they gave you before? It sounds nice, but it means nothing, until you fill in the claim with your own words, the words the advertisers didn't use. Since each of us fills in the claim differently, the ad and the product can become all things to all people, and not promise a single thing.

Unfinished words abound in advertising because they appear to promise so much. More importantly, they can be joined with powerful visual images on television to appear to be making significant promises about a product's effectiveness without really making any promises. In a television ad, the aspirin product that claims fast relief can show a person with a headache taking the product and then, in what appears to be a matter of minutes, claiming complete relief. This visual image is far more powerful than any claim made in unfinished words. Indeed, the visual image completes the unfinished words for you, filling in with pictures what the words leave out. And you thought that ads didn't affect you. What brand of aspirin do you use?

Some years ago, Ford's advertisements proclaimed "Ford LTD—700 percent quieter." Now, what do you think Ford was claiming with these unfinished words? What was the Ford LTD quieter than? A Cadillac? A Mercedes Benz? A BMW? Well, when the FTC asked Ford to substantiate this unfinished claim, Ford replied that it meant that the inside of the LTD was 700 percent quieter than the outside. How did you finish those unfinished words when you first read them? Did you even come close to Ford's meaning?

Combining Weasel Words

A lot of ads don't fall neatly into one category or another because they use a variety of different devices and words. Different weasel words are often combined to make an ad claim. The claim, "Coffee-Mate gives coffee more body, more flavor," uses Unfinished Words ("more" than what?) and also uses words that have no specific meaning ("body" and "flavor"). Along with "taste" (remember the Winston ad and its claim to taste good), "body" and "flavor" mean nothing because their meaning is entirely subjective. To you, "body" in coffee might mean thick, black, almost bitter coffee, while I might take it to mean a light brown, delicate coffee. Now, if you think you understood that last sentence, read it again, because it said nothing of objective value; it was filled with weasel words of no specific meaning: "thick," "black," "bitter," "light brown," and "delicate." Each of those words has no specific, objective meaning, because each of us can interpret them differently.

Try this slogan: "Looks, smells, tastes like ground-roast coffee." So, are you now going to buy Taster's Choice instant coffee because of this ad? "Looks," "smells," and "tastes" are all words with no specific meaning and depend on your interpretation of them for any meaning. Then there's that great weasel word "like," which simply suggests a comparison but does not make the actual connection between the product and the quality. Besides, do you know what "ground-roast" coffee is? I don't, but it sure sounds good. So, out of seven words in this ad, four are definite weasel words, two are quite meaningless, and only one has any clear meaning.

Remember the Anacin ad—"Twice as much of the pain reliever doctors recommend most"? There's a whole lot of weaseling going on in this ad. First, what's the pain reliever they're talking about in this ad? Aspirin, of course. In fact, any time you see or hear an ad using those words "pain reliever," you can automatically substitute the word "aspirin" for them. (Makers of acetaminophen and ibuprofen pain relievers are careful in their advertising to identify their products as nonaspirin products.) So, now we know that Anacin has aspirin in it. Moreover, we know that Anacin has twice as much aspirin in it, but we don't know twice as much as what. Does it have twice as much aspirin as an ordinary aspirin tablet? If so, what is an ordinary aspirin tablet, and how much aspirin does it contain? Twice as much as Excedrin or Bufferin? Twice as much as a chocolate chip cookie? Remember those Unfinished Words and how they lead you on without saying anything.

Finally, what about those doctors who are doing all that recommending? Who are they? How many of them are there? What kind of doctors are they? What are their qualifications? Who asked them about recommending pain relievers? What other pain relievers did they recommend? And there are a whole lot more questions about this "poll" of doctors to which I'd like to know the answers, but you get the point. Sometimes, when I call my doctor, she tells me to take two aspirin and call her office in the morning. Is that where Anacin got this ad?

Read the Label, or the Brochure

Weasel words aren't just found on television, on the radio, or in newspaper and magazine ads. Just about any language associated with a product will contain the doublespeak of advertising. Remember the Eli Lilly case and the doublespeak on the information sheet that came with the birth control pills. Here's another example.

In 1983, the Estée Lauder cosmetics company announced a new product called "Night Repair." A small brochure distributed with the product stated that "Night Repair was scientifically formulated in Estée Lauder's U.S. laboratories as part of the Swiss Age-Controlling Skincare Program. Although only nature controls the aging process, this program helps control the signs of aging and encourages skin to look and feel younger." You might want to read these two sentences again, because they sound great but say nothing.

First, note that the product was "scientifically formulated" in the company's laboratories. What does that mean? What constitutes a scientific formulation? You wouldn't expect the company to say that the product was casually, mechanically, or carelessly formulated, or just thrown together one day when the people in the white coats didn't have anything better to do. But the word "scientifically" lends an air of precision and promise that just isn't there.

It is the second sentence, however, that's really weasely, both syntactically and semantically. The only factual part of this sentence is the introductory dependent clause—"only nature controls the aging process." Thus, the only fact in the ad is relegated to a dependent clause, a clause dependent on the main clause, which contains no factual or definite information at all and indeed purports to contradict the independent clause. The new "skincare program" (notice it's not a skin cream but a "program") does not claim to stop or even retard the aging process. What, then, does Night Repair, at a price of over $35 (in 1983 dollars) for a .87-ounce bottle do? According to this brochure, nothing. It only "helps," and the brochure does not say how much it helps. Moreover, it only "helps control," and then it only helps control the "*signs* of aging," not the aging itself. Also, it "encourages" skin not to *be* younger but only to "look and feel" younger. The brochure does not say younger than what. Of the sixteen words in the main clause of this second sentence, nine are weasel words. So, before you spend all that money for Night Repair, or any other cosmetic product, read the words carefully, and then decide if you're getting what you think you're paying for.

Other Tricks of the Trade

Advertisers' use of doublespeak is endless. The best way advertisers can make something out of nothing is through words. Although there are a lot of visual images used on television and in magazines and newspapers, every advertiser wants to create that memorable line that will stick in the public consciousness. I am sure pure joy reigned in one advertising agency when a study found that children who were asked to spell the word "relief" promptly and proudly responded "r-o-l-a-i-d-s."

The variations, combinations, and permutations of doublespeak used in advertising go on and on, running from the use of rhetorical questions ("Wouldn't you really rather have a Buick?" "If you can't trust Prestone, who can you trust?") to flattering you with compliments ("The lady has taste." "We think a cigar smoker is someone special." "You've come a long way baby."). You know, of course, how you're *supposed* to answer those questions, and you know that those compliments are just leading up to the sales pitches for the products. Before you dismiss such tricks of the trade as obvious, however, just remember that all of these statements and questions were part of very successful advertising campaigns.

A more subtle approach is the ad that proclaims a supposedly unique quality for a product, a quality that really isn't unique. "If it doesn't say Goodyear, it can't be polyglas." Sounds good, doesn't it? Polyglas is available only from Goodyear because Goodyear copyrighted that trade name. Any other tire manufacturer could make exactly the same tire but could not call it "polyglas," because that would be copyright infringement. "Polyglas" is simply Goodyear's name for its fiberglass-reinforced tire.

Since we like to think of ourselves as living in a technologically advanced country, science and technology have a great appeal in selling products. Advertisers are quick to use scientific doublespeak to push their products. There are all kinds of elixirs, additives, scientific potions, and mysterious mixtures added to all kinds of products. Gasoline contains "HTA," "F–130," "Platformate," and other chemical-sounding additives, but nowhere does an advertisement give any real information about the additive.

Shampoo, deodorant, mouthwash, cold medicine, sleeping pills, and any number of other products all seem to contain some special chemical ingredient that allows them to work wonders. "Certs contains a sparkling drop of Retsyn." So what? What's "Retsyn"? What's it do? What's so special about it? When they don't have a secret ingredient in their product, advertisers still find a way to claim scientific validity. There's "Sinarest. Created by a research scientist who actually gets sinus headaches." Sounds nice, but what kind of research does this scientist do? How do you know if she is any kind of expert on sinus medicine? Besides, this ad doesn't tell you a thing about the medicine itself and what it does.

Advertising Doublespeak Quick Quiz

Now it's time to test your awareness of advertising doublespeak. (You didn't think I would just let you read this and forget it, did you?) The following is a list of statements from some recent ads. Your job is to figure out what each of these ads really says.

Domino's Pizza: "Because nobody delivers better."
Sinutab: "It can stop the pain."
Tums: "The stronger acid neutralizer."
Maximum Strength Dristan: "Strong medicine for tough sinus colds."
Listermint: "Making your mouth a cleaner place."
Cascade: "For virtually spotless dishes nothing beats Cascade."
Nuprin: "Little. Yellow. Different. Better."
Anacin: "Better relief."
Sudafed: "Fast sinus relief that won't put you fast asleep."
Advil: "Better relief."
Ponds Cold Cream: "Ponds cleans like no soap can."
Miller Lite Beer: "Tastes great. Less filling."
Philips Milk of Magnesia: "Nobody treats you better than MOM (Philips Milk of Magnesia)."
Bayer: "The wonder drug that works wonders."
Cracker Barrel: "Judged to be the best."
Knorr: "Where taste is everything."
Anusol: "Anusol is the word to remember for relief."
Dimetapp: "It relieves kids as well as colds."
Liquid Drano: "The liquid strong enough to be called Drano."
Johnson & Johnson Baby Powder: "Like magic for your skin."
Puritan: "Make it your oil for life."
Pam: "Pam, because how you cook is as important as what you cook."
Ivory Shampoo and Conditioner: "Leave your hair feeling Ivory clean."
Tylenol Gel-Caps: "It's not a capsule. It's better."
Alka-Seltzer Plus: "Fast, effective relief for winter colds."

The World of Advertising

In the world of advertising, people wear "dentures," not false teeth; they suffer from "occasional irregularity," not constipation; they need deodorants for their "nervous wetness," not for sweat; they use "bathroom tissue," not toilet paper; and they don't dye their hair, they "tint" or "rinse" it. Advertisements offer "real counterfeit diamonds" without the slightest hint of embarrassment, or boast of goods made out of "genuine imitation leather" or "virgin vinyl."

In the world of advertising, the girdle becomes a "body shaper," "form persuader," "control garment," "controller," "outerwear enhancer," "body garment," or "anti-gravity panties," and is sold with such trade names as "The Instead," "The Free Spirit," and "The Body Briefer."

A study some years ago found the following words to be among the most popular used in U.S. television advertisements: "new," "improved," "better," "extra," "fresh," "clean," "beautiful," "free," "good," "great," and "light." At the same time, the following words were found to be among the most frequent on British television: "new," "good-better-best," "free," "fresh," "delicious," "full," "sure," "clean," "wonderful," and "special." While these words may occur most frequently in ads, and while ads may be filled with weasel words, you have to watch out for all the words used in advertising, not just the words mentioned here.

Every word in an ad is there for a reason; no word is wasted. Your job is to figure out exactly what each word is doing in an ad—what each word really means, not what the advertiser wants you to think it means. Remember, the ad is trying to get you to buy a product, so it will put the product in the best possible light, using any device, trick, or means legally allowed. Your own defense against advertising (besides taking up permanent residence on the moon) is to develop and use a strong critical reading, listening, and looking ability. Always ask yourself what the ad is *really* saying. When you see ads on television, don't be misled by the pictures, the visual images. What does the ad say about the product? What does the ad *not* say? What information is missing from the ad? Only by becoming an active, critical consumer of the doublespeak of advertising will you ever be able to cut through the doublespeak and discover what the ad is really saying.

Professor Del Kehl of Arizona State University has updated the Twenty-third Psalm to reflect the power of advertising to meet our needs and solve our problems. It seems fitting that this chapter close with this new Psalm.

The Adman's 23rd

The Adman is my shepherd;

I shall ever want.

He maketh me to walk a mile for a Camel;

He leadeth me beside Crystal Waters In the High Country of Coors;

He restoreth my soul with Perrier.

READING WRITING

This Text: Reading

1. Lutz's essay is now almost 20 years old, yet it still feels relevant. What about his essay rings the most true?
2. Does Lutz have a clear thesis here? If so, can you locate it? How would you summarize his main argument?
3. Has advertising changed in the last 20 years? Are ads now savvier?

Your Text: Writing

1. Write an essay in which you read a series of ads through a Lutzian lens. Use his terminology to offer a semiotic and rhetorical reading.
2. Write a comparison/contrast essay in which you analyze an ad you find particularly manipulative with one you find reasonable and straightforward. Give specific analytic examples of how the two ads differ from each other.

Techno-Optimism: 10 Reasons There's a Bright Future for Journalism

Mark Glaser

A longtime journalist, Mark Glaser is the executive editor for Mediashift, *a PBS blog about the changing nature of journalism. Here he writes about why journalists should be optimistic about the future.*

THERE'S BEEN A LOT OF DEBATE lately about the future of newspapers, the future of TV, the future of radio—the future of journalism itself—in the face of drastic change brought by technology and the Internet. I've asked MediaShift readers whether they thought journalism's metaphorical cup was half empty or half full and most people saw a pretty bright future.

As you might imagine, I share their enthusiasm for the future, and wouldn't be writing this blog if I didn't believe we will end up in a better place. But I'm also a hardened realist and natural skeptic, and I know there are painful months and years ahead for the (dwindling number of) people working in traditional media. Not everything new and shiny will be good for us, and there are plenty of ethical and technological pitfalls ahead.

But rather than dwell on the negative, rail against change, or damn the upstarts at Google and Craigslist, I'd like to take a walk on the sunny side of life in new media, consider the positive aspects of all that is happening, and how we could end up in a renaissance era for journalism. While I do believe large media companies will have the most difficult time adapting to the changes, they can learn a lot from the successful business models of smaller sites such as TMZ or The Smoking Gun (both owned by media companies).

10 Reasons There's a Bright Future for Journalism

1. More access to more journalism worldwide. One of the undersung advantages of the Internet is that it gives us access to content from newspapers, TV channels, blogs and podcasts from around the world. No longer are we limited to our local media for news of the world. Now we can go directly to that corner of the world to get a local angle from far away. No one has figured out how to sell advertising that would be relevant to all those international readers, but that doesn't mean they won't figure it out eventually.

2. Aggregation and personalization satisfies readers. Tired of being programmed to, we now have the tools online to program our own media experience. Whether that's through Google News or personalizing My Yahoo or an RSS newsfeed reader, we can get quick access to the media outlets and journalism we want on one web page. Some newspaper executives have railed against Google News, but the vast majority are working on their own ways of aggregating content from other sources or offering up personalized versions of their sites (see mywashingtonpost.com). It's a more open way of doing journalism than saying "we have all the answers here."

3. Digital delivery offers more ways to reach people. Before the web became popular, traditional media offered up just one way to get their content—in a print publication, by watching TV or listening to the radio. Now you can get their content online, in email newsletters, on your mobile phone and in any way that digital bits and bytes can be delivered. That's journalism unbound from traditional format constraints.

4. There are more fact-checkers than ever in the history of journalism. Maybe it's true that professional fact-checking has taken a big hit in the layoffs at mainstream media outlets, but it's also true that bloggers and free-thinkers online have provided an important check and balance to reporting. They might have an axe to grind or a political bias, but if they uncover shoddy reporting, plagiarism or false sourcing, it's a good thing for journalists and the public.

5. Collaborative investigations between pro and amateur journalists. The Internet allows ad-hoc investigations to take place between professional reporters and amateur sleuths. The Sunlight Foundation gave tools to citizen journalists so they could help find out which members of U.S. Congress were employing their spouses. The *Los Angeles Times* and various amateur investigators worked together to unmask the LonelyGirl15 video actress as Jessica Rose. Many more of these collaborative investigations are possible thanks to easy communication online and experiments such as NewAssignment.net.

6. More voices are part of the news conversation. In the past, if you wanted to voice your opinion, correct a fact or do your own reporting, you had to work at a mainstream news organization. Now, thanks to the rising influence of independent bloggers and online journalists, there are more outsiders and experts exerting influence over the news agenda. Not only does that mean we have a more diverse constellation of views, but it also takes the concentrated agenda-setting power out of a few hallowed editorial boardrooms.

7. Greater transparency and a more personal tone. Thanks to blogs and the great wide pastures of the web, reporters can go onto media websites and explain their conflicts of interest in greater detail, leading to more transparency. Plus, online writing tends to be more personal, giving reporters, editors and news anchors the chance to be more human and connect with their audience in deeper ways.

8. Growing advertising revenues online. While old-line media people complain that online ads aren't bringing in enough revenues to replace what's lost in the transition from the old advertising formats, that doesn't mean all is lost. Almost every forecast for online advertising shows double-digit percentage increases in revenues over the next five years, and it's hard to believe none of that will trickle down to media companies. What might well happen is that media concentration will lessen, and more of the revenues will be spread out to smaller independent sites than just the big conglomerates.

9. An online shift from print could improve our environmental impact. Very few people consider just how much our love for print newspapers and magazines harms the environment. It's true that publishers are trying to use more recycled paper, but use of online media has a much less drastic ecological impact. Choosing online over print actually saves trees, which in turn means that media companies that transition wisely could be helping to reduce global warming. Many people expect that some type of reusable, flexible e-ink readers will eventually replace ink-on-dead-tree publications.

10. Stories never end. Perhaps one of the weakest points about traditional journalism is that there's rarely any follow-ups on big stories. It usually takes a professional reporter having to go back and report what's happened since the big story. But online, stories can live on for much longer in flexible formats, allowing people to update them in comments or add more facts as they happen. Wikinews is one example of user-generated news stories that can be updated and edited by anyone.

What do you think? What other reasons do you think journalism has a bright future ahead? Or are you a techno-pessimist who thinks none of this will presage better days for journalism?

READING WRITING

This Text: Reading

1. What does Glaser think about the future of journalism?
2. Why do you think he is concerned with newspapers and journalism? Do you share his interest or concern?
3. What advantages do newspapers have over the Internet? Disadvantages?

This Text: Writing

1. Write a short paper comparing the front pages of an electronic version of the front page of a newspaper.
2. Spend an afternoon taking notes on a newspaper site that updates. In what ways is the newspaper taking advantage of new technology? Is it undermining or enhancing the newspaper?
3. Read a few bloggers linked on the newspaper page and some other bloggers. Write about the differences and similarities in tone.
4. Take one of the above assignments and re-think it as if it were electronic. What things could you link to? Does this detract or enhance your paper?

The Google Suite

Google is now a verb, joining only a select few companies whose products have entered the language—Kleenex, Xerox, and Frisbee to name a few (and Facebook soon to join them). Its prominence in our lives was unimaginable when it began as a modest search engine in the 1990s. But in a sense, Google's growth stands as a symbol for the way the Internet is now featured in our lives. It now boasts the most popular web-based e-mail, increasingly popular office, calendar, and map applications, and another dozen or so more specialized applications.

While most of the world's attention has focused on Google's positives, an increasing amount of criticism has challenged Google's motto: "Don't be evil." Privacy experts worry about Google's hold on people's private information. Some critics have criticized its interactions with the Chinese government, given their record with human rights, in particular their openly stated goals of censoring some information available to its citizens. Others do not approve of the Google Books project, claiming it tramples over the rights of authors.

For others, the concerns are more cultural and intellectual, focusing on the way we now gather information. Many of you, born after card catalogs and the *Reader's Guide to Periodicals*, find out almost all of your information through Google. Even your professors use Google to find information in a hurry. In this suite, we have three writers who are examining Google from a variety of perspectives. Virginia Heffernan examines the conceptual intelligence that Google employs when suggesting searches. Nicholas Carr asks the question "Is Google making us stupid?" and Siva Vaidhyanathan responds, "not exactly."

The Google Alphabet: Googlealphabet

Virginia Heffernan

IF YOU HAVE ASKED Google to "show suggestions" in your browser toolbar, you know the keen comfort of discovering you're not alone in asking the Internet questions it's not quite equipped to answer, including, "Am I pregnant?" and "Am I crazy?" You start typing "Am I—" and like an impatient therapist Google Suggest interrupts you with a drop-down list of concepts seemingly culled from the unconsciousness of the human race. Google doesn't let you wallow in your eccentricities. "What's that? Are you— oh, lemme take a wild guess here—crazy? Well, now, that's original. . . ."

But if, instead of persisting with your weird questions, you stop at letter No. 1, dropping only "A" in your Google search, you don't have to face your issues. You go shopping. Type "A" and Google proposes Amazon. "J" gets you JC Penney. "T" is for Target. These sites, and 23 others, are Google's first suggestions for each letter of the alphabet. Tuning into "A"—or "B" or "Z"—on Google is like tuning into network TV in prime time: you get to join millions of people and do what they're doing. (Or maybe what Google wants most people to do. Google Suggest builds its hierarchies from a mysterious house blend of "searches you've done, searches done by users all over the world, sites in our search index and ads in our advertising network.") You find the big, broad sites that Google is now officially programmed to find.

So, if you start your search with "L," you might be swooningly looking to seduce someone with "love quotes," Google's sixth suggestion, but why not pre-empt the agonizing and make Google's first stop instead: good old Lowe's? "Bring the Ultimate Tailgate Party Home," read Lowe's home page not long ago. That's a love quote if ever there was one.

Or start off with "Q" and ignore both "quotes about love" and "quotes about life," the also-rans for "Q." (The first stop for "quotes about love" netted me Chuck Palahniuk's bruising "your heart is my pinata," anyway.) If you click the top choice, you'll find yourself on QVC, where for four or six easy payments you can have a KitchenAid Artisan mixer, enormous Cinnabon-scented candles or a Joan Rivers Call of the Wild animal-print watch. That watch looks amazing.

And, seriously, stop brooding on "H1N1 symptoms." If you're "H"-inclined, look no further than the steel-frame VersaTube sheds and garages at Home Depot. (Not the No. 1 suggestion, admittedly, but does anyone really head to Hotmail—via Google, no less—anymore?) And Best Buy has some vast Panasonic high-def TVs for sale; I bet you can run your Internet on those 65-inch screens, which would let you visit bestbuy.com and shop for your next HDTV on one of these HDTVs.

"U" was a good reminder that the only government agency that wins Google's love is the United States Postal Service. The U.S.P.S. is the oldest organization by about 200 years to make the Google alphabet. And now's a good time to point out that the Web designers for USPS.com have done a terrific job: you can easily buy stamps, schedule pickups, change your address and put your mail on hold with a few clicks. The designers of the maddening and jargony site for the Internal Revenue Service—"I.R.S." is No. 5 of Google's "I" suggestions—should look to their betters.

EBay is where my "E" always takes me, and I'm trying to quit, so I have to lay off "E" for a while. Best of luck to those of you who can use eBay in moderation. Kohl's, to my surprise, surpasses Kmart on the "K" suggestion list. And the hard Scrabble letters like "X" and "Z" turn up many results in the Internet age of lightning-extreme neologisms: Xbox 360 tops the "X" list ("Xanax" is not far behind), while Zillow and Zappos led the Z-words.

It's gratifying to travel only the Web's most-traveled roads. While sprinting around the Google alphabet, I'm alive to the great 21st-century American preoccupations: social life (Facebook, MySpace), entertainment (Netflix, YouTube, Pandora), real estate (Realtor, Zillow) and, above all, shopping. Things that don't crack the Google alphabet: religion, gambling, sex, politics, food and dieting—much of the stuff we're often told we're obsessed with.

There are only two pure information sites in the Google top 26: Dictionary.com and IMDB.com. Neither is the kind of highly wrought content gala—newspaper, magazine, aggregator—that people in the heyday of "portals" once predicted would be everyone's first stop on the Web. (Wikipedia is third after Wal-Mart and weather for "W"; CNN is second after Craigslist. Neither Time magazine nor The Drudge Report crack the Top 10 for "T" or "D.")

In all, Google's 26-stop tour of the Web would have you believe that the top-ranking American pastime is shopping for furniture and electronics and dishes and more. Shopping for home stuff is what we're supposed to do, I mean, when we're not on Realtor and Zillow shopping for homes themselves. Or maybe we're just, restlessly, still looking for a home on the Web. Are we crazy?

Is Google Making Us Stupid

Nicholas Carr

"DAVE, STOP. STOP, WILL YOU? Stop, Dave. Will you stop, Dave?" So the supercomputer HAL pleads with the implacable astronaut Dave Bowman in a famous and weirdly poignant scene toward the end of Stanley Kubrick's *2001: A Space Odyssey*.

Bowman, having nearly been sent to a deep-space death by the malfunctioning machine, is calmly, coldly disconnecting the memory circuits that control its artificial "brain." "Dave, my mind is going," HAL says, forlornly. "I can feel it. I can feel it."

I can feel it, too. Over the past few years I've had an uncomfortable sense that someone, or something, has been tinkering with my brain, remapping the neural circuitry, reprogramming the memory. My mind isn't going—so far as I can tell—but it's changing. I'm not thinking the way I used to think. I can feel it most strongly when I'm reading. Immersing myself in a book or a lengthy article used to be easy. My mind would get caught up in the narrative or the turns of the argument, and I'd spend hours strolling through long stretches of prose. That's rarely the case anymore. Now my concentration often starts to drift after two or three pages. I get fidgety, lose the thread, begin looking for something else to do. I feel as if I'm always dragging my wayward brain back to the text. The deep reading that used to come naturally has become a struggle.

I think I know what's going on. For more than a decade now, I've been spending a lot of time online, searching and surfing and sometimes adding to the great databases of the Internet. The Web has been a godsend to me as a writer. Research that once required days in the stacks or periodical rooms of libraries can now be done in minutes. A few Google searches, some quick clicks on hyperlinks, and I've got the telltale fact or pithy quote I was after. Even when I'm not working, I'm as likely as not to be foraging in the Web's info-thickets' reading and writing e-mails, scanning headlines and blog posts, watching videos and listening to podcasts, or just tripping from link to link to link. (Unlike footnotes, to which they're sometimes likened, hyperlinks don't merely point to related works; they propel you toward them.)

For me, as for others, the Net is becoming a universal medium, the conduit for most of the information that flows through my eyes and ears and into my mind. The advantages of having immediate access to such an incredibly rich store of information are many, and they've been widely described and duly applauded. "The perfect recall of silicon memory," *Wired*'s Clive Thompson has written, "can be an enormous boon to thinking." But that boon comes at a price. As the media theorist Marshall McLuhan pointed out in the 1960s, media are not just passive channels of information. They supply the stuff of thought, but they also shape the process of thought. And what the Net seems to be doing is chipping away my capacity for concentration and contemplation. My mind now expects to take in information the way the Net distributes it: in a swiftly moving stream of particles. Once I was a scuba diver in the sea of words. Now I zip along the surface like a guy on a Jet Ski.

I'm not the only one. When I mention my troubles with reading to friends and acquaintances—literary types, most of them—many say they're having similar experiences. The more they use the Web, the more they have to fight to stay focused on long pieces of writing. Some of the bloggers I follow have also begun mentioning the phenomenon. Scott Karp, who writes a blog about online media, recently confessed that he has stopped reading books altogether. "I was a lit major in college, and used to be [a] voracious book reader," he wrote. "What happened?" He speculates on the answer: "What if I do all my reading on the web not so much because the way I read has changed, i.e. I'm just seeking convenience, but because the way I THINK has changed?"

Bruce Friedman, who blogs regularly about the use of computers in medicine, also has described how the Internet has altered his mental habits. "I now have almost totally lost the ability to read and absorb a longish article on the web or in print," he wrote earlier this year. A pathologist who has long been on the faculty of the University of Michigan Medical School, Friedman elaborated on his comment in a telephone conversation with me. His thinking, he said, has taken on a "staccato" quality, reflecting the way he quickly scans short passages of text from many sources online. "I can't read *War and Peace* anymore," he admitted. "I've lost the ability to do that. Even a blog post of more than three or four paragraphs is too much to absorb. I skim it."

Anecdotes alone don't prove much. And we still await the long-term neurological and psychological experiments that will provide a definitive picture of how Internet use affects cognition. But a recently published study of online research habits, conducted by scholars from University College London, suggests that we may well be in the midst of a sea change in the way we read and think. As part of the five-year research program, the scholars examined computer logs documenting the behavior of visitors to two popular research sites, one operated by the British Library and one by a U.K. educational consortium, that provide access to journal articles, e-books, and other sources of written information. They found that people using the sites exhibited "a form of skimming activity," hopping from one source to another and rarely returning to any source they'd already visited. They typically read no more than one or two pages of an article or book before they would "bounce" out to another site. Sometimes they'd save a long article, but there's no evidence that they ever went back and actually read it. The authors of the study report:

> It is clear that users are not reading online in the traditional sense; indeed there are signs that new forms of "reading" are emerging as users "power browse" horizontally through titles, contents pages and abstracts going for quick wins. It almost seems that they go online to avoid reading in the traditional sense.

Thanks to the ubiquity of text on the Internet, not to mention the popularity of text-messaging on cell phones, we may well be reading more today than we did in the 1970s or 1980s, when television was our medium of choice. But it's a different kind of reading, and behind it lies a different kind of thinking—perhaps even a new sense of the self. "We are not only what we read," says Maryanne Wolf, a developmental psychologist at Tufts University and the author of *Proust and the Squid: The Story and Science of the Reading Brain*. "We are how we read." Wolf worries that the style of reading promoted by the Net, a style that puts "efficiency" and "immediacy" above all else, may be weakening our capacity for the kind of deep reading that emerged when an earlier technology, the printing press, made long and complex works of prose commonplace. When we read online, she says, we tend to become "mere decoders of information." Our ability to interpret text, to make the rich mental connections that form when we read deeply and without distraction, remains largely disengaged.

Reading, explains Wolf, is not an instinctive skill for human beings. It's not etched into our genes the way speech is. We have to teach our minds how to translate the symbolic characters we see into the language we understand. And the media or other technologies we use in learning and practicing the craft of reading play an important part in shaping the neural circuits inside our brains. Experiments demonstrate that readers of ideograms, such as the Chinese, develop a mental circuitry for reading that is very different from the circuitry found in those of us whose written language employs an alphabet. The variations extend across many regions of the brain, including those that govern such essential cognitive functions as memory and the interpretation of visual and auditory stimuli. We can expect as well that the circuits woven by our use of the Net will be different from those woven by our reading of books and other printed works.

Sometime in 1882, Friedrich Nietzsche bought a typewriter—a Malling-Hansen Writing Ball, to be precise. His vision was failing, and keeping his eyes focused on a page had become exhausting and painful, often bringing on crushing headaches. He had been forced to curtail his writing, and he feared that he would soon have to give it up. The typewriter rescued him, at least for a time. Once he had mastered touch-typing, he was able to write with his eyes closed, using only the tips of his fingers. Words could once again flow from his mind to the page.

But the machine had a subtler effect on his work. One of Nietzsche's friends, a composer, noticed a change in the style of his writing. His already terse prose had become even tighter, more telegraphic. "Perhaps you will through this instrument even take to a new idiom," the friend wrote in a letter, noting that, in his own work, his "'thoughts' in music and language often depend on the quality of pen and paper."

"You are right," Nietzsche replied, "our writing equipment takes part in the forming of our thoughts." Under the sway of the machine, writes the German media scholar Friedrich A. Kittler, Nietzsche's prose "changed from arguments to aphorisms, from thoughts to puns, from rhetoric to telegram style."

The human brain is almost infinitely malleable. People used to think that our mental meshwork, the dense connections formed among the 100 billion or so neurons inside our skulls, was largely fixed by the time we reached adulthood. But brain researchers have discovered that that's not the case. James Olds, a professor of neuroscience who directs the Krasnow Institute for Advanced Study at George Mason University, says that even the adult mind "is very plastic." Nerve cells routinely break old connections and form new ones. "The brain," according to Olds, "has the ability to reprogram itself on the fly, altering the way it functions."

As we use what the sociologist Daniel Bell has called our "intellectual technologies"— the tools that extend our mental rather than our physical capacities—we inevitably begin to take on the qualities of those technologies. The mechanical clock, which came into common use in the 14th century, provides a compelling example. In *Technics and Civilization,* the historian and cultural critic Lewis Mumford described how the clock "disassociated time from human events and helped create the belief in an independent world of mathematically measurable sequences." The "abstract framework of divided time" became "the point of reference for both action and thought."

The clock's methodical ticking helped bring into being the scientific mind and the scientific man. But it also took something away. As the late MIT computer scientist Joseph Weizenbaum observed in his 1976 book, *Computer Power and Human Reason: From Judgment to Calculation,* the conception of the world that emerged from the widespread use of timekeeping instruments "remains an impoverished version of the older one, for it rests on a rejection of those direct experiences that formed the basis for, and indeed constituted, the old reality." In deciding when to eat, to work, to sleep, to rise, we stopped listening to our senses and started obeying the clock.

The process of adapting to new intellectual technologies is reflected in the changing metaphors we use to explain ourselves to ourselves. When the mechanical clock arrived, people began thinking of their brains as operating "like clockwork." Today, in the age of software, we have come to think of them as operating "like computers." But the changes, neuroscience tells us, go much deeper than metaphor. Thanks to our brain's plasticity, the adaptation occurs also at a biological level.

The Internet promises to have particularly far-reaching effects on cognition. In a paper published in 1936, the British mathematician Alan Turing proved that a digital computer, which at the time existed only as a theoretical machine, could be programmed to perform the function of any other information-processing device. And that's what we're seeing today. The Internet, an immeasurably powerful computing system, is subsuming most of our other intellectual technologies. It's becoming our map and our clock, our printing press and our typewriter, our calculator and our telephone, and our radio and TV.

When the Net absorbs a medium, that medium is re-created in the Net's image. It injects the medium's content with hyperlinks, blinking ads, and other digital gewgaws, and it surrounds the content with the content of all the other media it has absorbed. A new e-mail message, for instance, may announce its arrival as we're glancing over the latest head-lines at a newspaper's site. The result is to scatter our attention and diffuse our concentration.

The Net's influence doesn't end at the edges of a computer screen, either. As people's minds become attuned to the crazy quilt of Internet media, traditional media have to adapt to the audience's new expectations. Television programs add text crawls and pop-up ads, and magazines and newspapers shorten their articles, introduce capsule summaries, and crowd their pages with easy-to-browse info-snippets. When, in March of this year, *The New York Times* decided to devote the second and third pages of every edition to article abstracts, its design director, Tom Bodkin, explained that the "shortcuts" would give harried readers a quick "taste" of the day's news, sparing them the "less efficient" method of actually turning the pages and reading the articles. Old media have little choice but to play by the new-media rules.

Never has a communications system played so many roles in our lives—or exerted such broad influence over our thoughts—as the Internet does today. Yet, for all that's been written about the Net, there's been little consideration of how, exactly, it's reprogramming us. The Net's intellectual ethic remains obscure.

About the same time that Nietzsche started using his typewriter, an earnest young man named Frederick Winslow Taylor carried a stopwatch into the Midvale Steel plant in Philadelphia and began a historic series of experiments aimed at improving the efficiency of the plant's machinists. With the approval of Midvale's owners, he recruited a group of factory hands, set them to work on various metalworking machines, and recorded and timed their every movement as well as the operations of the machines. By breaking down every job into a sequence of small, discrete steps and then testing different ways of performing each one, Taylor created a set of precise instructions—an "algorithm," we might say today—for how each worker should work. Midvale's employees grumbled about the strict new regime, claiming that it turned them into little more than automatons, but the factory's productivity soared.

More than a hundred years after the invention of the steam engine, the Industrial Revolution had at last found its philosophy and its philosopher. Taylor's tight industrial choreography—his "system," as he liked to call it—was embraced by manufacturers throughout the country and, in time, around the world. Seeking maximum speed, maximum efficiency, and maximum output, factory owners used time-and-motion studies to organize their work and configure the jobs of their workers. The goal, as Taylor defined it in his celebrated 1911 treatise, *The Principles of Scientific Management*, was to identify and adopt, for every job, the "one best method" of work and thereby to effect "the gradual substitution of science for rule of thumb throughout the mechanic arts." Once his system was applied to all acts of manual labor, Taylor assured his followers, it would bring about a restructuring not only of industry but of society, creating a utopia of perfect efficiency. "In the past the man has been first," he declared; "in the future the system must be first."

Taylor's system is still very much with us; it remains the ethic of industrial manufacturing. And now, thanks to the growing power that computer engineers and software coders wield over our intellectual lives, Taylor's ethic is beginning to govern the realm of the mind as well. The Internet is a machine designed for the efficient and automated collection, transmission, and manipulation of information, and its legions of programmers are intent on finding the "one best method"—the perfect algorithm—to carry out every mental movement of what we've come to describe as "knowledge work."

Google's headquarters, in Mountain View, California—the Googleplex—is the Internet's high church, and the religion practiced inside its walls is Taylorism. Google, says its chief executive, Eric Schmidt, is "a company that's founded around the science of measurement," and it is striving to "systematize everything" it does. Drawing on the terabytes of behavioral data it collects through its search engine and other sites, it carries out thousands of experiments a day, according to the Harvard Business Review, and it uses the results to refine the algorithms that increasingly control how people find information and extract meaning from it. What Taylor did for the work of the hand, Google is doing for the work of the mind.

The company has declared that its mission is "to organize the world's information and make it universally accessible and useful." It seeks to develop "the perfect search engine," which it defines as something that "understands exactly what you mean and gives you back exactly what you want." In Google's view, information is a kind of commodity, a utilitarian resource that can be mined and processed with industrial efficiency. The more pieces of information we can "access" and the faster we can extract their gist, the more productive we become as thinkers.

Where does it end? Sergey Brin and Larry Page, the gifted young men who founded Google while pursuing doctoral degrees in computer science at Stanford, speak frequently of their desire to turn their search engine into an artificial intelligence, a HAL-like machine that might be connected directly to our brains. "The ultimate search engine is something as smart as people—or smarter," Page said in a speech a few years back. "For us, working on search is a way to work on artificial intelligence." In a 2004 interview with *Newsweek*, Brin said, "Certainly if you had all the world's information directly attached to your brain, or an artificial brain that was smarter than your brain, you'd be better off." Last year, Page told a convention of scientists that Google is "really trying to build artificial intelligence and to do it on a large scale."

Such an ambition is a natural one, even an admirable one, for a pair of math whizzes with vast quantities of cash at their disposal and a small army of computer scientists in their employ. A fundamentally scientific enterprise, Google is motivated by a desire to use technology, in Eric Schmidt's words, "to solve problems that have never been solved before," and artificial intelligence is the hardest problem out there. Why wouldn't Brin and Page want to be the ones to crack it?

Still, their easy assumption that we'd all "be better off" if our brains were supplemented, or even replaced, by an artificial intelligence is unsettling. It suggests a belief that intelligence is the output of a mechanical process, a series of discrete steps that can be isolated, measured, and optimized. In Google's world, the world we enter when we go online, there's little place for the fuzziness of contemplation. Ambiguity is not an opening for insight but a bug to be fixed. The human brain is just an outdated computer that needs a faster processor and a bigger hard drive.

The idea that our minds should operate as high-speed data-processing machines is not only built into the workings of the Internet, it is the network's reigning business model as well. The faster we surf across the Web—the more links we click and pages we view—the more opportunities Google and other companies gain to collect information about us and to feed us advertisements. Most of the proprietors of the commercial Internet have a financial stake in collecting the crumbs of data we leave behind as we flit from link to link—the more crumbs, the better. The last thing these companies want is to encourage leisurely reading or slow, concentrated thought. It's in their economic interest to drive us to distraction.

Maybe I'm just a worrywart. Just as there's a tendency to glorify technological progress, there's a countertendency to expect the worst of every new tool or machine. In Plato's Phaedrus, Socrates bemoaned the development of writing. He feared that, as people came to rely on the written word as a substitute for the knowledge they used to carry inside their heads, they would, in the words of one of the dialogue's characters, "cease to exercise their memory and become forgetful." And because they would be able to "receive a quantity of information without proper instruction," they would "be thought very knowledgeable when they are for the most part quite ignorant." They would be "filled with the conceit of wisdom instead of real wisdom." Socrates wasn't wrong—the new technology did often have the effects he feared—but he was shortsighted. He couldn't foresee the many ways that writing and reading would serve to spread information, spur fresh ideas, and expand human knowledge (if not wisdom).

The arrival of Gutenberg's printing press, in the 15th century, set off another round of teeth gnashing. The Italian humanist Hieronimo Squarciafico worried that the easy availability of books would lead to intellectual laziness, making men "less studious" and weakening their minds. Others argued that cheaply printed books and broadsheets would undermine religious authority, demean the work of scholars and scribes, and spread sedition and debauchery. As New York University professor Clay Shirky notes, "Most of the arguments made against the printing press were correct, even prescient." But, again, the doomsayers were unable to imagine the myriad blessings that the printed word would deliver.

So, yes, you should be skeptical of my skepticism. Perhaps those who dismiss critics of the Internet as Luddites or nostalgists will be proved correct, and from our hyperactive, data-stoked minds will spring a golden age of intellectual discovery and universal wisdom. Then again, the Net isn't the alphabet, and although it may replace the printing press, it produces something altogether different. The kind of deep reading that a sequence of printed pages promotes is valuable not just for the knowledge we acquire from the author's words but for the intellectual vibrations those words set off within our own minds. In the quiet spaces opened up by the sustained, undistracted reading of a book, or by any other act of contemplation, for that matter, we make our own associations, draw our own inferences and analogies, foster our own ideas. Deep reading, as Maryanne Wolf argues, is indistinguishable from deep thinking.

If we lose those quiet spaces, or fill them up with "content," we will sacrifice something important not only in our selves but in our culture. In a recent essay, the playwright Richard Foreman eloquently described what's at stake:

> I come from a tradition of Western culture, in which the ideal (my ideal) was the complex, dense and "cathedral-like" structure of the highly educated and articulate personality—a man or woman who carried inside themselves a personally constructed and unique version of the entire heritage of the West. [But now] I see within us all (myself included) the replacement of complex inner density with a new kind of self—evolving under the pressure of information overload and the technology of the "instantly available."

As we are drained of our "inner repertory of dense cultural inheritance," Foreman concluded, we risk turning into "'pancake people'—spread wide and thin as we connect with that vast network of information accessed by the mere touch of a button."

I'm haunted by that scene in *2001*. What makes it so poignant, and so weird, is the computer's emotional response to the disassembly of its mind: its despair as one circuit after another goes dark, its childlike pleading with the astronaut—"I can feel it. I can feel it. I'm afraid"—and its final reversion to what can only be called a state of innocence. HAL's outpouring of feeling contrasts with the emotionlessness that characterizes the human figures in the film, who go about their business with an almost robotic efficiency. Their thoughts and actions feel scripted, as if they're following the steps of an algorithm. In the world of *2001*, people have become so machinelike that the most human character turns out to be a machine. That's the essence of Kubrick's dark prophecy: as we come to rely on computers to mediate our understanding of the world, it is our own intelligence that flattens into artificial intelligence.

No, Google Is Not Making Us Stupid

Siva Vaidhyanathan

In the summer of 2007 technology writer Nicholas Carr contributed a provocative cover article to *The Atlantic Monthly* called "Is Google Making us Stupid?" In it, Carr made the case that persistent dependence on the Web for intellectual resources and activity is fundamentally rewiring the minds of many people—his included. "And what the Net seems to be doing is chipping away my capacity for concentration and contemplation," Carr wrote. "My mind now expects to take in information the way the Net distributes it: in a swiftly moving stream of particles. Once I was a scuba diver in the sea of words. Now I zip along the surface like a guy on a Jet Ski."

Carr promised that soon we would have in-depth psychological and neurological experiments to support or disprove the hypothesis that Web use undermines one's ability to sustain thought. He cited a handful of preliminary studies that show people altering their habits of reading on-line. But Carr's concerns went beyond that. He was worried that the more we consume on-line—snippets and links and videos and songs and animations and more snippets of text each sending us to another at rapid speed—the less we will be capable of sitting and reading, say, an extended discourse on how Google is affecting our lives.[1]

THE GOOGLE SUITE

If the empirical data upon which Carr relied was thin and preliminary, his theoretical foundation was all too thick. Despite conflating the general experience of using on-line media and the form and function of Google, Carr raised in that article many of the same concerns I have in his book, *The Shallows*: Google is based on technocracy and thus extends the rein of technocracy by making us comfortable with it. Google feeds on and then feeds our technofundamentalist belief in technological progress. And Google was designed to supplement thought while recording the traces of our thought and leveraging that data in the service of more efficient consumption. But Carr took one step I can't take. He proposed that the practice of participating in this crazy, teeming new environment designed to overstimulate somehow fundamentally and irreversibly alters the pathways of our minds.

For this Carr deployed the spectre of HAL, the computer in *2001: A Space Odyssey*, who wails that his mind is going as Dave, the human, unplugs the memory circuits. Carr also invokes Marshall McLuhan, the grandfather of a particular brand of media theory that posits that dominant communicative technologies mold consciousness and thus create different types of people, such as "typographical man," born when, thanks to the printing, people began to keep account of their worlds through linear and replicable pages. McLuhan argued that humans who lived before or outside writing and printing had and have different manners of thought and collective consciousness as a result of these technologies. Those of us who grew up reading lines on a printed page have much more structured and linear modes of thought. Those of us born into electronic media environments undergo a "retribalization," or a return to a premodern mode of thought.[2]

All of these historical assertions are, of course, untestable nonsense. Once you overdetermine the categories—the modes of thought, in this case—you can simply fit whatever small sets you collect of documented behavior into those categories and pronounce a "new man" or a "new era." Such historical and anthropological taxonomy has about as much validity as astrology. The plasticity of a human mind, a well-documented phenomenon, means that human brains not only alter over time and with experience, they can keep on changing. So if you are as worried as Nicholas Carr that the Web is short-circuiting your capacities to think, you can just retrain your mind to think better. Training, though, is different from Lamarkian mutation.

Overusing or abusing any tool or technique can leave you numb or foggy. So it's not surprising that people report increased distraction in their lives since they adopted a number of technologies that have raised the cultural metabolism of daily life. But Carr makes too strong a claim for deep, biological change via technology. He commits the error of technological determinism.

A year later, futurist Jamais Cascio wrote in the *Atlantic* a rejoinder of sorts to Carr. In this article, Cascio proclaimed that electronic media are part of the great technological advances that we humans now use to simulate evolution. Instead of relying on the slow winnowing power of natural selection and reproductive advantage, we now invent things that help us deal with life. Google and the Web are on that list, Cascio argues. He posits that the noisiness of our digital, connected lives actually trains us to think better by training us to discriminate among stimuli. We may feel distracted and overwhelmed by stimuli, but that's just a function of the inadequacy of our filtering methods and technologies. If Google were better at filtering, as it likely will be, we would live happier, smarter, more sustainable lives. Nonetheless, Cascio argues, electronic media operate as "intelligence augmentation," making us smarter, not dumber.[3]

As with Carr, Cascio is half right. He is correct in asserting that technologies (along with social norms and laws) have liberated us from the eternal cycle of Darwinian pressures. We now invent our way out of life-threatening situations. And even the geeks may breed. Sociologist Lester Frank Ward made this same argument in 1883 in response to Herbert Spencer's then-dominant endorsement of social Darwinism.[4] And Cascio is correct to argue, along with Stephen Johnson, that many media forms today, especially video games, are so intellectually demanding that they are demonstrably making us more capable of sustained engagement and tactical, if not philosophical, thought.[5]

Cascio, though, commits an error similar to Carr's. They both assume technology necessarily and unidirectionally molds us. However, Cascio assumes that technologies lead us to something certain. For him, everything "will" happen. The future is certain, determined, and he knows what it will looks like. Cascio is, after all, a futurist by trade. He assumes technologies drive our abilities and desires, instead of the other way around or, more accurately, work in concert with us. According to Cascio's brand of technological determinism, we are always getting better, always rising, never polluting or poisoning or fattening or numbing ourselves into submission.

Cascio hints at one of the more profound changes to our lives that Google has wrought. When he argues that our filters should and will be stronger, that we would soon resign our powers to edit and ignore to an algorithm, he was flashing on some real and alarming changes that Google has been implementing in its systems of late. Bluntly: Google might not be making us stupid. But we are making Google smarter, because of all the information about our individual interests and proclivities that we allow it to harvest.

The consequences of allowing Google to filter the abundance of information for us by giving it information about us include a narrowing of our focus on the things that matter to each of us and the potential fracture of our sense of collective knowledge.

READING WRITING

This Text: Reading

1. Why did we include this suite in media rather than technology?
2. All three writers take different takes on Google—what do they agree on? Disagree?
3. Do you view Google as something good, bad, or neither? Why?
4. Have you ever used another search engine besides Google? What are the differences?

This Text: Writing

1. Write a paper on someone famous through their top 25 Google links. Where do the links lead you? What does this say about the subject? Google?
2. Google search your name or someone close to you and write about what you find there.
3. Take a research subject such as "the first amendment" and Google it and do a more formal research subject. How do the results compare from Google, the research database, and books?

READING BETWEEN THE LINES

Classroom Activities

1. Find an event or occurrence—a Supreme Court decision, a major decision or action made by the President, a law passed or not passed by Congress—and find an article from a conservative newspaper or magazine, a liberal one, and one that seems to be moderate. Compare how they evaluate the decision or action. What are their criteria? Can you tell what they value based on how they argue their point?

2. Watch and tape an episode of the local news. Do some sign-reading first. What impressions do you get from the set itself? How do you know it's a news set? What are the anchors wearing? Why is that important? What about the symbols—both in the "field" and the graphics section? How might this differ from a newspaper's coverage?

3. Share your experiences with dealing with a reporter, either from a school newspaper, a television station, or local newspapers. What are some common elements of these perceptions? Do you find yourself wishing the reporters handled themselves differently? In what way?

4. As a class, come up with a code of ethics, a set of ideas that all media should live by. Now critique it. What practical restrictions would this place on media outlets? How would it change the interpretation of the first amendment (freedom of speech)? How would it affect the way you receive news?

5. If you were a reporter, what type of reporter would you want to be? Why? What do you think the rewards of being a member of the media are?

6. Looking at some advertisements, either print or broadcast, what trends do you notice? Have these trends changed over time? What human characteristics do you think advertising appeals to? Do you think advertisers know you well enough to appeal to you? To the general public?

7. Notice the signs of advertisements. What elements do you see again and again?

8. Write a code of ethics for advertisers, advising them of the tactics they should or should not use when selling products to the public. If put into place, how would this change advertising as we know it?

Essay Ideas

1. Read a week of editorial pages from a local newspaper. What are some things you notice? How do columnists use particular words? What do they stand for?

2. Using the rhetorical triangle assignment at the beginning of the chapter, write an analysis of an advertisement.

3. Examine some of the signs of an advertisement.

4. Put yourself in the shoes of an advertiser for a particular product. Write an ad campaign for that product taking into account target audience, signs, and the medium you would use to advertise it.

5. What issues on campus could be covered better (or at all) by the local media? Why do you think they are not covered now?

Visualizing Writing

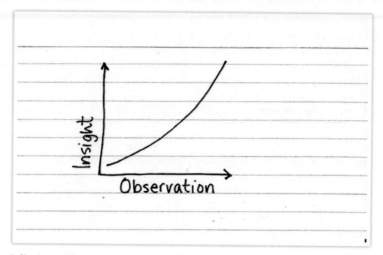

A final word from Jessica Hagy's *Indexed* about the connections between seeing and thinking.

10 Writing about Technology

HEY, WHERE DID THE CHAPTER GO?

In the table of contents, you were promised a technology chapter, and we're going to give you one—just not here. For years, we wanted to put our technology chapter entirely on the Web. Part of the reason was that so many of our essays in previous versions were actually a pretty even mix of material gathered from printed and electronic sources. But we noticed that more and more of the printed sources we like, including those from *The New York Times*, *The Washington Post*, and other more traditional media outlets, are investing as much (or more) energy in their Web portals as their printed versions. A big change came from Time Warner, who decided in recent years to foreground their Web presence. Now *The New York Times* has followed suit. In fact, two of the most important cultural magazines in the United States—*Slate* and *Salon*—exist solely in cyberspace. So now, when doing a chapter on "technology," it makes more sense to place readings on that topic within the space that has changed that term forever.

One of the more academic reasons for placing material on the Web is that it also mirrors how we increasingly interact with academic material. Although professors and students consult books routinely for studying, so much of our reading comes through the Web or electronic databases. Many teachers and students also use programs like Blackboard and WebCt to respond to work on discussion boards or hand in assignments. In many classes, these sites become a clearinghouse of information. But not only that—we increasingly see the Web as our first place to find information, whether it be academic, trivia, entertainment, or geographic. In fact, we often are upset when we cannot find information we want on the Web.

HOW THIS WORKS WITH OUR BOOK.

Much if not most of the material we have gathered here has appeared either online in a periodical or electronic database. We already have material on technology in our book, including a new suite directly engaging the battle between bloggers and journalists, and individual articles about technology as well. What this Web-based chapter allows us to do is expand the book beyond its printed pages, giving us a chance to link you to resources we could not fit here, including media outlets, writing resources, and material like photo essays. It also allows us to be more

Sometimes adopting to new technology is difficult.

precise in our use of technology. In a literal sense, technology is the subchapter behind all of our chapters—it is various forms of technology that allow artists and companies to create and us to read or watch and buy. In the chapter on the Web, we have made more specific links between the idea of technology and our individual chapters, hoping to broaden our use of technology. Please see our website at http://www.pearsonhighered.com/silverman. For more on technology, go techno yourselves. Check us out on Twitter and Facebook where we will be posting interesting articles and making up-to-date connections between what we write about in the book and what's happening in that text that is the world.

Credits

Text Credits

Photo Credits

Falling Water, Frank Lloyd Wright © Courtesy of Madelynn Ringo.
Scale comparison © Courtesy of Professor Liz Swanson.
Fence comparison © Courtesy of Professor Liz Swanson.
Spec vs. Mod Home © Courtesy of Professor Liz Swanson.
Material Natures © Courtesy of Professor Liz Swanson.
Cloud Gate © Courtesy of Professor Liz Swanson.
Photo of University of Cork © Courtesy of Professor Jonathan Silverman.
Photo of Oslo Quad © Courtesy of Professor Jonathan Silverman
Photo of Trinity College, Dublin © Courtesy of Professor Dean Rader
Photo of Pace University, NYC © Courtesy of Tom Henthrone and Kristen di Gennaro
Photo of University of Bergen, Norway © Courtesy of Professor Jonathan Silverman
Photo of Frances King School of English © Courtesy of Professor Jonathan Silverman
Photo of Copenhagen © Courtesy of Professor Dean Rader
UVA © Matt S. Hedstrom
© Courtesy of Professor Jonathan Silverman
IMG 1092 © Courtesy of Professor Jonathan Silverman
Univeristat © Courtesy of Professor Jonathan Silverman
Bergen auto © Courtesy of Professor Jonathan Silverman
Photo of Oslo Library © Courtesy of Professor Jonathan Silverman
Photo of University of London © Courtesy of Professor Jonathan Silverman
Bad Lieutenant 7 © Courtesy of Professor Dean Rader
Photo of University College Cork © Courtesy of Professor Jonathan Silverman
Photo of University of Cork #2 © Courtesy of Professor Jonathan Silverman
Photo of University of Cork #3 © Courtesy of Professor Jonathan Silverman
"Please" Do Not Park Here © Courtesy of Barrett Anderson
President Obama bumper sticker © Courtesy of Professor Dean Rader
Stupid Comics © 1998 by Jim Mahfood. "True Tales of Amerikkkan History Part II: the
    True Thanksgiving . . ." Stupid comics. © 1998 Jim Mahfood
Cartoon Mascot suit © Thom Little Moon
Cartoon Mascot suit © LALO ALCARAZ (c) 2002 Dist. by Universal Press Syndicate.
    Reprinted with permission. All rights reserved.
Obama, USA © Courtesy of Jan Davidson
Repomen poster © Courtesy of Judith Taylor
I, Robot © Moviestore Collection Ltd/Photofest
Dark Knight © Moviestore Collection Ltd/Photofest
Twilight: New Moon © Photos 12/Photofest
Star Wars © Pictorial Press Ltd/Photofest
Avatar © Photos 12/Photofest
Baby © Courtesy of Professor Dean Rader
Be Good © Courtesy of Professor Jonathan Silverman
Bob Wills Day © Courtesy of Professor Dean Rader
Filadelfia © Courtesy of Professor Dean Rader
French Hot Dog © Courtesy of Professor Dean Rader
Gravel Road © Courtesy of Professor Jonathan Silverman
Hollywood © Courtesy of Professor Jonathan Silverman
Horse path © Courtesy of Professor Jonathan Silverman
No Camping © Courtesy of Professor Dean Rader

Keeley at the *Blog of Unnecessary Quotations:* http://www.unnecessaryquotes.com/
Inserting movie reel © Courtesy of Mitch Shuldman
Indexed: Made, not born © Courtesy of Jessica Hagy at http://thisisindexed.com/
"How to Use an Apostrophe" © Courtesy of Matthew Inman
Field © Courtesy of Professor Dean Rader
Pathwork farm © Courtesy of Professor Dean Rader
Fall foliage © Courtesy of Professor Dean Rader
Halfdome with full moon © Courtesy of Professor Dean Rader
Road in the monument valley © Courtesy of Professor Dean Rader
Winter road © Courtesy of Professor Dean Rader
Ducks © Courtesy of Professor Dean Rader
Big bunny postcard © Courtesy of Professor Dean Rader
B&W family photo © Courtesy of Professor Dean Rader
Cemetary © Courtesy of Professor Dean Rader
Empty Kansas field © Courtesy of Professor Dean Rader
Desert © Courtesy of Professor Dean Rader
Lake © Courtesy of Professor Dean Rader
Main Street Christmas © Courtesy of Professor Dean Rader
Dyess © Courtesy of Professor Jonathan Silverman
Rural road and house © Courtesy of Professor Jonathan Silverman
Book cover © Courtesy of Professor Dean Rader
Tractor © Courtesy of Professor Dean Rader

Index

S

T

V

W

Z